attorney general ... gsu

OXFORD PAPE

A Dictionar

Law
Enforcement

Graham Gooch served in the police service for thirty years, mainly as a detective. The first twenty years of service were spent with the Metropolitan Police in divisions and the Specialist Operation Department. He was appointed detective superintendent in the Lancashire Constabulary and served there for ten years as a Senior Investigating Officer, with a tour as head of policy and criminal justice support. During that time he read law at the University of Central Lancashire and was awarded a first degree and a Master's degree. On leaving the police service he took up a lecturing post at the university and, from its inception, taught on and now leads the degree course in policing and criminal investigation. Apart from teaching at undergraduate and postgraduate level, he reviews criminal law textbooks for a number of publishers and writes a weekly column in the Police Review to prepare candidates for the National Investigators Examination.

Michael Williams has been involved with the investigation and prosecution of serious crime since joining the Royal Hong Kong Police (as it then was) in 1977. He later held commissioned rank in the Royal Australian Air Force Police and in the British Army Intelligence Corps (TA) before qualifying as a legal practitioner. Michael is called as a Barrister in the Supreme Court of Queensland and the High Court of Australia and is admitted as a Solicitor, with higher court advocacy rights, in England and Wales. He is a former Senior Crown Prosecutor and Revenue and Customs Prosecutor in England and Wales, Legal Adviser to the Australian Federal Police, and Crown Counsel in Queensland, and is now an Advocate with the General Medical Council.

Oxford Paperback Reference

The most authoritative and up-to-date reference books for both students and the general reader.

ABC of Music
Accounting
Allusions
Animal Behaviour
Archaeology
Architecture and Landscape Architecture
Art and Artists
Art Terms
Arthurian Legend and Literature*
Astronomy
Battles*
Better Wordpower
Bible
Biology
British History
British Place-Names
Buddhism
Business and Management
Card Games
Catchphrases
Celtic Mythology
Chemistry
Christian Art
Christian Church
Chronology of English Literature
Century of New Words
Classical Literature
Classical Myth and Religion
Classical World*
Computing
Contemporary World History
Countries of the World
Dance
Dynasties of the World
Earth Sciences
Ecology
Economics
Encyclopedia
Engineering*
English Etymology
English Folklore
English Grammar
English Language
English Literature
English Surnames
Euphemisms
Everyday Grammar
Finance and Banking
First Names
Food and Drink
Food and Nutrition
Foreign Words and Phrases
Geography
Humorous Quotations
Idioms
Internet
Islam
Kings and Queens of Britain
Language Toolkit
Law
Law Enforcement*
Linguistics
Literary Terms
Local and Family History
London Place-Names
Mathematics
Medical
Medicinal Drugs
Modern Design
Modern Quotations
Modern Slang
Music
Musical Terms
Musical Works
Nicknames
Nursing
Ologies and Isms
Philosophy
Phrase and Fable
Physics
Plant Sciences
Plays*
Pocket Fowler's Modern English Usage
Political Quotations
Politics
Popes
Proverbs
Psychology
Quotations
Quotations by Subject
Reverse Dictionary
Rhymes*
Rhyming Slang
Saints
Science
Scientific Quotations
Shakespeare
Ships and the Sea
Slang
Sociology
Space Exploration
Statistics
Superstitions
Synonyms and Antonyms
Weather
Weights, Measures, and Units
Word Histories
World History
World Mythology
World Place-Names
World Religions
Zoology

**forthcoming*

A Dictionary of

Law Enforcement

GRAHAM GOOCH
MICHAEL WILLIAMS

OXFORD
UNIVERSITY PRESS

Great Clarendon Street, Oxford OX2 6DP

Oxford University Press is a department of the University of Oxford.
It furthers the University's objective of excellence in research, scholarship,
and education by publishing worldwide in

Oxford New York

Auckland Cape Town Dar es Salaam Hong Kong Karachi
Kuala Lumpur Madrid Melbourne Mexico City Nairobi
New Delhi Shanghai Taipei Toronto

With offices in

Argentina Austria Brazil Chile Czech Republic France Greece
Guatemala Hungary Italy Japan Poland Portugal Singapore
South Korea Switzerland Thailand Turkey Ukraine Vietnam

Published in the United States
by Oxford University Press Inc., New York

Adapted from *A Dictionary of Law* (Oxford, 2003)
First published 2007

British Library Cataloguing in Publication Data
Data available

Library of Congress Cataloging in Publication Data
Data available

Typeset by SPI Publisher Services, Pondicherry, India
Printed in Great Britain
on acid-free paper by Clays, St. Ives, Bungay

ISBN 978-0-19-280702-1

1

Preface

Increasingly, law enforcement is a multi-agency activity: professionals from diverse agencies work together in the investigation of crime and the prosecution, punishment, and rehabilitation of offenders. Effective partnerships require participants to understand not only the particular language of their own organization and the common language of the law, but also that of the organizations with whom they interact.

This dictionary, produced by two writers who, between them, have over 60 years' experience in the investigation and prosecution of serious crime, both in England and Wales and overseas, draws on some entries from the *Oxford Dictionary of Law*; amended and expanded, where necessary, to meet the needs of the law enforcement community. In the main, however, the entries are entirely new and specific to that community. Its aim is to provide a clear definition of each term, together with a more detailed explanation where necessary. Key cases and statutory provisions are cited, as appropriate.

The work is designed to provide a convenient quick reference source for all those involved with law enforcement and the criminal justice system, or for those affected by or interested in those areas, but especially:

- All those involved in the prevention and investigation of crime, including: civilian and military police officers and officers of the Serious and Organised Crime Agency, HM Revenue and Customs, HM Immigration Service, National Health Service Counter Fraud, Department of Trade and Industry, Department of Work and Pensions, and the various local government Trading Standards and Environmental Health Agencies.
- All those who owe a duty to the court and whom the courts expect to have a basic knowledge of the law and legal procedure: crime scene examiners, forensic scientists and experts in other fields, and interpreters involved in both the investigative and court processes.
- Justices' clerks and legal advisers.
- Probation officers, members of Youth Offender Teams, Drug Action Teams, and Community Safety Working Groups, and others involved with the pre-sentence process and the rehabilitation of offenders.
- Those agencies and individuals responsible for the protection of children and vulnerable persons.

Not least, however, the writers have attempted to provide a key reference source for students in further and higher education and those studying for a professional or vocational qualification in subjects related to law enforcement and criminal justice.

In the last decade, the distinction between civil and criminal law has become ever more blurred, and investigators are now routinely involved in proceedings brought before the civil courts. Hence, this work encompasses such proceedings. Also included are the more common medical, firearms, and ballistic terms encountered in those fields, and particularly in expert reports. Basic criminology terms are incorporated for the benefit of those embarking on the academic study of crime and criminal behaviour.

Appendices to the work list many of the abbreviations and acronyms in common usage throughout the law enforcement community, those non-imprisonable offences that are designated as recordable, and, reflecting the crucial importance of the disclosure of unused material within the criminal process, the Code of Practice issued pursuant to s 23 of the Criminal Procedure and Investigations Act 1996 and the disclosure guidelines issued by the Attorney-General in April 2005.

An asterisk (*) before a word indicates that the word is further explained in its own entry. Some entries simply refer the user to another, indicating that the word is either a synonym or is explained fully within that entry. In line with the convention adopted in the drafting of legislation and following the Interpretation Act 1978, the use of the pronoun 'he' (rather than 'he or she') has been adopted purely to simplify the construction of sentences; it does not imply that the subject matter relates exclusively or primarily to men.

The law is as stated on 11 October 2006.

MTW
GG

April 2007

Contents

abandonment 1. The act of giving up a legal right, particularly a right of ownership of property. Property that has been abandoned is *res nullius* (a thing belonging to no one), and a person taking possession of it therefore acquires a lawful *title. An item is regarded as abandoned when it can be established that the original owner has discarded it and is indifferent as to what becomes of it: such an item cannot be the subject of a *criminal damage or *theft charge. However, property placed by its owner in a dustbin is not abandoned, having been placed there for the purpose of being collected as refuse. **2.** The offence contrary to s 1 of the Children and Young Persons Act 1933, of a *parent or *guardian leaving a child under the age of 16 to its fate. A child is not regarded as abandoned if the parent knows and approves steps someone else is taking to look after it. The court may allow a child to be adopted without the consent of its parents if they are *guilty of abandonment. *See also* CHILD CRUELTY.

abatement 1. (of debts) The proportionate reduction in the payment of *debts that takes place if a person's assets are insufficient to settle with his creditors in full. If obtained dishonestly by deception it amounts to a criminal offence under s 2 (1)(c) of the Theft Act 1978. **2.** (of nuisances) The termination, removal, or destruction of a *nuisance. A person injured by a nuisance has a right to abate it. In doing so, he must not do more damage than is necessary and, if removal of the nuisance requires entry on to the property from which it emanates, he may have to give notice to the wrongdoer. A *local authority can issue an abatement notice to control statutory nuisances.

abduction 1. The wrongful taking away of a person. The offences connected with the abduction of women contained within the Sexual Offences Act 1956 were repealed by the Sexual Offences Act 2003 (*see* SEXUAL OFFENCES) and replaced with a series of non-gender specific offences aimed at the protection of both children and adults, including those with a mental disorder impeding choice. *See also* CHILD ABDUCTION; KIDNAPPING; PEOPLE TRAFFICKING. **2.** (in *international law) The seizure of a person in one country for the purpose of taking him to another country for *trial avoiding extradition procedures. It is a breach of *international law including *human rights. The injured state can take action against the seizing state. Countries vary in their attitude to receiving such prisoners. UK courts will not accept *jurisdiction over a person brought into the country in this way. US courts are ambivalent; the US Supreme Court has held that circumvention of an extradition treaty will not per se cause denial of jurisdiction. Israeli courts will and do accept jurisdiction, as in the famous case of Adolf Eichman who was abducted from Argentina by Israeli government agents.

abet *See* AID AND ABET.

abolitionism A radical perspective in criminology, which sees crime as the same as other non-criminalized social problems and advocates the abolition of prisons and *punishment systems for dealing with crime.

abominable crime The term used in s 61 of the Offences Against the Person Act 1861 (now repealed) to describe the felonies of sodomy and bestiality. *See* BUGGERY; SEXUAL OFFENCES.

abortion The termination of a pregnancy: a miscarriage or the premature expulsion of a foetus from the womb before the normal period of gestation is complete. It is an offence to induce or attempt to induce an abortion unless the terms of the Abortion Act 1967, as reformulated by

a

the Human Fertilisation and Embryology Act 1990, and the Abortion Regulations 1991, as amended by the Abortion (Amendment) (England) Regulations 2002 (SI 2002/887), are complied with. The pregnancy can only be terminated by a registered medical practitioner, and two registered medical practitioners must agree that it is necessary, e.g. because (1) continuation of the pregnancy would involve a risk to the life or physical or mental health of the pregnant woman (or of other children of hers) that is greater than the risk of terminating the pregnancy, or (2) there is a substantial risk that the child will be born with a serious physical or mental handicap. However, doctors are not obliged to perform abortions if they can prove that they have a conscientious objection to doing so. A husband cannot prevent his wife having a legal abortion if she so wishes. *Compare* CHILD DESTRUCTION.

absconding The failure of a person to surrender to the *custody of a court in order to avoid legal proceedings. Under the Bail Act 1976, absconding by a person released on bail is an offence. *See also* BAIL; SURRENDER TO CUSTODY.

absence (in court procedure) The non-appearance of a party to *litigation or a person summoned to attend as a witness.

absent-mindedness *See* AUTOMATISM.

absolute discharge *See* DISCHARGE.

absolute privilege The *defence that a statement cannot be made the subject of an action for *defamation because it was made in *Parliament, in papers ordered to be published by either House of Parliament, in judicial proceedings or a fair and accurate newspaper or broadcast report of judicial proceedings, or in an official communication between certain officers of state. Under the Defamation Act 1996, the defence is also available for those reporting proceedings of the *European Court of Justice. Under certain circumstances defined by the 1996 Act the absolute privilege accorded to statements or proceedings in Parliament may be waived (**waiver of privilege**) to permit evidence to be adduced in an action for defamation. *Compare* QUALIFIED PRIVILEGE.

absolute right A right set out in the *European Convention on Human Rights that cannot be interfered with lawfully, no matter how important the public interest in doing so might be. Absolute rights include *freedom of thought, conscience, and religion and the prohibitions on *torture, *inhuman treatment or punishment, and *degrading treatment or punishment, and punishment without law. *Compare* QUALIFIED RIGHT.

abstracting electricity The offence contrary to s 13 of the Theft Act 1968 of dishonestly using, wasting, or diverting electricity. The offence is triable *either way; on conviction on indictment it is punishable with up to five years' imprisonment and/or a fine. It may be committed by someone who bypasses his electricity meter or reconnects a disconnected meter. *Joyriding in a lift (or some similar abuse) might also constitute wasting electricity.

abuse of position of trust An offence contrary to ss 16 to 19 of the Sexual Offences Act 2003, which provide that it is an offence for a person aged 18 or over intentionally to behave in certain *sexual ways in relation to a child aged under 18, where he is in a *position of trust in respect of the child. The sections re-enact and amend the offence of abuse of position of trust provided by ss 3 and 4 of the Sexual Offences (Amendment) Act 2000. The prohibited behaviour in each of the sections is identical to that prohibited by the child sex offences in ss 9 to 12 of the 2003 Act (*see* CHILD ABUSE), except that for the abuse of position of trust offences, the child may be 16 or 17. In cases where the child is aged 16 and over, ss 23 and 24 of the Act provide defences where the defendant is lawfully married to the child and where the couple were engaged in a lawful sexual relationship prior to the defendant being placed in the position of trust.

abuse of process A *tort where damage is caused by using a legal process for an ulterior collateral purpose (*see also* MALICIOUS PROSECUTION). Actions that are obviously frivolous, vexatious, or in bad faith can be stayed or dismissed by the court as an abuse of process.

The discretion of the court to stay proceedings for abuse of process applies where the defendant would not receive a fair *trial, and/or where it would be unfair for the defendant to be tried: *R v Beckford* [1996] 1 Cr App R 94. The latter will include cases where the prosecution have manipulated or misused the process of the court so as to deprive the defendant of a protection provided by the law or to take unfair advantage of a technicality (*R v Derby Crown Court, ex p Brooks* (1985) 80 Cr App R 164) and where it would be contrary to the public interest in the integrity of the *criminal justice system that a trial should take place: *R v Mullen* [1999] 2 Cr App R 143. The discretion applies not only to existing criminal proceedings, but also to the question whether proceedings should be brought in the first instance. However, it may be exercised only in exceptional circumstances (*A-G's Reference (No 1 of 1990)* (1992) 95 Cr App R 296) and not as a form of disciplinary disapproval of the prosecution: *R v Norwich Crown Court, ex p Belsham* (1992) 94 Cr App R 382. The issue can be raised in either the *Crown Court or the *magistrates' court.

In *R v Horseferry Road Magistrates' Court, ex p Bennett* [1994] 1 AC 42, the House of Lords decided that a court had a *discretion to stay any criminal proceedings on grounds of abuse of process where it would be impossible to give the accused a fair trial; or where it would amount to a misuse of process because it offends the court's sense of justice and propriety to be asked to try the accused in the circumstances of the particular case. There are a number of bases upon which an abuse of process argument may be founded. These include delay, breach of a promise not to prosecute, agents of the prosecution contributing to the offence (*see* ENTRAPMENT), and abuse of executive power.

abusive behaviour *See* THREATENING BEHAVIOUR.

acceptable behaviour contract (ABC) A voluntary agreement made between people involved in anti-social behaviour and the local police, the housing department, the registered social landlord, or the perpetrator's school. They are flexible in terms of content and format. *See also* ANTI-SOCIAL BEHAVIOUR ORDER; HARASSMENT.

acceptance Agreement to the terms of an *offer that, provided certain other requirements are fulfilled, converts the offer into a legally binding contract. The validity of an acceptance is governed by four principal rules. (1) It must take place while the offer is still in force, i.e. before it has lapsed or been revoked. (2) It must be on the same terms as the offer. An acceptance made subject to any variation is treated as a counteroffer. (3) It must be unconditional, thus an acceptance subject to contract is not a valid acceptance. (4) It must be communicated to the offeror. Acceptance by letter is treated as communicated when the letter is posted, but telex is equated with the telephone, so that communication takes place only on receipt. However, when the offer consists of a promise to confer a benefit on whoever may perform a specified act, the offeror waives the requirement of communication as a separate act. If, for example, he offers a reward for information, a person able to supply the information is not expected to accept the offer formally. The act of giving the information itself constitutes the acceptance, the communication of the acceptance, and the performance of the contract.

acceptance of a bill The written agreement by the person on whom a *bill of exchange is drawn (the drawee) that he will accept the order of the person who draws it upon him (the drawer). The acceptance must be written on the bill and signed. The signature of the drawee without additional words is sufficient, although generally the word 'accepted' is used as well. Upon acceptance the drawee becomes the acceptor and the party primarily liable upon the bill.

ACCESS Mnemonic for Shepherd's model of investigation as a cycle. The key words are Assess, Collect, Collate, Evaluate, Survey, Summary.

a

access Formerly, the opportunity to visit a child that was granted (at the discretion of the court) to its *parent when the other parent had the care and control of the child after divorce or when a custodianship order was in force. Since the Children Act 1989 came into force the concept of access has been replaced by that of *contact. *See also* SECTION 8 ORDERS.

accession 1. The formal agreement of a country to an international *treaty. The term is applied to the agreement of a country to become a member state of the European Union. Member states accede to the Treaty of Rome or any other EU treaty by signing **accession agreements**. **2.** The process of a member of the royal family succeeding to the throne, which occurs immediately on the death or abdication of the previous sovereign.

access land *Land to which the public have access for the purposes of open-air recreation under the Countryside and Rights of Way Act 2000. It includes land shown as open country (mountain, moor, heath, or down) on a map in conclusive form issued by an appropriate countryside body (the Countryside Agency or the Countryside Council for Wales), or as common land, or land situated more than 600 metres above sea level, or land that has been dedicated as access land.

accessory One who is a party to a crime that is actually committed by someone else. An accessory (sometimes referred to as a **secondary party**) is one who either successfully incites someone to commit a crime (**counsels or procures**) or helps him to do so (*see also* AID AND ABET). Liability is governed by the Accessories and Abettors Act 1861, as amended by the Criminal Law Act 1977. An accessory is subject to the same *punishments and orders as the principal offender (*see also* COMMON DESIGN). It is an offence contrary to s 4 of the Criminal Law Act 1977 to assist a person whom one knows has committed an offence for which the *penalty is fixed by law or for which a previously unconvicted person can be sentenced to imprisonment for a term of five years or more, with the intention of impeding his apprehension or prosecution. *See also* IMPEDING APPREHENSION OR PROSECUTION.

accident An unlooked-for mishap or an untoward event which is not expected or designed: *Fenton v Thorley* [1903] AC 443. On a charge of *murder, the *defence of accident may provide a complete defence or serve to reduce the offence to one of *manslaughter. *See also* FATAL ACCIDENT; MISTAKE; ROAD TRAFFIC ACCIDENT.

accident record book A record kept by the police of details of the accidents they have investigated. Access to this is usually requested by *solicitors acting in subsequent *litigation relating to *road traffic accidents. The Association of Chief Police Officers Traffic Committee has issued guidelines on charges for such reports.

accomplice One who is a party to a crime, either as a *principal or as an *accessory. *See also* CORROBORATION.

account monitoring order An order made under para 2(1) of sch 6A to the Terrorism Act 2000 or s 370 of the Proceeds of Crime Act 2002 requiring certain types of financial institution to provide certain information held by them relating to a customer for the purposes of an investigation.

accounts A statement of a company's financial position. All *registered companies must present accounts (in the form prescribed by the Companies Act 1985) annually at a *general meeting. These consist of a *balance sheet and a *profit-and-loss account with *group accounts (if appropriate) attached. They are accompanied by a *directors' report and an auditor's report. All limited companies must deliver copies of their accounts to the *Companies Registry (where they are open to public inspection), but companies that are classified (on the basis of turnover, balance sheet total, and number of members) as 'small' or 'medium-sized' enjoy certain exemptions. Members are entitled to be sent copies of the accounts.

accredited person A person employed under a *community safety accreditation scheme such as local authority street wardens, football stewards, etc. The Police

Reform Act 2002 gives such persons a range of police powers and creates an offence of assaulting them. *See also* ASSAULT.

accusatorial procedure (adversarial procedure) A system of criminal justice in which conclusions as to liability are reached by the process of *prosecution and *defence. It is the primary duty of the *prosecutor and defence to press their respective viewpoints within the constraints of the rules of evidence while the *judge acts as an impartial umpire, who allows the facts to emerge from this procedure. *Common-law systems usually adopt an accusatorial procedure. *See also* BURDEN OF PROOF. *Compare* INQUISITORIAL PROCEDURE.

accused One charged with a criminal offence. *See also* DEFENDANT.

acquiescence Express or implied *consent. In law, care must be taken to distinguish between mere knowledge of a situation and positive consent to it. For example, in the *defence of **volenti non fit injuria* an injured party will not be regarded as having consented to a risk simply because he knew that the risk existed.

acquis communautaire [French] The body of *Community legislation by which all EU member states are bound.

acquisitive offence A criminal offence, such as *theft, aimed at acquiring property for the offender. Studies show the incidence of this type of offence increases in times of economic downturn.

acquittal A decision by a court that a defendant accused of a crime is innocent. A court must acquit a defendant following a *verdict of *not guilty or a successful *plea of **autrefois acquit* or **autrefois convict*. Once acquitted, a defendant cannot be retried for the same crime, except that the Criminal Justice Act 2003 provides that where a person has been acquitted of a serious offence and there is new and compelling evidence that the person has committed the offence, he can by leave of the Court of Appeal be retried for the offence. An acquittal in a criminal court does not bind civil courts (e.g. a person acquitted of *rape can be sued for trespass to the person).

action 1. A proceeding in which a party pursues a legal right in a civil court. *See also* IN PERSONAM; IN REM. **2.** The assembly of moving parts in a *firearm that feed the *cartridge into the *chamber, lock and seal the chamber, fire the cartridge, unlock the chamber, extract and eject the empty cartridge case. Types of action include: (1) **blowback**, where, in an automatic or semi-automatic firearm, the residual pressure of the expanding gases which discharge the bullet from the barrel blow the *breechblock open; and (2) **bolt**, where breech closure is achieved manually by longitudinal movement of the breechblock parallel to the axis of the *bore. *See also* DOUBLE ACTION.

action plan order A type of community sentence order made under s 69 of the Powers of Criminal Courts (Sentencing) Act 2000 requiring a person aged under 16 (reduced from 18 by the Criminal Justice Act 2003, although the provision will apply in modified form in the case of offenders aged 16 and 17 until 4 April 2007) to comply with a three month plan relating to his actions and whereabouts and to comply with the directions of a responsible officer (e.g. *probation officer). It aims to provide an intensive and individually tailored response to offending behaviour which will address the causes of that behaviour. It is intended to combine *punishment, rehabilitation, and reparation.

activity requirement A requirement that may be imposed by a court dealing with an offender aged 16 or over as part of a *community order, *custody plus order, *suspended sentence order, or an *intermittent custody order. The offender must undertake the particular activities specified by the court. These may include undertaking training and education, counselling in debt and financial management, and mediation between the offender and the victim or persons affected by the offending if those persons consent. The specified time for the requirement may be between 20 and 60 days (s 201, Criminal Justice Act 2003, replacing a similar provision in the Powers of Criminal Court (Sentencing) Act 2000).

a

act of God An event due to natural causes (storms, earthquakes, floods, etc.) so exceptionally severe that no-one could reasonably be expected to anticipate or guard against it.

Act of Parliament (statute) A *document that sets out legal rules and has (normally) been passed by both Houses of *Parliament in the form of a *Bill and agreed to by the *Crown (*see* ROYAL ASSENT). Under the Parliament Acts 1911 and 1949, however, passing of public Bills by the *House of Lords can be dispensed with, except in the case of Bills to extend the duration of Parliament or to confirm provisional orders. Subject to these exceptions, the Lords can delay Bills passed by the *House of Commons; it cannot block them completely. If the Commons pass a money Bill (e.g. one giving effect to the Budget) and the Lords do not pass it unaltered within one month, it may be submitted direct for the royal assent. Any other Bill may receive the royal assent without being passed by the Lords if the Commons pass it in two consecutive sessions and at least one year elapses between its second reading in the first session and its third reading in the second.

Every modern Act of Parliament begins with a **long title**, which summarizes its aims, and ends with a **short title**, by which it may be cited in any other document. The short title includes the calendar year in which the Act receives the royal assent (e.g. The Competition Act 1998). An alternative method of citation is by the calendar year together with the Chapter number allotted to the Act on receiving the assent or, in the case of an Act earlier than 1963, by its regnal year or years and Chapter number. Regnal years are numbered from the date of a sovereign's accession to the throne, and an Act is attributed to the year or years covering the session in which it receives the royal assent. (*See also* ENACTING WORDS.) An Act comes into force on the date of royal assent unless it specifies a different date or provides for the date to be fixed by ministerial order.

Acts of Parliament are classified by the Queen's Printer as public general Acts, local Acts, and personal Acts. **Public general Acts** include all Acts (except those confirming provisional orders) introduced into Parliament as public Bills. **Local Acts** comprise all Acts introduced as private Bills and confined in operation to a particular area, together with Acts confirming provisional orders. **Personal Acts** are Acts introduced as private Bills and applying to private individuals or estates. Acts are alternatively classified as **public Acts** or **private Acts** according to their status in courts of law. A public Act is *judicially noticed (i.e. accepted by the courts as a matter of general knowledge). A private Act is not, and must be expressly pleaded by the person relying on it. All Acts since 1850 are public unless they specifically provide otherwise.

act of state An act, often involving force, of the executive of a state, or committed by an agent of a sovereign power with its prior approval or subsequent *ratification, that affects adversely a person who does not owe allegiance to that power. The courts have power to decide whether or not particular conduct constitutes such an act, but if it does, they have no jurisdiction to award any remedy.

actual bodily harm (ABH) Any hurt or injury calculated to interfere with the health or comfort of the victim. *Assault causing actual bodily harm is an *either way offence (contrary to s 47, Offences Against the Person Act 1861) carrying a maximum *punishment of five years' imprisonment. The hurt need not be serious or permanent in nature, but it must be more than trifling. It is enough to show that pain or discomfort has been suffered, even though no bruising is evident. The harm is not restricted to physical harm but includes psychiatric harm (*R v Ireland* [1998] AC 147 (HL)). This includes neurotic disorders but not fear or anxiety. Psychiatric injury must be proved by *expert evidence.

actuarialism In *penology a means of predicting persistent offending behaviour in individuals by risk calculation. The theory is that those identified as potentially persistent offenders can be sentenced to long terms of imprisonment thereby achieving reduction in crime levels.

actus reus [Latin: a guilty act] The essential element of a crime that must be proved to secure a conviction, as opposed to the mental state of the accused (*see* MENS REA). In most cases the *actus reus* will simply be an act (e.g. appropriation of property is the act of *theft) accompanied by specified circumstances (e.g. that the property belongs to another). Sometimes, however, it may be an *omission to act (e.g. failure to prevent death may be the *actus reus* of *manslaughter) or it may include a specified consequence (e.g. death being the consequence required for the *actus reus* of *murder or *manslaughter). In certain cases the *actus reus* may simply be a state of affairs rather than an act (e.g. being unfit to drive through drink or drugs when in charge of a motor vehicle on a road).

address for service The address, which a party to court proceedings gives to the court and/or the other party, to which all the formal *documents relating to the proceedings should be delivered. Notices delivered at that address (which may be, for example, the address of his *solicitors) are binding on the party concerned.

adduce To put forward (in evidence).

adipocere White deposit, found on some decomposed bodies, caused by post-mortem conversion of fat by enzymes and micro-organisms.

adjective law The part of the law that deals with practice and procedure in the courts. *Compare* SUBSTANTIVE LAW.

adjournment (in court procedure) The postponement or suspension of the hearing of a case until a future date. The hearing may be adjourned to a fixed date or *sine die* (without day), i.e. for an indefinite period.

adjudication The formal *judgment or decision of a court or tribunal.

ad litem [Latin: for the suit] A grant *ad litem* is the appointment by a court of a person to act on behalf of an estate in court proceedings, when the estate's proper representatives are unable or unwilling to act. A guardian *ad litem* is the former name for a *children's guardian.

administration 1. An insolvency procedure invoked against a company that is or is likely to become insolvent. It is brought about by an *administration order. **2.** The process of carrying out duties imposed by a trust in connection with the property of a person of unsound mind or a *bankrupt.

administration of poison *See* POISON.

administration order An order made by the court under the Insolvency Act 1986, directing that, during the period for which it is in force, the affairs, business, and property of a company shall be managed by a person appointed by the court (known as the **administrator**). In order for the court to grant such an order it must be satisfied that the company cannot or is unlikely to be able to pay its *debts when due *and* that the order is likely to allow (1) the survival of the company, or (2) the approval of a *voluntary arrangement, or (3) a more favourable realization of its assets than would be possible under a *winding-up or through an arrangement with *creditors.

The Insolvency Act does not specify a period for the duration of the order: it remains in force until the administrator is discharged, by the court, having achieved the purpose(s) for which the order was granted or having decided that the purpose cannot be achieved.

While the order is in force the company may not be wound up; no steps may be taken to enforce any security over the company's *property or to repossess *goods in the company's possession, except with the leave of the court, and no other proceedings or other legal processes may be initiated or continued, against the company or its property, except with the court's leave.

administrative powers Discretionary powers of an executive nature that are conferred by *legislation on government ministers, public and *local authorities, and other bodies and persons for the purpose of giving detailed effect to broadly defined policy. Examples include powers to acquire *land compulsorily, to grant or refuse *licences or consents, and to determine the precise nature and extent of services to be provided. Administrative

a

powers are found in every sphere of public administration, including town and country planning, the regulation of public health and other environmental matters, the functioning of the welfare services, and the control of many trades, professions, and other activities. Their exercise is subject to judicial control by means of the doctrine of **ultra vires*.

administrative receiver A *receiver who takes control of all (or substantially all) of a company's assets. *See also* INSOLVENCY PRACTITIONER.

administrative tribunal A body established by or under *Act of Parliament to decide claims and disputes arising in connection with the administration of legislative schemes, normally of a welfare or regulatory nature. Examples are *employment tribunals and rent assessment committees. They exist outside the ordinary courts of law, but their decisions are subject to judicial control by means of the doctrine of **ultra vires* and by *judicial review in cases of *error of law on the face of the record. *Compare* DOMESTIC TRIBUNAL.

admissibility of evidence The principles determining whether or not particular items of evidence may be received by the court. The central principle of admissibility is *relevance. All irrelevant evidence is inadmissible, but evidence that is legally relevant may also be inadmissible if it falls within the scope of one of the *exclusionary rules of evidence. *See also* CONDITIONAL ADMISSIBILITY; MULTIPLE ADMISSIBILITY.

admissibility of records In civil cases *documents containing information (records) are admissible as evidence of the facts stated in them. Before the introduction of the Civil Evidence Act 1995, such documents and records were admissible only if they came within an exception to the rules prohibiting the use of *hearsay evidence. Since 1995 the hearsay rules in civil cases have been abolished and accordingly these records are admissible. In criminal cases the hearsay rules in relation to business documents have been relaxed, although not completely abolished, by s 117 of the Criminal Justice Act 2003 (replacing similar provisions introduced by the Criminal Justice Act 1988). Under s 117, business and other documents are admissible if they have been created, received or processed by a person in the course of a trade, business, profession or other occupation, or as the holder of a paid or unpaid office; and the person who supplied the information had or may reasonably be supposed to have had personal knowledge of the matters dealt with. In the case of a document prepared for the purposes of pending or contemplated proceedings, it must also be shown that the person who supplied the information contained within the document is either unavailable or, having regard to the length of time since he supplied the information and all other circumstances, cannot reasonably be expected to have any recollection of the matters dealt with in the document.

admission (in criminal proceedings) A statement admitting an offence or a fact that constitutes legally acceptable evidence of the offence or fact. Admissions may be informal or formal. An informal admission is called a *confession. A formal admission may be made either before or at the hearing, but if not made in court, it must be in writing and signed by the defendant or his legal adviser. An admission may be made in respect of any fact about which *oral evidence could be given and is *conclusive evidence of the fact admitted at all criminal proceedings relating to the matter, although it may be withdrawn at any stage with the permission of the court. A *plea of *guilty to a *charge read out in court is a formal admission. *See also* CAUTION.

admonition A reprimand from a *judge to a defendant who has been discharged from the further prosecution of an offence.

adoptive relationship A legal relationship created as a result of an adoption order (see s 67 of the Adoption and Children Act 2002). A male adopter is known as the **adoptive father**, a female adopter as the **adoptive mother**, and other relatives as **adoptive relatives**. The laws of *affinity are, however, not altered by the new adoptive relationship.

adrenaline A hormone produced by the adrenal glands that elevates heart and respiration rates; also called **epinephrine**.

adult In criminal proceedings, the definition of 'adult' is simply a function of the definition of juvenile—i.e. an adult is any person aged 18 or over. In the context of sentencing, however, the term is sometimes used to mean those who have reached the age of 21, the age at which an offender becomes liable to imprisonment rather than detention in a young offender institution.

adulteration The mixing of other substances with food. It is an offence of *strict liability under the Food Act 1984 to sell any food containing a substance that would endanger health. It is also an offence to mix dangerous substances into food with the intention of selling the mixture.

advance information Before an accused charged with an *either way offence is called upon to make a decision regarding *mode of trial, he is entitled to advanced *disclosure of the *prosecution case. Generally, the prosecutor will provide a summary of the facts and matters which the prosecutor proposes to adduce by way of evidence, but it may be by way of a copy of those parts of every written statement relating to those facts and matters. The advance disclosure provisions do not apply to summary offences, although in response to the fair trial provisions of the *European Convention on Human Rights, advance information is generally provided in such cases. The procedure for furnishing advance information is laid down in r 21 of the *Criminal Procedure Rules.

adversary procedure (adversarial system) *See* ACCUSATORIAL PROCEDURE.

adverse inference *See* DEFENCE STATEMENT; RIGHT OF SILENCE.

adverse occupation Occupation of *premises by a trespasser to the exclusion of the owner or lawful occupier. *Trespassing itself is not usually a criminal offence, but if the premises are residential and were being occupied, the trespasser (whether or not he used force in order to enter) commits the *summary offence of 'adverse occupation', contrary to s 7 of the Criminal Law Act 1977 if he refuses to leave when asked to do so by the displaced *residential occupier or a protected intending occupier (or by someone, including a *constable, acting on behalf of them). A protected intending occupier includes a purchaser, someone let in by the *local authority, Housing Corporation, or a housing association with written evidence of his claim to the premises, or someone holding a *lease, *tenancy, or *licence with two years to run. Under the Criminal Justice and Public Order Act 1994, such a person may obtain an interim possession order. This differs from an ordinary possession order in that it is much quicker, may be heard in the absence of those on the property, and involves the police in enforcement. It is only available for buildings and ancillary *land and not against those, such as *gypsies and New Age Travellers, who occupy open land (for which, *see* UNAUTHORIZED CAMPING). Once the proper procedure has been followed and the applicant has shown a good case for possession, an order will require those on the land to leave within 24 hours. Remaining on the premises or reentry within 12 months is a *summary offence, contrary to s 76 of the Criminal Justice and Public Order Act 1994 and punishable by a *fine at level 5 and/or six months' imprisonment. It is also an offence contrary to s 75 of the 1994 Act to make false or misleading statements in making or resisting such an order. Similar penalties apply on summary conviction, but on *indictment a maximum of two years' imprisonment and/or a fine may be imposed.

Usually it is a summary offence for a stranger or the *landlord to use violence to gain entry to premises when it is known that there is someone on those premises opposed to such an entry. However, a displaced residential occupier or a protected intending occupier who has asked the person to leave may call on the police for assistance. By virtue of s 6 of the Criminal Law Act 1977, it is not an offence if a constable, a displaced residential occupier, or a protected intending occupier (or their agents) uses force to secure entry. *See* FORCIBLE ENTRY.

a

adverse possession The occupation of *land to which another person has *title with the intention of possessing it as one's own. The adverse possessor must occupy the land as if he were entitled to it to the exclusion of all others, and must intend to occupy it as his own. Both these factors must be evidenced by the use made of the land; e.g. cultivation, fencing, etc. Equivocal acts, such as use of the land for grazing animals from time to time or allowing children to play on the land, will not be sufficient. After 12 years' adverse possession, the original owner's title becomes statute-barred by the Limitation Act 1980, and he cannot recover his land from the adverse possessor. The adverse possessor becomes the lawful owner (a **squatter's title**), and is entitled to be registered as such. The law on adverse possession is frequently used to cure small discrepancies in the plan attached to a transfer of land, and the actual position of boundaries on the ground, but it can also be used to obtain ownership of large areas of land. *See also* SQUATTER.

adverse witness A witness who gives evidence unfavourable to the party who called him. If the witness's evidence is merely unfavourable he may not be impeached (i.e. his credibility may not be attacked) by the party calling him, but contradictory evidence may be called. If, however, the witness is *hostile he may be impeached by introducing evidence that shows his untruthfulness.

advice on evidence A written opinion identifying the issues raised in a case and advising what evidence it will be necessary to call at the *trial.

Advisory, Conciliation and Arbitration Service (ACAS) A statutory body that was established under the Employment Protection Act 1975; the composition and functions of ACAS are now governed by pts IV and VI of the Trade Union and Labour Relations (Consolidation) Act 1992. ACAS was set up to promote the improvement of industrial relations and the development of collective bargaining. In its conciliation function it may intervene, with or without the parties' consent, in a trade dispute to offer facilities and assistance in negotiating a settlement. It employs **conciliation officers** who may assist parties to an application to an *employment tribunal to reach a settlement. Earlier *legislation removed the necessity for binding settlements of employment disputes to involve an ACAS conciliation officer: settlements can now be made when the individual has had independent legal advice from a qualified lawyer.

ACAS does not itself arbitrate in trade disputes, but with the consent of both parties it may refer a dispute to the Central Arbitration Committee or to an independent arbitrator. ACAS may give free advice to *employers, *employees, and their respective representatives on matters of employment or industrial relations. It issues *codes of practice giving guidance on such matters as disciplinary procedures and disclosure of information to trade unions. It may also conduct inquiries into industrial relations problems, either generally or in relation to particular businesses, and publish the results after considering the views of parties directly affected. ACAS can charge for its services when it considers that this is appropriate. The law on conciliation generally is contained in the Employment Tribunals Act 1996.

advocate One who exercises a *right of audience and argues a case for a client in legal proceedings. In *magistrates' courts and the *county courts both *barristers and *solicitors have the right to appear as advocates. Formerly, only barristers held rights of audience in the *Crown Court, the *High Court, the *Court of Appeal, and the *House of Lords. However, the provisions of the Courts and Legal Services Act 1990 allow solicitors with appropriate experience or training to qualify for rights of audience similar to those of barristers. In many tribunals there are no rules concerning representation, and laymen may appear as advocates. Advocates no longer enjoy immunity from law suits for *negligence in relation to civil or criminal litigation. *See also* DESIGNATED CASE WORKER.

Advocate General An assistant to the judge of the *European Court of Justice whose function is to assist the court by presenting opinions upon every case brought before it. The Advocate General acts as an **amicus curiae* in putting forward arguments based upon his own view of the interests of the European Union, although it is not open to any of the parties to the legal action to submit observations on his opinion.

aetiology The study of the causes of behaviour, diseases, and events.

affidavit A sworn written statement used mainly to support certain applications and, in some circumstances, as evidence in court proceedings. The person who makes the affidavit must swear or *affirm that the contents are true before a person authorized to take oaths in respect of the particular kind of affidavit.

affinity The relationship created by marriage between a husband and his wife's blood relatives or between a wife and her husband's blood relatives. Some categories of people related by affinity are forbidden to marry each other (*see* PROHIBITED DEGREES OF RELATIONSHIPS). The relationship of blood relatives is known as *consanguinity. *See also* INCEST.

affirm 1. To confirm a legal decision, particularly (of an *appeal court) to confirm a judgment made in a lower court. **2.** To promise in solemn form to tell the truth while giving evidence or when making an *affidavit. Under the Oaths Act 1978, any person who objects to being sworn on *oath, or in respect of whom it is not reasonably practicable to administer an oath, may instead affirm. Affirmation has the same legal effects as the taking of an oath.

affray The offence, contrary to s 3 of the Public Order Act 1986, of intentionally using or threatening, other than by words alone, unlawful violence. The offending conduct must be such as would have caused a reasonable person to fear for his safety, though no such person need be present. The offence can be committed in private as well as in *public places. It is punishable on indictment with up to three years' imprisonment and/or a fine or, on summary conviction, by imprisonment for a term not exceeding six months or by a fine. *See also* ASSAULT; RIOT; VIOLENT DISORDER.

agent provocateur A person who actively entices, encourages, or persuades someone to commit a crime that would not otherwise have been committed for the purpose of securing his *conviction (*see* ENTRAPMENT). In such a case the agent provocateur will be regarded as an *accomplice in any offence that the accused commits as a result of this intervention.

age of consent The age at which a person can legally consent to sexual intercourse, or to an act that would otherwise constitute a *sexual offence. Under the Sexual Offences Act 2003, children under the age of 13 are not capable in law of giving consent to any form of sexual activity and any such conduct is treated as an offence of *strict liability. *See also* CHILD ABUSE; CONSENT.

age of criminal responsibility The age at which children are considered to have acquired sufficient maturity to take responsibility for their own criminal actions. In English law the age of criminal responsibility is 10 years. It is an irrebuttable presumption that a child under that age cannot commit a criminal offence. In *international law a defendant at the *International Criminal Court must have been at least 18 years of age at the time of the offence alleged.

aggravated assault *See* ASSAULT.

aggravated burglary *See* BURGLARY.

aggravated damages *Damages that are awarded when the conduct of the defendant or the surrounding circumstances increase the injury to the claimant by subjecting him to humiliation, distress, or embarrassment, particularly in such torts as *assault, *false imprisonment, and *defamation.

aggravated supply The offence of supplying drugs is aggravated for the purpose of sentencing where a person of the age of 18 years or over supplies drugs in the vicinity of a school or uses a courier under the age of 18 years. The Drugs Act 2005 inserted a new subsection into s 4 of the

Misuse of Drugs Act 1971, which affects sentencing but does not create an offence.

aggravated trespass *See* TRESPASS.

aggravated vehicle-taking The offence arises when a *mechanically propelled vehicle has been unlawfully taken, and between the time of it being taken and recovered it has been driven dangerously on a *road or other *public place; or owing to the driving of the vehicle an *accident resulting in injury to any person or to *property was caused; or *damage was caused to the vehicle (s 12A, Theft Act 1968, inserted by the Aggravated Vehicle Taking Act 1992). Any person who has taken the vehicle or has driven it or allowed themselves to be carried in it knowing it to have been taken without consent commits the offence.

aggression (in *international law) According to the General Assembly Resolution (3314) on the Definition of Aggression 1975, the use of armed force by one state against the *sovereignty, territorial integrity, or political independence of another state or in any way inconsistent with the Charter of the United Nations. The Resolution lists examples of aggression, which include the following: (1) invasion, attack, military occupation, or *annexation of the territory of any state by the armed forces of another state; (2) bombardment or the use of any weapons by a state against another state's territory; (3) armed *blockade by a state of another state's ports or coasts; (4) the use of a state's armed forces in another state in breach of the terms of the agreement on which they were allowed into that state; (5) allowing one's territory to be placed at the disposal of another state, to be used by that state for committing an act of aggression against a third state; (6) sending armed bands or guerrillas to carry out armed raids on another state that are grave enough to amount to any of the above acts.

The first use of armed force by a state in contravention of the UN Charter is prima facie evidence of aggression, although the final decision in such cases is left to the Security Council, who may also classify other acts as aggression. The Resolution declares that no consideration whatsoever can justify aggression, that territory cannot be acquired by acts of aggression, and that wars of aggression constitute a crime against international peace.

In drafting the Statute of the *International Criminal Court the states involved could not agree on a definition of aggression. As a compromise the Statute has created an offence of aggression but the ICC cannot enforce it until a definition is agreed.

See also HUMANITARIAN INTERVENTION; MARTENS CLAUSE; OCCUPATION; OFFENCES AGAINST INTERNATIONAL LAW AND ORDER; USE OF FORCE; WAR; WAR CRIMES.

agreement (in *international law) *See* TREATY.

agrément [French: assent] The formal diplomatic notification by a *state that the diplomatic agent selected to be sent to it by another state has been accepted, i.e. is *persona grata* and can consequently become accredited to it. The *agrément* is the reply to a query by the sending state, which precedes the sent diplomat's formal nomination and accreditation. This type of mutual exchange by two states over their diplomatic representation is called *agréation*. *See also* PERSONA NON GRATA.

agricultural motor vehicle A *motor vehicle which is constructed or adapted for use off roads for the purpose of agriculture, horticulture, or forestry and which is primarily used for one or more of those purposes, not being a dual-purpose vehicle (reg 3(2), Road Vehicles (Construction and Use) Regulations 1986 (SI 1986/1078)).

aid and abet To assist in the performance of a crime either before or during (but not after) its commission. Aiding usually refers to material assistance (e.g. providing the tools for the crime), and abetting to lesser assistance (e.g. acting as a lookout or driving a car to the scene of the crime). Aiders and abettors are liable to be tried as *accessories. Mere presence at the scene of a crime is not regarded as aiding and abetting. It is unnecessary to have a criminal motive to be *guilty of aiding and abetting: knowledge that one is assisting the criminal is sufficient. *See also* IMPEDING APPREHENSION OR PROSECUTION.

air-force law *See* SERVICE LAW.

Air Force Prosecuting Authority *See* ROYAL AIR FORCE PROSECUTING AUTHORITY.

airspace The portion of the atmosphere above a particular *land area. In English law and *international law, the ownership of land includes ownership of the airspace above it, by application of the maxim *cujus est solum ejus est usque ad coelum* [Latin: whose is the soil, his it is even to heaven]; outer space, however, is not considered to be subject to ownership. Civil aircraft flying at a reasonable height over land do not commit *trespass, but *damages can be obtained if material loss or damage is caused to people or property.

(In *international law) National airspace, including airspace above the *internal waters and the *territorial waters, is under complete and exclusive sovereignty of the subjacent state. As a result, apart from aircraft in distress, any use of national airspace by non-national aircraft requires the official consent of the state concerned. This can be granted unilaterally or more commonly (in respect of commercial flights) through a bilateral treaty, usually on conditions of reciprocity.

air weapon Defined by the Firearms Act 1968, s 1(3)(b) as being 'an air rifle, airgun or air pistol'; extended by the Firearms (Amendment) Act 1997 to include weapons powered by compressed carbon dioxide.

alcohol Spirits, wine, beer, cider, or any other fermented, distilled or spirituous liquor, but not including: (a) alcohol which is of a strength not exceeding 0.5 per cent at the time of the sale or supply in question; (b) perfume; (c) flavouring essences recognized by the Commissioners for *Her Majesty's Revenue and Customs as not being intended for consumption as or with dutiable alcoholic liquor; (d) the aromatic flavouring essence commonly known as Angostura bitters; (e) alcohol which is, or is included in, a medicinal product; (f) denatured alcohol; (g) methyl alcohol; (h) naphtha; or (i) alcohol contained in liqueur confectionery (s 191, Licensing Act 2003). Under the Act, the retail sale of alcohol or its supply by or on behalf of a club, or to the order of a club member, are *licensable activities.

alcohol treatment requirement Where a court is satisfied that an offender is dependent on *alcohol and that his dependency may be susceptible to treatment, as part of a *community order or *suspended sentence order it may impose a requirement that he receive a period of treatment, of not less than six months, to reduce or eliminate his dependency on alcohol. The requirement may not be imposed unless the offender agrees to comply with the requirement (s 212, Criminal Justice Act 2003, replacing a similar provision in the Powers of Criminal Court (Sentencing) Act 2000).

alibi [from Latin: elsewhere] A *defence to a criminal charge alleging that the defendant was not at the place at which the crime was committed and so could not have been responsible for it. If the defendant claims to have been at a particular place at the time of the crime, evidence in support of an alibi may only be given if the defendant has supplied particulars of it to the prosecution not later than seven days after committal, unless the Crown Court considers that there was a valid reason for not supplying them.

alien A person who, under the law of a particular state, is not a citizen of that state. Aliens are usually classified as **resident aliens** (domiciled in the host country) or **transient aliens** (temporarily in the host country on business, study, etc.). They are normally subject to certain civil disabilities, such as being ineligible to vote. For the purposes of UK statute law an alien is defined by the British Nationality Act 1981 (in force from 1 January 1983) as a person who is neither a *Commonwealth citizen, nor a *British protected person, nor a citizen of the Republic of Ireland. At common law, a distinction is drawn between friendly and **enemy aliens**. The latter comprise not only citizens of hostile states but also all others voluntarily living in enemy territory or carrying on business there; they are subject to additional disabilities. *See also* ALLEGIANCE; DUE DILIGENCE.

a

allegation Any statement of fact in a statement of case, *affidavit, or *indictment. It is the duty of the party who makes an allegation to adduce evidence in support of it at *trial, under the principle of 'he who asserts must prove'.

allegiance The duty of obedience owed to a head of state in return for his protection. It is due from all citizens of that state and its dependencies and also from any *alien present in the state (including enemy aliens under licence; e.g. internees). A person who is declared by the British Nationality Act 1981 not to be an alien but who has a primary citizenship conferred by a state other than the UK is probably governed by the same principles as aliens so far as allegiance is concerned.

alleygating A crime reduction method consisting of installing gates at the ends of alleyways behind houses to restrict access. *See* DEFENSIBLE SPACE.

allocation of trial venue *See* MODE OF TRIAL.

alternative dispute resolution (ADR) Any of a variety of techniques for resolving civil disputes without the need for conventional litigation. It may include a **mini-trial** (a shortened and simplified form of court hearing), informal methods of *arbitration, and structured forms of conciliation using a specially trained mediator acting as a go-between.

alternative verdict A *verdict of *not guilty of the offence actually charged but *guilty of some lesser offence not specifically charged. Such a verdict is only permitted when there is insufficient evidence to establish the more serious offence but the evidence given is sufficient to prove the lesser offence. If, for example, in a *murder case there is evidence that the defendant lacked *malice aforethought, an alternative verdict of *manslaughter may be returned.

amendment 1. Changes made to *legislation, for the purpose of adding to, correcting, or modifying the operation of the legislation. **2.** An alteration of a *treaty adopted by the consent of the *high contracting parties and intended to be binding upon all such parties. An amendment may involve either individual provisions or a complete review of the treaty.

amicus curiae [Latin: friend of the court] *Counsel who assists the court by putting arguments in support of an interest that might not be adequately represented by the parties to the proceedings (such as the public interest) or by arguing on behalf of a party who is otherwise unrepresented. *See also* SPECIAL ADVOCATE.

ammunition A generic term for the assembly of the *bullet or *projectile, the *propellant, the *igniter or *primer, and the *cartridge case. Section 57(2) of the Firearms Act 1968 provides that 'ammunition' means ammunition for any *firearm and includes grenades, bombs, and other like missiles, whether capable of use with a firearm or not, and also includes prohibited ammunition (defined by s 5(2)). Subject to certain exemptions, it is an offence contrary to s 1(1)(b) of the 1968 Act to possess, purchase, or acquire, any ammunition (other than (a) cartridges containing five or more shot, none of which exceeds 0.36 inch in diameter; (b) ammunition for an air gun, air rifle, or air pistol; and (c) blank cartridges not more than one inch in diameter) without holding a firearm certificate in force at the time, or otherwise than as authorized by such a certificate, or in quantities in excess of those so authorized.

amnesty An act erasing from legal memory some aspect of criminal conduct by an offender. It is most frequently granted to groups of people in respect of political offences and is wider than a *pardon, which merely relieves an offender of *punishment. *International law often places a duty on states to prosecute international crimes. Thus an amnesty in these circumstances is not permissible under customary international law and would not prevent prosecution in a third state.

Amsterdam Treaty The EU treaty signed in Amsterdam in 1997 (in force from 1 May 1999), which amended provisions of the *Treaty of Rome (European Community Treaty) and the *Maastricht Treaty (Treaty on European Union). Among other effects, the Amsterdam Treaty increased the powers of the *European Parliament by extending the co-decision procedure to all areas covered by qualified majority voting and enabled the Social Chapter to be incorporated into the Treaty of Rome.

anarchy The absence of government. Anarchist criminologists believe in social order without a state to control it, order being maintained by voluntary association and self-regulation. Anarchist *terrorists are opposed to all forms of government.

angary The right of belligerent states to make use of (or destroy if necessary) neutral property on their own or on enemy territory or on the open sea, for the purpose of offence and defence. Traditionally, the right (*jus angariae*) was restricted to the belligerent laying of an *embargo on and seizing neutral merchant ships in its harbours and compelling them and their crews to transport troops, ammunition, and provisions to certain places on payment of freight in advance. However, all sorts of neutral property, including vessels or other means of transport, arms, ammunition, provisions, or other personal property, may be the object of the modern right of angary, provided the articles concerned are serviceable to military ends and wants.

animal *See* CLASSIFICATION OF ANIMALS.

animal cruelty The offence, under the Protection of Animals Acts 1911–2000, of causing any unnecessary suffering to any domestic or captive animal, including farm animals. Other statutes which serve to criminalize the ill-treatment of animals include: the Performing Animals (Regulation) Act 1925, the Pet Animals Act 1951, the Cock Fighting Act 1952, the Abandonment of Animals Act 1960, and the Protection Against Cruel Tethering Act 1988. *See also* BESTIALITY; DISQUALIFICATION FROM KEEPING ANIMALS.

animal rights activist A member of a worldwide movement of individual activists, academics, and groups who campaign or engage in direct action against the use of non-human animals in animal testing, the meat, dairy, and fur farming industries, and in entertainment and sports. The more militant groups (e.g. the 'Animal Liberation Front') carry out raids to release animals from laboratories and farms and engage in the destruction of property and intimidation of people connected with those facilities.

animus [Latin: spirit] (in legal contexts) Intention, as in combinations such as: *animus furandi*—the intention to steal; *animus manendi*—the intention to remain in one place (for the purposes of the law relating to *domicile).

annexation (in *international law) The acquisition of legal *sovereignty by one state over the territory of another, usually by *occupation or conquest. Annexation is now generally considered illegal in *international law, even when it results from a legitimate use of force (e.g. in self-defence). It may subsequently become legal, however, by means of recognition by other states. The annexing state is not bound by pre-existing obligations of the state annexed.

annuity A sum of money payable annually for as long as the beneficiary (**annuitant**) lives, or for some other specified period (e.g. the life of another person (*pur autre vie*) or the minority of the annuitant). An annuity left by will is treated as a pecuniary legacy. An annuity may be charged on, or directed to be paid out of, a particular fund or it may be unsecured. A **joint annuity**, in which money is payable to more than one annuitant, terminates on the death of the last survivor. Dishonestly obtaining an annuity or better terms by deception is a criminal offence under the Theft Act 1968.

anomie (anomy) The state of a person or group of people who lack any ethical or social guidance to regulate their behaviour. Lawlessness.

anonymity The condition in which an individual's true identity is unpublished. The general rule protecting the anonymity of complainants of a *rape offence was established by s 4(1) of the Sexual Offences (Amendment) Act 1976. It provides that once an allegation of a 'rape offence' has been made, neither the complainant's name nor their address nor a still or moving picture of them may be published or

a

broadcast. The definition of a 'rape offence' was amended by the Sexual Offences Act 2003 to encompass all of the offences of *penetration created by that Act. Complainants of other *sexual offences are similarly protected by s 1 of the Sexual Offences Amendment Act 1992. The provisions of the Youth Justice Act 1999 which unify the two regimes by extending the 1992 Act to cover 'rape offences' have not yet been brought into force. Defendants in sex cases are not afforded the benefit of anonymity. *See also* REPORTING RESTRICTIONS.

antecedents An accused or convicted person's previous *convictions or history of bad *character. Formerly, such evidence was admissible only after *conviction for the purpose of determining *sentence, but under the Criminal Justice Act 2003, evidence of the defendant's bad character may be admitted under certain conditions for the purpose of determining guilt. *See also* CONVICTION, EVIDENCE OF.

anti-abortion group An organization opposed to *abortion, often on religious grounds. Some anti-abortion groups commit acts of *terrorism against abortion providers and supporters of the 'pro-choice' movement.

anti-globalization terrorism *Terrorist groups who oppose the increasing integration of the world into a single free market on the basis that it is contrary to individual and national interests. They target multinational corporations, international financial organisations, and US interests.

Anti-Social Behaviour Order (ASBO) An order imposed by the court where it is necessary to protect people in the area from the consequences of the defendant's behaviour or future anti-social behaviour. Section 2 of the Crime and Disorder Act 1998 defines anti-social behaviour as that which causes or is likely to cause *harassment, alarm or distress to one or more people who are not in the same household as the perpetrator. Powers to impose the orders were introduced by s 1 of the 1998 Act and were strengthened and extended by the Police Reform Act 2002, which introduced orders made on conviction in criminal proceedings, orders in county court proceedings and interim orders, and the Anti-Social Behaviour Act 2003. An order may be on complaint from a *local authority or chief officer of police for the area or where an offender is convicted of a relevant offence. It may be made against any person who has attained the age of 10 years and is effective for a minimum of two years. The restrictions that can be made are very wide and are defined only as 'those necessary to protect persons...from further anti-social acts by him' and typically contain conditions prohibiting certain specific anti-social acts or entry into defined areas. Breach of an ASBO is a criminal offence. *See also* ACCEPTABLE BEHAVIOUR CONTRACT.

Anton Piller order *See* SEARCH ORDER.

anus The terminal portion of the intestine. Sexual intercourse without *consent where there is penetration of the anus amounts to *rape.

aorta The main artery of the body running from the heart and down the body next to the spine.

apnoea The state of not breathing. Breathing may stop as a result of illness or traumas including poisoning, drowning, or electrocution. Apnoea stops the supply of oxygenated blood to the organs, especially the brain. If breathing is not restored within a few minutes permanent brain damage will result and eventually death. Prompt intervention with artificial respiration using techniques such as mouth-to-mouth resuscitation may restore breathing and save life.

a posteriori [Latin: from the later (i.e. from effect to cause)] Describing or relating to reasoning based on deductions from observation or known facts, i.e. inductive reasoning. *Compare* A PRIORI.

appeal An application for the judicial examination by a higher tribunal of the decision of any lower tribunal. In modern English practice most appeals are dealt with by way of *rehearing, in which the appellate tribunal notionally rehears the case tried before the lower tribunal, usually using a transcript or note of the evidence before the lower tribunal instead of hearing the witnesses in person. It may in general make any order that the lower tribunal could have made, but there are some statutory restrictions upon this power; e.g. in criminal cases the *Court of Appeal may not impose a more severe sentence than the *trial court. Appellate tribunals are usually reluctant to overrule the decisions of lower tribunals on questions of fact even when they have the power to do so, and consequently most of the argument on appeals tends to be directed towards legal errors allegedly committed at the trial. In some cases (e.g. appeals by *case stated from magistrates' courts) the appeal may by law be confined to questions of law. Appeal may be contrasted with **review**, in which the higher tribunal is confined to an examination of the *record of the lower tribunal's proceedings. *See also* APPELLATE JURISDICTION.

appellant A person who makes an *appeal to a court that has the jurisdiction to hear appeals, such as the *Court of Appeal.

Appellate Committee *See* HOUSE OF LORDS.

appellate jurisdiction The power of a *judge to hear *appeals from a previous court decision. Appellate jurisdiction in the *criminal courts is determined by the nature of the criminal offence in question. Criminal appeals following *summary conviction are to the *Crown Court for *committals for sentencing and for appeals by the defendant against *conviction and/or *sentence. Appeals from *magistrates' courts are to the *High Court or Divisional Court of the *Queen's Bench Division if an appeal by the *prosecution or *defence is by way of *case stated on a point of law. Appeals from the Crown Court can be by the prosecution or defence by way of *case stated but only if the Crown Court had previously heard the appeal from the magistrates' court. Higher appeals are restricted to those from the High Court or Divisional Court of the Queen's Bench Division by either the prosecution or the defence on a point of law of general public importance and only with permission. Criminal appeals from *trials on indictment are to the Court of Appeal (Criminal Division) by the defendant against conviction and/or sentence. The prosecution can apply to the Court of Appeal for an *acquittal to be quashed where the offence on the indictment was a serious offence and there is new and compelling evidence that the defendant committed the offence. References to the Court of Appeal (Criminal Division) may also be made (1) by the *Attorney-General due to an unduly light sentence, (2) by the Attorney-General on a point of law following acquittal (although the earlier acquittal will not be affected), or (3) by the *Home Secretary for consideration following conviction. A further appeal to the *House of Lords is only available to the defence or prosecution on a point of law of general public importance and with permission.

The House of Lords determines appeals primarily from the Court of Appeal but can hear appeals from the High Court under the *leapfrog procedure (House of Lords).

applying the proviso *See* PROVISO.

appointed day The date specified in an *Act of Parliament (or in a commencement order) for its coming into force.

appropriation *See* THEFT.

approximation of laws The process by which member states of the *European Union change their national laws to enable the free market to function properly. It is required by the *Treaty of Rome. *Compare* HARMONIZATION OF LAWS.

a priori [Latin: from the previous (i.e. from cause to effect)] Describing or relating to reasoning that is based on abstract ideas, anticipates the effects of particular causes, or (more loosely) makes a presumption that is true as far as is known, i.e. deductive reasoning. *Compare* A POSTERIORI.

arachnoid One of the layers of the *meninges—the membrane covering of the brain.

arbitrage A form of financial trading in which dealers buy and sell currency or securities to make a profit from the

a

differences in exchange rates and security prices at different markets or times.

arbitrary punishment *See* PUNISHMENT.

archive An area of a *computer drive that is used to store files (often in a compressed format) that are not used often or files that may be downloaded from a file library by Internet users.

Area Child Protection Committee A committee that advises and reviews local practice and procedure for inter-agency cooperation and training with regard to children in need of protection by *local authorities. It is made up of representatives from the various professions and agencies concerned with children.

armed conflict A resort to armed force between states or protracted armed violence between governmental authorities and organized armed groups or between groups within a state.

armed forces, jurisdiction over visiting forces *Jurisdiction over armed forces of foreign countries visiting the UK. It is regulated by the NATO status of forces agreement. Where the act is an offence under the law of both the sending and host states, jurisdiction will belong to the sending state where the offence is solely against the property or personnel of the sending state or in the execution of official duty, otherwise jurisdiction will belong to the host state. Jurisdiction can be waived in any case.

Army Prosecuting Authority (APA) A body which provides advice to *service police on the investigation and prosecutions of offences and determines whether there is sufficient evidence for the case to proceed and if it is in the public interest to proceed. It will then decide whether there should be a district court martial (a *Judge Advocate and three military members with a sentencing limit of two years' imprisonment) or a General *Court Martial (a Judge Advocate and five members but with no sentencing limits save that imposed by statute). The APA was established under the Armed Forces Act 1996 and came into existence on 1 April 1997. It acts independently of the military chain of command and is subject to the general superintendence of the *Attorney-General. The Armed Forces Act 2006 will see the establishment of a joint-service prosecuting authority that will combine the APA, the *Royal Air Force Prosecuting Authority, and the *Naval Prosecuting Authority. *See also* SERVICE LAW.

arraign To begin a criminal *trial on indictment by calling the defendant to the bar of the court by name, reading the indictment to him, and asking him whether he is *guilty or not. The defendant then pleads to the indictment, and this completes the arraignment.

array *See* CHALLENGE TO JURY.

arrest The *detention and restraint of a person under lawful authority. Arrest may be made under the authority of a *warrant issued by a *magistrate or *judge. Summary arrest without a warrant is permissible under certain circumstances at *common law or under the Police and Criminal Evidence Act 1984 (PACE). At common law any person may arrest any person who is committing a *breach of the peace or where a breach of the peace is apprehended or where there has been a breach of the peace and there is fear that it will be renewed. Under s 24 PACE (as substituted by the Serious Organized Crime and Police Act 2005) a *constable may arrest any person he suspects is, has, or is about to commit an offence provided that certain conditions are fulfilled. These are that the constable has reasonable grounds for believing that that arrest is necessary: to ascertain his name and address; to prevent the person in question causing or suffering harm to himself or another or causing loss or damage to property; to prevent him obstructing the *highway or committing an offence against public decency (where people about their normal business cannot avoid him); to protect a child or vulnerable person from him; to allow the prompt and effective investigation of the offence or of the conduct of the person in question; or to prevent the prosecution of the offence from being hindered by the disappearance of the person in question. A person other than a constable may arrest anyone whom he has reasonable grounds for suspecting is or has committed an *indictable offence. The power can be exercised only where it is not reasonably practicable for a constable to make the arrest and it is necessary to prevent the person in question: causing or suffering physical injury to himself or another; causing loss or damage to property; or making off before a constable can assume responsibility for him.

When an arrest is made, the accused must be told that he is being arrested and given the ground for his arrest. A constable has power to search the person he is arresting for any property that may be used in evidence against him. Anyone making or assisting in an arrest may use as much force as reasonable in the circumstances. *Resisting lawful arrest may involve the crime of *assault or *obstructing a police officer. A person who believes he has been wrongfully arrested may petition for *habeas corpus and may sue the person who arrested him for *false imprisonment. *See also* BAIL; CAUTION; CITIZEN'S ARREST; DETENTION; REMAND.

arrestable offence At one time a category of offence for which specific powers of *arrest existed. Arrestable, non-arrestable, and serious arrestable offences were abolished by the Serious Organized Crime and Police Act 2005.

arrested development For the purposes of the Mental Health Act 1983, a form of *mental disorder comprising mental impairment and severe mental impairment. **Mental impairment** implies a lack of intelligence that does not amount to severe mental impairment but that nevertheless requires or will respond to medical treatment. **Severe mental impairment** is a lack of intelligence and social functioning associated with aggressive or severely irresponsible conduct.

arrest of judgment A motion by a defendant in criminal proceedings on *indictment, between the *conviction and the *sentence, that *judgment should not be given on the ground of some objection arising on the face of the *record, such as a defect in the indictment itself. Such motions are extremely rare in modern practice.

arson The *intentional or *reckless destruction or damaging of property by fire without a lawful excuse. There are two forms of arson corresponding to the two forms of *criminal damage in the Criminal Damage Act 1971. Arson carries a maximum *sentence of life imprisonment.

article A clause in a *document. The plural, **articles**, is often used to mean the entire document, e.g. *articles of association.

Article 234 reference A provision of the *Treaty of Rome entitling national courts to refer matters of EU law to the *European Court of Justice for a determination. The case ultimately returns to the national court for a final judgment. Such a procedure is known as a '234 reference'. Article 234 (formerly 177) is a provision of the Treaty that empowers the ECJ to decide such issues as how the Treaty of Rome should be interpreted and whether or not the *European Commission or other bodies have acted properly.

articles of association Regulations for the management of *registered companies. They form, together with the provisions of the *memorandum of association, the company's constitution.

articulated bus A bus so constructed that (a) it can be divided into two parts, both of which are vehicles and one of which is a *motor vehicle, but cannot be so divided without the use of facilities normally available only at a workshop; and (b) passengers carried by it can at all times pass from either part to the other (reg 3(2), Road Vehicles (Construction and Use) Regulations 1986 (SI 1986/1078)).

articulated vehicle A heavy motor car or motor car, not being an *articulated bus, with a trailer so attached that part of the trailer is superimposed on the drawing vehicle and, when the trailer is uniformly loaded, not less than 20 per cent of the weight of its load is borne by the drawing vehicle (reg 3(2), Road Vehicles (Construction and Use) Regulations 1986 (SI 1986/1078)).

asphyxia The lack of oxygen to cells of the body generally caused by obstruction of airways, e.g. by strangulation or misplaced food that has gone into the windpipe (trachea).

asphyxiation The act of inducing *asphyxia.

aspiration The introduction of foreign material, such as vomit, into an airway.

assault An *intentional or *reckless act that causes someone to be put in fear of immediate physical harm. Actual physical contact is not necessary to constitute an assault (e.g. pointing a firearm at someone is an assault), but the word is often loosely used to include both threatening acts and physical violence (*see* BATTERY). Assault is a form of *trespass to the person and a crime as well as a *tort: an **ordinary** (or **common**) **assault**, as described above, is a *summary offence punishable by a *fine at level 5 on the standard scale and/or up to six months' imprisonment. There are a number of statutory offences which deal with assaults on particular categories of public servant. These include assaults on:

- a *constable (which includes a prison officer: s 8, Prisons Act 1952): s 89, Police Act 1996;
- a *Community Support Officer: s 46, Police Reform Act 2002;
- an officer of *Her Majesty's Revenue and Customs: s 32, Commissioner for Revenue and Customs Act 2005;
- designated staff of the *Serious Organized Crime Agency: s 51, Serious Organized Crime and Police Act 2005;
- a member of an international *joint investigation team: s 57, Serious Organized Crime and Police Act 2005;
- a traffic officer: s 10, Traffic Management Act 2004;
- a *court security officer: s 57, Courts Act 2003.

Certain kinds of more serious assault are known as **aggravated assaults** and carry stricter penalties. Examples of these are assault with intent to *resist lawful arrest (s 38, Offences Against the Person Act 1861: two years' imprisonment), assault occasioning *actual bodily harm (s 37, Offences Against the Person Act 1861: five years' imprisonment), and assault with intent to rob (s 8, Theft Act 1968: life imprisonment). *See also* AFFRAY; SEXUAL ASSAULT.

assault by penetration An offence under s 2 of the Sexual Offences Act 2003, the essence of which is the intentional *penetration of the *vagina or *anus of another person, who does not *consent to it and whom the accused does not reasonably believe consents to it. The penetration may be with a part of the offender's body, e.g. a finger, or a fist, or with anything else, e.g. a dildo or a sharp object. Unlike *rape, it can be committed by a male or female. The section is intended for use in the unusual situation when it is not possible to prove penile penetration, e.g. where a victim is drugged or blindfolded. Under the old law it was encompassed by the offence of *indecent assault. The offence is triable only on *indictment and carries a maximum *sentence of life imprisonment.

assault rifle A military *firearm that is chambered for ammunition of reduced size or propellant charge and has the capacity to switch between *semi-automatic and fully automatic fire. It is characterized by having a *pistol grip to enable the weapon to be more easily controlled when in fully automatic mode or when firing other than from the shoulder. Perhaps the best known examples are the Kalashnikov AK 47 and the Colt M16 ('Armalite') *See also* AUTOMATIC WEAPON; RIFLE.

assets Physical *property and/or *rights that have a monetary value and are capable of being those of a *juristic person or a natural person (i.e. a human being). They can comprise real assets (*real property) and personal assets (*personal property). In respect of a juristic person, such as a corporation, assets include fixed or capital assets (those identified as being held and used on a continuing basis in the business activity, e.g. machinery) and current or circulating assets (those not intended to be used on a continuing basis in the business activity but realized in the course of trading).

Assets Recovery Agency (ARA) A Non-Ministerial Department that reports to the *Home Secretary but is operationally independent. The Agency was set up by the Proceeds of Crime Act 2002 on 24 February 2003.

The Agency has three strategic aims: to disrupt organized criminal enterprises through the recovery of criminal *assets, thereby alleviating the effects of crime on communities; to promote the use of financial investigation as an integral part of criminal investigation, within and outside the Agency, domestically and internationally, through training and continuing professional development; and to operate the Agency in accordance with its vision and values.

Assets Recovery Strategy A cross-government plan which aims, among other things, to make greater use of the investigation of criminal *assets in the fight against crime, and to recover money that has been made from crime or which is intended for use in crime. It impacts on all parts of the *criminal justice system, including law enforcement agencies, prosecution authorities and government departments.

assize 1. An assize court or council. In modern times assizes were sittings of *High Court judges travelling on *circuits around the country with commissions from the *Crown to hear cases. These commissions were either of oyer, terminer, and general gaol delivery, empowering the judges to try the most serious criminal cases, or of *nisi prius*, empowering them to try civil actions. These assizes were abolished by the Courts Act 1971, and the criminal jurisdiction of assizes was transferred to the Crown Court. At the same time, the High Court was empowered to hear civil cases anywhere in England and Wales without the need for a special commission. **2.** A statute or *ordinance, e.g. the Assize of Clarendon, Novel Disseisin.

Association of Chief Police Officers (ACPO) A private company limited by guarantee and funded by a combination of a Home Office grant, contributions from each of the 44 *police authorities, membership subscriptions, and by the proceeds of its annual exhibition. Its members are *police officers who hold the rank of Commander, Deputy Assistant Commissioner, Assistant Commissioner, and Commissioner in London, and Chief Constable, Deputy Chief Constable, or Assistant Chief Constable, in provincial forces of England, Wales and Northern Ireland, national police agencies and certain other forces in the UK, the Isle of Man and the Channel Islands, and certain senior non-police staff. There are presently 280 members of ACPO.

ACPO was set up to undertake works in developing policing policies centrally, on behalf of the Service as a whole, rather than in 44 forces separately. ACPO aims to:

- assist chief officers to provide excellence in the leadership of the Service;
- ensure a professional and ethical service is delivered to all communities; and
- provide professional advice to Government, police authorities, and other appropriate organizations and individuals.

ACPO works towards these aims by trying to ensure that:

- appropriate policy standards are set and maintained;
- police staff are trained to these standards;
- police staff are properly equipped;
- the service case for adequate resources and staff rewards is formulated and promoted;
- good policing practice is identified, evaluated, disseminated, and built upon;
- regular dialogue takes place between the Association and its tripartite partners, representatives of communities, and relevant professional organizations;
- the Service's views are communicated to relevant audiences in order to inform and influence;
- operational policing activity is properly coordinated when events involve several *police forces and require a common approach.

ACPO liaises with Government and the *Cabinet Office in the face of civil emergencies and *terrorist activities.

Association of Police Authorities (APA) A body set up in 1997 to represent police authorities in England, Wales, and Northern Ireland, nationally and locally. It influences policy on policing and it supports local police authorities by providing training, publications, and research.

a

assumption Something that is believed to be true without proof. Under the provisions of the Proceeds of Crime Act 2002, if the court finds that the defendant has a '*criminal lifestyle' it must make four assumptions: first that any property transferred to him at any time after the relevant day was obtained by him as a result of his general criminal conduct and at the earliest time he appears to have held it; secondly, that any property held by him at any time after the date of conviction was obtained by him as a result of his general criminal conduct and at the earliest time he appears to have held it; thirdly, that any expenditure incurred by him at any time after the relevant day was met from property obtained as a result of his general criminal conduct; and, fourthly, that for the purpose of valuing any property obtained by him, he obtained it free of any other interests in it. *See also* CONFISCATION.

assurance *See* INSURANCE.

assured shorthold tenancy A special kind of *assured tenancy at the end of which the *landlord is entitled to recover *possession without having to show one of the usual grounds for possession of an assured tenancy. This kind of tenancy was introduced by the Housing Act 1988, replacing **protected shorthold tenancies**. Under the 1988 Act the landlord was obliged to give the tenant notice before the grant of the tenancy that it was an assured shorthold tenancy. However, under the Housing Act 1996, from 28 February 1997 the requirement for the landlord to serve a notice is removed, and all new tenancies are automatically assured shortholds unless otherwise agreed. If a landlord wants to give the tenant security under an assured tenancy, this must be specifically created; if this is not done, the tenancy is an assured shorthold without security of tenure. A tenant can apply to a rent assessment committee if he thinks the rent of the tenancy is excessive. The committee can fix a new rent if they think that the rent is significantly higher than that of other assured tenancies in the area. However, government regulations may restrict this right in certain areas or in certain circumstances.

The landlord may obtain possession at any time when he would have been entitled to do so contractually, by giving two months' notice and specifying that the tenancy is an assured shorthold tenancy. No order for possession may be made in the first six months of the tenancy.

assured tenancy A form of *tenancy under the Housing Act 1988 that is at a market rent but gives security of tenure. The *premises may be furnished or unfurnished. This kind of tenancy replaces *protected tenancies except those in existence before the Housing Act 1988 came into force. Former assured tenancies under the Housing Act 1980 (where different provisions applied) are converted into the new kind of assured tenancy.

To qualify as an assured tenancy, the premises must be let as a separate dwelling, within certain rateable value limits. There are certain exceptions, such as when the landlord lives in another part of the same premises. Under the Housing Act 1996, from 28 February 1997 all new residential tenancies are *assured shorthold tenancies without security of tenure, unless a notice is specifically served stating that the parties are creating an assured tenancy.

The rent is an open market rent agreed between the landlord and tenant, and it is not registered. However, the landlord must give the tenant notice if he intends to increase the rent, and the tenant can then apply to a rent assessment committee if he thinks the increase is excessive. The rent assessment committee determines the rent at the current market value. There are limits on the frequency of rent increases.

The landlord can only regain possession on certain statutory grounds. These include: non-payment of rent; that the landlord formerly lived in the dwelling and requires it again for his own use; that the tenant is a *nuisance neighbour or may become a nuisance; and that alternative accommodation is available (the court has discretion in this last case).

When the tenant of an assured tenancy dies, his spouse has a right, in certain circumstances, to take over the tenancy as successor to the deceased tenant. An assured tenant cannot usually assign the tenancy without the landlord's consent.

asthma A complaint in which air passages are constricted and contain thick mucus which makes breathing difficult. Sufferers usually carry inhalers of such drugs as 'Ventalin'. Urgent medical attention should be called to anyone suffering from asthma and who is having difficulty breathing. Sufferers are very badly affected by narcotic drugs.

asylum Refuge granted by a state, at its discretion, to a person from another state. There is no 'right' to asylum. It is an old concept and is much wider than refugee status to which the term is frequently misapplied. A person seeking asylum does not have to be in fear of persecution. A person seeking to enter another country for fear of persecution is a refugee and not an asylum seeker. Their status is defined in the Geneva Convention relating to the Status of Refugees 1951. This can include refuge in the territory of a foreign country (**territorial asylum**) or in a foreign embassy (**diplomatic asylum**). The latter is particularly contentious as it is a derogation from the sovereignty of the territorial state; moreover, diplomatic asylum may only be granted in cases of an alleged political offence and not in cases involving common-law crimes. Diplomatic asylum is well recognized in Latin American states. Conventions relating to it include the Havana Convention of 1928, the Montevideo Convention of 1933, and the Caracas Convention of 1954. The Nationality, Immigration and Asylum Act 2002 introduced a new asylum system, based on a network of induction, accommodation, and reporting centres as well as existing National Asylum Support Service accommodation and providing for reporting and residence requirements to be imposed on all asylum seekers. It allows for the discontinuation of support to asylum seekers who fail without reasonable cause to report as required and contains provisions making certain categories of person ineligible for support unless provision is made in regulations to the contrary (e.g. those who have refugee status in another EU member state and persons unlawfully in the UK); and additionally prohibits, subject to certain exceptions, the provision of support to asylum seekers who fail to make their asylum claim as soon as reasonably practicable after their arrival in the UK. The 2002 Act also contains a number of measures designed to simplify the process of removing those who have no right to stay in the UK. Section 15 of the Immigration, Asylum and Nationality Act 2006 imposes civil penalties in the form of fines on *employers of adults (i.e. persons over the age of 16) who have no leave to enter or remain in the UK; or whose leave is invalid, has expired, or prevents them from accepting employment. However, by s 21, if the employer knowingly employs an adult in those circumstances, he commits an offence which is punishable on *indictment to imprisonment for a term not exceeding two years or on *summary conviction for a term not exceeding twelve months. Sections 27 to 31 of the Act increase the powers of immigration, *Her Majesty's Revenue and Customs, and *police officers to obtain information, including fingerprints and other biometric information, and to search passengers arriving in the UK. *See also* IMMIGRATION; POLITICAL ASYLUM.

atheroma A fatty deposit on walls of arteries. When it occurs in the blood vessel of the heart it is often the cause of *myocardial infarction (heart attack).

atlas The top bone of the spine immediately below the skull.

attachment A court order for the *detention of a person and/or his *property. Attachment can be used by the courts for the *punishment of *contempt of court. However, the most common form of attachment is **attachment of earnings**, by which a court orders the payment of judgment debts and other sums due under court orders (e.g. maintenance) by direct deduction from the *debtor's earnings. Payment is usually in instalments, and the debtor's *employer is responsible for paying these to the court. *See also* GARNISHEE PROCEEDINGS.

a

attack on aid mission It is a *war crime under the Statute of the *International Criminal Court to attack personnel, installations, materials, units, or vehicles involved in humanitarian assistance or peacekeeping. A separate subsection in the Statute provides identical offences for international and non-international armed conflict.

attack on civilian object It is an offence against the Statute of the *International Criminal Court intentionally to attack civilian objects, in the context of international armed conflict. The offence will not be committed where the object has a military as well as a civil use, e.g. bridges and power stations.

attack on civilian population In the context of international and non-international armed conflict it is a *war crime under the Statute of the *International Criminal Court intentionally to attack civilian populations and individuals not involved in conflict. The *mens rea* of the offence requires proof that the perpetrator acted with the purpose of attacking civilians. *Collateral damage must be considered. If the collateral damage is excessive then the offence may be complete: if it is not excessive the offence is not made out.

attack on person and object bearing protective emblems *See* PROTECTIVE EMBLEMS.

attack on specially protected object In the context of international and non-international armed conflict, it is a *war crime under the Statute of the *International Criminal Court to attack specially protected civilian objects. These include buildings dedicated to religion, education, art, science or charitable purposes, historic monuments, hospitals, and places where the sick and wounded are collected. The protection does not apply if the object is used for a military purpose.

attempt (in criminal law) Any act that is more than merely preparatory to the intended commission of a crime; this act is itself a crime. For example, shooting at someone but missing could amount to attempted *murder, but merely buying a *revolver would not. One may be *guilty of attempting to commit a crime that proves impossible to commit (e.g. attempted theft from an empty handbag).

attendance centre order A *community sentence which may be imposed by the court under s 60 of the Powers of Criminal Courts (Sentencing) Act 2000, in cases where a person aged under 16 (reduced from 21 by the Criminal Justice Act 2003) has been convicted of an offence punishable with imprisonment. It involves attendance at a centre run by the police or the *Youth Offending Team, for two or three hours on a Saturday. The aggregate number of hours for which an offender can be ordered to attend may not be less than 12 (except in the case of a young person under the age of 14) or more than 24.

The order is only available in respect of an offence committed by an adult before 4 April 2005 (4 April 2007 in respect of a person aged 16 or 17). Offences committed by those aged 16 or over after those dates fall to be dealt with under the *community order provisions introduced by pt 12 of the Criminal Justice Act 2003.

attendance centre requirement A requirement that may be imposed by the court as part of a *community order, *custody plus order, *suspended sentence order, or an *intermittent custody order on offenders aged between 16 and 24. The requirement may be imposed for an offence which is not punishable by imprisonment. The regime typically involves discipline, physical training, and training in social skills. An Attendance Centre Requirement can be specified for between 12 and 36 hours with a maximum of three hours per attendance and one attendance per day (s 214, Criminal Justice Act 2003, amending s 60, Powers of Criminal Courts (Sentencing) Act 2000).

attorney A person who is appointed by another and has authority to act on behalf of another. *See also* POWER OF ATTORNEY.

Attorney-General (A-G) The principal law officer of the *Crown. The Attorney-General is usually a Member of Parliament to the ruling party and holds ministerial office, although he is not normally a member of the *Cabinet. He is the chief legal adviser of the Government, answers questions relating to legal matters in the *House of Commons, and is politically responsible for the *Crown Prosecution Service, *Director of Public Prosecutions, *Treasury Solicitor, *Revenue and Customs Prosecutions Office, and *Serious Fraud Office. He is the leader of the English *Bar and presides at its general meetings. The consent of the Attorney-General is required to bring proceedings for certain criminal offences, principally ones relating to offences against the state and public order and corruption. The Attorney-General sometimes appears in court as an *advocate in cases of exceptional public interest, but he is not now allowed to engage in private practice. He has the right to terminate any criminal proceedings by entering a *nolle prosequi*. *See also* SOLICITOR GENERAL.

Attorney-General's Reference Where a person tried on *indictment has been acquitted (whether on all or part of the indictment), the *Attorney-General may, under s 36(1) of the Criminal Justice Act 1972, seek the opinion of the *Court of Appeal on a point of law which has arisen in the case. The purpose of the procedure is to clarify the law and not reverse the verdict in the case.

auction A method of *sale in which parties are invited to make competing offers (**bids**) to purchase an item. The auctioneer, who acts as the agent of the *seller until fall of the hammer, announces completion of the sale in favour of the highest bidder by striking his desk with a hammer (or in any other customary manner). Until then any bidder may retract his bid and the auctioneer may withdraw the *goods. The seller may not bid unless the sale is stated to be subject to the seller's right to bid. Merely to advertise an auction does not bind the auctioneer to hold one. However, if he advertises an auction without reserve and accepts bids, he will be liable if he fails to knock the item down to the highest outside bidder. An auctioneer who discloses his agency promises to a *buyer that he has authority to sell and that he knows of no defect to the seller's *title; he does not promise that the buyer of a specific *chattel will get a good title.

auction ring A group of buyers who agree not to compete against each other at an *auction with a view to purchasing articles for less than the open-market value. The profit earned thereby is shared among the members of the ring, or a second 'knock-out' auction is held in private by the members of the ring with the article being sold to the highest bidder and the profit shared among the members. Under the Auctions (Bidding Agreements) Acts 1927 and 1969 it is a criminal offence for a dealer to participate in an auction ring and a seller is given the right to set aside the contract of sale if one of the purchasers is a dealer in a ring.

audit exemption Exemption from the requirement to file audited *accounts, which (since 11 August 1994) can be claimed by small companies with a turnover of under £90000 per annum and a balance-sheet total under £1.4 million.

auditor A person appointed to examine the *books of account and the *accounts of a *registered company and to report upon them to company members. An **auditor's report** must state whether or not, in the auditor's opinion, the accounts have been properly prepared and give a true and fair view of the company's financial position. The Companies Acts 1985 and 1989 set out the qualifications an auditor must possess and also certain rights to enable him to fulfil his duty effectively.

authentication A distinct procedural step at the conclusion of a *treaty at which the definitive text of the treaty is established as correct and authentic and not subject to further modification.

authority 1. Power delegated to a person or body to act in a particular way. The person in whom authority is vested is usually called an *agent and the person conferring the authority is the *principal. **2.** A governing body, such as a *local authority, charged with power and duty to perform certain functions. **3.** A judicial decision or other source of law used as a ground for a legal proposition. *See also* PERSUASIVE AUTHORITY.

a

authorized capital (nominal capital) The total value of the shares that a *registered company is authorized to issue in order to raise capital. The authorized capital of a company limited by shares (*see* LIMITED COMPANY) must be stated in the *memorandum of association, together with the number and nominal value of the shares. For example, an authorized capital of £20000 may be divided into 20000 shares of £1 (the **nominal value**) each. If the company has issued 10000 of these shares, it is said to have an **issued capital** of £10000 and retains the ability, without an increase in capital, to issue further shares in future. If the company has received the full nominal value of the shares issued, its *paid-up capital equals its issued capital. Where a company has not yet called for payment of the full nominal value, it has **uncalled capital. Reserve capital** is that part of the uncalled capital that the company has determined (by *special resolution) shall not be called up except upon a *winding-up.

autoeroticism The practice of solitary sexual acts frequently involving self-induced partial *asphyxiation, which sometimes causes death and because of the circumstances can be mistaken for *suicide.

autoloading weapon *See* SEMI-AUTOMATIC WEAPON.

automatic reservation A *reservation to the acceptance by a state of the compulsory *jurisdiction of the *International Court of Justice. This is made under the optional clause of the Statute of the Court, which permits an accepting state to unilaterally claim the right to determine the scope of its reservation.

automatic teller machine (ATM) A *computer terminal available to the public to dispense cash and other banking services when a valid ATM/*debit/*credit card is inserted and verified by entering a Personal Identification Number.

automatic weapon Any of a variety of weapons using gas pressure, recoil, etc., after the first shot is fired to eject the fired case, load the next *cartridge from the *magazine, fire and eject that cartridge, and repeat the process continuously until *ammunition is exhausted or pressure on the trigger is released. The term is often misapplied to semi-automatic actions.

automatism Unconscious *involuntary conduct caused by some external factor. A person is not criminally liable for acts carried out in a state of automatism, since his conduct is altogether involuntary. Examples of such acts are those carried out while sleepwalking or in a state of concussion or hypnotic trance, a spasm or reflex action, and acts carried out by a diabetic who suffers a *hypoglycaemic episode. Automatism is not a *defence, however, if it is self-induced (e.g. by taking drink or drugs). When automatism is caused by a disease of the mind, the defence may be treated as one of *insanity. Mere absent-mindedness, even when brought about by a combination of, e.g. depression and diabetes, is not regarded as a defect of reason under the defence of insanity. It may, however, be grounds for concluding that the accused was not capable of having the necessary **mens rea* at the time of the offence.

autopsy (post-mortem) The examination of a body after death in order to establish the cause of death. Autopsies are frequently requested by *coroners. *See also* INQUEST.

autrefois acquit [French: previously acquitted] A *special plea in bar of *arraignment claiming that the defendant has previously been acquitted by a court of competent *jurisdiction of the same (or substantially the same) offence as that with which he is now charged or that he could have been convicted on an earlier *indictment of the same (or substantially the same) offence. When this plea is entered the *judge determines the issue. If the plea is successful, generally it bars further proceedings on the indictment (*but see* DOUBLE JEOPARDY). The plea may be combined with one of *not guilty. *See also* NEMO DEBET BIS VEXARI.

autrefois convict [French: previously convicted] A *special plea in bar of *arraignment claiming that the defendant has previously been convicted by a court of competent *jurisdiction of the same (or substantially the same) offence as that with which he is now charged or that he could have been convicted on an earlier *indictment of the same (or substantially the same) offence. When this plea is entered the *judge determines the issue. If the plea is successful it bars further proceedings on the indictment. The plea may be combined with one of *not guilty. *See also* NEMO DEBET BIS VEXARI.

avow To declare as a thing one can vouch for; to admit or confess.

award *See* ARBITRATION.

backed for bail Describing a warrant for *arrest issued by a *magistrate or by the *Crown Court to a *police officer, directing him to release the accused, upon arrest, on *bail under specified conditions.

bad character *See* CHARACTER.

bail The release of a person by the police or a court with a duty to surrender at a court or police station at a fixed future date and time. To fail to surrender at the time and place appointed is an offence.

Bail is granted in a number of circumstances: **1. Street bail** is granted by a *constable to a person who has been arrested but not taken to a police station. The person bailed has a duty to surrender at a police station at a given time. The main use of this type of bail is at times when the custody office at the police station is busy and it is more efficient for the person to appear at the police station at a more convenient time to be dealt with. **2.** Bail may also be granted by police to people who have been arrested and detained at a police station for an offence but inquiries are not complete. Continued police detention is only justified if it is *necessary*. If a detained person is to be released while further inquiries are made the release must be on bail. Where there is sufficient evidence to *charge a person with an offence but further consideration is to be given by the *Crown Prosecution Service as to whether charging is appropriate, the detained person will be bailed by police to return to the police station at a prescribed time. In such cases the custody officer may require sureties and impose conditions on the bail. Once a person has been charged with an offence the custody officer must order his release with a requirement to appear at court. In theory the release can be with or without bail but in practice the person is almost invariably released on bail. There are exceptional circumstances where a person who has been charge is not bailed but is taken to court in *custody. Those circumstances are where the person's name and address cannot be ascertained; there is likelihood of failure to appear in court; where the offence is imprisonable, commission of a further offence is likely; where the offence is non-imprisonable, there is a risk of injury to another or loss or damage to property, or risk of interference with the administration of justice or the investigation of offences; or for the defendant's own protection. The custody officer can require sureties and impose the same conditions on the bail as a court can, except for residence in a *bail hostel or requirement for a medical report. **3.** A *magistrates' court or the *Crown Court may grant bail to a person held in legal custody while awaiting *trial or the determination of an *appeal against a criminal *conviction. Generally, there is a presumption in favour of bail unless there are substantial grounds to believe that the accused will abscond, commit further offences, or interfere with witnesses or otherwise obstruct the course of justice (sch 1, Bail Act 1976). However, if he was already on bail for an offence at the time of the offence that brings him back before the court, then the court may not grant bail unless it is satisfied that there is no significant risk of his committing a further offence whilst on bail (s 14, Criminal Justice Act 2003). If the accused is charged with murder, attempted murder, manslaughter, rape, or attempted rape and has a previous conviction for such an offence, a court may only grant bail if there are 'exceptional circumstances' to justify it. Section 19(4) of the Criminal Justice Act 2003 added paras 6A to 6C to the Bail Act 1976, sch 1, pt I. These provide that an accused aged 18 or over who has been charged with an imprisonable offence will not be granted bail, unless the court is satisfied that there is no significant risk of his committing an offence while on bail, where there is drug test evidence that the person has a specified Class A drug in his body; either he is charged with an offence of *possession or possession with intent to supply a specified Class A drug, and the offence relates to, or the court is satisfied that there are substantial grounds for believing that the misuse of a specified Class A drug caused or contributed to the offence with which he is charged or that offence was motivated wholly or partly by his intended misuse of a specified Class A drug; and he does not agree to undergo an assessment (carried out by a suitably qualified person) of whether he is dependent upon or has a propensity to misuse any specified Class A drugs, or he has undergone such an assessment but does not agree to participate in any relevant follow-up which has been offered. It is open to the court to attach conditions to the grant of bail. Those conditions include: a requirement to give a security (a sum of money) for his surrender; a condition that he lives and sleeps at a specified address (*see also* FORFEITURE OF SECURITY FOR ATTENDANCE); a condition of residence in a *bail hostel; a *curfew; surrender of his *passport and any other travel documents; a condition that he report to a police station on specified days and at specified times; a condition not to contact witnesses; or a condition not to go to a particular place or within a certain distance of a particular address. **Electronic monitoring** is available as a condition of bail in support of a curfew condition for both adult and *juvenile offenders, although in the case of the latter it is restricted to those who are charged with imprisonable offences. Often the court also requires guarantors (known as **sureties**) to undertake to produce the accused or to forfeit the sum fixed by the court if they fail to do so. In these circumstances the bailed person is, in theory, released into the custody of the sureties (*see also* FORFEITURE OF RECOGNIZANCE). It is a criminal offence, contrary to s 9 of the 1976 Act, for a defendant who is granted bail to agree to indemnify his surety against any loss arising out of standing surety. The Bail (Amendment) Act 1993 confers upon the prosecution the right to appeal to the Crown Court against a decision by magistrates to grant bail in cases where the accused is charged with or convicted of an offence which is (or would be in the case of an adult) punishable by a term of imprisonment.

bail hostel Accommodation for persons of no fixed address who have been released on *bail.

bailiff 1. An officer of a court (usually a *county court) concerned with the service of the court's processes and the enforcement of its orders, especially warrants of execution authorizing the seizure of the *goods of a *debtor. The term is often loosely applied to a sheriff's officer. **2.** A judicial official in Guernsey (Royal Court Bailiff).

bail information officer *See* BAIL INFORMATION SCHEME.

bail information scheme A scheme whereby a bail information officer gathers information and provides it to the *Crown Prosecution Service to aid them in their *remand request to the court. Brief, factual details, usually consisting of a statement verifying that the defendant has an address he can stay at if given bail, are provided to the CPS as well as the defence solicitors who take this information into account in applications to the court. By informing remand decisions the scheme is aimed at reducing unnecessary remands in custody. Each prison that holds prisoners on remand must provide a bail information scheme (Prison Service Regulations PSO 6101).

bailment The transfer of the possession of *goods by the owner (the **bailor**) to another (the **bailee**) for a particular purpose. Examples of bailments are the hiring of goods, the loan of goods, the pledge of goods, and the delivery of goods for carriage, safe custody, or repair. Ownership of the goods remains in the bailor, who has the right to demand their return or direct their disposal at the end of the period (if any) fixed for the bailment or (if no period is fixed) at will. This right will, however, be qualified by any *lien the bailee may have over the goods. Bailment exists independently of contract. But if the bailor receives payment for the bailment (a **bailment for reward**) there is often an express contract setting out the rights and obligations of the parties.

A bailment for which the bailor receives no reward (e.g. the loan of a book to a friend) is called a **gratuitous bailment**.

balance of probabilities The *standard of proof in civil cases requiring only the slightest tip of the balance to decide who wins the case. (Compare the standard of proof in criminal cases requiring the prosecution to prove its case 'beyond reasonable doubt'.)

In criminal cases any evidential burden placed on the defence need be proved only on the balance of probabilities. For example it is an offence for a person to possess an *offensive weapon without lawful authority or reasonable excuse 'proof whereof shall lie on him'. The defendant need prove this only on the balance of probability.

balance sheet A *document presenting in summary form a true and fair view of a company's financial position at a particular time (e.g. at the end of its financial year). It must show the items listed in either of the two formats set out in the Companies Act 1985. Its purpose is to disclose the amount that would be available for the benefit of members if the company were immediately wound up and liabilities were discharged out of the proceeds of selling its *assets. *See also* ACCOUNTS.

ball cartridge A *cartridge containing a single *projectile and a propellant charge.

ballistics The science of propulsion, flight, and impact of *projectiles. It is divided into three categories: interior ballistics, the time between the start of *primer *ignition and the *bullet's exit from the *barrel; exterior ballistics, the bullet's movement from barrel exit to target impact; and terminal ballistics, the bullet's behaviour from the moment it enters its target until it stops moving.

Baltic Exchange An organization in the City of London that exists to find *ships for people with cargoes and cargoes for ship operators and a similar service for air cargoes. It also provides a market for the sale of second-hand ships. The Baltic Exchange is also the self-regulator for the freight shipping industry, publishing a code of ethics and mediating in disputes.

bankers' book A record as originally defined by the Bankers' Books Evidence Act 1879 to include ledgers, daybooks, cash books, account books, and all other books used in the ordinary business of the bank. Section 9(2) of the Act, as substituted by the Banking Act 1979, has now extended that definition to include those other records used in the ordinary business of a bank, building society, National Savings Bank, and the Post Office; whether they are in written form or are kept on microfilm, magnetic tape, or any other form of mechanical or electronic data retrieval mechanism. Paid cheques and paying-in slips retained by a bank after the conclusion of a banking transaction to which they relate do not fall within that definition: *Barker v Wilson* [1980] 1 WLR 884; *Williams v Williams* [1988] QB 161. A copy of an entry in a banker's book may be received in all legal proceedings as *prima facie evidence of such entry, and of the matters, transactions, and accounts therein recorded, provided it is shown that the book was one of the ordinary books of the bank, that the entry was made in the usual and ordinary course of business, that the book is in the custody and control of the bank, and that the copy has been examined with the original entry and is correct.

bank holiday A day that is declared a holiday for the clearing banks and is kept as a public holiday under the Banking and Financial Dealing Act 1971 or by *royal proclamation under this Act. In England and Wales there are currently eight bank holidays a year: New Year's Day (or, if that is a Saturday or Sunday, the following Monday), Good Friday, Easter Monday, May Holiday (the first Monday in May), Spring Bank Holiday (the last Monday in May), Summer Bank Holiday (the last Monday in August), and Christmas Day and the following day (or, if Christmas Day is a Saturday or Sunday, the following Monday and Tuesday).

bankruptcy The state of a person who has been adjudged by a court to be insolvent (*compare* WINDING-UP). The court orders the compulsory *administration of a bankrupt's affairs so that his *assets can be fairly distributed among his *creditors. To declare a *debtor to be bankrupt a creditor or the debtor himself must make an application (known as a **bankruptcy petition**) either to the *High Court or to a *county court. If a creditor petitions, he must show that the debtor owes him at least £750 and that the debtor appears unable to pay it. The debtor's inability to pay can be shown either by: (1) the creditor making a formal demand in a special statutory form, and the debtor failing to pay within three weeks; or (2) the creditor of a judgment debtor being unsuccessful in enforcing payment of a judgment debt through the courts. If the petition is accepted the court makes a *bankruptcy order. Within three weeks of the bankruptcy order, the debtor must usually submit a *statement of affairs, which the creditors may inspect. This may be followed by a *public examination of the debtor. After the bankruptcy order, the bankrupt's property is placed in the hands of the *official receiver. The official receiver must either call a creditors' meeting to appoint a *trustee in bankruptcy to manage the bankrupt's affairs, or he becomes trustee himself. The trustee must be a qualified *insolvency practitioner. He takes possession of the bankrupt's property and, subject to certain rules, distributes it among the creditors.

A bankrupt is subject to certain disabilities (*see* UNDISCHARGED BANKRUPT). Bankruptcy is terminated when the court makes an order of *discharge, but a bankrupt who has not previously been bankrupt within the preceding 15 years is automatically discharged after three years. *See also* VOLUNTARY ARRANGEMENT.

bankruptcy order A court order that makes a *debtor bankrupt. When the order is made, ownership of all the debtor's property is transferred either to a court officer known as the *official receiver or to a *trustee appointed by the *creditors. It replaced both the former **receiving order** and **adjudication order** in bankruptcy proceedings. *See also* BANKRUPTCY.

bankruptcy petition An application to the *High Court or *county court for a *bankruptcy order to be made against an insolvent *debtor. *See* BANKRUPTCY.

banning order *See* FOOTBALL HOOLIGANISM.

bar 1. A legal impediment. **2.** An imaginary barrier in a court of law. Only Queen's Counsel, officers of the court, and litigants in person are allowed between the bar and the *bench when the court is in session. **3.** A rail near the entrance to each House of Parliament beyond which nonmembers may not pass but to which they may be summoned (e.g. for reprimand).

Bar *Barristers, collectively. To be **called to the Bar** is to be admitted to the profession by one of the *Inns of Court.

barbiturates A group of sedative drugs. Now seldom prescribed for medicinal purposes because of the risk of addiction.

Bar Council (General Council of the Bar of England and Wales) The governing body of the *barristers' branch of the legal profession. It regulates the activities of all barristers, maintains standards within the *Bar, and considers complaints against barristers.

barotrauma An internal injury caused by sudden rapid change of air pressure as caused by an explosion. It may also be caused by rapid ascent in an aircraft when sinuses or the Eustachian tube are blocked by mucus.

barratry 1. Any act committed wilfully by the master or crew of a *ship to the detriment of its owner or charterer. Examples include *scuttling the ship and *embezzling the cargo. Illegal activities (e.g. carrying prohibited persons) leading to the *forfeiture of the ship also constitute barratry. **2.** The former *common-law offence (abolished by the Criminal Law Act 1967) of habitually raising or inciting disputes in the courts.

barrel The part of a *firearm through which the *bullet or shot passes from *breach to *muzzle.

barrister A legal practitioner admitted to plead at the *Bar. The primary function of barristers is to act as *advocates for parties in courts or tribunals, but they also undertake the writing of opinions and some of the work preparatory to a *trial. Their general *immunity from law suits in *negligence for criminal and civil litigation has been abolished. With certain exceptions a barrister may only act upon the instructions of a *solicitor, who is also responsible for the payment of the barrister's fee. Barristers have the right of audience in all courts: they are either *Queen's Counsel (often referred to as **leaders** or **leading counsel**) or *junior barristers.

baseline The line forming the boundary between the *internal waters of a state on its landward side and the territorial sea on its seaward side (*see* TERRITORIAL WATERS). Other coastal state zones (the contiguous zone, *exclusive economic zone, and exclusive fishing zone) are measured from the baseline.

Basic Command Unit (BCU) A geographical area within a *police force area, usually coterminous with a *local authority area under the command of a superintendent or *chief superintendent. The unit provides all the day-to-day policing service for that area.

basic input/output system (BIOS) A program that controls interaction between the various components of a *computer.

basic intent *See* INTENTION; INTOXICATION.

battered child A child subjected to physical violence or abuse by a *parent, *step-parent, or 'any other person with whom he is living. A battered child may be protected if the other parent (or person who is looking after him) applies for an *injunction under the Family Law Act 1996, but only if the child is living, or might reasonably be expected to live, with the applicant. The Act applies to children under 18. When a child is suffering, or likely to suffer, significant harm, a *local authority may apply for a *supervision order or *care order under the Children Act 1989. *See also* EMERGENCY PROTECTION ORDER.

battered spouse or cohabitant A person subjected to physical violence by their husband, wife, or *cohabitant (subsequently referred to as 'partner' in this entry). Battered partners (or those afraid of future violence) may seek protection in a number of ways. Under the Family Law Act 1996 they can apply to the court for a *non-molestation order, directing the other partner not to molest, annoy, or use violence against them, or for an *occupation order, entitling the applicant to remain in occupation of the matrimonial home and prohibiting, suspending, or restricting the abusive partner's right to occupy the house. Battered partners can apply for these orders if they are also applying for some other matrimonial relief (e.g. a divorce). The court must attach a *power of arrest to a non-molestation order or an occupation order if the abuser has used or threatened violence against his or her partner. This gives a *constable the power to arrest the abuser without *warrant if he or she is in breach of the order. In cases of emergency, an injunction without notice may be granted. A criminal prosecution for *assault or for *harassment under the Protection from Harassment Act 1997 may also be brought. Under the Housing Act 1985, *local authorities have a duty to supply emergency accommodation to those made homeless when they have left their homes because of *domestic violence.

Those who have been subjected to continued beatings by their partners over a period of time may plead *provocation or *diminished responsibility if charged with the *murder of their partner.

battery The intentional or reckless application of physical force to someone without his consent. Battery is a form of *trespass to the person and is a *summary offence (punishable with a *fine at level 5 on the standard scale and/or six months' imprisonment) as well as a *tort, even if no actual harm results. If actual harm does result, however, the *consent of the victim may not prevent the act from being criminal, except when the injury is inflicted in the course of properly conducted sports or games (e.g. rugby or boxing) or as a result of reasonable surgical intervention. *Compare* ASSAULT; GRIEVOUS BODILY HARM.

bear An investor who sells shares that he may not in fact have in the hope that the price will fall and he can later buy the shares at a lower price. The system works because there is a delay before settlement is required. At the end of this period the investor must settle the account. If the price has gone down he can buy at a lower price than that at which he sold, and make a profit. If the price has gone up he will still have to buy the shares but as the price is higher than that at which he sold them he will make a loss. The opposite of a bear is a *bull.

bearer The person in possession of a *bill of exchange or *promissory note that is payable to the bearer.

bearer bond A *bond which is not recorded in any register and ownership is demonstrated merely by possession of it. *Title is transferred by physical passage of the *document.

belief *See* KNOWLEDGE.

belligerent communities, recognition of The formal acknowledgment by a state of the existence of a civil *war between another state's central government and the peoples of an area within its territorial boundaries. Such recognition brings about the conventional operation of the rules of war, in particular those humanitarian restraints upon the combatants introduced by the *international law of armed force. Another result of recognition of belligerency is that both the rebels and the parent central government are entitled to exercise belligerent rights and are subject to the obligations imposed on belligerents. Following recognition, third states have the rights and obligations of *neutrality. *Compare* INSURGENCY.

bench 1. Literally, the seat of a *judge in court. The bench is usually in an elevated position at one side of the court room facing the seats of *counsel and *solicitors. **2.** A group of judges or *magistrates sitting together in a court, or all judges, collectively. Thus a lawyer who has been appointed a judge is said to have been **raised to the bench**.

bench warrant A *warrant for the *arrest of a person who has failed to attend court when summoned or *subpoenaed to do so or against whom an order of committal for *contempt of court has been made and who cannot be found. The warrant is issued during a sitting of the court.

benzodiazepines A group of common pharmaceutical drugs such as diazepam (Valium™), temazepam (Restoril™), and nitrazepam (Mogadon™). They are frequently abused.

best-evidence rule A rule requiring that a party must call the best evidence that the nature of the case will allow. Formerly of central importance, in modern law it is largely confined to a rule of practice, not a requirement of law, that the original of a private *document must be produced in order to prove its contents; if it cannot be produced its absence must be explained.

bestiality Anal or vaginal intercourse by a man or a woman with an animal. Intercourse with an animal is an offence contrary to s 69 of the Sexual Offences Act 2003. *See also* ANIMAL CRUELTY.

best value A requirement under the Local Government Act 1999 that *local authorities must have regard to economy, efficiency, and effectiveness when exercising their functions and must make arrangements to secure continuous improvement.

bias *See* NATURAL JUSTICE.

bid *See* AUCTION.

bifurcation Dividing in two. In *penology, the concept of classifying crimes into those serious offences for which imprisonment is absolutely necessary and all other offences which can be dealt with by community-based *punishment.

bigamy The act of going through a marriage ceremony with someone when one is already lawfully married to someone else. Bigamy is a crime, punishable by up to seven years' imprisonment; however, there is a defence if the accused honestly

b

and reasonably believed that his or her first spouse was dead or that their previous marriage had been dissolved or annulled or was void. There is also a special defence if the accused's spouse has been absent for at least seven years, and is therefore presumed by the accused to be dead, even if he does not have positive proof of the death. Even though a person is found *not guilty of the crime of bigamy, the bigamous marriage will still be void if that person had a spouse living at the time that the second marriage was celebrated.

bilateral contract (synallagmatic contract) A contract that creates mutual obligations, i.e. both parties undertake to do, or refrain from doing, something in exchange for the other party's *undertaking. The majority of contracts are bilateral in nature. *Compare* UNILATERAL CONTRACT.

Bill A draft of a proposed *Act of Parliament, which must (normally) be passed by both Houses before becoming an Act. Bills are either public or private, and the procedure governing their passing by Parliament depends basically on this distinction. In general, a **public Bill** is one relating to matters of general concern; it is introduced by the Government or by a private member (**private member's Bill**). In the *House of Commons the Government sets aside certain Fridays for debate on private member's Bills, and a ballot at the beginning of each session of Parliament determines the members whose Bills are to have priority on those days. A private member's Bill that is not supported by the Government stands little chance of successfully completing all stages and becoming an Act. The Government sometimes prefers a private member to sponsor a particularly controversial Bill that they themselves support; e.g. the Abortion Act 1967 was introduced by a private member (David Steel) and was successful because it had the support of the Government of the day. A public Bill, unless predominantly financial, can be introduced in either House (less controversial Bills are introduced in the *Lords first). The Bill is presented by the *minister or other member in charge, passed by being read three times, and then sent to the other House. Its first reading is a formality, but it is debated on second and third readings, between which it goes through a Committee stage and a Report stage during which amendments may be made. A Bill that has not become an Act by the end of the session lapses; if reintroduced in a subsequent session, it must go through all stages again.

A **private Bill** is one designed to benefit a particular person, *local authority, or other body, by whom it is presented. It is introduced on a petition by the promoter, which is preceded by public advertisement and by notice to those directly affected. Its Committee stage in the first House is conducted before a small group of members, and evidence for and against it is heard. Thereafter, it follows the procedure for public Bills.

A **hybrid Bill** is a Government Bill that is purely local or personal in character and affects only one of a number of interests in the same class. For example, a Government Bill to nationalize one only of several private-sector airlines would be hybrid. A hybrid Bill proceeds as a public Bill until after second reading in the first House, after which it is treated similarly to a private Bill.

bill of exchange An unconditional order in writing, addressed by one person (the **drawer**) to another (the **drawee**) and signed by the person giving it, requiring the drawee to pay on demand or at a fixed or determinable future time a specified sum of money to or to the order of a specified person (the **payee**) or to the bearer. If the bill is payable at a future time the drawee signifies his *acceptance, which makes him the party primarily liable upon the bill; the drawer and endorsers may also be liable upon a bill. The use of bills of exchange enables one person to transfer to another an enforceable right to a sum of money. A bill of exchange is not only transferable but also negotiable, since if a person without an enforceable right to the money transfers a bill to a *holder in due course, the latter obtains a good *title to it. Much of the law on bills of exchange is codified by the Bills of Exchange Act 1882 and the Cheques Act 1992.

bill of indictment A formal written accusation charging someone with an *indictable offence. Under r 14.2 of the *Criminal Procedure Rules, the prosecution must lodge an indictment with the *Crown Court within 28 days of the accused having been committed or sent for *trial (*see* COMMITTAL FOR TRIAL; SENDING OFFENCES FOR TRIAL) or within 28 days of a *notice of transfer being served. *See also* INDICTMENT; VOLUNTARY BILL PROCEDURE.

bill of lading A *document acknowledging the shipment of a consignor's *goods for carriage by sea (*compare* SEA WAYBILL). The bill serves three functions: it is a receipt for the goods, it summarizes the terms of the contract of carriage, and it acts as a document of *title to the goods. A bill of lading is also issued by a shipowner to a charterer who is using the ship for the carriage of his own goods.

bill of sale A *document by which a person transfers the *ownership of *goods to another. The Bills of Sale Acts 1878 and 1882 regulate the registration and form of bills of sale.

bind over To order a person to enter into a *recognizance to perform some act (e.g. attend court to give evidence) or to keep the peace and be of good behaviour. *Magistrates have powers to bind over under s 115 of the Magistrates' Courts Act 1980, under *common law, and under the Justices of the Peace Act 1361. The power to bind over under the 1980 Act is exercisable upon *complaint alleging behaviour causing a breach of the peace.

At common law and under the 1361 Act, any *court of record can bind over, with or without *sureties, any participant in the proceedings (including a witness), if it considers that the conduct of the person concerned is such that there might be a breach of the peace or that the behaviour has been **contra bonos mores*.

biological weapon A biological agent used as a weapon. Such weapons can be used against large populations by causing disease, contaminating water supplies, or by attacking food supplies by causing disease in farm animals or food plants. Biological weapons can also be used against individuals. There are five main groups of biological weapon agents: animals (e.g. Colorado Beetles dropped on enemy country to destroy the potato crop); viruses (e.g. smallpox); bacteria (e.g. anthrax); toxins (e.g. ricin); and rickettsia (e.g. typhus). The use of biological weapons is banned by the 1925 Geneva Protocol, and the manufacture, development, and stockpiling are banned by the Convention on the Prohibition of the Development, Production and Stockpiling of Bacteriological (Biological) and Toxin Weapons and on Their Destruction. Terrorists have used anthrax sent through the post in the USA, killing five people.

bit A bit (short for *binary digit*) is the smallest unit of data in a *computer. A bit has a single binary value, either 0 or 1. Computers generally store data and execute instructions in bit multiples called *bytes. In most computer systems, there are eight bits in a byte.

black eye Bruising around the circumference of the eye socket. It is most commonly caused by a blow to the area but can be caused by a blow on the bridge of the nose or by a fracture of the base of the skull, which causes blood to leak into the tissue around the eyes.

blackmail The offence contrary to s 21 of the Theft Act 1968 of making an unwarranted demand with menaces for the purpose of financial gain for oneself or someone else or financial loss to the person threatened. The menaces may include a threat of violence or of detrimental action, e.g. exposure of past immorality or misconduct. Blackmail is punishable by up to fourteen years' imprisonment. As long as the demand is made with menaces, it will be presumed to be unwarranted, unless the accused can show both that he thought he was reasonable in making the demand and that he thought it was reasonable to use the menaces as a means of pressure. Under s 40 of the Administration of Justice Act 1970, there is also a statutory offence of *harassment of debtors, which applies to behaviour intended to force a debtor to pay his debt. *See also* THREAT.

Black Rod, Gentleman Usher of the An official of the *House of Lords whose title derives from his staff of office—an ebony rod surmounted with a gold lion. The office originated as usher of the Order of the Garter in the 14th century; the parliamentary appointment dates from 1522. Black Rod is responsible for maintaining order in the House and summons members of the Commons to the Lords to hear a speech from the throne.

blasphemy Statements or writings that deny—in an offensive or insulting manner—the truth of the Christian religion, the Bible, the Book of Common Prayer, or the existence of God. Blasphemy is a crime at *common law, and if it is published there is no need to show an intention to shock or insult or an awareness that the publication is blasphemous. Prosecutions for blasphemy are now rare and it has been suggested that the crime be abolished.

blast The sudden and rapid increase in air pressure caused by an *explosion. It is a frequent cause of *barotrauma.

blockade The act of a belligerent power of preventing access to or egress from the *ports of its enemy by stationing a ship or squadron in such a position that it can intercept vessels attempting to approach or leave such ports. A neutral merchant vessel trying to break through a blockade is liable to capture and condemnation by the captor's prize court.

blood relationship *See* CONSANGUINITY.

blood specimen *See* SPECIMEN OF BLOOD.

blowback *See* ACTION.

blow fly One of the group of sarcophageous flies such as bluebottles and greenbottles. They breed on decomposing bodies and a study of their *maggots and *pupae can be used to determine the approximate time of death of a decomposed body.

bluejacking The sending of unsolicited messages to Bluetooth^{TM}-enabled devices, such as mobile phones and laptop *computers. Where the content is offensive or sexually explicit, it may amount to a criminal offence of *harassment. Under s 1 of the Malicious Communications Act 1988 it is an offence to send an indecent, offensive, or threatening letter, electronic communication, or other article to another person. *See also* BLUESNARFING.

bluesnarfing The theft of, or unauthorized access to, information from a Bluetooth^{TM}-enabled device such as a mobile phone or laptop *computer via a wireless connection. *See also* BLUEJACKING.

blunt force injury An injury such as a *contusion (bruise), abrasion (graze), or *laceration caused by being struck with an instrument such as a fist or club, or by hitting the floor.

board of inquiry A body convened by naval, army, or air force authorities to investigate and report upon the facts of any happening (e.g. the loss or destruction of service property), particularly for the purpose of determining whether or not disciplinary proceedings should be instituted.

bodily harm *See* ACTUAL BODILY HARM; ASSAULT; GRIEVOUS BODILY HARM.

bolt The mechanical part of a *firearm that blocks the rear of the *chamber while the *projectile is discharged, forcing all the expanding gas forward. In a bolt action firearm, the bolt is operated manually. In a *semi-automatic firearm, the bolt moves forward or backward, under pressure from the expanding gas or the recoil spring. When it moves forward it pushes a *cartridge from the *magazine into the chamber. When it moves backward, the *extractor pulls the spent *case from the chamber. Once the case is clear the *ejector propels the case out of the weapon. The *firing pin, *extractor, and sometimes the ejector are usually integral parts of the bolt. *See also* ACTION; BREECH BLOCK.

bomb hoax A deception in which one or more people are led to believe that an *explosion is likely to occur that will cause physical injury or damage to property. A bomb hoax may constitute *blackmail (if accompanied by a demand), *public nuisance, threats to damage property (an offence under s 2, Criminal Damage Act 1971), or wasting the time of the police (under s 5, Criminal Law Act 1967). Under s 51 of the Criminal Law Act 1977 it is an offence, punishable by imprisonment for up to five years and/or a fine, to place or send an object anywhere with the intention of leading someone to believe that it is likely to explode and cause harm. It is also an offence falsely to tell anyone that a bomb has been placed in a certain place or that some other object is liable to explode.

bona fide purchaser for value (BFPFV) Under s 3(2) of the Theft Act 1968 a person who in good faith pays a reasonable price for something and later discovers that it is stolen is not a thief BUT if he then destroys, sells, or pawns the article he will have assumed one of the rights of an owner and appropriated the property, thereby becoming a thief.

bond 1. A *deed by which one person (the **obligor**) commits himself to another (the **obligee**) to do something or refrain from doing something. If it secures the payment of money, it is called a **common money bond**; a bond giving security for the carrying out of a contract is called a **performance bond**. **2.** A *document issued by a government, *local authority, company, or other public body undertaking to repay long-term *debt with interest. **Bond issues** are issues of debt securities by a borrower to investors in return for the payment of a subscription price.

books of account Records that disclose and explain a company's financial position at any time and enable its *directors to prepare its *accounts. The books (which *registered companies are required to keep by the Companies Act 1985) should reveal, on a day-to-day basis, sums received and expended together with details of the transaction, *assets and *liabilities, and (where appropriate) *goods sold and purchased. Public companies must preserve their books for six years, private companies for three years. Company officers and *auditors (but not members) have a statutory right to inspect the books.

boot To start a *computer, more frequently used as 'reboot'.

boot disk A floppy disk or CD that contains the files needed to start an operating system. A special boot disk (often called a system rescue disk) can be created that will allow a *computer to boot even if it cannot boot from the hard disk.

bore The term used to describe the approximate diameter of a barrel before the rifling (*see* RIFLE) is cut.

borough An area of local government, abolished as such (except in *Greater London) by the Local Government Act 1972. A district (*see* DISTRICT COUNCIL) may, however, be styled a borough by royal charter. Originally, a borough was a fortified town; later, a town entitled to send a representative to *Parliament.

borstal An institution to which young offenders (aged 15 to 20 inclusive) could be sent before June 1983 instead of prison. Sentence to borstal has been replaced by *detention in a young offender institution. *See also* JUVENILE OFFENDER.

bottomry *See* HYPOTHECATION.

boundary (in *international law) An imaginary line that determines the territorial limits of a state. Such boundaries define the limitation of each state's effective *jurisdiction. They are three-dimensional in nature in that they include the *airspace and subsoil of the state, the *terra firma* within the boundary, and the maritime domain of the state's internal waters and territorial sea.

brain death The absence of functional brain activity. This is now the standard test for death. A series of tests have to be performed twice before a diagnosis can be given.

brain stem The part of the brain that connects with the spinal cord and contains the vital centres, which control heart rate and respiration.

b

breach of confidence The disclosure of confidential information without permission.

breach of contract An actual failure by a party to a contract to perform his obligations under that contract or an indication of his intention not to do so.

breach of statutory duty Breach of a *duty imposed on some person or body by a statute. The person or body in breach of the statutory duty is liable to any criminal *penalty imposed by the statute, but may also be liable to pay damages to the person injured by the breach if he belongs to the class for whose protection the statute was passed. Not all statutory duties give rise to civil actions for breach. If the statute does not deal with the matter expressly, the courts must decide whether or not *Parliament intended to confer *civil remedies. Most actions for breach of statutory duty arise out of statutes dealing with *safety at work.

breach of the peace (BoP) The state that occurs when harm is done or likely to be done to a person or (in his presence) to his property, or when a person is in fear of being harmed through an *assault, *affray, or other disturbance. At *common law, anyone may lawfully *arrest a person for a breach of the peace committed in his presence, or when he reasonably believes that a person is about to commit or renew such a breach. To breach the peace is a crime in Scotland; elsewhere, *magistrates may *bind over a person to keep the peace. *See also* ARREST; OFFENCE AGAINST PUBLIC ORDER.

breathalyzer A device, approved by the Secretary of State, that is used in the preliminary *breath test to measure the amount of *alcohol in a *driver's breath. A breathalyzer should not be used within 20 minutes after consuming alcohol or on a suspect who has just been smoking. *Constables must give instructions; testing suspects who have difficulty with breathing requires special care. *See also* BREATH TEST.

breath specimen *See* SPECIMEN OF BREATH.

breath test A preliminary test applied by a uniformed *police officer by means of a *breathalyzer to a *driver whom he suspects has *alcohol in his body in excess of the legal limit, has committed a traffic offence while the car was moving, or has driven a *motor vehicle involved in an accident. The test may be administered on the spot to someone either actually driving, attempting to drive, or in charge of a motor vehicle on a *road or *public place or suspected by the police officer of having done so in the above circumstances. If the test proves positive (*see* DRUNKEN DRIVING), the police officer may *arrest the suspect without a *warrant and take him to a police station, where further investigations may take place (*see* SPECIMEN OF BREATH). It is an offence under s 6 of the Road Traffic Act 1988 to refuse to submit to a breath test unless there is some reasonable excuse (usually a medical reason), and a police officer may arrest without warrant anyone who refuses the test. The offence is punishable by a fine, *endorsement (four points), and discretionary *disqualification. A police officer has the power to enter any place in order to apply the breath test to someone he suspects of having been involved in an accident in which someone else was injured or to arrest someone who refused the test or whose test was positive.

breech The rear portion of the *barrel of a *firearm that opens to allow *ammunition to be loaded.

breech block The part of the action of a *firearm that holds and locks the *cartridge in the *chamber during firing and usually contains the *firing pin. Although a *bolt is a breech block it is not normally so called.

bribery and corruption Offences relating to the improper influencing of people in certain positions of trust. The offences commonly grouped under this expression are now statutory. Under the Public Bodies Corrupt Practices Act 1889 (amended by the Prevention of Corruption Act 1916) it is an offence, if done corruptly (i.e. deliberately and with an improper motive), to give or offer to a member, officer, or servant of a public body any reward or advantage to do anything in relation to any matter with which that body is concerned; it is also an offence for a public servant or officer to corruptly receive or solicit such a reward. The Prevention of Corruption Act 1906 (amended by the 1916 Act) is wider in scope. It relates to agents, which includes not only those involved in the business of agency but also all *employees, including anyone serving under the *Crown or any public body. Under this Act it is an offence to corruptly give or offer any valuable *consideration to an agent to do any act or show any favour in relation to his principal's affairs; like the 1889 Act, it also creates a converse offence of receiving or soliciting by agents.

bridle way A way over which the public has a *right of way on foot and a right of way on horseback or leading a horse, with or without a right to drive animals along the way (s 329, Highways Act 1980 and s 192, Road Traffic Act 1988).

brief A *document by which a *solicitor instructs an *advocate to appear in court. Unless the client is receiving *legal aid, the brief must be marked with a fee that is paid to *counsel whether he is successful or not. A brief usually comprises a **backsheet**, typed on large brief-size paper giving the title of the case and including the solicitor's instructions, which is wrapped around the other papers relevant to the case.

British Association for Women in Policing (BAWP) An organization whose main objectives are to enhance the role and understanding of the specific needs of women and issues concerning women employed in the police service.

British citizenship One of three forms of citizenship introduced by the British Nationality Act 1981, which replaced citizenship of the UK and Colonies. The others are *British Overseas Territories citizenship and *British Overseas citizenship. *British National (Overseas) Citizens, formerly having different legal status, were included in this category by the British Overseas Territories Act 2002. British citizenship is the most common type of British *nationality, and the only one that automatically carries a right of abode in the UK. Of the various classes of British nationality and *British protected person status, all except British citizenship and British Overseas Territories citizenship are residual categories. This means that they will become extinct with the passage of time, as they can only be passed down to the national's children in exceptional circumstances, e.g. if the child would otherwise be stateless.

On the date on which the 1981 Act came into force (1 January 1983), the Act conferred British citizenship automatically on every existing citizen of the UK and Colonies who was entitled to the right of abode in the UK under the Immigration Act 1971 (*see* IMMIGRATION). As from that date, there have been four principal ways of acquiring the citizenship—by birth, by descent, by registration, and by naturalization. A person acquires it by birth only if he is born in the UK and his father or mother is either a British citizen or settled in the UK (i.e. resident there, and not restricted by the immigration laws as to length of stay). If born outside the UK, he acquires it by descent if one of his *parents has British citizenship (but not, normally, if that citizenship was itself acquired by descent). The British Nationality (Falkland Islands) Act 1983 makes special provisions to confer British citizenship on those people with connections with the Falkland Islands. The British Nationality (Hong Kong) Act 1997 gave additional rights to certain people from Hong Kong to acquire British citizenship 'by descent' or 'otherwise than with descent'. Registration may be applied for by a minor, but adults are eligible only if they have particular links with the UK. In some cases (e.g. British Dependent Territories citizens, British Overseas citizens, British protected persons, and British subjects with certain residential qualifications), it is a right; in others, it is at the discretion of the *Home Secretary. However, s 58(1) of the Immigration, Asylum and Nationality Act 2006 now precludes the registration as a citizen of any description of any person falling within the categories concerned unless the Home Secretary is satisfied that the person concerned is of good character.

The Nationality, Immigration and Asylum Act 2002 contains provisions which amend the 1981 Act and includes provision for citizenship ceremonies and a pledge, and imposes a requirement for *naturalization as a British citizen that the applicant has sufficient knowledge about life in the UK. The 2002 Act also amended the grounds for deprivation of citizenship, and provided replacement procedure for reviewing the deprivation decision with a new right of *appeal against deprivation. Under the amended provisions, the Home Secretary may by order deprive a person of a citizenship status if he is satisfied that the person has done anything seriously prejudicial to the vital interests of the UK, or a British overseas territory. Section 56 of the 2006 Act amends the wording so that the Home Secretary must be satisfied that deprivation of citizenship is conducive to the public good.

British Commonwealth *See* COMMONWEALTH.

British Crime Survey (BCS) A survey carried out in England for the Home Office. Its aim is to measure the amount of crime in England and Wales by asking people about crimes they have experienced in the last year. The BCS includes crimes that are not reported to the police, thus allowing the Government to have information on these unreported crimes. The BCS helps in the planning of crime prevention programmes by identifying those most at risk of different types of crime. It also looks at people's attitudes to crime, such as how much they fear crime and what measures they take to avoid it. The BCS also asks people about their attitude to the *Criminal Justice System, including the police and the courts. It is criticized by some criminologists because it only questions people over 16 years of age and excludes those in institutions. It also excludes crimes against the state, *victimless crimes, and crimes against children and organizations.

British Dependent Territories citizenship One of three forms of citizenship introduced by the British Nationality Act 1981 to replace citizenship of the UK and Colonies. It was renamed *British Overseas Territories citizenship by the British Overseas Territories Act 2002. On the date on which the British Nationality Act 1981 came into force (1 January 1983), it conferred citizenship automatically on a large number of existing citizens of the UK and Colonies on the grounds of birth, registration, or *naturalization in a *dependent territory or descent from a *parent or grandparent who had that citizenship on one of those grounds. On 1 July 1997, those who were British Dependent Territories citizens by virtue of a connection with Hong Kong ceased to be British Dependent Territories citizens. However, they were entitled to acquire a new form of British *nationality, known as *British National (Overseas), by registration.

British National (Overseas) A form of British *nationality that those who were *British Dependent Territories citizens by virtue of a connection with Hong Kong may acquire by registration. They ceased to be British Dependent Territories citizens on 1 July 1997.

British Overseas citizenship One of three forms of citizenship introduced by the British Nationality Act 1981 to replace citizenship of the UK and Colonies. On the date on which it came into force (1 January 1983), the Act conferred the citizenship automatically on every existing citizen of the UK and Colonies who did not qualify for either of the other new forms (*British citizenship and *British Dependent Territories citizenship). Acquisition as from that date has been by registration only, and this is confined almost completely to minors. A British Overseas citizen may become entitled to registration as a British citizen by virtue of UK residence.

British Overseas Territories citizenship Formerly, *British Dependent Territories citizenship. Nearly all persons falling into this category are now also *British citizens as a result of the British Overseas Territories Act 2002. For the purposes of the 1981 Act, British overseas territories are: Anguilla, British Antarctic Territory, Bermuda, British Indian Ocean Territory, British Virgin Islands, Cayman Islands, Falkland Islands, Gibraltar, Montserrat, St Helena and Dependencies (Ascension Island and Tristan da Cunha), Turk and

Caicos Islands, Pitcairn Island, South Georgia and South Sandwich Islands, and the Sovereign Base Areas on Cyprus.

British protected person One of a class of people defined as such by an order under the British Nationality Act 1981 or the Solomon Islands Act 1978 because of their connection with former protectorates, *protected states, and trust territories. A British protected person may become entitled to registration as a British citizen by reason of UK *residence.

British subject Under the British Nationality Act 1948, a secondary status that was common to all who were primarily citizens either of the UK and Colonies or of one of the independent Commonwealth countries. This status was also shared by a limited number of people who did not have any such primary citizenship, including former British subjects who were also citizens of Eire (as it then was) or who could have acquired one of the primary citizenships but did not in fact do so.

Under the British Nationality Act 1981 (which replaced the 1948 Act as from 1 January 1983), the status of British subject was confined to those who had enjoyed it under the former Act without having one of the primary citizenships; the expression *Commonwealth citizen was redefined as a secondary status of more universal application. The Act provided for minors to be able to apply for registration as British subjects and for British subjects to become entitled to registration as British citizens by virtue of UK residence.

brittle bone disease A *congenital disease that causes abnormally brittle bones. In children these bones frequently break and this can lead to incorrect allegations of *child abuse.

broadcasting, unauthorized An offence under the international *law of the sea where there is unauthorized broadcasting of radio or television to the general public from a *ship on the *high seas. The offence can be prosecuted by the flag state of the ship, the state of the person concerned, or the state where the broadcast is received.

Broadmoor A *special hospital at Crowthorne, near Camberley, in Berkshire. It treats dangerous and violent patients (previously known as criminal lunatics) who are sent to it.

Broken Windows *See* ZERO TOLERANCE.

brothel A place used for the purpose of female or male *prostitution. The term is not defined by statute. The leading *common law authority is *Gorman v Standen* [1964] 1 QB 294, in which it was defined as 'a house resorted to by more than one woman for the purposes of prostitution'. A contract for the hiring or letting of a brothel is void (as being contrary to public policy) and under ss 33A to 36 of the Sexual Offences Act 1956 (as amended by the Sexual Offences Act 2003) it is an offence for someone to keep or manage a brothel, for a *landlord to let *premises knowing that they are to be used as a brothel, or for a tenant or occupier of any premises to permit the premises to be used as a brothel. At common law, there is also the distinct offence of keeping a common **bawdy house**, although there appear to have been no prosecutions for the offence recorded in modern times. The term means a house or room, or set of rooms in any house, kept for the purposes of prostitution: *Singleton v Ellison* [1895] 1 QB 607. Section 3(1) of the Children and Young Persons Act 1933 makes it an offence for a person to allow a child aged over 3 and under 16 for which he has responsibility to reside in or frequent a brothel. *See also* DISORDERLY HOUSE.

bruise *See* CONTUSION.

Bryan Treaties (Bryan Arbitration Treaties) [named after William Jennings Bryan, US Secretary of State 1913–15] The series of *treaties, signed at Washington in 1914, that established permanent commissions of inquiry. Such inquiries were designed to resolve differences between the USA and a large number of foreign states. The treaties were not all identical, but had the following key features in common: the *high contracting parties agreed (1) to refer all disputes that diplomatic methods had failed to resolve to a Permanent International Commission for

b

investigation and report, and (2) not to begin hostilities before the report was submitted. *See also* INQUIRY.

buccal swab A swab taken from the lining of the buccal cavity (mouth). This is the principle method of taking cellular material from a living person for DNA analysis.

Budget *See* CHANCELLOR OF THE EXCHEQUER.

buffer An area of *computer memory, often referred to as a *cache, used to speed up access to devices. It is used for temporary storage of the data read from or waiting to be sent to a device such as a hard disk, CD-ROM, or printer.

buggery (sodomy) Anal intercourse by a man with another man or a woman or *bestiality by a man or a woman. The term is no longer used in law and the previous offences have been repealed and replaced in part by the Sexual Offences Act 2003. Anal intercourse without consent is an offence of *rape. Intercourse with an animal is a specific offence under s 69 of the 2003 Act.

bugging *See* ELECTRONIC SURVEILLANCE.

bull An investor who buys shares hoping that the price will go up and he can sell them at a profit. The opposite of a *bear.

bullet The *projectile discharged by a *firearm. It is usually made from hardened lead, sometimes enclosed in a jacket of cupronickel or other metal. The term is often incorrectly used to refer to the combination of bullet, *case, *powder, and *primer; such an item is correctly called a *cartridge.

bulletin board system (BBS) A system maintained by a host *computer for posting information, carrying on discussions, uploading and downloading files, chatting, and other online services. BBSs are generally created for a specific group of users and are usually topic-specific.

bullet splash The particles sprayed from a *bullet on its impact against metal or other hard material.

burden of proof The duty of a party to *litigation to prove a fact or facts in issue. Generally the burden of proof falls upon the party who substantially asserts the truth of a particular fact (the prosecution or the claimant). A distinction is drawn between the **persuasive** (or **legal**) **burden**, which is carried by the party who as a matter of law will lose the case if he fails to prove the fact in issue; and the **evidential burden** (**burden of adducing evidence** or **burden of going forward**), which is the duty of showing that there is sufficient evidence to raise an issue fit for the consideration of the *trier of fact as to the existence or non-existence of a fact in issue.

The normal rule is that a defendant is presumed to be innocent until he is proved *guilty; it is therefore the duty of the *prosecution to prove its case by establishing both the **actus reus* of the crime and the **mens rea*. It must first satisfy the evidential burden to show that its allegations have something to support them. If it cannot satisfy this burden, the *defence may submit or the *judge may direct that there is *no case to answer, and the judge must direct the *jury to acquit. The prosecution may sometimes rely on presumptions of fact to satisfy the evidential burden of proof (e.g. the fact that a woman was subjected to violence during sexual intercourse will normally raise a presumption to support a charge of *rape and prove that she did not consent). If, however, the prosecution has established a basis for its case, it must then continue to satisfy the persuasive burden by proving its case beyond reasonable doubt (*see also* PROOF BEYOND REASONABLE DOUBT). It is the duty of the judge to tell the jury clearly that the prosecution must prove its case and that it must prove it beyond reasonable doubt; if he does not give this clear direction, the defendant is entitled to be acquitted.

There are some exceptions to the normal rule that the burden of proof is upon the prosecution. The main exceptions are as follows. (1) When the defendant admits the elements of the crime (the *actus reus* and *mens rea*) but pleads a special defence, the evidential burden is upon him to create at least a reasonable doubt in his favour. This may occur, for example, in a prosecution for *murder in which the defendant raises a defence of *self-defence. (2) When the defendant pleads *coercion, *diminished responsibility, or *insanity, both the evidential and persuasive burden rest upon him. In this case, however, it is sufficient if he proves his case on a balance of probabilities (i.e. he must persuade the jury that it is more likely that he was insane than not). (3) In some cases statute expressly places a persuasive burden on the defendant; e.g. a person who carries an *offensive weapon in public is guilty of an offence unless he proves that he had lawful authority or a reasonable excuse for carrying it.

Under the Statute of the *International Criminal Court the burden of proof cannot be reversed and the standard is proof beyond reasonable doubt.

burglary The offence, under s 9 of the Theft Act 1968, of either entering a building, *ship, or inhabited vehicle (e.g. a caravan) as a trespasser with the intention of committing one of three specified crimes in it (**burglary with intent**) or entering it as a trespasser only but subsequently committing one of two specified crimes in it (**burglary without intent**). The three specified crimes for burglary with intent are (1) *theft; (2) inflicting *grievous bodily harm; and (3) causing *criminal damage (*see also* ULTERIOR INTENT). The two specified offences for burglary without intent are (1) stealing or attempting to steal; and (2) inflicting or attempting to inflict grievous bodily harm. Burglary is punishable by up to fourteen years' imprisonment. **Aggravated burglary**, in which the trespasser is carrying a *weapon of offence, *explosive, or *firearm, may be punished by a maximum sentence of *life imprisonment (s 10, Theft Act 1968). The former offence of burglary with intent to rape was repealed by the Sexual Offences Act 2003 and replaced with the offence of trespass with intent to commit any sexual offence (s 63), which carries a maximum sentence of ten years' imprisonment. *See also* MANDATORY MINIMUM SENTENCES.

burn An injury caused by heat. First degree burns affect only the surface of the skin. Second degree burns damage the full thickness of the skin. Third degree burns cause damage to deeper tissues as well as the skin.

business name The name, other than its own, under which a sole trader, partnership, or company carries on business. The choice of a business name is restricted by the Business Names Act 1985 and by the common law of *passing off. The true names and addresses of the individuals concerned must be disclosed in *documents issuing from the business and upon business *premises. Contravention of the Act may lead to a fine and to inability to enforce contracts. *See also* COMPANY NAME.

buyer The party to a contract for the *sale of goods who agrees to acquire ownership of the *goods and to pay the price. *See also* PURCHASER.

byelaw A form of *delegated legislation, made principally by *local authorities. District and London borough councils and to a limited extent Parish Councils have general powers to make byelaws for the good rule and government of their areas, and all local authorities have powers to make them on a wide range of specific matters (e.g. public health). Certain public corporations (such as the British Airports Authority) also make byelaws for the regulation of their *undertakings. A statutory power to make byelaws includes a power to rescind, revoke, amend, or vary them. By contrast with most other forms of delegated legislation, byelaws are not subject to any form of parliamentary control but take effect if confirmed by a government minister. It is common for central government to prepare draft byelaws that may be made by such authorities as choose to do so. Byelaws are, however, subject to judicial control by means of the doctrine of **ultra vires*.

byte In most *computer systems, a unit of data that is eight *bits long. A byte is the unit most computers use to represent a character such as a letter, number, or typographic symbol. Computer storage is usually measured in byte multiples. For example, a 1GB (gigabyte) hard drive holds a nominal one thousand million bytes of data.

cabbage In clothing manufacture, extra garments, in excess of the contracted number, made from the cloth provided for the contract and appropriated by the manufacturer as perquisite. Often given as an explanation for the sale of store branded items in markets.

Cabinet A body of *ministers (normally about 20) consisting mostly of heads of chief government departments but also including some ministers with few or no departmental responsibilities; it is headed by the *Prime Minister, in whose gift membership lies. As the principal executive body under the UK constitution, its function is to formulate government policy and to carry it into effect (particularly by the initiation of *legislation). The Cabinet has no statutory foundation and exists entirely by convention, although it has been mentioned in statute from time to time, e.g. in the Ministers of the Crown Act 1937, which provided additional salaries to 'Cabinet Ministers'. The Cabinet is bound by the convention of **collective responsibility**, i.e. all members should fully support Cabinet decisions; a member who disagrees with a decision must resign. If the government loses a vote of confidence, or suffers any other major defeat in the *House of Commons, the whole Cabinet must resign.

cabotage Transport services provided in one member state of the *European Union by a *carrier of another state. Article 71 (formerly 75) of the *Treaty of Rome provides that the Council of the European Union may lay down proposals in relation to the conditions under which non-resident carriers may operate transport services within a member state.

cache A cache is a temporary, high-speed storage area within a *computer. Two types of caching are commonly used: **memory caching** and **disk caching**. Caching is effective because most programs access the same data or instructions over and over. In some circumstances, experts can access the cache and thereby identify the usage history of the computer.

cadaver A dead human body.

cadaveric spasm An uncommon form of *rigor mortis that sets in instantaneously following death.

cadet, police A young person below the minimum age for appointment as a *constable (18½) under training by a *police force with a view to later appointment as a constable. Cadets may be employed full-time or as unpaid 'voluntary cadets'.

café coronary (*slang*) A term for a sudden death caused by a mass of food becoming stuck in the throat and blocking the *trachea. The victim is often intoxicated with *alcohol.

Caffey's syndrome The existence of multiple bony fractures of various ages in children caused by *child abuse—at one time thought to be caused by disease.

calibration check The automatic process by which the accuracy of an *evidential breath testing device is proved. A reading outside the range of 32–37μg/100*ml* in either of the two simulator checks will invalidate the procedure. In such circumstances, the evidence of any readings obtained from the person under test is inadmissible and should not be led.

calibre 1. Distance across the *bore measured from *land to opposite land. In the USA and UK this measurement is usually given in 0.00 or 0.000 of an inch. In Europe and Asia the measurement is generally expressed in millimetres. Commercial designation of a calibre need only be within several thousandths of an inch of the true bore diameter. **2.** In *ballistics, a unit expressing comparative dimensions; e.g. with a *bullet, if the length is three times the diameter it is described as three calibres long.

call A ceremony at which students of the *Inns of Court become *barristers. The name of the student is read out and he is 'called to the Bar' by the Treasurer of his Inn. Call ceremonies take place four times a year, once in each dining term.

calling the jury Announcing the names of those selected to serve on a *jury as a result of a ballot of the jury panel.

callus The scar tissues on healing bone, the existence or extent of which can indicate the period since the injury was inflicted.

Camden Assets Recovery Inter-Agency Network (CARIN) A *European Union network of practitioners and experts in the cross-border identification, freezing, seizure, and confiscation of the proceeds of crime. Based in The Hague, it was established in 2004 to enhance knowledge of methods and techniques in the field and brings together specialists from all European countries to exchange ideas, information, and draft policy. The UK is an active member of the group and will assume the Presidency in 2007.

camera*, sittings *in Legal proceedings conducted other than in open court. The general principle at *common law and in Article 6 of the *European Convention on Human Rights is that court proceedings should be held in public. The common law does allow the court to exclude the public and sit *in camera* where: there is a possibility of disorder; a witness would refuse to testify publicly; or, because of the effect of public hearing on possible future prosecutions. Statute allows the exclusion of the public in some Official Secrets Act *trials and excludes children unless they are witnesses or defendants. There are special restrictions on the public attending *youth courts.

Camic Breath Analyzer A first generation *evidential breath testing device. Its approval was revoked with effect from 1 January 2000 by the Breath Analysis Devices Revocation of Approval 1999. Although first generation evidential devices can no longer be used, a substantial proportion of the accumulated case law in relation to those devices is likely to be of application with regard to machines of the second generation. *See also* CAMIC DATAMASTER.

Camic Datamaster A second generation *evidential breath testing device. By the Breath Analysis Devices Approval 1998 (Road Traffic) the device was approved for use in England and Wales from 1 March 1998. *See also* CAMIC BREATH ANALYZER.

camping *See* UNAUTHORIZED CAMPING.

canard A hoax.

cannabinol A chemical obtained from cannabis resin. A controlled drug of Class C. *See also* CANNABIS.

cannabis A *controlled drug of Class C made from the leaves and flowers of the plant Cannabis sativa. The plant, also called hemp, is used legitimately to make rope and the seeds used to feed caged birds and as bait for fishing. Possession of the seeds and mature stems is not an offence. In addition to the offences applying to all controlled drugs there is a specific offence applying only to cannabis, cannabis resin, and prepared *opium: it is an offence for an *occupier, *landlord, or property manager to allow these substances to be smoked on *premises he occupies or manages (see CONTROLLED DRUG).

cannon-shot rule The rule by which a state has territorial *sovereignty of that coastal sea within three miles of *land. Its name derives from the fact that in the 17th century this limit roughly corresponded to the outer range of coastal artillery weapons and therefore reflected the principle *terrae dominum finitur, ubi finitur armorium vis* (the dominion of the land ends where the range of weapons ends). The rule is now not widely recognized: many nations have established a six or twelve-mile coastal limit. *See also* TERRITORIAL WATERS.

capacity of a child in criminal law *See* DOLI CAPAX.

capacity to contract Competence to enter into a legally binding agreement.

The main categories of persons lacking this capacity in full are minors, the mentally disordered, the drunk, and corporations other than those created by royal charter.

C

capillary The smallest blood vessel in the body which carries oxygenated, nutrition-laden blood from the small arteries (arterioles) to the cells and carries away the waste product of cell activity to the small veins (venules).

capital punishment Death (usually by *hanging) imposed as a *punishment for crime. Capital punishment for *murder was abolished in the UK under the Murder (Abolition of Death Penalty) Act 1965. The death penalty for the last remaining capital offences of *piracy and *treason was abolished by the Crime and Disorder Act 1998. The ratification by the UK of the Sixth Protocol to the *European Convention on Human Rights and the introduction of the *Human Rights Act 1998 has meant that the death penalty is now completely abolished, apart from special provisions in respect of acts in times of war. Its reintroduction would be a violation of the Human Rights Act and, at an international level, a breach of a treaty obligation.

capitulation 1. An agreement under which a body of troops or a naval force surrenders upon conditions. The arrangement is a bargain made in the common interest of the contracting parties, one of which avoids the useless loss that is incurred in a hopeless struggle, while the other, besides also avoiding loss, is spared all further sacrifice of time and trouble. A capitulation must be distinguished from an **unconditional surrender**, which need not be effected on the basis of an instrument signed by both parties and is not an agreement. **2.** A system of extraterritorial jurisdiction, based partly upon custom and partly upon treaties of unilateral obligation, in which cases relating to foreign citizens were tried before diplomatic or consular courts operating in accordance with the laws of the states concerned. The practice is now obsolete, being a clear breach of the right of sovereign equality between states.

caravan A mobile home. For the purpose of collective *trespass and *powers of search in anticipation of *violent disorder, any structure adapted for human habitation and capable of being moved from one place to another, either by being towed or being transported on a *motor vehicle or *trailer. *See also* UNAUTHORIZED CAMPING.

carbon-dating A method of calculating the time since death by measuring the amount of the radioactive isotope of Carbon (C^{14}) in once living material.

carbon dioxide (CO_2) A gaseous component of the atmosphere. A product of respiration and the combustion of hydrocarbons (e.g. petrol, coal, etc). It is the predominant 'greenhouse gas'. It is not poisonous but can cause suffocation by excluding air. It is heavier than air and can build up in vessels. It is used in fire extinguishers particularly for use on fires where there may be live electricity cables. At one time it was known as 'choke-damp' in the mining industry.

carbon monoxide (CO) A poisonous gas produced by the incomplete combustion of hydrocarbons (e.g. petrol, domestic gas, etc.). It is most frequently found where gas fires or water heaters are used in rooms where there is insufficient ventilation or the flues are blocked; also in car exhaust fumes where no catalytic converter is fitted. The gas attaches itself to *haemoglobin in the red blood cells and excludes oxygen. Victims frequently have cherry red facial colouring.

carboxyhaemoglobin *Haemoglobin to which *carbon monoxide has become attached.

cardiac Relating to the heart.

cardiac arrest The heart stops beating. The most common cause is coronary heart disease. Other causes include respiratory arrest, electrocution, drowning, choking, and trauma. Cardiac arrest can also occur without any known cause. Brain death starts four to six minutes after cardiac arrest. Cardiac arrest can be reversed if it is treated within a few minutes with an electric shock (defibrillation) to the heart to restore a normal heartbeat. The chances of survival reduce with every minute that passes without defibrillation.

cardiac massage The rhythmic pressing on the chest to restart blood circulation.

cardiactamponade (haemopericardium) The *pericardium, the sac containing the heart, fills with blood and because blood as a liquid is incompressible it prevents the heart from beating. Often caused by a stab wound passing into the heart and causing it to bleed.

cardiomyopathy The name of a group of heart diseases.

cardiopulmonary resuscitation (CPR) A first aid procedure consisting of mouth-to-mouth respiration and chest compression. CPR allows oxygenated blood to circulate to vital organs such as the brain and heart. CPR can keep a person alive until more advanced procedures (such as defibrillation) can treat the *cardiac arrest. CPR started immediately increases the likelihood of survival for victims of cardiac arrest.

card issuer A bank or other financial institution that issues *debit or *credit cards. The card issuer undertakes to pay the trader if the correct procedures have been followed.

card-not-present (CNP) A transaction using a *debit/*credit card where the trade does not have physical access to the card as in transactions conducted by telephone, mail order or the Internet.

card scheme A system for governing the issue, use and payment of *credit and *debit cards. Some schemes such as Visa or MasterCard are international card schemes whereas Switch is a domestic scheme.

card security code A three or four digit number printed on the reverse side of a *credit/*debit card on the signature strip. The number will be asked for by the trader in a *card-not-present transaction to ensure that the purchaser is in possession of the card and has not merely obtained the account number by illegitimate means such as reading a bill found in a bin.

care and control Formerly, the right to the physical possession and control of the day-to-day activities of a minor. *See* CARE OR CONTROL; PARENTAL RESPONSIBILITY; SECTION 8 ORDERS.

care contact order An order of the court allowing a *local authority to restrict *contact with a child in care (see CARE ORDER). Under the Children Act 1989 there is a presumption that children in care will have reasonable contact with their *parents (including unmarried parents) or those who have had care of them and a local authority must now seek a court order if it wishes to limit such contact.

careless and inconsiderate cycling The offence of riding bicycles, tricycles, and cycles having four or more wheels on a *road or other *public place without due care and attention or without reasonable consideration for other road users. This offence, defined by s 29 of the Road Traffic Act 1988 (as amended by the Road Traffic Act 1991), is a *summary offence for which the maximum *penalty is a *fine at level 3 on the standard scale. The test as to whether a defendant is *guilty of careless cycling is an objective one: what the prosecution have to prove is that the defendant has departed from the standard of a reasonable, prudent, and competent rider in all the circumstances of the case. *See also* DANGEROUS CYCLING; STOPPING AND REPORTING.

careless and inconsiderate driving The offence of driving a *motor vehicle on a *road or other *public place without due care and attention or without reasonable consideration for other road users. This is a *summary offence for which the maximum *penalty is a *fine at level 4 on the standard scale and it carries *endorsement of three to nine penalty points; *disqualification is discretionary. This offence, defined by s 3 of the Road Traffic Act 1988 (as amended by the Road Traffic Act 1991), replaces the former offences of careless driving and inconsiderate driving. The test as to whether a defendant is *guilty of careless driving is an objective one: what the prosecution have to prove is that the defendant has departed from the standard of a reasonable, prudent and competent *driver in all the circumstances of the case. *See also* CAUSING DEATH BY CARELESS DRIVING; STOPPING AND REPORTING.

care or control Protection and guidance of a minor or the discipline of such a child. A court has authority to make orders in care proceedings only if it is satisfied that (in addition to other specified conditions) the child is in need of care or is beyond parental control. In this context it is not necessary to show that all his day-to-day needs are being neglected. *See* CARE ORDER.

care order A court order placing a child under the care of a *local authority. Under the Children Act 1989 an application for a care order can only be made by a local authority, the NSPCC, or a person authorized by the Secretary of State. The court has the power to make a care order only when it is satisfied that a child is suffering or likely to suffer significant harm either caused by the care (or lack of care) given to it by its *parents, or because the child is beyond parental control (the so-called ***threshold criteria**). The phrase 'significant harm', as defined in the 1989 Act, means ill treatment (including sexual abuse and forms of treatment that are not physical) or the impairment of health (either physical or mental) or development (whether physical, intellectual, emotional, social, or behavioural). Once the court is satisfied that the threshold criteria have been satisfied, it must decide whether a care order would be in the best interests of the child. In so doing, it should scrutinize the *care plan drawn up in respect of the child. The court may, instead of making a care order, make a *supervision order or a *section 8 order. Since the coming into force of the *Human Rights Act 1998, the court must ensure that the granting of a care order will not be in breach of Article 8 (which guarantees a right to *family life); the court must be satisfied that any intervention by the state between parents and children is proportionate to the legitimate aim of protecting family life. A care order gives the local authority *parental responsibility for the child who is the subject of the order. Although parents retain their parental responsibility, in practice all major decisions relating to the child are made by the local authority. While the child is in care, the local authority cannot change the child's religion or surname or consent to an adoption order or appoint a *guardian. There is a presumption that parents will have reasonable contact with their children while in care; if the local authority wishes to prevent this, it must apply for a court order to limit such contact. A parent with parental responsibility, the child itself, or the local authority may apply to discharge a care order. No care order can be made with respect to a child who is over the age of 16. Under the Crime and Disorder Act 1998, the family proceedings court has the power to make a care order if a child is in breach of a *child safety order.

care plan A plan drawn up by a *local authority in respect of a child it is looking after. The purpose of a care plan is to safeguard and promote the welfare of the child in accordance with the local authority's duties under the Children Act 1989. The plan will address such matters as where the child is to be placed and the likely duration of such a placement, arrangements for contact between the child and its family, and what the needs of the child are and how these might be met. When a court is deciding whether or not to make a *care order or a *supervision order in respect of a child, the care plan is of crucial importance and must be scrutinized carefully.

care proceedings *See* CARE ORDER.

carjacking Taking a motor car from a person by force or threat of force. If the purpose is to steal the car, it would be charged as *robbery.

carnival of crime Carnival was originally the week before the start of Lent in the Christian calendar. It was a time of revelry and riotous amusement culminating on Shrove Tuesday (*Mardi gras*). It is now seen by criminologists as a manifestation of opposition to accepted standards of behaviour. Criminologists have argued that an overly organized economic world has provoked a widespread desire for extreme, oppositional forms of popular and personal pleasure. This desire has resulted in a cathartic 'second life' of illicit pleasures which are seen by society as criminal acts. There is evidence that carnival has spread from organized events to everyday life.

carotid artery The main blood vessel carrying blood to the head.

car park An area designed for or set aside for the parking of *motor vehicles. For the purposes of the Road Traffic Acts, a car park is not a *road, per se: the fact that the public has access to it does not of itself make such a place a road. Although a car park may be a 'public place' for the purposes of the Acts, that is a question of fact in every case.

carriage A wheeled passenger vehicle.

carriage by road Defined by Article 1(1) of Regulation (EEC) 3820/85 as 'any journey on roads open to the public of a vehicle whether laden or not used for the carriage of passengers or goods'.

carriage, drunk in charge of It is an offence contrary to s 12 of the Licensing Act 1872 to be in charge of any *carriage (and also, inter alia, any horse or cattle) on any *highway or other *public place when drunk. The section applies to cyclists (*Corkery v Carpenter* [1951] 1 KB 102). The prosecution must establish that the defendant was not merely under the influence of drink but 'drunk'. The *penalty is a *fine at level 1 on the standard scale or one month's imprisonment.

carriage of controlled waste It is an offence punishable with a *fine at level 5 for a person who is not a registered carrier to transport *controlled waste to or from any place in Great Britain in the course of any business of his or otherwise with a view to profit: s 1, Control of Pollution (Amendment) Act 1989, as amended by the Environmental Protection Act 1990.

carriage of explosives The action of carrying *explosives, regulated by the Carriage of Explosives by Road Regulations 1996 (SI 1996/2093), as amended.

carriage of goods This includes the transport or haulage of *goods (Road Traffic Act 1988, s 192).

carriage of radioactive material The transport of radioactive material by *road, governed by the Radioactive Material (Road Transport) Regulations 2002 (SI 2002/1093).

carriageway The part of the *highway used by vehicles (*compare* FOOTWAY). It is defined by s 329 of the Highways Act 1980 as 'a way constituting or comprised in a highway, being a way (other than a cycle track) over which the public have a right of way for the passage of vehicles'.

carrier One who transports persons or *goods from one place to another, either gratuitously or for reward. A **common carrier** is one who publicly undertakes to carry any goods or persons for payment on the routes he covers. Such a carrier is subject to three *common-law duties: (1) he must, if he has space, accept any goods of the type he carries or any person; (2) he must charge only a reasonable rate; and (3) he is strictly liable for all loss or damage to goods in the course of transit (*but see* INHERENT VICE). All other carriers are **private carriers**. They are not under any obligation to accept goods for carriage and owe only a duty of reasonable care in respect of the goods.

carrier's lien The right of a common *carrier to retain possession of *goods he has carried until he has been paid his freight or charge.

carrying capacity The number of passengers which can be carried in a public service vehicle is regulated by the Public Service Vehicle (Carrying Capacity) Regulations 1984 (SI 1984/1406).

cartel An agreement between belligerent states for certain types of non-hostile transactions, especially the treatment and exchange of prisoners.

car transporter A *trailer which is constructed and normally used for the purpose of carrying at least two other wheeled vehicles, as defined by reg 3(2) of the Road Vehicles (Construction and Use) Regulations 1986 (SI 1986/1078) (as amended).

cartridge A complete unit of *ammunition: *case, propellant powder, *primer, and *bullet. Commonly applied only to small arms ammunition, including *shotgun shells.

C

case 1. A court *action. **2.** A legal dispute. **3.** The arguments, collectively, put forward by either side in a court action. **4.** (action on the case) A form of action abolished by the Judicature Acts 1873–5. **5.** (*slang*) To keep watch on *premises with a view to stealing from them later. **6.** (in relation to firearms) The paper, metal or plastic container that holds all the other components of a *cartridge.

case law The body of law set out in judicial decisions, as distinct from *statute law. *See also* PRECEDENT.

case management hearing A pre-trial hearing to set, follow, or revise a timetable for the progress of the case, which may include a timetable for any hearing including the *trial, and to otherwise facilitate the effective management of the case in accordance with the *Civil Procedure Rules or the *Criminal Procedure Rules. *See also* CASE PROGRESSION OFFICER; PLEA AND CASE MANAGEMENT HEARING; PRELIMINARY HEARING; PREPARATORY HEARING.

Case Progression Officer (CPO) A member of court staff appointed to facilitate the effective management of cases in the *magistrates' court and in the *Crown Court, under r 3 of the *Criminal Procedure Rules, with responsibility for progressing the case, monitoring compliance with directions of the court, and ensuring that the court is kept informed of events that may affect the progress of that case.

case stated A written statement of the facts found by a *magistrates' court or tribunal (or by the *Crown Court in respect of an *appeal from a magistrates' court) submitted for the opinion of the *High Court (*Queen's Bench Divisional Court) on any question of law or *jurisdiction involved. Any person who was a party to the proceedings or is aggrieved by the decision can request the court or tribunal to state a case; if it wrongly refuses, it can be compelled to do so by a *mandatory order.

case to answer The situation where the *prosecution has put forward sufficient evidence to establish a *prima facie case. At the conclusion of the case for the prosecution and before the accused is called upon to present his case, the court must consider (either of its own volition or in response to a submission by the defence, whether there is a 'case to answer': the case presented by the prosecution must be sufficient, of itself, to support a conviction otherwise the accused must be acquitted. There may be no case to answer where, for example, there has been no evidence whatsoever adduced of an essential ingredient of the offence or where the evidence of a prosecution witness has been so discredited that no *jury could reasonably convict the accused on the basis of that evidence.

casino An establishment where gambling takes place. Casinos must be run as a club and be licensed under the Gaming Act 1968. Section 43 of the Act gives powers of entry to *police officers and Gaming Board inspectors. Licensing will become the responsibility of the *local authority and supervised by the Gambling Commission when the provisions of the Gambling Act 2005 come into effect.

casus belli [Latin: occasion for war] An event giving rise to *war or used to justify war. The only legitimate *casus belli* now is an unprovoked attack necessitating self-defence on the part of the victim.

catecholamine A drug causing a similar effect to *adrenaline.

categories of cases Under the Magistrates' Courts Act 1980 there are three categories of cases:

- those triable only on *indictment;
- those triable either on *indictment or *summarily (*'either way offences'); and
- those triable only summarily.

category 1 territories Those territories designated by Order of the Secretary of State for the purposes of pt 1 of the Extradition Act 2003 (*see* EXTRADITION). A territory may not be designated as a category 1 territory if a person found *guilty in the territory of a criminal offence may be sentenced to death for the offence under the general criminal law of the territory. As at 1 September 2006 the following territories had been so designated (by the Extradition Act 2003 (Designation of Part 1 Territories) Order 2003 (SI 2003/3333); the Extradition Act 2003 (Amendment to Designations) Orders 2004 (SI 2004/1898), 2005 (SI 2005/365), and (No 2) 2005 (SI 2005/2036)): Austria, Belgium, Cyprus, Czech Republic, Denmark, Estonia, Finland, France, Germany, Greece, Hungary, Ireland, Italy, Latvia, Lithuania, Luxembourg, Malta, the Netherlands, Poland, Portugal, Slovakia, Slovenia, Spain, and Sweden.

category 2 territories Those territories designated by Order of the Secretary of State for the purposes of pt 2 of the Extradition Act 2003 (*see* EXTRADITION). As at 1 September 2006 the following territories had been so designated (by art 2 of the Extradition Act 2003 (Designation of Part 2 Territories) Order 2003 (SI 2003/3334)): Albania, Andorra, Antigua and Barbuda, Argentina, Armenia, Australia, Austria, Azerbaijan, the Bahamas, Bangladesh, Barbados, Belize, Bolivia, Bosnia and Herzegovina, Botswana, Brazil, Brunei, Bulgaria, Canada, Chile, Colombia, Cook Islands, Croatia, Cuba, Cyprus, Czech Republic, Dominica, Ecuador, El Salvador, Estonia, Fiji, France, the Gambia, Georgia, Germany, Ghana, Greece, Grenada, Guatemala, Guyana, Hong Kong Special Administrative Region, Haiti, Hungary, Iceland, India, Iraq, Israel, Italy, Jamaica, Kenya, Kiribati, Latvia, Lesotho, Liberia, Liechtenstein, Lithuania, Luxembourg, Macedonia FYR, Malawi, Malaysia, Maldives, Malta, Mauritius, Mexico, Moldova, Monaco, Nauru, the Netherlands, New Zealand, Nicaragua, Nigeria, Norway, Panama, Papua New Guinea, Paraguay, Peru, Poland, Romania, Russian Federation, Saint Christopher and Nevis, Saint Lucia, Saint Vincent and the Grenadines, San Marino, Serbia and Montenegro, Seychelles, Sierra Leone, Singapore, Slovakia, Slovenia, Solomon Islands, South Africa, Sri Lanka, Swaziland, Switzerland, Tanzania, Thailand, Tonga, Trinidad and Tobago, Turkey, Tuvalu, Uganda, Ukraine, Uruguay, USA, Vanuatu, Western Samoa, Zambia, and Zimbabwe.

As at the same date, territories which are further designated (by art 2 of the Extradition Act 2003 (Designation of Part 2 Territories) Order 2003 (SI 2003/3334)) as those which are not required to satisfy the *prima facie case requirement of the 2003 Act are: Albania, Andorra, Armenia, Australia, Azerbaijan, Bulgaria, Canada, Croatia, Georgia, Iceland, Israel, Liechtenstein, Macedonia FYR, Moldova, New Zealand, Norway, Romania, Russian Federation, Serbia and Montenegro, South Africa, Switzerland, Turkey, Ukraine, and USA.

cattle, drunk in charge of *See* CARRIAGE, DRUNK IN CHARGE OF.

cattle trespass An early form of strict *liability for damage done by trespassing cattle or other livestock (but not dogs or cats), replaced in England by the Animals Act 1971. Under the 1971 Act, the owner of livestock that strays on another's *land and does damage to the land or any property on it is liable for the damage and any expenses incurred in keeping the livestock or ascertaining to whom it belongs.

causa causans [Latin: the effective cause]. *See* CAUSATION.

causation The relationship between an act and the consequences it produces. It is one of the elements that must be proved before an accused can be convicted of a crime in which the effect of the act is part of the definition of the crime (e.g. *murder). Usually it is sufficient to prove that the accused had **mens rea* (intention or recklessness) in relation to the consequences; the *burden of proof is on the *prosecution. In *tort it must be established that the defendant's tortious conduct caused or contributed to the damage to the claimant before the defendant can be found liable for that damage. Sometimes a distinction is made between the effective or immediate cause (**causa causans*) of the damage and any other cause in the sequence of events leading up to it (*causa sine qua non*). Simple causation problems are solved by the 'but for' test (would the damage have occurred but for the defendant's tort?), but this test is inadequate for cases of concurrent or cumulative causes (e.g. if the acts of two independent tortfeasors would each have been sufficient to produce the damage).

Sometimes a new act or event (**novus actus* (or *nova causa*) *interveniens*) may break the legal chain of causation and relieve the defendant of responsibility. Thus if a house, which was empty because of a *nuisance committed by the *local authority, is occupied by *squatters and damaged, the local authority is not responsible for the damage caused by the squatters. Similarly, if X stabs Y, who almost recovers from the wound but dies because of faulty medical treatment, X will not have 'caused' the death. It has been held, however, that if a patient is dying from a wound and doctors switch off a life-support machine because he is clinically dead, the attacker, and not the doctors, 'caused' the death. If death results because the victim has some unusual characteristic (e.g. a thin skull: *see* EGG-SHELL SKULL RULE) or particular belief (e.g. he refuses a blood transfusion on religious grounds) there is no break in causation and the attacker is still *guilty.

cause 1. A court *action. **2.** *See* CAUSATION.

causing death by careless driving whilst under the influence The offence committed by someone whose driving while unfit through drink or drugs or driving over the prescribed limit (*see* DRUNKEN DRIVING) results in the death of another person. For this offence, which was created by the Road Traffic Act 1991, the driving must be judged careless (*see* CARELESS AND INCONSIDERATE DRIVING) rather than dangerous (*compare* CAUSING DEATH BY DANGEROUS DRIVING); the maximum *punishment is five years' imprisonment and compulsory *disqualification (s 3A, Road Traffic Act 1988).

causing death by dangerous driving The offence committed by someone *guilty of *dangerous driving that results in the death of another person. The offence is defined by s 1 of the Road Traffic Act 1988 (as substituted by s 1 of the Road Traffic Act 1991) and replaces the former offence of causing death by reckless driving. If the danger is such that there is an obvious and serious risk of injury to another person or significant damage to property—and the *driver either recognizes the risk or fails to give any thought to the possibility that such a risk exists—this will constitute reckless *manslaughter in addition to causing death by dangerous driving. The maximum *penalty for causing death by dangerous driving is ten years' imprisonment and compulsory *disqualification for not less than two years.

causing or inciting or controlling prostitution The offence of organizing or encouraging the sale of sexual services. For the first time, ss 48 to 50 of the Sexual Offences Act 2003 introduce specific offences relating to causing inciting or controlling child prostitution. The prosecution need not show that the offender acted with a view to gain. It is a defence for the offender to show that he reasonably believed the child to be over 18 years of age provided that the child is over 13 years of age, but it is for him to make both the fact of belief and that it was reasonable a live issue. Where the child is under 13, a belief that he or she is over 18 is irrelevant. Sections 52 and 53 of the Act repeal and replace a number of offences that appeared in the Sexual Offences Act 1956 but leave untouched *legislation such as the Street Offences Act 1959 (*see* BROTHEL; KERB CRAWLING; SOLICITING). They are intended to increase the rate of *prosecution of those who recruit adults into prostitution, by force or otherwise, for gain. For all of the new offences, the prostitution or pornography itself does not need to take place for the offences to be committed. The causing or inciting or controlling must take place in the UK but the prostitution or pornography can take place, or be intended to take place, in any part of the world. Unlike some of the offences which they replace, the new offences are framed in gender neutral terms. The definition of '*prostitute' (s 51(1) and s 54(2)) is a wide one so as to bring within the protective ambit of the legislation not only a person who has offered or provided sexual services for payment or a promise of payment voluntarily but also one who has done so under compulsion. Such offer or provision need have taken place on only one occasion (*compare*

COMMON PROSTITUTE; SOLICITING). Payment is defined widely (s 51(3)) in terms of financial advantage including the discharge of an obligation to pay or the provision of *goods or services (including sexual services) gratuitously or at a discount. An additional element of the adult prostitution offences is that the offender must act in the expectation of gain for himself or a third person. Gain is expressed partly in terms of financial advantage. Financial advantage is widely defined by s 54(1). However, the definition of gain not only reproduces the definition of payment given in s 51(3) but adds a reference to the goodwill of any person which is, or appears likely in time, to bring financial advantage.

Section 48 makes it an offence for a person intentionally to cause or incite a child under 18 into prostitution or involvement in pornography in any part of the world. The offence is targeted at the recruitment into prostitution or pornography of a child who is not engaged in that activity at the time. Section 49 makes it an offence for a person intentionally to control any of the activities of a child that relate to the child's prostitution or involvement in pornography in any part of the world. For example a person in the UK might give directions over the telephone regarding the price that a child prostitute in Asia should charge for sexual services. Section 50 makes it an offence for a person to arrange or facilitate the involvement of a child in prostitution orpornography in any part of the world. For example, the offence is committed by a person in the UK who makes arrangements over the Internet for the filming of a child in a pornographic film in Europe. The three offences are triable *either way and each carries a maximum *penalty of fourteen years.

Section 52 makes it an offence for a person intentionally to cause or incite another person into prostitution anywhere in the world where he does so for or in expectation of gain for himself or for a third party. The person incited need not in fact have engaged in an act of prostitution; 'causes', however, implies that the person must have become a prostitute. Section 53 makes it an offence for a person intentionally to control another person's activities relating to prostitution, in any part of the world, where he does so for, or in the expectation of, gain for himself or a third party. Controlling an activity relating to a single act of prostitution suffices. The offence covers those who control the price that a prostitute charges for different sexual services, who require a prostitute to work in a particular place or to provide sexual services to a particular number of men each night. The adult offences are triable either way and carry a maximum penalty of seven years.

caution 1. (in criminal law) A warning that should normally be given by a *police officer or other investigator, in accordance with a *code of practice issued under the Police and Criminal Evidence Act 1984, when he has grounds for believing that a person has committed an offence and when arresting him. The caution is in the following terms: 'You do not have to say anything. But it may harm your defence if you do not mention when questioned something which you later rely on in court. Anything you do say may be given in evidence.' The caution must be given before any questions are put. If a person is not under arrest when a caution is given, the officer must say so; if he is at a police station the officer must also tell him that he is free to leave and remind him that he may obtain legal advice. The officer must record the caution in his pocket book or the interview record, as appropriate. *See* RIGHT OF SILENCE. **2.** A formal warning given by a police officer as an alternative to prosecution for adult offenders. A caution can be cited in court in any subsequent conviction of that person. The practice is governed by Home Office Circular 18/94. The cautioning system for *juvenile offenders was replaced by a system of Reprimands and Warnings by s 65 of the Crime and Disorder Act 1998. *See also* CONDITIONAL CAUTION.

caveat emptor [Latin: let the buyer beware] A *common-law maxim warning a purchaser that he could not claim that his purchases were defective unless he protected himself by obtaining express guarantees from the *vendor. The maxim has been modified by statute: under the Sale of Goods Act 1979 (a *consolidating statute), contracts for the *sale of goods have implied terms requiring the *goods to correspond with their description and any sample and, if they are sold in the course of a business, to be of satisfactory quality and fit for any purpose made known to the *seller. Each of these implied terms is a condition of the contract. However, in most commercial contracts the implied terms are excluded. This will usually be valid unless the exclusion is unreasonable or unfair under the law relating to *unfair contract terms. These statutory conditions do not apply to sales of *land, to which the maxim *caveat emptor* still applies as far as the condition of the property is concerned. However, a term is normally implied that the vendor must convey a good *title to the land, free from encumbrances that were not disclosed to the purchaser before the contract was made.

CE [French *Communauté européenne*: *European Community] A marking applied to certain products, such as toys and machinery, to indicate that they have complied with certain EU directives that apply to them, including *electromagnetic compatibility. A *CE* marking is not a quality mark, but it indicates that health and safety and other *legislation has been complied with. The manufacturer or first importer into the *European Union must apply the *CE* marking; *fines can be levied for breach of the rules.

CELEX [Latin *Communitatis Europae Lex*: European Community Law] A database of EU material of a legislative nature, such as directives, regulations, and treaties, including national legislation. It is possible to access this electronically through the online data service EURIS.

cell **1.** A small room in a police station custody suite built to *Home Office specification for accommodation of *detained persons. The condition and use of cells is regulated by PACE Code C 8. **2.** The microscopic units of which all animals and plants are composed. Cells are made of a nucleus and cytoplasm enclosed in a membrane (except red blood cells which do not have a nucleus).

censorship A body of law restricting publication and broadcasting of material. Article 10 of the *European Convention on Human Rights ensures the right to *freedom of expression but allows restrictions to the right when they are necessary in a democratic society, in the interests of national security, territorial integrity or public safety, for the prevention of disorder or crime, for the protection of health or morals, for protection of the reputation or rights of others, for preventing disclosure of information received in confidence, or for maintaining authority or impartiality of the judiciary (*Handyside v UK* (1997) 1 EHRR 737).

Central Criminal Court The principal *Crown Court for Central London, usually known from its address as the **Old Bailey**. The Lord Mayor of London and any City aldermen may sit as judges with *High Court or *circuit judges or *recorders. *See also* COMMON SERJEANT.

Centralized Analytical Team Collating Homicide Expertise Management (CATCHEM) A database containing details of murders of women and girls under 21 years and boys under 17 years to assist investigators and profilers. The database was originally maintained by Derbyshire Police but later transferred to the National Crime and Operations Faculty at *Centrex.

Central Jury Summoning Bureau (CJSB) A central body that uses a *computer system to select *jurors at random from electoral rolls. There is a link with the *Police National Computer which permits an automatic check against each person selected.

Central Police Training and Development Authority *See* CENTREX.

central processing unit (CPU) The 'brain' of a *computer. Sometimes referred to simply as the 'processor' or 'central processor', the CPU is where most calculations take place. In terms of computing power, the CPU is the most important element of a computer system.

Centrex The working name of the Central Police Training and Development

Authority. A non-departmental public authority set up by the Criminal Justice and Police Act 2001 to provide police training and to facilitate the provision of police training by other bodies. The stated aim is to develop policing by identifying good practice and sharing this knowledge nationally and internationally. This is achieved through the development and delivery of training and the provision of expert advice from written guidelines to analytical and operational support in the field.

CERD Committee The committee that supervises the Convention on the Elimination of all Forms of Racial Discrimination. The committee receives and examines annual reports from the 155 signatory states to the convention. It can also deal with complaints against states made by other states and individuals.

cerebral Relating to the brain.

cerebrospinal fluid The fluid which flows over the brain and spinal column. Samples of the fluid are sometimes taken at *autopsy for analysis.

cerebrovascular accident (CVA) Commonly called a 'stroke' (*arch* apoplexy), it involves bleeding from or blockage of a blood vessel in the brain. It may be fatal and may cause paralysis of one side of the body.

certificate of incorporation A *document issued by the Registrar of Companies after the *registration of a company, certifying that the company is incorporated (*see* INCORPORATION). For a *limited company, the certificate also certifies that the *company members have limited liability, and for a *public company the fact that it is a public company. The validity of the incorporation cannot thereafter be challenged.

certificate of insurance A certificate issued by an *insurance company to the person to whom an insurance policy is issued (the policyholder) in respect of use of a *motor vehicle on a *road. It must be in the form prescribed by sch 1 to the Motor Vehicles (Third Party Risks) Regulations 1972 (SI 1972/1217) and containing such particulars of any conditions subject to which the policy is issued and of any other maters as may be prescribed. By s 174(1) of the Road Traffic Act 1988, a policy of insurance shall be of no effect for the purposes of pt IV of the Act until there is delivered to the person insured a certificate of insurance in the prescribed form.

certified extract An extract from the register of a *magistrates' court, authenticated by the court or *clerk to the justices, which can be used to establish a *conviction, *acquittal, order of the court, etc.

certiorari [Latin: to be informed]. *See* QUASHING ORDER.

chain of evidence That which establishes the *continuity of an exhibit between seizure and production in court.

challenge to jury A procedure by which the *parties may object to the composition of a *jury before it is sworn. Before the Criminal Justice Act 1988 came into force a challenge could be **peremptory** (i.e. with no reason for the challenge being given) or **for cause**. Peremptory challenges were abolished by the Criminal Justice Act 1988, but the *prosecution can ask that a *juror 'stand by', in which case he rejoins the jury panel and may be challenged for cause when the rest of the panel has been gone through. Either party may challenge for cause. This may be **to the array**, in which the whole panel is challenged by alleging some irregularity in the summoning of the jury (e.g. bias or partiality on the part of the jury summoning officer); or **to the polls**, in which individual jurors may be challenged. Any challenge to jurors for cause is tried by the judge before whom the accused is to be tried.

chamber The rear section of the *barrel of a *firearm, which encloses and supports the *cartridge during firing. In a *revolver, chambers are located in the *cylinder.

chambers 1. The offices occupied by a *barrister or group of barristers. (The term is also used for the group of barristers practising from a set of chambers.) **2.** The private office of a *judge, *master, or *district judge. Most *interim proceedings are held in chambers (in private) and the public is not admitted, although *judgment may be given in open court if the matter is one of public interest.

Chancery Division The division of the *High Court of Justice created by the Judicature Act 1873–5 to replace the Court of Chancery. The work of the Division is principally concerned with matters relating to *real property, trusts, and the administration of estates, but also includes cases concerned with company law, *patents and other *intellectual property, and confidentiality cases. The effective head of the Division is the *Vice Chancellor, although the *Lord Chancellor is nominally its president.

change of name A natural person (i.e. a human being) may change his or her *surname simply by using a different name with sufficient consistency to become generally known by that name. A change is normally given formal publicity (e.g. by means of a statutory declaration, deed poll, or newspaper advertisement), but this is not legally necessary. A woman can also change her surname through operation of law on getting married. A young child, however, has no power to change his surname, nor does one *parent have such a power without the consent of the other. (An *injunction may be sought to prevent a parent from attempting to change a child's name unilaterally.) When a mother has remarried after *divorce or is living with another person, and wishes to change the name of the child to that of her new partner, a court order must be obtained and the welfare of the child will be the first and paramount consideration. A person's Christian name (i.e. a name given at baptism) can, under ecclesiastical law, be changed only by the bishop on that person's subsequent confirmation.

A *juristic person may change its name but may be subject to formal procedure before the change of name takes effect; e.g. for a company limited by *shares, a change of name is possible only on the passing of a *special resolution of the company at an extraordinary or annual *general meeting.

channel data format A system used to prepare information for webcasting.

Chapter VII The chapter of the *United Nations Charter that is headed: 'Action with respect to threats to the peace, breaches of the peace and acts of aggression' and includes Articles 39 to 51 of the Charter. Those who devised the UN Charter were acutely aware of the failure of the former Covenant of the League of Nations in respect of *collective security, namely (1) that it left it open to member states to respond, or not respond, to the call for military aid and (2) it provided no machinery or system for organizing League forces in advance or for coordinating such responses as members might make. Chapter VII addressed such problems by empowering the Security Council to orchestrate such collective actions under Articles 42 and 43. Under Articles 43 to 47 advance preparation of collective action was to be made through a Military Staff Committee. Article 51 creates a right to *self-defence for member states; controversially, it is held to have preserved the wider scope of self-defence in customary *international law. *See also* ENFORCEMENT ACTION.

character (in the law of evidence) **1.** The *reputation of a party or witness. In civil cases the reputation of a party is not admissible unless it is directly in issue, as it may be in an action for *defamation. In criminal cases the accused was protected from the prejudicial effect of the revelation of his previous *convictions or *misconduct except where the previous misconduct is so similar that it is probative of the new offence, where such evidence is essential background without which the account placed before the *jury would be incomplete or incomprehensible, or under the Criminal Evidence Act 1898, where the accused had asserted his own good character, attacked the character of a prosecution witness, or given evidence against a co-accused. Conversely, the accused had almost free rein to challenge the character and credibility of a prosecution witness. However, pt 11, ch 1 of the Criminal Justice Act 2003 completely overhauled the use of evidence of previous bad character. It abolished the *common law rules of *admissibility of evidence of misconduct, as well as exceptions to that prohibition, and repealed some of the previous statutory provisions relating to bad character. The 2003 Act adopts a different approach to non-defendants' and defendants' bad character. Non-defendants are given protection in statute for the first time against their bad character being exposed unless the substantial probative value test ('enhanced relevance test') is satisfied. On the other hand the 2003 Act has an inclusionary approach to evidence of the bad character of a defendant. A defendant's bad character evidence is not subject to the 'enhanced relevance test' but is admissible if it is relevant to an important matter in issue subject to the court's discretion to exclude. There is no requirement to seek leave of the court to adduce evidence of the bad character of the accused, although witnesses other than the accused do have that protection. A party wanting to adduce bad character evidence in criminal proceedings must comply with the notice requirements laid down in pt 35 of the *Criminal Procedure Rules. **2.** Loosely, the disposition of a party.

charge 1. The allegation of a criminal offence. The Police and Criminal Evidence Act 1984 directs that as soon as the police have sufficient evidence to charge a detained person, questioning must cease (with a few exceptions) and the person must be charged. (Charging may be delayed if the detained person is unfit to be dealt with or the person is being detained for a number of offences in which case charging can be delayed until they can all be charged together.) *See also* INDICTMENT. **2.** A 'written charge' may be served on an accused person who is not in police custody (s 29, Criminal Justice Act 2003). **3.** Instructions given by a *judge to a *jury.

chargeable gain A profit made on the disposal of an *asset, which may attract capital gains tax or corporation tax.

charge card A payment card, such as certain types of American Express card, which allows purchases or cash withdrawals up to a set limit with an obligation to settle the account in full at the end of each month. Generally, the cardholder pays an annual fee for the use of the card.

charge sheet A *document on which the charges against a person detained in police custody are stated: it forms part of the *custody record.

charging 1. The formal reading of a charge to a detained person. **2.** Serving a 'written charge' under s 29 of the Criminal Justice Act 2003.

charging guidelines *See* STATUTORY CHARGING SCHEME.

charging standard Standards agreed between the police services and the *Crown Prosecution Service in relation to offences against the person, public order and Road Traffic Act offences. The purpose of the joint standards is to ensure that the most appropriate charge is selected at the earliest possible opportunity.

charity A body (corporate or not) established for one of the charitable purposes specified by statute. A charity is subject to the control of the *High Court in the exercise of its *jurisdiction with respect to charities. With certain exceptions, all charities are required to be registered with the *Charity Commissioners.

Charity Commissioners A statutory body, now governed by the Charities Act 1993, generally responsible for the administration of charities. The Commissioners are responsible for promoting the effective use of charitable resources, for encouraging the development of better methods of administration, for giving charity *trustees information and advice on matters affecting charity, and for investigating and checking abuses. The Commissioners maintain a register of charities and decide whether or not a body should be registered; an *appeal from their decision may be made to the *High Court. Their Annual Reports (published by the Stationery Office) indicate how the Commissioners operate and how they are allowing the law of charity to develop.

charter A constitution, e.g. the Charter of the *United Nations.

chastisement Physical *punishment as a form of discipline. A *parent or *guardian has the *common-law right to inflict reasonable and moderate punishment on his children and may authorize someone **in loco parentis* to do so, such as a child carer, nanny, or school. State schools now prohibit this, although if parents have consented it is still lawful in private schools. A husband does not, however, have the right to chastise his wife, nor a wife her husband. Illegal chastisement may amount to one of the *offences against the person.

chattel Any property other than freehold *land (*compare* REAL PROPERTY). *Leasehold interests in land are called **chattels real**, because they bear characteristics of both real and *personal property. Tangible *goods are called **chattels personal**. The definition of 'personal chattels' in the Administration of Estates Act 1925, for the purposes of succession on *intestacy, excludes chattels used for business purposes at the intestate's death, money, and securities for money.

cheating An offence, under s 42 of the Gambling Act 2005, committed when a person cheats at gambling, or does anything for the purpose of enabling or assisting another person to cheat at gambling. For the purposes of s 42(1) it is immaterial whether a person who cheats improves his chances of winning anything, or wins anything.

cheating the public revenue To make a false statement (whether written or not) relating to *tax with intent to defraud the *Crown and *Her Majesty's Commissioners of Revenue and Customs, or to deliver or cause to be delivered a false *document relating to tax with similar intent, amounts to a *common law offence and is indictable as such: *R v Hudson* [1956] 2 QB 252; *R v Mavji* 84 Cr App R 34. Cheating may include any form of fraudulent conduct: a deception is not a necessary ingredient of the offence. The offence is satisfied by matters of omission. It is enough if one dishonestly fails to make *value-added tax or other tax returns and to pay the tax due.

cheque A *bill of exchange drawn on a banker payable on demand. Since a cheque is payable on demand it need not be presented to the drawee bank for acceptance. A cheque operates as a *mandate or order to the drawee bank to pay and debit the account of its customer, the drawer. The Cheques Act 1992 gave legal force to the words 'account payee' on cheques, making them non-transferable.

cheque guarantee card A card issued by a bank to one of its customers containing an *undertaking that any *cheque signed by the customer and not exceeding a stated sum will be honoured by the bank. This is normally subject to certain conditions; e.g. the cheque must be signed in the presence of the payee, the signature must correspond with a specimen on the card, and the payee must write the card number on the reverse of the cheque. The bank thus undertakes to the payee of the cheque that the cheque will be honoured regardless of the state of the customer's account with the bank. All cards in the UK Domestic Cheque Guarantee Card Scheme carry a hologram containing a portrait of William Shakespeare.

chicken hawk (*slang*) A *paedophile, especially one who uses the Internet to locate potential victims.

chief constable The chief officer of a *police force outside London.

chief inspector The police rank above inspector and below superintendent.

Chief Inspector of Constabulary Her Majesty's Inspectorate of Constabulary (HMIC) has the statutory duty of reporting on the effectiveness of all *police forces and *police authorities (s 55, Police Act 1996). There is a Chief Inspector of Constabulary and five Inspectors, appointed by the *Home Secretary, each with a team of staff officers and support staff in each of the four regional HMIC offices.

chief superintendent The police rank above superintendent.

Chief Surveillance Commissioner An individual appointed to perform a number of statutory functions under s 91 of the Police Act 1997. These responsibilities were extended by the Regulation of Investigatory Powers Act 2000 to cover oversight of pts II and III of that Act except where they relate to interception of communications and the intelligence services. The surveillance commissioners and the chief commissioner must have held high judicial office.

child 1. There is no definitive definition of a child: the term has been used for persons under the age of 14, under the age of 16, and sometimes under the age of 18 (an *infant). Each case depends on its context and the wording of the statute governing it. For the purposes of the Children and Young Persons Act 1933, 'child' means a person under the age of 14 years, unless the context otherwise requires. The Children and Young Persons Act 1969 contains a similar provision in respect of the majority of the provisions of that Act, while the Children and Young Persons Act 1963 provides that it shall be construed as one with the 1933 Act. It should be noted, however, that in some contexts (e.g. for purposes of children in care) 'child' is given an extended meaning: for the purposes of the Children Act 1989 and the Family Law Act 1996 a child is a person under the age of 18. For the purposes of the *special measures directions which may be made under the Youth Justice and Criminal Evidence Act 1999 to assist *vulnerable and intimidated witnesses to give evidence, a child witness is a witness who is under 17 when the direction is made. Another relevant definition for the purposes of the Youth Justice and Criminal Evidence Act 1999 relates to the giving of *unsworn evidence. A 'child' under the age of 14 who is competent to give evidence does so without taking an *oath or making an equivalent solemn *affirmation, i.e. unsworn. **2.** An offspring of *parents. In wills, statutes, and other legal *documents, the effect of the Family Law Reform Act 1987 is that there is a presumption that (unless the contrary intention is apparent) the word 'child' includes any illegitimate child (*see* ILLEGITIMACY). Adopted children are treated as the legitimate children of their adoptive parents. *See also* CHILD OF THE FAMILY.

child abduction The offence under s 2 (1) of the Child Abduction Act 1984 of taking or detaining a child under the age of 16 so as to remove him from, or keep him out of the control of, any person who has lawful control of the child. It is a defence to show that the defendant acted with lawful authority or reasonable excuse. Other offences such as *assault, *false imprisonment, and *kidnapping may also be committed when a person abducts a child.

child abuse The molestation of children by *parents or others (*see* BATTERED CHILD). If the molestation is of a sexual nature, the offender may be *guilty of *sexual assault or one of the 'child sex offences' contained within ss 9 to 15 of the Sexual Offences Act 2003. Under the Act, children under the age of 13 are not capable in law of giving *consent to any form of sexual activity and any such conduct is treated as an offence of *strict liability (*see also* SEXUAL OFFENCES; PAEDOPHILE). It is an offence to take or allow the taking of indecent photographs of a child under the age of 18 (s 45, Sexual Offences Act 2003, amending and expanding the offence at s 1(1) of the Protection of Children Act 1978), to distribute or show such photographs, to advertise that one intends to distribute or show them, or simply to possess them without legitimate reason (s 160, Criminal Justice Act 1988). Photographs on the Internet and *computers were brought within the definition of a 'photograph' by the Criminal Justice Act 1994. *See also* CAUSING OR INCITING OR CONTROLLING PROSTITUTION; INDECENT PHOTOGRAPHS OF CHILDREN; OBSCENE PUBLICATIONS; PAYING FOR SEXUAL SERVICES OF A CHILD.

child assessment order An order of the court made under s 43 of the Children Act 1989 when a *local authority or the NSPCC has concerns for a child's welfare in circumstances when the child's *parents are refusing to allow the child to be medically or otherwise examined. The order authorizes such an examination. If a local authority fears that a child is in immediate danger, or when it is denied access to a child, an *emergency protection order should be applied for rather than a child assessment order.

child being looked after by a local authority A child who is either the subject of a *care order or who is being provided with accommodation by the *local authority on a voluntary basis (*see* VOLUNTARY ACCOMMODATION). In respect of such a child, the local authority must seek, where possible, to promote *contact between the child and its *parents, relatives, and others closely connected with the child. Accommodation should be near where the child lives, and siblings should be accommodated together. A written plan should be drawn up before a child is placed; all the people involved in the plan, including the child (so far as is consistent with his age and understanding), should be consulted.

child cruelty An offence under s 1 of the Children and Young Persons Act 1933. A person aged 16 or over with responsibility for a child under the age of 16 is *guilty of an offence of child cruelty if he wilfully assaults, ill-treats, neglects (including by failing to provide adequate food, clothing, lodging, or medical aid), abandons or exposes him in a manner likely to cause him unnecessary suffering or injury to health, or causes or procures him to be so treated. The offence is triable *either way.

child curfew *See* DISPERSAL ORDER.

child destruction An act causing a viable unborn child to die during the course of pregnancy or birth. (A foetus is generally considered to be viable, i.e. capable of being born alive, if the pregnancy has lasted at least 24 weeks.) If carried out with the intention of causing death, and if it is proved that the act was not carried out in good faith in order to preserve the mother's life, the offence is subject to a maximum *punishment of *life imprisonment (s 1, Infant Life (Preservation) Act 1929). *Compare* ABORTION.

child, drunk while in charge of An offence under s 2(1) of the Licensing Act 1902 of being drunk in a *public place while having charge of a child apparently under the age of seven years.

child employee A child of compulsory school age (i.e. between 5 and 16 years) who undertakes paid work. Subject to certain exceptions, such employment is prohibited in Britain, and any employment under the age of 13 years is completely prohibited. Children are prohibited from working in industrial *undertakings, factories, or mines. There are narrow exceptions for work in theatres and films, sports, work experience and/or training, and light work, with strict conditions attached in each case. In many cases these exceptions require that prior authorization is obtained from a *local authority with respect to the proposed work (see, for example, the Children (Protection at Work) Regulations 2000).

In particular, children falling within some of the above exceptions must not work for more than two hours on any school day (outside school hours) or for more than twelve hours a week during term times. Work must not start before 7 am or after 7 pm. These restrictions can be relaxed for working time during school holidays and for children between 13 and 15 years of age. Night work by children is prohibited between 8 pm and 6 am, and children working more than 4½ hours daily are entitled to a 30-minute break from work. *Local authorities are also empowered to further regulate the employment of children under *byelaws.

child in care A child who is the subject of a *care order. It is important to note that not all children who are being looked after by a *local authority are the subjects of care orders; some of these children may be being accommodated by the local authority on a voluntary basis (*see* VOLUNTARY ACCOMMODATION). *See also* CHILD BEING LOOKED AFTER BY A LOCAL AUTHORITY.

child of the family A person considered under the Matrimonial Causes Act 1973, the Domestic Procedures and Magistrates' Courts Act 1978, and the Children Act 1989 to be the child of a married couple, although not necessarily born to or adopted by them, on the grounds that he or she has been treated by them as their own child. Courts have powers to make orders in favour of children of the family in all *family proceedings.

child pornography *See* CAUSING OR INCITING OR CONTROLLING PROSTITUTION; INDECENT PHOTOGRAPHS OF CHILDREN.

child prostitution *See* CAUSING OR INCITING OR CONTROLLING PROSTITUTION; PAYING FOR SEXUAL SERVICES OF A CHILD.

Child Protection Conference A conference that decides what action should be taken by the *local authority in respect of a child believed to be at risk of suffering harm. The conference comprises representatives of those bodies concerned with the child's welfare, including the NSPCC, social services, the police, the health and education authorities, and the probation service. *Parents have no absolute right to attend the Child Protection Conference but are usually excluded only in exceptional circumstances.

Children and Family Court Advisory and Support Service (CAFCASS) A service to provide courts with information about children coming before them, amalgamated from three former services, the Guardian ad Litem Service, the Family Court Welfare Service, and the Official Solicitor's children's department.

children, exclusion from court Children under the age of 14 years (other than an infant in arms) are excluded from courts unless present as a witness or justice requires their presence or the court consents (s 36, Children and Young Persons Act 1933). *See also* CAMERA, SITTINGS IN.

children in care *See* CHILD IN CARE; CARE ORDER.

children in need Those children designated by the Children Act 1989 as being in need of special support and provision by the *local authority. They include disabled children and children who are unlikely to maintain a reasonable standard of health or development without the provision of these special services.

children's certificate A certificate issued by a licensing authority permitting children (under 14) to be present in all or part of *licensed premises.

children's guardian A person appointed by the court to protect a minor's interests in proceedings affecting his interests (such as adoption, *wardship, or care proceedings), formerly known as a **guardian *ad litem***. Since the Children Act 1989 came into force the role of guardians has increased and they must ensure that the options open to the court are fully investigated. However, if a child is deemed capable of instructing a *solicitor on his own behalf, he may do so even if this conflicts with the interests of the guardian.

child safety order An order that enables *local authorities and courts to intervene when a child under the age of ten (who cannot be prosecuted in criminal proceedings by virtue of his age) behaves antisocially or disruptively. The order was introduced by the Crime and Disorder Act 1998 as part of a strategy to reduce youth crime and is founded on the belief that early intervention is more effective than waiting until a child is old enough to be dealt with under the youth justice system. Application for an order is made by a local authority under s 11 of the 1998 Act on the grounds that the child has committed or is in danger of committing an offence, or is in breach of a local child curfew scheme, or has acted in a manner likely to cause *harassment, alarm, or distress to a person not living in the same household as the child. The requirements imposed under the order are entirely a matter for the court and might include, for example, attendance at school or extracurricular activities, avoiding contact with disruptive and older children, and not visiting such areas as shopping centres unsupervised. The purpose of the requirements imposed is either to ensure that the child receives appropriate care, protection, and support and is subject to proper control, or to prevent the repetition of the kind of behaviour that led to the child safety order being made. Breach of the order may lead to the court making a *care order in respect of the child. *See also* PARENTING ORDER.

child soldiers It is an offence under the Statute of the *International Criminal

Court to conscript or enlist children under the age of fifteen in the armed forces or use them to participate actively in hostilities during international armed conflicts. It also prohibits conscription or enlistment into any army or group during non-international conflict. It is also an international crime for insurgents to recruit children.

child tax credit *See* TAX CREDIT.

child witness *See* VIDEO-RECORDED EVIDENCE; WITNESS.

chip *See* COMPUTER CHIP.

chip card A *debit or *credit card containing a microchip that can store or process information. It is an essential component of the 'chip and pin' payment system.

choke-damp *See* CARBON DIOXIDE.

choking Blocking the upper airway causing *asphyxia.

chop shop (*slang*) An establishment where stolen *motor vehicles are dismantled in order that the component parts may be sold.

chose A thing. Choses are divided into two classes. A **chose in possession** is a tangible item capable of being actually possessed and enjoyed, e.g. a book or a piece of furniture. A **chose in action** is a right (e.g. a right to recover a debt) that can be enforced by legal action.

chromosome The structure in the nucleus of a cell containing *deoxyribonucleic acid (DNA).

circuit judge Any of the *judges appointed under the provisions of the Courts Act 1971 from among those who have had a ten-year *Crown Court or *county court advocacy qualification, or who are *recorders, or who have held a full-time appointment of at least three years' duration in one of the offices listed in the Courts Act 1971. They sit in the county courts and the Crown Court and may, by invitation of the *Lord Chancellor, sit as *High Court judges. All judges of county courts and other judges of comparable status were made circuit judges in 1971.

circuit system The system of dividing England and Wales into regional **circuits** for the purpose of court administration. It is based upon the traditional regional groupings adopted by the *Bar and consists of the South-Eastern, Western, Midland and Oxford, Wales and Chester, Northern, and North-Eastern circuits. Each circuit is administered by a circuit administrator and supervised by two *presiding judges. *See also* CIRCUIT JUDGE.

circumcision In males—the removal of the foreskin of the penis for medical reasons or as a rite of Judaism or Islam. Male circumcision is lawful in the UK. In females—the excision of the clitoris, *labia majora*, or *labia minora*. Unless performed for medical reasons (rare), female circumcision is a criminal offence even if performed for cultural or religious reasons. It is an offence to aid, abet, counsel, or procure a girl to circumcise herself. It is also an offence to aid, abet, counsel, or procure a non-UK national to perform such an act outside the UK (Female Genital Mutilation Act 2003).

circumstantial evidence (indirect evidence) Evidence from which the *judge or *jury may infer the existence of a fact in issue but which does not prove the existence of the fact directly. Case law has described circumstantial evidence as evidence that is relevant (and, therefore, admissible) but that has little probative value. *Compare* DIRECT EVIDENCE.

cirrhosis An often fatal disease of the liver usually caused by long-term *alcohol abuse, less commonly caused by viral hepatitis.

citation The quoting of a legal case or authority. *See also* LAW REPORTS.

citator A reference book containing alphabetical or chronological lists of *cases or *legislation.

citizen's arrest An *arrest by anyone other than a *police officer. Under s 24A of the Police and Criminal Evidence Act 1984 (inserted by s 110, Serious Organized Crime and Police Act 2005), a person other than a *constable has the power to arrest, without *warrant, anyone who (a) has committed or is in the act of committing an *indictable offence, or (b) whom the person reasonably suspects to have committed or to be committing such an offence. However, the power is only exercisable if it appears to the person making the arrest that (a) it is not reasonably practicable for a constable to make it instead, and (b) that there are reasonable grounds for believing that the arrest is necessary to prevent the offender causing physical injury to himself or any other person, suffering physical injury, causing loss of or damage to property, or making off before a constable can assume responsibility for him. Every person has a duty at *common law to take reasonable steps, including arrest, to prevent a *breach of the peace that is being, or reasonably appears about to be, committed in his presence.

citizenship of the UK and Colonies *See* BRITISH CITIZENSHIP.

civil court A court exercising *jurisdiction over civil rather than criminal cases. In England the principal civil *courts of first instance are the *county courts and the *High Court. *Magistrates' courts have limited civil jurisdiction, mainly confined to matrimonial proceedings.

Civilian Enforcement Officer A person, not being a *constable, authorized by the *magistrates' courts committee to execute *warrants of *arrest, commitment, detention, or distress, issued by a *justice of the peace (s 125A, Magistrates' Courts Act 1980).

civilian with police powers A civilian granted powers previously reserved to *constables. The Police Reform Act 2002 enables *chief constables to designate *police authority *employees to be *Community Support Officers, *Investigating Officers, *Detention Officers, and *Escort Officers. (Contractors not employed by the police authority may be designated Detention and Escort Officers.) Each role is granted certain powers, set out in sch 4 to the Act.

civil law 1. The law of any particular state, now usually called *municipal law. **2.** Roman law. **3.** A legal system based on Roman law, as distinct from the English system of *common law. **4.** *Private law, as opposed to *public law, military law, and ecclesiastical law.

Civil Procedure Rules (CPR) The procedural code, which was enacted in 1998 and revoked the Rules of the Supreme Court with effect from 26 April 1999. The CPR, a result of the reforms proposed by Lord Woolf's *Access to Justice* (Final Report) 1996, now govern proceedings in the civil cases of the *Court of Appeal (Civil Division), the *High Court, and the *county courts. The CPR have been supplemented by *Practice Directions and pre-action protocols. They have no application in certain areas, including pt IV of the Mental Health Act 1983 and family and adoption proceedings.

civil recovery The scheme under pt 5 of the Proceeds of Crime Act 2002 that enables the *Asset Recovery Agency to use civil proceedings to recover property which is or represents property obtained through unlawful conduct.

Civil Recovery Unit (CRU) An agency responsible to the Scottish Ministers under pt 5 of the Proceeds of Crime Act 2002 for the implementation of *civil recovery and cash forfeiture in Scotland.

civil remedy *See* REMEDY.

civil wrong An infringement of a person's rights, for which the person wronged may sue for damages or some other civil remedy. Examples are *torts and *breaches of contract.

claim A demand for a *remedy or assertion of a right, especially the right to take a particular case to court (right of action). The term is used in civil litigation.

claimant A person applying for relief against another person in an action, suit, petition, or any other form of court proceeding. Before the introduction of the *Civil Procedure Rules in 1999, a claimant was called a **plaintiff.** *Compare* DEFENDANT.

classical criminology This approach to criminality, first described in the 18th century, is based on the notion that people are, by nature, self-seeking and thus liable to commit crime. But as there is a consensus in society that property and people should be protected, people freely enter into a contract with the state to preserve the peace. *Punishment must be used to deter individuals from violating the interests of others. Punishments must be proportional to the crime and not excessive. It was also held that punishment must not be used for reformation because this would restrict the right of the individual and breach the social contract. It was held that there should be as little law as possible, and it should be implemented strictly in accordance with due process. All people were held to be equal in the eyes of the law and responsible for their own actions. Thus their circumstances could not be considered as mitigating factors.

classification of animals At *common law animals were formerly classified as wild by nature (*ferae naturae*) or tame by nature (*mansuetae naturae*), referring to the species in general rather than the individual animal. The owner of a wild animal was strictly liable for any damage it caused. The owner of a tame animal was liable for damage it caused if he knew that it had a vicious tendency abnormal in the species (the **scienter rule**). Special rules applied to damage done by cattle (*see* CATTLE TRESPASS) and dogs. The common law classifications have been largely replaced by modern statutes.

For purposes of civil liability in England, animals are classified as belonging to a dangerous or a non-dangerous species (Animals Act 1971). A dangerous species is one not commonly domesticated in the British Isles, fully grown members of which are likely to cause severe damage. The keeper of an animal of a dangerous species is strictly liable for any damage it causes. Liability for damage done by other animals arises either under the Animals Act, if the animal was known by its keeper to have characteristics not normally found in that species, or only normally found in particular circumstances, which made it likely to cause that kind of damage; or under ordinary rules of *tort liability. Thus carelessly allowing a dog to stray on the highway can make the keeper liable in *negligence if it causes an accident, and excessive smell from a pig farm can be an actionable *nuisance. The 1971 Act also imposes *strict liability for damage done by trespassing livestock, which includes cattle, horses, sheep, pigs, goats, and poultry. The keeper of a dog that kills or injures livestock is liable for the damage, except when the livestock was injured while straying on the keeper's *land. If livestock is worried by a dog, the owner of the livestock (or the owner of the land on which the livestock lives) may kill or injure the dog to protect the livestock.

Dangerous wild animals may require a licence under the Dangerous Wild Animals Act 1976. Keeping dogs of a species bred for fighting is an offence under the Dangerous Dogs Act 1991. The use of *guard dogs is controlled by the Guard Dogs Act 1975. Other statutes protect various species, control importation of animals, and deal with animal diseases. *See also* ANIMAL CRUELTY; COCKFIGHTING.

clause 1. A sub-division of a *document. A clause of a written contract contains a term or provision of the contract. Clauses are usually numbered consecutively (1, 2, etc.); sub-clauses may follow a clause, numbered 1.1, 1.1.1, etc. **2.** A section of a *Bill.

clavicle The collar bone.

clearance A certificate acknowledging a *ship's compliance with customs requirements.

clear-up rate A measure of the number of crimes 'solved' by the police, used as an indicator of the performance of the police. The figure is made up of the sum of *primary detections and *secondary detections.

clearway A *road where stopping is prohibited. The Various Trunk Roads (Prohibition of Waiting) (Clearways) Order 1963 (SI 1963/1172, made under ss 1 and 6 of the Road Traffic Regulation Act 1984) forbids vehicles to stop on the main *carriageway of certain named roads unless, with police permission, for building, road or public utility works, fire, ambulance or police purposes, postal collections and deliveries, local authority cesspool and refuse vehicles, to close gates and barriers, to avoid accidents, or in circumstances beyond the *driver's control. Local clearways orders may also apply.

clerk to the justices (justices' clerk, magistrates' clerk) A person designated and appointed by the *Lord Chancellor, under s 27 of the Courts Act 2003, as *justices' clerk to one or more *local justice areas. A person may be so designated only if he has a five year *magistrates' court qualification, is a *barrister or *solicitor who has served for not less than five years as an assistant to a justices' clerk, or has previously been a justices' clerk. The Lord Chancellor may also designate and appoint a person to be an assistant to a justices' clerk (a **legal adviser**). An assistant clerk must have certain minimum qualifications (see Justices' Clerks (Qualification of Assistants) Rules 1979 (SI 1979/570), as amended).

The functions of a justices' clerk and his assistants include giving advice to any or all of the *magistrates of the magistrates' court about matters of law (including procedure and practice) on questions arising in connection with the discharge of their functions. The advice should be given publicly in open court. If advice is provided after the magistrates have retired to consider their decision and the clerk cites authority which was not cited in open court, he should inform the *advocates in the case and give them the opportunity to make further submissions to the magistrates. Since the magistrates are the ultimate arbiters of both law and fact there is no obligation on them to heed that advice, but they will usually do so. No action lies against a justices' clerk or an assistant clerk in respect of that which he does or omits to do whilst acting in the execution of his duty.

See also MAGISTRATES' COURT.

client A person who employs a *solicitor to carry out legal business on behalf of himself or someone else. The relationship between a solicitor and his client is a *fiduciary one and any other transactions between them may be affected by *undue influence. A solicitor's client cannot consult a *barrister directly but only through his solicitor: the solicitor is therefore the barrister's client.

client/server An architecture in which one *computer can get information from another. The client is the computer that asks for access to data, software, or services. The server, which can be anything from a personal computer to a mainframe, supplies the requested data or services for the client.

client/server network A network in which one or more *computers are servers, and the others are clients, as opposed to a peer-to-peer network, in which any node can be a client and server.

closed circuit television link *See* LIVE TELEVISION LINK.

close tail A surveillance operation in which the target is kept constantly within view.

closure notice A notice issued under s 1 of the Anti-Social Behaviour Act 2003 by a police superintendent to the *occupier/owner of *premises stating his intention to apply to *magistrates for a *closure order under s 2 of the Act.

closure order 1. An order under s 179A of the Licensing Act 1964 (s 161, Licensing Act 2003) made by a *police officer of at least the rank of inspector ordering the immediate closure of *licensed premises where there is disorder or there is likely to be disorder on or in the vicinity of and related to the licensed premises. In regard to non-licensed premises where intoxicating liquor is being illegally sold, the police can apply to *magistrates for a closure order. **2.** An order under s 2 of the Anti-Social Behaviour Act 2003 made by magistrates ordering the closure of *premises that have been used in connection with the unlawful use, production or supply of a Class A *controlled drug and the premises are associated with the occurrence of disorder or serious nuisance. **3.** An order under s 40 of the Anti-Social Behaviour Act 2003 made by the chief executive of a *local authority ordering the closure of specified licensed premises during a specified period.

clotting *See* COAGULATION.

club An association regulated by rules that bind its members according to the law of contract. Club property is either vested in *trustees for the members (**members' club**) or owned by a proprietor (often a company limited by guarantee; *see* LIMITED COMPANY) who operates the club as a business for profit (**proprietary club**). The committee is usually liable for club *debts in the case of a members' club; the proprietor in the case of a proprietary club.

club premises certificate A certificate granted under s 60 of the Licensing Act 2003 permitting supply of *alcohol in qualifying clubs.

cluster 1. *Computers running Microsoft Windows™ allocate space to files in units called clusters. Each cluster contains from 1 to 64 contiguous sectors, depending on the type and size of the disk. A cluster is the smallest unit of disk space that can be allocated for use by a file. **2.** A group of computers that are networked together and used as a single unit to run parallel programs.

co-accused A person charged in the same proceedings as another. A co-accused can only be called by the *prosecution to give evidence for the prosecution if he has ceased to be a co-accused (by having pleaded *guilty or otherwise being no longer liable to be convicted of any offence in the proceedings). An accused person is competent but not compellable for a co-accused but becomes compellable once he ceases to be a co-accused.

coach A large *bus with a maximum gross weight of more than 7.5 tonnes and with a maximum speed exceeding 60mph (reg 3(2), Road Vehicles (Construction and Use) Regulations 1986 (SI 1986/1078).

coagulation The clotting of blood at sites of blood vessel damage, brought about by chemicals (factors) in the blood.

cocaine A Class A controlled drug produced from the leaves of the coca plant. Usually found as a white or colourless crystalline powder.

cockfighting The placing of two cock fowls in a ring for the purpose of their fighting. It is an offence under the Protection of Animals Act 1911 to arrange, attend, or advertise any animal fights. The Cockfighting Act 1952 creates a specific offence of possessing instruments for use in cockfighting. Section 36 of the Town Police Clauses Act 1847 and s 47 of the Metropolitan Police Act 1839 create offences of keeping *premises for the fighting and baiting of animals.

code A complete written formulation of a body of law (e.g. the *Code Napoléon* in France, the Queensland Criminal Code 1899). A code of English law does not exist, but a few specialized topics have been dealt with in this way by means of a *codifying statute (e.g. the Sale of Goods Act 1893, re-enacted with modifications by the Sale of Goods Act 1979).

Code for Crown Prosecutors A Code issued under s 10 of the Prosecution of Offences Act 1985, giving guidance on the general principles to be applied when making decisions about *prosecutions. It applies not only to the *Crown Prosecution Service but also, by virtue of s 36(2) of the Commissioners for Revenue and Customs Act 2005, to the *Revenue and Customs Prosecutions Office. The Code is a public *document and is available on the CPS website: <http://www.cps.gov.uk>. *See also* FULL CODE TEST; THRESHOLD TEST.

Code of Conduct The code for the conduct of *police officers laid down by the Police (Conduct) Regulations 2004 (SI 645/2004) which replaced earlier statutory regulations and the former Discipline Code.

code of practice A body of rules for practical guidance only, or that sets out professional standards of behaviour, but does not have the force of law, e.g. the Highway Code. Under the provisions of the Fair Trading Act 1973, the *Director General of Fair Trading has the duty of encouraging trade associations to prepare and distribute to their members codes of practice for guidance in safeguarding and promoting the interests of UK consumers. Several such codes have been approved by the Director General. Codes of practice have also been published by ACAS, the Health and Safety, Equal Opportunities, and Racial Equality Commissions, and the Secretary of State for Work and Pensions, providing guidance to *employers, *employees, and their representatives on the fulfilment of their statutory obligations in relevant fields. Codes of practice under the Police and Criminal Evidence Act 1984 regulate, inter alia, searches and the *interrogation of suspects by the police.

Generally, failure to comply with a code of practice does not automatically expose the party in breach to *prosecution or any civil remedy. It may, however, be relied on as evidence tending to show that he has not fulfilled some relevant statutory requirement.

Code of Practice for Victims A code issued by the *Home Secretary, under s 32 of the Domestic Violence, Crime and Victims Act 2004, as to the services to be provided to a victim of criminal conduct, including the family of a victim who has died as a result of such conduct. Some of the key requirements of the code are:

- A right to information about the progress of the investigation within specified time scales, including the right to be notified of any *arrests and court cases.
- Assignment of a dedicated family liaison *police officer to bereaved relatives.
- A right to clear information from the *Criminal Injuries Compensation Authority on eligibility for compensation under the Scheme.
- A right to be informed regarding *Victim Support and either to be referred on to them or offered their service.

The Code is a public *document and is available on the Home Office website: <http://www.homeoffice.gov.uk>.

codes of practice, access to A person brought to a police station under *arrest or arrested at the station must be informed of the right to consult the PACE Codes of Practice at any stage during the period in custody.

coercion A defence available only to married women who have committed a crime (other than *murder or *treason) in the presence of, and under pressure from, their husbands. Its scope is unclear but may be wider than that of *duress in that it may cover economic and moral as well as physical pressure, though unlike duress it has to be proved (*see* BURDEN OF PROOF). If a wife is acquitted on grounds of coercion, her husband may be liable for the offence in question through his wife's innocent agency and/or for a crime involving a *threat.

cognitive interview A form of *investigative interview intended to help victims and witnesses put themselves mentally at the scene of a crime. *See also* CONVERSATION MANAGEMENT; ENHANCED COGNITIVE INTERVIEW.

cohabitants *See* COHABITATION.

cohabitation Living together as husband and wife. Married persons generally have a right to expect their spouses to live with them. Unmarried people living together as husband and wife (**cohabitants**) do not usually have the status of a married couple (*see also* COMMON-LAW MARRIAGE). But under the **cohabitation rule** the resources and requirements of an unmarried couple living together are aggregated for the purposes of claiming social security benefits (*see* INCOME SUPPORT) and *tax credits even in the absence of a sexual relationship.

co-imperium Joint rule by two or more states of an entity that has a distinct international status (*compare* CONDOMINIUM). An example is the occupation and rule of Germany after 1945 by the four victorious powers.

collateral damage (in armed conflict) The unintended damage and destruction of targets or personnel not considered as lawful military targets. For instance, civilians unintentionally killed when military targets are bombed or accidental bombing of medical facilities.

collateral intrusion The unintentional gathering of intelligence material with intended material e.g. background conversation recorded with intended speech.

Collection A division of *Her Majesty's Revenue and Customs under the command of a *Collector.

collective harassment A term inserted into s 7 of the Protection from Harassment Act 1997 by s 44 of the Criminal Justice and Police Act 2001 to make those who aid, abet, counsel, and procure acts of harassment liable for the conduct that they have brought about.

collective security The centralized system of international rules, now embodied in the Charter of the *United Nations, that governs the collective resort to force under the authority of the United Nations for the purpose of maintaining or restoring international peace and security. An example is the action by the international community during the Gulf War of 1991. It should be noted that the precise legal justification of this conflict is uncertain, the UN Security Council Resolution 678 stating only that its legal basis was under *Chapter VII of the UN Charter. *See also* ENFORCEMENT ACTION.

collective trespass *See* TRESPASS.

Collector An officer of *Her Majesty's Revenue and Customs in charge of a division called a *Collection.

colluding trader A trader who knowingly accepts stolen *credit/*debit cards. He is often detected by the number of transactions using stolen cards for sums just below the *floor limit.

collusion An improper agreement or bargain between parties that one of them should bring proceedings against the other.

colon Part of the large bowel between the caecum and rectum, the main function of which is to absorb water from its contents back into the blood stream.

colony A territory that forms part of the *Crown's dominions outside the UK. Although it may enjoy internal self-government, its external affairs are controlled by the UK Government.

comity (comitas gentium) [Latin: the courteousness of nations] Neighbourly gestures or courtesies extended from one state to another, or others, without accepting a legal obligation to behave in that manner. Comity is founded upon the concept of sovereign equality among states and is expected to be reciprocal. It is possible for such practices, over a period of time and with common usage, to develop into rules of customary *international law, although this requires such behaviour to acquire a binding or compelling quality. *See* CUSTOM; OPINIO JURIS.

Command Papers *Documents that the Government, by royal command, presents to *Parliament for consideration. They include **white papers** and **green papers**. The former contain statements of policy or explanations of proposed *legislation; the latter are essentially discussion documents. For reference purposes they have serial numbers, with (since 1869) prefixes. The prefixes are **C** (1870–99), **Cd** (1900–18), **Cmd** (1919–56), **Cmnd** (1957–86) and **Cm** (1986–).

commission 1. Authority to exercise a power or a direction to perform a duty; e.g. a commission of a *justice of the peace. **2.** A body directed to perform a particular duty. Examples are the *Charity Commissioners and the *Law Commission. **3.** A sum payable to an *agent in return for his performing a particular service. This may, for example, be a percentage of the sum for which he has secured a contract of sale of his principal's property. The circumstances in which a commission is payable depend on the terms of the contract between principal and agent. The terms on which commission is paid to a *commercial agent are set down in EU Directive 86/653. **4.** Authorization by a court or a *judge for a witness to be examined on *oath by a court, judge, or other authorized person, to provide evidence for use in court proceedings. In civil proceedings, under r 32.8 of the *Civil Procedure Rules, the procedure may be used when the witness is unlikely to be able to attend the hearing (e.g. because of illness). A person from whom evidence is to be obtained following an order under this rule is referred to as a '**deponent**' and the evidence is referred to as a '**deposition**'. If the witness is still unable to attend when the court hearing takes place, the written evidence is read by the court. A similar procedure is also available to obtain evidence from a witness outside the *jurisdiction under r 32.23 of the Civil Procedure Rules.

Commissioner 1. Rank of chief officer of the City of London Police and Metropolitan Police Service. **2.** (in the EU) *See* EUROPEAN COMMISSION.

commissioner for oaths A person appointed by the Lord *Chancellor to administer *oaths or take *affidavits. By statute, every *solicitor who holds a *practising certificate has the powers of a commissioner for oaths, but he may not exercise these powers in a proceeding in which he is acting for any of the parties or in which he is interested. Thus when an affidavit must be sworn, the client cannot use his own solicitor but must go to another solicitor to witness the swearing.

Commissioners for Her Majesty's Revenue and Customs *See* HER MAJESTY'S REVENUE AND CUSTOMS.

Commission for Racial Equality A body appointed by the *Home Secretary under the Race Relations Act 1976 with the general function of working towards the elimination of *racial discrimination by promoting equality of opportunity and good relations between different racial groups. It keeps the working of the Act under review, investigates alleged contraventions and, when necessary, issues and applies for *injunctions to enforce non-discrimination notices. It is due to be replaced by the Commission for Equality and Human Rights in 2007 when the Equality Act 2006 comes into force.

Commission of Human Rights *See* EUROPEAN COMMISSION OF HUMAN RIGHTS.

Commission of the European Communities *See* EUROPEAN COMMISSION.

commissions rogatoires *See* LETTER OF REQUEST.

committal for sentence An alternative to passing *sentence themselves whereby *magistrates may in some circumstances commit an offender to the *Crown Court to be sentenced. The Powers of Criminal Courts (Sentencing) Act 2000 provides powers to commit for sentence: adult offenders summarily convicted after *trial of an offence triable *either way (s 3); adult offenders convicted of an either way offence as a result of a *guilty *plea indicated before the *mode of trial procedure (s 4); an offender in breach of a Crown Court *suspended sentence, probation order, or conditional discharge to be dealt with for the breach (ss 13(5), 120 and sch 3, para 10(3)); a prisoner who commits an imprisonable offence between the date of his early release and the expiry of the full term of his sentence (s 116(3)). In order to commit an adult offender summarily convicted after trial of an offence triable either way the magistrates must be of the opinion that the offence (in combination where appropriate with other offences) is so serious that the proper *punishment exceeds its powers or that in the case of a violent or *sexual offence a custodial sentence longer than it can impose is necessary to protect the public from serious harm (s 3(2)). Under s 70 of the Proceeds of Crime Act 2002 a magistrates' court must commit a defendant convicted of an offence to the Crown Court when the prosecutor asks the court to do so to enable the Crown Court to consider a *confiscation order under s 6 of the Act.

committal for trial Committal proceedings have traditionally been the means by which a *magistrates' court determines whether there is sufficient evidence against an accused in respect of an *indictable offence to justify sending him to the *Crown Court to stand *trial on indictment. Major changes to the nature of committal were brought about by the Criminal Procedure and Investigation Act 1996, which limited the evidence that could be considered to documentary evidence tendered by the *prosecution together with any exhibits. It abolished the right of the *defence to call evidence of its own or to require prosecution witnesses to attend to give evidence orally. It also introduced a new procedure for taking depositions from reluctant witnesses in advance of committal proceedings (*see* DEPOSITION). Section 51 of the Crime and Disorder Act 1998 abolished committal proceedings for cases triable on indictment only and provided for such offences, together with certain related offences, to be sent by the magistrates' court directly to the Crown Court. Schedule 3 to the Criminal Justice Act 2003 makes provision for the abolition of committal proceedings for offences triable *either way. However, those provisions have yet to be brought into force. *See also* OFFENCE TRIABLE EITHER WAY; SENDING OFFENCES FOR TRIAL.

committal in civil proceedings A method of enforcing *judgment by obtaining an order that a person be committed to prison. It is most commonly sought when the person has committed a *contempt of the court (e.g. by disobedience of an order of the court). In modern practice it is very occasionally available to enforce an order for the payment of a *debt.

committal proceedings *See* COMMITTAL FOR TRIAL; NOTICE OF TRANSFER.

Committee Against Torture The committee of ten states with expertise in human rights set up to monitor and supervise the United Nations *Convention Against Torture, and other Cruel, Inhuman, or Degrading Treatment or Punishment 1984.

common approach path (CAP) The designated route into and out of a crime scene so designated in order to minimize disturbance to the surrounding area.

common assault *See* ASSAULT.

common battery The criminal offence of *battery where no *actual bodily harm is caused. It is a summary offence punishable with a fine at level 5 and/or six months' imprisonment.

common carrier *See* CARRIER.

common design The intention assumed to be shared by those engaged in a joint illegal enterprise: each party is liable for anything done during the pursuance of that enterprise, including any unexpected consequences that arise. If, however, one of the parties does something that was not agreed beforehand, the others may not be held responsible for the consequences of this act. *See also* ACCESSORY.

common land *Land subject to rights of common. The Commons Registration Act 1965 provides for the registration with *local authorities of all common land in England and Wales, its owners, and claims to rights of common over it. Subject to the investigation by Commons Commissioners of disputed cases, and to exceptions for land becoming or ceasing to be common land, registration provides conclusive evidence that land is common land and also of the rights of common over it. Rights could be lost by failure to register.

common law 1. The part of English law based on rules developed by the royal courts during the first three centuries after the Norman Conquest (1066) as a system applicable to the whole country, as opposed to local customs. The Normans did not attempt to make new law for the country or to impose French law on it; they were mainly concerned with establishing a strong central administration and safeguarding the royal revenues, and it was through machinery devised for these purposes that the common law developed. Royal representatives were sent on tours of the shires to check on the conduct of local affairs generally, and this involved their participating in the work of local courts. At the same time there split off from the body of advisers surrounding the king (the *curia regis*) the first permanent royal court—the Court of Exchequer, sitting at Westminster to hear disputes concerning the revenues. Under Henry II (reigned 1154–89), to whom the development of the common law is principally due, the royal representatives were sent out on a regular basis (their tours being known as circuits) and their functions began to be exclusively judicial. Known as *justiciae errantes* (wandering justices), they took over the work of the local courts. In the same period there appeared at Westminster a second permanent royal court, the Court of Common Pleas. These two steps mark the real origins of the common law. The judges of the Court of Common Pleas so successfully superimposed a single system on the multiplicity of local customs that, as early as the end of the 12th century, reference is found in court records to the custom of the kingdom. In this process they were joined by the judges of the Court of Exchequer, which began to exercise *jurisdiction in many cases involving disputes between subjects rather than the royal revenues, and by those of a third royal court that gradually emerged—the Court of King's Bench. The common law was subsequently supplemented by *equity, but it remained separately administered by the three courts of common law until they and the Court of Chancery (all of them sitting in Westminster Hall until rehoused in the Strand in 1872) were replaced by the *High Court of Justice under the Judicature Acts 1873–5. **2.** Rules of law developed by the courts as opposed to those created by statute. **3.** A general system of law deriving exclusively from court decisions.

common-law marriage 1. A marriage recognized as valid at *common law although not complying with the usual requirements for marriage. Such marriages are only recognized today if (1) they are celebrated outside England and there is no local form of marriage reasonably available to the parties or (2) they are celebrated by military chaplains in a foreign territory (or on a *ship in foreign waters), and one of the parties to the marriage is serving in the Forces in that territory. The form of marriage is a declaration that the parties take each other as husband and wife. **2.** Loosely, the situation of two unmarried people living together as husband and wife (*see* COHABITATION). In law such people are treated as unmarried, although recently they have been recognized as equivalent to married persons for purposes of protection against battering and for some provisions of the Rent Acts (such as succession to statutory tenancies).

common prostitute A person who is a prostitute and 'who engages for reward in acts of lewdness with all and sundry': *R v Morris-Lowe* [1985] 1 WLR 29. A person who offers or provides sexual services to another person in return for payment, or promise of payment on a single occasion does not fall within the meaning of the term. *Compare* PROSTITUTE.

Common Serjeant The title held by one of the *circuit judges at the *Central Criminal Court. It was formerly an ancient office of the City of London, first mentioned in its records in 1291. Serjeants-at-law were the highest order at the English Bar from the 13th or 14th century until the King's Counsel took priority in the 17th century. Until 1873 the judges of the common law courts were appointed from the serjeants; the order of serjeants was dissolved in 1877. The title remains, however, for a circuit judge who has a ten-year *Crown Court qualification and who has been appointed a Common Serjeant by the Crown.

Commonwealth (British Commonwealth) A voluntary association consisting of the UK and many of its former colonies or dependencies (e.g. protectorates) that have attained full independence and are recognized by *international law as separate countries. The earliest to obtain independence (e.g. Australia and Canada) did so by virtue of the Statute of Westminster 1931, but the majority have been granted it individually by subsequent Independence Acts. Some (such as Australia and Canada) are still technically part of the *Crown's dominions; others (e.g. India) have become republics. All accept the Crown as the symbol of their free association and the head of the Commonwealth.

Commonwealth citizen A wide, secondary status of citizenship, redefined by s 37 of the British Nationality Act 1981, as amended by the British Overseas Territories Act 2002, to include every person who is either a British citizen (*see* BRITISH CITIZENSHIP), a *British Overseas citizen, a *British National (Overseas), a *British subject (in its current sense), or a citizen of one of the independent Commonwealth countries listed in sch 3 to the 1981 Act.

Commonwealth citizen, access to The right of *Commonwealth citizens in police detention to communicate with their High Commission, have it informed of their detention, and receive visits from consular staff, under PACE Code C 7.

communications protocol A standard way of regulating data exchange between *computers, including the rules for data transmission and the formatting of messages. Some communications protocols are TCP/IP, DECnet, AppleTalk, SNA, and IPX/SPX.

C

Communities Against Drugs (CAD) A funding stream whereby *Crime and Disorder Reduction Partnerships are awarded funds to work with the Police and Drug Action Teams to develop action against drug markets and drug related crime, and to strengthen communities to resist drug use.

community home An institution for the accommodation and maintenance of children and young persons in care. Community homes are provided by *local authorities and voluntary organizations under s 53 of the Children Act 1989. A local authority may be liable for the acts of children in community homes.

Community law (EU law) The law of the *European Union (as opposed to the national laws of the member states). It consists of the treaties establishing the EU (together with subsequent amending treaties), *Community legislation, and decisions of the *European Court of Justice. Any provision of the treaties or of Community legislation that is directly applicable or directly effective in a member state forms part of the law of that state and prevails over its national law in the event of any inconsistency between the two.

Community Legal Service (CLS) A body which brings together *solicitors, Citizens Advice Bureaux, Law Centres, *local authority services, and other organizations in local partnerships to provide the widest possible access to information and advice so that people can resolve actual or potential disputes and enforce their rights effectively. The emphasis is on early preventative intervention. Subject to certain financial eligibility criteria, the CLS provides publicly funded advice and assistance in specified types of cases. It replaced the Legal Aid Board. *See also* LEGAL AID.

Community legislation Laws made by the *Council of the European Union or the *European Commission. Each body has legislative powers, but most legislation is made by the Council, based on proposals by the Commission, and usually after consultation with the *European Parliament. The role of the Parliament in the legislative process was strengthened under the *Single European Act 1986 and the *Maastricht Treaty. Community legislation is in the form of regulations, directives, and decisions. **Regulations** are of general application, binding in their entirety, and directly applicable in all member states without the need for individual member states to enact these domestically (*see* COMMUNITY LAW). **Directives** are addressed to one or more member states and require them to achieve (by amending national law if necessary) specified results. They are not directly applicable—they do not create enforceable Community rights in member states until the state has legislated in accordance with the directive: the domestic statute then creates the rights for the citizens of that country. A directive cannot therefore impose legal obligations on individuals or private bodies, but by its **direct effect** it confers rights on individuals against the state and state bodies, even before it has been implemented by changes to national law, by decisions of the European court. **Decisions** may be addressed either to states or to persons and are binding on them in their entirety. Both the Council and the Commission may also make **recommendations**, give **opinions**, and issue **notices**, but these are not legally binding.

community liaison Arrangements made by each local *police authority, in consultation with the *chief constable, as required by s 96 of the Police Act 1996, for obtaining the views of people in that area about matters concerning the policing of the area and their cooperation with the police in preventing crime in that area (separate provisions apply in relation to the Metropolitan Police Area).

community orders A scheme for community penalties in respect of offenders aged 16 or over introduced by ch 2, pt 12 of the Criminal Justice Act 2003 (CJA 2003) (replacing the orders provided by the Powers of Criminal Courts (Sentencing) Act 2000, as amended by the Criminal Justice and Court Services Act 2000).

The scheme applies in respect of offences committed on or after 4 April 2005, save that, so far as they apply where a person aged 16 or 17 is convicted of an offence, they will come into force on 4 April 2007. Under the new provisions, a court may impose a single order with a combination of the following requirements:

- *unpaid work requirement (s 199, CJA 2003)
- *activity requirement (s 201, CJA 2003)
- *programme requirement (s 202, CJA 2003)
- *prohibited activity requirement (s 203, CJA 2003)
- *curfew requirement (s 204, CJA 2003), generally in conjunction with an *electronic monitoring requirement (s 177 (3), CJA 2003)
- *exclusion requirement (s 205, CJA 2003), generally in conjunction with an electronic monitoring requirement (s 177(3), CJA 2003)
- *residence requirement (s 206, CJA 2003)
- *mental health treatment requirement (s 207, CJA 2003)
- *drug rehabilitation requirement (s 209, CJA 2003)
- *alcohol treatment requirement (s 212, CJA 2003)
- *supervision requirement (s 213, CJA 2003)
- (in the case of an offender aged under 25) *attendance centre requirement (s 214, CJA 2003)

Under s 179 and sch 8 to the 2003 Act, an offender who breaches a community order or commits an offence whilst subject to such an order may have that order amended so as to include more onerous conditions or revoked, in which case the court may impose any *punishment that could originally have been imposed for the offence. In the case of a wilful and persistent disregard for the order, an offender aged over 18 originally convicted of a non-imprisonable offence may be sentenced to a term of imprisonment not exceeding 51 weeks. *See also* REPARATION ORDER.

community policing A philosophy that the police should work with the community through partnerships and problem solving to address problems of crime and disorder.

community punishment and rehabilitation order Although s 35(2) of the Powers of the Criminal Courts (Sentencing) Act 2000 prevents a court imposing both a *community punishment and a *community rehabilitation order for the same offence, s 51(1) of the Act provides that where the court is dealing with an offender who has attained the age of 16 and who has been convicted of a criminal offence, the court may make a community punishment and rehabilitation order (formerly known as a **combination order**). The effect of the order is that the offender is under the supervision of a *probation officer (or member of a *youth offending team if he is under 18 years of age) for a period which must be between twelve months and three years; and is required to perform unpaid work for a specified number of hours, which must be between 40 and 100 hours.

Such an order can only be made if the court is of the view that it is desirable so to do in the interests of securing the rehabilitation of the offender or of protecting the public from harm by preventing him from committing further offences. The order is only available in respect of an offence committed before 4 April 2005 (4 April 2007 in respect of a person aged 16 or 17). Offences committed after those dates fall to be dealt with under the *community order provisions introduced by pt 12 of the Criminal Justice Act 2003.

community punishment order An order made under s 46 of the Powers of the Criminal Courts (Sentencing) Act 2000 that requires an offender (who must consent and be aged at least 16) to perform unpaid work for between 40 and 240 hours under the supervision of a *probation officer. Formerly known as a **community service order**, it was renamed under the Criminal Justice and Court Services Act 2000. Such an order replaces any other form of *punishment (e.g. imprisonment); it is usually based on a pre-sentence report and is carried out within twelve months (unless extended). The order is only available in respect of an offence committed before 4 April 2005 (4 April 2007 in respect of a person aged 16 or 17). Offences committed after those dates fall to be dealt with under the *community order provisions introduced by pt 12 of the Criminal Justice Act 2003.

C

community rehabilitation order An order, formerly known as a **probation order**, made under s 41 of the Powers of Criminal Courts (Sentencing Act 2000), placing an offender under the supervision of a *probation officer for a period of between six months and three years, imposed (only with the consent of the offender) instead of a sentence of imprisonment. Such orders may be imposed on any offender over the age of 16; they are most commonly imposed on first offenders, young offenders, elderly offenders in need of support, and offenders whose crimes are not serious. The order is only available in respect of an offence committed before 4 April 2005 (4 April 2007 in respect of a person aged 16 or 17). Offences committed after those dates fall to be dealt with under the *community order provisions introduced by pt 12 of the Criminal Justice Act 2003.

The order contains conditions for the supervision and behaviour of the offender during the rehabilitation period, including where he should live, when and how often he should report to his local probation officer, and a requirement that he should notify the probation officer of any change of address. The order may also require him to live in an approved probation hostel (for those offenders employed outside the hostel) or an approved probation home (for offenders not employed outside). An order may also be made that the offender should attend a specified **day-training centre**, designed to train him to cope with the strains of modern life, for a period of up to 60 days.

A community rehabilitation order has the same legal effect as a *discharge. If the offender is convicted of a further offence while undergoing community rehabilitation, he may be punished in the normal way for the original offence (for which the order was made) as though he had just been convicted of that offence. If he does not comply with the conditions specified in the community rehabilitation order, he may be fined or the court may make a *community punishment order or order for attendance at a day centre or it may punish him for the original offence as though he had just been convicted of it.

Community rehabilitation orders may also be imposed on offenders who, though not insane, are suffering from some mental problem. A medical practitioner or chartered psychologist may be specified in such orders.

community safety accreditation scheme A system introduced by the Police Reform Act 2002 whereby commissioners and *chief constables may give suitably trained security staff, traffic wardens, street and community wardens, limited but targeted powers to deal with anti-social behaviour, disorder, and nuisance.

community safety partnerships Collaboration by every *local authority and corresponding *police force, as required by ss 5 and 6 of the Crime and Disorder Act 1998, with a range of organizations to develop a local strategy to tackle the problems of crime and disorder. The resulting community safety partnership is required to routinely conduct a crime audit to determine the key priorities for immediate and long-term action and, thereafter, to produce a three year strategy (the *community safety plan), stating the partnership's priorities for its local area.

community safety plan The three year plan produced by a *community safety partnership outlining the local policing priorities and strategy for the reduction of crime and disorder in the area.

community sentence A *sentence imposed as an alternative to imprisonment. The Criminal Justice Act 2003 introduced a largely new regime of community sentences. Section 147 of the Criminal Justice Act 2003 defines community sentence as a *community order or one or more *youth community orders (*curfew order, *exclusion order, *attendance centre order, *supervision order, or *action plan order).

These youth community orders will still be made under the Powers of Criminal Courts (Sentencing) Act 2000, although all the provisions have been amended so as to make them available only in the case of offenders under 16 years of age. The provisions of the 2000 Act that provide for *community rehabilitation orders, *community punishment orders, *community punishment and rehabilitation orders, *drug treatment and testing orders, and *drug abstinence orders are all repealed but will continue to apply to offences committed before 4 April 2005, and, in modified form, will apply to offences committed by persons aged 16 or 17 on conviction until 4 April 2007.

Community Support Officer An *employee of a *police authority who is not a *constable but patrols the streets and is given some police powers as listed in sch 4 to the Police Reform Act 2002.

Community Trade Mark (CTM) A *trade mark that is registered for the whole of the *European Union. It can be obtained by application to national trade mark offices or the Community Trade Mark Office at Alicante, Spain. The *European Commission adopted the Regulation for the Community Trade Mark, Regulation 40/94, on 20 December 1993; UK *legislation was included in the Trade Marks Act 1994. Marks are registered for a period of ten years and may be renewed on payment of fees.

compact disk—read-only memory or media-recordable (CD-ROM) A disk from which data can be read but not added to.

compact disk—recordable (CD-R) A disk to which data can be written but not over-written or erased.

compact disk—rewritable (CD-RW) A disk from which data can be read and to which data can be written, overwritten or erased.

Companies House *See* COMPANIES REGISTRY.

companies register The official list of companies registered at the *Companies Registry (*see* REGISTRATION OF A COMPANY).

Companies Registry (Companies House) The office of the Registrar of Companies (*see* REGISTRATION OF A COMPANY). Companies with a registered office in England or Wales are served by the registry at Cardiff; those in Scotland by the registry in Edinburgh. Certain *documents lodged there are open to inspection. These documents include the *accounts of limited companies, the annual return, any *prospectus, the *memorandum and *articles of association, and particulars of the *directors, the secretary, the *registered office, some types of company charge, and notices of liquidation.

company An association formed to conduct business or other activities in the name of the association. Most companies are incorporated (*see* INCORPORATION) and therefore have a legal personality distinct from those of their members. Incorporation is usually by registration under the Companies Act 1985 (*see* REGISTRATION OF A COMPANY) but may be by private Act of Parliament (**statutory company**) or by royal charter (**chartered company**). Shareholders and *directors are generally protected when the company goes out of business. *See* DISQUALIFICATION OF COMPANY DIRECTORS; FOREIGN COMPANY; LIMITED COMPANY; PRIVATE COMPANY; PUBLIC COMPANY; UNLIMITED COMPANY.

company member A person who holds *shares in a company or, in the case of a company that does not issue shares (such as a company limited by guarantee), any of those who have signed the *memorandum of association or have been admitted to membership by the *directors. *See* LIMITED COMPANY.

company name The title of a *registered company, as stated in its *memorandum of association and in the *companies register. The names with which companies can be registered are restricted (*see also* BUSINESS NAME). The name must appear clearly in full outside the *registered office and other business *premises, upon the company seal, and upon certain *documents issuing from the company, including notepaper and invoices. Non-compliance is an offence and fines can be levied. Under the Insolvency Act 1986, it may be an offence for a *director of a company that has gone into insolvent liquidation to reuse the company name. *See also* CHANGE OF NAME; LIMITED COMPANY.

C

company secretary An officer of a company whose role will vary according to the nature of the company but will generally be concerned with the administrative duties imposed upon the company by the Companies Act (e.g. delivering *documents to the *Companies Registry). Under the Companies Act 1985 every company is required to have a company secretary. A sole *director cannot also be the company secretary, and in the case of a *public company the company secretary must be qualified to act as such.

Comparative Case Analysis (CCA) An application on the *Police National Computer which provides *police forces with an effective method of comparing crimes of a similar nature, especially those committed on a regional, national, or international basis, with a view to identifying the people responsible.

compellable witness A person who may lawfully be required to give evidence. In principle every person who is competent to be a witness is compellable (*see* COMPETENCE). In criminal prosecutions the spouse of the accused is generally competent and, under the 1999 amendments to the Police and Criminal Evidence Act 1984, may in some circumstances be compellable; e.g. when the offence charged is an assault upon the spouse or someone under the age of 16, the spouse is compellable as well as competent. The spouse is always compellable for the defence.

compensation A monetary payment to compensate for loss or *damage. When someone has committed a criminal offence that caused personal injury, loss, or damage, and he has been convicted for this offence or it was taken into consideration when sentencing for another offence, s 130 of the Powers of Criminal Courts (Sentencing) Act 2000 allows the court to make a compensation order requiring the offender to pay compensation to the person suffering the loss (with interest, if need be). *Magistrates' courts may make orders in respect of compensation. The court must take into account the offender's means and should avoid making excessively high orders or orders to be paid in long-term instalments. If the offender cannot afford to pay both a *fine and compensation, priority should be given to payment of compensation. A compensation order may be made for funeral expenses or bereavement in respect of death resulting from an offence other than a death due to a *motor-vehicle accident. Potential claimants and maximum compensation for bereavement are the same as those under the Fatal Accidents Act 1976 (*see* FATAL ACCIDENT). An order may only be made in respect of injury, loss, or damage (other than loss suffered by a person's dependants in consequence of his death) due to a motor-vehicle accident if (1) it is for damage to property occurring while it was outside the owner's possession in the case of offences under the Theft Act 1968, or (2) the offender was uninsured to use the vehicle and compensation is not payable under the *Motor Insurers' Bureau agreement in which case the maximum compensation that can be awarded by the court is £300. A court that does not award compensation must give reasons. Victims of *criminal injury may apply for compensation under the *Criminal Injuries Compensation Scheme. Under the Theft Act 1968, a *restitution order in monetary terms may be made when the stolen *goods are no longer in existence; this kind of order is equivalent to a compensation order. Compensation orders may be made in addition to, or instead of, other sentences. A court must order a *parent or *guardian of an offender under the age of 17 to pay a compensation order on behalf of the offender unless the parent or guardian cannot be found or it would be unreasonable to order him to pay it. Where 'sample charges' are preferred the court cannot award compensation for offences not charged or taken into consideration.

A person who has been wrongfully convicted of a criminal offence may apply to the *Home Secretary for compensation, which is awarded upon the assessment of an independent assessor.

compensation for damage by police Financial restitution paid for damage caused by police to private property during searches of *premises. When police cause damage in the course of entering and searching premises compensation is unlikely to be paid if the entry and search are lawful. Where the wrong premises are searched by mistake there should be presumption that compensation should be paid (PACE Code B Note 6A).

competence (of witnesses) The legal capacity of a person to be a witness. Since the abolition in the 19th century of certain ancient grounds of incompetence, every person of sound mind and sufficient understanding has been competent, subject to certain exceptions. For example, a child may be sworn as a witness only if he understands the solemnity of the occasion and that the taking of an *oath involves an obligation to tell the truth over and above the ordinary duty of doing so. However, under the Youth Justice and Criminal Evidence Act 1999, a child below the age of 14 years may only give *unsworn evidence. Since the Police and Criminal Evidence Act 1984 and the subsequent 1999 amendments, the spouse of an accused is generally a competent witness for the *prosecution (subject to some exceptions) and *compellable for the accused (subject to some exceptions).

complainant A person who alleges that a crime has been committed. A complainant alleging *rape, attempted rape, incitement to rape, or being an accessory to rape is allowed by statute to remain anonymous; evidence relating to her previous sexual experience cannot be given (unless the court especially rules otherwise). *See also* SEXUAL HISTORY.

complaint 1. The initiating step in civil proceedings in the *magistrates' court, consisting of a statement of the *complainant's allegations. The complaint is made before a *justice of the peace or, if the complaint is not required to be on *oath, before a *clerk to the justices, who may then issue an originating process directed to the defendant. **2.** An allegation of a crime. A complaint made by the victim of a *sexual offence directly after the commission of the offence is admissible as evidence of the consistency of the complainant's story.

complaint against police Defined by s 65 of the Police Act 1996 as 'a complaint about the conduct of a member of a *police force which is submitted (a) by a member of the public, or (b) on behalf of a member of the public and with his written consent'. Complaints must be recorded and investigated in accordance with pt IV of the 1996 Act.

Complementary Metal-Oxide Semi-Conductant (CMOS) A low power chip, commonly holding the BIOS preference of the *computer during power-down.

composite trailer A combination of a *converter dolly and a *semi-trailer as defined by reg 3(2) of the Road Vehicles (Construction and Use) Regulations 1986 (SI 1986/1078).

compound *See* COMPOUNDING; COMPOUNDING AN OFFENCE.

compounding Settling out of court in a customs and excise case. Section 152(a) of the Customs and Excise Management Act 1979 allows the Commissioners of HM Revenue and Customs to '...compound any proceedings for an offence or for the *condemnation of any thing being forfeited under the customs and excise Acts'. In effect this allows the Commissioners to enter into an agreement with an offender to settle the matter out of court as an alternative to initiating legal proceedings in cases where there is sufficient evidence that would support criminal proceedings with a realistic prospect of *conviction. There is no power to impose a settlement and the offender is under no obligation to accept an offer. If an agreement to compound cannot be reached, the offence may be prosecuted in the normal manner. In addition to offences contrary to the Customs and Excise Management Act 1979 has also been applied to cover:

- VAT offences by virtue of s 72(12) of the Value Added Tax Act 1994;

- insurance premium tax offences by virtue of sch 7, para 11 to the Finance Act 1994;
- landfill tax offences by virtue of sch 5, para 17 to the Finance Act 1996; and
- *intrastat offences by virtue of the Statistics of Trade (Customs and Excise) (Amendment No 2) Regulations 1993 (SI 1993/3015).

compounding an offence The offence of accepting or agreeing to accept *consideration for not disclosing information that might assist in convicting or prosecuting someone who has committed an offence for which the *penalty is fixed by law or where an adult not previously convicted could be sentenced to a term of imprisonment of five years or more (consideration here does not include reasonable *compensation for loss or injury caused by the offence). There is also a special statutory offence of advertising a reward for stolen *goods on the basis that 'no questions will be asked' or that the person producing the goods 'will be safe from inquiry'.

compulsory powers Powers, held by persons authorized by the *Director of the Serious Fraud Office, the *Director of Public Prosecutions, and the *Director of the Revenue and Customs Prosecutions Office, under s 2 of the Criminal Justice Act 1987 (CJA) and s 62 of the Serious Organized Crime and Police Act 2005 (SOCPA), to require a person to answer questions, provide information, or produce *documents for the purposes of an investigation. The powers under the 1987 Act may only be used for the purposes of an investigation of a suspected offence which appears on reasonable grounds to the Director of the Serious Fraud Office to involve serious or complex *fraud and where there is good reason to do so for the purpose of investigating the affairs, or any aspect of the affairs of any person. The powers under the 2005 Act may be exercised where there are reasonable grounds to believe that an offence listed in s 61 of the Act has been committed and that any person has information (whether or not contained in a document) which relates to a matter relevant to the investigation of that offence, and that there are reasonable grounds for believing that information which may be provided by that person in compliance with a disclosure notice is likely to be of substantial value (whether or not by itself) to that investigation. They are exercised by service of a **disclosure notice**. The majority of such notices are issued to banks, financial institutions, accountants, and other professionals, who may, in the ordinary course of their business, hold information or documents relevant to a suspected fraud. In most instances those institutions and persons owe duties of confidence to their clients and, whilst they may be willing to assist an investigation, cannot do so while such duties of confidence remain.

Section 2(4) CJA 1987 and s 66(2) SOCPA 2005 allow for a *justice of the peace to issue a search *warrant if, on an information on *oath laid by the investigating authority, he is satisfied, inter alia, that a person has been required by a disclosure notice to produce relevant documents but has not done so, or that it is not practicable to give a disclosure notice requiring their production, or that giving such a notice might seriously prejudice the investigation of an offence. Such a warrant provides authority to an appropriate person named in it to enter and search the *premises specified, using such force as is reasonably necessary; to take possession of any documents (including any *computer disk or other electronic storage device) appearing to be documents of a description specified, or to take any other steps which appear to be necessary for preserving, or preventing interference with, any such documents; to take copies of or extracts from any such documents; to require any person on the premises to provide an explanation of any such documents or information or to state where any such documents or information may be found; and to require any such person to give such assistance as may reasonably be required for the taking of copies or extracts.

Powers under the 1987 and 2005 Acts are known as 'compulsory powers' because a person commits an offence if, without reasonable excuse, he fails to comply with a disclosure notice (s 2(13) CJA 1987, s 67(1) SOCPA 2005), or makes a statement which he knows is, or is reckless as to whether it is, false or misleading (s 2(14) CJA 1987, s 67(2) SOCPA 2005). However, a person may not be required to answer any privileged question (i.e. a question relating to information to which *legal privilege applies), to provide any privileged information, or to produce any privileged document. A statement made by a person in response to a disclosure notice may not be used unless the proceedings are for the offence of giving false or misleading information in response to the notice (s 2(14) CJA 1987, s 65(2) SOCPA 2005), or when giving evidence in proceedings for some other offence, the person adduces evidence relating to the interview or a question about it is asked by him, in which case he can then be *cross-examined on any inconsistencies.

compulsory winding-up A procedure for *winding up a company by the court based on a petition made under circumstances listed in the Insolvency Act 1986. The main grounds for this type of petition are that the company is unable to pay its *debts or that the court is of the opinion that it is in the interests of the company that a *just and equitable winding-up should be made. The winding-up is conducted by a *liquidator. *See also* WINDING-UP.

computer An electronic device for processing and storing binary data.

computer chip A small piece of semiconducting material (usually silicon) on which an integrated circuit is embedded. *Computers consist of many chips placed on electronic boards called printed circuit boards. There are different types of chips. For example, *central processing unit chips (also called microprocessors) contain an entire processing unit, whereas memory chips contain blank memory.

computer crime *See* COMPUTER FRAUD; CYBERCRIME; HIGH TECHNOLOGY CRIME.

computer documents (in the law of evidence) A *document produced by a *computer. In civil cases a computer document is admissible under the general rules of evidence as evidence of any fact recorded in it of which direct oral evidence would be admissible. In criminal cases information recorded and processed by a computer which has been entered by a person, whether directly or indirectly, is *hearsay: to be admissible, it must be brought within one of the exceptions to the rule against hearsay provided by chapter 2 of pt II of the Criminal and Justice Act 2003. Where there is no human intervention in the processing of computer information (e.g. where the computer has been programmed to automatically record information) then the information produced is *real evidence and is treated accordingly.

computer fraud A *computer-related crime involving alteration of computer input in an unauthorized way; destroying, suppressing, or stealing output; making unapproved changes to stored information; or amending or misusing programs to obtain a benefit, financial or otherwise. *See also* CYBERCRIME; HIGH TECHNOLOGY CRIME.

computer misuse *See* CRACKING; HACKING.

computer virus *See* VIRUS.

concealing indictable offences The offence under s 5 of the Criminal Law Act 1967 of accepting or agreeing to accept *consideration for not disclosing information that might assist in convicting or prosecuting someone who has committed an *indictable offence for which an adult could be sentenced to five years' or more imprisonment or the *penalty is fixed by law (consideration here does not include reasonable *compensation for loss or injury caused by the offence). There is also a special statutory offence of advertising a reward for stolen *goods on the basis that 'no questions will be asked' or that the person producing the goods 'will be safe from inquiry' (s 23, Theft Act 1968).

concealment *See* NON-DISCLOSURE.

concealment of securities The offence, contrary to s 20 of the Theft Act 1968 and punishable by up to seven years' imprisonment, of dishonestly concealing, destroying, or defacing any **valuable security**, will, or any *document issuing from a court or government department for the purpose of gain for oneself or causing loss to another. Valuable securities include any documents concerning rights over property, authorizing payment of money or the delivery of property, or evidencing such rights or the satisfying of any obligation.

C

Concerted Inter-Agency Criminal Finances Action Group (CICFA) A group formed in June 2002 that consists of senior representatives of the main government agencies involved in asset recovery (law enforcement, *prosecutors, and courts administration). Its role is to monitor performance in relation to confiscation and to consider measures to increase the efficiency of the enforcement process. *See also* JOINT ASSET RECOVERY DATABASE; CONFISCATION ENFORCEMENT TASK FORCE.

conclusive evidence Evidence that must, as a matter of law, be taken to establish some fact in issue and that cannot be disputed. For example, the *certificate of incorporation of a company is conclusive evidence of its incorporation.

concurrent sentence A *sentence to be served at the same time as one or more other sentences, when the accused has been convicted of more than one offence. Concurrent sentences are usually terms of imprisonment, and in effect the accused serves the term of the longest sentence. Alternatively the court may impose **consecutive sentences**, which follow on from each other.

concussion A group of symptoms including amnesia, confusion, nausea caused by head injury.

condemnation proceedings Appellate proceedings brought under ss 144 to 148 and 150 to 155 of the Customs and Excise Management Act 1979 to challenge the seizure of *goods by *Her Majesty's Revenue and Customs pursuant to s 141 of the Act. Proceedings are commenced by sending a valid Notice of Claim to HMRC within one month of the date of seizure.

condition A major term of a contract. It is frequently described as a term that goes to the root of a contract or is of the **essence of a contract**, as opposed to a **warranty**, which is a term of minor importance. Breach of a condition constitutes a fundamental *breach of the contract and entitles the injured party to treat it as discharged, whereas breach of warranty is remediable only by an action for *damages, subject to any contrary provision in a contract.

conditional admissibility The *admissibility of evidence whose *relevance is conditional upon the existence of some fact that has not yet been proved. The courts permit such evidence to be given conditionally, upon proof of that fact at a later stage of the *trial. Such evidence is sometimes said to have been received **de bene esse*.

conditional caution A *caution which is given in respect of an offence committed by the offender and which has conditions attached to it with which the offender must comply. It is an alternative to *prosecution for adult offenders. Conditional cautions are a disposal introduced by ss 22 to 27 of the Criminal Justice Act 2003. A conditional caution may be appropriate where a *Crown Prosecutor considers that while the public interest justifies a prosecution, the interests of the suspect, victim, and community may be better served by the suspect complying with suitable conditions aimed at rehabilitation or reparation. These may include restorative processes. Failure to comply with the conditions leads to prosecution for the offence.

conditional discharge *See* DISCHARGE.

conditional sale agreement A contract of sale under which the price is payable by instalments and *ownership is not to pass to the *buyer (although he is in possession of the *goods) until specified conditions relating to the payment of the price or other matters are fulfilled. The *seller retains ownership of the goods as security until he is paid. A conditional sale agreement is a *consumer-credit agreement; it is regulated by the Consumer Credit Act 1974 if the buyer is an individual, the credit does not exceed £25 000, and the agreement is not otherwise exempt.

condominium **1.** Joint *sovereignty over a territory by two or more states (the word is also used for the territory subject to joint sovereignty). For example, the New Hebrides Islands in the South Pacific were a Franco-British condominium until 1980. Sovereignty is joint, but each jointly governing power has separate jurisdiction over its own subjects. *Compare* CO-IMPERIUM. **2.** Individual ownership of part of a building (e.g. a flat in a block of flats) combined with common ownership of the parts of the building used in common.

confederation A formal association of states loosely bound by a treaty, in many cases one establishing a central governing mechanism with specified powers over member states but not directly over citizens of those states. In a confederation, the constituent states retain their national sovereignty and consequently their right to *secession. *Compare* FEDERAL STATE.

conference **1.** A meeting of members of the *House of Lords and the *House of Commons appointed to attempt to reach agreement when one House objects to amendments made to one of its *Bills by the other. **2.** A meeting between an *advocate and a *solicitor to discuss a case in which they are engaged. If the *barrister involved is a *Queen's Counsel, the meeting is called a **consultation**.

confession An *admission, in whole or in part, made by an accused person of his guilt. A confession is one of the exceptions to the rule against *hearsay. Its admissibility is governed by s 76 of the Police and Criminal Evidence Act 1984, which requires the *prosecution, if called upon to do so, to prove beyond a reasonable doubt that the confession was not obtained by oppression of the person who made it or as a result of anything that was likely to render the confession unreliable. Under s 78 of the Act, a confession may also be ruled to be inadmissible if it appears to the court that, having regard to all the circumstances, including the circumstances in which the confession was obtained, its admission would have such an adverse effect on the fairness of the proceedings that the court ought not to admit it (e.g. if the defendant has been denied access to legal advice). Under s 76A of the 1984 Act (introduced by the Criminal Justice Act 2003), a confession made by an *accused may be used as evidence for a *co-accused if it is relevant to a matter in issue in the proceedings.

confidence trick A trick, device, or swindle that takes advantage of a victim's trust or gullibility in order to unlawfully obtain money or other property.

confidential communication The mere fact that a communication is confidential does not in itself make it inadmissible; it will only be so if it is within the scope of an evidentiary *privilege, such as legal professional privilege or public-interest privilege.

confirmation bias The limiting of an interview with a suspect to points which tend to confirm or verify the interviewer's preconceived hypothesis of the offence being investigated.

Confiscation Enforcement Task Force (CETF) An inter-agency group established by the *Concerted Inter-Agency Criminal Finances Action Group in 2003 in order to clear a backlog of *confiscation orders and improve efficiency in the enforcement of new orders. The CETF deals only with orders made under the Criminal Justice Act 1988 and the Drug Trafficking Act 1994 and does not enforce orders made under the Proceeds of Crime Act 2002. The task force is made up of *Her Majesty's Revenue and Customs and police financial investigators, and *Crown Prosecution Service and * Revenue and Customs Prosecutions Office lawyers, on attachment.

confiscation order An order that requires a convicted defendant to pay a sum that the court thinks fit. A confiscation order may only be made by the *High Court or *Crown Court. The limited power of the *magistrates' court under earlier confiscation *legislation is abolished. Under the Proceeds of Crime Act 2002, a confiscation order may be made following any conviction in the Crown Court. Where the conviction takes place in the magistrates' court a confiscation order can only be made if the defendant

C

is either committed to the Crown Court for sentence or committed to the Crown Court for sentence and confiscation under s 70 of the Act. Section 6 of the Act empowers the Crown Court to order a convicted defendant to pay a sum of money representing the defendant's benefit from either his 'general criminal conduct' or his 'particular criminal conduct'. Confiscation is by reference to the defendant's criminal conduct where he is identified by the court on conviction as having a *criminal lifestyle. The amount is the amount of the defendant's benefit from his criminal conduct unless the amount available for confiscation is considered by the court and found to be less than the benefit in question, in which case the order must be made in that lesser amount. For offences committed before 24 March 2003, confiscation proceedings must be brought in the High Court under the Criminal Justice Act 1988 or Drug Trafficking Act 1994.

confrontation, identification by A means of identifying a suspect by showing him directly to a witness. It can be used only if it is not possible to arrange a parade, group identification, or video identification. It does not require the consent of the suspect (PACE Code C 3.23).

congenital Present from birth; often used to refer to an abnormality.

congestion The distension of small blood vessels caused by blocking of vessels that should take the blood away.

conjunctiva The transparent film over the eye and inner eyelids.

conjunctivitis Inflammation of the *conjunctiva.

Connexions Service The Government's support scheme for all young people aged 13 to 19 in England. The service aims to provide integrated guidance and access to personal development opportunities for this group and to help them make a smooth transition to adulthood and working life.

conquest The acquisition by military force of enemy territory followed by its formal annexation after the cessation of hostilities. It does not include the acquisition of *land as a term of a peace *treaty. The acquisition of territory after a *war in the absence of any peace treaty, because the defeated state has ceased to exist, is known as debellatio or **subjugation**. Conquest is not now regarded as a legitimate means of acquiring territory, and hence conferring valid title, as Article 2(4) of the UN Charter expressly prohibits aggressive war and Article 5(3) of General Assembly Resolution 3314 (XXIX) of 1975 effectively nullifies any legal title acquired in this way.

conscience, freedom of The human right guaranteed by Article 9 of the *European Convention on Human Rights.

consecutive sentence *See* CONCURRENT SENTENCE.

consent Deliberate or implied affirmation; compliance with a course of proposed action. Consent is essential in a number of circumstances. For example, contracts and marriages are invalid unless both parties give their consent. Consent must be given freely, without duress or deception, and with sufficient legal competence to give it (*see also* INFORMED CONSENT). In criminal law, issues of consent arise mainly in connection with offences involving violence and *dishonesty. For public policy reasons, a victim's consent to conduct which foreseeably causes him bodily harm is no defence to a charge involving an *assault, *wounding, or *homicide. For the purposes of the Sexual Offences Act 2003, 'a person consents if he agrees by choice and has the freedom and capacity to make that choice'. This general definition is supplemented by evidential (s 75) and conclusive (s 76) presumptions about consent which endeavour to make clear the circumstances in which consent is not, or is unlikely to be, present. Under the Act, children under the age of 13 are not capable in law of giving consent to any form of sexual activity and any such conduct is treated as an offence of *strict liability. *See also* AGE OF CONSENT; BATTERY; CONVEYANCE; SEXUAL OFFENCES.

consent, stop and search powers Even if a person voluntarily consents to a search, *police officers may not search a person unless a power to do so exists (PACE Code A 1.5).

consideration An act, forbearance, or promise by one party to a contract that constitutes the price for which he buys the promise of the other. Consideration is essential to the validity of any contract other than one made by *deed.

Consolidated Criminal Practice Direction A consolidation of existing *Practice Directions, Practice Statements, and Practice Notes that govern proceedings in the Court of Appeal (Criminal Division), the *Crown Court, and the *magistrates' courts. *See also* CRIMINAL PROCEDURE RULES.

consolidating statute A statute that repeals and re-enacts existing statutes relating to a particular subject. Its purpose is to state their combined effect and so simplify the presentation of the law. It does not aim to alter the law unless it is stated in its long title to be a consolidation with amendments. An example of a consolidating statute is the Trade Union and Labour Relations (Consolidation) Act 1992. *Compare* CODIFYING STATUTE. *See also* INTERPRETATION OF STATUTES.

conspiracy An agreement between two or more people that a course of conduct will be pursued that will necessarily amount to, or involve, the commission of an offence by at least one of the conspirators. The agreement is itself a statutory crime, usually punishable in the same way as the offence agreed on, even if it is not carried out. **Mens rea*, in the sense of knowledge of the facts that make the action criminal, is required by at least two of the conspirators, even if the crime agreed upon is one of *strict liability. One may be *guilty of conspiracy even if it is impossible to commit the offence agreed on (e.g. when two or more people conspire to take money from a safe but, unknown to them, there is no money in it). A person is, however, *not guilty of conspiracy if the only other party to the agreement is his (or her) spouse or a child under the age of criminal responsibility. Nor is there liability when the acts are to be carried out in furtherance of a trade dispute and involve only a summary and non-imprisonable offence. Incitement to conspire and attempt to conspire are no longer crimes.

Criminal conspiracy at *common law is now limited to: (1) conspiracy to *defraud; (2) conspiracy to corrupt public morals (*see* CORRUPTION OF PUBLIC MORALS); and (3) conspiracy to outrage public decency. There is doubt whether the last two still exist.

constable 1. An office held under the *Crown giving certain powers over other citizens in the enforcement of law and keeping the peace. All *police officers hold the office of constable. **2.** The titular commander of a royal castle.

constabulary A body of *constables. A *police force outside London. Some provincial police forces have changed their names from 'Constabulary' to 'Police'.

constituency An area of the UK for which a representative is elected to membership of the *House of Commons or the *European Parliament.

constitution The rules and practices that determine the composition and functions of the organs of central and local government in a state and regulate the relationship between the individual and the state. Most states have a written constitution, one of the fundamental provisions of which is that it can itself be amended only in accordance with a special procedure. The constitution of the UK is largely unwritten. It consists partly of statutes, for the amendment of which by subsequent statutes no special procedure is required (*see* ACT OF PARLIAMENT), but also, to a very significant extent, of *common law rules and constitutional conventions.

construction *See* INTERPRETATION.

Construction and Use Regulations The common name for the Road Vehicles (Construction and Use) Regulations 1986 (SI 1986/1078) and the Pedal Cycles (Construction and Use) Regulations 1983 (SI 1983/1176). The Regulations are secondary *legislation made pursuant to s 41 of the Road Traffic Act 1988, relating to the use of motor vehicles and trailers on roads, their construction and equipment, and the conditions under which they may be so used.

constructive Describing anything that is deemed by law to exist or to have happened, even though that is not in fact the case.

C

consul A *diplomatic agent commissioned by a sovereign state to reside in a foreign city, to represent the political and trading interests of the sending state, and to assist in all matters pertaining to the commercial relations between the two countries. *See also* DIPLOMATIC MISSION.

consular agreement A bilateral agreement stating that when a citizen of a country with which an agreement exists is taken into police detention, the embassy or consulate of that country must be informed of the detention and the reason for it, unless the detained person is a political refugee. The countries with which such agreements exist are listed in PACE Code C, Annex F.

Consultancy Service Index An index maintained by the Department of Health of child care workers or former child care workers about whom concerns exist relating to their suitability to work in the child care field. The index should be checked by *local authorities and voluntary care agencies before employing people to work with children.

consumer A private individual acting otherwise than in a course of a business. Consumers are often given greater legal protection when entering into contracts, e.g. by having a right to avoid certain unfair terms or to cancel the contract (*see* CONSUMER PROTECTION; DISTANCE SELLING). Many regulations define 'consumer' in a particular manner.

consumer-credit agreement A *personal-credit agreement in which an individual (the *debtor) is provided with credit not exceeding £25000. Unless exempted, consumer-credit agreements are regulated by the Consumer Credit Act 1974, which contains provisions regarding the seeking of business, entry into agreements, matters arising during the currency of agreements, default and termination, security, and judicial control. A loan to an individual businessman for business purposes can be a consumer-credit agreement. The Consumer Credit Act 2006, which is to be brought into effect in 2007 and 2008, is likely to make changes in this area, including the removal of the financial limit.

consumer-credit business Any business that comprises or relates to the provision of credit under *consumer-credit agreements regulated by the Consumer Credit Act 1974 (which is to be amended by the Consumer Credit Act 2006). With certain exceptions, e.g. *local authorities, a *licence is required to carry on a consumer-credit business.

consumer-credit register The register kept by the *Director General of Fair Trading, as required by the Consumer Credit Act 1974 (which is to be amended by the Consumer Credit Act 2006), relating to the licensing or carrying on of *consumer-credit businesses or *consumer-hire businesses. The register contains particulars of undetermined applications, *licences that are in force or have at any time been suspended or revoked, and decisions given by the Director under the Act and any *appeal from them. The public is entitled to inspect the register on payment of a fee.

consumer goods *Goods normally supplied for private use or consumption. The Unfair Contract Terms Act 1977 provides that if consumer goods prove defective when used otherwise than exclusively for business purposes as a result of negligence of a manufacturer or distributor, that person's business liability cannot be excluded or restricted by any guarantee under which the goods are sold. Under the Consumer Protection Act 1987, suppliers of all consumer goods must ensure that the goods comply with the *general safety requirement. Otherwise they commit a criminal offence.

consumer-hire agreement An agreement made by a person with an individual, a partnership, or with some other unincorporated body (the **hirer**) for the *bailment of *goods to the hirer. Such an agreement must not be a *hire-purchase agreement, must be capable of subsisting for more than three months, and must not require the hirer to make payments exceeding £25000. The concept thus does not include a hiring by a company. Consumer-hire agreements, unless exempted, are regulated by the Consumer Credit Act 1974 (which is to be amended by the Consumer Credit Act 2006). *Compare* CONSUMER-CREDIT AGREEMENT.

consumer-hire business Any business that comprises or relates to the *bailment of *goods under *consumer-hire agreements regulated by the Consumer Credit Act 1974 (which is to be amended by the Consumer Credit Act 2006). With certain exceptions, e.g. *local authorities, a *licence is required to carry on a consumer-hire business.

consumer protection The protection, especially by legal means, of *consumers (those who contract otherwise than in the course of a business to obtain *goods or services from those who supply them in the course of a business). It is the policy of current *legislation to protect consumers against *unfair contract terms. In particular they are protected against terms that attempt to exclude or restrict the seller's implied *undertakings that he has a right to sell the goods, that the goods conform with either description or sample, and that they are of satisfactory quality and fit for their particular purpose (Unfair Contract Terms Act 1977). EU Directive 93/13 renders unfair terms in consumer contracts void; it is implemented in the UK by the Unfair Terms in Consumer Contracts Regulations 1999 (SI 1999/2083). The Office of Fair Trading runs a special unfair terms unit, which investigates cases in this field. There is also provision for the banning of unfair *consumer trade practices (Fair Trading Act 1973). Consumers (including individual businessmen) are also protected when obtaining credit (Consumer Credit Act 1974; to be amended by the Consumer Credit Act 2006) and there is provision for the imposition of standards relating to the safety of goods under the Consumer Protection Act 1987 and the General Product Safety Regulations 1994. There are, in addition, many legislative measures that are product-specific, such as toy safety regulations. For tort liability under the Consumer Protection Act, *see* PRODUCT LIABILITY.

Consumer Protection Advisory Committee (CPAC) A body set up under the Fair Trading Act 1973 to assess proposals for new criminal offences to protect *consumers.

C

consumer trade practice Any practice carried on in connection with the supply of *goods (by sale or otherwise) or services to *consumers. These practices include the terms or conditions of supply and the manner in which they are communicated to the consumers, the promotion of the supply of goods or services, the methods of salesmanship employed in dealing with consumers, the way in which goods are packed, or the methods of demanding or securing payment for goods or services. Consumer trade practices are controlled by the Minister and the *Office of Fair Trading.

contact (in family law) The opportunity for a child to communicate with a person with whom that child is not resident. The degree of contact may range from a telephone call to a long stay or even a visit abroad, and the court may formalize such arrangements by making a contact order (*see* SECTION 8 ORDERS). A *parent being visited by a child may exercise *parental responsibility during the child's visit. The question of contact after a child has been adopted is becoming a contentious issue. *See also* CARE CONTACT ORDER.

contact order *See* SECTION 8 ORDERS.

contamination of goods An *indictable offence under s 38 of the Public Order Act 1986 concerned with contaminating goods, threatening to contaminate *goods, claiming to have contaminated goods, or possession of certain articles with intent to cause alarm, injury, or economic loss.

contempt of court 1. (civil contempt) Disobedience to a court *judgment or process, e.g. breach of an *injunction or improper use of discovered *documents. If the injunction is served on the defendant with a **penal notice** attached, breach of the injunction can result in the defendant being jailed. **2.** (criminal contempt) Conduct that obstructs or tends to obstruct the proper administration of justice. At *common law criminal contempt includes the following categories. (1) Deliberately interfering with the outcome of particular legal proceedings (e.g. attempting improperly to pressurize a party to settle legal proceedings) or bribing or intimidating witnesses, the *jury, or a *judge. (2) **Contempt in the face of the court**, e.g. using threatening language or creating a disturbance in court. (3) Scandalizing the court by 'scurrilous abuse' of a judge going beyond reasonable criticism or attacking the integrity of the administration of justice. (4) Interfering with the general process of administration of justice (e.g. by disclosing the deliberations of a jury), even though no particular proceedings are pending.

Under the Contempt of Court Act 1981 it is a statutory contempt to publish to the public, by any means, any communication that creates a substantial risk that the course of justice in particular legal proceedings will be seriously impeded or prejudiced, if the proceedings are active. Such publications constitute **strict-liability contempt**, in which the intention to interfere with the course of justice is not required, but there are various special defences. It is also contempt under the Act to obtain or disclose any particulars of jury discussions and to bring into court or use a tape recorder without permission. The Act also protects (subject to certain exceptions) sources of information against disclosure in court. Contempt of court is a criminal offence punishable by a jail sentence and/or a fine of any amount ordered by the court.

continental shelf The sea bed and the soil beneath it that is adjacent to the coast of a maritime state and outside the limits of the state's *territorial waters. The 1958 Geneva Convention on the Continental Shelf limits the extent of the shelf to waters less than 200 metres deep or, beyond that limit, to waters that are of such a depth that exploitation of the natural resources of the sea bed is possible. The coastal state is granted exclusive sovereign rights of exploitation over mineral resources and non-moving species in its continental shelf, provided that this causes no unreasonable interference to navigation, fishing, or scientific research. The 1982 Conference on the Law of the Sea extends the continental shelf, in some cases, to a distance of 200 nautical miles from the *baselines around the coast from which the breadth of the territorial sea is measured. It also makes special provisions for delimiting the continental shelf between states with adjacent or opposite coastlines, but does not lay down rules of law for such delimitation. Rocks that cannot sustain human habitation do not have a continental shelf. *See also* LAW OF THE SEA.

continuity The state of being continuous; an unbroken succession; a logical sequence.

continuous bail *Bail granted by a *magistrates' court directing the accused to appear at every time and place to which the proceedings may from time to time be adjourned, as opposed to a direction to appear at the end of a fixed period of remand.

contraband 1. *Goods whose import or export is forbidden. **2.** (contraband of war) Goods (such as munitions) carried by a neutral vessel (ship or aircraft) during wartime and destined for the use of one belligerent power against the other (or capable of being so used). Arms and other goods of a military nature were traditionally referred to as **absolute contraband**, while goods having peaceful uses, but nevertheless of assistance to a belligerent, were **conditional contraband**. The distinction, though formally retained, has effectively been abolished. Belligerent states are expected to issue contraband lists in order to exercise the right of capture. Goods being carried to enemy territory in an enemy ship are contraband even if they belong to a neutral power. The other belligerent is entitled to seize and confiscate such goods. *See also* SEARCH OF SHIP.

contra bonos mores [Latin: against good morals] It is a matter of controversy to what extent the criminal law should, or does, prohibit immoral conduct merely on the ground of its immorality. The tendency in recent years has been to limit legal intervention in matters of morals to acts that cause harm to others. However, there are still certain offences regarded as essentially immoral (e.g. *incest). There are also offences of conspiring to corrupt public morals (although *corruption of public morals is not in itself criminal) and of outraging (or conspiring to outrage) public decency, although the scope of these offences is uncertain. *See also* CONSPIRACY; OBSCENE PUBLICATIONS.

contract A legally binding agreement. Agreement arises as a result of offer and acceptance, but a number of other requirements must be satisfied for an agreement to be legally binding. (1) There must be *consideration (unless the contract is by *deed). (2) The parties must have an intention to create legal relations. This requirement usually operates to prevent a purely domestic or social agreement from constituting a contract. (3) The parties must have *capacity to contract. (4) The agreement must comply with any formal legal requirements. In general, no particular formality is required for the creation of a valid contract. It may be oral, written, partly oral and partly written, or even implied from conduct. Certain transactions are, however, valid only if effected by deed (e.g. transfers of shares in British ships) or in writing (e.g. *promissory notes, contracts for the sale of interests in *land, and guarantees that can at law only be enforced if evidenced in writing). (5) The agreement must be legal (*see* ILLEGAL CONTRACT). (6) The agreement must not be rendered void either by some *common-law or statutory rule or by some inherent defect, such as operative mistake (*see* VOID CONTRACT). Certain contracts, though valid, may be liable to be set aside by one of the parties on such grounds as misrepresentation or the exercise of undue influence (*see* VOIDABLE CONTRACT).

contrecoup An injury to the brain on the opposite side to where a blow was struck to the head. It is caused when the brain bounces off the initial impact site and impacts against the opposite side of the skull.

controlled drugs Dangerous *drugs that are subject to criminal regulation. In the Misuse of Drugs Act 1971 these are grouped in three classes: A, B, and C. Class A is the most dangerous and includes *opium and its natural and synthetic derivatives (e.g. *morphine and heroin), *cocaine, and *Ecstasy. Class B includes amphetamine; and C—the supposedly least dangerous class—includes anabolic steroids, *benzodiazepine antidepressants, and (as at January 2004) *cannabis. It is an offence to possess a controlled drug (s 5 of the 1971 Act): to supply or offer it to another (s 4 of the 1971 Act); or to intentionally supply or offer to supply any article (other than a hypodermic syringe or part thereof) which may be used or adapted to be used in the administration of a controlled drug (s 9A of the 1971 Act, inserted by s 34 of the Drug Trafficking Offences Act 1986). Possession of drugs of classes A or B are *indictable offences. The defendant is liable on a charge of possession for the most minute quantity of the drug and without proof of **mens rea*, unless he can prove that he did not believe or suspect that it was a controlled drug. In the case of an *occupier or someone concerned in the management of *premises, it is an offence to knowingly permit the premises to be used for the production or supply of a controlled drug, the preparation of opium for smoking, or the administration or use of any controlled drug (s 8 of the 1971 Act, as amended by s 28 of the Criminal Justice and Police Act 2001). It is a particular offence to smoke or otherwise use prepared opium or to frequent a place used for the purpose of opium smoking (s 9 of the 1971 Act). Importation or exportation of a controlled drug is a breach of the prohibition imposed by the s 3 of the 1971 Act and is charged as one of the offences provided by the Customs and Excise Management Act 1979.

controlled waste Various forms of waste, including household waste, as defined by the Controlled Waste Regulations 1992 (SI 1992/588, as amended).

contusion The leakage of blood from *capillaries and other small blood vessels usually caused by blunt force.

convention 1. A *treaty, usually of a multilateral nature. The *International Law Commission prepares draft conventions on various issues for the progressive development of *international law. **2.** A written *document adopted by international organizations for their own regulation.

Convention Against Torture and Other Cruel, Inhuman or Degrading Treatment or Punishment 1984, UN The convention obliges states to take all measures to prevent *torture within their own state and by any person within their *jurisdiction. The convention has been ratified by 117 states and 66 others are signatories.

C

conventional encryption A form of encryption in which the sender and receiver of *computer data share with each other a secret key to decode messages sent between them. Conventional encryption, also called *private key encryption, is different from *public key encryption in which both sender and receiver have the public key, but each has a private key which is not shared.

conversation management A structured interview with a witness or suspect using the *PEACE framework.

conversion The tort of wrongfully dealing with a person's *goods in a way that constitutes a denial of the owner's rights or an assertion of rights inconsistent with the owner's. Wrongfully taking *possession of goods, disposing of them, destroying them, or refusing to give them back are acts of conversion. Mere *negligence in allowing goods to be lost or destroyed was not conversion at *common law, but is a ground of liability under the Torts (Interference with Goods) Act 1977. The claimant in conversion must prove that he had *ownership, possession, or the right to immediate possession of the goods at the time of the defendant's wrongful act (*see also* JUS TERTII). Subject to some exceptions, it is no defence that the defendant acted innocently.

converter dolly A wheeled chassis placed between a *semi-trailer and its drawing vehicle as defined broadly by reg 3(2) of the Road Vehicles (Construction and Use) Regulations 1986 (SI 1986/1078).

conveyance Any vehicle, vessel, or aircraft manufactured or subsequently adapted to carry one or more people. *See also* AGGRAVATED VEHICLE-TAKING; INTERFERING WITH VEHICLES; TAKING A CONVEYANCE WITHOUT CONSENT.

conviction 1. In criminal proceedings, a finding of *guilty, or an *acquittal on the ground of insanity. *See also* SUMMARY CONVICTION **2.** (for the purposes of the Rehabilitation of Offenders Act 1974) Any finding (except one of insanity), either in criminal proceedings or in care proceedings, that a person has committed an offence or carried out the act for which he was charged. *See also* SPENT CONVICTION.

conviction, evidence of (in criminal proceedings) Evidence that a person has been convicted or acquitted of an offence on a previous occasion may be proved by a certificate of *conviction or *acquittal, together with proof that the person before the court and the person named in the certificate are one and the same (s 73, Police and Criminal Evidence Act 1984). *See also* ANTECEDENTS.

cookie A set of data that a website server gives to a browser the first time the user visits the site, that is updated with each return visit. The remote server saves the information the cookie contains about the user and the user's browser does the same, as a text file stored in the Netscape or Explorer system folder.

coopering The practice of transferring goods from one vessel to another at sea. It is often used by those engaged in *smuggling.

copyright The exclusive right to reproduce or authorize others to reproduce artistic, dramatic, literary, or musical works. It is conferred by the Copyright, Designs and Patents Act 1988, which also extends to sound broadcasting, cinematograph films, and television broadcasts (including cable television). Copyright lasts for the author's lifetime plus 70 years from the end of the year in which he died; it can be assigned or transmitted on death. EU Directive 93/98 requires all *European Union member states to ensure that the duration of copyright is the life of the author plus 70 years. Copyright protection for sound recordings lasts for 50 years from the date of their publication; for broadcasts it is 50 years from the end of the year in which the broadcast took place. Directive 91/250 requires all EU member states to protect *computer *software by copyright law. The principal remedies for breach of copyright (known as **piracy**) are an action for *damages and *account of profits or an *injunction. It is a criminal offence knowingly to make or deal in articles that infringe a copyright. *See also* HACKING.

cordon, for terrorism investigation The demarcation of an area by police for the purpose of investigating *terrorist offences by use of tape or other means under powers given by s 33 of the Terrorism Act 2000. Normally the authority to do so must be given by a *police officer of at least the rank of superintendent but in an emergency any officer may authorize the cordon pending the authority of a superintendent.

coronary Relating to the heart.

coronary thrombosis A blockage of an artery in the heart by a blood clot.

coroner An officer of the *Crown whose principal function is to investigate deaths suspected of being violent or unnatural. He will do this either by ordering an *autopsy and if that does not reveal death by natural causes will conduct an *inquest. The coroner also holds inquests on *treasure (s 7, Treasure Act 1996). Coroners are appointed by the Crown from among medical practitioners, *barristers, or *solicitors of not less than five years' standing (s 2 Coroners Act 1988).

corporate crime The acts or omissions of a company or other formal body that are punishable in criminal courts. Such acts or omissions are usually for the benefit of the organization at the behest of an individual or group of individuals at management level within the organization. It was held in *HL Bolton (Engineering) Co Ltd v TJ Graham & Sons Ltd* [1956] 3 All ER 624 that 'The state of mind of these people is the state of mind of the company and is treated by the law as such'. These acts or omissions may be to the detriment of other *employees, customers, consumers, or the public at large.

corporate personality *See* INCORPORATION.

corporation (body corporate) An entity that has legal personality, i.e. it is capable of enjoying and being subject to legal rights and duties (*see* JURISTIC PERSON) and possesses the capacity of succession. A **corporation aggregate** (e.g. a company registered under the Companies Acts) consists of a number of members who fluctuate from time to time. A **corporation sole** (e.g. the *Crown) consists of one member only and his or her successors. *See also* INCORPORATION.

corpus delicti [Latin: the body of the offence] The facts and circumstances constituting a breach of the law.

Correctional Services Board (CSB) The body responsible for setting the overarching strategy for the Prison Service, National Probation Service, and the *Youth Justice Board for England and Wales. It is chaired by the Minister for Community and Custodial Provision.

corroboration Evidence that confirms the accuracy of other evidence 'in a material particular'. In general, English law does not require corroboration and any fact may be proved by a single item of credible evidence. The obligation to warn the *jury of the dangers of acting on uncorroborated evidence of *accomplices or of *complainants in cases of sexual offences has been abolished: the *judge now has a discretion to indicate the dangers of a jury relying on particular evidence. Corroboration remains mandatory in cases of *treason and *perjury and for *opinion evidence as to some matters, e.g. *speeding.

corrupt and illegal practices Offences defined by the Representation of the People Act 1983 in connection with conduct at parliamentary or local elections. Corrupt practices, which include bribery and intimidation, are the more serious of the two. The most frequent illegal practice is spending by a candidate in excess of the amount authorized for the management of his campaign.

corruption *See* BRIBERY AND CORRUPTION.

corruption of public morals Conduct 'destructive of the [moral] fabric of society'. It is uncertain if such acts are crimes, although those who published 'directories' of *prostitutes or magazine advertisements encouraging readers to meet the advertisers for homosexual purposes have been found *guilty of conspiring to corrupt public morals. *See also* CONSPIRACY; CONTRA BONOS MORES.

cortex The outer area of an organ.

corticosteroids A group of drugs used to treat allergic reactions and inflammation.

costal cartilage The ends of the ribs that join the sternum, They become ossified in later life.

costs Sums payable for legal services. The power of criminal courts to award costs is contained in Prosecution of Offences Act 1985. *See also* WASTED COSTS ORDER.

Council for the Advancement of Communication with Deaf People *See* INTERPRETER.

councillor (in local government) *See* LOCAL AUTHORITY.

Council of Europe A European organization for cooperation in various areas between most European (not just EU) states. The assembly of the Council of Europe elects the judges of the *European Court of Human Rights.

counsel A *barrister, barristers collectively, or anyone advising and representing *litigants. *See also* ADVOCATE.

counsel or procure *See* ACCESSORY.

count *See* INDICTMENT.

counterfeit card A fake *debit/*credit card that has been reprinted, embossed, and encoded so that it has the appearance of a genuine card.

county council A *local authority whose area is a county. A county council has certain exclusive responsibilities (e.g. education, fire services, highways, and refuse disposal) and shares others (e.g. recreation, town and country planning) with the *district councils in its area.

county court Any of the civil courts forming a system covering all of England and Wales, originally set up in 1846. The area covered by each court does not invariably correspond to the local government county boundary. Each court has a *circuit judge and a *district judge. *See also* APPELLATE JURISDICTION.

coup A coup injury is caused when the head is stopped suddenly, e.g. by hitting a wall or floor, and the brain rushes forward and is injured by hitting the side of the skull and rubbing against the inner ridges of the skull. *See also* CONTRECOUP.

course of criminal activity Conduct forms part of a course of criminal activity for the purposes of the Proceeds of Crime Act 2002 if the defendant has benefited from the conduct and either: in the proceedings in which he was convicted he was convicted of three or more other offences, each of three or more of them constituting conduct from which he has benefited; or, in the period of six years ending with the day when those proceedings were commenced he was convicted on at least two separate occasions of an offence constituting conduct from which he has benefited.

court 1. A body established by law for the administration of justice by *judges or *magistrates. **2.** A hall or building in which a court is held. **3.** The residence of a sovereign. The sovereign and her (or his) family and attendants or officials of state.

court board A body established in each *local justice area by s 4 of the Courts Act 2003 to scrutinize, review, and make recommendations about the way in which the *Lord Chancellor is discharging his general duty in relation to the courts in its area, and to consider the business plans relating to those courts. Each board has a minimum of seven members and these must include one *judge, two *magistrates, two people with knowledge or experience of the local courts, and two people who are representative of the local community. *See also* LOCAL CRIMINAL JUSTICE BOARD.

court legal advisor *See* CLERK TO THE JUSTICES.

court martial A court convened within the armed forces to try offences against *service law. It consists of a number of serving officers, who sit without a jury and are advised on points of law by a legally qualified *judge advocate. Army and air-force courts martial are similar. The Armed Forces Act 1996 (effective from 1 April 1997) updated the laws in this field; in particular, it reinforced the independence of courts martial. A **general court martial** must consist of a president of the rank of major/squadron leader or above and four members, at least two of whom must be of the rank of captain/flight lieutenant or above. Up to two members may be warrant officers (i.e. non-commissioned). A **district court martial** must consist of a president of the rank of major/squadron leader or above and two members, at least one of whom has held commissioned rank for at least two years. Up to one member may be a warrant officer. A **field general court martial** may only be convened in active service conditions, and may exceptionally consist of two officers. Naval courts martial must consist of between five and nine officers of the rank of lieutenant or above who have held commissioned rank for at least three years, although up to two members may be warrant officers. The members of the court may not all belong to the same ship or shore establishment. The president of a naval court martial must be of the rank of captain or above, and when a senior officer is to be tried there are further rules as to the court's composition. In all cases members of another branch of the armed forces of equivalent minimum rank may serve on army, air-force, or naval courts martial. Courts martial's findings of *guilty, and their *sentences, are subject to review by the Defence Council or any officer to whom they delegate. Since 1951 there has been a Courts-Martial Appeal Court, which consists of the *Lord Chief Justice and other members of the *Supreme Court. After first petitioning the Defence Council for the quashing of his *conviction, a convicted person may *appeal to the Court against the conviction and (from 1 April 1997) against sentence. Either he or the Defence Council may then appeal to the *House of Lords.

When a member of the armed forces is charged in the UK with conduct that is an offence under both service law and the ordinary criminal law the *trial must in certain serious cases (e.g. *treason, *murder, *manslaughter, and *rape) be held by the ordinary criminal courts (and is in practice frequently held by them in other cases). Provision exists to ensure that a person cannot be tried twice for the same offence. (*See also* STANDING CIVILIAN COURT.)

The Armed Forces Act 2006 will replace the service discipline Acts and harmonize the tri-services approach to service discipline. The Act provides for offenders to be dealt with summarily by a commanding officer (CO) or tried by court martial. Instead of (as at present) courts-martial being set up to deal with particular cases, the Act provides for a standing court martial, called the 'Court Martial', which may sit in more than one place at the same time. Those charged with offences under the Act that the CO intends to deal with summarily have a right to elect trial by the Court Martial and to appeal the outcome of a summary hearing to the Summary Appeal Court or the outcome of a court martial to the Court Martial Appeal Court.

Court of Appeal A court created by the Judicature Acts 1873–5, forming part of the *Supreme Court of Judicature. The Court exercises *appellate jurisdiction over all judgments and orders of the *High Court and most determinations of judges of the *county courts. In some cases the Court of Appeal is the *court of last resort, but in most cases its decisions can be appealed to the *House of Lords, with permission of the Court of Appeal or the House of Lords. The Court is divided into a **Civil Division** (presided over by the *Master of the Rolls) and a **Criminal Division** (presided over by the *Lord Chief Justice). The ordinary judges of the Court are the *Lords Justices of Appeal, but other specific office holders and High Court judges may, by invitation, also sit in the Court.

court of first instance 1. A court in which any proceedings are initiated. **2.** Loosely, a court in which a case is tried, as opposed to any court in which it may be heard on *appeal.

Court of First Instance The first court of *appeal from decisions of the *European Commission. The Court is the judicial body at first instance of the European Communities. Since 1994 it has dealt with all actions brought by individuals and *undertakings against measures of the Community institutions. More specifically, the Court of First Instance has jurisdiction to hear and determine actions for annulment, for failure to act and for damages brought by natural and legal persons against the Community institutions. The Court of First Instance also has jurisdiction to hear and determine disputes between the Community and its officials and other servants. It also decides cases concerning public or private law contracts concluded by the Community if they contain an arbitration clause. Its judgment may be the subject of an appeal, limited to points of law, to the *European Court of Justice.

Court of Justice of the European Communities *See* EUROPEAN COURT OF JUSTICE.

court of last resort A court from which no *appeal (or no further appeal) lies. In English law the *House of Lords is usually the court of last resort (although some cases may be referred to the *European Court of Justice). However, in some cases the *Court of Appeal is by statute the court of last resort.

court of record (in common law jurisdictions) A court that keeps permanent records of its proceedings. Judgments of a *trial court of record are normally subject to appellate review. In modern practice the principal significance of such courts is that they have the power to punish for *contempt of court. The *House of Lords, *Court of Appeal, *High Court, and *Crown Court are examples of superior courts of record. The *county court is the only remaining inferior court of record, others having been abolished by the Courts Act 1971.

court of summary jurisdiction *See* MAGISTRATES' COURT.

court order *See* ORDER.

court security officer A person appointed by the *Lord Chancellor and designated as a court security officer. Such an officer may search any person wishing to enter a court building and restrain, remove, and exclude any person for the purpose of maintaining order, enabling court business to be carried on without interference or delay, or securing the safety of any person in the court building. He may also remove any person from a court room at the request of a *judge or *justice of the peace.

cover An assumed identity adopted by an investigator during an undercover operation.

cover note A note signed by or on behalf of an *insurance company and issued to the proposer while the proposal is being considered by the insurance company. The note provides interim cover to use a *motor vehicle.

covert human intelligence source (CHIS) An informant or undercover *police officer employed in a role defined by s 26 of the Regulation of Investigatory Powers Act 2000 as being a person who establishes or maintains a covert relationship with a person for the covert purpose of obtaining or gaining access to information; or covertly discloses information obtained by use of such a relationship. The use of a CHIS may be authorized by a superintendent or, in other bodies, as set out in SI 2000/2417. The authorizing officer must be satisfied that conduct/use is proportionate to what is sought to be achieved and that arrangements are in place to ensure levels of management and oversight; that records contain statutory particulars and are available only on a need to know basis. *See also* SURVEILLANCE.

covert surveillance Surveillance carried out in a manner that is calculated to ensure that persons who are subject to the surveillance are unaware that it is taking place. *See also* SURVEILLANCE.

crack A derivative of *cocaine produced by mixing cocaine with baking soda and water, heating the solution and then drying and splitting the substance into pellet-sized chunks. Crack has ten times the stimulant effect of unprocessed cocaine. Also known as rock or crack rock.

cracked trial A *trial that has been listed for a *not guilty hearing on a particular day but does not proceed, either because the defendant pleads *guilty to the whole or part of the *indictment, or an alternative charge, or because the *prosecution offer no evidence.

cracking The process of accessing *computer content, services, accounts, or networks belonging to another party, without authorization, or attempting to penetrate the electronic security measures designed to protect against such access, in order to destroy, corrupt, or modify stored information. The term was coined by 'hackers' to differentiate themselves from those who gain unauthorized access with malicious intent. *See also* HACKING.

cranium The skull, other than the *mandible.

crank (*slang*) The street name for methamphetamine (not to be confused with *crack).

crazing The irregular cracks in glass due to rapid, intense heat. Their presence may indicate the use of an accelerant in a fire.

credit 1. The agreed deferment of payment of a *debt. Under the Consumer Credit Act 1974 (which is to be amended by the Consumer Credit Act 2006), credit also includes any other form of financial accommodation, including a cash loan. It does not include the charge for credit but does include the total price of *goods hired to an individual under a *hire-purchase agreement less the aggregate of the deposit and the total charge for credit. **2.** (in the law of evidence) The credibility of a witness. It must be inferred by the *trier of fact from the witness's demeanour and the evidence in the case. A witness may be cross-examined as to credit (i.e. **impeached**) by reference to bias, or any physical or mental incapacity affecting the credibility of his evidence. In criminal proceedings, evidence of the **bad character** of a person other than the defendant is admissible only if it is important explanatory evidence, has substantial probative value to a matter in issue in the proceedings which is of substantial importance in the context of the case as a whole, or all parties agree to it being admissible (s 100, Criminal Justice Act 2003). *See also* SEXUAL HISTORY.

credit card A plastic card, issued by a bank or finance organization, that enables its holder to obtain *credit when making purchases. The use of credit cards usually involves three contracts. (1) A contract between the company issuing the credit card and the cardholder whereby the holder can use the card to purchase *goods and, in return, promises to pay the credit company the price charged by the supplier. The holder normally receives monthly statements from the credit company, which he may pay in full within a certain number of days with no interest charged; alternatively, he may make a specified minimum payment and pay a high rate of interest on the outstanding balance. (2) A contract between the credit company and the supplier whereby the supplier agrees to accept payment by use of the card and the credit company agrees to pay the supplier the price of the goods supplied less a discount. (3) A contract between the cardholder and the supplier, who agrees to supply the goods on the basis that payment will be obtained from the credit company.

credit limit 1. The maximum *credit allowed to a *debtor. **2.** (under the Consumer Credit Act 1974) The maximum debit balance allowed on a running-account credit agreement during any period.

creditor 1. One to whom a debt is owed. *See also* LOAN CREDITOR. **2.** (under the Consumer Credit Act 1974) The person providing credit under a *consumer-credit agreement or the person to whom his rights and duties under the agreement have passed by assignment or operation of law.

creditors' committee A committee that may be appointed by *creditors to supervise the trustee appointed to handle the affairs of a bankrupt. A committee consists of between three and five creditors and their duty is to see that the distribution of the bankrupt's assets is carried out as quickly and economically as possible. *See also* BANKRUPTCY.

credit sale agreement A contract for the *sale of goods under which the price is payable by instalments but the contract is not a *conditional sale agreement, i.e. ownership passes to the buyer. A credit sale agreement is a *consumer-credit agreement; it is regulated by the Consumer Credit Act 1974 if the buyer is an individual, the credit does not exceed £25000, and the agreement is not otherwise exempt.

crepitations The sound made by lungs containing excess fluid.

crepitus The sound of the broken ends of bones grating against each other.

cricoid cartilage The cartilage ring in the larynx. They are often broken during strangulation.

crime An act (or sometimes a failure to act) that is deemed by statute or by the *common law to be a public wrong and is therefore punishable by the state in criminal proceedings. Every crime consists of an **actus reus* accompanied by a specified **mens rea* (unless it is a crime of *strict liability), and the prosecution must prove these elements of the crime beyond reasonable doubt (*see* BURDEN OF PROOF). Some crimes are serious wrongs of a moral nature (e.g. *murder or *rape); others interfere with the smooth running of society (e.g. parking offences). Most *prosecutions for crime are brought by the police (although they can also be initiated by private people); some require the consent of the *Attorney-General. Crimes are customarily divided into *indictable offences (for *trial by *judge and *jury) and *summary offences (for trial by *magistrates); some are hybrid (*see* OFFENCE TRIABLE EITHER WAY). The *punishments for a crime include *life imprisonment (e.g. for murder), imprisonment for a specified period, *suspended sentences of imprisonment, *conditional discharges, *probation, *binding over, and *fines; in most cases judges have discretion in deciding on the *punishment (*see* SENTENCE). Some crimes may also be civil wrongs (*see* TORT); e.g. *theft and *criminal damage are crimes punishable by imprisonment as well as torts for which the victim may claim *damages.

Crime and Disorder Reduction Partnerships Partnerships established by the Crime and Disorder Act 1998, between the police, *local authorities, probation service, health authorities, the voluntary sector, and local residents and businesses. The Act also places new obligations on local authorities, the police, police authorities, health authorities, and probation committees (amongst others) to cooperate in the development and implementation of a strategy for tackling crime and disorder in their area.

Crime Liaison Officer (CLO) *See* MUTUAL ASSISTANCE.

crime pattern analysis (CPA) A generic term for a number of related analytical disciplines, which look for linkages between crimes to reveal similarities and differences. It can help to reveal the relationships between crimes and link them to possible offenders. It identifies where prevention and diversion measures will be the most effective.

crime prevention The act of preventing the commission of criminal offences by both reducing opportunity for offending and deterrence.

crimes against humanity (in *international law) Serious crimes committed against civilian populations as part of a widespread and systematic attack. The Statute of the *International Criminal Court lists the serious crimes as: *murder, extermination, enslavement, *deportation or forcible transfer, unlawful deprivation of liberty, *torture, *rape and other serious sexual violence, collective persecution, enforced disappearances, apartheid and other similar inhumane acts causing great suffering or serious injury. *See also* WAR CRIME.

crimes against peace *See* WAR CRIME.

crime scene investigator (CSI) An *employee of a *police force specially trained and employed to examine and record crime scenes, recover, package, and store physical evidence, and give evidence of those findings in court. Typically CSIs also maintain intelligence indices on *modi operandi*, tool marks, footwear marks, etc.

Criminal Assets Bureau (CAB) An agency of the Irish Government that performs similar functions in Republic of Ireland as the *Assets Recovery Agency does in England, Wales, and Northern Ireland.

Criminal Case Management Framework (CCMF) A framework intended to provide guidance to those who are engaged in any criminal case, as to their functions and as to what the court will expect of them at the various stages of a case. The Framework is based on practices developed by the police, *Crown Prosecution Service, lawyers, and the courts. It is supported in decisions of the *Court of Appeal Criminal Division. It also includes references to new practices for charging and for witness management that are being delivered through the *Criminal Case Management Programme (CCMP). *See also* CRIMINAL PROCEDURE RULES.

Criminal Case Management Programme (CCMP) A programme which introduced new practices for charging and for witness management, intended to give victims and witnesses better support and secure more convictions before the courts. The programme is made up of three key components: the *Statutory Charging scheme, the *Effective Trial Management Programme (ETMP), and the *'No Witness, No Justice' project.

Criminal Cases Review Commission (CCRC) An independent body established under the Criminal Appeal Act 1995. The Commission's role is to review and investigate suspected miscarriages of justice in England, Wales, and Northern Ireland and to refer a *conviction, *verdict, finding, or *sentence to the appropriate court of *appeal when it considers that there is a real possibility that it would not be upheld.

criminal conviction certificate A certificate given to those who request details of information held about their criminal records. The certificate is obtained from the *Criminal Records Bureau.

criminal court A court exercising *jurisdiction over criminal rather than civil cases. In England all criminal cases must be initiated in the *magistrates' courts. *Summary offences and some *indictable offences are also tried by magistrates' courts; the more serious indictable offences are committed to the *Crown Court for *trial.

criminal damage The offence contrary to s 1 of the Criminal Damage Act 1971 of intentionally or recklessly destroying or damaging any property belonging to another without a lawful excuse. It is punishable by up to ten years' imprisonment. There is also an aggravated offence, punishable by a maximum sentence of *life imprisonment, of damaging property (even one's own) in such a way as to endanger someone's life, either intentionally or recklessly. Related offences are those of threatening to destroy or damage property and of possessing anything with the intention of destroying or damaging property with it. *See also* ARSON.

Criminal Defence Service (CDS) The Criminal Defence Service for England and Wales was created by the Access to Justice Act 1999 to replace the previous system of criminal legal aid provided for by the Legal Aid Act 1988. The service, which came into being in April 2001, provides those facing criminal *charges with such access to 'advice and assistance', 'advocacy assistance', and 'representation' as the interests of justice require. Advice and assistance includes general advice, negotiation, seeking the opinion of a *barrister, and preparing a written case. It is not available after charge or *summons and does not cover representation in court. Advocacy assistance covers case preparation and initial representation in certain proceedings in both the *magistrates' court and the *Crown Court. It also may cover representation for those who have failed to pay a civil *fine or obey a civil court order of the magistrates' court and are at risk of imprisonment and applications for *anti-social behaviour orders. Representation covers case preparation and legal representation at *trial, including pre-trial issues such as *bail. It also covers advice regarding the merits of an *appeal against a *verdict or *sentence of the magistrates' court or the Crown Court, or a decision of the *Court of Appeal.

Public funding is only available in cases that meet the 'interests of justice test' (sometimes called the 'means test'). Factors relevant to that determination include whether in the event of conviction, the accused is likely to receive a term of imprisonment, lose his livelihood, or suffer serious damage to his reputation; and whether the proceedings involve consideration of a complex issue of law. With the coming into effect of the Criminal Defence Service Act 2006, from 2 October 2006 criminal legal aid, other than advice and representation at the police station, is also subject to a means test.

See also LEGAL AID; PUBLIC DEFENDER SERVICE.

criminal geographic targeting An investigative aid originally developed in the 1990s by Detective Inspector Kim Rossmo, PhD, of the Vancouver Police Department. It is based on an analysis of the locations of a connected series of offences, the characteristics of the neighbourhoods in which they have occurred, and the psychological profile of the offender, in an attempt to determine the most probable areas in which the offender might reside or work.

Criminal Injuries Compensation Authority (CICA) The authority which administers the *Criminal Injuries Compensation Scheme.

Criminal Injuries Compensation Scheme A state scheme governed by the Criminal Injuries Compensation Act 1995 for awarding payments from public funds to victims who have sustained *criminal injury, on the same basis as civil *damages would be awarded (*see also* COMPENSATION). Damage to property is not included in the scheme. The scheme is administered by a board that may refuse or reduce an award (1) if the claimant fails to cooperate in providing details of the circumstances of the injury or in assisting the police to bring the wrongdoer to justice, or (2) because of the claimant's activities, unlawful conduct, or conduct in connection with the injury. Dependants of persons dying after sustaining criminal injury may also claim awards. The board may apply for a *county court order directing a convicted offender wholly or partly to reimburse the board for an award made. *See also* RIOT.

criminal injury (for purposes of the *Criminal Injuries Compensation Scheme) Any crime involving the use of violence against another person. Such crimes include *rape, *assault, *arson, poisoning, and *criminal damage to property involving a risk of danger to life; traffic offences other than a deliberate attempt to run the victim down are not included. The injury sustained includes pregnancy, disease, and mental distress attributable either to fear of immediate physical injury (even to another person) or to being present when another person sustained physical injury.

Criminal Investigation Department (CID) A body of detectives within a *police force. At one time the department was largely independent of the uniform branch of a police force with its own management structure. It is now largely integrated in the main management structure of the force. The term is no longer used in some police forces but is widely used in common parlance.

criminalistic Relating to criminals or their habits.

criminalistics Alternative term for *forensic science, especially in the USA.

Criminal Justice System (CJS) A system intended to maintain social control, enforce laws, and administer justice, which is characterized by: (1) explicit rules (laws) created by legislative authority; (2) designated officials to interpret and enforce the rules; and, (3) provision for *punishment for those who offend and commit acts against the rules and society at large and compensation for those who are the victims of crime. In England and Wales, the CJS is made up of several separate agencies and departments which are responsible for various aspects of the work of maintaining law and order and the administration of justice. The main agencies are:

- police services;
- public prosecution agencies, including: *Crown Prosecution Service, *Revenue and Customs Prosecution Office, and the *Serious Fraud Office;
- *Criminal Defence Service;
- HM Courts Service (*magistrates' courts and the *Crown Court);
- *Court of Appeal, Criminal Division;
- National Offender Management service (comprising the Prison Service and the National Probation Service);
- *Criminal Cases Review Commission;
- *Criminal Injuries Compensation Authority.

The *Home Office, *Attorney-General's Office, and the Department for Constitutional Affairs (formerly the Lord Chancellor's Department) are the three main government departments with responsibility for the CJS, setting the policy framework, objectives, and targets.

Criminal Justice Unit (CJU) A single administrative unit, introduced following the Glidewell Review in 1998, co-locating police and *Crown Prosecution Service staff in order to maximize efficiency and eliminate duplications. CJUs offer police investigators ready access to early legal advice by CPS lawyers.

criminal libel *See* LIBEL.

criminal lifestyle For the purpose of the Proceeds of Crime Act 2002 a defendant is deemed to have a criminal lifestyle if the offence (or any of the offences) concerned either is specified in sch 2 to the Act; or, constitutes activity forming part of a *course of criminal activity; or, is an offence committed over a period of at least six months and the defendant has benefited from the conduct which constitutes the offence—provided that in the latter two instances the defendant obtains *relevant benefit of not less than £5000.

Criminal Procedure and Investigations Act 1996 Part I of the Act provides a statutory scheme of pre-trial disclosure, placing a clear and continuing duty on the prosecution to disclose any material that 'might reasonably be considered capable of undermining the case for the prosecution...or of assisting the case for the accused' (a test modified by the Criminal Justice Act 2003 after much criticism of the subjective, 'in the prosecutor's opinion' test that was originally enacted). For the first time, the Act requires the defence to disclose the nature of the defence in cases tried on *indictment, although that limited disclosure is voluntary in cases tried summarily. Part II of the Act, inter alia, imposes a duty upon the *Home Secretary to prepare a *code of practice to regulate the conduct of the police in relation to unused material, which is to be disclosed by the prosecution. *See also* DEFENCE STATEMENT; DISCLOSURE OF UNUSED MATERIAL.

Criminal Procedure Rules (CPR) The Criminal Procedure Rules 2005 (SI 2005/384) took effect on 4 April 2005. They apply to all courts within the criminal jurisdiction and provide the courts with explicit powers to actively manage the preparation of criminal cases waiting to be heard: to avoid delay, and to promote certainty. This includes the court identifying 'real issues' at an early stage; identifying the needs of witnesses and giving any direction or taking any step to progress the case. Parties are placed under an obligation to inform the court and each other at once of any significant failure to take any procedural steps required under the CPR. *See also* CIVIL PROCEDURE RULES; CONSOLIDATED CRIMINAL PRACTICE DIRECTION.

criminal profiling A method of suspect identification that attempts to identify the offender's emotional and psychological characteristics. Also known as *offender profiling or psychological profiling.

criminal record certificate Certificate of criminal convictions, or lack thereof, issued under the Police Act 1997 to prospective *employers/*employees seeking work with vulnerable people.

Criminal Records Bureau (CRB) An executive agency of the Home Office. It provides access to criminal record information for *employers in the public, private, and voluntary sectors to identify prospective *employees who may be unsuitable for certain work, especially that involving contact with children or other vulnerable members of society. *See also* CONSULTANCY SERVICE INDEX.

crop mark An anomaly in vegetation suggestive of something being buried beneath the surface. The vegetation may be more or less lush than the surrounding area depending upon the nature of what is buried.

cross-appeals *Appeals by both parties to court proceedings when neither party is satisfied with the *judgment of the lower court. For example, a defendant may appeal against a judgment finding him liable for *damages, while the claimant may appeal in the same case on the ground that the amount of damages awarded is too low.

cross-contamination That which occurs when items intended for scientific examination are inadvertently allowed to come into contact. It may occur due to improper evidence handling procedures.

cross-examination The questioning of a witness by a party other than the one who called him to testify. It may be **to the issue**, i.e. designed to elicit information favourable to the party on whose behalf it is conducted and to cast doubt on the accuracy of evidence given against that party; or **to credit**, i.e. designed to cast doubt upon the credibility of the witness. *Leading questions may be asked during cross-examination. *See also* CREDIT.

Crown The office (a *corporation sole) in which supreme power in the UK is legally vested. The person filling it at any given time is referred to as the **sovereign** (a **king** or **queen**: *see also* QUEEN). The title to the Crown is hereditary and its descent is governed by the Act of Settlement 1701 as amended by His Majesty's Declaration of Abdication Act 1936 (which excluded Edward VIII and his descendants from the line of succession). The majority of governmental powers in the UK are now conferred by statute directly on ministers, the judiciary, and other persons and bodies, but the sovereign retains a limited number of common law functions (known as *royal prerogatives) that, except in exceptional circumstances, can be exercised only in accordance with ministerial advice. In practice it is the minister, and not the sovereign, who today carries out these common law powers and is said to be the Crown when so doing.

At *common law the Crown could not be sued in *tort, but the Crown Proceedings Act 1947 enabled civil actions to be taken against the Crown. It is still not possible to sue the sovereign personally.

Crown Court A court created by the Courts Act 1971 to take over the *jurisdiction formerly exercised by *assizes and *quarter sessions, which were abolished by the same Act. It is part of the *Supreme Court of Judicature. The Crown Court has an unlimited jurisdiction over all criminal cases tried on *indictment and also acts as a court for the hearing of *appeals from *magistrates' courts. Unlike the courts it replaced, the Crown Court is one court that can sit at any centre in England and Wales designated by the *Lord Chancellor. *See also* THREE-TIER SYSTEM.

Crown Court Rule Committee An advisory Non-Departmental Public Body, created by virtue of s 86 of the Supreme Court Act 1981 which confers the power to make *Crown Court Rules for the purpose of regulating and prescribing the practice and procedure to be followed by the *Crown Court. The function of the Crown Court Rule Committee is to examine any proposed amendments to those Rules.

Crown Court Rules Rules regulating the practice and procedure of the *Crown Court. The rules are made by the *Crown Court Rule Committee under a power conferred by the Courts Act 1971. The majority have been incorporated into the *Criminal Procedure Rules 2005.

Crown prerogative *See* ROYAL PREROGATIVE.

Crown privilege *See* PUBLIC INTEREST IMMUNITY.

Crown Prosecution Service (CPS) An organization created by the Prosecution of Offences Act 1985 to conduct the majority of criminal *prosecutions. Its head is the *Director of Public Prosecutions, who is answerable to *Parliament through the *Attorney-General. The CPS is independent of the police and is organized on a regional basis, each region having a **Chief Crown Prosecutor**. It also advises *police forces on matters related to criminal offences.

Crown Prosecutor A *barrister or *solicitor employed by the *Crown Prosecution Service. As a minister of justice assisting in the administration of justice, a Crown Prosecutor is personally responsible for conducting *prosecutions fairly in accordance with the *common law duty of a prosecutor. All Crown Prosecutors are required to exercise individual and independent judgment, subject to the direction of the *Director of Public Prosecutions and the superintendence of the *Attorney-General, in advising the police and reviewing cases in accordance with the *Code for Crown Prosecutors. *See also* REVENUE AND CUSTOMS PROSECUTOR.

Crown road A *road defined in s 131 of the Road Traffic Regulation Act 1948 as other than a *highway, to which the public has access by permission granted by the appropriate *Crown authority, or otherwise granted on behalf of the Crown. Generally, a Crown road will fall within the definition of a 'road' within the meaning of the Road Traffic Act 1988 and the Road Traffic Regulation Act 1984.

Crown servant Any person in the employment of the *Crown (this does not include *police officers or local government *employees).

Cruse Cruse Bereavement Care is a *charity that exists to promote the well-being of bereaved people and to enable anyone bereaved by death to understand their grief and cope with their loss. The organization provides counselling and support to families and friends of those bereaved by violent death and natural and man-made disasters.

cryptography The process of securing binary data that is sent through the internet or other public networks by encrypting it in a way that makes it unreadable to anyone not holding the mathematical key to decrypt the information.

curfew condition *See* BAIL.

curfew order A *youth community order made under s 37 of the Powers of Criminal Courts (Sentencing) Act 2000 that requires a convicted offender to remain at a specified place at particular times and generally includes an *electronic tagging requirement to enable the offender's whereabouts to be monitored. The maximum duration of an order is six months. The periods of curfew must be specified; they must not be less than two hours or more than twelve hours. Before making a curfew order, the court must seek information regarding the attitude of anyone likely to be affected by the enforced presence of the offender at the place specified in the order.

As originally enacted, the provision applied to offenders under the age of 18 but will not apply to those aged 16 or 17 years after 4 April 2007. Rule 48.1 of the *Criminal Procedure Rules makes provision as to the service of notice of the curfew order on the defendant and on the person responsible for electronically monitoring compliance, and where any *community order additional to the curfew order has been made, as to service of a copy of the notice served on the person responsible for electronically monitoring compliance on the local probation board or *youth offending team responsible for the offender.

curfew requirement A requirement that may be imposed by the court as part of a *community order, *custody plus order, *suspended sentence order, or an intermittent custody order that requires a convicted offender to remain at a specified place at particular times. It is generally accompanied by an *electronic tagging requirement to enable the offender's whereabouts to be monitored. The periods of curfew must be specified; they must not be less than two hours or more than twelve hours. Before imposing a curfew requirement, the court must seek information regarding the attitude of anyone likely to be affected by the enforced presence of the offender at the place specified in the order.

In the case of a requirement imposed as part of a *community order or *suspended sentence order, the maximum duration of a curfew requirement is six months. A *custody plus order which imposes a curfew requirement may not exceed the first six months of the licence period. An intermittent custody order which imposes such a requirement must not specify a period that would cause the aggregate number of days on which the offender is subject to the requirement to exceed 182 (s 204, Criminal Justice Act 2003, replacing a similar provision in the Powers of Criminal Court (Sentencing) Act 2000).

curry house coronary *See* CAFÉ CORONARY.

curtilage The *land within which a building is set and which belongs to it.

custody 1. Imprisonment or confinement. The current policy behind the use of custody was established in the Criminal Justice Act 1991 and consolidated by ss 79 to 80 of the Powers of Criminal Courts (Sentencing) Act 2000. Sections 152 and 153 of the Criminal Justice Act 2003 reproduce the combined effect of the earlier provisions in the 2000, modified to take into account the provisions of the 2003 Act. There is a twin-track approach, under which long custodial *sentences will be levied on very serious crimes, particularly those of violence, but custody may be replaced with *community sentences or *youth community orders. Section 152 of the 2003 Act lays down a 'custody threshold' that has to be surmounted before any court can impose a custodial sentence, and s 153 imposes limits on the length of any custodial sentence given (*see also* PRE-SENTENCE REPORT). In response to calls for a structured framework to deal with the large number of offenders who persist in low-level criminality of the type that rarely attracts lengthy terms of imprisonment, the 2003 Act also introduces a completely new system for dealing with sentences of imprisonment for a term of less than twelve months. Subject to certain conditions, pt 12 of the 2003 Act empowers the sentencing court to make an intermittent custody order (although such orders were withdrawn on 20 November 2006), a *custody plus order, or a *suspended sentence order in appropriate cases. These orders couple terms of actual or suspended imprisonment with some of the requirements that may be attached to a *community order. **2.** (in family law) Formerly, the bundle of rights and responsibilities that parents (and sometimes others) had in relation to a child. 'Custody', which featured in various statutes, has now been replaced by the concept of *parental responsibility introduced by the Children Act 1989.

custody for offenders under 21 An offender under the age of 21 cannot be sentenced to imprisonment; instead he may be sentenced to *detention in a young offender institution under s 96 of the Powers of Criminal Courts Sentencing Act 2000 (18 to 20 year olds); a *detention and training order under s 100 of the Act (offenders under 18); or *long-term detention, under s 91 of the Act (offenders under 18).

If found *guilty of *murder, an offender aged 18 to 20 must be sentenced to 'custody for life' (s 93); an offender aged 10 to 17 is sentenced to be 'detained during Her Majesty's pleasure' (s 90). Section 94 of the Act provides that where an offender aged 18 to 20 is convicted of an offence which carries discretionary *life imprisonment in the case of an adult offender, the *Crown Court may impose custody for life. When the prospective repeal of s 94 (by ss 74 and 75 of the Criminal Justice and Court Services Act 2000) takes effect, offenders aged 18 to 20 who would have been sentenced to 'custody for life' will be sentenced to 'life imprisonment'.

custody officer A *police officer of at least the rank of sergeant or an officer of *Her Majesty's Revenue and Customs appointed to carry out duties concerning the reception, detention, and treatment of detained persons in accordance with the Police and Criminal Evidence Act 1984.

custody officer (secure training centre) A person employed under the provisions of pt 11 of the Criminal Justice and Public Order Act 1994 to work in contracted-out *secure training centres for offenders aged 12 to 14.

custody plus order A *sentence which may be imposed on *conviction for a criminal offence. It replaces custodial sentences of less than twelve months and provides for a further period of supervision in the community after the offender is released. Section 181 of the Criminal Justice Act 2003 provides that, in general, all prison sentences of less than twelve months should consist of a short period of custody (the 'custodial period') followed by a longer period on licence (the 'licence period') during which the offender must comply with the requirements imposed by the court as part of the custody plus order. The orders were to have been introduced in November 2006 but have been delayed pending further consultation.

The following requirements may be attached to the order:

- *unpaid work requirement (s 199, CJA 2003);
- *activity requirement (s 201, CJA 2003);
- *programme requirement (s 202, CJA 2003);
- *prohibited activity requirement (s 203, CJA 2003);
- *curfew requirement (s 204, CJA 2003), together with an *electronic monitoring requirement (s 177(3), CJA 2003);
- *exclusion requirement (s 205, CJA 2003), together with an *electronic monitoring requirement (s 177(3), CJA 2003);
- * supervision requirement (s 213, CJA 2003);
- (in the case of an offender aged under 25) *attendance centre requirement (s 214, CJA 2003).

The custodial period must be between two and thirteen weeks and the licence period at least 26 weeks. In the case of consecutive sentences, the total term for two or more offences is limited to 65 weeks, with a maximum custodial period of 26 weeks.

custody record A record kept by the *custody officer at a detention facility of every person brought there under *arrest or arrested there having attended voluntarily. Whilst not required by the Police and Criminal Evidence Act 1984 (PACE), the *Home Office advises that it would be wise to open a custody record for persons detained but not under arrest, e.g. people detained for court on a production order. PACE prescribes a very long list of matters that should be recorded on the custody record relating to the reception, detention, and treatment of a person throughout their time in police or other detention. The custody record must be available for inspection by a detained person or his solicitor.

custom A practice that has been followed in a particular locality in such circumstances that it is to be accepted as part of the law of that locality. In order to be recognized as customary law it must be reasonable in nature and it must have been followed continuously, and as if it were a right, since the beginning of *legal memory. Legal memory began in 1189, but proof that a practice has been followed within living memory raises a presumption that it began before that date. Custom is one of the four sources of *international law. Its elaboration is a complex process involving the accumulation of state practice, i.e. (1) the decisions of those who advise the state to act in a certain manner, (2) the practices of international organizations, (3) the decisions of international and national courts on disputed questions of international law, and (4) the mediation of jurists who organize and evaluate the amorphous material of state activity. One essential ingredient in transforming mere practice into obligatory customary law is **opinio juris*.

Customs and Excise, HM *See* HER MAJESTY'S REVENUE AND CUSTOMS.

customs duty A charge or toll payable on certain *goods exported from or imported into the UK. Customs duties are charged either in the form of an *ad valorem* *duty, i.e. a percentage of the value of the goods, or as a specific duty charged according to the volume of the goods. All goods are classified in the Customs Tariff but not all goods are subject to duty. The *Commissioners of Revenue and Customs administer and collect customs duties. Membership of the *European Union has required the abolition of import duties between member states and the establishment of a Common External Tariff. *Compare* EXCISE DUTY.

customs officer An officer of *Her Majesty's Revenue and Customs appointed by the Commissioners under s 2 of the Commissioners for Revenue and Customs Act 2005.

cut A lay term for a break in the surface of the skin. *Pathologists describe cuts caused by blunt force as *lacerations and cuts caused by sharp instruments as *incisions.

cutis anserine **(goose pimples)** Raised bumps of skin around body hairs which involuntarily rise when the person is cold or experiences strong emotions.

cut-throat defence A *defence in criminal proceedings where a defendant gives evidence on his own behalf, thereby strengthening the *prosecution case against his co-defendant.

cutting agent A substance that is not a drug which is mixed with a drug to dilute it to increase profitability, e.g. the addition of lactose to heroin.

cyberattack An attack on, or by means of, information technology. *See also* CYBERCRIME; HIGH TECHNOLOGY CRIME.

cybercrime A broad term used to describe criminal activity associated with *computers, computer networks, or the Internet. These can either be the target of the offence, such as when the offender steals information from or causes damage to the system, or a tool by which the offence is facilitated, such as fraud or the distribution of child pornography. *See also* HIGH TECHNOLOGY CRIME.

cyberculture The culture that has formed among those who use the Internet and other networks to communicate, and have formed social groups which meet and interact online and may never meet in real life. Cyberculture has its own customs, etiquette, mythology, and ethics.

cybersmearing Use of the Internet or networked *computer system to defame or criticize an organization or individual. Where the content is offensive or sexually explicit, it may amount to a criminal offence of *harassment. Under s 1 of the Malicious Communications Act 1988 it is an offence to send an indecent, offensive or threatening letter, electronic communication, or other article to another person.

cyberspace The electronic space created by *computers connected together in networks such as the Internet.

cyberstalking The harassment of a victim via electronic means.

cyberterrorism A form of *terrorism which seeks to exploit or attack electronic information systems.

cycle A bicycle, tricycle, or similar machine.

cycle, drunk in charge of An offence under s 12 of the Licensing Act 1872 to be in charge of a cycle whilst drunk (see *Corkery v Carpenter* [1951] 1 KB 102). The prosecution must establish that the defendant was not merely under the influence of drink but 'drunk'. The *penalty is a fine of level 1 on the standard scale or one month's imprisonment.

cycle track A route over which riders of pedal cycles have a right of way. It is an offence under the Cycle Tracks Acts 1984 to place a *motor vehicle on a cycle track.

cylinder That part of a *revolver which holds a number of *cartridges and moves. It rotates in order that successive cartridges are correctly aligned and locked in position for firing.

damage 1. In the offence of *criminal damage, the term 'damage' is not statutorily defined. Generally it has been held that its meaning is sufficiently wide to embrace injury, mischief, or harm done to property. It is not necessary that the damage renders the property useless or prevents it from fulfilling its normal function. The courts have held that temporary functional derangement is sufficient and this is demonstrated in a number of instances. Urinating in the back of a taxi, jumping on a policeman's cap, drawing on the pavement with water-soluble paint, and blocking a cell toilet and flushing it to cause flooding have all been held to amount to damage for the purposes of the Criminal Damage Act 1971. **2.** Loss or harm. Not all forms of damage give rise to a right of action; e.g. an *occupier of *land must put up with a reasonable amount of noise from his neighbours (*see* NUISANCE), and the law generally gives no compensation to relatives of an accident victim for grief or sorrow, except in the limited statutory form of damages for bereavement (*see* FATAL ACCIDENT). Damage for which there is no remedy in law is known as *damnum sine injuria*. Conversely, a legal wrong may not cause actual damage (*injuria sine damno*). If the wrong is actionable without proof of damage (such as *trespass to *land) and no damage has occurred, the claimant is entitled to nominal damages. Most *torts, however, are only actionable if damage has been caused (*see* NEGLIGENCE). In *libel and some forms of *slander, damage to *reputation is presumed.

damages A sum of money awarded by a court as *compensation for a *tort or a *breach of contract. Damages are usually a lump-sum award. The general principle is that the claimant is entitled to full compensation (*restitutio in integrum*) for his losses. **Substantial damages** are given when actual damage has been caused, but **nominal damages** may be given for breach of contract and for some torts (such as *trespass) in which no damage has been caused, in order to vindicate the claimant's rights. Damages may be *aggravated by the circumstances of the wrong. In exceptional cases in tort (but never in contract) *exemplary damages may be given to punish the defendant's wrongdoing.

Damages obtained as a result of a cause of action provided by the *Human Rights Act 1998 will be provided on the basis of the principles of *just satisfaction developed by the *European Court of Human Rights.

dangerous animals *See* CLASSIFICATION OF ANIMALS.

dangerous cycling The offence, contrary to s 28 of the Road Traffic Act 1988, of riding a cycle dangerously on a *road. It would seem that dangerous cycling should be interpreted in the same manner as dangerous driving; i.e. in such a way as to fall far below the standard that would be expected of a competent and careful cyclist, or in a manner that would be considered obviously dangerous by a competent and careful cyclist. This offence is defined by the Road Traffic Act 1991 and has replaced the old offence of reckless driving (defined in the Road Traffic Act 1988). The maximum *penalty is a *fine at level 4 on the standard scale. *See also* CARELESS AND INCONSIDERATE CYCLING; STOPPING AND REPORTING.

dangerous driving The offence of driving a *motor vehicle in such a way as to fall far below the standard that would be expected of a competent and careful *driver, or in a manner that would be considered obviously dangerous by a competent and careful driver. This offence is defined by s 2 of the Road Traffic Act 1988, as substituted by the Road Traffic Act 1991 and has replaced the old offence of reckless driving. The maximum *penalty is a *fine at level 5 on the standard scale or six months' imprisonment; *disqualification is compulsory. *See also* CAUSING DEATH BY DANGEROUS DRIVING; CARELESS AND INCONSIDERATE DRIVING; STOPPING AND REPORTING.

dangerous offender An offender who is considered to pose a significant risk to the public of serious harm. Chapter 5 of pt 12 of the Criminal Justice Act 2003 introduced a new scheme of custodial *sentences for 'dangerous offenders' which came into effect on 4 April 2005. It consists of two new sentences: imprisonment or detention for public protection (ss 225 and 226), and extended sentences (ss 227 and 228). Crucial to the operation of the scheme is the question whether the offender poses 'a significant risk to the public of serious harm occasioned by the commission by him of further specified offences'. In answering that question, s 229 obliges the court to take into account all information available about the nature and circumstances of the offence, and permits it to take into account any other information relating to the pattern of behaviour of which the offence forms part and any other information about the offender.

The new provisions will replace those for imposing longer than commensurate custodial sentences upon offenders convicted of violent or *sexual offences (ss 79(2)(b) and 80(2)(b), Powers of Criminal Courts (Sentencing) Act 2000); the power to impose a discretionary life sentence upon an offender with a specified minimum period (s 82A, Powers of Criminal Courts (Sentencing) Act 2000); and the extended sentence provisions under s 85 of the Powers of Criminal Courts (Sentencing) Act 2000, affecting the period of supervision on licence of a person dealt with for a violent and sexual offence. Offenders being sentenced after the commencement date in respect of offences committed before that date will continue to be subject to the former regime.

Under s 225, a court may impose imprisonment for public protection where an offender aged 18 or over is convicted of a 'serious offence' (a violent or sexual offence specified in sch 15 to the Act and punishable either with *life imprisonment or a determinate sentence of at least ten years' imprisonment) and the court believes that the commission by him of further specified offences poses a significant risk to members of the public. If the offence is punishable with life imprisonment and the court considers that the seriousness of the offence is such as to justify the imposition of a sentence of imprisonment for life, then the court must impose such a sentence. A court which imposes a sentence of imprisonment for public protection must fix a minimum term to be served in accordance with s 82A, Powers of Criminal Courts (Sentencing) Act 2000. Once the offender has served the minimum term, he may require his case to be referred to the Parole Board, who may direct his release under s 28 of the Crime (Sentences) Act 1997 if they are satisfied that it is no longer necessary for the protection of the public that he should be confined. In the case of an offender aged under 18, s 226 of the Act operates in much the same manner, save that the sentence is detention for life (or, as the case may be, for an indeterminate period) under s 91, Powers of Criminal Courts (Sentencing) Act 2000.

Extended sentences under ss 227 and 228 of the 2003 Act may be imposed on adult offenders convicted of a 'specified violent offence' or 'specified sexual offence' which is not a 'serious offence'. In the case of those under 18, an extended sentence of detention may be imposed. In both instances, the court must consider that there is a significant risk to the public of serious harm occasioned by the commission by the offender of further 'specified offences', whether or not they are 'serious offences'. The extension period may be up to five years for a 'specified violent offence' and up to eight years for a 'specified sexual offence'.

database An organized collection of information held on a computer. Databases are usually protected by *copyright in the UK under the Copyright Designs and Patents Act 1988 and EU Directive 96/9 (implemented by the Copyright and Rights in Databases Regulations 1997 (SI 1997/3032)). Copyright protects the structure, order, arrangement on the page or screen, and other features of the database in addition to the information in the database itself.

data protection Safeguards relating to personal data, i.e. personal information about individuals that is stored on a computer and on 'relevant manual filing systems'. The principles of data protection, the responsibilities of data controllers (formerly data users under the Data Protection Act 1984), and the rights of data subjects are governed by the Data Protection Act 1998, which came into force on 1 March 2000.

The 1998 Act extends the operation of protection beyond computer storage, replaces the system of registration with one of notification, and demands that the level of description by data controllers under the new Act is more general than the detailed coding system required under the Data Protection Act 1984. Under the 1998 Act, the eight principles of data protection are: (1) The information to be contained in personal data shall be obtained, and personal data shall be processed, fairly and lawfully. (2) Personal data shall be held only for specified and lawful purposes and shall not be used or disclosed in any manner incompatible with those purposes. (3) Personal data held for any purpose shall be relevant to that purpose and not excessive in relation to the purpose(s) for which it is used. (4) Personal data shall be accurate and, where necessary, kept up to date. (5) Personal data held for any purpose shall not be kept longer than necessary for that purpose. (6) Personal data shall be processed in accordance with the rights of data subjects. (7) Appropriate technical and organizational measures shall be taken against unauthorized and unlawful processing of personal data and against accidental loss or destruction of, or damage to, personal data. (8) Personal data shall not be transferred to a country or territory outside the *European Community area unless that country or territory ensures an adequate level of protection for the rights and freedoms of data subjects in relation to the processing of personal data.

Data controllers must now notify their processing of data (unless they are exempt) with the **Information Commissioner** via the telephone, by requesting, completing, and returning a notification form, or by obtaining such a form from the website <http://www.dpr.gov.uk/notify/1.html>. Notification is renewable annually; a data controller who fails to notify his processing of data, or any changes that have been made since notification, commits a criminal offence.

The Information Commissioner can seek information (via an information notice) and ultimately take enforcement action (via an enforcement notice) against data controllers for non-compliance with their full obligations under the 1998 Act. *Appeals against decisions of the Information Commissioner may be made to the **Data Protection Tribunal**, which comprises a chairperson and two deputies (who are legally qualified) and lay members (representing the interests of the data controllers and the data subjects). There are other strict liability criminal offences under the 1998 Act other than non-notification. They include (1) obtaining, disclosing (or bringing about the disclosure), or selling (or advertising for sale) personal data without consent of the data controller; (2) obtaining unauthorized access to data; (3) asking another person to obtain access to data; and (4) failing to respond to an information and/or enforcement notice.

Data subjects have considerable rights conferred on them under the 1998 Act. They include: (1) the right to find out what information is held about them; (2) the right to seek a court order to rectify, block, erase, and destroy personal details if these are inaccurate, contain expressions of opinion, or are based on inaccurate data; (3) the right to prevent processing where such processing would cause substantial unwarranted damage or substantial distress to themselves or anyone else; (4) the right to prevent the processing of data for direct working; (5) the right to compensation from a data controller for damage or damage and distress caused by any breach of the 1998 Act; and (6) the right to prevent some decisions about data being made solely by automated means, where those decisions are likely to affect them significantly.

dawn raid 1. An offer by a person or persons to buy a substantial quantity of *shares in a *public company at above the market value, the offer remaining open for a very short period (usually hours). Because of the speed required, smaller shareholders may have little opportunity to avail themselves of the offer. Rules restrict the speed at which such acquisitions can be made. **2.** An unannounced visit by officials of the *European Commission or the UK *Office of Fair Trading investigating *cartels or other breaches of the competition rules under Articles 81 and 82 of the *Treaty of Rome or under the Competition Act 1998.

d

dealer list A list compiled by a drug dealer typically listing customers, amounts and prices. Such a list can be admissible at *trial if the *jury is properly directed that it must demonstrate future intent and not merely past dealing. *Police officers are permitted to give *expert evidence to interpret the meaning of entries in dealer lists and notes.

death The cessation of life. It can only be diagnosed by a registered medical practitioner or trained paramedic. The time between death and the body being examined is the post-mortem interval. This can be estimated by body temperature in the first 24 hours. After that various methods can be used by various experts: the degree of decomposition by taphonomists; the invasion of insects by entomologists; the examination of the bones by forensic anthropologists; and examination of chemical isotopes such as radio-carbon dating. Timing of death is notoriously unreliable.

death penalty *See* CAPITAL PUNISHMENT.

de bene esse [Latin: of well-being] Denoting a course of action that is the best that can be done in the present circumstances or in anticipation of a future event. An example is obtaining a *deposition from a witness when there is a likelihood that he will be unable to attend the court hearing.

debit card A card issued by a bank or other financial institution that allows the holder to pay for *goods or services. Unlike a *credit card, funds are taken immediately from the holder's account. The use of a debit card involves three contracts, similar to those that apply to the use of a credit card.

debt 1. A sum of money owed by one person or group to another. **2.** The obligation to pay a sum of money owed.

debtor 1. One who owes a debt. **2.** (under the Consumer Credit Act 1974) The individual receiving credit under a *consumer-credit agreement or the person to whom his rights and duties under the agreement have passed by assignment or operation of law.

debtor-creditor agreement A *consumer-credit agreement regulated by the Consumer Credit Act 1974 (which is to be amended by the Consumer Credit Act 2006). It may be (1) a *restricted-use credit agreement to finance a transaction between the *debtor and a supplier in which there are no arrangements between the *creditor and the supplier (e.g. when a loan is paid by the creditor direct to a dealer who is to supply the debtor); (2) a restricted-use credit agreement to refinance any existing indebtedness of the debtor's to the creditor or any other person; or (3) an unrestricted-use credit agreement (e.g. a straight loan of money) that is not made by the creditor under arrangements with a supplier in the knowledge that the credit is to be used to finance a transaction between the debtor and the supplier.

debtor-creditor-supplier agreement A *consumer-credit agreement regulated by the Consumer Credit Act 1974 (which is to be amended by the Consumer Credit Act 2006). It may be (1) a *restricted-use credit agreement to finance a transaction between the *debtor and the *creditor, which may or may not form part of that agreement (e.g. a purchase of *goods on credit); (2) a restricted-use credit agreement to finance a transaction between the debtor and a supplier, made by the creditor and involving arrangements between himself and the supplier; or (3) an unrestricted-use credit agreement that is made by the creditor under pre-existing arrangements between himself and a supplier in the knowledge that the credit is to be used to finance a transaction between the debtor and the supplier.

decapitation Removal of the head.

decarceration A policy of replacing imprisonment as the main sanction for criminal offences with community *punishments.

decelerate To reduce speed.

deception A false representation, by words or conduct, of a matter of fact (including the existence of an intention) or law that is made deliberately or recklessly to another person. Deception itself is not a crime, but there are eight indictable offences in which deception is involved: (1) obtaining property (s 15, Theft Act 1968); (2) obtaining a wrongful credit (s 15A, Theft Act 1968); (3) obtaining an overdraft, an *insurance policy, an annuity contract, or the opportunity to earn money (or more money) in a job or to win money by betting (s 16, Theft Act 1968); (4) obtaining any services (e.g. of a *driver or typist or the hiring of a car) (s 1, Theft Act 1978); (5) securing the remission of all or part of an existing liability to make payment (whether one's own or another's) with intent to make permanent default in whole or in part (s 2, Theft Act 1978); (6) causing someone to wait for or forego a debt owing to him (s 2, Theft Act 1978); (7) obtaining an exemption from or abatement of liability to pay for something (e.g. obtaining free or cheap travel by falsely pretending to be a senior citizen) (s 2, Theft Act 1978); (8) procuring the execution of a valuable security (s 20, Theft Act 1968). All the foregoing offences will be repealed when the Fraud Act 2006 comes into force and the word deception will no longer appear in *legislation. It is not an offence, however, to deceive someone in any other circumstances, provided there is no element of *forgery or *false accounting.

declaration (in the law of evidence) An oral or written statement not made on *oath. The term is often applied to certain types of out-of-court statement that are admissible as an exception to the rule against *hearsay evidence; e.g. *declaration against interest, declaration concerning pedigree, declaration concerning public or general rights, and *declaration in course of duty. *See also* STATUTORY DECLARATION.

declaration against interest A *declaration by a person who has subsequently died which he knew, when he made it, would be against his pecuniary or proprietary interest. At common law, it could be tendered to the court as an exception to the rule against *hearsay evidence. However, the rule was abolished by s 118(2) of the Criminal Justice Act 2003.

declaration in course of duty A *declaration by a person who has subsequently died made while pursuing a duty to record or report his acts. At *common law, it could be tendered to the court as an exception to the rule against *hearsay evidence. However, the rule was abolished by s 118 (2) of the Criminal Justice Act 2003.

declaration of incompatibility *See* HUMAN RIGHTS ACT.

declaratory judgment A *judgment that merely states the court's opinion on a question of law or declares the rights of the parties, without normally including any provision for enforcement. A claim for declaration may, however, be combined with one for some substantive relief, such as damages.

declaratory theory The proposition that a state has capacity (and personality) in *international law as soon as it exists in fact (that is, when it becomes competent in *municipal law). This capacity is generated spontaneously from the assertion by the community that it is a judicial entity. When socially organized, the new state is internally legally organized, and hence competent to act in such a way as to engage itself in international responsibility. Thus, according to this theory, recognition does not create any state that did not already exist. *See* INTERNATIONAL LEGAL PERSONALITY.

decompilation (reverse engineering) The process of taking computer *software apart. Under EU Directive 91/250, computer software is protected by *copyright throughout the *European Union. However, a very limited right to decompilation is given in that Directive for the defined purpose of writing an interoperable program, under certain very strict conditions. Any provision in a contract to exclude this limited right will be void. In the UK this Directive is implemented by the Copyright (Computer Programs) Regulations 1992.

decree 1. A law. **2.** A court order.

decriminalize The process of removing criminal sanctions from any activity either by removing any prohibition of the activity or by moving responsibility for enforcement to a non-criminal process. This has been used, for example, in the enforcement of parking restrictions. It is seen as a way of reducing pressure on the *criminal justice system but has been criticized because the safeguards for those accused are not always present in the administrative process.

deduction (in employment law) Sum deducted from an *employee's wages. The Employment Rights Act 1996 provides strict rules on what can be deducted from wages. Permitted deductions include those for income tax, national insurance, and pension contributions (for *employees who have agreed to be part of an *employer's pension scheme). Deductions are also allowed when there has been an overpayment of wages or expenses in the past, when there has been a strike and wages are withheld, or when there is a court order, such as an order from the Child Support Agency or a court attachment of earnings order. There are special rules for those in retail employment. These provide, for example, that deductions of up to 10 per cent may be made from gross wages for cash shortages or stock deficiencies.

deed A written document that must make it clear on its face that it is intended to be a deed and validly executed as a deed. Before 31 July 1990, all deeds required a seal in order to be validly executed, but this requirement was abolished by the Law of Property (Miscellaneous Provisions) Act 1989. A deed executed since that date by an individual requires only that it must be signed by its maker in the presence of a witness, or at the maker's direction and in the presence of two witnesses, and delivered. Deeds executed by companies require the signature of a *director and secretary, or two directors, of the company; alternatively, if the company has a seal, the deed may be executed by affixing the company seal. *See also* DEED POLL.

deed of arrangement A written agreement between a *debtor and his *creditors, when no *bankruptcy order has been made, arranging the debtor's affairs either for the benefit of the creditors generally or, when the debtor is insolvent, for the benefit of at least three of the creditors. A deed of arrangement is regulated by statute and must be registered with the Department of Trade and Industry within seven days. It may take a number of different forms: it may be a composition, an assignment of the debtor's property to a *trustee for the benefit of his creditors, or an agreement to wind up the debtor's business in such a way as to pay his debts. The debtor usually agrees to such an arrangement in order to avoid bankruptcy. A similar arrangement can be agreed after a *bankruptcy order is made, but this is regulated in a different way (*see* VOLUNTARY ARRANGEMENT).

deed of covenant A *deed containing an *undertaking to pay an agreed amount over an agreed period. Certain tax advantages could be obtained through the use of covenants, particularly in the case of four-year covenants in favour of *charities. This was superseded by gift aid in April 2000.

deed of gift A *deed conveying property from one person (the **donor**) to another (the **donee**) when the donee gives no *consideration in return. The donee can enforce a deed of gift against the donor. Gifts made other than by deed are not generally enforceable.

deed poll A *deed to which there is only one party; e.g. one declaring a *change of name.

deemed Supposed. In the construction of some documents (particularly statutes) an artificial construction is given to a word or phrase that ordinarily would not be so construed, in order to clarify any doubt or as a convenient form of drafting shorthand.

de facto [Latin: in fact] Existing as a matter of fact rather than of right. The Government may, for example, recognize a foreign government *de facto* if it is actually in control of a country even though it has no legal right to rule.

defamation The *publication of a statement about a person that tends to lower his *reputation in the opinion of right-thinking members of the community or to make them shun or avoid him. Defamation is usually in words, but pictures, gestures, and other acts can be defamatory. In English law, a distinction is made between defamation in permanent form (*see* LIBEL) and defamation not in permanent form (*see* SLANDER). The remedies in *tort for defamation are *damages and *injunction.

default Failure to do something required by law, usually failure to comply with mandatory rules of procedure. If a defendant in civil proceedings is in default (e.g. by failing to file a defence), the claimant may obtain **judgment in default**. If the claimant is in default, the defendant may apply to the court to dismiss the action.

defect (in a product) A fault in a product as defined in the Consumer Protection Act 1987. A defect exists in products under the Act when the safety of the products is not what people generally are entitled to expect. In determining what people are entitled to expect, reference should be made to the way in which the *goods are marked, any warnings issued with them, and the time of supply. The Act implements EU Directive 85/374 on *product liability.

defective goods *Goods sold that are not of satisfactory quality and are therefore in breach of the implied term under s 14 of the Sale of Goods Act 1979. If the goods are dangerous it is also a criminal offence under the Consumer Protection Act 1987 and the General Product Safety Regulations 1994 (SI 1994/2328). Action may also lie in *tort against the *seller in contract or the manufacturer in *negligence. *See also* PRODUCT LIABILITY.

defective product *See* PRODUCT LIABILITY.

defence (in civil and criminal proceedings) An issue of law or fact that, if determined in favour of the defendant, will relieve him of liability wholly or in part. *See also* GENERAL DEFENCES.

defence statement (in criminal proceedings) A *document setting out: the nature of the accused's *defence, including any particular defences on which he intends to rely; indicating the matters of fact on which he takes issue with the *prosecution case; setting out, in the case of each such matter, why he takes such issue; and indicating any point of law which he wishes to take, any authority on which he intends to rely for that purpose; and particulars of any *alibi evidence that the accused proposes to adduce. When the case is to be tried in the *Crown Court, the defence is required (by s 5 of the Criminal Procedure and Investigations Act 1996, as amended by the Criminal Justice Act 2003) to serve a defence statement within fourteen days of the date on which the prosecution complies with its duty to make initial disclosure under s 3 of the Act. If the defence fails to serve a statement, sets out inconsistent defences in a statement, or puts forward a defence at *trial that is inconsistent with any defence set out, then the court or, with the leave of the court, the prosecution may 'make such comment as appears appropriate'. The jury may also 'draw such inferences as appear proper in deciding whether the accused is guilty of the offence' (an **adverse inference**). Where the case is to be tried in a *magistrates' court or *youth court, s 6 of the Act provides for voluntary service of such a statement. *See also* CRIMINAL PROCEDURE AND INVESTIGATIONS ACT 1996; DISCLOSURE OF UNUSED MATERIAL.

defence wound An injury incurred by a victim whilst defending himself. Defence injuries often take the form of *lacerations and *contusions to the hands and outer aspects of the forearms.

defendant A person against whom court proceedings are brought. In criminal proceedings, the term is often used interchangeably with **accused**. *Compare* CLAIMANT.

defensible space As a way of designing out crime, space is created around vulnerable *premises or communities to keep out intruders. An example of this is *alleygating where gates are erected at the ends of alleyways behind houses and access is permitted only to residents.

deferred debt (in bankruptcy proceedings) A *debt that by statute is not paid until all other debts have been paid in full.

deferred sentence The postponement of passing *sentence. Section 1 of the Powers of Criminal Courts (Sentencing) Act 2000 empowers a court to defer passing sentence on an offender for a period of up to six months from *conviction for the offence. The court may only defer sentencing if the convicted person consents and if the court considers that it is in the interests of justice to do so. The purpose of a deferral is to enable the court to assess any change in the offender's conduct or circumstances during that time. Where sentence is deferred by a *magistrates' court, the offender may still be committed to the *Crown Court at the end of the period of deferment. Section 278 of the Criminal Justice Act 2003 amended s 1 of the 2000 Act so as to empower the court to require the offender to undertake reparative activities during the deferment period.

defibrillation A medical procedure in which electric shocks are delivered to the heart to stop extremely rapid and irregular heartbeat and restore a regular sinusoidal rhythm.

defrauding Any act that deprives someone of something that is his or to which he might be entitled or that injures someone in relation to any proprietary right. It is a crime (a form of *conspiracy at *common law) to conspire to defraud someone. *See also* CHEATING; DECEPTION; DISHONESTY.

degrading treatment or punishment Treatment that arouses in the victim a feeling or fear, anguish, and inferiority capable of humiliating and debasing the victim and possibly breaking his physical or moral resistance. The prohibition on degrading treatment or punishment as set out in Article 3 of the *European Convention on Human Rights is now part of UK law as a consequence of the *Human Rights Act 1998. This right is an *absolute right; such treatment can never be justified as being in the public interest, no matter how great that public interest might be. Public authorities have a limited but positive duty to protect this right from interference by third parties.

dehydration Lack of water in the body. Commonly caused by starvation or neglect. Also occurs in *hypothermia.

de jure [Latin: by law] As a matter of legal right. *Compare* DE FACTO.

delegated legislation (subordinate legislation) *Legislation made under powers conferred by an *Act of Parliament (an enabling statute, often called the parent Act). The bulk of delegated legislation is governmental: it consists mainly of *Orders in Council and instruments of various names (e.g. orders, regulations, rules, directions, and schemes) made by ministers (*see also* GOVERNMENT CIRCULARS). Its primary use is to supplement Acts of Parliament by prescribing the detailed and technical rules required for their operation; unlike an Act, it has the advantage that it can be made (and later amended if necessary) without taking up parliamentary time. Delegated legislation is also made by a variety of bodies outside central government, examples being *byelaws and the codes of conduct of certain professional bodies (*see also* ORDERS IN COUNCIL).

Most delegated legislation (byelaws are the main exception) is subject to some degree of parliamentary control, which may take any of three principal forms: (1) a simple requirement that it be laid before *Parliament after being made (thus ensuring that members become aware of its existence but affording them no special method or opportunity of questioning its substance); (2) a provision that it be laid and, for a specified period, liable to annulment by a resolution of either House (**negative resolution** procedure); or (3) a provision that it be laid and either shall not take effect until approved by resolutions of both Houses or shall cease to have effect unless approved within a specified period (**affirmative resolution** procedure). In the case of purely financial instruments, any provision for a negative or affirmative resolution refers to the House of Commons alone.

All delegated legislation is subject to judicial control under the doctrine of **ultra vires*. Delegated legislation is interpreted in the light of the parent Act, so particular words are presumed to be used in the same sense as in that Act. This rule apart, it is governed by the same principles as those governing the *interpretation of statutes.

See also STATUTORY INSTRUMENT; SUBDELEGATED LEGISLATION.

delegation 1. The grant of authority to a person to act on behalf of one or more others, for agreed purposes. **2.** *See* VICARIOUS LIABILITY.

delinquent 1. A person who commits offences. **2.** Describing offending behaviour.

delivery The transfer of *possession of property from one person to another. Under the Sale of Goods Act 1979, a *seller delivers *goods to a *buyer if he delivers them physically, if he makes **symbolic delivery** by delivering the document of title to them (e.g. a *bill of lading) or other means of control over them (e.g. the keys of a warehouse in which they are stored), or if a third party who is holding them acknowledges that he now holds them for the buyer. In **constructive delivery**, the seller agrees that he holds the goods on behalf of the buyer or the buyer has possession of the goods under a *hire-purchase agreement and becomes owner on making the final payment.

demanding with menaces *See* BLACKMAIL.

de minimis non curat lex [Latin: the law does not take account of trifles] It will not, for example, award damages for a trifling nuisance. The *de minimis* rule applies in a number of other areas, including EU competition law.

denial A defence mechanism whereby a person, community, or state faced with a fact that is uncomfortable or painful to accept, such as wrong-doing, rejects it instead, insisting that it is not true despite what may be overwhelming evidence. The subject may deny that it occurred (simple denial), admit that it occurred but deny its seriousness (minimization), or admit both the event and its seriousness but deny responsibility (transference).

denial of service attack (DoS) An attack directed against a website, e-Business, or large computer network intended to disrupt the operation of the system by preventing the normal flow of electronic communication. The attack may be launched as a form of either *blackmail or *vandalism. Generally, a DoS attack takes one of four forms:

- overload of system or network resources;
- disruption of configuration information, such as routing information;
- disruption of physical network components;
- disruption of the operation of a key service by the introduction of malicious software (e.g. *viruses, *worms, *Trojan horses).

denying quarter A *war crime under the Statute of the *International Criminal Court where a commander gives an order that no quarter be given, for example 'take no prisoners'. 'Quarter' means not killing an enemy who has surrendered.

dependent state A member of the community of states with qualified or limited status. Such states possess no separate statehood or *sovereignty: it is the parent state alone that possesses *international legal personality and has the capacity to exercise international rights and duties.

dependent territory A territory (e.g. a colony) the government of which is to some extent the legal responsibility of the government of another territory.

deportation 1. The removal from a state of a person whose initial entry into that state was illegal (*compare* EXPULSION). In the UK this is authorized by the Immigration Act 1971 (as amended by the Immigration and Asylum Act 1999) in the case of any person who does not have the right of abode there (*see* IMMIGRATION). He may be ordered to leave the country in four circumstances: if he has overstayed or broken a condition attached to his permission to stay; if another person to whose family he belongs is deported; if (he being 17 or over) a court recommends deportation on his conviction of an offence punishable with imprisonment (*see* RECOMMENDATION FOR DEPORTATION ON CONVICTION); or if the Secretary of State thinks his deportation to be for the public good. The Act enables *appeals to be made against deportation orders. Normally, they are either direct to the *Immigration Appeal Tribunal or to that tribunal after a preliminary appeal to an adjudicator. The Immigration Act 1988 restricts this right of appeal in the case of those who have failed to observe a condition or limitation on their leave to enter the UK. The Immigration and Asylum Act 1999 gives additional powers to order those present in the UK without permission to leave, either when they have overstayed or obtained leave to remain by deception or when they were never granted leave to remain. An asylum seeker may not be deported, although a deportation order may be made against him before determination of his claim. Under s 22 of the Antiterrorism, Crime and Security Act 2001, *enforcement action may be taken in respect of a suspected international *terrorist despite the fact that (whether temporarily or indefinitely) the action cannot result in his removal from the UK because of a point of law which wholly or partly relates to an international agreement, or a practical consideration. **2.** In some circumstances the forcible evacuation of the whole or part of the civilian populations may be a *crime against humanity under the Statute of the *International Criminal Court. However temporary deportation may be lawful in time of peace if it is for the benefit of the population to avoid natural disasters. In time of war, the Fourth Geneva Convention allows an occupying power to evacuate the civilian population if the security of the population or military imperative demand. However, in this case they must be returned as soon as possible. Where there is no lawful reason the deportation does not have to be from one country to another, it can be from one area of a country to another as in *Prosecutor v Krstic* (2 August 2001) Case No IT98-33, which involved the removal of Bosnian Muslims from Srebenica to other parts of Bosnia.

depose To make a *deposition or other written statement on oath. *See also* COMMISSION.

deposition A statement made on *oath before a *magistrate or court official by a witness and usually recorded in writing.

In committal proceedings before the *magistrates' court (*see* COMMITTAL FOR TRIAL), evidence by way of a deposition may be taken (under s 97A of the Magistrates' Courts Act 1980) in advance of the committal proceedings where a person 'is likely to be able to make a written statement containing material evidence' on behalf of the *prosecutor and 'the person will not voluntarily make the statement'. If a magistrate is satisfied of those conditions, then a summons, or if necessary a warrant, can be issued. The court does not need to be convened for the deposition to be taken and neither the defendant nor his legal representative need be notified or be present. Once taken, the deposition is admissible in subsequent committal proceedings by virtue of s 5C of the 1980 Act.

In civil cases the court may order an examiner of the court to take depositions from any witnesses who are (for example) ill or likely to be abroad at the time of the hearing. At the taking of the deposition the witness is examined and cross-examined in the usual way, and the examiner notes any objection to admissibility that may be raised. The deposition is not admissible at the *trial without the consent of the party against whom it is given, unless the witness is still unavailable. *See also* COMMISSION.

deprave To make morally bad. The term is used particularly in relation to the effect of *obscene publications. A person is considered to have been depraved if his mind is influenced in an immoral way, even though this does not necessarily result in any act of depravity.

derivative An asset that is traded. The term includes futures, forwards, and options which are financial instruments based on a real asset such as metals or currency.

derivative title A claim of *sovereignty over a territory, that territory having previously belonged to another sovereign state. Derivation of *title to territory involves the transfer (*cession) of title from one sovereign state to another.

dermis A thick layer of skin under the outer surface (*epidermis) containing small blood vessels, nerve endings, smooth muscle, and connective tissues.

derogation The lessening or restriction of the authority, strength, or power of a law, right, or obligation. Specifically: **1.** (in the *European Convention on Human Rights) A provision that enables a signatory state to avoid the obligations of some but not all of the substantive provisions of the rest of the Convention. This procedure is provided by Article 15 of the Convention and is available in time of *war or other public emergency threatening the life of the nation. Although Article 15 is not brought into domestic law by the *Human Rights Act 1998, the Act exempts public authorities from compliance with any articles (or parts of articles) where a derogation is in place. **2.** (in EU law) An exemption clause that permits a member state of the *European Union to avoid a certain directive or regulation. Sometimes member states are allowed a longer than normal time to implement an EU directive.

desertion An offence against *service law committed by a member of the armed forces who leaves or fails to attend at his unit, ship, or place of duty. He must either intend at the time to remain permanently absent from duty without lawful authority or subsequently form that intention. One who absents himself without leave to avoid service overseas or service before the enemy is also *guilty of desertion.

designated case worker Staff of the *Crown Prosecution Service who are not *barristers or *solicitors but who are permitted to undertake all work in *magistrates' courts other than *trials, *proofs in absence in *either way cases, *committals for trial, *case management hearings, *Newton hearings, contested *bail hearings and proceedings for *sending offences to the Crown Court for trial. The Commissioners for Revenue and Customs Act 2005 makes provision for the Director of the *Revenue and Customs Prosecutions Office to appoint designated case workers, although he has not as yet exercised that power.

designated civilian A civilian granted powers previously reserved to *constables. Section 38 of the Police Reform Act 2002 allows chief *police officers to designate certain police powers to *police authority *employees who are not constables when employed as *community support officers, *investigating officers, *detention officers, or *escort officers. Detention officers and escort officers who are contractors may also be designated.

design right Legal protection for the external appearance of an article, including its shape, configuration, pattern, or ornament. A design right is distinct from a *patent, which protects the internal workings of the article. The right entitles the owner to prevent others making articles to the same design. Design rights in the UK are either registered (*see* REGISTERED DESIGN) or unregistered. Registered designs must have aesthetic appeal; they are protected under the Registered Designs Act 1949 as amended and last for a maximum of 25 years provided renewal fees are paid. Unregistered designs, which came into existence in 1989, are protected under the Copyright, Designs and Patents Act 1988. Unregistered design protection is for only fifteen years. Design protection is not available for parts of articles that simply provide a fit or match to another article, such as a car-body panel.

destroy An offence under the Criminal Damage Act 1971 which goes further than *damage. In practical terms it is unnecessary as it is not possible to destroy something without damaging it. A defendant would not be charged with 'destroying property' as it would leave open an argument that he intended only to damage it.

detention Depriving a person of his liberty against his will following *arrest. The Police and Criminal Evidence Act 1984 closely regulates police powers of detention and detained persons' rights. Detention of adults without *charge is allowed only when it is necessary to secure or preserve evidence or to obtain it by questioning; it should only continue beyond 24 hours (to 36 hours) in respect of *indictable offences when a superintendent or more senior officer reasonably believes it to be necessary. *Magistrates' courts may then authorize a further extension without charge for up to 36 hours, which can be extended for another 36 hours, but the overall detention period cannot exceed 96 hours.

If the ground for detention ceases, or if further detention is not authorized, the detainee must either be released or be charged and either released on *bail to appear before a court or taken before the next available court. An arrested person held in *custody may have one person told of this as soon as practicable, though if an indictable offence is involved and a senior *police officer reasonably believes that this would interfere with the investigation, this can be delayed for up to 36 hours. The detainee has a broadly similar right of access to a *solicitor. *Terrorism suspects may be detained for up to seven days on a magistrate's authority.

detention and training order Section 100 of the Powers of Criminal Courts (Sentencing) Act 2000 provides for a detention and training order for 12 to 17 year olds. In the case of an offender under the age of 15 at the time of *conviction, the court may not make an order unless it is satisfied that he is a 'persistent offender' (*see* PERSISTENT YOUNG OFFENDER.). At present, there is no power to make such an order in respect of an offender under the age of 12, the necessary order not having been made by the Secretary of State. Should the power become available, it will only be available if the court is satisfied that 'only a custodial sentence would be adequate to protect the public from further offending'.

The order may be made for four, six, eight, ten, twelve, or eighteen months but cannot exceed the maximum term of imprisonment that the *Crown Court could impose on an adult offender convicted of the same offence (s 101 of the 2000 Act). The period of detention under such an order is one-half of the total term of the order. When that portion is complete, the offender is subject to supervision by a probation officer, social worker, or a member of a *youth offending team for the remaining term of the order. *See also* DETENTION IN A YOUNG OFFENDER INSTITUTION; JUVENILE OFFENDER; LONG-TERM DETENTION.

detention in a young offender institution The detention of offenders aged 18, 19, and 20, under s 96 of the Powers of Criminal Courts (Sentencing) Act 2000, in a young offender institution. For those under that age, it has been replaced by a *detention and training order. The term of detention may never exceed the maximum term of imprisonment that could be imposed for the offence in the case of an offender aged 21 or over. The minimum is 21 days. *See also* DETENTION AND TRAINING ORDER; JUVENILE OFFENDER; LONG-TERM DETENTION.

detention officer A person who is not a *constable and is employed or contracted by a *police force to assist the *custody officer with people detained at a police station. They may be designated by the chief officer to take *fingerprints, conduct searches of detained people and take *non-intimate samples from them.

deterrence *See* PUNISHMENT.

deviance Behaviours, attitudes, and demeanours that differ significantly from the norms, standards, ethics, and expectations of society and are often classed as criminal or anti-social.

deviancy amplification A concept that holds that the reaction to deviant behaviour by the police, press, and politicians may increase the deviant behaviour rather than reduce it.

diabetes mellitus Illness caused by lack of functioning of the pancreas, producing too little insulin. If correct medication is not taken the patient can fall into a coma; it can be mistaken for drunkenness. Medical attention should be sought immediately if diabetic coma is suspected.

diamorphine (heroin) (*slang*: big H, blactar, brown sugar, dope, horse, mud, skag, smack) A narcotic drug composed of two molecules of *morphine. It is used pharmaceutically to relieve extreme pain. It is very addictive and is a major drug of abuse. Pharmaceutical diamorphine is a colourless liquid in glass vials for injection. Illicit diamorphine (heroin) is a powder which can vary from white to dark brown or a tar-like substance. The drug can be taken by injection into a vein ('mainlining') or muscle, smoked in a pipe or cigarette, or heated on a piece of metal foil and inhaled ('chasing the dragon'), or snorted as a powder. When the drug is administered the user gets an immediate feeling of euphoria ('rush'). This soon wears off and the person wants more of the drug and quickly becomes addicted to it. It is classified as Class A by the Misuse of Drugs Act 1971. All offences involving Class A drugs are *indictable and carry penalties of up to *life imprisonment.

diatom Microscopic single celled organism found in naturally occurring water. There are *c.*100 000 species. Different species live in sea water and fresh water; some species are found more in puddles than lakes. Thus in cases of *drowning an examination of any diatoms found in the lungs may give an indication of the type of water in which the deceased person drowned.

diazepam A sedative drug of the *benzodiazepine group. Trade name Valium™.

dictum [Latin: a saying] An observation by a judge with respect to a point of law arising in a case before him. *See also* OBITER DICTUM.

diffuse axonal injury (DIA) A severe injury of the brain often resulting in the victim going into a persistent vegetative state. It is caused by rapid acceleration or deceleration of the brain causing the axons of the nerves within to tear. It is frequently caused in high speed road traffic collisions.

digital signature Data appended to a unit of data held on a computer, or a cryptographic transformation of a data unit, that allows the recipient of the data unit to prove its source and integrity and protects against forgery. The International Standards Organization defined this means of identification and protection. An *electronic signature, as defined by the Electronic Communications Act 2000, has a similar effect in relation to a commercial agreement.

diminished responsibility An abnormal state of mind that does not constitute *insanity but is a special defence to a charge of *murder. The abnormality of mind (which need not be a brain disease) must substantially impair the mental responsibility of the accused for his acts, i.e. it must reduce his powers of control, judgment, or reasoning to a condition that would be considered abnormal by the ordinary man. It may be caused by disease, injury, or mental subnormality, and is liberally interpreted to cover such conditions as depression or *irresistible impulse. If the defendant proves the defence, he is convicted of *manslaughter. *See also* BATTERED SPOUSE OR COHABITANT.

diplomatic agent One of a class of state officials who are entrusted with the responsibility for representing their state and its interests and welfare and that of its citizens or subjects in the *jurisdiction of another state or in international organizations. Diplomatic agents can be generally classified into two groups: (1) heads of mission and (2) members of the staff of the mission having diplomatic rank. *See also* DIPLOMATIC IMMUNITY; DIPLOMATIC MISSION.

diplomatic immunity The freedom from legal proceedings in the UK that is granted to members of *diplomatic missions of foreign states by the Diplomatic Privileges Act 1964. This Act incorporates some of the provisions of the Vienna Convention on Diplomatic Relations (1961), which governs diplomatic immunity in *international law. The extent of the immunity depends upon the status of the member in question, as certified by the Secretary of State. If he is a member of the mission's diplomatic staff, he is entitled to complete criminal immunity and to civil immunity except for actions relating to certain private activities. A member of the administrative or technical staff has full criminal immunity, but his civil immunity relates only to acts performed in the course of his official duties. For domestic staff, both criminal and civil immunity are restricted to official duties.

Similar immunities are granted to members of *Commonwealth missions by the Diplomatic and other Privileges Act 1971, and to members of certain international bodies under the International Organisations Acts 1968 and 1981. Under the Diplomatic and Consular Premises Act 1987, the Secretary of State may remove diplomatic status from diplomatic or consular *premises that are being misused.

diplomatic mission A body composed of government officers representing the interests and welfare of their state who have been posted abroad (by the sending state) and operate within the *jurisdiction of another state (the receiving state). This mission will be accorded protection by the receiving state in accordance with the rules of *diplomatic immunity. *See also* DIPLOMATIC AGENT.

diplomatic privilege The immunity given to members of *diplomatic missions and diplomatic couriers from arrest and prosecution for any criminal offence. The *premises and diplomatic bags of the mission are inviolable and cannot be entered unless privilege is waived. The law on diplomatic privilege is laid down in the Vienna Convention on Diplomatic Relations 1961 and brought into UK law by the Diplomatic Privileges Act 1964 and subsequent Acts. It is an offence under the Criminal Law Act 1977 to trespass on the premises of a foreign mission.

direct effect (in EU law) *See* COMMUNITY LEGISLATION.

direct evidence (original evidence) 1. A statement made by a witness in court offered as proof of the truth of any fact stated by him. *Compare* HEARSAY EVIDENCE. **2.** A statement of a witness that he perceived a fact in issue with one of his five senses or that he was in a particular physical or mental state. *Compare* CIRCUMSTANTIAL EVIDENCE.

direct examination *See* EXAMINATION-IN-CHIEF

direction to jury The duty of a *judge to instruct a *jury on a point of law (e.g. the definition of the crime charged or the nature and scope of possible *defences). Failure to carry out this instruction correctly may be grounds for an *appeal if a miscarriage of justice is likely to have occurred as a result of the misdirection.

directives of the EU *See* COMMUNITY LEGISLATION.

directly applicable law Any provision of the law of the *European Community that forms part of the national law of a member state. *See* COMMUNITY LAW; COMMUNITY LEGISLATION.

directly effective law *See* COMMUNITY LAW; COMMUNITY LEGISLATION.

director An officer of a company appointed by or under the provisions of the *articles of association. Directors may have a contract of employment with the company (**service directors** and **managing directors**) or merely attend board meetings (**non-executive directors**). (*See also* SHADOW DIRECTOR.) Contracts of employment can be inspected by *company members; long-term contracts may require approval by ordinary resolution. Usually, general management powers are vested in the directors acting collectively, although they may delegate some or all of these powers to the managing director. Directors act as agents of their company, to which they owe *fiduciary duties (in the performance of which they must consider the interests of both company members and *employees) and a *duty of care. Transactions involving a conflict between their duty and their personal interests are regulated by the Companies Acts. Directors can be dismissed by *ordinary resolution despite the terms of the articles or any contract of employment, but dismissal in these circumstances is subject to the payment of *damages for *breach of contract. Under the Company Directors Disqualification Act 1986, directors may be disqualified for *fraudulent trading or *wrongful trading and conduct that makes them unfit to be concerned in the management of companies. *See also* DISQUALIFICATION OF COMPANY DIRECTORS.

Remuneration of directors for their services may be due under a contract of employment or determined by the general meeting. Particulars appear in the *accounts.

Director of Public Prosecutions (DPP) The head of the *Crown Prosecution Service (CPS), who must be a lawyer of at least ten years' general qualification. The DPP is appointed by the *Attorney-General and discharges his functions under the superintendence of the Attorney-General. The DPP, through the CPS, is responsible for the conduct of all criminal *prosecutions instituted by the police and he may intervene in any criminal proceedings when it appears to him to be appropriate. Some statutes require the consent of the DPP to prosecution.

Director of the Revenue and Customs Prosecutions Office The head of the *Revenue and Customs Prosecutions Office (RCPO), who is appointed by the *Attorney-General and discharges his functions under the superintendence of the Attorney-General. The Director is responsible for the institution and conduct of criminal proceedings in England and Wales relating to a criminal investigation by *Her Majesty's Revenue and Customs and for providing advice in relation to such investigations. He may delegate those functions to a *Revenue and Customs Prosecutor. The Director must have a ten year general qualification within the meaning of s 71 of the Courts and Legal Services Act 1990.

Director of the Serious Fraud Office The head of the *Serious Fraud Office (SFO), who is appointed by the *Attorney-General under s 1 of the Criminal Justice Act 1987 and discharges his functions under the superintendence of the Attorney-General, both in his capacity as Attorney-General for England and Wales and Attorney-General of Northern Ireland. He is responsible for the institution and conduct of offences of serious and complex *fraud in England and Wales and Northern Ireland. He may delegate those functions to a SFO lawyer qualified in those jurisdictions.

disabling statute A statute that disqualifies a person or persons of a specified class from exercising a legal right or freedom that he or they would otherwise enjoy.

disbar To expel a *barrister from his *Inn of Court. The sentence of disbarment is pronounced by the Benchers of the barrister's Inn, subject to a right of *appeal to the *judges who act as visitors of all the Inns of Court.

discharge The release of a convicted defendant without imposing a *punishment on him. A discharge may be absolute or conditional. In an **absolute discharge** the defendant is not punished for the offence. His conviction may, however, be accompanied by a *compensation order or by *endorsement of his driving licence or *disqualification from driving. A **conditional discharge** also releases the defendant without punishment, provided that he is not convicted of any other offence within a specified period (usually three years). If he is convicted within that time, the court may sentence him for the original offence as well. Three conditions are required for the court to order a discharge: (1) that a *community rehabilitation order is not appropriate; (2) that the punishment for the offence must not be fixed by law; and (3) that the court thinks it inadvisable to punish the defendant in the circumstances.

disclosure **1.** (in criminal law) *See* ADVANCE INFORMATION; DISCLOSURE OF UNUSED MATERIAL. **2.** (in contract law) *See* NON-DISCLOSURE; UBERRIMAE FIDEI. **3.** (in company law) A method of protecting investors that relies on the company disclosing and publishing information, which is then evaluated by the investors, their advisers, and the press. (*See also* STOCK EXCHANGE.) A method of regulating the conduct of *directors and promoters by requiring them, on *fiduciary principles or by statutory provisions, to disclose to the company any relevant information, e.g. an interest in a contract with the company.

disclosure and inspection of documents (in civil court proceedings) Disclosure by a party to civil litigation of the *documents in his *possession, *custody, or power relating to matters in question in the action and their subsequent inspection by the opposing party; before the introduction of the *Civil Procedure Rules in 1999, this procedure was called **discovery and inspection of documents**. For the purposes of disclosure, documents extend beyond paper to include anything upon which information is capable of being recorded and retrieved (e.g. tapes, computer disks). In the absence of disclosure and/or inspection, the court has power to direct that **general** or **specific disclosure** and/or inspection be made. *See also* FAILURE TO MAKE DISCLOSURE; NON-DISCLOSURE.

disclosure notice *See* COMPULSORY POWERS.

disclosure of information *See* ADVANCE INFORMATION; DISCLOSURE OF UNUSED MATERIAL.

disclosure of interest The duty of *local authority members to disclose (at the time or by prior notice to the authority) any pecuniary interest they or their spouses have in any matter discussed at a local authority meeting. They must also abstain from speaking and voting on it. Breach of the duty is a criminal offence.

disclosure of unused material The disclosure to the *defence of material which does not form part of the *prosecution case. For criminal proceedings issued after 1 April 1997, the Criminal Procedure and Investigations Act 1996 (as amended by the Criminal Justice Act 2003) sets out detailed rules on the disclosure to the defence of material ('unused material') which does not form a part of the prosecution case, and, in cases tried on *indictment, requires the defence to serve a statement setting out the nature of the accused's defence, including any particular defences on which he intends to rely and indicating the matters of fact on which he takes issue with the prosecution. In cases tried summarily, the defendant may make a defence statement. As originally enacted, the test for disclosure of unused material was a subjective one: the prosecution was required to disclose any material which 'in the prosecutor's opinion' might undermine the prosecution case or assist that of the accused. The test was modified by the Criminal Justice Act 2003 to require the *prosecutor to disclose material that 'might reasonably be considered capable of undermining the case for the prosecution against the accused, or of assisting the case for the accused'. *See also* CRIMINAL PROCEDURE AND INVESTIGATIONS ACT 1996; defence statement; public interest immunity.

Police officers and others who are charged with the duty of conducting an investigation as defined in the Act are required to have regard to the 1996 Act; the Code of Practice issued pursuant to s 23(1) of the Act (reproduced at **Appendix 3**); the Attorney-General's Guidelines on Disclosure (reproduced at **Appendix 4**) and, in matters to be tried on indictment, the Protocol for the Control and Management of Unused Material In The Crown Court (reproduced at **Appendix 5**).

In criminal proceedings, an expert instructed by the prosecution is required to comply with the disclosure provisions of the 1996 Act. The *Attorney-General has issued a booklet entitled 'Disclosure: Expert's Evidence and Unused Material-Guidance Booklet for Experts', designed to provide a practical guide to disclosure for such witnesses, reproduced at Annex K to the *CPS Disclosure Manual (see <http://www.cps.gov.uk/legal/section20/chapter_a_annex_k.html>). *See also* EXPERT EVIDENCE.

disclosure order An order made by a *magistrates' court requiring the person to whom it is directed to supply the name, date of birth or national insurance number, and address of the person to whom a *warrant relates. A magistrates' court issuing a warrant of arrest, commitment, detention, or distress in connection with the enforcement of a *fine or other order imposed or made on *conviction may, if it is satisfied that it is necessary to do so for the purposes of executing a warrant, make a disclosure order (s 125CA, Magistrates' Court Act 1980, inserted by s 28, Domestic Violence, Crime and Victims Act 2004).

discontinuance of action *See* NOTICE OF DISCONTINUANCE.

discount house A financial institution that specializes in buying *bills of exchange, treasury bills, etc., at a price lower than the face value. The bearer thus obtains cash without having to wait for the due date and the discount house holds the security until the due date and gets the full face value.

discovery (in *international law) A method of acquiring territory in which good *title can be gained by claiming previously unclaimed *land (*terra nullius*). In the early days of European exploration it was held that the discovery of a previously unknown land conferred absolute title to it upon the state by whose agents the discovery was made. However, it has now long been established that the bare fact of discovery is an insufficient ground of proprietary right.

discovery and inspection of documents *See* DISCLOSURE AND INSPECTION OF DOCUMENTS.

discretion The power, held by *police officers as holders of the office of *constable, to decide whether and how, within legal bounds, they enforce the law. The part of discretion most often used is the power not to take action. Other professionals in the *criminal justice system also have the power of discretion in the performance of their professional roles. In particular, *prosecutors have the discretion not to initiate or continue with proceedings if it is not in the public interest to prosecute. *See also* JUDICIAL DISCRETION.

discretionary area of judgment A concept used in some cases in the domestic courts when reviewing decisions of public authorities under the *European Convention on Human Rights. The concept allows the courts to defer on democratic grounds to the decisions of elected bodies. It follows from the fact that the concept of the *margin of appreciation is not applicable in the domestic courts.

discrimination Treating one or more members of a specified group unfairly as compared with other people. Discrimination may be illegal on the ground of sex, sexual orientation, race, religion, disability, or *nationality. *See also* HUMAN RIGHTS ACT; RACIAL DISCRIMINATION.

dishonesty An element of liability in *theft, *abstracting electricity, *deception, *handling stolen *goods, and some related offences. To convict of such offences the *magistrates or *jury must be satisfied that what was done was dishonest by the standards of ordinary decent people and that the defendant realized this at the time: *R v Ghosh* [1982] All ER 689.

disk imaging *See* IMAGING.

disorderly house A *brothel or a place staging performances or exhibitions that tend to corrupt or deprave and outrage common decency. It is an offence at *common law to keep a disorderly house. Brothel keeping is normally prosecuted under ss 33–5 of the Sexual Offences Act 1956, but the common law offence is useful for dealing with establishments offering 'peep shows', sado-masochistic activities and, in certain circumstances, those *premises occupied by lone *prostitutes.

dispersal order An order under s 30 of the Anti-Social Behaviour Act 2003 to disperse a group of two or more young people under 16 who are unsupervised in *public places after 9 pm and return them to their homes. They are only available where an authorization has been made by an officer of at least the rank of superintendent regarding a designated area. In order to make such an authorization, the officer must have reasonable grounds for believing (a) that any members of the public have been intimidated, harassed, alarmed, or distressed as a result of the presence or behaviour of groups of two or more persons in public places in any locality in his police area, and (b) that anti-social behaviour is a significant and persistent problem in that locality.

The power of a *constable in uniform or *Community Support Officer to give directions is also subject to the requirement that he has reasonable grounds for believing that the presence or behaviour of a group of two or more persons in any public place in the relevant locality has resulted, or is likely to result, in any members of the public being intimidated, harassed, alarmed, or distressed. If so, the constable may give one or more of the following directions: (a) a direction requiring the persons in the group to disperse (either immediately or by such time as he may specify and in such ways as he may specify), (b) a direction requiring any of those persons whose place of residence is not within the relevant locality to leave it or any part of it (either immediately or by such time as he may specify and in such way as he may specify), and (c) a direction prohibiting any of those persons whose place of residence is not within the relevant locality from returning to it or any part of it for such period (not exceeding 24 hours) from the beginning of the direction as he may specify. The direction may be given orally, to any person individually or to two or more persons together, and may be withdrawn or varied by the person who gave it. Such a direction may not be given in respect of a group of persons (a) who are engaged in conduct which is lawful under s 220 of the Trade Union and Labour Relations (Consolidation) Act 1992, or (b) who are taking part in a public procession within the meaning of s 11 of the Public Order Act 1986, in respect of which appropriate written notice has been given or is not required.

Section 30 of the 2003 Act allows the police to return young people under 16 who are unsupervised in public places in areas covered by an authorization after 9pm to their homes.

displacement The movement of incidents of crime from one location to another as a result of police action in the former location.

disposition The tendency of a party (especially the accused) to act or think in a particular way. Evidence of the accused's disposition may generally not be given unless it is based upon admissible evidence of *character.

disqualification Depriving someone of a right because he has committed a criminal offence or failed to comply with specified conditions. Disqualification is usually imposed in relation to activities requiring a *licence, and in particular for traffic offences.

disqualification from driving A ban from driving following *conviction for a road traffic offence. It may be either obligatory or discretionary. Where a person is convicted of an offence involving obligatory disqualification, the court must order him to be disqualified for a minimum period of twelve months (s 34(1), Road Traffic Offenders Act 1988) in the absence of *special reasons. There is no statutory maximum period of disqualification. The following offences carry obligatory disqualification: *causing death by dangerous driving; *dangerous driving; driving or attempting to drive when unfit through drink or drugs or with excess alcohol in breath, blood, or urine (*see* DRUNKEN DRIVING); and failing to provide a specimen of breath, blood, or urine for analysis. If an offender is convicted of a second drunken driving offence within a ten year period then the minimum period of disqualification is increased to three years.

In the case of an offence carrying discretionary disqualification, the court may impose a disqualification, but is under no obligation to do so (s 34(2), Road Traffic Offenders Act 1988). There is no limit on the period of disqualification that may be imposed.

Many road traffic offences are endorsable; i.e. the court must order that the fact of conviction together with the number of **penalty points** applicable to the offence, are recorded on the offender's licence unless there are special reasons for not so doing (*see also* ENDORSEMENT). Penalty points for the most important offences are as follows:

- three to eleven points: any offence involving obligatory disqualification for which disqualification was not ordered because of special reasons or mitigating circumstances;
- ten points: being in charge when unfit or with excess alcohol in the body (*see*

DRUNKEN DRIVING); failing to provide a *specimen of breath;

- five to ten points: failing to stop after a *road traffic accident; failing to report an accident;
- three to nine points: *careless and inconsiderate driving;
- eight points: taking a *conveyance;
- six to eight points: *driving without insurance;
- seven points: *driving while disqualified;
- four points: failing to provide a specimen for a preliminary *breath test;
- three points: *speeding (if a fixed penalty); leaving a car in a dangerous position (*see* OBSTRUCTION);
- two points: *driving without a licence; driving under age.

If an offender accrues twelve penalty points or more in a three year period then he stands to be disqualified under the so-called 'totting-up' system (s 35, Road Traffic Offenders Act 1988). Such an offender must be disqualified for at least six months unless there are grounds for 'mitigating the normal circumstances of the conviction'. Unlike *special reasons, these need not be connected with the offence itself but may be personal to the offender, such as the hardship which disqualification would cause. If the offender has already been disqualified within the three years before the latest endorsable conviction, the minimum disqualification is for one year; if he has been disqualified more than once, the minimum is two years. Mitigating circumstances are still permitted (to prevent disqualification or shorten the period), but only upon proof of exceptional hardship. The effect of a disqualification under the penalty points procedure is to wipe the offender's licence clean. If he is subsequently convicted of a road traffic offence, previously endorsed points are not taken into consideration, but the fact of a penalty points disqualification is relevant to any future points disqualification. Under the Road Traffic (New Drivers) Act 1995, if a *driver is convicted of an endorsable offence and accumulates six or more penalty points within two years of passing a driving test, his licence is revoked and he must retake the test.

In certain circumstances, s 36 of the Road Traffic Offenders Act 1988 requires the court to order that the offender remain disqualified until he passes a driving test or extended driving test. Sections 34A to 34C of the 1988 Act establish awareness courses for offenders convicted of drink-driving offences and provide an incentive to drivers to attend such courses by reducing the period of disqualification for those who do. After an extended experimental period, the scheme now operates permanently in all areas. A person who has been disqualified from driving may apply to have the disqualification removed after two years or half the period of disqualification (whichever is longer) or, when he has been disqualified for ten years or more, after five years (s 42, Road Traffic Offenders Act 1988).

The *Crown Court has power to disqualify, for such period as it thinks fit, where a *motor vehicle was used for the purpose of committing or facilitating the commission of an offence, or where a person is convicted of any offence (ss 147 and 146, Power of Criminal Courts (Sentencing) Act 2000).

Section 301 of the Criminal Justice Act 2003 provides that instead of committing an offender to *custody for non-payment of a *fine, it may disqualify him from driving for a period of up to twelve months. The disqualification ceases to have effect if the fine is paid in full.

See also DRIVING WHILE DISQUALIFIED.

disqualification from keeping animals Section 1 of the Protection of Animals (Amendment) Act 1954 empowers a court to disqualify a person who has been convicted of causing unnecessary suffering to an animal from keeping any animal for a specified period. *See also* ANIMAL CRUELTY.

disqualification of company directors A person who has been convicted of an *indictable (including *either way) offence connected with the formation, management, liquidation, or receivership of a company may be disqualified from being a company *director or from being involved in the setting up of a company (ss 1 and 2, Company Directors Disqualification

Act 1986). The usual maximum period of disqualification is five years (*magistrates' court) and fifteen years (*Crown Court).

disqualification order An order made under the Criminal Justice and Courts Services Act 2000 which gives a sentencing court a power to disqualify an offender from working or applying for work with children. The offender must have been convicted of a *sexual or violent offence committed against a child and been sentenced to twelve months' or more imprisonment. These orders should not be confused with *restraining orders issued under the Sexual Offences Act 2003.

distance selling The sale of *goods or services to a consumer in which the parties do not meet, such as sale by mail order, telephone, digital TV, email, or the Internet. The EU distance selling Directive 976/7, implemented from October 2000 in the UK by the Consumer Protection (Distance Selling) Regulations 2000 (SI 2000/2334), contains the relevant law. In particular, consumers have rights to certain information about the contract to be entered into and, in many cases, the right to cancel the contract within a certain period, often seven working days from the day after receipt of the goods. The right applies whether the goods are defective or not, but it does not apply in certain important categories (such as *auctions, betting, goods specifically made for a consumer, and food that will deteriorate).

distinguishing a case The process of providing reasons for deciding a case under consideration differently from a similar case referred to as a *precedent.

distrain To seize *goods by way of distress.

distressing letters *See* OBSCENE AND THREATENING COMMUNICATION.

distributor denial of service attack (DDoS) *See* DENIAL OF SERVICE ATTACK.

district council A *local authority whose area is a district. A district council has certain exclusive responsibilities (e.g. housing and local planning) and shares others (e.g. recreation, town and country planning) with the council of the county to which the district belongs. Some responsibilities (e.g. education and the personal social services) belong to the district council if the district is metropolitan, but to the county council if it is not. If a district has the style of *borough, its council is called a borough council and its chairman the mayor.

district judge (county court) A judicial officer appointed by the *Lord Chancellor from *solicitors of not less than seven years' standing. The district judge supervises interim (*interlocutory) and post-judgment stages of the case, but can also try cases within a financial limit defined by statute. District judges were formerly known as **district registrars**.

district judge (magistrates' court) A *barrister or *solicitor of not less than seven years' standing, appointed by the *Lord Chancellor to sit in a *magistrates' court on a full-time salaried basis: formerly (before August 2000) called a **stipendiary magistrate**. Metropolitan district judges (magistrates' court) sit in magistrates' courts for Inner London; other magistrates sit in large provincial centres. They have power to perform any act and to exercise alone any jurisdiction that can be performed or exercised by two *justices of the peace, except the grant or transfer of any *licence. In other respects their powers are the same as other justices.

diversion The process of dealing with offenders other than through the formal criminal justice process.

Divisional Court A court consisting of not less than two *judges of one of the Divisions of the *High Court. There are Divisional Courts of each of the Divisions. Their function is to hear *appeals in various matters prescribed by statute; they also exercise the supervisory jurisdiction of the High Court over inferior courts. Most of this jurisdiction is exercised by the *Queen's Bench Division, which also hears applications for *judicial review and appeals by *case stated from *magistrates' courts. The *Chancery Division hears appeals in *bankruptcy matters and the *Family Division hears appeals from magistrates' courts in matters of family law.

Divisions of the High Court *See* CHANCERY DIVISION; FAMILY DIVISION; QUEEN'S BENCH DIVISION.

divorce The legal termination of a marriage and the obligations created by marriage, other than by a decree of nullity or presumption of death.

DNA fingerprinting (genetic fingerprinting) A scientific technique in which an individual's genetic material (DNA) is extracted from cells in a sample of tissue and analyzed to produce a graphic chart that is unique to that person. The technique may be used as *evidence of identity in a criminal or civil case and has been notably successful in both paternity and *rape cases. **DNA samples** (e.g. of hair) may be taken without consent from suspects in detention following arrest for a *recordable offence (s 63, Police and Criminal Evidence Act 1984, as amended by s 10 of the Criminal Justice Act 2003). *See also* NON-CONSENSUAL DNA ANALYSIS.

doctrine of incorporation The doctrine that rules of *international law automatically form part of municipal law. It is opposed to the **doctrine of transformation**, which states that international law only forms a part of municipal law if accepted as such by statute or judicial decisions. It is not altogether clear which view English law takes with respect to rules of customary international law. As far as international *treaties are concerned, the sovereign has the power to make or ratify treaties so as to bind England under international law, but these treaties have no effect in municipal law (with the exception of treaties governing the conduct of war) until enacted by *Parliament. However, *judges will sometimes consider provisions of international treaties (e.g. those relating to *human rights) in applying municipal law. It has been said that directives of the *European Community have the force of law in member states, but practice varies widely (*see* COMMUNITY LEGISLATION).

doctrine of recent possession *See* RECENT POSSESSION, DOCTRINE OF.

document Something that records or transmits information, typically in writing on paper. For the purposes of providing evidence to a court, documents include books, maps, plans, drawings, photographs, graphs, discs, tapes, soundtracks, and films (*see also* COMPUTER DOCUMENTS). Some legal documents are only valid if they meet certain requirements. Documents that are to be used in court proceedings must be disclosed to the other party in a procedure known as *disclosure and inspection of documents. In court, the original of a document must be produced in most cases. In the case of a public document a particular kind of copy must be produced; e.g. a copy of a statute must be a government printer's copy, and a copy of a *byelaw must be certified by the clerk to the *local authority concerned. The authenticity of private documents must be proved by the evidence of a witness. In practice this procedure is often avoided or simplified by each party admitting the authenticity of particular documents prior to the court hearing. *See also* PAROL EVIDENCE; PRODUCTION OF DOCUMENTS.

documentary evidence Evidence in written rather than oral form. The admissibility of a document depends upon (1) proof of the authenticity of the document and (2) the purpose for which it is being offered in evidence. If it is being offered to prove the truth of some matter stated in the document itself it will be necessary to consider the application of the rule against hearsay (*see* HEARSAY EVIDENCE) and its many exceptions.

document of title to goods A *document, such as a *bill of lading, that embodies the *undertaking of the person holding the *goods (the bailee) to hold the goods for whoever is the current holder of the document and to deliver the goods to that person in exchange for the document.

dog *See* CLASSIFICATION OF ANIMALS; GUARD DOG.

dog worrying livestock An offence under the Dogs (Protection of Livestock) Act 1953 committed by the owner or person in charge of a dog which worries livestock on agricultural *land. Worrying includes attacking and chasing cattle, sheep, goats, swine, horses, or poultry. In the case of sheep, protection is enhanced by the Wildlife and Countryside Act to prohibit a dog being at large (that is to say not on a lead or otherwise under close control) in a field or enclosure in which there are sheep. The 1953 Act also permits a farmer whose livestock is being attacked or chased to shoot the dog without any obligation to compensate the owner; neither will the farmer be liable for criminal damage to the dog.

doli capax [Latin: capable of wrong] A child under the age of ten is deemed incapable of committing any crime. Above the age of ten children are *doli capax* and are treated as adults, although they will usually be tried in special *youth courts (with the exception of *homicide and certain other grave offences) and subject to special *punishments. Formerly, there was a rebuttable presumption that a child between the ages of ten and fourteen was also *doli incapax* (incapable of wrong). This presumption has now been abolished. *See* JUVENILE OFFENDER.

domain name An Internet address, which may be protected under *trade mark law.

domestic premises A private residence, used wholly for living accommodation, together with its garden, yard, and attached buildings (such as garages and outhouses).

domestic tribunal A body that exercises *jurisdiction over the internal affairs of a particular profession or association under powers conferred either by statute (e.g. the disciplinary committee of the *Law Society) or by contract between the members (e.g. the disciplinary committee of a trade union). The decisions of these tribunals are subject to judicial control under the doctrine of **ultra vires* and, if they are statutory, when there is an *error of law on the face of the record. *Compare* ADMINISTRATIVE TRIBUNAL.

domestic violence Any criminal offence arising out of physical, sexual, psychological, emotional, or financial abuse by one person against a current or former partner in a close relationship, or against a current or former family member. This includes all forms of violent and controlling behaviour and includes familial elder abuse, sibling abuse, parent abuse, and in-law abuse, regardless of gender or age of either the victim or defendant. *See also* BATTERED SPOUSE OR COHABITANT.

domicile The country that a person treats as his permanent home and to which he has the closest legal attachment. A person cannot be without a domicile and cannot have two domiciles at once. He acquires at birth a **domicile of origin**. Normally, if his father is then alive, he takes his father's domicile; if not, his mother's. He retains his domicile of origin until (if ever) he acquires a **domicile of choice** in its place. A domicile of choice is acquired by making a home in a country with the intention that it should be a permanent base. It may be acquired at any time after a person becomes 16 and can be replaced at will by a new domicile of choice.

Dominions Formerly, the group of UK colonies that, by virtue of the Statute of Westminster 1931, were the first to become fully independent. The Dominions were Australia, Canada, New Zealand, and South Africa. (Also Newfoundland—now part of Canada—and the Irish Free State—now the Republic of Ireland.) Apart from the Republic of Ireland these, together with many other former colonies, are now collectively known as the *Commonwealth.

doorstep conditions A condition of *bail that requires a person on bail with curfew and place of residence conditions to present himself to a *police officer at the door of the prescribed *premises at any time during the curfew period.

double action 1. The firing mechanism in a *revolver in which a continuous pull on the *trigger will revolve the *cylinder to place a *cartridge in the firing position, cock and then release the hammer to fire the weapon. The trigger must be released before the cycle can be repeated. **2.** In some *semi-automatic pistols, a mechanism by means of which continuous pressure on the trigger cocks then releases the hammer to fire the first shot.

double criminality *See* DUAL CRIMINALITY.

double jeopardy The principle that no one should be tried more than once for the same offence. There are four exceptions to the principle. First, the *prosecution has a right to *appeal by way of *'case stated' to the Divisional Court against *acquittal in summary cases on the ground that the decision 'is wrong in law or is in excess of jurisdiction' (ss 28, 111, Magistrates' Courts Act 1980; s 28, Supreme Court Act 1981). Secondly, retrial is permissible if 'the interests of justice so require' following a successful appeal by the defendant against *conviction (s 7, Criminal Appeal Act 1968). Thirdly, 'tainted acquittals' can be challenged where there has been an offence of interference with, or *intimidation of, a *juror or witness (s 54, Criminal Procedure and Investigations Act 1996). Fourthly, a person acquitted of *murder, *manslaughter, and other serious offences (listed in pt 1 of sch 5 to the Criminal Justice Act 2003) may on the order of the *Court of Appeal be retried for the offence if there is new and compelling evidence. *See also* AUTREFOIS ACQUIT.

Drago doctrine The doctrine that states cannot employ force in order to recover *debts incurred by other states. Thus the fact that a state has *defaulted on its debt to *aliens or to another state does not legalize the use of military intervention by these *creditors in order to reclaim monies they are owed.

driver For purposes of the Road Traffic Acts, anyone who uses the ordinary controls of a vehicle (i.e. steering and brakes) to direct its movement. This includes anyone steering a car when the engine is off or when being towed by another vehicle.

driving licence An official authority to drive a *motor vehicle, granted upon passing a two-stage driving test (the theory test and the practical test). A renewable provisional driving *licence, valid for twelve months, may be granted to learner *drivers, but the holder of a provisional licence may not drive a motor car on a public road unless accompanied by a qualified driver and unless he displays 'L' plates on the front and rear of the vehicle. Once a driver has passed the practical test he is subject to a probationary period of two years.

A full licence may also be issued to anyone who has held a full licence issued in Great Britain, Northern Ireland, the Isle of Man, or the Channel Islands within ten years before the date on which the licence is to come into force. Under the Motor Vehicles (Driving Licences) Regulations 1999 (SI 1999/2864), a person resident in the UK who holds a valid EEA or Community licence issued in the *European Economic Area or *European Community may drive cars and motorcycles for as long as his foreign licence remains valid, or until age 70. Those countries are:

Austria
Belgium
Cyprus
Czech Republic
Denmark
Estonia
Finland
France
Germany
Greece
Hungary
Iceland
Ireland
Italy
Latvia
Liechtenstein
Lithuania
Luxembourg
Malta
Netherlands
Norway
Poland
Portugal
Slovakia
Slovenia
Spain
Sweden

Under the Driving Licences (Exchangeable Licences) Orders 1984 (SI 1984/672), those who hold a valid licence from the following countries may drive in the UK and apply to exchange their licence for a domestic one up to five years after taking up residence:

Australia
Barbados
British Virgin Islands
Canada
Republic of Cyprus
Hong Kong
Gibraltar
Japan
Republic of Korea
Malta
Monaco
New Zealand
Singapore
South Africa
Switzerland
Zimbabwe

Holders of licences issued in countries other than those above can drive any category of small vehicle shown on the licence for up to twelve months from the time the person becomes resident in the UK. To allow continuous driving entitlement a provisional GB licence must have been obtained and a driving test(s) passed before the twelve-month period elapses.

A full licence is normally granted until the applicant's 70th birthday. After the age of 70, licences are granted for three-year periods. Where the licence is in the form of a photocard, that card must be surrendered no less often than every ten years. It is reissued, free of charge, bearing a more current photograph.

An applicant for a driving licence must disclose any disability and may be asked to produce his medical records or have a medical examination. An applicant will not normally be granted a licence if he is suffering from certain types of disability, including epilepsy, sudden attacks of disabling giddiness or fainting, or a severe mental illness or defect. In the case of epilepsy, however, he may still be granted a licence if he can show that he has been free of all attacks for at least two years or that he has only had attacks during sleep for more than three years. If an applicant for a licence has diabetes or a heart condition, is fitted with a heart pacemaker, has been treated within the previous three years for drug addiction, or is suffering from any other disability (e.g. loss or weakness of a limb) that would affect his driving, the grant of a licence is usually discretionary. It is an offence contrary to s 174 of the Road Traffic Act 1988 to knowingly make a false statement in order to obtain a driving licence. The offence carries a *fine at level 4 on the standard scale.

Under s 164 of the Road Traffic Act 1988, a *police officer may require a driver to show his driving licence or produce it personally at a specified police station within five days. He may also ask to see the licence of someone whom he believes was either driving a vehicle involved in an accident or had committed a motoring offence. Failure to produce one's licence in these circumstances carries a fine at level 3 on the standard scale. *See also* DRIVING WITHOUT A LICENCE.

Under the Road Traffic (New Drivers) Act 1995, a driver who is convicted of an *endorsable offence and who has accumulated six or more penalty points (*see* DISQUALIFICATION FROM DRIVING) within two years of passing a driving test will have his licence revoked and must retake the test.

driving-test order An order by the court that a person who has been convicted of an offence that is subject to *disqualification should be disqualified from driving until he passes a test showing that he is fit to drive. The order should only be made where there is reason to suspect that the person is not fit to drive; e.g. because he is very old or unwell, and has shown evidence of incompetence in his driving. It is not meant as a *punishment but to protect the public. *See* DISQUALIFICATION FROM DRIVING.

driving while disqualified An offence committed by the *driver of a *motor vehicle on a public *road when he is disqualified from driving (*see* DISQUALIFICATION FROM DRIVING). This is an endorsable offence (carrying six penalty points) and the courts have discretion to impose a further period of disqualification.

driving while unfit *See* DRUNKEN DRIVING.

driving without a licence An offence contrary to s 87 of the Road Traffic Act 1988 committed by the *driver of a *motor vehicle on a public *road without a *driving licence or provisional driving licence valid for the vehicle he is driving. The offences are punishable by a *fine and *endorsement (three to six penalty points).

driving without insurance An offence contrary to s 143 of the Road Traffic Act 1988 committed by a *driver who uses or allows someone else to use a *motor vehicle on a public *road without valid *third-party insurance. The offence is one of *strict liability (except when an *employee is using his *employer's vehicle) and applies even if, for example, the insurance company who issued the insurance suddenly goes into liquidation. The offence is punishable by a *fine, *endorsement (six to eight penalty points), and *disqualification at the discretion of the court.

drown To die by suffocation caused by immersion in water.

drugs *See* CONTROLLED DRUGS.

drug abstinence order An order requiring an offender to abstain from misusing specified Class A drugs and to submit to regular drug testing. Section 58A of the Powers of Criminal Courts (Sentencing Act) 2000 empowers a court to make a drug abstinence order in respect of an offender aged 18 or over, provided that it is satisfied that he is dependent on or has the propensity to misuse specified Class A drugs and either the offence which brought him before the court is a 'trigger offence' (as defined in sch 6 to the Criminal Justice and Court Services Act 2000) or else misuse of the Class A drug caused or contributed to the offence. The order must be for a specified period of between six months and three years and may be made in conjunction with a *community rehabilitation order. The order is only available in respect of an offence committed before 4 April 2005.

drug intervention order An order requiring a person to attend drug counselling. With effect from 1 October 2006, ss 1G and 1H of the Crime and Disorder Act 1998 (inserted by s 142(1) of the Serious Organized Crime and Police Act 2005) provide for a drug intervention order to be attached to *anti-social behaviour orders issued to adults whose anti-social behaviour is drug related. A person who fails, without reasonable excuse, to comply with any requirement included in the order is *guilty of a *summary offence and liable on *conviction to a *fine not exceeding level 4 on the standard scale.

Drug Liaison Officer (DLO) *See* MUTUAL ASSISTANCE.

drug rehabilitation requirement A requirement that may be imposed by the court as part of a *community order or suspended sentence order in respect of an offender aged 16 or over, provided that it is satisfied that he is dependent on or has the propensity to misuse drugs and that he requires or may be susceptible to treatment. The requirement must be imposed for a period of at least six months but cannot be made unless the offender expresses his willingness to comply with its conditions (s 209, Criminal Justice Act 2003, replacing s 52, Powers of Criminal Courts (Sentencing) Act 2000 so far as that section relates to offenders aged 16 and over).

Offenders are required to submit to regular drug testing, to attend an intensive treatment and rehabilitation programme, and to have their progress reviewed regularly by the courts. Offenders may be brought before the court to be re-sentenced if they fail to comply with any part of the requirement.

drug treatment and testing order An order requiring an offender to submit to regular drug testing, to attend an intensive treatment and rehabilitation programme, and to have his progress reviewed regularly by the courts. Section 52 of the Powers of Criminal Courts (Sentencing Act) 2000 empowers a court to make a drug treatment and testing order in respect of an offender aged 16 or over, provided that it is satisfied that he is dependent on or has the propensity to misuse drugs and that he requires or may be susceptible to treatment. The order must be made for a period of between six months and three years. It cannot be made unless the offender expresses his willingness to comply with its requirements. Offenders are supervised by the Probation Service and may be brought before the court to be re-sentenced if they fail to comply with the order. The order is only available in respect of an offence committed by an adult before 4 April 2005 (4 April 2007 in respect of a person aged 16 or 17). Offences committed by those aged 16 or over after those dates fall to be dealt with under the *community order provisions introduced by pt 12 of the Criminal Justice Act 2003.

drunken driving Driving (*see* DRIVER) while affected by *alcohol. Drunken driving covers two separate legal offences. (1) **Driving while unfit**. It is an offence contrary to s 4 of the Road Traffic Act 1988 (as amended) to drive or attempt to drive a *motor vehicle on a *road or *public place when one's ability to drive properly is impaired by alcohol or drugs. Drugs include medicines (such as insulin for diabetics), and the offence appears to be one of *strict liability. It is also an offence to be in charge of a motor vehicle on a road or in a public place while unfit to drive because of drink or drugs, but the defendant will be acquitted if he can show that there was no likelihood of his driving the vehicle in this condition (e.g. if he arranged for someone else to drive him if he became drunk). A *police officer can *arrest without a *warrant anyone whom he reasonably suspects is committing or has been committing either of these offences; he may also (except in Scotland) enter any place where he believes the suspect to be, using force if necessary. (2) **Driving over the prescribed limit**. It is an offence contrary to s 4 of the Road Traffic Act 1988 (as amended) to drive or attempt to drive or to be in charge of a motor vehicle on a road or in a public place if the level of alcohol in one's breath, blood, or urine is above the specified prescribed limit (35 micrograms of alcohol in 100 millilitres (ml) of breath; 80 milligrams (mg) of alcohol in 100 ml of blood; 107 mg of alcohol in 100 ml of urine—roughly equivalent to 2½ pints of beer, or five glasses of wine, or five single whiskies). It is also an offence to be in charge of a motor vehicle on a road or in a public place when the proportion of alcohol is more than the prescribed limit, subject to the same *defence as in being in charge while unfit. Both these offences are offences of strict liability: it is therefore not a defence to show that one did not know that the drink was alcoholic or that it exceeded the prescribed limit. The normal way in which offences involving excess alcohol levels are proved is by taking a *specimen of breath for laboratory analysis, but this is not necessary if the offence can be proved in some other way (e.g. by evidence of how much a person drank before driving). There is no power to arrest a person on suspicion of committing or having committed an offence of this sort before administering a preliminary *breath test.

Most charges involving drinking and driving are brought under the offence of driving over the prescribed limit rather than driving while unfit, but the powers to administer a breath test or to take a specimen of breath for analysis apply to both offences. The penalties for either of these offences are a *fine and/or imprisonment, *endorsement, and obligatory *disqualification (in cases of driving or attempting to drive) or discretionary disqualification (in cases of being in charge) (*see* DISQUALIFICATION FROM DRIVING) Under the **totting-up system**, the discretionary disqualification offences carry ten penalty points and the compulsory disqualification offences carry three to eleven penalty points (which are only imposed if there are special reasons preventing disqualification). *See also* CAUSING DEATH BY CARELESS DRIVING WHILST UNDER THE INFLUENCE; OFFENCE RELATING TO ROAD TRAFFIC.

drunkenness *Intoxication resulting from imbibing an excess of *alcohol. It is an offence contrary to s 12 of the Licensing Act 1872 to be drunk in a *public place.

dual criminality The rule in *extradition procedures that, in order for the request to be complied with, the crime for which extradition is sought must be a crime in both the requesting state and the state to which the fugitive has fled.

dualism *See* MONISM.

due diligence The legal obligation of states to exercise all reasonable efforts to protect *aliens and their property in the host state. Such aliens must have been permitted entry into the host state. If there is a failure or lack of due diligence, the state in default is held responsible and liable to make compensation for injury to the alien or to the alien's estate.

duodenum The first part of the small intestine running from the stomach.

dura mater The thick white outer layer of the *meninges, the membrane that surrounds the brain.

duress Pressure, especially actual or threatened physical force, put on a person to act in a particular way. Acts carried out under duress usually have no legal effect; e.g. a contract obtained by duress is *voidable. In criminal law, when the defendant's power to resist is destroyed by a threat of death or serious personal injury, he will have a defence to a criminal charge, although he has the **mens rea* for the crime and knows that what he is doing is wrong. Duress is not a defence to a charge of *murder as a principal (i.e. to someone who actually carries out the murder himself), although it is still a defence to someone charged with *aiding and abetting murder. The threat need not be immediate; it is sufficient that it is effective; e.g. a threat in court to kill a witness may constitute duress and thus be a defence to a charge of *perjury, even though it cannot be carried out in the courtroom. However, the defence is unavailable to someone who failed to take available alternative action to avoid the threat. *See also* COERCION; NECESSITY; SELF-DEFENCE.

during Her (or His) Majesty's pleasure A phrase colloquially used to describe the period of *detention imposed upon a defendant found *not guilty by reason of *insanity. Such a person was consequently known as a **pleasure patient**. The defendant must still be admitted to a hospital specified by the *Home Secretary (either a local psychiatric hospital or a *special hospital) and remain there until otherwise directed, but the phrase 'during Her Majesty's pleasure' is no longer used in the statute.

Dutch courage *See* INTOXICATION.

duty 1. A legal requirement to carry out or refrain from carrying out any act. *Compare* POWER. **2.** A payment levied by the state, particularly on certain *goods and transactions. Examples are *customs duty, *excise duty, and stamp duty.

duty of care The legal obligation to take reasonable care to avoid causing *damage. There is no *liability in *tort for *negligence unless the act or omission that causes damage is a breach of a *duty of care owed to the *claimant. There is a duty to take care in most situations in which one can reasonably foresee that one's actions may cause physical damage to the person or property of others. The duty is owed to those people likely to be affected by the conduct in question. Thus doctors have a duty of care to their patients and users of the *highway have a duty of care to all other road users. But there is no general duty to prevent other persons causing damage or to rescue persons or property in danger, liability for careless words is more limited than liability for careless acts, and there is no general duty not to cause economic loss or psychiatric illness. In these and some other situations, the existence and scope of the duty of care depends on all the circumstances of the relationship between the parties. Most duties of care are the result of judicial decisions, but some are contained in statutes, such as the Occupiers' Liability Act 1957 (*see* OCCUPIER'S LIABILITY).

duty solicitor A *solicitor who attends by rota at a *magistrates' court in order to assist defendants who are otherwise unrepresented.

duty to prosecute A duty under *international law for states to prosecute people who commit *international crimes.

dying declaration An oral or written statement by a person on the point of death concerning the cause of his death. A dying declaration is admissible at a *trial for the *murder or the *manslaughter of the declarant as an exception to the rule against *hearsay evidence, provided that he would have been a competent witness had he survived (*see* COMPETENCE). However, the rule was abolished by s 118 (2) of the Criminal Justice Act 2003.

dysrhythmia An abnormality in any physiological rhythm, especially of the heart or brain.

Early Administrative Hearing (EAH) The first hearing in the *magistrates' court of a case triable only on *indictment that must be sent. to the *Crown Court for *trial (*see* SENDING OFFENCES FOR TRIAL), or any other case in which a *not guilty *plea is anticipated (e.g. when the defendant has denied the offence in interview). Under s 50 of the Crime and Disorder Act 1998, such a hearing may be conducted by a single justice who, on adjourning the hearing, may remand the accused in *custody or on *bail. Also, it may be conducted by a *clerk to the justices or an assistant clerk, although the defendant then may not be remanded in custody or, without his consent and the consent of the *prosecutor, remanded on bail on conditions other than those, if any, previously imposed. Any requirement under pt I of the Police and Criminal Evidence Act 1984 for a person to be brought before a magistrates' court is satisfied if the person appears or is brought before a clerk to the justices at an EAH. *See also* PLEA BEFORE VENUE.

early complaint *See* RECENT COMPLAINT.

Early First Hearing (EFH) The first hearing of a case in the *magistrates' court in which a *guilty *plea is anticipated (e.g. when the defendant has admitted the offence in interview). In the event of a *not guilty plea being entered, cases will be transferred to an *Early Administrative Hearing court.

easement A right enjoyed by the owner of *land (the dominant tenement) to a benefit from other land (the servient tenement). An easement benefits and binds the land itself and therefore continues despite any change of *ownership of either dominant or servient tenement, although it will be extinguished if the two tenements come into common ownership (*compare* QUASI-EASEMENT). It may be acquired by statute (e.g. local Acts of Parliament), expressly granted (e.g. by *deed giving a *right of way), arise by implication (e.g. an easement of support from an adjoining building), or be acquired by *prescription. (*See also* PROFIT À PRENDRE.) An easement can exist as either a legal or an equitable interest in land. Under s 62 of the Law of Property Act 1925, when land is conveyed, all easements appertaining to it automatically pass with it without the necessity for express words in the *conveyance.

ecchymosis A large *contusion (bruise).

ecolabel A label with the *European Union logo that is used on products that comply with environmental requirements in particular directives.

e-commerce Transactions for *goods or services where the *buyer and *seller are not in the same location and the business is transacted by electronic means such as the Internet.

ecstasy (*slang*: E, XTC, vitamin E, candy, mind candy, nikEs, blue nikEs, yellow bananas, mitsubishis, 007s, double stacks) An hallucinogenic drug MDMA (3,4 methylenedioxymethamphetamine). Taken in tablet form it releases the brain chemical serotonin. The drug is mood elevating, giving users heightened feelings of empathy, emotional warmth, and self-acceptance. It is widely used in dance clubs. It causes *dehydration and can have serious side effects including death, even on first use.

effective remedy A right contained in Article 13 of the *European Convention on Human Rights but not incorporated directly by the *Human Rights Act 1998. The Article stipulates that the state must provide systems that give *effective remedies for violations and arguable claims of violations of the other rights contained in the Convention. This article requires that such systems can both determine such claims and provide for redress for those violations that are substantiated.

Effective Trial Management Programme (ETMP) A programme of managing cases in and out of court, aimed at reducing the number of ineffective *trials by improving case preparation and case progression The ETMP incorporates key *Criminal Justice System agencies such as the *Crown Prosecution Service, police, *magistrates, and *Crown Court, and also members of the judiciary and the *defence.

eggshell skull rule The rule that a *tortfeasor or assailant cannot complain if the injuries he has caused turn out to be more serious than expected because his victim suffered from a pre-existing weakness, such as an unusually thin skull. A tortfeasor or assailant must take his victim as he finds him.

either way offence *See* OFFENCE TRIABLE EITHER WAY.

ejaculation The projection of semen from the penis.

ejector A device on *breech loading small arms that removes the empty *cartridge case after firing. Usually, it is a small protuberance within the *receiver against which the case, having been extracted (*see* EXTRACTOR), strikes and is thrown clear.

***ejusdem generis* rule** *See* INTERPRETATION OF STATUTES.

electricity *See* ABSTRACTING ELECTRICITY.

electrocardiogram A printout from an electronic device which measures the electrical activity in the heart. It is used to detect evidence of heart attacks or abnormal rhythms. The machines are carried in ambulances as well as in hospitals.

electrocution Injury or death caused by electric current passing through the body.

electroencephalogram A printout from an electronic device for measuring and recording electrical activity in the brain.

electromagnetic compatibility The capability of electromagnetic products, such as *computer equipment, machines, etc., to be used together without special modification. The EU electromagnetic compatibility Directive 89/336, which is now part of English law, sets out the minimum requirements to ensure that the use of computers, etc., does not cause interference with other electromagnetic products. *See also* CE.

electronic data interchange (EDI) The use of electronic data-transmission networks to exchange information. Significant commercial contracts set out the terms on which such information is supplied, and much commerce is now done on this basis (known as **paperless trading**), either through a closed network called an **intranet**, to which only members of a limited group have access, or through an open network, i.e. the Internet. Some international legal rules have been agreed in this field, including the Uniform Rules of Conduct for Interchange of Trade Data by Teletransmission.

Electronic Fund Transfer at Point of Sale (EFTPOS) Payment for *goods by *payment card at the *point of sale.

electronic monitoring *See* BAIL.

electronic monitoring requirement A requirement as part of a *youth community order for securing the electronic monitoring of the offender's compliance with any other requirements imposed by the order, under s 36B of the Powers of Criminal Courts (Sentences) Act 2000 (as amended by the Criminal Justice Act 2003). Section 177(3) of the 2003 Act requires a court which imposes a *curfew requirement or *exclusion requirement on an adult offender also to impose an electronic monitoring requirement (as defined by s 215 of the 2003 Act) unless it is either impracticable or inappropriate in the particular circumstances of the case to do so.

electronic purse A *payment card on which credit is stored to pay for *goods and services. The value of any purchase is deducted from the balance stored on the card. The card can usually be reloaded.

electronic signature An item of data incorporated into or associated with an electronically transmitted *document or contract for use in establishing the authenticity of the communication. Under the Electronic Communications Act 2000 electronic signatures are recognized in legal proceedings and as having legal effect. An electronic signature can be purchased from such bodies as the Post Office and Chamber of Commerce on production of relevant identification documents. *See also* DIGITAL SIGNATURE.

electronic surveillance *See* PROPERTY INTERFERENCE; SURVEILLANCE.

electronic tagging The attachment of an electronic device to a person subject to a curfew as a condition of *bail or requirement of a *community order, or an *exclusion order or requirement which allows authorities to monitor his position to ensure compliance with the order. *See* ELECTRONIC MONITORING REQUIREMENT.

eligible witness *See* VULNERABLE AND INTIMIDATED WITNESS.

embargo The detention of *ships in *port: a type of *reprisal. Ships of a *delinquent state may be prevented from leaving the ports of an injured state in order to compel the delinquent state to make *reparation for the wrong done. *See also* ANGARY.

embezzlement The dishonest appropriation by an *employee of any money or *property given to him on behalf of his *employer. Before 1969 there was a special offence of embezzlement; it is now, however, classified as a form of *theft.

embolism A frequent cause of sudden death, it involves blockage of an artery usually by a blood clot that has moved from elsewhere. If the embolism lodges in an artery in the heart, lungs, or brain it is often fatal.

emergency powers Powers conferred by government regulations during a state of emergency. Part 2 of the Civil Contingencies Act 2004 allows Ministers to make such regulations if an emergency event or situation has occurred, is occurring, or is about to occur either inside or outside the UK. An emergency event or situation is one which threatens serious damage to human welfare in the UK, or *war or *terrorism which threatens serious such damage to the country. The regulations made may confer on government departments, the armed forces, and others all powers necessary to secure the supply and distribution of necessities and the maintenance of public peace and safety.

emergency protection order A court order made under ss 44 et seq of the Children Act 1989 that gives a *local authority or the NSPCC the right to remove a child to suitable accommodation for a maximum of eight days (with a right to apply for a seven-day extension) if there is reasonable cause to believe a child is suffering or is likely to suffer significant harm unless the order is made. The order gives the applicant *parental responsibility in so far as it promotes the welfare of the child. In some cases it may be preferable to remove the abuser from the home rather than the child. The Children Act 1989 provides for the inclusion of an *exclusion requirement in an emergency protection order. The effect of this is to exclude the abuser from the family home. The order may only be made when another person in the same household as the child consents to the exclusion order and is able and willing to care properly for the child. *See also* SECTION 47 INQUIRY.

emoluments A person's earnings, including salaries, fees, wages, profits, and benefits in kind (e.g. company cars). They are subject to income tax under sch E to the Income and Corporation Taxes Act 1988.

empanel To swear a *jury to try an issue.

employee A person who works under the direction and control of another (the *employer) in return for a wage or salary. *See also* CHILD EMPLOYEE.

employer A person who engages another (the *employee) to work under his direction and control in return for a wage or salary. Companies are **associated employers** if one of them controls the other or others or if they are themselves controlled by the same company.

employer's liability The *liability of an *employer for breach of his duty to provide for his *employees competent fellow-workers, safe equipment, a safe place of work, and a safe system of work, including adequate supervision. Liability can be in *tort for *damages for *negligence and for *breach of statutory duty under statutes providing for *safety at work; there are also criminal penalties. On the principle of *vicarious liability, third parties may hold an employer responsible for certain wrongs committed by his employee in the course of his employment.

Employment Appeal Tribunal (EAT) A statutory body established to hear *appeals from *employment tribunals. The EAT consists of a *High Court *judge as chairman and two or four lay members who have special knowledge or experience as *employers' or *employees' representatives. They can only hear appeals on questions of law, issues of fact being in the exclusive *jurisdiction of employment tribunals. The EAT may allow or dismiss an appeal or, in certain circumstances, remit the case to the employment tribunal for further hearing. It does not generally order either party to pay the other's costs, except when the appeal is frivolous, *vexatious, or improperly conducted. The parties may be represented at the hearing by anyone they choose, who need not have legal qualifications. The EAT cannot enforce its own decisions; thus, for example, when an employer fails to comply with an order for *compensation that the EAT upholds, separate application must be made to the court to enforce the order. A party may appeal to the *Court of Appeal from a decision of the EAT, but only with the leave of the EAT or the Court of Appeal. The Employment Tribunals Act 1996 (effective from 22 August 1996) sets out the jurisdiction of the EAT.

employment tribunal (ET) Any of the bodies established under the employment protection *legislation, consolidated by the Employment (formerly Industrial) Tribunals Act 1996, to hear and rule on certain disputes between *employers and *employees or trade unions relating to statutory terms and conditions of employment. (Originally called **industrial tribunals**, they (and the 1996 Act) were renamed under the Employment Rights (Dispute Resolution) Act 1998.) The tribunals hear, inter alia, complaints concerning unfair dismissal, redundancy, equal pay, maternity rights, and complaints of unlawful deductions from wages under the Employment Rights Act 1996 (pt II). Tribunals sit in local centres in public and usually consist of a legally qualified chairman and two independent laymen, although chairmen are permitted to sit alone, without lay members, for certain types of case (e.g. deductions from wages claims), cases where the parties agree in writing, and uncontested cases. An ET differs from a civil court in that it cannot enforce its own awards (this must be done by separate application to a court) and it can conduct its proceedings informally. Strict rules of evidence need not apply and the parties can present their own case or be represented by anyone they wish at their own expense. The tribunal has wide powers to declare a dismissal unfair and to award *compensation, which is the usual remedy, but they also have power to order the reinstatement or re-engagement of a dismissed employee.

In cases involving allegations of sexual misconduct, employment tribunals are empowered to make a **restricted reporting order**, which prevents identification of anyone pursuing or affected by the allegations until the tribunal's decision is promulgated. There is also a power to remove identifying information in such cases from the decisions and other public *documents.

Before conducting a full hearing of the case, the tribunal may consider (on either party's application or on its own initiative) what the parties have said in the written complaint to the tribunal (the **originating application**) and the answer to it (the **notice of appearance**) in a **prehearing assessment**. If this assessment suggests that either party is unlikely to succeed, the tribunal may warn that party that he may be ordered to pay the other's costs if he insists on pursuing his case to a full hearing. When a full hearing takes place, the tribunal will not award costs to the successful party unless the other has been warned of this likelihood at a prehearing assessment or has acted *vexatiously, frivolously, or unreasonably in bringing or defending the proceedings. An *appeal on a point of law arising from any decision by an employment tribunal may be heard by the *Employment Appeal Tribunal.

e

EMV EMVCo™ is a company owned by MasterCard™ and Visa™ which maintains the agreed standards on chip payment. The original parties were Europay™, MasterCard™, and Visa™.

enabling statute A statute that confers rights or powers upon any body or person. For example the Police and Criminal Evidence Act 1984 confers on the *Home Secretary power to make *codes of practice to give guidance on how the Act should be implemented.

enacting words The introductory words in an *Act of Parliament that give it the force of law. They follow immediately after the long title and date of *royal assent, unless preceded by a preamble, and normally run: 'Be It Enacted by the Queen's most Excellent Majesty, by and with the advice and consent of the Lords Spiritual and Temporal, and Commons, in this present Parliament assembled, and by the authority of the same, as follows...'. A special formula is used in cases when the Parliament Acts 1911 and 1949 apply (*see* ACT OF PARLIAMENT).

enactment An *Act of Parliament, a Measure of the General Synod, an order, or any other piece of subordinate *legislation, or any particular provision contained in any of these (e.g. a particular section or article). *Delegated legislation is not an enactment for the purposes of the Local Government Act 1992.

endorsement 1. The procedure in which the particulars of a driving offence are noted on a person's *driving licence. When the court orders endorsement for an offence carrying obligatory or discretionary *disqualification but the *driver is not disqualified, the endorsement also contains particulars of the number of penalty points imposed for the purposes of **totting up**. When the court orders disqualification, only the particulars of the offence are noted. The courts can order endorsement upon a conviction for most traffic offences (the main exceptions being parking offences) and in many cases they must order an endorsement, unless there are special reasons (e.g. a sudden emergency) why they should not. A person whose licence is to be endorsed must produce it for the court; if he does not do so, his licence may be suspended. *See also* DISQUALIFICATION FROM DRIVING. **2.** The signature of the holder on a *bill of exchange, which is an essential step in negotiating or transferring a bill payable to order. The endorsement must be completed by delivering the bill to the transferee. An **endorsement in blank** is the bare signature of the holder and makes the bill payable to bearer. A **special endorsement** specifies the person to whom (or to whose order) the bill is payable (e.g. 'Pay X or order'). An endorser, by endorsing a bill, takes on certain obligations to the holder or a subsequent endorser.

endothelium Single celled lining of blood and other vessels. These cells may be present in semen and therefore a possible source of DNA where the semen sample contains no spermatozoa, usually as a result of a vasectomy.

enemy flags, insignia, and uniforms, misuse of The use of an enemy's flags, insignia, and uniforms is contrary to the *international law of *war if used during an attack, but may be permissible during the lead-up to hostilities.

enforcement action Any action, authorized by the *United Nations Security Council, to enforce *collective security under *Chapter VII (i.e. Articles 39 to 51) of the UN Charter. As such it stands as one of the very few legal justifications for *use of force in *international law. Strictly, any enforcement action can only be justified under Article 42 of the Charter, which requires agreement by member states to place their armed forces at the disposal of the UN. However, although the theory of enforcement action would seem to be that of concerted action by members under Article 42, such a limitation is not expressly stated in the Charter. Article 39 was worded so widely as to allow the Security Council, using the implied powers allowed for by that Article, to bypass this problem and authorize that member states voluntarily furnish armed forces to be under the unified command of one member state. Upon the basis of such implied power, an enforcement action was justified under Security Council recommendations under Article 39 in order to defend Korea (1950).

Enforcement Concordat A document issued by the Cabinet Office giving guidance to regulatory authorities on enforcement of consumer protection laws.

engross To prepare a fair copy of a *deed or other legal *document ready for execution by the parties.

enhanced cognitive interview A method of interviewing witnesses that uses cognitive techniques within a planned structure to overcome problems caused by inappropriate sequencing of questions, which hinders memory retrieval. *See also* COGNITIVE INTERVIEW.

enlarge bail To extend the *bail to a later date.

enter (in the law of *burglary) To make an entry as a trespasser. At common law to enter to the slightest degree is sufficient. The entry need be neither effective nor substantial. Entry may not be actual entry by the offender; entry by an innocent agent (e.g. a child under the age of ten), trained animal, or by an instrument (e.g. a fishing rod used to hook property, or the muzzle of a gun) would amount to entry.

entomology The study of insects. It is useful in *forensic pathology for determining the time since death by studying the stage of development of *blowflies in a decomposing body.

entrapment Deliberately trapping a person into committing a crime in order to secure his *conviction, as by offering to buy *drugs. English courts do not recognize a *defence of entrapment as such, since the defendant is still considered to have a free choice in his acts. Under the Police and Criminal Evidence Act 1984, entrapment may be a reason for making certain evidence inadmissible on the ground that the admission of the evidence would have such an adverse effect on the fairness of the proceedings that the court ought not to admit it. The question of the admissibility of evidence obtained through entrapment is in some doubt as a consequence of the cases now being decided under the *Human Rights Act 1998. Entrapment may also be used as a reason for *mitigating a sentence. *See also* AGENT PROVOCATEUR.

entry without warrant Entry by a *police officer onto private *premises without the authority of a *warrant. This is in general unlawful except with the *occupier's consent (which is revocable), but it is permitted by statute for the purpose of arresting for certain offences (*see* INDICTABLE OFFENCE) and in certain circumstances to search premises (*see* POWER OF SEARCH); it is also allowed at *common law to stop an actual or apprehended *breach of the peace.

entry wound An injury caused by a weapon, usually a *bullet, as it enters the body.

environmental criminology That part of criminology that is concerned with the study of crime as it relates to location. Developed as *geographic profiling as a means of crime reduction and detection.

epidermis The outer layer of the skin.

epilepsy A group of disorders caused by abnormal electrical activity in the brain. It is not a mental illness. It manifests itself in varying degrees of severity. The sufferer may have seizures varying from nothing more than having a vacant look to a dramatic seizure in which the sufferer falls to the floor and has uncontrollable fits. Stopping the medication of an epileptic can have very serious consequences. Medical advice should be sought whenever a person suffering from epilepsy is taken into custody.

equality of arms A requirement that there be a fair balance between the opportunities afforded the *parties involved in *litigation (e.g. each party should be able to call witnesses and cross-examine the witnesses called by the other party). In some circumstances this may require the provision of financial support to allow a person of limited means to pay for legal representation. The concept was created by the *European Court of Human Rights in the context of the right to a *fair trial (Article 6).

equal treatment The requirement, enshrined in the *Treaty of Rome, that nationals of one EU state moving to work in another EU state must be treated in the same way as those workers of the state to which they have moved. There must be *free movement of workers throughout the *European Union and no discrimination in relation to pay, social security, and tax benefits.

equitable 1. Recognized by or in accordance with the rules of *equity: applied to distinguish certain concepts used in both *common or *statute law and in equity. **2.** Describing a right or concept recognized by the Court of Chancery. **3.** Just, fair, and reasonable. For example, a *document may have two meanings, one strict and the other (the equitable construction) more benevolent.

equity 1. That part of English law originally administered by the *Lord Chancellor and later by the Court of Chancery, as distinct from that administered by the courts of *common law. The common law did not recognize certain concepts (e.g. *uses and trusts) and its remedies were limited in scope and flexibility, since it relied primarily on the remedy of *damages. In the Middle Ages *litigants were entitled to petition the king, who relied on the advice of his Chancellor, commonly an ecclesiastic, to do justice in each case. By the 15th century, petitions were referred directly to the Chancellor, who dealt with cases on a flexible basis: he was more concerned with the fair result than with rigid principles of law. Moreover, if a defendant refused to comply with the Chancellor's order, he would be imprisoned for contempt of the order until he chose to comply. In the 17th century conflict arose between the common-law judges and the Chancellor as to who should prevail; James I resolved the dispute in favour of the Chancellor. General principles began to emerge, and by the early 19th century the Court of Chancery was more organized and its *jurisdiction, once flexible, had ossified into a body of *precedent with fixed principles which were stated in the form of maxims of equity. Under the Judicature Acts 1873–5, with the establishment of the *High Court of Justice to administer both common law and equity, the Court of Chancery was abolished (though much of its work is still carried out by the *Chancery Division). The Judicature Acts also provided that in cases in which there was a conflict between the rules of law and equity, the rules of equity should prevail. The main areas of equitable jurisdiction now include *trusts, equitable interests over property, relief against *forfeiture and penalties, and equitable remedies. Equity is thus a regulated scheme of legal principles, but new developments are still possible: recent examples of its creativity include the *freezing injunction and the *search order. **2.** A *share in a *limited company.

***erga omnes* obligations** [Latin: towards all] (in *international law) Obligations in whose fulfilment all states have a legal interest because their subject matter is of importance to the international community as a whole. It follows from this that the breach of such an obligation is of concern not only to the victimized state but also to all the other members of the international community. Thus, in the event of a breach of these obligations, every state must be considered justified in invoking (probably through judicial channels) the responsibility of the guilty state committing the internationally wrongful act. It has been suggested that an example of an *erga omnes* obligation is that of a people's right to *self-determination.

error A mistake of law in a *judgment or order of a court or in some procedural step in legal proceedings.

error of law on the face of the record A mistake of law that is made by an inferior court or tribunal in reaching a decision and is apparent from the record of its proceedings. The decision can be quashed by the *High Court in *judicial review proceedings by the remedy of a *quashing order except in the case of a *domestic tribunal with purely contractual powers. *See also* ULTRA VIRES.

escape The *common-law offence of escaping from lawful *custody. The custody may be in prison or a police station, or even in the open air. The escaper need not have been charged with any offence, provided his *detention is lawful (e.g. he may be detained to provide a *specimen of breath). Nor is it necessary for him to commit any act of breaking out. It is an offence contrary to s 39 of the Prison Act 1952 to help the escape of a prisoner and to permit a prisoner who is detained in relation to a criminal matter to escape. *See also* PRISON BREAK.

escort officer A person other than a *constable employed by a *police authority or contractor and designated by the Chief Officer to carry out duties in relation to escorting and guarding people under arrest or in police detention using powers under the Police Reform Act 2002.

espionage *See* SPYING.

espousal of claim The action by which a state undertakes to gain redress of a grievance on behalf of one of its subjects or citizens. *See also* EXHAUSTION OF LOCAL REMEDIES.

estate agent A person who introduces prospective *buyers and *sellers of property to each other. Such a person may be a member of a professional body but must, in any event, under the Estate Agents Act 1979, take out *insurance cover to protect money received as deposits from clients. The Property Misdescription Act 1991 prohibits estate agents from making false or misleading statements about property in the course of their business; making such statements is punishable by a *fine of up to £5000 or possibly by imprisonment. *See also* MISDESCRIPTION.

estreat [from Old French *estrait*: extract] **1.** An extract from a record relating to *recognizances and *fines. **2.** To *forfeit a recognizance, especially one given by the *surety of someone admitted to *bail, or to enforce a fine.

ethnic cleansing *See* ETHNIC MINORITY.

ethnic minority A group numerically inferior to the rest of the population of a state whose members are nationals of that state and possess cultural, religious, or linguistic characteristics distinct from those of the total population and show, if only implicitly, a sense of solidarity, directed towards preserving their own social customs, religion, or language. The attempted extirpation of an ethnic minority by the forces of the majority within a state (known as **ethnic cleansing**) can be regarded as a crime against humanity (*see* WAR CRIMES) justifying humanitarian intervention.

EU law *See* COMMUNITY LAW.

euro *See* EUROPEAN MONETARY UNION.

Eurojust A *European Union body, established in 2002 to improve the investigation and *prosecution of serious cross-border and organized crime and cooperation between the competent authorities of the member states, in particular by facilitating the execution of international *mutual legal assistance and the implementation of *extradition requests. It brings together *prosecutors and *judges from across Europe and is the first permanent network of judicial and prosecuting authorities to be established anywhere in the world.

European Arrest Warrant (EAW) A *warrant that is valid throughout the member states of the *European Union, which authorizes the *arrest of criminal suspects and convicted fugitives who have been sentenced to imprisonment for a term of at least four months; and their transfer for *trial or *detention. Part 3 of the Extradition Act 2003 (which implemented the EU Council Framework

Decision on the European Arrest Warrant of 13 June 2002) provides that *extradition requests to EU Member States are now dealt with under the EAW procedure. In domestic law, the warrant is known as a **Part 3 warrant**. The procedure applies only if the person sought is suspected of an offence that carries a maximum *sentence of at least twelve months or has been sentenced to a term of imprisonment of at least four months. *Dual criminality must apply, unless the offence is one of the 32 designated by sch 2 to the 2003 Act and carries a maximum sentence of three years' imprisonment. A warrant may be issued by a *District Judge (Magistrates' Court) on the application of a *constable or other person designated by the Extradition Act 2003 (Part 3 Designation) Order 2003 (SI 2003/3335) if a domestic warrant has been issued for the person and there are reasonable grounds for believing that the person has committed an extradition offence or is unlawfully at large following *conviction.

European Atomic Energy Community (Euratom) The organization set up under the *Treaty of Rome (1957) by the six members of the *European Coal and Steel Community and effective from 1 January 1958. Euratom was formed to create the technical and industrial conditions necessary to establish the nuclear industries and direct them to peaceful use to obtain a single energy market. *See* EUROPEAN COMMUNITY.

European Central Bank (ECB) A central bank of the *European Union to which member states who have adopted *European Monetary Union are committed by the *Maastricht Treaty. The ECB was set up in 1998 and became active in 1999, as the governor of economic and monetary policy throughout the Union. It works closely with the central banks of the states participating in EMU.

European Coal and Steel Community (ECSC) The first of the European Communities, established by the Paris Treaty (1951) and effective from 1952. The treaty expired in 2002 and the community was subsumed into the economic community. The ECSC created a common market in coal, steel, iron ore, and scrap between the member states, and it coordinated policies of the member states in these fields. The original members were Belgium, France, West Germany, Italy, Luxembourg, and the Netherlands. These six countries, in 1957, signed the *Treaty of Rome setting up the European Economic Community. *See* EUROPEAN COMMUNITY.

European Commission (Commission of the European Communities) An organ of the *European Union formed in 1967, having both executive and legislative functions. It is composed of twenty **Commissioners**, who must be nationals of member states and are appointed by member states by mutual agreement (two Commissioners each from the five largest member states—France, Germany, Italy, Spain, and the UK; one each from the remaining members); their appointment must be approved by the *European Parliament. Each Commissioner assumes responsibility for a particular field of activity and oversees the department (**Directorate General**) devoted to that field. Once appointed, the Commissioners must act in the interests of the EU; they are not to be regarded as representatives of their countries and must not seek or take instructions from any government or other body. Each Commissioner is appointed for a (renewable) four-year period. The Commission's executive functions include administration of Community funds and ensuring that Community law is enforced (*see* EUROPEAN COURT OF JUSTICE). Its legislative functions consist primarily of submitting proposals for *legislation to the *Council of the European Union, in some cases on the orders of the Council and in others on its own initiative (*see also* EUROPEAN PARLIAMENT). It also has legislative powers of its own, partly under the *Treaty of Rome and partly by virtue of delegation by the Council, but only on a limited range of subjects (*see* COMMUNITY LEGISLATION).

European Community (EC) An economic and political association of European states that originated as the **European Economic Community**. It was created by the *Treaty of Rome in 1957 with the broad object of furthering economic development within the Community by the establishment of a **Common Market** and the approximation of the economic policies of member states. Its more detailed aims included eliminating *customs duties internally and adopting a common customs tariff externally, the following by member states of common policies on agriculture and transport, promoting the free movement of labour and capital between member states, and outlawing within the Community all practices leading to the distortion of competition. Two of its institutions, the *European Parliament and the *European Court of Justice, were shared with the *European Coal and Steel Community (established in 1951) and the *European Atomic Energy Community (Euratom; established in 1957); the separate executive and legislative bodies of these three **European Communities** were merged in 1967 (see EUROPEAN COMMISSION; COUNCIL OF THE EUROPEAN UNION).

The *Single European Act 1986, given effect in the UK by the European Communities (Amendment) Act 1986, contains provisions designed to make 'concrete progress' towards European unity, including measures to establish a *Single Market for the free movement of *goods, services, capital, and persons within the Community: the Single Market came into operation on 1 January 1993. In February 1992 the member states signed the Treaty on European Union (*see* MAASTRICHT TREATY). This amended the founding treaties of the Communities by establishing a *European Union based upon the three Communities; renamed the EEC the European Community; and introduced new policy areas with the aim of creating closer economic, political, and monetary union between member states. The Treaty came into force on 1 November 1993; it was amended by the *Amsterdam Treaty.

The original members of the EC were Belgium, France, Germany, Italy, Luxembourg, and the Netherlands. The UK, the Republic of Ireland, and Denmark joined in 1972, Greece in 1981, Spain and Portugal in 1986, and Austria, Sweden, and Finland in 1995 (in 1994 Norway voted by referendum not to join). A further ten countries joined in 2004 and brought total membership to 25. Bulgaria and Romania will be admitted in 2007. The changes in UK law necessary as a result of her joining were made by the European Communities Act 1972.

European Community Treaty *See* TREATY OF ROME.

European Convention on Human Rights (ECHR; Convention for the Protection of Human Rights and Fundamental Freedoms) A convention, originally formulated in 1950, aimed at protecting the *human rights of all people in the member states of the *Council of Europe. Part 1 of the Convention, together with a number of subsequent protocols, define the freedoms that each signatory state must guarantee to all within its *jurisdiction, although states may derogate from the Convention in respect of particular activities (*see* DEROGATION). The Convention established a **Commission on Human Rights** and a **Court of Human Rights** in Strasbourg. The Commission may hear complaints (known as **petitions**) by one state against another. It may also hear complaints by an individual, group, or *non-governmental organization claiming to be a victim of a breach of the Convention, provided that the state against which the complaint has been made declares that it recognizes the authority of the Commission to receive such petitions. The Commission cannot deal with any complaint, however, unless the applicant has first tried all possible remedies in the national courts (in England he must usually first *appeal to the *House of Lords). All complaints must be made not later than six months from the date on which the final decision against the applicant was made in the national courts. The Commission will only investigate a complaint if it is judged to fulfil various conditions that make it admissible. If the Commission thinks there has been a breach of the Convention, it places itself at the disposal of the parties in an attempt to achieve a friendly settlement. If this fails, the Commission sends a report on the case to the Committee of Ministers of the Council of Europe. The case may then be brought before the

Court within three months by either the Commission or one of the states concerned (an individual victim cannot take the matter to the Court himself). No case can be brought before the Court, however, unless the state against which the complaint is made has accepted the Court's jurisdiction. The Court then has power to make a final ruling, which is binding on the parties, and in some cases to award compensation. If the matter is not taken to the Court, a decision is made instead by the Committee of Ministers.

The Convention has established a considerable body of jurisprudence. As of 2 October 2000 the Convention and its terms were transformed into English law as the *Human Rights Act 1998.

European Convention on State Immunity An international convention of 1972 setting out when and how member states of the *European Community (now the *European Union) may *sue or be sued (by other states or by individuals). It is in force only in those EU states that have signed up to the convention. *See also* IMMUNITY.

European Council A body consisting of the heads of government of the member states of the *European Union. It is not a formal organ of the EU (*compare* COUNCIL OF EUROPE), but meets three times a year to consider major developments of policy. It inspired, for example, the *European Monetary System.

European Court of Human Rights *See* EUROPEAN CONVENTION ON HUMAN RIGHTS.

European Court of Justice (ECJ; Court of Justice of the European Communities) An institution of the *European Union that has three primary judicial responsibilities. It interprets the treaties establishing the *European Community; it decides upon the validity and the meaning of *Community legislation; and it determines whether any act or omission by the *European Commission, the *Council of Europe, or any member state constitutes a breach of *Community law.

The Court sits at Luxembourg. It consists of fifteen judges appointed by the member states by mutual agreement and assisted by six *Advocates General. Proceedings before the Court involve written and oral submissions by the parties concerned. Proceedings against the Commission or the Council may be brought by the other of these two bodies, by any member state, or by individual persons; proceedings to challenge the validity of legislative or other action by either Commission or Council are known as proceedings for **annulment**. Proceedings against a member state may be brought by the Commission, the Council, or any other member state. *Appeals from the *Court of First Instance go to the ECJ. The decisions of the Court are binding and there is no appeal against them.

The Court also has power, at the request of a court of any member state, to give a preliminary ruling on any point of Community law on which that court requires clarification.

European Currency Unit (ECU) A currency medium and unit of account of the *European Monetary System, which was replaced by the euro in 1999 (*see* EUROPEAN MONETARY UNION). Its value was calculated from the values of the currencies of individual member states of the *European Union. The ECU was not a unit of currency as such, although some prices were quoted in ECU by the *European Commission and other bodies. The ECU was used in the Exchange Rate Mechanism, and some bonds were issued by member states in ECUs.

European Economic Area (EEA) A free-trade area encompassing the fifteen member states of the *European Union and the member states (excluding Switzerland) of the *European Free Trade Association, i.e. Norway, Iceland, and (from 1 May 1995) Liechtenstein. The EEA Agreement, which contains many provisions similar to the *Treaty of Rome, was signed in 1992 and came into force on 1 January 1994. The EEA has its own institutions, such as the EFTA Court of Justice and the EFTA Surveillance Authority, and many of the EU *Single Market directives and other legislative measures apply within it, although it does not have a budget.

European Economic Community *See* EUROPEAN COMMUNITY.

European Free Trade Association (EFTA) A trade association formed in 1960 between Austria, Denmark, Norway, Portugal, Sweden, Switzerland, and the UK. Finland, Iceland, and Liechtenstein joined later. The UK, Denmark, Portugal, Austria, Finland, and Sweden left on joining the *European Union (or its earlier communities). EFTA is a looser association than the EU, dealing only with trade barriers rather than generally coordinating economic policy. EFTA is governed by a council in which each member has one vote; decisions must normally be unanimous and are binding on all member countries. EFTA has bilateral agreements with the EU. All tariffs between EFTA and EU countries were abolished finally in 1984 and a free-trade area now exists between EU and EFTA member states (*see* EUROPEAN ECONOMIC AREA).

European Monetary System (EMS) A financial system formed in March 1979 to develop closer cooperation in monetary policy among members of the *European Community in advance of the liberalization of capital. It included the Exchange Rate Mechanism to stabilize exchange rates between member states as a precursor to *European Monetary Union. Directive 88/361 removed restrictions on the movement of capital between people resident in the member states. Article 102A of the Single European Act 1986 inserted a new Article (now called Article 98) into the Treaty of Rome to refer to the EMS. The UK has been a party to the EMS since its inception and participated in the ERM from 1990 to 1992.

European Monetary Union (EMU) The establishment of a common currency for member states of the *European Union. The *Maastricht Treaty specified three stages for achieving EMU, starting with participation in the Exchange Rate Mechanism. The second stage created the European Monetary Institute, which coordinated the economic and monetary policy of member states. The third stage, achieved by January 1999, locked member states into a fixed exchange rate, activated the *European Central Bank, and introduced the single currency, the **euro** (divided into 100 cents), for all non-cash transactions (national currencies continued in use for cash transactions). In 2002 euro notes and coins came into circulation in those states within the system (i.e. all member states except the UK, Denmark, and Sweden).

European Parliament An institution of the *European Union, formerly called the **Assembly of the European Communities.** Members of the European Parliament (**MEPs**) are drawn from member states of the EU but group themselves politically rather than nationally. There are 732 seats of which the UK has 77. In the case of the UK, MEPs are elected under the European Assembly Elections Act 1978 for constituencies comprising two or more UK parliamentary constituencies.

The European Parliament's power and influence derive chiefly from its power to amend, and subsequently to adopt or reject, the EU's budget. The Parliament is consulted by the *Council of Europe on legislative proposals put to the Council by the *European Commission; it gives opinions on these after debating reports from specialist committees, but these opinions are not binding. However, its powers in the legislative process were extended under the *Single European Act 1986 and the *Maastricht Treaty by the introduction of the cooperation, codecision, and assent procedures. The Parliament may also put questions to the Council and the Commission and, by a motion of censure requiring a special majority, can force the resignation of the whole Commission (but not of individual Commissioners). Under the Maastricht Treaty it can now veto the appointment of a new Commission.

The European Parliament holds its sessions in Strasbourg, but its Secretariat-General is in Luxembourg and its committees meet in Brussels. The elected Parliament serves a term of five years, after which elections are held.

European Union (EU) The 25 nations (Austria, Belgium, Cyprus, the Czech Republic, Denmark, Estonia, Finland, France, Germany, Greece, Hungary, Ireland, Italy, Latvia, Lithuania, Luxembourg, Malta, the Netherlands, Poland, Portugal, Slovakia,

Slovenia, Spain, Sweden, and the UK) that have joined together to form an economic community with common monetary, political, and social aspirations. Bulgaria and Romania will join in 2007. The EU came into being on 1 November 1993 according to the terms of the *Maastricht Treaty. It comprises the three European Communities (see EUROPEAN COMMUNITY), extended by the adoption of a common foreign and security policy (CFSP), which requires cooperation between member states in foreign policy and security, and cooperation in justice and home affairs.

Europol The *European Union law enforcement organization based in The Hague, Netherlands. It was established by the *Maastricht Treaty on European Union of 7 February 1992 for the purpose of improving the effectiveness and cooperation between the competent authorities of the member states in preventing and combating serious international organized crime and terrorism, with an emphasis on targeting criminal organizations. The Europol Convention was ratified by all member states and came into force on 1 October 1998.

Europol started limited operations in January 1994 in the form of the **Europol Drugs Unit (EDU)**. Progressively, other important areas of criminality were added and, in January 2002, its mandate extended to deal with all serious forms of international crime as listed in the annex to the Europol Convention. The primary function of Europol is to: facilitate the exchange of information between *Europol liaison officers, in accordance with national law (*see* MUTUAL ASSISTANCE; MUTUAL LEGAL ASSISTANCE); provide operational analysis in support of operations; generate strategic reports (e.g. threat assessments) and crime analysis on the basis of information and intelligence supplied by member states and third parties; and provide expertise and technical support for investigations and operations carried out within the EU, under the supervision of the member states concerned.

Europol Drugs Unit (EDU) *See* EUROPOL.

Europol Liaison Officers (ELO) Personnel seconded to *Europol by European member states as representatives of their national law enforcement agencies.

euthanasia Originally meaning quiet and easy death, the term is now generally applied to deliberately killing a person suffering from an incurable and extremely painful illness at the request of that person. This is permitted in some countries, but in England is still *murder.

evading a liability An offence under s 2 of the Theft Act 1978 penalizing those who dishonestly avoid or reduce a monetary liability which they have incurred.

eviction The removal of a *tenant or any other *occupier from occupation. Under the Protection from Eviction Act 1977 the eviction of a *residential occupier, other than by proceedings in the court, is a criminal offence. It is also an offence to harass a residential occupier to try to persuade him to leave (*see* HARASSMENT OF OCCUPIER). Many tenants have statutory protection and the *landlord must prove to a court that he has appropriate grounds for *possession. Under the Housing Act 1988 a tenant may claim damages for unlawful eviction. *See also* TRESPASS.

The Protection from Harassment Act 1997 allows the court to impose a *restraining order against a tenant who is harassing a neighbour, which might require the harasser to be evicted (*see* HARASSMENT; NUISANCE NEIGHBOURS).

evidence That which tends to prove the existence or non-existence of some fact. It may consist of *testimony, *documentary evidence, *real evidence, and, when admissible, *hearsay evidence. The law of evidence comprises all the rules governing the presentation of facts and proof in proceedings before a court, including in particular the rules governing the *admissibility of evidence and the *exclusionary rules. *See also* CIRCUMSTANTIAL EVIDENCE; CONCLUSIVE EVIDENCE; DIRECT EVIDENCE; EXTRINSIC EVIDENCE; PRIMARY EVIDENCE; SECONDARY EVIDENCE; VIDEO-RECORDED EVIDENCE.

evidence in rebuttal Evidence offered to counteract (**rebut**) other evidence in a case. There are some restrictions on the *admissibility of evidence in rebuttal, e.g. if it relates to a collateral question, such as the *credit of a witness.

evidence obtained illegally Evidence obtained by some means contrary to law. At *common law, if evidence was obtained illegally (e.g. as a result of a search of *premises without a search *warrant), it was not inadmissible but the court might exclude it as a matter of *discretion. Section 78 of the Police and Criminal Evidence Act 1984 provides that the court may refuse to allow evidence on which the *prosecution proposes to rely if the admission of the evidence would have such an adverse effect on the fairness of the proceedings that the court ought not to admit it. The *Human Rights Act 1998 and the cases now being decided under its provisions have left the previous law in some doubt. *See also* CONFESSION.

evidence of character *See* CHARACTER.

evidence of disposition *See* DISPOSITION.

evidence of identity That which tends to prove the identity of a person. A person's identity may be proved by *direct evidence (even though it may involve an expression of *opinion) or by *circumstantial evidence. *Secondary evidence of an out-of-court identification by a witness (e.g. that he picked the accused out of an identification parade) may also be given to confirm the witness's testimony. In criminal cases, if the evidence of identity is wholly or mainly based on visual identification the jury must be specially warned of the danger of accepting the evidence; any *corroboration must be pointed out to them by the judge. In criminal cases this issue must be dealt with under the detailed provisions of PACE Code D. Failure to follow this procedure and its accompanying safeguards may render the evidence of identity inadmissible. *See also* DNA FINGERPRINTING.

evidence of opinion *See* OPINION EVIDENCE.

evidential breath testing device A device approved by the Secretary of State under s 7(1)(a) of the Road Traffic Act 1988 that measures the *alcohol content of air from a *driver's lungs (alveolar air). *See also* CAMIC BREATH ANALYZER; CAMIC DATAMASTER; SPECIMEN OF BREATH.

evidential presumption *See* CONSENT.

examination The questioning of a witness on *oath or *affirmation. In court, a witness is subject to *examination-in-chief, *cross-examination, and *re-examination. In some circumstances a witness may be examined prior to the court hearing (*see* COMMISSION).

examination-in-chief (direct examination) The questioning of a witness by the party who called him to give evidence. *Leading questions may not be asked, except on matters that are introductory to the witness's evidence or are not in dispute or (with permission of the judge) when the witness is *hostile. The purpose of examination-in-chief is to elicit facts favourable to the case of the party conducting the examination. It is followed by a *cross-examination by the opposing party.

examining justices *Justices of the peace sitting upon a preliminary inquiry into whether or not there is sufficient evidence to send an accused person from the *magistrates' court to the *Crown Court for *trial on indictment.

Exchequer The department within Government that receives and controls the national revenue.

excise duty A charge or toll payable on certain *goods produced and consumed within the UK. Payments for *licences, e.g. for the sale of spirits, are also classed as excise duty. *Compare* CUSTOMS DUTY.

excluded material Material listed in s 12 of the Police and Criminal Evidence Act 1984 which consists of: personal records; human tissue or fluid taken for the purpose of diagnosis or medical treatment; and journalistic material held in confidence. Access to this material by the police can only be obtained if before the Act was passed a *warrant could have been issued authorizing the search for such material. These circumstances are so rare that effectively access to the material is impossible without consent of the person possessing the material.

exclusion and restriction of contractual liability *See* EXEMPTION CLAUSE.

exclusion and restriction of negligence liability The Unfair Contract Terms Act 1977 provides that a person cannot exclude or restrict his business *liability for death or injury resulting from *negligence. Nor can he exclude or restrict his liability for other loss or damage arising from negligence, unless any contract term or notice by which he seeks to do so satisfies the requirement of reasonableness (as defined in detail in the Act). For the purposes of this provision, negligence means the breach of any contractual or *common-law duty to take reasonable care or exercise reasonable skill or of the common duty of care imposed by the Occupiers' Liability Acts 1957 and 1984. There are similar provisions in relation to consumer contracts in the Unfair Terms in Consumer Contracts Regulations 1999 (SI 1999/2083).

exclusionary rules Rules in the law of evidence prohibiting the proof of certain facts or the proof of facts in particular ways. Although all irrelevant evidence must be excluded, the rules are usually restricted to relevant evidence, e.g. the rule against *hearsay evidence. Exclusionary rules may be justified in various ways; e.g. by the desirability of excluding material that is of little evidentiary weight or that may be unfairly prejudicial to an accused person.

exclusion order 1. An order prohibiting an offender from entering a place specified in the order for a specified period of up to two years in the case of an offender aged 16 or over or three months if the offender has not yet attained that age, made under s 40A of the Powers of the Criminal Courts (Sentencing) Act 2000 (as amended by the Criminal Justice Act 2003). The order is available in respect of both youth and adult offenders for offences committed prior to 4 April 2005 and for offences committed by persons aged 16 or 17 on conviction until 4 April 2007. Thereafter, it will be available only as a *youth community order. The order may specify different places for different periods or days and may include an *electronic monitoring requirement to ensure compliance with the exclusion order. Breach of an exclusion order is dealt with under the procedure set out in sch 3 to the 2000 Act. *See also* EXCLUSION REQUIREMENT. **2.** An order prohibiting an offender convicted of an offence of violence from entering *licensed premises without the express consent of the *licensee for a specified period of between three months and two years, made under s 1 of the Licensed Premises (Exclusion of Certain Persons) Act 1980. **3.** An order of the Secretary of State under the Prevention of Terrorism (Temporary Provisions) Act 1989 (now repealed) excluding a named person from Great Britain, Northern Ireland, or the UK in order to prevent terrorist acts aimed at influencing policy or opinion concerning Northern Ireland. *See also* TERRORISM.

exclusion requirement 1. A requirement in an *emergency protection order or an interim *care order that a person who is suspected of having abused a child is excluded from the child's home. A *power of arrest may be attached to the order. **2.** A requirement that may be imposed by a court dealing with an offender aged 16 or over as part of a *community order, *custody plus order, *suspended sentence order, or an intermittent custody order which prohibits the offender from entering a specified place for a specified period (s 205, Criminal Justice Act 2003). The order may specify different places for different periods or days. *See also* EXCLUSION ORDER.

excusable homicide The killing of a human being that results in no criminal *liability, either because it took place in lawful *self-defence or by misadventure (an accident not involving *gross negligence).

execution 1. The process of carrying out a *sentence of death imposed by a court. *See also* CAPITAL PUNISHMENT. **2.** The completion of the formalities necessary for a written *document to become legally valid. In the case of a *deed, for example, this comprises the signing and delivery of the document.

executive agency An independent agency, operating under a chief executive, that is responsible for delivering a service according to the policy of a central government department. Examples are the Benefits Agency and the Passport Agency. The intention is that central government should become purely policy-making, the services it is responsible for being delivered by executive agencies.

exemplary damages (punitive damages, vindictive damages) *Damages given to punish the defendant rather than (or as well as) to compensate the claimant for harm done. Such damages are exceptional in *tort, since the general rule is that damages are given only to compensate for loss caused. They can be awarded in some tort actions: (1) when expressly authorized by statute; (2) to punish oppressive, arbitrary, or unconstitutional acts by government servants; (3) when the defendant has deliberately calculated that the profits to be made out of committing a tort (e.g. by publishing a defamatory book) may exceed the damages at risk. In such cases, exemplary damages are given to prove that 'tort does not pay'. Exemplary damages cannot be given for *breach of contract.

exemption clause A term in a contract purporting to exclude or restrict the *liability of one of the *parties in specified circumstances. The courts do not regard exemption clauses with favour. If such a clause is ambiguous, they will interpret it narrowly rather than widely. If an exclusion or restriction is not recited in a formal contract but is specified or referred to in an informal *document, such as a ticket or a notice displayed in a hotel, it will not even be treated as a term of the contract (unless reasonable steps were taken to bring it to the notice of the person affected at the time of contracting). The Unfair Contract Terms Act 1977 and Unfair Terms in Consumer Contracts Regulations 1999 (SI 1999/2083) contain complex provisions limiting the extent to which a person can exclude or restrict his business liability towards consumers. In addition, the 1977 Act subjects certain types of exemption clause to a test of reasonableness, even in a business-to-business transaction. The Office of Fair Trading runs an unfair terms unit to monitor such clauses and enforce the 1999 Regulations. Other statutes forbidding the exclusion or restriction of particular forms of liability are the Defective Premises Act 1972, the Consumer Protection Act 1987, and the Road Traffic Act 1988. *See also* EXCLUSION AND RESTRICTION OF NEGLIGENCE LIABILITY; INTERNATIONAL SUPPLY CONTRACT.

exempt supply A supply that is outside the scope of *value-added tax. Examples include sales of *land, the supply of certain financial and *insurance services, and the services performed in the course of employment. *See also* ZERO-RATED SUPPLY.

exequatur A certificate issued by a host state that admits and accords recognition to the official status of a *consul, authorizing him to carry out consular functions in that country. The sending state grants the consular official a commission or patent, which authorizes the consul to represent his state's interests within the host state.

ex gratia [Latin: done as a matter of favour] An *ex gratia* payment is one not required to be made by a legal duty.

exhaustion of local remedies The rule of customary *international law that when an *alien has been wronged, all municipal remedies available to the injured party in the host country must have been pursued before the alien appeals to his own government to intervene on his behalf. This is a customary precondition to any *espousal of claim by a state on behalf of a national based upon foreign soil.

exhaustion of rights A free-trade principle which holds that, once *goods are put on the market, owners of *intellectual property rights in those goods, who made the goods or allowed others to do so under their rights, may not use national intellectual property rights to prevent an import or export of the goods. Within the

*European Union these rules derive from Articles 28 to 30 (formerly 30 to 36) of the *Treaty of Rome. *See also* FREE MOVEMENT.

exhibit 1. A physical object or *document produced in a court, shown to a witness who is giving evidence, or referred to in an *affidavit. Exhibits are marked with an identifying number, and in *jury *trials the jury is normally permitted to take exhibits with them when they retire to consider their verdict. Physical objects produced for the inspection of the court (e.g. a *murder weapon) are referred to as *real evidence. **2.** To refer to an object or document in an *affidavit.

exhumation Removing a body from a proper or clandestine *grave. The recovery of a body from a proper grave or tomb can only be carried out on the authority of the *Home Secretary.

exit wound An injury caused by a weapon, usually a *bullet, as it leaves the body.

ex officio [Latin: by virtue of holding an office] Thus, the *Lord Chief Justice is *ex officio* a member of the *Court of Appeal.

***ex officio* magistrate** A *magistrate by virtue of holding some other office, usually that of mayor of a city or borough. Most *ex officio* magistrateships were abolished by the Justices of the Peace Act 1968 and the Administration of Justice Act 1973, but *High Court judges are *justices of the peace *ex officio* for the whole of England and Wales and the Lord Mayor and aldermen are justices *ex officio* for the City of London.

ex parte [Latin: from (by, for, or on behalf of) one party] **1.** A legal proceeding brought by one person in the absence of and without notification to other parties (*see e.g.* PUBLIC INTEREST IMMUNITY). Since the introduction of the *Civil Procedure Rules in 1999, this phrase is no longer used in civil proceedings, having been replaced by **without notice**. *See* WITHOUT NOTICE APPLICATION. **2.** When used preceding a name in the *citation of a case, the term indicates that the party whose name follows is the party on whose application the case is heard.

expert evidence Evidence from witnesses who are experts in a particular field. It is a rule of the *common law that on a subject requiring special knowledge and competence and likely to fall outside the experience of the *judge and *jury (or *magistrates in *summary trials), evidence is admissible from witnesses who have the necessary expertise in the subject. Qualification to give expert evidence is a matter of competence and may be acquired by study or practice, or a combination of both; although, ultimately, the question of whether a witness is competent to give such evidence is a matter for the court. The topics upon which expert evidence has been received are legion: ranging from a drugs squad *police officer giving evidence in relation to the street value of drugs, to medical practitioners giving their opinion as to the extent and likely cause of injuries. The categories of expert opinion that may be admitted by the court are not closed: '[i]t would be entirely wrong to deny to the law of evidence the advantages to be gained from new techniques and . . . advances in science' (*per* Steyn LJ, in *R v Clarke (RL)* [1995] 2 Cr App R 425).

At common law, a witness could not give his opinion on an 'ultimate issue' (i.e. the question that the court had to decide) but this rule, which was not very strictly applied in practice, was abolished in respect of civil cases by the Civil Evidence Act 1972. Although the rule has not been abolished formally for the purpose of criminal proceedings, it is clear that an expert can give such evidence, although the judge should make it clear to the jury that they are not bound by the expert's opinion and that the issue is for them to decide (*R v Stockwell* (1993) 97 Cr App R 260).

In both civil and criminal proceedings, it is the duty of an expert to assist the court on the matters within his expertise. This duty overrides any obligation to the person from whom he has received instructions or by whom he is paid (pt 33, *Criminal Procedure Rules; pt 35, *Civil Procedure Rules; *National Justice Cia Naviera SA v Prudential Assurance Co Ltd, The Ikarian Reefer* [1993] 2 Lloyd's Rep 68; *R v Bowman* [2006] EWCA Crim 417). He must provide the court with objective, impartial opinion on matters within his expertise, and must not mislead by omission nor assume the role of an *advocate. He must consider all material facts, including those which might detract from his opinion, and should make it clear when a question or issue falls outside his expertise and when he is not able to reach a definite opinion, e.g. because he has insufficient information (*R v Harris* [2006] 1 Cr App R 5; *AB (A Minor) (Medical Issues: Expert Evidence)* [1995] 1 FLR 181). If, after producing a report, an expert changes his view on any material matter, such change of view must be communicated to all the *parties without delay.

The following matters are necessary inclusions in an expert report (pt 33, Criminal Procedure Rules; *R v Bowman* [2006] EWCA Crim 417):

- details of the expert's relevant academic and professional qualifications, experience, and any limitations upon that expertise;
- a statement setting out the substance of all the instructions received (whether written or oral), questions upon which an opinion is sought, the materials provided and considered, and the *documents, statements, evidence, information, or assumptions which are material to the opinions expressed or upon which those opinions are based;
- information relating to who has carried out measurements, examinations, tests, etc., and the methodology used, and whether or not such measurements, etc., were carried out under the expert's supervision;
- where there is a range of opinion in the matters dealt with, a summary of the range of opinion, the reasons for the opinion given, any material facts or matters which detract from that opinion, and any points which can fairly be made against it;
- a summary of the conclusions reached;
- relevant extracts of literature;
- a statement to the effect that the expert has complied with his duty to the court to provide independent assistance by way of objective unbiased opinion, in relation to matters within his expertise and an acknowledgment that the expert will inform all parties and where appropriate the court in the event that his opinion changes on any material issues; and
- the same declaration of truth that is contained in a witness statement.

In complex matters it is useful if the report contains a glossary of technical terms.

Expert evidence may not be adduced in a criminal trial, by either the *prosecution or the *defence, unless the party that intends to rely on it has served a copy of the 'statement in writing of any finding or opinion which he proposes to adduce' (i.e. a copy of the expert witness's report); and, on request, a 'copy of the record of any observation, test, calculation or other procedure' on which the report is based (r 24(1), Criminal Procedure Rules). However, the rule does not apply if, either: the evidence is to be the subject of an application for leave to adduce it under s 41 of the Youth Justice and Criminal Evidence Act 1999 (*see* SEXUAL HISTORY); or the party proposing to rely on it has reasonable grounds for believing that its disclosure might lead to the intimidation, or attempted intimidation, of any person on whose evidence he intends to rely in the proceedings, or otherwise to the course of justice being interfered with.

Under r 33.7 of the Criminal Procedure Rules, where more than one accused wants to introduce expert evidence on an issue at trial, the court may direct that such evidence is to be given by a single joint expert.

See also DISCLOSURE OF UNUSED MATERIAL.

expert opinion *See* OPINION EVIDENCE.

explosion The violent release of a large amount of energy as a gas generating heat and noise.

explosive Any substance made in order to achieve an *explosion that causes damage or destruction or intended to be used in that way by a person who possesses it. If someone committing *burglary has an explosive with him, he is *guilty of aggravated burglary, punishable with a maximum of *life imprisonment. The Explosive Substances Act 1883 creates special offences of (1) causing an explosion that is likely to endanger life or cause serious damage to property (even if no harm or damage is actually done); (2) attempting to cause such an explosion; and (3) making or possessing an explosive with the intention of using it to endanger life or to seriously damage property. Under the Offences Against the Person Act 1861, it is an offence to injure anyone by means of an explosion, to send or deliver an explosive to anyone, or to place an explosive near a building, ship, or boat with the intention of causing physical injury. These crimes cover most acts of *terrorism.

ex post facto [Latin: by a subsequent act] Describing any legal act, such as a statute, that has retrospective effect.

exposure It is an offence under the Sexual Offences Act 2003 for a person of either sex intentionally to expose his genitals with the intention that someone will see them and be alarmed or distressed. The offence replaces offences under the Vagrancy Act 1824 and the Town Police Clauses Act 1847 which applied only to exposure by men.

expressio unius est exclusio alterius *See* INTERPRETATION OF STATUTES.

express term A provision of a contract, agreed to by the *parties, that is either written or spoken. Such a provision may be classified as a *condition, a *warranty, or an innominate term.

expropriation The taking by the state of private *property for public purposes, normally without *compensation. The right to expropriate is known in some legal systems as the right of **eminent domain**. In the UK, expropriation requires statutory authority except in time of *war or apprehended war (*see* ROYAL PREROGATIVE).

***ex proprio motu* (*ex mero motu*)** [Latin: of his own motion] Describing acts that a court may perform on its own initiative and without any application by the *parties.

expulsion The termination by a state of an *alien's legal entry and right to remain. This is often based upon the ground that the alien is considered undesirable or a threat to the state. *Compare* DEPORTATION.

extended sentence A *sentence longer than the maximum prescribed for a particular offence, which was formerly imposed on persistent offenders under certain circumstances. The power to impose extended sentences was abolished by the Criminal Justice Act 1991. *See* DANGEROUS OFFENDERS; MANDATORY MINIMUM SENTENCES.

extortion A *common-law offence committed by a public officer who uses his position to take money or any other benefit that is not due to him. If he obtains the benefit by means of menaces, this may also amount to *blackmail.

extortionate credit bargains A bargain that requires the *debtor or a relative to make payments that are grossly exorbitant or otherwise grossly contravene ordinary principles of fair dealing under ss 137 to 140 of the Consumer Credit Act 1974. The debtor can take proceedings in the *county court to have the bargain renegotiated.

extractor In *small arms, a device for withdrawing a *cartridge case from the *chamber. In *automatic and *semiautomatic weapons, the extractor may take the form of a 'claw' attached to the *breech block, which engages the case's extractor groove when the *breech is closed; or may be a movable portion of the *barrel's rear face.

extradition The formal surrender by one country to another, of an individual accused or convicted of a serious criminal offence committed outside the territory of the extraditing state and within the *jurisdiction of the requesting state. This is distinct from *deportation where the country in which the person is present initiates the removal process. The Extradition Act 2003 deals with extradition to and from the UK to the territories designated for such purposes and implements the Framework Decision of 13 June 2002 on the *European Arrest Warrant (EAW) and the surrender procedures between member states of the *European Union. The Act creates two extradition zones. *Category 1 territories are those member states that have implemented the EAW within domestic *legislation and have been so designated by order made by the Secretary of State. *Category 2 territories are *Commonwealth and other states with which the UK has extradition arrangements. Prior to the 2003 Act, there could be no extradition for crimes incidental to and forming part of political disturbances (the 'political offence exception'). However, that rule has been abolished under the new scheme. However, the principles of *speciality and *dual criminality continue to apply, albeit with exceptions. The Framework Decision contains a list of 32 categories of offence to which the dual criminality test does not apply.

Under pt 1 of the Act, a streamlined procedure is available for the extradition of persons to category 1 territories. On receipt of a warrant (a 'Part 1 warrant') issued by the judicial authority in the requesting territory, a *District Judge (Magistrates' Court) is required to determine only that the offence is an 'extradition offence' for the purpose of the Act; that none of the bars to extradition apply (speciality, the rule against *double jeopardy; extraneous considerations; passage of time or hostage-taking considerations); and whether the person's extradition would be compatible with his rights under the *European Convention on Human Rights.

Part 2 of the Act retains the principle that responsibility for extradition is shared between the judiciary, which determines whether the criteria for return set out in the law are satisfied, and the Secretary of State, who ultimately determines whether the person is to be surrendered. A *District Judge (Magistrates' Court) must satisfy himself that the request meets the requirements of the 2003 Act, including *dual criminality and, where appropriate, *prima facie evidence of guilt (the judge may rely upon 'information', rather than 'evidence' from designated countries: *see* CATEGORY 2 TERRITORIES); that none of the bars to extradition apply (the rule against double jeopardy; extraneous considerations; passage of time or hostage-taking considerations); and that the person's extradition would be compatible with his Convention rights. The Secretary of State must then consider, *inter alia*, whether extradition is prohibited because: the person could face the death penalty (unless an adequate written assurance is received from the requesting state that the death penalty will not be imposed, or will not be carried out, if imposed); or (except in certain limited circumstances) there are no speciality arrangements with the requesting country.

Under pt 3 of the 2003 Act, extradition requests to EU member states are now dealt with under the EAW procedure. Other outgoing extradition requests are made under the *royal prerogative. They can be made to any country but almost all are made to the UK's existing extradition partners in accordance with the relevant multilateral or bilateral arrangements. As a matter of policy, the UK will extradite its own nationals, including those suspected of fiscal offences, providing other bars to extradition do not apply.

See also FUGITIVE OFFENDER.

extradition treaty A bilateral or multilateral *treaty under the terms of which a state agrees to deport a *fugitive offender to the state where the offence was committed or to the fugitive's state of *nationality (*see* EXTRADITION).

extradural haemorrhage Bleeding in the space between the skull and the covering of the brain. It is usually caused by fracture of the skull.

extrajudicial divorce A *divorce granted outside a court of law by a non-judicial process (such as a *ghet or a *talaq). An extrajudicial divorce will not be recognized in the UK if it takes place in the UK, Channel Islands, or Isle of Man. *See also* OVERSEAS DIVORCE.

extraordinary resolution A decision reached by a majority of not less than 75 per cent of *company members voting in person or by proxy at a *general meeting. It is appropriate in situations specified by the Companies Act 1985, e.g. *voluntary winding-up. At least 14 days' notice must be given of the intention to propose an extraordinary resolution; if the resolution is to be proposed at the annual general meeting, 21 days' notice is required.

extraterritoriality A theory in *international law explaining *diplomatic immunity on the basis that the *premises of a foreign mission form a part of the territory of the sending state. This theory is not accepted in English law (thus a *divorce granted in a foreign embassy in England is not obtained outside the British Isles for purposes of the Recognition of Divorces Act 1971). Diplomatic immunity is based either on the theory that the diplomatic mission personifies—and is entitled to the immunities of—the sending state or on the practical necessity of such immunity for the functioning of diplomacy.

extrinsic evidence Evidence of matters not referred to in a *document offered in evidence to explain, vary, or contradict its meaning. Its admissibility is governed by the *parol evidence rule.

ex turpi causa non oritur actio [Latin: no action can be based on a disreputable cause] The principle that the courts may refuse to enforce a claim arising out of the claimant's own illegal or immoral conduct or transactions. Hence parties who have knowingly entered into an *illegal contract may not be able to enforce it and a person injured by a fellow-criminal while they are jointly committing a serious crime may not be able to *sue for *damages for the injury.

facial reconstruction A technique in which modelling material is affixed to a skull to recreate its appearance in life. The technique is used to assist in the identification of skeletal remains.

fact An event or state of affairs known to have happened or existed. It may be distinguished from law (as in *trier of fact) or, in the law of evidence, from opinion (*see* OPINION EVIDENCE). The **facts in issue** are the main facts that a *party carrying the persuasive *burden of proof must establish in order to succeed; in a wider sense they may include subordinate or collateral facts, such as those affecting the *credit of a witness or the *admissibility of evidence. *See also* FACTUM.

factor An agent entrusted with the *possession of *goods (or *documents of title representing goods) for the purposes of sale. A factor is likely to fall within the definition of a *mercantile agent in the Factors Act 1889 and to have the powers of a mercantile agent. A factor has a *lien over the goods entrusted to him that covers any claims against the *principal arising out of the agency.

factoring A service to companies whereby a third party firm immediately pays the company a high percentage (usually about 80 per cent) of *debts owing to it immediately and then claims the full amount from the *debtor. This improves the cash-flow for the company. Factoring companies also offer services such as debt-collection, sales accounting, and protection against bad debts.

factors A group of chemicals in the blood that control coagulation.

factum [Latin: fact] **1.** A *fact or statement of facts. For example, a *factum probans* (pl. *facta probantia*) is a fact offered in evidence as proof of another fact, and a *factum probandum* (pl. *facta probanda*) is a fact that needs to be proved. **2.** An act or deed. *See also* NON EST FACTUM.

failure to account for objects, substances, or marks Failure by a detained person to account for any object, substance, or mark, found on him at the time of his *arrest, which a *constable reasonably believes may be attributable to his participation in the offence, and for which the constable has asked him to account. If the detained person fails or refuses to account for them, any court in subsequent proceedings may draw such inferences as appear proper (s 36, Criminal Justice and Public Order Act 1994).

failure to account for presence at the scene of an offence Failure by a detained person to account for his presence at a place at or about the time of the offence, which an investigator reasonably believes may be attributable to his participation in the offence and for which the investigator has asked him to account. If the detained person fails or refuses to account for his presence, any court in subsequent proceedings may draw such inferences as appear proper (s 37, Criminal Justice and Public Order Act 1994).

failure to make disclosure (in civil proceedings) Failure of a party to disclose *documents as required by a disclosure direction (*see* DISCLOSURE AND INSPECTION OF DOCUMENTS). This will lead to an application to the court for an order compelling disclosure.

fair trading *See* DIRECTOR GENERAL OF FAIR TRADING.

fair trial A right set out in Article 6 of the *European Convention on Human Rights and now part of UK law as a consequence of the *Human Rights Act 1998. The right to a fair trial applies in civil and criminal proceedings and includes the right to a public hearing (subject to some exceptions) by an independent and impartial tribunal established by law. In criminal cases there are the following specified rights: the *presumption of innocence; the right to be told the details of the case; to have time and facilities to prepare a *defence and to instruct lawyers (with financial support where necessary); to call witnesses and examine the witnesses for the *prosecution; and to have the free assistance of an *interpreter. *See also* EQUALITY OF ARMS.

f

false accounting An offence contrary to s 17 of the Theft Act 1968, punishable by up to seven years' imprisonment, committed by someone who dishonestly falsifies, destroys, or hides any account or *document used in accounting or who uses such a document knowing or suspecting it to be false or misleading. The offence must be committed for the purpose of gain or causing loss to another. There is also an offence (also punishable by up to seven years' imprisonment) committed by a company *director who publishes or allows to be published a written statement he knows or suspects is misleading or false in order to deceive members or *creditors of the company (s 19, Theft Act 1968). *See also* FORGERY.

false imprisonment Unlawful restriction of a person's freedom of movement, not necessarily in a prison. Any complete deprivation of freedom of movement is sufficient, so false imprisonment includes unlawful *arrest and unlawfully preventing a person leaving a room or a shop. The restriction must be total: it is not imprisonment to prevent a person proceeding in one direction if he is free to leave in others. False imprisonment is a form of *trespass to the person, so it is not necessary to prove that it has caused actual *damage. It is both a criminal offence at *common law and a *tort. *Damages, which may be *aggravated or *exemplary, can be obtained in tort and the writ of *habeas corpus is available to restore the imprisoned person to liberty.

false-memory paradigm The result of giving people an account of things they have not in fact experienced or witnessed. They are repeatedly interviewed about the event and come to believe that they did experience or witness the event and give the interviewer an account of the event.

false pretence The act of misleading someone by a false representation, either by words or conduct. The former offence of obtaining *property by false pretences is now known as obtaining property by *deception.

false statement *See* PERJURY.

false trade description A description of *goods made in the course of a business that is false in respect of certain facts (*see* TRADE DESCRIPTION). Under the Trade Descriptions Acts 1968 and 1972 it is an offence to apply a false trade description to goods either directly, by implication, or indirectly (e.g. by tampering with a car's milometer or painting over rust on the bodywork). It is also an offence to supply or offer to supply goods to which a false trade description is attached. These offences are triable either summarily or on *indictment (in which case they carry a maximum two years' prison sentence). They are offences of *strict liability, although certain specified *defences are allowed (e.g. that the defendant relied on information supplied by someone else). The Acts are supplemented by the Fair Trading Act 1973.

falsification of accounts *See* FALSE ACCOUNTING.

familial sex offences A group of offences under the Sexual Offences Act 2003 prohibiting sexual activity amongst family members. These offences replace the *incest offences of previous *legislation.

family A group of people connected by a close relationship. For legal purposes a family is usually limited to relationships by blood, marriage, civil partnership, or adoption, although sometimes (e.g. for social security purposes) statute expressly includes other people, such as common-law wives (*see* COMMON-LAW MARRIAGE). The courts have interpreted the word 'family' to include unmarried couples living as husband and wife in permanent and stable relationships.

family assistance order A court order under the Children Act 1989 that a *probation officer, or an officer of a local authority, should advise, assist, and befriend a particular child or a person closely connected with the child (such as a *parent) in order to provide short-term support for the family. The order can only be made with the consent of the person it concerns (other than the child) and has effect for up to six months.

Family Division The division of the *High Court concerned with *family proceedings and non-contentious probate matters. Until 1971, it was known as the Probate, Divorce and Admiralty Division. It may hear some *appeals (*see* APPELLATE JURISDICTION). The chief judge of the Division is called the **President**.

family life A right set out in Article 8 of the *European Convention on Human Rights and now part of UK law as a consequence of the *Human Rights Act 1998. The right to family life extends beyond formal relationships and legitimate arrangements. This right is a *qualified right; as such, the public interest can be used to justify an interference with it providing that this is prescribed by law, designed for a legitimate purpose, and proportionate. Public authorities have a limited but positive duty to protect family life from interference by third parties. The right to found a family (the right to procreation) is contained in Article 12 of the Convention.

family name *See* SURNAME.

family proceedings All court proceedings under the inherent *jurisdiction of the *High Court that deal with matters relating to the welfare of children. Before 1989 the court's powers to make orders concerning children varied, depending on the level of the court and the proceedings involved. The Children Act 1989, together with the Family Proceedings Rules 1991 (SI 1991/1247), rationalized the court's powers and created a unified structure of the *High Court, *county courts, and *magistrates' courts. The ambit of family proceedings is very wide, including proceedings for *divorce, domestic violence (*see* BATTERED SPOUSE OR COHABITANT), children in care (*see* CARE ORDER), adoption, and *wardship and applications for a parental order under s 30 of the Human Fertilization and Embryology Act 1990 (see SECTION 30 ORDER).

fatal accidents Formerly, at *common law, the death of either *party extinguished the right to bring an action in *tort. In addition, a person who caused death was not liable to compensate the deceased's relatives and others who suffered loss because of the death. Both rules have now been abolished by statute.

By the Law Reform (Miscellaneous Provisions) Act 1934, a right of action by (or against) a deceased person survives his death and can be brought for the benefit of (or against) his estate. Thus if a person is killed in a motor accident due to the *negligence of the *driver, an action can be brought against the driver in the name of the deceased; any *damages obtained become part of the deceased's estate. Actions for defamation of a deceased person and claims for certain types of loss are excluded from the Act and do not survive death.

The Fatal Accidents Act 1976, amended by the Administration of Justice Act 1982, confers the right to recover damages for loss of support on the dependants of a person who has been killed in an accident, if the deceased would have been able to recover damages for injury but for his death. The class of dependants who may *sue is defined by statute and includes such persons as spouses, former spouses, *parents, children, brothers, and sisters. The main purpose of the action is to compensate dependants for loss of the financial support they could have expected to receive from the deceased. However, **damages for bereavement** may be claimed, on the death of a spouse or an unmarried minor child, by the surviving spouse of the former or the parents of the latter; other relatives have no claim. The amount awarded is currently fixed at £10 000. Funeral expenses can be recovered if incurred.

fat embolism A blockage of a blood vessel, often in the lungs or kidney, caused by a piece of fat. This is often the result of injuries such as a fracture of a bone or crushing. In cases of assault it may cause death some time after the event.

fear of crime The anxiety of becoming a victim of crime. The fear may be genuine and well founded but is often irrational and not supported by analysis of the true situation. For example, there may be a common fear that older people cannot go out in safety because of the likelihood of being robbed, whereas in reality they are the sector of the population least likely to be victimized in this way. Such irrational fear is often directed towards strangers and leads to popular and media calls for stronger laws and police powers.

f

febrile Of, or relating to, or characterized by fever.

federal state A state formed by the amalgamation or union of previously autonomous or independent states. A newly created federal state is constitutionally granted direct power over the subjects or citizens of the formerly independent states. As such, the new federal state becomes a single composite international legal person. Those former entities that comprise it have consented to subsume their former sovereignty into that of the federal state, although they retain their identity in *municipal law. Examples of federal states include Australia, the USA, and Switzerland. *Compare* CONFEDERATION.

felony Formerly, an offence more serious than a *misdemeanour. Since 1967 the term has been abandoned (although it is retained in pre-1967 statutes that are still in force) and the law formerly relating to misdemeanours now applies to felonies. *See also* INDICTABLE OFFENCE; SUMMARY OFFENCE.

femur The long bone in the upper leg, the longest bone in the body. It is useful in skeletal remains for determining the height of the person and, broadly, the age at death.

ferae naturae *See* CLASSIFICATION OF ANIMALS.

fibula The thinner of the two bones in the lower leg.

fiction An assumption that something is true irrespective of whether it is really true or not. In English legal history, fictions were used by the courts during the development of forms of court action. They enabled the courts to avoid cumbersome procedures, to make remedies available when they would not be otherwise, and to extend their *jurisdiction. For example, the action of trover was originally based on the defendant's finding the claimant's *goods and taking them for himself. In time, it became unnecessary to prove the 'finding': a remedy was granted on the basis only of proving that the goods were the claimant's and that the defendant had taken them.

fiduciary [from Latin *fiducia*: trust] **1.** A person, such as a *trustee, who holds a position of trust or confidence with respect to someone else and who is therefore obliged to act solely for that person's benefit. **2.** In a position of trust or confidence. Fiduciary relationships include those between trustees and their beneficiaries, company promoters and *directors and their shareholders, *solicitors and their clients, and *guardians and their wards.

file A collection of related data that is identified, stored, accessed, and retrieved by a *computer by reference to a unique name (the 'filename'). A file may contain a computer program (or part thereof), a text document, or a collection of data. The smallest unit of disk space that can be allocated for use by a file is known as a *cluster. When a user 'deletes' a file, the computer's operating system only deletes references to the file, rather than erasing the file itself. Hence, the 'deleted' file remains on the hard drive (or other data storage device) and can often be recovered for *forensic purposes.

final act A *document containing a formal summary of the proceedings of an international conference. The signature appended to the final act is not regarded as binding on the signatory state with regard to the treaties it refers to. For the document to be binding, a separate signature is required followed by *ratification. In rare circumstances, the final act can constitute a *treaty.

final warning scheme A scheme introduced by s 37 of the Crime and Disorder Act 1998 aimed at diverting children and young people from their offending behaviour before they enter the court system. The scheme was designed to do this by: ending repeat *cautioning and providing a progressive and effective response to offending behaviour; providing appropriate and effective interventions to prevent reoffending; and ensuring that young people who do reoffend after being warned are dealt with quickly and effectively by the courts.

The final warning scheme introduced a system of *reprimands and final warnings for 10 to 17 year old offenders. Depending on the seriousness of the offence, a reprimand is normally given for a first offence and a final warning for a second offence. If a young person who has been given a final warning commits a further offence he *must be charged*. The only exception is where it is at least two years since the previous warning and the offence is not so serious as to require a charge to be brought, in which case a second final (*sic*) warning may be given. A final warning goes further than an old style caution. Following a final warning, the police have a statutory duty to refer the *young offender to the *youth offending team (YOT). The YOT in turn has a statutory duty to carry out an assessment of the young offender and in most cases to provide an intervention programme aimed at preventing reoffending. Compliance with the intervention programme is voluntary. However, if a young person goes to court, the final warning and any failure to participate in an intervention programme may be cited in the same way as previous convictions. Furthermore, if the young offender has received a final warning within the past two years the court can only give a conditional discharge in exceptional circumstances and should give reasons if they do so.

Finance Bill A parliamentary *Bill dealing with taxation matters, usually introduced each year to enact the Budget proposals.

Financial Services Authority (FSA) The UK government body responsible for overseeing and regulating the finance industry. The Financial Services and Markets Act, which came into force on 1 December 2001, gave the FSA its statutory powers.

financial year For statutes referring to finance, the period fixed by a statute of 1854 as the twelve calendar months ending on 31 March. Annual public accounts are made up for this period. For income-tax purposes, the year runs to 5 April. Companies and other bodies are free to choose their own financial years for accounting purposes.

fine 1. A sum of money that an offender is ordered to pay on *conviction. A fine may be imposed for any offence except one which carries mandatory *life imprisonment. Most *summary offences are punishable by a fine with a fixed maximum, in accordance with a standard scale of five levels. These are currently (2006) as follows: level 1—£200; level 2—£500; level 3—£1000; level 4—£2500; level 5—£5000. Under s 164 of the Criminal Justice Act 2003, before fixing a fine, a court must inquire into the financial circumstances of the offender and the amount of the fine fixed by the court should, in addition, reflect the seriousness of the offence. Section 129 of the Powers of Criminal Courts (Sentencing) Act 2000 provides various sanctions for non-payment of a fine, to commit the offender to prison in certain circumstances (*see also* DISQUALIFICATION FROM DRIVING). Section 35 of the Crime (Sentences) Act 1997 and sch 5 to the Courts Act 2003 put in place additional powers to aid the enforcement of fines. Sometimes provision is made for imprisonment in cases of failure to pay the fine. A fine may also be imposed instead of, or in addition to, any other *punishment for someone convicted on *indictment or committed to the *Crown Court for *sentence (*see* COMMITTAL FOR SENTENCE). This fine is **at large**, i.e. the amount is at the discretion of the *judge.

The maximum fine that can be imposed by a *magistrates' court on a person under the age of 18 (see JUVENILE OFFENDER), is

£1000. The limit for those under 14 is £250. In the case of an offender under the age of 16, under s 137 of the Powers of Criminal Courts (Sentencing) Act 2000, the court must order that the fine be paid by the *parent or *guardian of the offender unless his parent or guardian cannot be found or it would be unreasonable in the circumstances to expect his parent or guardian to pay it. **2.** A lump-sum payment by a *tenant to a *landlord for the grant or renewal of a *lease.

f

fingerprints The marks left on material by secretions from the skin showing the pattern of ridges that occur on the fingers, palms, and feet of people. These unique marks were described by Dr Nehemiah Grew (1641–1712) to the Royal Society in 1684 but not used until the 19th century for identifying individuals in prisons; they were first used in a criminal *trial in 1902. They remain an effective means of crime detection.

fingertip bruising An oval area of *bruising caused by the fingertips when gripping another person forcefully. It is often seen on the arms and on the neck in strangulation cases. It is frequently seen in *child abuse cases.

firearm Generally, any weapon from which a *projectile is expelled by the action of expanding powder gases. For the purposes of the Firearms Act 1968, any potentially lethal weapon with a *barrel that can fire a shot, *bullet, or other missile or any weapon classified as a *prohibited weapon (even if it is not lethal). Illegal possession of a prohibited weapon carries a maximum sentence of ten years' imprisonment.

The 1968 Act creates various offences in relation to firearms. The main offences include: (1) buying or possessing a firearm without a *licence; (2) buying or hiring a firearm under the age of 17 or selling a firearm to someone under 17 (similar offences exist under the Crossbows Act 1987 in relation to crossbows); (3) possessing a firearm under the age of 14; (4) supplying firearms to someone who is drunk or insane; (5) carrying a firearm and suitable *ammunition in a *public place without a reasonable excuse; (6) *trespassing with a firearm; (7) possessing a firearm with the intention of endangering life; (8) using a firearm with the intention of resisting or preventing a lawful *arrest; (9) having a firearm with the intention of committing an *indictable offence; (10) possessing a firearm or ammunition after having previously been convicted of a crime; and (11) having a firearm in one's possession at the time of committing or being arrested for such offences as *rape, *burglary, robbery, and certain other offences. The Firearms Act 1982 extends the provisions of the 1968 Act to imitation firearms that can be easily converted to firearms, and the Firearms (Amendment) Act 1988 strengthened controls over some of the more dangerous types of firearms, *shotguns, and ammunition.

The Firearms (Amendment) Act 1997 bans all *handguns above 0.22 calibre. The public may own and use less powerful *pistols in secure gun clubs. The pistols may not be removed from the clubs without prior permission of the police. The Act also provided for the establishment of licensed gun clubs, tightened police licensing procedures, and introduced stronger police powers to suspend or revoke certificates. Anyone who uses a handgun must have a licence. The police have powers to revoke certificates when good reasons for possessing the gun no longer exist.

Under the Theft Act 1968 someone who has with him a firearm or imitation firearm while committing *burglary is *guilty of *aggravated burglary. For the purposes of this Act, a firearm may include an airgun, air pistol, or anything that looks like a firearm. *See also* OFFENSIVE WEAPON; DANGEROUS OFFENDER; MANDATORY MINIMUM SENTENCE.

firearms discharge residue (FDR) The particles of the propellants of a *bullet left after it has been discharged. The particles escape from the weapon when it is fired and can be found on the clothing and on the person of the firer. The residue falls off quite quickly and should be collected as soon as possible after the firing.

fire damage An *occupier of *land or buildings is not liable for a fire that begins there accidentally (Fires Prevention (Metropolis) Act 1774). *Liability is imposed if the fire is caused by *negligence, *nuisance, or a non-natural *user of the land, or if the fire, having started accidentally, is negligently allowed to spread.

firing pin The part of the mechanism of a *small arm which strikes the *primer to start *ignition and explode the *propellant charge. In a *revolver or *pistol the firing pin is an integral part of the *hammer; in a rifle it generally forms part of the *bolt or *breechblock.

first description The first description of an offender given by a witness. This must be recorded by police and disclosed (*see* DISCLOSURE OF UNUSED MATERIAL). Before any *identification procedure the suspect or his *solicitor must be provided with details of the first description.

first offender A person with no previous *conviction by a criminal court. A court of summary *jurisdiction (*see* MAGISTRATES' COURT) is not empowered to send a person to prison for a first offence, unless it is satisfied that there is no other appropriate method of dealing with that person. *See also* SENTENCE.

fitness for purpose A standard that must be met by one who sells *goods in the course of a business. When the *buyer makes known to the *seller any particular purpose for which the goods are being bought, there is an implied condition that the goods are reasonably fit for that purpose, except when the circumstances show that the buyer does not rely (or that it is unreasonable for him to rely) on the skill or judgment of the seller.

fixation The preserving or setting of body organs in a solution of formaldehyde. It is often used where a person has been on a life support system for some time before dying. In those cases the brain becomes very watery and cannot be examined properly. The brain is put in a 'hammock' and suspended in formaldehyde for several days to set it, thus delaying the *pathologist's examination.

fixed penalty notice A notice given to a person who has committed a specified 'penalty offence' entitling that person to discharge any *liability to *conviction by payment of a prescribed amount of money. Originally the notices were used only for traffic offences but are now issued for a range of *nuisance (*see* PENALTY NOTICE FOR DISORDER) and criminal offences. It is expected that the scheme will be extended some time in 2007 to include offences such as *assault, *threatening behaviour, and possession of certain *controlled drugs. *Police officers, traffic wardens, *Community Support Officers, and *local authority officers may issue the notices.

fixture 1. A *chattel that has been annexed to *land or a building so as to become a part of it, in accordance with the maxim *quicquid plantatur solo, solo cedit* (whatever is annexed to the soil is given to the soil). *Annexation normally involves actual affixation, but a thing resting on its own weight can be regarded as annexed if it can be shown that it was intended to become part of the land or to benefit it. Fixtures become the property of the freeholder, subject to certain rights of removal (as, for example, in the case of trade fixtures and certain agricultural fixtures). A *vendor of land may retain the right to fixtures as against the purchaser by express provision in the contract. **2.** The final agreed details of a shipping agreement between the owner of a cargo and the ship owner.

flag of convenience The national flag of a state flown by a *ship that is registered in that state but is owned by a national of another state. A state whose law allows this practice can grant, in return for financial considerations, *nationality and the right to fly its national flag to virtually any ship without stipulating any requirements, such as those relating to the safety of the ship and crew, the nationality of the vessel's owner, or the country of construction. Before a state is justified in extending its nationality to a ship, or permitting a ship to fly its flag, it seems that there must be some effective link connecting the ship with the state. Hence a flag of convenience may only be validly granted when a genuine link exists, though what constitutes such a link remains unclear. *See also* FLAG STATE JURISDICTION.

flag of truce A white flag displayed to indicate a willingness to negotiate during *armed conflict. The envoy is protected by the flag of truce under Article 32 of the Hague Convention. The side displaying the flag of truce is prohibited from attacking whilst displaying the flag.

flagrante delicto [Latin: in the commission of an offence] The phrase is most commonly applied to the situation in which a person finds his or her spouse in the act of committing adultery. Someone who kills his or her spouse in this situation may have a defence of *provocation.

f

flag state jurisdiction The rule whereby, exceptions applying, a *ship on the *high seas is subject only to the *jurisdiction of the flag state, i.e. that state permitting it the right to sail under its flag (*see* FLAG OF CONVENIENCE).

flail chest A condition describing the destruction of the structure of the chest wall caused by multiple rib fractures.

floating charge *See* CHARGE.

floating rate An interest rate that is fixed at a percentage above a variable rate. For example, the interest rate on a mortgage set at 2 per cent above the Bank of England base rate.

floor limit The highest value of *payment card transaction that a merchant may conduct without seeking authorization from the card issuer. Merchants who have accepted stolen cards have their floor limits reduced. *See also* COLLUDING TRADER.

flotation A process by which a *public company can, by an issue of *securities (*shares or debentures), raise capital from the public. It may involve a **prospectus issue**, in which the company itself issues a *prospectus inviting the public to acquire securities; an **offer for sale**, in which the company sells the securities on offer to an **issuing house**, which then issues a prospectus inviting the public to purchase the securities from it; or a **placing**, whereby an issuing house arranges for the securities to be taken up by its own or another's clients in the expectation that they will ultimately become available to the public on the open market.

flotation test A test conducted during the *autopsy of a newborn baby where the lungs were put in a bowl of water. If they floated it was assumed that the baby had breathed after birth and had therefore lived. The method is discredited by some pathologists.

f.o.b. contract (free on board contract) A type of contract for the international *sale of goods in which the *seller's duty is fulfilled by placing the goods on board a *ship. There are different types of f.o.b. contract: the *buyer may arrange the shipping space and the procurement of a *bill of lading and nominate the ship to the seller; he may nominate a general ship and leave it to the seller to place the goods on board and to procure a bill of lading; or the seller may be asked to make all the shipping arrangements for which the buyer will pay. The risk of accidental loss or *damage normally passes to the buyer when the goods are loaded onto the ship. Insurance during the sea transit is the responsibility of the buyer. F.o.b. is a defined *incoterm in *Incoterm* 2000.

foetus An unborn child more than eight weeks after conception (*compare* embryo—less than eight weeks). A foetus does not have a separate existence from its mother and cannot be the victim of *homicide or *assault charges. Separate offences of *abortion and *child destruction exist to protect unborn children.

folk devil A group of people stigmatized as a threat to society by the populace and media at any time and blamed for the ills of society. Such groups as the unemployed, single mothers, *asylum seekers, and 'inner city youth' have all at some time been categorized in this way, and stiffer *legislation to take action against them has been called for.

fontanelle The soft spot on the top of a young baby's skull where the bones have not yet joined.

Food Standards Agency (FSA) An independent government department set up with the aim of protecting the public's health and consumer interests in relation to food. The FSA provides advice and information to the public and government on food safety and protects consumers through effective food enforcement and monitoring.

football banning order *See* FOOTBALL HOOLIGANISM.

football hooliganism A form of disorderly behaviour in which participants are supporters of one or more football clubs, and which most often occurs at, or immediately before or after, a football match. The Sporting Events (Control of Alcohol, etc.) Act 1985 contains finable offences of possessing *alcohol, being drunk, or causing or permitting the carriage of alcohol on trains and vehicles capable of carrying nine or more passengers; the vehicle must be carrying two or more passengers to or from a 'designated sporting event' (mainly Football League club and international fixtures), and normal scheduled coach or train services are excluded. A *constable who reasonably suspects that a relevant offence is being or has been committed may stop the vehicle or train and search it or the suspected offender. It is also an offence to be drunk or to possess alcohol or (unless lawful authority is proved) fireworks and similar objects (but not matches or lighters) in the viewing area within two hours before, during, or one hour after the event, or while trying to enter.

Admission to a designated football match is controlled under the Football Spectators Act 1989. Once inside the venue, spectators are subject to the provisions of the Football (Offences) Act 1991 intended to control disorderly behaviour. The 1991 Act creates three *summary only offences: throwing of missiles (s 2), indecent or racist chanting (s 3), and going on to the playing area (s 4). Under s 14A of the Football Spectators Act 1989 (as amended by the Football (Disorder) Act 2000 and the Football Disorder (Amendment) Act 2002), a **banning order** may be made to prohibit an offender from attending a football match in England and Wales. If the order is made in addition to a *sentence of immediate *custody, it must last for a specified period of between six and ten years; otherwise it must be made for a specified period of between three and five years. Unless there are exceptional circumstances, the offender is required to surrender his *passport to prevent him travelling to a football match abroad. On the application of the *prosecutor, the court may also make an order under s 35 of the Public Order Act 1986, requiring the offender to attend at a police station in order to have his photograph taken.

Under s 14B of the 1989 Act, a civil application for a banning order (brought by complaint to a *magistrates' court) may be made by the chief officer of police for the area in which the respondent resides if it appears that the respondent has at any time caused or contributed to any violence or disorder in the UK or elsewhere. Provided that the court is satisfied that there are reasonable grounds to believe that making a banning order would help to prevent violence or disorder at or in connection with any regulated football matches, it must make a banning order in respect of the respondent for a specified period of between three and five years. *See also* OFFENCES AGAINST PUBLIC ORDER.

footpath (under the Highways Act 1980) Any *highway (other than a *footway) over which the public have a *right of way on foot only.

footway (under the Highways Act 1980) Any way over which the public have a *right of way on foot only and which is part of a *highway that also comprises a way for the passage of vehicles. *Compare* FOOTPATH.

footwear marks The marks left by footwear at a crime scene. The marks may be impressed, e.g. in soil or snow, or transfer surface marks, where the footwear has transferred dust, damp, or other contaminant to a surface. Casting, photographing, or electrostatic lifting devices may recover the marks for comparison with the shoes of a suspect or to link scenes.

forbearance A deliberate failure to exercise a legal right (e.g. to *sue for a *debt). A forbearance to sue at a *debtor's request may be *consideration for some fresh promise by the debtor. A promise not to enforce a claim that is bad in law may still be consideration if the claim is believed to be valid. A requested forbearance, even if it is not binding, may have more limited effects either at *common law or in *equity (e.g. in certain circumstances it may not be revoked without reasonable notice).

f

forced labour A situation where people are compelled to work against their will. Generally forced labour is a breach of human rights under Article 4 of the *European Convention on Human Rights. There are exceptions where work may be compulsory, as in national service, work carried out as a community *punishment or part of imprisonment, in times of national emergency, and in some member states where trainee lawyers have to take cases pro bono as part of their training.

forcible entry A *common-law offence (as amended by various statutes) that applied under certain circumstances when force was used to gain entry to *premises. The common-law offence has been replaced by a statutory *indictable offence of using or threatening violence against people or property in order to secure entry into premises (s 6, Criminal Law Act 1977). The offence only applies if there is someone present on the premises who is opposed to the entry and the offender knows of this. The fact that the offender is the legal owner or *occupier of the premises is not in itself a *defence. However, there is a special defence if the offender can prove that he was at the relevant time a displaced *residential occupier or protected intending occupier who requires the property for his residence and has a qualifying freehold or *leasehold interest, *tenancy, or *licence and was seeking to gain entry or to pass through premises that form an access to his own place of residential occupation. These provisions do not apply to *landlords seeking to regain possession and it is a *summary offence to make false statements when claiming to be a protected occupier. It is not an offence, however, for a person unlawfully evicted from his own home to use force to re-enter, subject to the common-law rule that the force must not be excessive. The police may use force to enter with lawful authority. *See also* ADVERSE OCCUPATION.

foreign bill Any *bill of exchange other than an *inland bill. The distinction is relevant to the steps taken when the bill has been dishonoured.

foreign company A company incorporated outside Great Britain but having a place of business within Great Britain. Foreign companies are subject to provisions of the Companies Acts relating to registration, accounts, name, etc. *See* OVERSEAS COMPANY.

foreign enlistment The offence under the Foreign Enlistment Act 1870 of enlisting oneself or others (except with the licence of the Crown) for armed service with a foreign state that is at *war with a state with which the UK is at peace. A foreign state for this purpose includes part of a province or persons exercising or assuming powers of government. It is also an offence under the Act (again, except with licence) to build or equip any *ship for such service or to fit out any naval or military expedition for use against a state with which the UK is at peace. The Act does not apply to civil wars.

foreign law (in *private international law) Any legal system other than that of England. A foreign legal system may be the system of a foreign state (one recognized by public *international law) or of a law district. Thus the law of Scotland, Northern Ireland, the Channel Islands, and Isle of Man, and the law of each of the American or Australian states and territories or Canadian provinces is a separate foreign law. When an element of foreign law arises in an English court, it is usually treated as a question of *fact, which must be proved (usually by expert evidence) in each case. The English courts retain an overriding power to refuse to enforce (or even to recognize) provisions of foreign law that are against English public policy, foreign penal or revenue laws, or laws creating discriminatory disabilities or status. *See also* COMMUNITY LAW.

foreign travel order An order (introduced by s 114 of the Sexual Offences Act 2003) made by a *magistrate on the application of the chief officer of police for an area in which the defendant lives, or to which he may travel, to prohibit the defendant from travelling outside the UK for a period of up to six months. The defendant must have been previously convicted of a qualifying offence (*sexual offences against or involving children) and he has acted in such a way as to give reasonable belief that it is necessary to make the order for the purpose of protecting children in general or a particular child from serious sexual harm from the defendant outside the UK. *See also* SEXUAL OFFENCES PREVENTION ORDER.

forensic Of or for use in a court of law. Frequently misused to apply narrowly to forensic science.

forensic accountant An accountant who specializes in examining and analyzing the *accounts of companies and individuals for use in court proceedings.

forensic anthropologist A scientist who specializes in the examination, identification, and analysis of bones. From this they can assist in determining the sex, age, and race of the deceased, the post-mortem interval, and cause of death. Forensic anthropologists have been used extensively in examining mass *graves that have resulted from *genocide.

forensic archaeologist A scientist who specializes in the finding and recovery of buried bodies for *forensic purposes.

forensic entomologist A scientist who studies insects for *forensic purposes. When a body dies it becomes inhabited by insects, which lay their eggs on the body; the eggs hatch to become *larvae which feed on the flesh. The larvae pupate and then emerge as adult insects (imago). By studying the stages of insect present in the body and the number of generations, the forensic entomologist can assist in determining the post-mortem interval (time since death).

Forensic Science Service A UK government-owned company, previously a government agency, which is the market leader in the supply of forensic science services to *police forces in England and Wales, although it now has to compete against other forensic science providers (such as Forensic Alliance).

Forensic Science Society An international professional body with members in over 60 countries. It publishes a peer reviewed journal (*Science & Justice*), awards qualifications and prizes, arranges scientific conferences in the UK and abroad, and is engaged in setting standards and accreditation in forensic sciences.

forensic scientist A scientist of any discipline who carries out scientific examinations for *forensic purposes.

foresight Awareness at the time of doing an act that a certain consequence may result. In the case of some crimes (e.g. *murder or *wounding with intent) an *intention by the accused to bring about a certain consequence must be proved before he can be found *guilty; foresight is not enough (*see also* ULTERIOR INTENT) unless it is proved that death or serious bodily harm are a virtual certainty as a result of the defendant's actions and that the defendant appreciated that such was the case (*R v Woollin* [1999] 1 AC 82). However, conviction for many crimes (including *wounding) requires only that the accused foresaw a specified consequence as likely or possible. In all cases where foresight suffices for *liability, the court may not assume that the defendant had foresight merely because the particular consequence that occurred was the natural and likely consequence of his acts. *See also* RECKLESSNESS.

forfaiting A method of providing fixed-rate financing for international trade transactions. In recent years, it has assumed an important role for exporters who desire cash instead of deferred payments, especially from countries where protection against credit, economic and political risks has become more difficult. It provides the exporter with cash at the time of shipment, and on a non-recourse basis.

The importer's bank guarantees a series of *promissory notes or *bills of exchange, which cover repayment of a supplier's credit, provided by the exporter to the importer, for a period of from 180 days to seven years. The notes are initially given to the exporter at the time of shipment and become its property. The notes represent the unconditional and irrevocable commitment of the *buyer and/or its bank to pay the notes at maturity. Once the exporter becomes the bona fide owner of the notes, it can sell them to a third party at a discount from their face amounts, for immediate cash payment. This sale is without recourse to the exporter, and the buyer of the notes assumes all of the risks. The buyer's security is the guarantee of the importer's bank.

forfeiture Deprivation of *property by a criminal court following *conviction for a criminal offence. Forfeiture should not be confused with confiscation following *conviction or *civil recovery: it is not intended to recover the proceeds of criminal conduct. There are three main situations in which a criminal court may order forfeiture of property.

(1) Under the Customs and Excise Management Act 1979 *goods can be forfeited if they: have been improperly imported; were found on a person entering or leaving the UK contrary to a prohibition; are items for signalling to smugglers; are *ships, aircraft, or vehicles that have been constructed, altered, or fitted for the purpose of concealing goods; are aircraft, *ships, vehicles, animals, or containers of any sort used to convey, handle, deposit, or conceal goods that are liable to forfeiture. *Her Majesty's Revenue and Customs (HMRC) can then apply to a court to have the property forfeited and condemned. The proceedings are against the goods (*in rem*) rather than against a person (*in personam*). This means that there does not have to have been a conviction and it is not necessary to show that the person whose goods are concerned was involved in any improper importation, or even knew what was happening (see *Customs & Excise Commissioners v Air Canada* [1991] 2 QB 446). Goods forfeited by a court are condemned and disposed of at the discretion of HMRC Commissioners. For example, in the *Air Canada* case the aircraft was returned on payment of £50 000.

(2) Under s 27 of the Misuse of Drugs Act 1971, as amended, following conviction for a drug trafficking or lifestyle offence (including *conspiracy or incitement), and within 28 days of sentencing, a court can order the forfeiture of anything related to the offence for which he has been convicted. Thus if a person is convicted of possessing drugs with intent to supply any cash they have cannot be forfeited under this section because it relates to past conduct and not the offence which imputes future conduct.

(3) The Powers of Criminal Courts (Sentencing) Act 2000 gives courts wide powers following conviction to order forfeiture of anything that was seized from the offender or in his possession or under his control at the time he was apprehended or when a *summons was issued. The article must have been either the subject of a charge of unlawful possession, or have been used for the purpose of committing or facilitating the commission of any offence, or was intended for that purpose. The section includes forfeiture of cars where the *driver has committed a drink/drive offence, *dangerous driving, and failing to stop/report an accident. However, the court must take into account the value of the property and the likely effect on the offender of making the order. The order must be considered part of the overall sentence. Property in the possession of police which has been forfeited is dealt with under the Police (Property) Act 1997. *See also* CONFISCATION ORDER.

forfeiture of recognizance Where a person has stood *surety for the attendance of a defendant at court and he fails to attend court in answer to his *bail, the surety is ordered to appear at court to show cause why the *recognizance should not be *estreated. The court can then order that some or all of the sum of the surety be forfeited.

forfeiture of security for attendance Where a person has put up a security for the attendance at court of a person on *bail and that person does not attend, the court can order the forfeiture of all or some of the security.

forgery The offence of making a 'false instrument' in order that it may be accepted as genuine, thereby causing harm to others. Under the Forgery and Counterfeiting Act 1981, an 'instrument' may be a *document, a stamp issued by the Post Office or the Inland Revenue, or any device (e.g. magnetic tape) in which information is recorded or stored. An instrument is considered to be 'false' if, for example, it purports to have been made or altered (1) by or on the authority of someone who did not in fact do so; (2) on a date or at a place when it was not; or (3) by someone who is non-existent. In addition to forgery itself, it is a criminal offence under the Act to copy or use a false instrument, knowing or believing it to be false. It is also an offence merely to have in one's possession or control any one of certain specified false instruments with the intention of passing them off as genuine. It is also an offence to make or possess any material that is meant to be used to produce any of the specified false instruments. These specified instruments include money or postal orders, stamps, *share certificates, *passports, *cheques, cheque cards and *credit cards, and copies of entries in a register of births, marriages, or deaths. All the above offences are punishable on *indictment by up to ten years' imprisonment and upon *summary trial to a *fine at level 5 on the standard scale and/or six months' imprisonment.

The Act also deals with the offences of **counterfeiting currency** (notes or coin), with or without the intention of passing it off as genuine; possessing counterfeit currency; passing it off; making or possessing anything which can be used for counterfeiting; and importing or exporting counterfeit currency. It is also an offence to reproduce any British currency note (e.g. to photocopy a £5 note), even in artwork, and, under certain circumstances, to make an imitation British coin. Some of these offences are subject to the same penalties as forgery.

forward market A *derivative market in forward contracts which are agreements to buy or sell a commodity (metals, coffee, etc.), currency or financial bonds at a future date for an agreed price. Once agreed these contracts cannot be traded (*compare* FUTURES MARKET).

foster child A child who is cared for by someone other than its natural or adopted *parents or a person having *parental responsibility (*see* FOSTER PARENT). *Local authorities are obliged by law to supervise the welfare of foster children within their area and to inspect and control the use of *premises as foster homes. Foster children do not include children who are looked after by relatives or *guardians or boarded out by a local authority or voluntary organization.

foster parent A person looking after a *foster child. Foster parents have no legal rights over the children they foster, who may be removed from their care by their *parents or legal *guardian. They may, however, apply to have the child made a *ward of court or apply for a residence order (*see* SECTION 8 ORDERS) when a child has lived with them for three years (or within that period if the *local authority gives its consent), which will invest them with *parental responsibility. If the child has been living with them for at least twelve months they may apply to adopt him.

fracture A break or crack of a bone or cartilage.

fraenulum *See* FRENULUM.

franchise 1. (in constitutional law) A special right conferred by the *Crown on a subject. Also known as a **liberty**, it is exemplified by the right to hold a market or fair or to run a ferry. **2.** (in constitutional law) The right to vote at an election. To qualify to vote at a parliamentary or local government election, a person must be a *Commonwealth citizen or a citizen of the Republic of Ireland, must be aged 18 or over, must be shown on the register of electors governing the election (*see* ELECTOR) as resident on the qualifying date in the parliamentary *constituency or local government area concerned, and must not be subject to any legal incapacity to vote. Those incapacitated are peers and peeresses in their own right (for parliamentary elections only, and not including peers of Ireland), persons serving *sentences of imprisonment, persons convicted during the preceding five years of certain offences relating to elections or to the bribery of public officials, and persons who are incapable of understanding the nature of their acts. **3.** (in commercial law) A *licence given to a manufacturer, distributor, trader, etc., to enable them to manufacture or sell a named product or service in a particular area for a stated period. The holder of the licence (**franchisee**) usually pays the grantor of the licence (**franchisor**) a *royalty on sales, often with a lump sum as an advance against royalties. The franchisor may also supply the franchisee with a brand identity as well as finance and technical expertise. Franchises are common in the fast-food business, petrol stations, travel agents, etc. A franchise contract in the *European Union must comply with Regulation 4087/88, which sets out which provisions are permitted and which are banned under EU competition law.

fraud A false *representation by means of a statement or conduct made knowingly or recklessly in order to gain a material advantage. If the fraud results in injury to the deceived party, he may claim damages for the *tort of deceit. A contract obtained by fraud is voidable on the grounds of fraudulent *misrepresentation. In relation to crime, see CHEATING; CONSPIRACY; CYBERCRIME; DEFRAUDING; DISHONESTY; FALSE PRETENCE; FORGERY.

fraud on the minority An improper exercise of voting power by the majority of members of a company. It consists of a failure to cast votes for the benefit of the company as a whole and makes a resolution voidable. Examples are the ratification of an expropriation of company property by the *directors (themselves the majority shareholders) and alteration of the *articles of association to allow the compulsory purchase of members' *shares when this is not in the company's interests. Actual or threatened fraud on the minority may give rise to a derivative action.

fraudulent conveyance A transfer of *land made without valuable *consideration and with the intent of defrauding a subsequent purchaser. An example of fraudulent *conveyance is when A, who has contracted to sell to B, conveys the land to his associate C in order to escape the contract with B. Under the Law of Property Act 1925, B is entitled to have the conveyance to C set aside by the court.

fraudulent evasion An offence under s 170 of the Customs and Excise Management Act 1979 which prohibits evasion of payment of *duty on imported *goods or evasion of a prohibition or restriction on the import/export of goods. Under s 170 (1), it must be shown that the accused knowingly performed certain acts with intent to defraud Her Majesty or with intent to evade a relevant prohibition or restriction. In relation to knowingly harbouring goods, it is usually enough to show that goods which were subject to duty were found in the possession of the accused. Under s 170(2), the word 'fraudulent' means dishonest conduct 'deliberately intended to evade the prohibition or restriction with respect to, or the duty chargeable on, goods as the case may be': per Lord Lane CJ in *Attorney-General's Reference (No 1 of 1981)* [1982] QB 848. The offence includes more than merely entering the UK with goods concealed and with no intention of declaring them; it extends to any offending conduct which was directed and intended to lead to the prohibited importation. Offences under s 170 are continuing offences because, by definition, the evasion of a prohibition or restriction often involves a continuing series of events and is rarely limited to the moment of importation itself; 'it includes anyone who acquires possession of goods unlawfully removed from a warehouse, or anyone who hides goods on which duty has not been paid, or anyone who carries goods the importation of which is forbidden': per Griffiths LJ in *R v Neal* 77 Cr App R 283. *See also* CONTROLLED DRUGS.

fraudulent misrepresentation *See* MISREPRESENTATION.

fraudulent receipt of programme Receipt of a programme included in a broadcasting or cable programme service provided from a place in the UK with intent to avoid payment of any charge applicable to the reception of the programme. It is a *summary offence, contrary to s 297 of the Copyright, Designs and Patents Act 1988. Section 297A of the Act (inserted by the Conditional Access (Unauthorised Decoders) Regulations 2000 (SI 2000/1175)) creates an offence triable *either way concerned with certain commercial activities in relation to unauthorized decoders (that is apparatus to enable receipt of encrypted transmissions).

fraudulent trading The carrying on of business with the intention of defrauding *creditors or for any other fraudulent purpose, e.g. accepting advance payment for *goods with no intention of either supplying them or returning the money. Such conduct is a criminal offence and the court may order those responsible to contribute to the company's assets on a *winding-up. *See also* WRONGFUL TRADING.

fraudulent use of telecommunication systems The offence, contrary to s 125 of the Communications Act 2003, of obtaining an electronic communications service (other than a programme included in a broadcasting or cable programme service provided from a place in the UK) with intent to avoid payment of a charge applicable to the provision of that service. It is also an offence, contrary to s 126 of the Act, for a person to have in his possession or under his control anything which may be used for obtaining such a communications service, provided he has the requisite intention; and for a person to supply or offer to supply anything which may be so used, where he knows or believes that the person supplied has the requisite intention. The three offences are triable *either way, and the maximum *penalty is, on *conviction on *indictment, imprisonment for a term not exceeding five years or a *fine or both and, on *summary conviction, imprisonment for a term not exceeding six months or a fine not exceeding the statutory maximum or both. *See also* FRAUDULENT RECEIPT OF PROGRAMME.

freedom from encumbrance The freedom of *property from the binding rights of parties other than the owner. In contracts for the *sale of goods, unless the *seller makes it clear that he is contracting to transfer only such *title as he or a third person may have, there is an implied *warranty that the goods are free from any charge or encumbrance not disclosed or known to the buyer before the contract was made.

freedom of association A right set out in Article 11 of the *European Convention on Human Rights and now part of UK law as a consequence of the *Human Rights Act 1998 which protects **freedom of peaceful assembly**, including the right to form and join trade unions and similar bodies. It is a *qualified right; as such, the public interest can be used to justify an interference with it providing that this is prescribed by law, designed for a legitimate purpose, and proportionate. The right of those in the armed forces, the police, and the administration of the state is protected only to the extent that any interference with this right must be prescribed by law. The right of assembly does not extend to purely social gatherings, e.g. youths gathering in a shopping centre.

freedom of expression A right set out in Article 10 of the *European Convention on Human Rights and now part of UK law as a consequence of the *Human Rights Act 1998 which allows an individual to hold opinions and receive and impart information without interference. 'Freedom of expression constitutes one of the essential foundations of a democratic society, one of the basic conditions for its progress and for the development of every man ... it is applicable not only to "information" or "ideas" that are favourably received or regarded as inoffensive or as a matter of indifference, but also to those that offend, shock or disturb ... such are the demands of that pluralism, tolerance and broadmindedness without which there is no "democratic society".' (European Court of Human Rights in *Handyside v UK* Series A No 24, (1979) 1 EHRR 737.) Convention jurisprudence gives different weight to different kinds of expression. The most important expression—political speech—therefore is likely to be protected to a much greater extent than the least important—commercial speech.

Freedom of expression is a *qualified right; as such, the public interest can be used to justify an interference with it providing that this is prescribed by law, designed for a legitimate purpose, and proportionate.

freedom of thought, conscience, and religion A right set out in Article 9 of the *European Convention on Human Rights and now part of UK law as a consequence of the *Human Rights Act 1998 which allows an individual to change and manifest his religion or belief. While freedom of thought itself is an *absolute right, and as such not subject to public-interest limitations, the right to manifest one's beliefs or religion is a *qualified right; therefore the public interest can be used to justify an interference providing that this is prescribed by law, designed for a legitimate purpose, and proportionate.

free elections A duty of the state to hold free elections at reasonable intervals by secret ballot, under conditions that will ensure the free expression of the opinion of the people in the choice of the legislature. This duty does not apply to local elections (*local authorities are not the *legislature but the European Parliament is), and there is no duty to use any particular system of voting (proportional representation or first past the post). The duty is set out in Article 3 of the First Protocol to the *European Convention on Human Rights and is now part of UK law as a consequence of the *Human Rights Act 1998.

free movement The movement of *goods, persons, services, and capital within an area without being impeded by legal restrictions. This is a basic principle of the *European Community, whose treaty insists on the free movement of goods (involving the elimination of *customs duties and quantitative restrictions between member states and the setting up of a Common External Tariff) as well as the free movement of services, capital, and persons (including workers and those wishing to establish themselves in professions or to set up companies). *See also* EXHAUSTION OF RIGHTS.

free on board *See* F.O.B. CONTRACT.

freezing injunction An *injunction, now consolidated in statute, that enables the court to freeze the *assets of a defendant (whether resident within the *jurisdiction of the English court or not). This prevents the defendant from removing his assets abroad and thus makes it worthwhile to sue such a defendant. The remedy is draconian and has become very popular, both in the commercial world and outside it; any person seeking the remedy, however, must himself disclose all material information to the court. Before the introduction of the Civil Procedure Rules in 1999, freezing injunctions were known as **Mareva injunctions**, from the case *Mareva Compania Naviera SA v International Bulkcarriers SA* [1975] 2 Lloyd's Rep 509.

freight 1. The profit derived by a shipowner or hirer from the use of the *ship by himself or by letting it to others, or for carrying *goods for others. **2.** The amount payable under a contract (of affreightment) for the *carriage of goods by sea.

frenulum (fraenulum) The loose tissue joining the upper and lower gums to the back of the lip. A tear in the frenulum is frequently a sign of *child abuse.

friction ridges The ridges in the surface of the fingers, palms, and feet which make the patterns of *fingerprints.

frottage *See* FROTTEURISM.

frotteur A person who practises *frotteurism.

frotteurism [from French *frotter*: to rub] The act of achieving sexual gratification by rubbing one's body, especially the genital area, against another person. Typically, such contact occurs in crowded situations, such as on trains or buses, where the individual rubs up against a stranger. If done without consent, the act may amount to *sexual assault.

frustration of contract The unforeseen termination of a contract as a result of an event that either renders its performance impossible or illegal or prevents its main purpose from being achieved. Frustration would, for example, occur if the *goods specified in a *sale of goods contract were destroyed (impossibility of performance); if the outbreak of a *war caused one party to become an enemy *alien (illegality); or if X were to hire a room from Y with the object (known to Y) of viewing a procession and the procession was cancelled (failure of main purpose). Unless specific provision for the frustrating event is made, a frustrated contract is automatically discharged and the position of the parties is, in most cases, governed by the Law Reform (Frustrated Contracts) Act 1943. Money paid before the event can be recovered and money due but not paid ceases to be payable. However, a party who has obtained any valuable benefit under the contract must pay a reasonable sum for it. The Act does not apply to certain contracts for the sale of goods, contracts for the *carriage of goods by sea, or contracts of *insurance.

fugitive offender A term applied to a person subject to *extradition proceedings. At one time such people were not entitled to *bail. However, since the coming into force of the Crime (International Cooperation) Act 2003 and the Extradition Act 2003 there is a presumption of bail for unconvicted fugitives but not for those already convicted by the foreign court. *See also* EXTRADITION.

full age *See* MAJORITY.

full code test A two-stage test, under the *Code for Crown Prosecutions, applied by a *prosecutor when determining whether an offender is to be charged with an offence. The first stage is consideration of the evidence. If the case does not pass the evidential stage it must not go ahead no matter how important or serious it may be. If the case does pass the evidential stage, the prosecutor must proceed to the second stage and decide if a prosecution is needed in the public interest. *See also* THRESHOLD TEST.

full powers A *document produced by the competent authorities of a state designating a person (or body of persons) to represent the state for negotiating, adopting, or authenticating the text of a *treaty, for expressing the consent of the state to be bound by a treaty, or for accomplishing any other act with respect to a treaty. *See also* SIGNATURE OF TREATY.

full representation *See* COMMUNITY LEGAL SERVICE.

fundamental breach *See* BREACH OF CONTRACT.

fungibles Instruments that are equivalent, substitutable, and interchangeable in law. Where the subject of the obligation is *a* thing of a given class, the thing is said to be fungible, i.e. the delivery of any object which answers to the generic description will satisfy the terms of the obligation. For example if an investor buys a hundred bottles of vintage wine which are kept in a warehouse with thousands of others, it is impossible to say which bottles belong to the investor—the bottles are fungibles.

futures market A *derivative market in futures contracts which require the delivery of a specified quality and quantity of a commodity, currency, or financial instrument in a specified future month, if not liquidated before the contract matures. These contracts can be, and frequently are, traded.

gag Placing an article across or in the mouth to prevent speech or noise.

gall bladder A small bladder under the liver in which bile is stored. If at *autopsy the gall bladder is empty it is likely that the person ate a meal shortly before death. If the stomach is also empty it may indicate that the deceased ate a meal and then vomited shortly before death.

game Wild animals or birds hunted for sport or food. The Game Acts define these as including hares, pheasants, partridges, grouse, heath or moor game, black game, and bustards. The right to game belongs basically to the *occupier, although in leases it is frequently reserved to the *landlord rather than the *tenant. *See also* POACHING.

gaming (gambling) Playing a game in order to win money or anything else of value, when winning depends on luck. There are various restrictions upon gaming, depending on whether it takes place in controlled (i.e. licensed or registered) or uncontrolled *premises. If the premises are uncontrolled, it is illegal to play a game that involves playing against a bank or a game in which each player does not have an equal chance or the chance of winning is weighted in favour of someone other than the players (e.g. a promoter or organizer), unless the game takes place in a private house in the course of ordinary family life. Thus one cannot play roulette with a zero in uncontrolled premises, but one may play such games as bridge, whist, poker, or cribbage. It is also illegal (subject to one or two exceptions) to game when a charge is made for the gaming or a levy is charged on the winnings. Gaming in any street or any place to which the public has access is illegal, except for dominoes, cribbage, or any game specially authorized in a pub (provided the participants are over 18). If the premises are controlled (either by the grant of a licence or by registration as a gaming club), the restrictions applying to uncontrolled premises apply unless they have been permitted by regulation. Thus casino-type games may be played on controlled premises for commercial profit if permission has been obtained, but only by members of licensed or registered clubs and their guests. There are also restrictions relating to playing on Sundays, and no one under 18 may be present when gaming takes place. It is illegal to use, sell, or maintain gaming machines without a certificate or *licence.

When the Gaming Act 2005 comes into force gaming will be defined as playing a game of chance for a prize. A 'game of chance' includes: a game that involves both an element of chance and an element of skill; a game that involves an element of chance that can be eliminated by superlative skill; and a game that is presented as involving an element of chance. It does not include a sport.

gaming contract A contract involving the playing of a game of chance by any number of people for money or money's worth. A **wagering contract** is one involving two parties only, each of whom stands to win or lose something of value according to the result of some future event (e.g. a horse race) or to which of them is correct about some past or present fact; neither party can have any interest in the contract except his stake. In general, gaming and wagering contracts are by statute null and void and no action can be brought to recover any money paid or won under them.

garnishee A person who has been warned by a court to pay a *debt to a third party rather than to his *creditor. *See* GARNISHEE PROCEEDINGS.

garnishee proceedings A procedure by which a judgment creditor may obtain a court order against a third party who owes money to, or holds money on behalf of, the judgment debtor. The order requires the third party to pay the money (or part of it) to the judgment creditor. For example, if the judgment debtor has £1000 in a bank account and judgment has been entered against him for £500, the court may order the bank to pay £500 direct to the judgment creditor.

garrotte To strangle by means of a ligature. It was at one time used as a means of judicial execution in Spain.

gastric Relating to the stomach.

gastrointestinal Relating to the digestive system.

gearing The ratio between debt capital plus borrowing and the equity. Small companies that take over larger companies may do so by borrowings secured on the capital value of the company being purchased. This leads to very high gearing. Such companies are very vulnerable particularly if interest rates go up.

GEMAC A mnemonic for the phases of an interview. The key words are Greeting, Explanation, Mutual Activity, and Close.

gender reassignment A physiological and ultimately surgical procedure, under medical supervision, for the purpose of changing a person's sexual characteristics. The process is undertaken by *transsexuals (estimated to number some 5000 in the UK). Initially discrimination in the workplace with respect to a person's sexual orientation or transsexualism was outside the ambit of the Sex Discrimination Act 1975. The definition of sex within that Act referred to discrimination on grounds of biological gender and hence covered discrimination only between men and women. As a result of a series of test cases taken before both the *European Court of Justice and the *European Court of Human Rights, the UK Sex Discrimination Act must now be construed to include both sexual orientation and transsexualism within its definition. However, with respect to transsexualism, as gender reassignment is an ongoing process, it was necessary to introduce supporting regulations, to clarify the protections to be given at the workplace to a transsexual undergoing this process. The Sex Discrimination (Gender Reassignment) Regulations 1999 (SI 1999/1102) bring UK law into line with the decision of the ECJ in *P v S and Cornwall County Council* [1996] ECR I-2143, the case in which discrimination on grounds of gender reassignment was ruled to be contrary to *European Community law.

The Regulations provide protection against discrimination by *employers at all stages of the reassignment process, starting when an individual indicates an intention to begin reassignment. The Regulations also cover recruitment procedures, vocational training, and discrimination with respect to pay (*see* EQUAL PAY). The Sex Discrimination Act as amended by the Regulations outlaws direct discrimination and provides for *employees who are absent from work to undergo treatment to be treated no less favourably than they would be if the absence was due to sickness or personal injury. The protection is extended to post-operative treatment on a transsexual's return to work. A defence to a claim of unlawful treatment is also provided in relation to the employment in question, if being a man or woman is a genuine occupational qualification for the job. This could arise, for example, if an employee recruited to a sex-specific post begins the gender reassignment process, or if the job involves the holder of the post to perform intimate physical body searches, or if the nature or location of the establishment makes it impracticable for the holder of the job to live elsewhere than on the *premises provided by the employer and the issue of decency and privacy must be taken into consideration.

The Department for Work and Pensions (formerly Employment) has produced a guide to the implementation of these Regulations. It offers further assistance to employers on such issues as: whether or not an employee should be redeployed following treatment, the amount of time off necessary for surgical procedures, and the expected point or phase of change of name and personal details and the required amendments to records and systems. Further assistance given relates to confidentiality issues: informing line managers, colleagues, and clients. The guide also offers advice on agreeing a procedure between the employee and employer regarding a changing in dress code and agreeing when individuals will start using single-sex facilities at the workplace in their new gender.

Under the Sexual Offences Act 2003 the definition of penis includes a part surgically reconstructed, in particular through gender reassignment therapy. Thus female to male transsexuals can commit *rape. Similarly surgically constructed vaginae are such for the purposes of rape or penetrative assault.

gene A piece of *DNA in a chromosome in a cell which controls a particular inherited feature.

general and special damages A classification of *damages awarded for a *tort or a *breach of contract, the meaning of which varies according to the context. **1.** General damages are given for losses that the law will presume are the natural and probable consequence of a wrong. Thus it is assumed that a *libel is likely to injure the reputation of the person libelled, and damages can be recovered without proof that the claimant's reputation has in fact suffered. Special damages are given for losses that are not presumed but have been specifically proved. **2.** General damages may also mean damages given for a loss that is incapable of precise estimation, such as *pain and suffering or loss of *reputation. In this context special damages are damages given for losses that can be quantified, such as out-of-pocket expenses or earnings lost during the period between the injury and the hearing of the action.

General Assembly (of the UN) *See* UNITED NATIONS.

general defences *Common-law defences to any common-law or statutory crimes; with one exception (*insanity), these defences relate to *involuntary conduct. A defendant should be acquitted when the *magistrates or *jury have a reasonable doubt as to whether he was entitled to a general defence. By contrast, **special defences** are confined to individual offences, are usually of statutory origin, and usually place a *burden of proof on the defendant to show that he acted reasonably. *See also* AUTOMATISM; IMPOSSIBILITY; MISTAKE; SELF-DEFENCE.

general issue A *plea in which every allegation in the opposite party's pleading is denied. In civil proceedings it is no longer permitted. Instead, each allegation must be specifically admitted or denied. In criminal cases the defendant pleads the general issue by pleading *not guilty.

general meeting A meeting of *company members whose decisions can bind the company. Certain **reserved powers**, specified by the Companies Act, can only be exercised by a general meeting. These include alteration of the *memorandum and *articles of association, removal of a *director before his term of office has expired, *alteration of share capital, the appointing of an *auditor other than upon a casual vacancy, and putting the company into *voluntary winding-up. Powers may also be reserved by the articles of association of a particular company. Powers other than reserved powers are usually delegated in the articles to the directors. The general meeting can overrule the directors' decision in relation to these delegated powers by *special resolution, but this will not affect the validity of acts already done; it could also, while exercising reserved powers, dismiss the directors or alter the articles and thus the delegation. General meetings are either *annual general meetings or *extraordinary general meetings. Unless the articles of association provide or the court orders otherwise, at least two company members must be present personally.

general participation clause A clause in the *Hague Conventions of 1899 and 1907. The clause, concerning the conduct of hostilities, stipulates that the Conventions shall be binding upon the belligerents only so long as all belligerents are parties to the Convention. The effect of this clause was to significantly weaken the effectiveness of the Hague Convention rules.

general power of investment A power, introduced by the Trustee Act 2000, that allows a *trustee to make any kind of investment that he could make if he were absolutely entitled to the *assets of the trust fund. Previously, trustees were only permitted to make certain authorized investments. This much wider general power of investment may be expressly excluded in the trust instrument. There are still some restrictions on investments in *land. In exercising the general power of investment, the trustees are required by the Act to consider criteria relating to the suitability of the proposed investment to the trust and the need for diversification of investment within the unique circumstances of the trust. Trustees are also required by the Act to review the investments from time to time with the same standard criteria in mind. Before investing, the trustee must obtain and consider proper advice, unless he reasonably considers it unnecessary or inappropriate to do so.

general principles of law According to the Statute of the *International Court of Justice, the source for rules of *international law can be found in what it terms 'General Principles of Law'. The majority of Western jurists consider that these principles should be based on those underlying the municipal legal systems of civilized states, especially those of Europe and the USA. These jurists also consider the general principles to be a law-creating source that is independent of either *treaties or *custom. Due to their possible bias towards certain Western capitalist countries, these propositions have proved highly contentious in the Third World and Socialist countries, which have endeavoured to limit the scope of the principles.

general safety requirement A standard of safety that *consumer goods must meet in order to comply with the Consumer Protection Act 1987 and the General Product Safety Regulations 1994 (SI 1994/2328). The *goods are required to be reasonably safe having regard to all the circumstances, e.g. the way the goods are marketed, including any instructions or warnings about their use; their compliance with published safety standards for goods of that kind; and whether reasonable steps could be taken to make them safer. Suppliers of consumer goods who fail to meet the safety requirement commit an offence.

general verdict **1.** (in a civil case) A *verdict that is entirely in favour of one or other party. **2.** (in a criminal case) A verdict either of *guilty or *not guilty. *Compare* SPECIAL VERDICT.

genetic fingerprinting *See* DNA FINGERPRINTING.

Geneva Conventions A series of international *conventions on the laws of war, the first of which was formulated in Geneva in 1864. The 1864 and 1906 Conventions protect sick and wounded soldiers; the Geneva Protocol of 1925 prohibits the use of gas and bacteriological warfare; the three Conventions of 1929 and the four Conventions of 1949 protect sick and wounded soldiers, sailors, and prisoners of war, and the 1949 Conventions protect, in addition, certain groups of civilians. The First Protocol of 1977 supplements the 1949 Conventions, extending protection to wider groups of civilians, regulating the law of bombing, and enlarging the category of wars subject to the 1949 Conventions (to include, for example, civil wars). The 1949 Conventions are accepted by many states and are generally considered to embody customary *international law that relates to war. Grave breaches of the Conventions are the subject of universal jurisdiction giving any country the right to punish grave breaches regardless of where the crime was committed or the *nationality of the perpetrator or victim. *See also* HAGUE CONVENTIONS; MARTENS CLAUSE.

genocide Conduct aimed at the destruction of a national, ethnic, racial, or religious group. Genocide, as defined in the United Nations Convention on the Prevention and Punishment of the Crime of Genocide 1948, includes not only killing members of the group, but also causing them serious physical or psychological harm, imposing conditions of life that are intended to destroy them physically or measures intended to prevent childbirth, or forcibly transferring children of the group to another group, if these acts are carried out with the intention of destroying the group as a whole or in part. Destruction of a cultural or political group does not amount to genocide. The Genocide Convention 1948 declares that genocide is an international crime; the parties to the Convention undertake to punish not only acts of genocide committed within their *jurisdiction but also complicity in genocide and *conspiracy, *incitement, and attempts to commit genocide. The Convention has been enacted into English law by the Genocide Act 1969. It is generally considered that the Convention embodies principles of customary *international law that bind all nations, including those that are not parties to the Convention. Genocide is an offence under the Statute of the *International Criminal Court. *See also* WAR CRIMES; HUMANITARIAN INTERVENTION.

geographic profiling An investigative methodology used in the investigation of series crimes which uses analysis of the crime sites to determine the most probable location of the offender's residence. *See also* DRAGNET.

ghet A Jewish religious *divorce, executed by the husband delivering a bill of divorce (which must be handwritten according to specific detailed rules) to his wife in the presence of two witnesses. In theory a ghet does not require a court procedure, but in practice it is usually executed through a court because of the many complexities of the relevant religious law. Under s 1 of the Divorce (Religious Marriages) Act 2002, on the application of either party, the court may order that a decree of divorce is not to be made absolute until a declaration made by both parties that they have taken such steps as are required to dissolve the marriage in accordance with those usages is produced to the court. *See also* EXTRAJUDICIAL DIVORCE.

Ghosh test The test for *dishonesty in *theft. Following the decision in *R v Ghosh* [1982] 2 All ER 689 the *jury should if necessary be directed to apply a two part test. First, was what the defendant did dishonest by the ordinary standards of reasonable honest people; and, if so, did the defendant realise that what he did was dishonest by those (rather than his own) standards.

gift A gratuitous transfer or grant of property.

gipsy (gypsy) A person of a nomadic way of life with no fixed abode. Formerly, *local authorities had a duty to provide sites for gipsies resorting to their areas. (The strict definition of gipsy as a member of the Romany race did not apply for this purpose, but the term did not include travelling showmen or New Age travellers.) Under the Criminal Justice and Public Order Act 1994 this duty is abolished, although local authorities may provide sites if they wish. *See also* TRESPASS; UNAUTHORIZED CAMPING.

Glasgow Coma Scale (GCS) A way of describing levels of consciousness by testing eye opening, verbal response, and movement. The highest score (fully awake) is 15 and the lowest 3.

glue sniffing *See* INTOXICATION.

going public The process of forming a *public company or of reregistering a *private company as a public company.

golden handshake A payment, usually very large, made to a *director or other senior executive who is forced to retire before the expiry of an employment contract (e.g. because of a takeover or merger) as compensation for loss of office. It is made when a contract does not allow payment in lieu of notice. Part of the payment may be tax-free.

golden hello A lump-sum payment to entice an *employee of senior level to join a new *employer. Whether or not the payment is tax-free depends on the nature of the payment.

golden rule *See* INTERPRETATION OF STATUTES.

golden share *See* SHARE.

good behaviour A term used in an order by a *magistrate or by a *Crown Court upon *sentencing. The person named in the order should 'be of good behaviour' towards another person (the *complainant). The court may order that the person named enter into a *recognizance, and if he does not comply with the order he may be imprisoned for up to six months. The procedure may be used against anyone who has been brought before the court if there is a fear that he may cause a *breach of the peace or if he is the subject of a complaint by someone (which need not be based on the commission of a criminal offence).

good faith Honesty. An act carried out in good faith is one carried out honestly. Good faith is implied by law into certain contracts, such as those relating to commercial agency. *See also* UBERRIMAE FIDEI.

good offices A technique of peaceful settlement of an international dispute, in which a third party, acting with the consent of the disputing states, serves as a friendly intermediary in an effort to persuade them to negotiate between themselves without necessarily offering the disputing states substantive suggestions towards achieving a settlement. *See also* CONCILIATION; MEDIATION.

goods Personal *chattels or items of *property. *Land is excluded, and the statutory definition in the Sale of Goods Act 1979 also excludes *choses in action and money. It includes emblements and things attached to or forming part of land that are agreed to be severed before sale or under a contract of sale.

goods vehicle A *motor vehicle or *trailer constructed or adapted for use for the carriage or haulage of *goods or burden of any description (reg 3(2), Road Vehicles (Construction and Use) Regulations 1986 (SI 1986/1078)).

goodwill The advantage arising from the *reputation and trade connections of a business, in particular the likelihood that existing customers will continue to patronize it. Goodwill is a substantial item to be taken into account on the sale of a business; it may need to be protected by prohibiting the vendor from setting up in the same business for a stated period in competition with the business he has sold.

government circulars *Documents circulated by government departments on behalf of ministers, setting out principles and practices for the exercise of ministerial powers delegated to others. These may provide mere administrative guidelines or they may be intended to have legislative effect (i.e. as *delegated legislation), in which case any purported exercise of the delegated powers is invalid unless it complies with them. *See* ULTRA VIRES.

Government Communications Headquarters (GCHQ) An intelligence and security organization that reports to the Foreign Secretary and works closely with the UK's other intelligence agencies (commonly known as MI5 and MI6). Its primary customers are the Ministry of Defence, the Foreign and Commonwealth Office, and law enforcement authorities, but it also serves a wide range of other government departments. It has two missions: signals intelligence (Sigint) and Information Assurance. **Sigint** work protects the vital interests of the nation: GCHQ provides information to support government decision-making in the fields of national security, military operations, and law enforcement. The intelligence it provides is concerned largely with *terrorism and also contributes to the prevention of serious crime. **Information Assurance** helps keep the government communication and information systems safe from *hackers and other threats. It also helps those responsible for the UK's critical national infrastructure (power, water, communications, etc.) to keep their networks safe from interference and disruption.

government department An organ of central government responsible for a particular sphere of public administration (e.g. the Treasury). It is staffed by permanent civil servants and is normally headed by a minister who is politically responsible for its activities and is assisted by one or more junior ministers, usually responsible for particular aspects of departmental policy.

government-in-exile A government established outside its territorial *jurisdiction. Following the German defeat of Poland in 1939, the Polish government transferred its operations to London and thereby became a government-in-exile.

grant 1. The creation or transfer of the ownership of property (e.g. an estate or interest in *land) by written instrument; e.g. the grant of a lease. **2.** A *grant of representation. **3.** The allocation of money, powers, etc., by *Parliament or the *Crown for a specific purpose.

g

grants in aid Central government grants towards *local authority expenditure, comprising specific grants for particular services (e.g. the police) and rate support grants to augment income generally.

granulation tissue The tissue that grows during repair of injuries in the skin.

grave An excavation in the ground where a body is buried.

Gray's Inn One of the four *Inns of Court, situated in Holborn. The earliest claims for its existence are *c*.1320.

Greater London A local government area consisting of the 32 **London boroughs** (12 inner and 20 outer), the *City of London, and the Inner and Middle Temples. A Greater London Council was established by the Local Government Act 1972 but abolished by the Local Government Act 1985 with effect from 1 April 1986. London borough councils, which are unitary (single-tier) authorities, are elected every fourth year, counting from 1982 (*see also* LOCAL AUTHORITY). In 1998 Londoners voted in favour of government proposals to elect a Mayor of London and a *London Assembly to operate from 2000; the Greater London Authority Act 1999 enacted these proposals (*see also* GREATER LONDON AUTHORITY). The City of London is distinct in both constitution and functions. The Temples have limited independent functions (e.g. public health), but are administered in many respects by the City's Common Council.

Greater London Authority A body created by the Greater London Authority Act 1999 and consisting of the Mayor of London and the *London Assembly. Its principal purposes are to promote economic development and wealth creation, social development, and the improvement of the environment in Greater London. The London Development Agency was created to further the first of these aims.

green paper *See* COMMAND PAPERS.

grievous bodily harm (GBH) Serious injury which can be either physical or psychiatric. Under the Offences Against the Person Act 1861 there are several offences involving grievous bodily harm. Under s 20, it is an offence, punishable by up to five years' imprisonment, to wound or inflict (by direct or indirect acts) grievous bodily harm upon anyone intending or being reckless as to whether some harm (albeit slight) might be caused. Under s 18 of the Act, it is an offence, punishable by a maximum sentence of *life imprisonment, to wound or cause grievous bodily harm to anyone with the intention of causing grievous bodily harm or of resisting or preventing lawful *arrest. 'Causing' in this offence includes indirect acts, such as pulling a chair away from a person so that he falls and breaks his arm. If a person intends to cause grievous bodily harm but his victim actually dies, he is guilty of *murder, even though he did not intend to kill him. Causing grievous bodily harm may also be an element in some other offence, e.g. *burglary. The courts have held that 'grievous bodily harm' means quite simply 'serious harm'. What amounts to grievous bodily harm for the purposes of charging the offences is laid down in the *charging standards. *See also* WOUNDING WITH INTENT.

gross indecency A sexual act that may include masturbation, indecent physical contact, or even indecent behaviour without any physical contact. Prior to the enactment of the Sexual Offences Act 2003, it was an offence for a man to commit an act of gross indecency with another man unless both parties were over 18, consented to the act, and it was carried out in private.

gross negligence A high degree of *negligence, manifested in behaviour substantially worse than that of the average reasonable man. Causing someone's death through gross negligence is a form of *manslaughter if the accused's conduct fell well below acceptable standards (*see R v Adomako* [1995] 1 AC 171).

ground penetrating radar (GPR) A technique for finding buried bodies or objects by transmitting a short pulse of electromagnetic energy into the ground and analyzing the reflected signal.

group accounts *Accounts required by law to be prepared by a *registered company that has a *subsidiary company. Group accounts deal with the financial position of the company and its subsidiaries collectively.

group action A procedure in which a large number of claims arising out of the same event, or against the same defendant, are dealt with together (e.g. proceedings by the victims of a plane crash for *damages for personal injury). The court exercises more direct control over the *interim (interlocutory) proceedings in such cases than is normal.

group identification An identification procedure where a suspect is viewed by a witness while amongst a group of people in an informal setting. It may be held if a suspect refuses to participate in a formal identification procedure or one is impracticable. The procedure is regulated under PACE Code of Practice D.

guarantee 1. A secondary agreement in which a person (the **guarantor**) is liable for the *debt or default of another (the principal debtor), who is the party primarily liable for the debt. A guarantee requires an independent *consideration and must be evidenced in writing. A guarantor who has paid out on his guarantee has a right to be indemnified by the principal debtor. *Compare* INDEMNITY. **2.** *See* WARRANTY.

guarantee company *See* LIMITED COMPANY.

guard dog A dog kept specifically for the purpose of protecting people, property, or someone who is guarding people or property. Under the Guard Dogs Act 1975 it is a summary offence punishable by fine to use a guard dog, or to allow its use, unless either it is secured and cannot roam the *premises freely or a handler is controlling it. The Act does not, however, affect civil liability for injuries or damage caused by the dog, which depends on the law of *tort. In some cases the owner may be criminally liable for injury caused by a guard dog; e.g. if it kills someone, the owner may be guilty of *manslaughter by gross negligence or of constructive manslaughter. *See also* CLASSIFICATION OF ANIMALS.

guardian One who is formally appointed to look after a child's interests when the *parents of the child do not have *parental responsibility for him or have died. Appointment can be made either by the courts during *family proceedings, if it is considered necessary for the child's welfare, or privately by any parent with parental responsibility. Under the Children Act 1989 a private appointment does not have to be by deed or will but merely made in writing, dated, and signed by the person making it. A guardian automatically assumes parental responsibility for the child.

guardian *ad litem* *See* CHILDREN'S GUARDIAN.

guardianship order An order, made under the Mental Health Act 1983, placing a person over the age of 16 who has been convicted of an offence and who is suffering from any of certain types of mental illness under the guardianship of a local social services authority or an approved person. It has been proposed by the *Law Commission that it should no longer be possible to appoint an individual as *guardian.

guillotine A *House of Commons procedure for speeding up the passing of *legislation: a means whereby government can control the parliamentary timetable and limit debate. The number of days allowed for a *Bill's Committee and Report stages is limited by an allocation-of-time order moved by the government; the total time available is then allotted between particular portions of the Bill. When the time limit for any portion is reached, debate on it ceases and all outstanding votes are taken forthwith.

guilty 1. An admission in court by an accused person that he has committed the offence with which he is charged. If there is more than one charge he may plead guilty to some and *not guilty to others. **2.** A *verdict finding that the accused has committed the offence with which he was charged or some other offence of which he can be convicted on the basis of the evidence in the case. *See also* CONVICTION.

g

guilty knowledge The knowledge of facts or circumstances required for a person to have **mens rea* for a particular crime. Knowledge is usually actual knowledge, but when a person deliberately ignores facts that are obvious, he is sometimes considered to have 'constructive' knowledge.

guilty mind *See* MENS REA.

gunboat diplomacy The settling of disputes with weaker states by the threat of *use of force. The phrase derives from the Victorian colonial empire, in which gunboats and other naval vessels were often utilized in order to coerce local rulers to accept the terms and trade of British merchants.

gynaecology Branch of medicine dealing with the female genital tract.

gypsy *See* GIPSY.

habeas corpus A prerogative *writ used to challenge the validity of a person's *detention, either in official *custody (e.g. when held pending *deportation or *extradition) or in private hands. Deriving from the *royal prerogative and therefore originally obtained by petitioning the sovereign, it is now issued by the Divisional Court of the *Queen's Bench Division, or, during vacation, by any *High Court *judge. If on an application for the writ the court or judge is satisfied that the detention is prima facie unlawful, the custodian is ordered to appear and justify it, failing which release is ordered.

hacking A deliberate, unauthorized intrusion into a *computer, computer network, or communications system. Generally the term is confined to *nuisance attacks or the acquisition of information, rather than serious, malicious assaults. Offenders include disgruntled *employees, computer enthusiasts treating the medium as a challenge, and those engaged in industrial espionage and information warfare. Gaining unauthorized access to either a single computer or to a computer system is a *summary offence under the Computer Misuse Act 1990. Under this Act it is also an offence, triable summarily or on *indictment, to engage in hacking with the intention of committing another offence (e.g. *theft, diverting funds), or to destroy, corrupt, or modify computer-stored information or programs while hacking. *See also* CRACKING; DATA PROTECTION; PHARMING; PHREAKING.

haematoma A collection of blood outside a blood vessel and in the tissues (bruise).

haemoglobin A chemical contained in the red cells in the blood to which oxygen attaches to be carried round the body. The chemical even more readily attracts carbon monoxide. This gives the red cells a brighter colour, which accounts for the cherry red skin colour of people suffering from carbon monoxide poisoning. Congenital defects such as sickle cell disease can occur and cause abnormality of the cell functioning.

haemopericardium The presence of blood in the *pericardial cavity which surrounds the heart. If too much blood enters the pericardial cavity it can stop the heart beating (a cardiac tamponade) because the blood is, as all liquids are, incompressible. It is often seen where the victim has been stabbed in the chest and the knife has entered the pericardial cavity.

haemophilia An hereditary disease almost exclusively of men which prevents blood from clotting and causes abnormal bleeding. There may be problems in taking blood samples from sufferers and urgent medical attention should be sought for a sufferer who is bleeding.

haemoptysis The coughing up of blood or blood-stained sputum. Haemoptysis is usually frothy, alkaline, and bright red.

haemorrhage The escape of blood from blood vessels—bleeding.

haemothorax The presence of blood in the chest cavity. Often caused by stab wounds to the chest or injury to the chest caused in a road traffic collision.

Hague Conventions The Hague Conventions for the Pacific Settlement of International Disputes: a series of international conventions on the laws of *war (three in 1899 and thirteen in 1907). The 1899 Conventions established a Permanent Court of Arbitration, which was active before the Permanent Court of International Justice and the *International Court of Justice functioned. The Hague Conventions are still in force but their provisions are often inapplicable to modern warfare. *See also* GENERAL PARTICIPATION CLAUSE; GENEVA CONVENTIONS; MARTENS CLAUSE.

Hague Rules *See* BILL OF LADING; INTERNATIONAL CARRIAGE.

half blood *See* CONSANGUINITY.

hallucinogenic drugs *See* PSYCHOTROPHIC DRUGS.

Hamburg Rules *See* BILL OF LADING; INTERNATIONAL CARRIAGE.

hammer In a *firearm, a device that strikes the *firing pin or *cartridge primer to detonate the powder.

handgun A *pistol or *revolver. *See also* FIREARM.

h

handling stolen goods Dishonestly receiving *goods that one knows or believes to be stolen or undertaking, arranging, or assisting someone to retain, remove, or dispose of stolen goods. Under s 22 of the Theft Act 1968, this is an offence subject to a maximum sentence of fourteen years' imprisonment. 'Stolen goods' include not only goods that have been the subject of *theft but also anything that has been obtained by *blackmail or *deception. The theft or other crime may have occurred at any time and anywhere in the world, provided the handling occurs in England or Wales. There is also a provision to extend the concept of stolen goods to the proceeds of their sale. Thus if A steals goods, sells them for £3000, and gives part of the money to B, B is *guilty of handling if he knows the money represents the proceeds of the sale of stolen goods. If A then buys a car with the rest of the £3000 and C agrees to dispose of the car for A, knowing or believing that it was bought with the proceeds of sale of stolen goods, C will also be *guilty of handling, since he has 'undertaken to dispose of stolen goods'. The crime is therefore very widely defined; it also covers, for instance, forging or providing new *documents and number plates for stolen cars and contacting and negotiating with dealers in stolen property (fences). *See also* DISHONESTY.

hang To strangle with a ligature where the pressure is applied to the neck by the weight of the body. Hanging occurs accidentally in cases of *autoeroticism where the person seeks to obtain enhanced sexual pleasure by restricting the blood supply to the brain but slips and the hanging causes death. In these cases a polythene bag is often placed over the head and there are frequently signs that the person has been masturbating.

Hansard The name by which the Official Report of Parliamentary Debates is customarily referred to (after the Hansard family, who—as printers to the *House of Commons—were concerned with compiling reports in the 19th century). Reporting was taken over by the Government in 1908, and separate reports for the House of Commons and the *House of Lords are published by the Stationery Office in daily and weekly parts. They contain a verbatim record of debates and all other proceedings (e.g. question time). *Members of Parliament have the right to correct anything attributed to them, but may not make any other alterations. In certain circumstances Hansard may be used to discover the will of *Parliament, as an aid to judicial statutory interpretation when *legislation is unclear. *Compare* JOURNALS.

harassment 1. Words, conduct, or other actions, generally repeated or persistent and directed at a specific person, that tend to annoy or cause harassment, alarm, or distress to another person. A person who harasses another may incur liability for a tort or a variety of criminal offences. The Protection from Harassment Act 1997 (as amended by the Domestic Violence, Crime and Victims Act 2004 and the Serious Organized Crime and Police Act 2005) creates a statutory *tort of harassment (s 3) and two criminal offences (s 2 and s 4). Section 1 prohibits a person from pursuing a course of conduct (i.e. conduct on more than one occasion) which amounts to the harassment of another and which he knows or ought to know amounts to harassment of the other. The term is not defined, although s 7 provides that it includes causing a person alarm or distress. The more serious s 4 offence is committed where fear of violence was caused on at least two occasions. Sections 5 and 5A allow criminal courts to impose *restraining orders on defendants who have been convicted of criminal harassment offences or on those acquitted of such offences where it is necessary to do so to prevent another from harassment by him. Breach of a restraining order or an *injunction imposed under s 3 are imprisonable offences. **2.** It is an offence under s 5 of the Public Order Act 1986 to use disorderly, threatening, abusive or insulting words or behaviour, or display any writing, sign, or other visible representation which is threatening, abusive, or insulting and there by cause any person harassment, alarm, or distress. A more serious offence of intentionally causing harassment, alarm, or distress (s 4A) was inserted into the 1986 Act by the Criminal Justice and Public Order Act 1994. Both offences may be committed in a public or private place (with certain exceptions relating to a dwelling). Section 31 of the Crime and Disorder Act 1998 provides racially or religiously aggravated versions of both offences. **3.** Where someone is being harassed by a person they are married to or have been married to, by a former cohabitant, by a relative or if they have a child in common or have lived in the same household for a period then they are regarded as 'associated persons' and can obtain 'non-molestation orders' under ss 42 to 63 of the Family Law Act 1996. Courts can attach a power of *arrest to these orders, so allowing the police to enforce them.

See also ACCEPTABLE BEHAVIOUR CONTRACT; ANTI-SOCIAL BEHAVIOUR ORDER; HARASSMENT OF A PERSON IN HIS HOME; HARASSMENT OF DEBTORS; HARASSMENT OF OCCUPIER; NUISANCE NEIGHBOURS; STALKING; THREATENING BEHAVIOUR.

harassment of a person in his home Behaviour by a person in another person's home which is intended to persuade the resident not do something that he is entitled or required to do or to do something that he is not obliged to do. Under s 42 of the Criminal Justice and Police Act 2001, a police *constable has the power to direct a person to move away from another person's home if that person is present for the purpose of *harassment. The section was amended by the Serious Organized Crime and Police Act 2005 so as to make it an offence for a person, where he is subject to a direction to leave the vicinity, to return within a specified period of up to three months. The 2005 Act also inserts a new s 42A to criminalize behaviour of broadly the same kind as that which currently enables the police to issue a direction under s 42.

harassment of debtors Behaviour designed to force a *debtor or one believed to be a debtor to pay his debt. This is a criminal offence under s 40 of the Administration of Justice Act 1970 and is punishable by *fine, if the debt is based on a contract and the nature or frequency of the acts subject the debtor (or members of his household) to alarm, distress, or humiliation. Harassment also includes false statements that the debtor will face criminal proceedings or that the *creditor is officially authorized to enforce payment, and using a *document that the creditor falsely represents as being official. The offence may overlap with the crime of *blackmail, but it will also cover cases in which the creditor believes he is entitled to act as he does (which might not amount to blackmail).

harassment of occupier The offence of a *landlord (or his agent) using or threatening violence or any other kind of pressure to obtain possession of his property from a *tenant (the residential occupier) without a court order. The offence is found in s 1 of the Protection from Eviction Act 1977 and includes interfering with the tenant's peace or comfort (or that of the tenant's household), withdrawing or not providing services normally required by the tenant (e. g. cutting off gas or electricity, even when the bills have not been paid), and preventing the tenant from exercising any of his rights or taking any legal or other action in respect of his *tenancy. The Act does not apply, however, to a displaced residential owner, as opposed to a landlord (*see also* FORCIBLE ENTRY). *See also* HARASSMENT; NUISANCE NEIGHBOURS.

harbouring Hiding a criminal or suspected criminal. This will normally constitute the offence of *impeding apprehension or prosecution. *See also* ESCAPE.

Hare Psychopathy Checklist—Revised (PCL-R) A means of measuring severe personality disorders and delivering a numerical score.

h

harmonization of laws The process by which member states of the *European Union make changes in their national laws, in accordance with *Community legislation, to produce uniformity, particularly relating to commercial matters of common interest. The *Council of Europe has, for example, issued directives on the harmonization of company law and of units of measurement. *Compare* APPROXIMATION OF LAWS.

hate crime A lay term for criminal acts that are motivated by hatred of the victims on the basis of their race, religion, or sexual orientation.

h

hawala An underground banking system based on trust which enables money to be made available internationally without the physical transfer of funds. In its most basic variant, the transferor lodges a sum of money with a hawala broker (known as a **hawaladar**) who then contacts another broker in the recipient's location with instructions for the disposition of the funds (less a small commission), promising to settle the debt at a later date. The unique feature of the system is that no promissory instruments are exchanged between the hawala brokers and no records are produced of individual transactions; only a running tally of the amount owed one broker by the other is kept. Settlements of debts between hawala brokers can take a variety of forms, and need not take the form of direct cash transactions. The system is extensively used by *terrorists to fund operations and by organized criminal groups to launder the *proceeds of crime.

hawaladar *See* HAWALA.

headings Words prefixed to sections of a statute. They are treated in the same way as *preambles and may be used to assist in resolving an ambiguity.

heads of state, immunity The freedom, under customary *international law, of heads of state, heads of government, and ministers from criminal jurisdiction for public and private acts committed while in office or before. (See *The Arrest Warrant of 11 April 2000 (Democratic Republic of Congo v Belgium)*, ICJ Reports, 2002). The position after they have left office is not quite so clear. The *Arrest Warrant* case suggests that they have immunity for public acts done whilst in office. However, if a head of state or minister ordered *torture while in office he would be liable under the Torture Convention. In the case of the former president of Chile, General Pinochet, the House of Lords decided that he had no immunity to prevent him being *extradited for torture charges relating to matters while he was in office.

Health and Safety Commission (HSC) A body responsible for furthering the general purposes of the Health and Safety at Work Act 1974, e.g. by advising and promoting research and training. It also appoints a Health and Safety Executive, which shares with *local authorities responsibility for enforcing the Act and operates for this purpose through such inspectorates as the Factories and Nuclear Installations Inspectorates. *See also* SAFETY AT WORK.

Health and Safety Executive (HSE) A body responsible for health and safety in many industries including nuclear installations, mines, factories, farms, hospitals, schools, offshore gas and oil installations, the gas grid, the movement of dangerous *goods and substances, and railways for the benefit of the workers in those industries and the public who are affected by them. The HSE is a prosecuting authority for offences breaching health and safety laws. *Local authorities are responsible to HSE for enforcement in offices, shops, and other parts of the services sector.

health records Records kept by the National Health Service about patients. Under the Access to Health Records Act 1990, from 1 November 1991 most patients were given the right to see their health records. The patient does not have to give a reason for wanting access and can authorize someone else, such as his *solicitor, to obtain access on his behalf. It is a policy of the Department of Health that individuals are permitted to see what has been written about them and that health-care providers should make arrangements to allow patients to see, if they wish, records other than those covered by the 1990 Act. This Act has been amended by the Data Protection Act 1998 (*see also* DATA PROTECTION).

hearing The *trial of a case before a court. Hearings are usually in public but the public may be barred from the court in certain circumstances (*see* IN CAMERA).

Hearing Officer An officer of the *European Court of Justice whose role was established in 1982 after criticism of the administrative nature of the decision-making process of the Commission in competition law cases. His terms of reference were published in the Commission's XXth Report on Competition Policy. He organizes and chairs hearings, decides the date, duration, and place of hearings, seeks to ensure protection of the interests of defendants, and supervises the preparation of minutes of hearings. He will, in addition, prepare his own report of a hearing and make recommendations as to the future conduct of the matter.

hearsay evidence Evidence of the statements of a person other than the witness who is testifying and statements in *documents adduced to prove the truth of what is asserted in the oral statement or document. The mischief of hearsay evidence lies in the inherent danger of unreliability through repetition and the fact that the demeanour of the person who made the original assertion cannot be assessed and nor can he be challenged in *cross-examination. Accordingly, at *common law such evidence was generally held to be inadmissible (the **rule against hearsay**) other than in exceptional circumstances: e.g. *dying declarations, *declarations of deceased persons, *recent complaint, evidence given in former *trials, *depositions, *admissions, and *confessions. In civil cases, the Civil Evidence Act 1995 abolished the rule against hearsay. The 1995 Act provides that what in civil litigation would formerly have been called 'hearsay evidence' may be used when a notice of the intention to rely on that evidence is given. It is for the court to decide at trial what weight to put on any particular evidence, whether it is hearsay or not. Statutory intervention has also served to relax the rule in criminal cases in the belief that tribunals of fact 'should be trusted to give appropriate evidence the weight it deserves when they exercise their judgement' (*Justice for All* (2002) Cm 5563). In criminal cases, ch 2 of the Criminal Justice Act 2003 expressly preserves certain common law categories of admissibility of hearsay evidence (s 118) but also provides (s 114) for such evidence to be admissible, subject to the court's general discretion to exclude it (s 126) if: all parties to the proceedings agree to its admission; or the court is satisfied that it is in the interests of justice for it to be admissible; or if the evidence falls within one of the categories of admissibility (sometimes called 'gateways') provided under the Act. The principle gateways of admissibility relate to cases where a witness is unavailable (s 116) and business and other documents (s 117, replacing similar provisions introduced by the Criminal Justice Act 1988). Additional requirements limiting the admissibility of multiple hearsay (i.e. when evidence contains at least two separate out-of-court statements, each of which is offered for its truth) are laid down in s 121 of the 2003 Act. A party wanting to adduce hearsay evidence in criminal proceedings must comply with the notice requirements laid down in pt 34 of the *Criminal Procedure Rules. *See also* ADMISSIBILITY OF RECORDS.

heavy motor car A *mechanically propelled vehicle, not being a *locomotive, a *motor tractor, or a motor car, which is constructed itself to carry a load or passengers and the weight which unladen exceeds 2 540 kg (reg 3(2), Road Vehicles (Construction and Use) Regulations 1986 (SI 1986/1078)).

hedge, high A row of two or more trees or shrubs exclusively or mostly evergreen or semi-evergreen which are more than two metres high. If a 'high hedge' because of its height spoils reasonable enjoyment of neighbouring domestic *land because it restricts access to that land or forms a barrier to light then action can be taken under pt 8 of the Anti-social Behaviour Act 2003 to have it lowered.

hedgerow A row of shrubs or small trees bordering a field or lane. Hedging of ancient origin is protected under the

Hedgerow Regulations 1997. Farmers are required to notify local authorities of their intention to uproot a hedgerow, allowing time for a protection order to be issued; the notification period is currently 42 days. Failure to comply with the regulations is punishable by an unlimited fine.

help at court *See* COMMUNITY LEGAL SERVICE.

hereditament (historically) Any *real property capable of being passed to an heir. **Corporeal hereditaments** are tangible items of property, such as *land and buildings. **Incorporeal hereditaments** are intangible rights in land, such as *easements and *profits *à prendre*.

Her Majesty's Revenue and Customs (HMRC) A non-ministerial government department, formed on 18 April 2005 following the merger of the Inland Revenue (IR) and HM Customs and Excise (HMCE). Under the Commissioners for Revenue and Customs Act 2005, the Queen appoints Commissioners who exercise statutory functions on behalf of the Crown and appoint officers of Revenue and Customs, who work under their directions.

The department brings together the direct taxes and other duties that were previously administered by IR and the indirect taxes and customs functions that were dealt with by HMCE. It is responsible for, inter alia, the administration and collection of direct taxes (including income tax, National Insurance, and corporation tax); capital taxes (such as capital gains tax and inheritance tax); indirect taxes (including *value-added tax, insurance premium tax, petroleum revenue tax, excise duties, stamp duty land tax); and environmental taxes such as air passenger duty and the climate change levy. HMRC is also the agency with primary responsibility for import and export controls for *goods and services.

heroin *See* DIAMORPHINE.

hide and die syndrome A pattern of behaviour seen in death from *hypothermia in which the victim hides in a cupboard or other confined space either to seek warmth or because of the confusion caused by hypothermia.

high contracting parties The representatives of states who have signed or ratified a *treaty. From the point of view of *international law it is immaterial where the treaty-making power resides (e.g. in a head of state, a senate, or a representative body): this is a question determinable by the constitutional law of the particular contracting state concerned. Other nations are entitled only to demand from those with whom they contract a *de facto* capacity to bind the society that they represent. The *House of Lords has held that the determination of who the high contracting parties are is to be based upon the terms of the individual treaty in question. Thus the signatories, as well as the parties, can be considered to be high contracting parties.

High Court of Justice A court created by the Judicature Acts 1873–5, forming part of the *Supreme Court of Judicature. Under pt 7 of the *Civil Procedure Rules, which sets out the rules for starting proceedings, the High Court is restricted to (1) personal injury claims of £50000 or more, (2) other claims exceeding £15000, (3) specialist High Court claims that are required to be placed on a specialist list (e.g. the Commercial List), and (4) claims that are required by statute to be commenced in the High Court. The High Court has *appellate jurisdiction in civil and criminal matters. It is divided into the three Divisions: the *Queen's Bench Division, Chancery Division, and *Family Division.

High Potential Development Scheme (HPD) A personal development scheme for *police officers aimed at developing officers with identified high potential for accelerated appointment to senior ranks.

high seas The seas beyond *territorial waters, i.e. the seas more than twelve miles from the coasts of most countries. The English courts have *jurisdiction to try offences committed by anyone anywhere on the high seas in a British *ship. They also have jurisdiction to try offences committed anywhere in the world on board a British-controlled aircraft while it is in flight. Sometimes these offences amount to the special crimes of *hijacking or *piracy.

The high seas as defined by Article 86 of the UN Convention on the Law of the Sea 1982 exclude the exclusive economic zone. However, the freedoms of all states to fly over, navigate, lay submarine cables, etc., in the exclusive economic zone, as stated in the earlier Geneva Convention on the High Seas 1958, have been preserved in Article 58(1) of the UN Convention. *See also* LAW OF THE SEA.

high technology crime A crime which involves the use of information or communications technology. Use of the term varies widely between investigative and prosecution agencies, however the following are generally held to fall within the definition of the term:

- computer intrusions (e.g. malicious *hacking);
- unauthorized modification of data, including destruction of data;
- *denial-of-service (DoS) attacks;
- the creation and distribution of malicious software (e.g. *viruses, *worms, *trojans).

See also COMPUTER FRAUD; CYBERCRIME.

highway A *road or other way over which the public may pass and repass as of right. Highways include *footpaths, *bridle ways, * carriageways, and cul-de-sacs. Navigable rivers are also highways. A highway is created either under statutory powers or by dedication (express or implied) by a landowner and acceptance (by use) by the public. Once a highway has been created, it does not cease to be a highway by reason of disuse. Obstructing a highway is a public nuisance (*see also* OBSTRUCTION), and misuse of the public right to pass and repass over a highway is a trespass against the owner of the subsoil of the highway.

hijacking Seizing or exercising control of an aircraft in flight by the use or threat of force (the term derives from the call 'Hi Jack,' used when illegal alcohol was seized from bootleggers during Prohibition in the USA). Hijacking is prohibited in *international law by the Tokyo Convention 1963, which defines the conditions under which *jurisdiction may be assumed over hijackers, but does not oblige states to exercise such jurisdiction and does not create an obligation to *extradite hijackers. There is also a Hague Convention of 1970 and a Montreal Convention of 1971 creating the offences of unlawfully seizing or exercising control of an aircraft by force or threats and of *sabotaging aircraft; these conventions provide for compulsory jurisdiction as well as extradition. In English law, hijacking and similar offences are governed by the Hijacking Act 1971, the Protection of Aircraft Act 1973, and the Aviation Security Act 1982.

hire 1. To enter into a contract for the temporary use of another's *goods, or the temporary provision of his services or labour, in return for payment. In the case of goods, the person hiring them is a bailee (*see* BAILMENT). **2.** The act of hiring. The payment made under a contract of hire.

hire purchase A method of buying *goods in which the purchaser takes possession of them as soon as he has paid an initial instalment of the price (a **deposit**) and obtains *ownership of the goods when he has paid all the agreed number of subsequent instalments and exercises his option to purchase the goods. A **hire-purchase agreement** differs from a *credit sale agreement and a sale-by-instalments contract because in these transactions ownership passes when the contract is signed. It also differs from a contract of *hire, because in this case ownership never passes. Hire-purchase agreements were formerly controlled by government regulations that stipulated the minimum deposit and the length of the repayment period. These controls were removed in July 1982. Hire-purchase agreements were also formerly controlled by the Hire Purchase Act 1965, but most are now regulated by the Consumer Credit Act 1974 (which is to be amended by the Consumer Credit Act 2006). In this Act a hire-purchase agreement is regarded as one in which goods are bailed in return for periodical payments by the bailee; ownership passes to the bailee if he complies with the terms of the agreement and exercises his option to purchase.

A hire-purchase agreement often involves a finance company as a third party. The seller of the goods sells them outright to the finance company, which enters into a hire-purchase agreement with the hirer. In this situation there is generally no direct contractual relationship between the seller and the buyer.

histology The study of the structure of tissue. At *autopsy the *pathologist will take small samples from each organ for histology.

holder The person in possession of a *bill of exchange or *promissory note. He may be the payee, the endorsee, or the bearer. A holder may *sue on the bill in his own name. When value (which includes a past *debt or *liability) has at any time been given for a bill, the holder is a **holder for value**, as regards the acceptor and all who were parties to the bill before value was given. A **holder in due course** is one who has taken a bill of exchange in good faith and for value, before it was overdue, and without notice of previous dishonour or of any defect in the *title of the person who negotiated or transferred the bill. He holds the bill free from any defect of title of prior parties and may enforce payment against all parties liable on the bill.

holding out Conduct by one person that leads another to believe that he has an authority that does not in fact exist. By the doctrine of *estoppel, the first person may be prevented from denying that the authority exists. For example, a person who wrongly represents himself as being a partner in a firm will be as liable as if he were in fact a partner to anyone who gives credit to the firm on the faith of the representation.

Home Authority Principle A scheme intended to help *local authorities work together with businesses to provide consistent and coordinated trading standards and food enforcement services across the UK. It assists businesses that have outlets in more than one local authority and distribute *goods and/or services beyond the boundaries of one local authority.

The Home Authority Principle helps effective communication between authorities and businesses and ensures the consistent application of *legislation and advice. *Local Authorities Coordinators of Regulatory Services supports and acts as a steward of the Home Authority Principle by providing framework advice and guidance on its operation, monitoring its use and where possible resolving disputes and providing an extensive database of companies, brand names, and local authority contact information to facilitate effective communications.

The Home Authority Principle provides a single point of contact for businesses to access local authority experience and advice and creates a more coordinated approach to business locally and nationally.

The Home Authority Principle is widely recognized and supported by local authority food and trading standards services throughout the UK and by government departments. It is referenced in a document called the *Enforcement Concordat.

homeless person A person who has no living accommodation that he is entitled to occupy, or is unlawfully excluded from his own living accommodation, or whose accommodation is mobile and cannot be placed in a location where he is permitted to reside in it (Housing Act 1996). Certain homeless people (e.g. the elderly or infirm or those with dependent children) have a statutory right to permanent *local authority accommodation or, if they became homeless intentionally, to temporary accommodation.

Home Office Large Major Enquiry System (HOLMES) A computerized database used in the investigation of major crimes and other police operations where large amounts of data have to be processed. Now in its second generation as HOLMES2 it makes the investigation process of a major inquiry easier than previous manual systems of filing and retrieving data which proved incapable of handling very large inquiries. It helps investigating officers to identify and plot lines of inquiry and keep track of evidence. HOLMES2 also has a Casualty Bureau function to help coordinate the aftermath of major incidents such as *terrorist attacks, floods, or train crashes.

Home Office Road Traffic Form 1 (HORT/1) A form, commonly known as a 'producer', given to *motor vehicle *drivers who are unable to produce their driving licence, insurance, and test certificate when stopped. The form has to be taken to a nominated police station with the *documents within seven days.

Home Office Scientific Development Branch A body which works closely with UK *police forces and other law enforcement agencies, the prison service, and a range of other government departments to provide them with science and technology based solutions. It was formerly known as the Police Scientific Development Branch.

Home Secretary The minister in charge of the Home Office, who is responsible throughout England and Wales for law and order generally (including matters concerning the police and the prison and security services) and for a variety of other domestic matters, such as *nationality, *immigration, race relations, *extradition, and *deportation. He also advises the sovereign on the exercise of the *prerogative of mercy.

homicide The act of killing a human being. **Unlawful homicide**, which constitutes the crime of *murder, *manslaughter, or *infanticide, can only be committed if the victim is an independent human being (*see* ABORTION), and the act itself causes the death (*see* CAUSATION). A British citizen may be tried for homicide committed anywhere in the world. **Lawful homicide** occurs when somebody uses reasonable force in preventing crime or arresting an offender, in *self-defence or defence of others, or (possibly) in defence of his property, and causes death as a result. *See also* EXCUSABLE HOMICIDE.

honorarium A payment or reward made to a person for services rendered by him voluntarily.

honour killing The deliberate preplanned *murder, usually of a woman, by or at the behest of members of her family motivated by a perception that she has brought shame on the family.

hors de combat [French: out of action] Members of armed forces who are rendered unable to fight by reason of sickness, wounds, detention, or any other cause and are protected by the *Geneva Convention.

hospital order An order of the *Crown Court or a *magistrates' court, made under ss 37 to 43 of the Mental Health Act 1983, authorizing the detention in a specified hospital (for a period of twelve months, renewable by the hospital managers) of an offender suffering from *mental disorder who has been convicted of an imprisonable offence. Unless a *restriction order has also been made, discharge while an order is in force may be authorized by the managers or the doctor in charge or directed by a *Mental Health Review Tribunal.

hostage A person who is held as a security. Under the Taking of Hostages Act 1982, it is an offence, punishable in the English courts by a maximum *sentence of *life imprisonment, to take anyone as a hostage against his will anywhere in the world and to threaten to kill, injure, or continue to hold him hostage in order to force a state, international governmental organization, or person to do or not to do something. This is an *extraditable offence, but prosecutions may only be brought with the consent of the Attorney-General. *See also* HIJACKING; KIDNAPPING; TERRORISM.

hostile witness An *adverse witness who wilfully refuses to testify truthfully on behalf of the party who called him. A hostile witness may, with the permission of the court, be cross-examined by that party, e.g. by putting to him a *previous statement that is inconsistent with his present testimony.

hot pursuit, right of The right of a coastal state to pursue a foreign *ship within its *territorial waters (or possibly its contiguous zone) and there capture it if the state has good reason to believe that this vessel has violated its laws. The hot pursuit may—but only if it is uninterrupted—continue onto the *high seas, but it must terminate the moment the pursued ship enters the territorial waters of another state, as such pursuit would involve an offence to the other state; in these circumstances *extradition should be employed instead.

housebreaking Before the Theft Act 1968 an offence of forcing one's way into someone else's house to steal. It is now covered by the offence of *burglary.

House of Commons The representative chamber of *Parliament (also known as the **Lower House**), composed of 659 ***Members of Parliament** (**MPs**) elected for 529 single-member *constituencies in England, 72 in Scotland, 40 in Wales, and 18 in Northern Ireland (see FRANCHISE). The total number of MPs may within certain limits be varied as a result of constituency changes proposed by the *boundary commissions.

A number of people are disqualified from membership. They include those under 21, civil servants, the police and the regular armed forces, most clergy (but not Non-conformist ministers), aliens, those declared bankrupt, convicted prisoners and people *guilty of corrupt or illegal practices, the holders of most judicial offices (but not lay *magistrates), and the holders of a large number of public offices listed in the House of Commons Disqualification Act 1975. Public offices that disqualify include stewardship of the Chiltern Hundreds and the Manor of Northstead. The number of members who may hold ministerial office is limited to 95. The House of Lords Act 1999 removed an earlier disqualification on hereditary peers from voting and from being elected members of the House of Commons. The Removal of Clergy Disqualification Bill, when enacted, will permit all clergy to be MPs.

The House is presided over by the **Speaker**, who is elected from among themselves by the members at the beginning of each Parliament. The Speaker is responsible for the orderly conduct of proceedings, which must be supervised with complete impartiality, and is the person through whom the members may collectively communicate with the sovereign. The **Leader of the House** is a government minister responsible for arranging the business of the House in consultation with the Opposition.

House of Commons Commission A body established in 1978 to supervise the staffing of the House. It consists of the Speaker, the Leader of the House, and four other members, one of whom is appointed by the Leader of the Opposition.

House of Lords The second chamber of *Parliament (also known as the **Upper House**), which scrutinizes *legislation and has judicial functions. The House of Lords Act 1999 substantially changed the constitution of the House by excluding hereditary peers from a place in the House as of right, although for a transitional period 92 were allowed to remain on merit. Of these, 75 were elected by their own political party or by cross-bench (usually non-party-political) groups. A further 15 hereditary peers were elected to act as Deputy Speakers or Committee chairmen. Two hereditary royal appointments were also retained: the Earl Marshal and the Lord Great Chamberlain. The other members of the Lords were (as at July 2001) life peers (592) or bishops (26), comprising the Archbishops of Canterbury and York, the Bishops of London, Durham, and Winchester, and 21 other Anglican bishops selected according to seniority of appointment. Long-term reform of the Lords is currently being debated; a white paper published in November 2001 proposed the following composition of the Lords: 120 members to be elected by the public, 120 non-party-political members to be selected by the *House of Lords Appointments Commission, up to 332 members to be nominated by party leaders, and 16 bishops.

The House is presided over by a Speaker chosen by members of the House and its business is arranged, in consultation with the Opposition, by a government minister appointed **Leader of the House**. The Lords is the final court of *appeal in the UK in both civil and criminal cases, although it refers some cases to the *European Court of Justice for a ruling. In its judicial capacity the Lords formally adopts opinions delivered by an **Appellate Committee** (of which there are two), and it is a constitutional convention that the only peers who may participate in the proceedings of the committee are the Lord Chancellor, the

*Lords of Appeal in Ordinary, and others who have held high judicial office. *See also* SUPREME COURT.

House of Lords Appointments Commission A body that recommends people for appointment as non-party-political life peers and vets all nominations for membership of the *House of Lords. Set up by the Government following the House of Lords Act 1999, which modernizes the Lords, the Commission is an independent non-departmental public body staffed by civil servants.

housing action trust (HAT) A statutory trust set up for a particular area with the objects to secure: the repair and improvement of housing in the area; its proper and effective management; greater diversity of kinds of tenure of the housing; and the improvement of social and living conditions in the area generally. In their areas, HATs can be given power to exercise most of the functions of a housing authority and the planning control and public-health functions of *local authorities. Local authority housing can be transferred to a HAT by government order if a majority of the tenants agree. A HAT must achieve its objects as quickly as possible and is then dissolved and its property disposed of. HATs were introduced by the Housing Act 1988.

housing association A non-profit-making organization whose main purpose is to provide housing. A fully mutual housing association is excepted from the *assured tenancy provisions. The Housing Corporation can make grants to housing associations registered by them.

housing association tenancy A *tenancy in which the *landlord is a *housing association, a *housing trust, or the *Housing Corporation. The Housing Act 1996 gave certain housing association tenants a right to buy their homes, and they may be able to obtain a grant towards the purchase price.

housing benefit A benefit payable by *local authorities to those with no or very low incomes who pay rent for their housing. There are two types: rent rebates, paid to the local authority's own needy *tenants, and rent allowances, paid to tenants other than their own (e.g. housing association tenants).

Housing Corporation A body with functions under the Housing Associations Act 1985 and the Housing Act 1988. These include maintaining a register of *housing associations, promoting and assisting the development of—and making and guaranteeing loans to—registered housing associations and unregistered self-build societies, and providing dwellings for letting or sale.

Housing Ombudsman An official appointed, under the Housing Act 1996, to deal with complaints against registered social landlords (not including *local authorities). The first Housing Ombudsman was appointed with effect from 1 April 1997; he is in charge of the *Independent Housing Ombudsman.

housing trust A trust set up to provide housing, or whose funds are devoted to charitable purposes and which in fact uses most of its funds for the provision of housing. If it is a fully mutual housing association, it is exempted from the assured tenancy provisions. *See also* HOUSING ACTION TRUST.

human assisted reproduction Techniques to bring about the conception and birth of a child other than by sexual intercourse between the parties. It includes artificial insemination by the husband (AIH) or by a donor (DI), in vitro fertilization (IVF), and egg and embryo donation. Such methods mean it is no longer possible to base legal parentage solely on genetic links. Under the terms of the Human Fertilization and Embryology Act 1990, the legal mother is the woman who has given birth to the child, regardless of genetic parentage, unless the child is subsequently adopted or a *section 30 order is made. However, the Act is not retrospective and the position of children conceived or born before the Act came into force has yet to be resolved. The legal father is generally the genetic father except when the latter is a donor whose sperm is used for licensed treatment under the 1990 Act, or when the donor's sperm is used after his death. If a wife conceives as a result of assisted reproduction, her husband may be regarded as the child's legal father, even if he is not the genetic father, as long as he consented to her treatment. However, this does not hold for all purposes. For example, in a recent case it was ruled that a peer's 'son' born by donor insemination could not inherit his father's title when it was found after the peer's death that his wife had been impregnated by sperm from a third party (rather than from her husband) at the relevant clinic.

It is an offence to use female germ cells from an embryo or foetus, or to make use of embryos created from such germ cells, for the purpose of providing a fertility service. Such practice is already banned by the *Human Fertilization and Embryology Authority. The offence is triable only on *indictment and is punishable with up to ten years' imprisonment.

Human Fertilization and Embryology Authority A body, established under the Human Fertilization and Embryology Act 1990, that monitors, controls, and reviews research involving the use of embryos and issues licences for such research and for treatment in *human assisted reproduction. It must also maintain a register of persons whose gametes are kept or used for such purposes and of children born as a result. Children over the age of 18 can apply to the Authority for information concerning their ethnic and genetic background.

human immunodeficiency virus (HIV) A virus that causes an infection that gradually destroys the immune system, resulting in infections that are hard for the body to fight. If not treated the condition progresses to AIDS. Pathologists are loathe to undertake autopsies on HIV positive subjects and will do so only in a specially equipped mortuary using stringent safeguards.

humanitarian intervention The interference of one state in the affairs of another by means of armed force with the intention of making that state adopt a more humanitarian policy, usually the protection of *human rights of *minority groups. Despite debate, such intervention is not recognized as legal under the UN Charter. However, states continue to rely on humanitarian grounds as justification for military action; examples of humanitarian intervention include Vietnam's invasion of Cambodia (1978), the declaration by the USA, the UK, Russia, and France of an air exclusion zone in southern Iraq in an effort to protect the Shia Marsh Arabs (1992), and military actions to protect the Muslim population of Kosovo (1999).

human rights Rights and freedom to which every human being is entitled. Protection against breaches of these rights committed by a state (including the state of which the victim is a national) may in some cases be enforced in *international law. It is sometimes suggested that human rights (or some of them) are so fundamental that they form part of *natural law, but most of them are best regarded as forming part of treaty law.

The United Nations Universal Declaration of Human Rights (1948) spells out most of the main rights that must be protected but it is not binding in *international law. There are two international covenants, however, that bind the parties who have ratified them: the 1966 International Covenant on Civil and Political Rights and the International Covenant on Economic, Social and Cultural Rights. The *United Nations has set up a Commission on Human Rights, which has power to discuss gross violations of human rights but not to investigate individual complaints. The Human Rights Committee, set up in 1977, has power to hear complaints from individuals, under certain circumstances, about alleged breaches of the 1966 Covenant on Civil and Political Rights. There are also various regional conventions on human rights, some of which have established machinery for hearing individual complaints. The best known of these is the *European Convention on Human Rights (enacted in English law as the *Human Rights Act 1998) and the Inter-American Convention on Human Rights (covering South America).

Human Rights Act *Legislation, enacted in 1998, that brought the *European Convention on Human Rights into domestic law for the whole of the UK on 2 October 2000. In the past the use of the Convention was limited to cases where the law was ambiguous and public authorities had no duty to exercise administrative discretion in a manner that complied with the Convention.

The Act creates a statutory general requirement that all *legislation (past or future) be read and given effect in a way that is compatible with the Convention. Section 3 provides that all legislation, primary and secondary, whenever enacted, must be read and given effect in a way that is compatible with Convention rights *wherever possible*.

The Act requires public authorities—including courts—to act compatibly with the Convention unless they are prevented from doing so by statute. This means that the courts have their own primary statutory duty to give effect to the Convention unless a statute positively prevents this. Section 7 gives the *victim of any act of a public authority that is incompatible with the Convention the power to challenge the authority in court using the Convention, to found a cause of action or as a *defence. The Act introduces a new ground of illegality into proceedings brought by way of *judicial review, namely, a failure to comply with the Convention rights protected by the Act, subject to a 'statutory obligation' defence. Secondly, it will create a new cause of action against public bodies that fail to act compatibly with the Convention. Thirdly, Convention rights will be available as a ground of defence or *appeal in cases brought by public bodies against private bodies (in both criminal and civil cases). Section 7(5) imposes a limitation period of one year for those bringing proceedings.

However, only persons classified as 'victims' by the Act are able to enforce the duty to act compatibly with the Convention in proceedings against the authority, and only victims will have standing to bring proceedings by way of judicial review. Most private litigants, at least in private law proceedings, will count as victims.

The Convention rights that have been incorporated into the Act are: Articles 2 to 12, 14, 16, 17, 18; Articles 1 to 3 of the First Protocol; and Articles 1 and 2 of the Sixth Protocol (individual rights are subjects of entries in this dictionary). *See* ABSOLUTE RIGHT; QUALIFIED RIGHT.

The Act requires any court or tribunal determining a question that has arisen in connection with a Convention right to take into account the jurisprudence of the Strasbourg organs (the *European Court and Commission of Human Rights and the Committee of Ministers). This jurisprudence must be considered 'so far as, in the opinion of the court or tribunal, it is relevant to the proceedings in which that question has arisen', whenever the judgment, decision, or opinion to be taken into account was handed down.

Section 19 provides that when legislation is introduced into *Parliament for a second reading, the introducing minister must make a statement, either (1) to the effect that, in his view, the legislation is compatible with the Convention, or (2) that although the legislation is not compatible with the Convention, the Government still wishes to proceed. If it is not possible to read legislation so as to give effect to the Convention, then the Act does not affect the validity, continuing operation, or enforcement of the legislation. In such circumstances, however, s 4 empowers the high courts to make a **declaration of incompatibility**. Section 10 and sch 2 provide a 'fast-track' procedure by which the Government can act to amend legislation in order to remove incompatibility with the Convention when a declaration of incompatibility has been made.

The Act gives a court a wide power to grant such relief, remedies, or orders as it considers just and appropriate, provided they are within its existing powers. *Damages may be awarded in civil proceedings, but only if necessary to afford *just satisfaction; in determining whether or not to award damages and the amount to award, the court must take account of the principles applied by the European Court of Human Rights.

Sections 12 and 13 provide specific assurances as to the respect that will be afforded to *freedom of expression and *freedom of thought, conscience, and religion: these are 'comfort clauses' for sections of the press and certain religious organizations.

The Act does not make Convention rights directly enforceable against a private litigant, nor against a quasi-public body with some public functions if it is acting in a private capacity. But in cases against a private litigant, the Act still has an effect on the outcome, because the court will be obliged to interpret legislation in conformity with the Convention wherever possible; must exercise any judicial discretion compatibly with the Convention; and must ensure that its application of *common law or *equitable rules is compatible with the Convention.

h

human shield The use of civilians or prisoners of *war to deter an enemy from attacking certain targets. It is an offence under the Statute of the *International Criminal Court to use civilians and other protected persons as human shields. Such offences were committed in Yugoslavia and in Iraq where the army put civilians onto military and government buildings to prevent them being attacked.

humerus The long bone of the upper arm.

hydrogen cyanide An extremely poisonous gas used as a *war gas by France in World War I, Japan in World War II, and by Iraq in attacks on the Kurdish population in the 1980s. It was the active ingredient of Zyklon-B, used in Nazi extermination camps at Auschwitz-Berkenau and Majdanek to murder about 1 million people, mainly Jews. Other sources of cyanide are fires involving plastics and acrylic nail varnish removers.

hymen A thin sheet of tissue at the entrance to the vagina present in most female children. At one time it was thought that an intact hymen was evidence of virginity. The hymen can be torn by activities such as horse riding and cycling but can also be torn by penetration by a penis or other object.

hyoid A horseshoe shaped cartilaginous structure in the larynx. It ossifies later in life. It is the only bone in the body that does not articulate with another bone. The horns of the hyoid are often broken in strangulation.

hyper A prefix denoting raised level, e.g. hypertension means high blood pressure.

hyperglycaemia A raised level of blood sugar usually found in diabetics due to lack of insulin.

hypo A prefix denoting low level or value, e.g. hypotension means low blood pressure.

hypoglycaemia The condition of having a low level of blood sugar caused by too much insulin.

hypostasis The red colouration of the skin in dead bodies where the blood settles within the body due to gravity. The areas in contact with the surface on which it is laid stay white. It may be useful in indicating whether the body has been moved after death.

hypothecation **1.** An authority given to a banker, usually as a **letter of hypothecation**, to enable the bank to sell *goods or *property that have been pledged to it as security for a loan. It applies only when the goods remain in the possession of the pledgor. **2.** An authority from the Treasury for *police forces to keep money raised from fixed *penalties for driving above the speed limit to cover the cost of enforcement.

hypothermia A condition of having a body *temperature of less than 30 degrees Celsius. It is often fatal. In final stages the sufferer becomes confused and feels hot, sometimes ripping his clothes off and knocking furniture over. It can give the appearance of suspicious death.

hypoxia The lack of oxygen in the blood.

identification procedure A procedure used by police to test the ability of witnesses to identify a person they have seen on a previous occasion—usually the perpetrator of an offence. The procedures are regulated by the PACE Code D. Where the identity of a suspect is not known the witnesses can be taken to an area to see if they can spot the suspect. If the suspect is sufficiently identified and available he should be arrested and a formal identification procedure carried out. The preferred method, which must be the first option, is a *video identification. A video identification is when the witness is shown moving images of a known suspect, together with similar images of others who resemble the suspect. Moving images must be used unless: the suspect is known but not available; or the identification officer does not consider that replication of a physical feature can be achieved or that it is not possible to conceal the location of the feature on the image of the suspect. The identification officer may then decide to make use of video identification but using still images. The second method is an identification parade, where the witness sees the suspect in a line of others who resemble the suspect. The next procedure is a group identification where the witness sees the suspect in an informal group of people. The least favoured procedure is confrontation with the suspect. The suspect's consent is not required for this procedure.

identity (in the law of evidence) *See* EVIDENCE OF IDENTITY.

idiopathic A medical term which means that the cause of the disease is unknown or at best uncertain.

ignition (in a *firearm) The setting on fire of the propellant powder charge by the *primer.

ignorance of the law *See* MISTAKE.

ignorantia juris non excusat [Latin: ignorance of the law is no excuse] Ignorance is no defence against criminal or other proceedings arising from its breach. The Statutory Instruments Act 1946 modifies the rule slightly (*see* STATUTORY INSTRUMENT). *See also* MISTAKE.

ignoring traffic signals Failing to comply with traffic signs, traffic lights, or road markings. A number of different offences are included in this category, all concerned with breaches of the rules relating to traffic signals as laid down in the Highway Code. All these offences are subject to a *fine, *endorsement (carrying three penalty points under the totting-up system), and *disqualification at the discretion of the court. Sometimes charges may also be brought under the head of *careless and inconsiderate driving or *dangerous driving, depending on the circumstances. It is also an offence contrary to s 35 of the Road Traffic Act 1988 not to comply with road directions given by a uniformed *police officer acting in the course of his duties or engaged in a traffic census or survey.

Prosecutions for ignoring traffic signals or police directions are subject to a *notice of intended prosecution.

ileum The last part of the small intestine.

illegal contract A contract that is prohibited by statute (e.g. one between traders providing for minimum resale prices) or is illegal at *common law on the grounds of *public policy. An illegal contract is totally void, but neither party (unless innocent of the illegality) can recover back any money paid or property transferred under it (*see* EX TURPI CAUSA NON ORITUR ACTIO). Related transactions may also be affected. A related transaction between the same parties (e.g. if X gives Y a *promissory note for money due from him under an illegal contract) is equally tainted with the illegality and is therefore void. The same is true of a related transaction with a third party (e.g. if Z lends

X the money to pay Y) if the original illegality is known to him. In certain circumstances, illegal contracts may be saved by *severance.

illegal practices *See* CORRUPT AND ILLEGAL PRACTICES.

illegitimacy The status of a child born out of wedlock. Although evidence of illegitimacy is readily available from the entry in the birth register relating to the child's *parents, it is usual for a short form of birth certificate to be issued, which makes no mention of the parents. Entry in the register of the name of a man who is not married to the mother (which may only be done with the consent of the mother) is evidence of his paternity.

The effect of the Family Law Reform Act 1987 is that, for nearly all purposes, children are to be treated alike, whether or not their parents are married to one another. The parents of illegitimate children have much the same rights, duties, and responsibilities in relation to them as they have for their legitimate children. The father of an illegitimate child is under a duty to maintain the child in the same way as his duty to maintain legitimate children but does not automatically have *parental responsibility for that child. Illegitimate children are able to inherit property under wills (unless the contrary intention is apparent) and on *intestacy in the same way as if they were legitimate. However, the Family Law Reform Act 1987 did not remove all distinctions between legitimate and illegitimate children, notably in relation to entitlement to *British citizenship and succession to the throne of England and to titles of honour.

It is now becoming more usual to use the term 'child of unmarried parents' for children born out of wedlock, rather than 'illegitimate child'.

imaging The process of copying the complete contents and structure of a data storage device, such as a *computer hard drive, without altering the original in any way. Two images of the device are generally produced, one for evidential purposes and the second as a 'working copy' which is examined for evidential material. Where necessary, a properly verified and unaltered image can be produced in evidence in lieu of the original data storage device.

imitation firearm An object that has the appearance of being a *firearm. Some offences, by their definition, apply to 'imitation firearms': e.g. the offence of possession of a firearm or imitation firearm with intent to cause fear of violence, contrary to s 16A of the Firearms Act 1968. Offences which do not include 'imitation firearms' by definition may nonetheless extend to them by virtue of the Firearms Act 1982, which applies the provisions of the 1968 Act (with certain exceptions) to imitation firearms which have the appearance of being, or are readily convertible into, firearms to which s 1 of the 1968 Act applies.

Section 57(4) of the 1968 Act provides that the term 'imitation firearm' means 'any thing which has the appearance of being a firearm (other than such a weapon as is mentioned in section 5(1)(b) of [the] Act) whether or not it is capable of discharging any shot, bullet or other missile'. Weapons in s 5(1)(b) are one category of *prohibited weapons, that is, a weapon designed or adapted for the discharge of any noxious liquid, gas, or other thing. This means that an offence requiring 'possession' or 'having with' a firearm or imitation firearm requires a 'thing' which is separate and distinct from a person. Accordingly, putting a hand inside a jacket and using fingers to force out the material to give the impression of a firearm falls outside the scope of such offences, as a person's bodily parts are not a 'thing': *R v Bentham* [2005] UKHL 18.

immigration The act of entering a country other than one's native country with the intention of living there permanently. Immigration into the UK is subject to control under the Immigration Acts 1971 and 1988, as amended by the Immigration and Nationality Act 1999, the Nationality, Immigration and Asylum Act 2002, and the Immigration, Asylum and Nationality Act 2006. With some exceptions, this control extends to all potential entrants except those to whom the Acts give the **right of abode** in the UK. As originally enacted, the Act gave the right of abode to all citizens of the UK and Colonies who either owed their status to their own (or a parent's or grandparent's) birth, registration, or naturalization in the UK or were or became at any time settled in the UK and had at that time been ordinarily resident there for at least five years. Commonwealth citizens had the right of abode if one of their parents was a citizen of the UK and Colonies by reason of birth in the UK. A person having the right of abode was termed a **patrial**. As from 1 January 1983 the Act was amended by the British Nationality Act 1981 to confine the right of abode to British citizens as defined by that Act (*see* BRITISH CITIZENSHIP) and to *Commonwealth citizens enjoying it before the Act came into force; the term patrial was discarded. With minor exceptions, a person subject to immigration control may not enter or remain in the UK except with leave, which may be granted either indefinitely or for a limited period; if leave is granted for a limited period, an immigrant is subject to further conditions (e.g. conditions restricting employment). The 1971 Act itself gave indefinite leave to stay to those not entitled to the right of abode but who were lawfully settled in the UK when it came into force. Whether or not leave is needed, whether it should be granted, and whether a time limit and any other conditions should be imposed are decided initially by immigration officers acting in accordance with immigration rules made by the Secretary of State. *Appeals against the decisions of immigration officers are made to adjudicators at the ports of entry, and thence to the *Immigration Appeal Tribunal.

Under the Immigration (Carriers' Liability) Act 1987, the owners of *ships and aircraft are liable to pay a *penalty of £1000 in respect of any person who arrives in the UK on their ship or aircraft and who seeks leave to enter the UK without proper *documents (e.g. *passport or visa). Under the Asylum and Immigration Act 1996, from 27 January 1997 it has been a criminal offence for an *employer to employ anyone subject to immigration control. Breach of this Act leads to fines of up to £5000. Employers must ask new *employees taken on or re-employed after that date for evidence of residential status, such as

p
non-
breach

Immigratio nal appointed b under the Immigra *appeals against *imm portation decisions.

immoral contract A contract sexual immorality, such as a con *prostitution. Such contracts are *ille contracts on the grounds that they contravene *public policy.

immovables Tangible things that cannot be physically moved, particularly *land and buildings.

immunity Freedom or exemption from legal proceedings. Examples include the immunity of the sovereign personally from all legal proceedings (*see* ROYAL PREROGATIVE); the immunity of members of the *House of Commons and the *House of Lords from proceedings in respect of words spoken in debate (*see* PARLIAMENTARY PRIVILEGE); *judicial immunity; and the immunity from the *jurisdiction of national courts enjoyed by members of *diplomatic missions and by foreign sovereigns (*see* DIPLOMATIC IMMUNITY; SOVEREIGN IMMUNITY). Offenders who assist the *prosecution may be granted immunity from prosecution by the *Director of Public Prosecutions, *Director of the Revenue and Customs Prosecutions Office, *Director of the Serious Fraud Office, Director of Public Prosecutions for Northern Ireland, or their nominated *prosecutor under the provisions of s 71 of the Serious Organized Crime and Police Act 2005.

immunological response The reaction of the body to foreign bodies such as bacteria, viruses, or objects.

impeding apprehension or prosecution Giving assistance to a person one knows to be *guilty of an *indictable offence (one for which the sentence is fixed by law or on first *conviction an adult may be sentenced to five or more years' imprisonment) with the intention of preventing or delaying his *arrest or *prosecution (e.g.

gain a... impersonate a ... public officials, a voter, ... ing property, services, or certain ... advantages through impersonation may amount to a crime of *deception.

implementation The process of bringing any piece of *legislation into force. EU directives, which are not directly applicable (*see* COMMUNITY LEGISLATION), are implemented at national level by member states by *Act of Parliament or regulation. In the UK this may be done by statute or by *statutory instrument or regulation.

implied condition A term or obligation implied by law in a contract, any breach of which will entitle the innocent party not only to *damages but to treat the contract as discharged (*see* CONDITION). In a contract of *sale of goods there are implied conditions that the *seller has the right to sell the *goods, that the goods will correspond with the contract description, and, in the case of sales in the course of business, that the goods are of *satisfactory quality and fit for the *buyer's declared purpose.

implied contract A contract not created by express words but inferred by the courts either from the conduct of the *parties or from some special relationship existing between them.

implied malice **Mens rea* that the law considers sufficient for a crime, although there is no intention to commit that crime. The term is usually now used only ... *murder, referring to the ...ause *grievous bodily harm ...FORETHOUGHT).

...ust A trust that arises either ...resumed but unexpressed in... the settlor or by operation of ...ity imposes an obligation to cre... trusts by inference from the ...cluding the conduct or relation... the *parties. An implied trust ...e subdivided into or overlap with ...ng trusts and constructive trusts.

...ossibility A *general defence that ...s when compliance with the criminal ... is physically impossible. This is most ...ely to arise in the context of crimes ... *omission. Thus one cannot be found guilty of failing to report a road traffic accident of which one was unaware. However, under the Criminal Attempts Act 1981 one may be convicted of attempting the impossible (*see* ATTEMPT).

impossibility of performance The impossibility of carrying out a contract, which occurs, for example, when it relates to subject matter that does not exist. The event making fulfilment impossible may arise either before or after the contract is made. In the former case (e.g. if X agrees to sell Y a horse that, unknown to either, is already dead) the contract is void for *mistake. In the latter case (e.g. if the horse dies between contract and performance) the contract will be discharged under the doctrine of *frustration of contract.

imprisonment *See* CUSTODY; SENTENCE; FALSE IMPRISONMENT; LIFE IMPRISONMENT.

imputability The principle that internationally illegal acts or omissions contributing to the damage to foreign property, and caused in some way by organs of the state apparatus, are attributable to the state and therefore incur that state's responsibility. Thus, there must have been state participation in the act before there can be *state responsibility for it.

imputation An attack on the *character of another person adduced in evidence by a defendant or made by him during questioning under caution before being charged or at the time of being charged. Where such an attack is made, the defendant's own bad character can be admitted in evidence under s 101 of the Criminal Justice Act 2003.

in camera [Latin: in the chamber] In private. A court hearing must usually be public but the public may be barred from the court or the hearing may continue in the *judge's private room in certain circumstances; e.g. when it is necessary for public safety or when a child gives evidence in a case involving indecency. *See also* CAMERA, SITTINGS IN.

incapacity benefit A state benefit that replaced invalidity benefit and sickness benefit in April 1995. It is paid at three basic rates, the two highest of which are taken into account as taxable income. Short-term incapacity benefit is payable at the lower rate for the first 28 weeks of incapacity and at the higher rate for the 29th to 52nd weeks. Long-term benefit is payable, at the highest rate, after 52 weeks. Those claiming the benefit must complete a questionnaire about the activities they can engage in; after 28 weeks they must undergo a medical test to assess their capacity for work-related activities as well as submitting a questionnaire. Doctors must certify in all cases the material supplied.

incapacity (incompetence) A lack of full legal *competence in any respect; e.g. the incapacity of *mentally disordered persons to conclude valid contracts (*see* CAPACITY TO CONTRACT). A person suffering from incapacity is frequently referred to as a **person under disability**.

incest Prohibited sexual relations with certain categories of family members. Under the Sexual Offences Act 1956, it was an offence for a man to have vaginal sexual intercourse with a woman he knew to be his mother, daughter, sister, half-sister, or granddaughter or for a woman over the age of 16 to have vaginal sexual intercourse with a man she knew to be her father, son, brother, half-brother, or grandfather. The Sexual Offences Act 2003 introduced completely separate offences dealing with child and adult family members (ss 25 to 26 and 64 to 65, respectively) which cover not only vaginal sexual intercourse but a wide range of sexual activity. The prohibited degrees of relationship are extended to encompass adopted children and adult carers living in the same household.

inchoate Incomplete. Certain acts, although not constituting a complete offence, are nonetheless prohibited by the criminal law because they constitute steps towards the complete offence. These inchoate offences include *incitement, *attempt, and *conspiracy. One may be *guilty of inciting someone to commit the crime of incitement or of attempting to incite, but one cannot be guilty of incitement to conspire or of attempting to conspire.

incision A cut in the skin caused by a sharp object.

incitement Persuading or attempting to persuade someone else to commit a crime. If the other person then actually carries out the criminal act, the inciter becomes a participator in the crime and is *guilty of *aiding and abetting it. If the other person does not carry out the crime, the person who attempted to persuade him to do so may nonetheless be guilty of the crime of incitement. Incitement may be by means of suggestion, persuasion, threats, or pressure, by words or by implication; e.g. advertising an article for sale to be used to commit an offence may constitute incitement to commit that offence.

income support An income-related benefit payable under the Social Security Acts to persons over 16 whose income and savings do not exceed a prescribed amount, and who are not working 16 or more hours a week, and (if applicable) whose spouses or cohabitants (*see* COHABITATION) are not working 24 hours or more a week, and who are incapable of or unavailable for work (e.g. because they are disabled or a lone parent). It replaced supplementary benefit from April 1988. Since October 1996 the unemployed who would formerly have been recipients of income support have received instead a *jobseeker's allowance.

incompetence *See* INCAPACITY.

inconsiderate driving *See* CARELESS AND INCONSIDERATE DRIVING.

incorporation 1. The formation of an association that has **corporate personality**, i.e. a personality distinct from those of its members. A *corporation (such as a company) has wide legal capacity (subject to the doctrine of **ultra vires*): it can own property and incur *debts. *Company members have no liability to company *creditors for such debts (though they may be under some liability to their company). An incorporated company has its own *rights and *liabilities, and legal proceedings in respect of them should be brought by and against it in its own name. It can be convicted of crimes; when **mens rea* is a requirement of the offence, the *mens rea* of the officers responsible may be attributed to the company. A company is usually incorporated by *registration under the Companies Act 1985 but there are other methods (e.g. by royal charter or private Act of Parliament). *See also* CERTIFICATE OF INCORPORATION; LIFTING THE VEIL. **2.** *See* DOCTRINE OF INCORPORATION.

incorporation by reference Reference to named contract terms, e.g. on the back of a railway ticket, saying where the terms can be seen for those who want to read them. This will often be sufficient to incorporate the terms by reference into the contract, although the other party may not have taken the opportunity to read the terms.

incorporeal hereditament *See* HEREDITAMENT.

incoterm An international trade term. Incoterms, the best known of which are c.i.f. and *f.o.b., are used as an international shorthand in commercial agreements. A glossary of these terms, the latest edition of which is *Incoterms 2000*, is published by the International Chamber of Commerce. It sets out definitions of the various incoterms, which deal with such matters as which party to a contract is responsible for transport of the *goods, who insures them in transit, and who arranges payment of *customs duties.

incriminate 1. To charge with a criminal offence. **2.** To indicate involvement in the commission of a criminal offence. A witness in court need not answer a question if, in the *judge's opinion, the answer might expose him to the danger of criminal prosecution. A witness does not have this protection when his answer might lead only to civil action against him.

indecent assault An *assault or *battery in circumstances of indecency. The offence was replaced by *sexual assault in the Sexual Offences Act 2003.

indecent exposure An offence under the Vagrancy Act 1824 and now replaced by the offence of *exposure by the Sexual Offences Act 2003. It is an offence contrary to s 66 of the 2003 Act for a person intentionally to expose his genitalia intending that someone will see them and be alarmed or distressed.

indecent photographs of children An image of a child involved in sexual activity or in a sexually provocative pose. A person who takes, makes, shows, distributes, advertises, or possesses an indecent 'photograph or pseudo-photograph' of a child commits an offence. A 'pseudo-photograph' is an image, created by *computer graphics or any other means, that resembles a photograph and can include electronically stored data that can be converted into such images. A 'child' means a person under the age of 18 (raised from 16 by s 45 of the Sexual Offences Act 2003), although it will be possible to convict a person of making a pseudo-photograph where the dominant impression conveyed is that the person shown is a child, notwithstanding that some of the physical characteristics shown are those of an adult. It is a defence if a photograph was of a child aged 16 or over, and at the time of the offence charged the accused and child were married, or were living together as partners in an enduring family relationship. For the purposes of the relevant *legislation, the word 'indecent' is not defined and is a matter for the *trier of fact. However, it is generally taken to mean any image of a child, apparently under 18 years of age, involved in sexual activity or posed to be sexually provocative.

Section 1 of the Protection of Children Act 1978 provides that it is an offence for a person (a) to take, or permit to be taken, or to make, any indecent photograph or pseudo-photograph of a child; or (b) to distribute or show such indecent photographs or pseudo-photographs; or (c) to have in his possession such indecent photographs or pseudo-photographs, with a view to their being distributed or shown by himself or others (a view only to show them to himself is insufficient: *R v ET* 163 JP 349 (CA)); or (d) to publish or cause to be published any advertisement likely to be understood as conveying that the advertiser distributes or shows such indecent photographs or pseudo-photographs, or intends to do so. Section 1B of the Act contains an exemption from criminal proceedings where the indecent image is made pursuant to an authorization given by a relevant authority for the purposes of the prevention, detection, or investigation of crime or for the purposes of criminal proceedings in any part of the world. The authorization must be in writing and specific in its terms. Section160 of the Criminal Justice Act 1988 makes it an offence for a person to have any indecent photograph or pseudo-photograph of a child in his possession. A *defence is provided if the accused can show that that he had a legitimate reason for having the image in his possession; or that he had not himself seen the image and did not know, nor had any cause to suspect, it to be indecent; or that the image was sent to him without any prior request made by him or on his behalf and that he did not keep it for an unreasonable time.

Both offences are triable *either way and require the consent of the *Director of Public Prosecutions before proceedings are instituted. The maximum *penalty for an offence under the 1978 Act is ten years' imprisonment (if committed on or after 11 January 2001; otherwise three years); and for an offence under the 1988 Act, five years' imprisonment (if committed on or after 11 January 2001; otherwise the offence is *summary only, punishable with six months' imprisonment or a *fine not exceeding level 5 on the standard scale, or both).

See also CAUSING OR INCITING OR CONTROLLING PROSTITUTION.

indefeasible Incapable of being made *void.

indemnity An agreement by one person (X) to pay to another (Y) sums that are owed, or may become owed, to him by a third person (Z). It is not conditional on the third person defaulting on the payment, i.e. Y can sue X without first demanding payment from Z. If it is conditional on the third person's default (i.e. if Z remains the principal *debtor and must be sued for the money first) it is not an indemnity but a *guarantee. Unlike a guarantee, an indemnity need not be evidenced in writing.

independent contractor A person or firm engaged to do a particular job of work, as opposed to a person under a contract of employment. An independent contractor is his own master, bound to do the job he has contracted to do but having a discretion as to how to do it. A taxi-driver, for example, is the independent contractor of the passenger who hires him. A person who uses an independent contractor is not generally vicariously liable for *torts committed by the contractor, but may be in exceptional cases; situations in which *vicarious liability may be incurred include those in which the contractor is employed in particularly hazardous activities, or to perform statutory duties, or to work on or over (but not merely near) the *highway, or is specifically authorized to commit a *negligent act.

Independent Housing Ombudsman A body set up under the Housing Act 1996, under the control of the *Housing Ombudsman, to ensure protection for *housing association tenants against *landlord mismanagement and to attempt to resolve disputes for housing association tenants.

Independent Police Complaints Commission (IPCC) A non-departmental public body, funded by the *Home Office, but by law entirely independent of the police, interest groups, and political parties and whose decisions on cases are free from government involvement. The statutory powers and responsibilities of the IPCC, chief *police officers, and *police authorities are set out in the Police Reform Act 2002. This guarantees the independence of the Commission, outlines its role as guardian of the police complaints system as a whole, and gives the IPCC a duty to raise public confidence. The IPCC became operational on 1 April 2004 with wide powers to radically change the way complaints against the police are handled in England and Wales. The IPCC may manage or supervise the police investigation into a case or investigate independently, usually in the more serious cases.

i

index maps Maps kept in the *Land Registry showing the position and extent of every registered estate in *land. The index maps can be searched to find out if a particular piece of land has an estate registered in respect of it.

indictable offence An offence that may be tried on *indictment, i.e. by *jury in the *Crown Court. Most serious *common-law offences are indictable (e.g. *murder, *rape) and many are created by statute. When statute creates an offence without specifying how it is to be tried, it is automatically an indictable offence. An *attempt to commit an indictable offence is itself an indictable offence; the same is not true for a *summary offence. Some indictable offences, if not very serious, may be tried either by *magistrates or on indictment (*see* OFFENCE TRIABLE EITHER WAY). Generally, there are no time limits applicable to indictable (including either way) offences. However, in the case of offences contrary to the customs and excise Acts, proceedings may not be commenced after the end of the period of twenty years beginning with the day on which the offence was committed (s 146A of the Customs and Excise Management Act 1979).

indictment A formal *document accusing one or more persons of committing a specified *indictable offence or offences. It is read out to the accused at the *trial. An indictment is in a particular form. It is headed with the name of the case and the place of trial. There is then a statement of offence, stating what crime has allegedly been committed, followed by particulars of offence, i.e. such details as the date and place of the offence, property stolen, etc. If the accused is charged with more than one offence, each allegation and charge appears in a separate paragraph called a **count**. Counts may, however, be **framed in the alternative**, i.e. two or more counts may charge different offences arising out of the same allegation of fact but the defendant may be convicted of only one of them; e.g. when a defendant is charged as a principal in one count and as an accessory in another in respect of the same incident. *See also* BILL OF INDICTMENT; TRIAL ON INDICTMENT.

indigenous peoples Those peoples and nations that have a historical continuity with pre-invasion and pre-colonial societies that developed on their territories and consider themselves distinct from other sectors of the societies now prevailing in those territories (or parts of them). Forming a non-dominant sector of the prevailing society, they exhibit a determination to preserve, develop, and transmit to future generations their ancestral territories, and their ethnic identity, as the basis of their continued existence as peoples, in accordance with their own cultural patterns, social institutions, and legal systems. Examples of indigenous peoples include the Sami (Lapps) in Scandinavia and the Cymry (Welsh) in the United Kingdom.

indirect evidence *See* CIRCUMSTANTIAL EVIDENCE.

inducement 1. The promise of some advantage (e.g. *bail) held out by a person in authority in relation to a *prosecution to a person suspected of having committed a criminal offence. At *common law a *confession made after an inducement was inadmissible. It may now render the confession unreliable, and therefore inadmissible, under the terms of the Police and Criminal Evidence Act 1984. **2.** *See* MISREPRESENTATION.

industrial tribunal *See* EMPLOYMENT TRIBUNAL.

Industry Hot Card File (IHCF) A list of lost and stolen *credit/*debit cards maintained by the banking industry and available to merchants to prevent fraud.

inevitable accident An accident that could not have been prevented by the exercise of ordinary care and skill.

infant (minor) Since 1969, a child under the age of 18. Certain *rights (such as rights of *parental responsibility, the right to make a child a *ward of court, and the right to withhold consent to marriage) only apply to *infants. Other rights (such as the right to marry with consent) are governed by different age limits, often 16. Infants have a limited *capacity to contract.

infanticide The killing of a child under 12 months old by its mother. If the mother can show that the balance of her mind was disturbed because of the effects of the childbirth or lactation, she will be found *guilty of infanticide, rather than *murder, and punished as though she was guilty of *manslaughter. Most cases of infanticide are dealt with by probation or *discharge. *See also* DIMINISHED RESPONSIBILITY.

infantile cortical hyperostosis A disease that causes new bone growth especially on the long bones. This can be confused with the new growth of bone following fracture and can lead to mistaken suspicion of *child abuse.

infarction The death of a clump of cells caused by lack of blood supply. It is frequently seen in *myocardial infarction where the cells affected are the muscles of the heart. It is a frequent cause of sudden death.

inferior (in *pathology) The lower part, e.g. of arms, legs, or organs.

inferior court Any of the courts that are subordinate to *superior courts, having a *jurisdiction limited to a particular geographical area, size of claim, or type of case. Their decisions are normally subject to *appeal to a superior court, and the exercise of their jurisdiction may be subject to control by a superior court. In England and Wales, *county courts and *magistrates' courts are inferior courts.

inflammation The swelling, reddening, and production of pus caused by the body moving fluid and specialist infection fighting cells from the blood into tissue in response to infection or foreign bodies.

informant *See* COVERT HUMAN INTELLIGENCE SOURCE.

information The formal means by which criminal investigation authorities provide evidence to the *magistrates' court in support of a request for a *warrant or *summons. There are three main types of information in English law: (1) those that formally allege offences and request the issue of a summons; (2) those that formally allege offences and request the issue of an arrest warrant; and (3) those that provide evidence in support of a request for the issue of a search warrant. Informations alleging offences must comply with the provisions of the Magistrates' Courts Act 1980. *See also* LAYING AN INFORMATION.

Information Commissioner's Office An independent public body set up to promote access to official information and to protect personal information. The office regulates and enforces the Data Protection Act, the Freedom of Information Act, the Privacy and Electronic Communications Regulations, and the Environmental Information Regulations. It provides guidance to organizations and individuals; rules on eligible complaints; and can take action to order compliance, using enforcement and decision notices, and *prosecution.

informed consent The doctrine that determines the information to be disclosed to a patient to render his *consent to treatment lawful. In the USA, the doctrine is based upon the 'prudent patient' criterion, i.e. the nature, depth, and amount of information is judged by the physician as that required by a prudent patient. In the UK the doctrine is based upon the 'prudent physician' criterion, i.e. the nature, depth, and amount of information is judged by the physician as that which is necessary for the patient. Failure to disclose such information will render any treatment unlawful.

informer A person who gives information to the police about crimes committed by others. An informer who is himself involved in the crimes may sometimes receive a lighter *sentence in return for cooperation with the police that leads to the *conviction of other offenders. However, the police may not employ their own informers to participate in crimes and then arrest the criminals, and a police informer who pretends to join a plot to commit a crime may himself be *guilty of *conspiracy. It is nevertheless generally thought that if a police informer pretends to help in committing a crime with the intention of frustrating it, he will not be considered an *accessory if he fails to prevent the crime taking place. *See also* COVERT HUMAN INTELLIGENCE SOURCE.

inherent vice An inherent *defect in certain *goods that makes them liable to *damage. Some fibres, for example, are liable to rot during shipment. If a *carrier or insurer of such goods has not been warned of the inherent vice, he will not be liable for damage resulting directly from the defect.

inheritance 1. The devolution of property on the death of its owner, either according to the provisions of his will or under the rules relating to *intestacy contained in the Administration of Estates Act 1925 as amended. **2.** Property that a beneficiary receives from the estate of a deceased person.

inheritance tax A tax introduced by the Finance Act 1986 to replace capital transfer tax. The tax is payable on the value of a person's estate on death added to the value of lifetime gifts in the seven years preceding death and on certain other lifetime gifts. There are a number of exemptions, including gifts between husband and wife, gifts to *charities and political parties, and gifts for national purposes or for the public benefit.

inhuman treatment or punishment Treatment that causes intense physical and mental suffering. The prohibition on inhuman treatment or punishment as set out in Article 3 of the *European Convention on Human Rights is now part of UK law as a consequence of the *Human Rights Act 1998. This right is an *absolute right; inhuman treatment or punishment can never be justified as being in the public interest, no matter how great that public interest might be. Public authorities have a limited but positive duty to protect this right from interference by third parties.

injunction A remedy in the form of a court order addressed to a particular person that either prohibits him from doing or continuing to do a certain act (a **prohibitory injunction**) or orders him to carry out a certain act (a **mandatory injunction**). For example, a prohibitory injunction may be granted to restrain a *nuisance or to stop the infringement of a *copyright or *trade mark. A mandatory injunction may be granted to order a person to demolish a wall that he has built in breach of covenant. The remedy is discretionary and will be granted only if the court considers it just and convenient to do so; it will not be granted if *damages would be a sufficient remedy. *See also* HARASSMENT.

Injunctions are often needed urgently. A temporary injunction (**interim** or **interlocutory injunction**) may therefore be granted at a special hearing pending the outcome of the main hearing of the case. If it is granted, the claimant must undertake to compensate the defendant for any damage he has suffered by the grant of the injunction if the defendant is successful in the main action. If judgment is given for the claimant in the main action, a **perpetual injunction** is granted. A person who fails to abide by the terms of an injunction is *guilty of *contempt of court. *See also* FREEZING INJUNCTION.

injury 1. Infringement of a right. **2.** Actual harm caused to people or property.

inland bill A *bill of exchange that is (or on the face of it purports to be) both drawn and payable within the British Islands or drawn within the British Islands upon some person resident there. All other bills are *foreign bills. Unless the contrary appears on the face of a bill, the holder may treat it as an inland bill.

The distinction is relevant to the steps taken when a bill has been dishonoured.

Inland Revenue *See* HER MAJESTY'S REVENUE AND CUSTOMS.

in loco parentis [Latin: in place of a parent] A phrase used loosely to describe anyone looking after children on behalf of the *parents, e.g. *foster parents or relatives. In law, however, only a *guardian or a person in whose favour a residence order is made stands *in loco parentis*; their rights and duties are determined by statutory provisions.

Inner Temple An *Inn of Court situated in the Temple between the Strand and the Embankment. The earliest recorded claim for its existence is 1440.

innocent passage *See* TERRITORIAL WATERS.

Inns of Court Ancient legal societies situated in central London; every *barrister must belong to one of them. These voluntary unincorporated associations have the exclusive right of call to the *Bar. The early history of the Inns is disputed, but they probably began as hostels in which those who practised in the *common law courts lived. These hostels gradually evolved a corporate life in which Benchers, barristers, and students lived together as a self-regulating body. From an early date they had an important role in legal education. In modern times four Inns survive: *Gray's Inn, *Inner Temple, *Lincoln's Inn, and *Middle Temple.

innuendo (in an action for *defamation) A statement in which the claimant explains the defamatory meaning of apparently innocent words that he alleges are defamatory. The claimant must set out in his particulars of claim the facts or circumstances making the words defamatory.

in personam [Latin: against the person] A phrase describing a court action or a claim made against a specific person or a right affecting a particular person or group of people (*compare* IN REM). The *maxim of equity, 'equity acts *in personam*', refers to the fact that the Court of Chancery issued its decrees against the defendant himself, who was liable to imprisonment if he did not enforce them.

inquest An inquiry into a death the cause of which is unknown. An inquest is conducted by a *coroner and often requires the decision of a *jury of seven to eleven *jurors. It must be held in the case of a sudden death whose cause is unknown or suspicious, a death occurring in prison, or when the coroner reasonably suspects that the death was caused by violent or unnatural means. Inquests are not, however, criminal proceedings; witnesses are usually cross-examined only by the coroner and the strict laws of evidence do not apply. If unlawful *homicide is suspected, and criminal proceedings are likely, the coroner will usually adjourn the inquest (and must do so if requested to by a chief *police officer). It is an offence to dispose of a body with the intention of preventing an inquest being held.

inquiry 1. The overall investigation of an offence or incident (compare **enquiry**: the action of an individual asking for information). **2.** An investigation of a matter of public concern conducted by a judge, e.g. the Stephen Lawrence Inquiry. **3.** (in *international law) An attempt to discover the facts surrounding an international incident that is the subject of a dispute between two or more *parties by means of an impartial investigative body. Such an investigation is intended to promote a successful resolution of the dispute. In *treaty law each of the *Bryan Treaties and a number of other treaties between South and Central American states provided for the establishment of permanent commissions of inquiry. In 1967, the UN General Assembly adopted a resolution supporting the institution of such impartial fact-finding and requested the Secretary-General to establish a register of experts whose services could be used by states in specific disputes. *See also* GOOD OFFICES; MEDIATION.

inquisition A *document containing the verdict of a coroner's *inquest. It consists of the **caption** (details of the *coroner, *jury, and the inquest hearing), the **verdict** (identification of the body and probable cause of death), and the **attestation** (signatures of the coroner and jurors).

An **open verdict** may be recorded when there is insufficient evidence of the cause of death.

inquisitorial procedure A system of criminal justice, in force in some European countries but not in England, in which the truth is revealed by an inquiry into the facts conducted by the judge. In this system it is the judge who takes the initiative in conducting the case, rather than the *prosecution or *defence; his role is to lead the investigations, examine the evidence, and interrogate the witnesses. *Compare* ACCUSATORIAL PROCEDURE.

in re [Latin: in the matter of] A phrase used in the headings of *law reports, together with the name of the person or thing that the case is about (e.g. cases in which wills are being interpreted). It is often abbreviated to *re*, in which form it is used in headings to letters, etc.

in rem [Latin: against the thing] **1.** Describing a *right that should be respected by other people generally, such as *ownership of *property, as distinct from a right **in personam*. **2.** Describing a court action that is directed against an item of property, rather than against a person or group of people. Actions *in rem* are a feature of the Admiralty Court.

insanity (in criminal law) A defect of reason, arising from mental disease, that is severe enough to prevent a defendant from knowing what he did (or what he did was wrong). A person accused of a crime is presumed sane and therefore responsible for his acts, but he can rebut this presumption and escape a *conviction if he can prove (*see* BURDEN OF PROOF) that at the time of committing the crime he was insane. For purposes of this *defence, insanity is defined by the **McNaghten Rules**. These were formulated by *judges after the *trial of Daniel McNaghten (1843), who killed the Prime Minister's secretary by mistake for the Prime Minister, under the delusion that the Government was persecuting him, and was acquitted on the grounds of insanity. According to the rules, the defendant must show that he is suffering from a defect of reason arising out of 'a disease of the mind'. This would usually include most psychoses, paranoia, and schizophrenic diseases, but psychopaths and those suffering from neuroses or subnormality would not normally fall within the terms of the rules. The defendant must also show that, as a result of the defect of reason, he either did not know the 'nature and quality' of his acts, i.e. he did not know what he was doing (e.g. if he put a child on a fire, thinking it was a log of wood) or he did not know that his acts were wrong, even if he knew their nature and quality (e.g. if he knew he was murdering, but did not know that this was wrong). If the defendant is suffering from an insane delusion, he is treated as though the delusion was true and will have a defence if there would normally be one on those facts (e.g. if he kills someone under the insane delusion that he is acting in *self-defence, since self-defence is a defence). Medical evidence may be brought, but the *jury are entitled to form their opinion on the facts. If found to be insane the defendant is given a **special verdict** of 'not guilty by reason of insanity' and may be admitted to hospital. In cases of *homicide, the accused must be sent to hospital (usually a *special hospital, such as Broadmoor). Because of the consequences of successfully pleading it, in practice insanity was usually only pleaded to avoid the death penalty. However, a defendant who puts his mental state in issue (e.g. by raising a defence of *diminished responsibility on a *murder charge) might have to change his *plea to *guilty to avoid being treated as pleading insanity (though he is entitled to *appeal against an insanity *verdict).

*Magistrates' courts are not empowered to return a *special verdict. They will either grant a complete *acquittal, if the defendant's evidence of mental abnormality amounts to a denial that he had any necessary **mens rea* for the crime, or they may make a *hospital order, if the crime with which he is charged is one for which they could usually imprison him.

If someone in *custody for trial is suffering from mental illness or severe subnormality, he may be detained in hospital and not brought to trial until he is fit. A person who is insane at the time of his trial, in the sense that he does not understand the charge and cannot properly instruct his lawyers, may be found *unfit to plead.

See also GENERAL DEFENCES; IRRESISTIBLE IMPULSE.

insider dealing Taking advantage of specific unpublished price-sensitive information to deal in *securities to make a profit or avoid a loss. Under pt V of the Criminal Justice Act 1993, as amended by the Insider Dealing (Securities and Regulated Markets) (Amendment) Order 2002 (SI 2002/1874), dealings by insiders and those who have acquired information from insiders may be a criminal offence. Improperly disclosing such information or encouraging others to deal is also prohibited.

insolvency practitioner A person appointed to officiate in the *winding-up of a company or in *bankruptcy proceedings. The Insolvency Act 1986 requires the appointment of a qualified practitioner to act as a *liquidator, an *administrative receiver, the supervisor of a *voluntary arrangement, or a *trustee in bankruptcy. Under the Act, a person is only authorized to act in such a capacity if he has met certain statutory requirements, including membership of an approved professional body (such as the Institute of Chartered Accountants of England and Wales or the Insolvency Practitioners Association).

inspector A police rank above sergeant and below chief inspector.

instrument A formal legal *document, such as a will, *deed, or *conveyance, which is evidence of (for example) *rights and *duties. The *European Convention on Human Rights is a **living instrument** in that it must be interpreted in the light of present-day conditions rather than by trying to ascertain the meaning of those who drafted it over 50 years ago. *See also* STATUTORY INSTRUMENT.

insufficient evidence A direction by a *judge to a *jury that, as a matter of law, the evidence does not entitle them to make a certain finding. For example, if there is insufficient evidence for a *conviction, the judge may direct the jury to return a *verdict of *not guilty.

insulin A hormone produced in the pancreas. It controls the levels of sugar in the blood. *Diabetes mellitus is the production of too little or no insulin.

insulting behaviour *See* THREATENING BEHAVIOUR.

insurance A contract in which one *party (the **insurer**) agrees for payment of a consideration (the **premium**) to make monetary provision for the other (the **insured**) upon the occurrence of some event or against some risk. For such contracts to be enforceable, there must be some element of uncertainty about the events insured against and the insured must have an insurable interest in the subject matter of the contract. (The term **assurance** has the same meaning as insurance but is generally used in relation to events that will definitely happen at some time or another (especially death), whereas insurance refers to events that may or may not happen.) There are two types of insurance: **indemnity insurance**, which provides an indemnity against loss and in which the measure of the loss is the measure of payment (e.g. a fire policy); and **contingency insurance**, which involves payment on a contingent event and in which the sum paid is not measured by the loss but stated in the policy (e.g. a life policy). A contract of insurance is one requiring the utmost good faith (*see* UBERRIMAE FIDEI) and is voidable if a party fails in preliminary negotiations to disclose a fact material to the risk (*see* NON-DISCLOSURE; VOIDABLE CONTRACT). Innocent or fraudulent *misrepresentation may also render the contract voidable, or the contract may be terminated for breach of an essential term (*see* WARRANTY). Particular types of insurance include *life assurance, fire insurance, motor-vehicle insurance (*see* THIRD-PARTY INSURANCE), marine insurance, liability insurance, and guarantee insurance. There is considerable statutory regulation of insurance business.

Insurers are either **insurance companies** or *Lloyd's underwriters. Insurance companies are regulated by statute, aimed, among other things, at ensuring the insurance companies have sufficient funds to meet all claims made on them. **Insurance**

brokers negotiate insurance contracts with insurance companies or Lloyd's underwriters on a commission basis and usually handle claims on their clients' behalf. In the event of a claim, the insured receives either the amount agreed in the policy or an appropriate sum that is calculated by an independent **insurance assessor**.

insurance broker *See* INSURANCE.

insurance company *See* INSURANCE.

insurance policy A formal *document issued by an insurer setting out the terms of a contract of *insurance. Insurance contracts are not required by law to be in writing. Before the issue of a policy an insurer may issue a **cover note**, which is itself a temporary contract of insurance.

insurgency A state of revolt against constituted authority by rebels who are not recognized as *belligerent communities. Hence, recognition by nation X of a state of insurgency in nation Y means that while the former nation acknowledges a state of rebellion or revolt in nation Y, it is not yet prepared to extend recognition of a state of belligerency to that nation. Such a decision is based upon the relative proportion and success of the rebellion or revolt within state Y.

intangible property *Property that has no physical existence: *choses in action and incorporeal *hereditaments.

intellectual property *Intangible property that includes *patents, *trade marks, *copyright, and registered and unregistered *design rights.

intelligent detection system A *computer system also known as a knowledge-based system or neural network, used by the banking industry to detect fraudulent *payment card use.

intention The state of mind of one who aims to bring about a particular consequence. Intention is one of the main forms of **mens rea*, and for some crimes the only form (e.g. in the crime of threatening to destroy someone's *property, with the intention that he should fear that the threat will be carried out). A person is assumed to intend those consequences of his acts that are inevitable, but cannot be presumed to intend a consequence merely because it is probable or natural. In the latter case, the *jury must decide, on all the available evidence, whether or not in fact the accused did intend the consequences. For purposes of the law of *murder, however, a person is presumed to intend to cause death if he foresees that it is a highly likely consequence of his acts. This is sometimes known as **oblique intention**. Intention is often contrasted with *recklessness and should not be confused with *motive. For some purposes, offences are divided into crimes of **basic intent** or **specific intent** (*see* INTOXICATION). *See also* ULTERIOR INTENT.

Intention to injure is also a constituent element of some *torts, particularly those dealing with business relations (e.g. *conspiracy, *intimidation, procuring *breach of contract).

intercostal muscle The muscle sheets found between the ribs.

interfering with trade or business The *tort of deliberately interfering with the trade or business of another person by unlawful means, thereby causing *damage to that person. *Liability in this tort is wider than in the tort of procuring *breach of contract, since it is not necessary to show that an existing contract has been interfered with or broken. The operation of the tort in trade disputes is limited by statute.

interfering with vehicles It is an offence, under s 9 of the Criminal Attempts Act 1981, punishable with up to three months' imprisonment and/or a *fine, for a person to interfere with a vehicle or anything it carries with the intention that he or someone else will steal the vehicle or any of its contents or take the vehicle without the owner's consent. It is also a *summary offence, under the Road Traffic Act 1988, to get onto a vehicle on a *road or in a *local authority car park or to tamper with its brakes or other part of its mechanism without lawful authority or reasonable cause. *See also* CONVEYANCE.

interfering with witnesses Attempting to prevent a witness from giving evidence or to influence the evidence he gives. Making improper threats against witnesses may amount to the *common-law offence of *perverting the course of justice; persuading a witness to tell a lie constitutes—in addition to this—the offence of *subornation of *perjury. It is also perverting the course of justice to put pressure upon a witness to give evidence or to pay him money to testify in a particular way. Sometimes interfering with witnesses may also amount to *contempt of court. There is also a separate common-law offence of **tampering with witnesses** when one uses threats to persuade them not to give evidence. *See also* INTIMIDATION; JURY TAMPERING.

interim *See* INTERLOCUTORY.

interim injunction (interlocutory injunction) *See* INJUNCTION.

interim proceedings (interlocutory proceedings) The preliminary stages in civil proceedings, such as statements of case and *disclosure of documents, which occur between the issue of the claim form and the *trial. Their principal functions are to define the issues that will have to be decided at the trial and to prevent surprise.

interim relief (interlocutory relief) A temporary remedy, such as an interim *injunction, granted to a claimant by a court pending the *trial.

interlineation Writing between the lines of a *document. The effect is the same as that of an alteration.

interlocutory During the course of proceedings. Before the introduction of the *Civil Procedure Rules in 1999, the term was applied to certain processes in civil proceedings occurring between initiation of the action and the final *judgment (e.g. interlocutory *injunction, interlocutory proceedings). Under the Rules, it has been replaced by the term **interim**.

internal waters All rivers, canals, lakes (excluding international ones), and land-locked seas, the waters of *ports, bays, and roadsteads, and the waters on the landward side of the *baseline of the territorial sea. Within its internal waters, a coastal state exercises civil and criminal *jurisdiction over foreign merchant *ships and also administrative functions, such as enforcing customs and fishing regulations. *Compare* TERRITORIAL WATERS.

international carriage The *carriage of persons or *goods between two or more nations, which is regulated by various international conventions. The international carriage of goods by sea is governed by the **Hague Rules** (1924), the **Hague–Visby Rules** (1968), and the **Hamburg Rules** (1978, not yet in force); that of goods by *road by the Geneva Convention (1956); and that of goods by rail by a convention of 1980. There are also conventions regulating the international carriage of passengers by sea, rail, and road. The UK is a party to various of these conventions and has legislated to give them legal effect; e.g. the Carriage of Goods by Sea Act 1971 covers the Hague–Visby Rules.

International Court of Justice A court at The Hague, consisting of fifteen judges elected for nine-year terms of office, that has power to determine disputes relating to *international law. It was set up by the *United Nations in succession to the Permanent Court of International Justice, and all members of the UN are automatically parties to the Statute of the Court. No state may be brought before the Court in contentious proceedings unless it has accepted its *jurisdiction, either by agreement in a particular case or by recognition of the authority of the Court in general, in respect of any dispute with another state accepting the general jurisdiction of the Court (the **principle of reciprocity**). The Court may also give advisory opinions, which do not bind the *parties but are of great *persuasive authority.

international crime An offence that is recognized by the international community as being so serious as to warrant international action. Even though the offences will be violations of the law of the state, the international community may prosecute where the state finds it impracticable to prosecute or the state is too inefficient or fearful of the consequences of prosecution within the state system.

International Criminal Court A permanent court to try individuals for the most serious offences of global concern. In July 1998, 160 nations decided to establish this court; the Statute of the Court came into force in 2003 after 60 countries ratified it. Crimes within the jurisdiction of the Court are *genocide, *war crimes, and *crimes against humanity, such as widespread or systematic extermination of civilians, enslavement, *torture, *rape, forced pregnancy, persecution on political, racial, ethnic, or religious grounds, and enforced disappearances. The Court's Statute lists and defines all these crimes to avoid ambiguity. The seat of the Court is at The Hague, in the Netherlands, but it is authorized to try cases in other venues when appropriate.

International Criminal Police Organization (Interpol) An international police organization, with 184 member countries. It was formed in 1923, and facilitates international police cooperation; it supports and assists other law enforcement organizations. It operates to facilitate international police cooperation even where diplomatic relations do not exist between particular countries. Action is taken within the limits of existing laws in different countries and in the spirit of the *Universal Declaration of Human Rights. Interpol's constitution prohibits 'any intervention or activities of a political, military, religious or racial character'.

international humanitarian law A term for the body of law once called the rules and customs of war. The laws deal with the grave or serious violations known as *war crimes.

international law (**jus gentium*, law of nations) The system of law regulating the interrelationship of sovereign states and their rights and duties with regard to one another. In addition, certain international organizations (such as the *United Nations), companies, and sometimes individuals (e.g. in the sphere of *human rights) may have rights or duties under international law. International law deals with such matters as the formation and recognition of states, acquisition of territory, *war, the *law of the sea and of space, *treaties, treatment of *aliens, human rights, *international crimes, and international judicial settlement of disputes. The usual sources of international law are (1) *conventions and treaties; (2) international *custom, in so far as this is evidence of a general practice of behaviour accepted as legally binding (*see* OPINIO JURIS); (3) the *general principles of law recognized by civilized nations.

International law is also known as **public international law** to distinguish it from *private international law, which does not deal with relationships between states.

International Law Commission (ILC) A body established in 1947 by General Assembly Resolution 174 (II) and acting under Article 13 of the *United Nations Charter. The ILC consists of 25 members of recognized competence in *international law who are elected for five-year periods by the General Assembly from a list of candidates nominated by the member states of the UN. The mission of the ILC is to promote the progressive development of international law by preparing draft conventions on subjects that have not yet been regulated by international law and by codifying the law. It produces annual reports of current problems.

international legal personality (in *international law) Entities who are endowed with *rights and *obligations under public international law are said to have international legal personality. The entities with this legal personality include states, international organizations, *non-governmental organizations, and to some limited extent private individuals and corporations within a state.

international minimum standard (in *international law) A minimum standard of treatment that must always be observed with regard to the treatment of foreign nationals. This standard consists of at least the *right to life, liberty, and free access to the courts and to the protection of *property (especially fair compensation for the nationalization of property). The international minimum standard has proved to be contentious with developing countries and Socialist states, who believe that it merely advances Western economic imperialism. *See also* ESPOUSAL OF CLAIM; EXPROPRIATION. *Compare* NATIONAL TREATMENT STANDARD.

international supply contract A contract for the *sale of goods made by parties whose places of business (or habitual residences) are in the territories of different states. The limitations imposed by the Unfair Contract Terms Act 1977 on the extent to which a person may exclude or restrict his *liability (e.g. by an *exemption clause) do not apply to such a contract if (1) when it is made, the *goods are in *carriage (or due to be carried) from one state to another; (2) the offer and its acceptance take place in different states; or (3) the goods are to be delivered in a state other than that in which the offer and acceptance take place. However, other statutes may apply to such contracts, and in many countries the Vienna Convention on the International Sales of Goods and world trade rules under the General Agreement on Tariffs and Trade (GATT) and the *World Trade Organization (WTO) will apply.

inter partes [Latin: between the parties] Proceedings for which all *parties have been served with notice and given the opportunity to attend. *Compare* EX PARTE.

interpleader A procedure used to decide how conflicting claims against the same person should be dealt with. It applies when there are two or more claims against the applicant (whether or not court proceedings have been issued) that conflict with each other, e.g. when two or more people claim the same *goods that are being held by the applicant. The court decides how the matter should be dealt with; it may, for example, direct that there should be a court action between the rival claimants.

interpretation (construction) The process of determining the true meaning of a written *document. It is a judicial process, effected in accordance with a number of rules and presumptions. So far as is relevant, the rules and presumptions applicable to *Acts of Parliament (*see* INTERPRETATION OF STATUTES) apply equally to private *documents, such as *deeds and wills.

Interpretation Act An Act of 1978 (originally 1889) that defines a number of common words and expressions and provides that the same definitions are to apply in all other Acts except those specifically indicating otherwise. For example, 'person' includes (in addition to an individual) any body of persons corporate or unincorporate. It also lays down that unless otherwise mentioned any word importing the masculine includes the feminine so that *legislation does not have to put he/she every time a pronoun is used.

interpretation clause A clause in a written *document that defines words and phrases used in the document itself. In an *Act of Parliament it is called an **interpretation section**. *See also* INTERPRETATION ACT.

interpretation of statutes The judicial process of determining, in accordance with certain rules and presumptions, the true meaning of *Acts of Parliament. The principal rules of statutory interpretation are as follows. (1) An Act must be construed as a whole, so that internal inconsistencies are avoided. (2) Words that are reasonably capable of only one meaning must be given that meaning whatever the result. This is called the **literal rule**. (3) Ordinary words must be given their ordinary meanings and technical words their technical meanings, unless absurdity would result. This is the **golden rule**. (4) When an Act aims at curing a defect in the law any ambiguity is to be resolved in such a way as to favour that aim (the **mischief rule**). (5) The ***ejusdem generis* rule** [Latin: of the same kind]: when a list of specific items belonging to the same class is followed by general words (as in 'cats, dogs, and other animals'), the general words are to be treated as confined to other items of the same class (in this example, to other *domestic* animals). (6) The ***expressio unius est exclusio alterius* rule** [Latin: the inclusion of the one is the exclusion of the other]: when a list of specific items is not followed by general words it is to be taken as exhaustive. For example, 'weekends and public holidays' excludes ordinary weekdays.

The *House of Lords has ruled against the existence of an alleged **social policy rule**, which would enable an ambiguous Act to be interpreted so as to best give effect to the social policy underlying it. Ambiguities may occasionally be resolved by referring to external sources; e.g. the intention of *Parliament in regard to a proposed Act, as revealed by ministers during its passage through Parliament, may be discovered by reference to *Hansard.

There are some general presumptions relating to the interpretation of statutes. They are presumed (1) not to bind the *Crown (including the sovereign personally); (2) not to operate retrospectively so far as *substantive (but not procedural) law is concerned; (3) not to interfere with vested rights (particularly without *compensation); (4) not to oust the *jurisdiction of the courts; and (5) not to *derogate from constitutional rights or *international law. But clear words or necessary implication may override these presumptions. A *consolidating statute is presumed not to be intended to alter the law, but this does not apply to codifying statutes, which may be concerned with clarifying law that was previously unclear. Penal and taxing statutes are subject to **strict construction**, i.e. if after applying the normal rules of interpretation it is still doubtful whether or not a *penalty or *tax attaches to a particular person or transaction, the ambiguity must be resolved in favour of the subject. *See also* INTERPRETATION ACT; INTERPRETATION CLAUSE.

interpreter A person providing interpretation services. Interpreters in criminal proceedings are expected to have knowledge of police and court procedures; ideally they will be selected from the **National Register of Public Service Interpreters**, or the **Council for the Advancement of Communication with Deaf People** Register of Sign Language. It is the responsibility of the police or investigating agency to arrange for interpreters for any part of an investigation, and for the requirements of the suspect, or person charged, while in *custody. The court is responsible for arranging the interpreter for the defendant at court, except where the first court appearance is within two days of the charge when the police or prosecuting agency will make the arrangements on its behalf. Normally, the interpreter used in the investigative stage will not be used in court proceedings. The *prosecution and *defence are responsible for arranging interpreters for their own witnesses. Generally, a separate interpreter is required for each defendant.

interregnum 1. The period between the death of a sovereign and the *accession of his or her successor. **2.** Temporary rule exercised during such a period. In the UK a sovereign's death does not result in an interregnum.

interrogation *See* INVESTIGATIVE INTERVIEWING.

interstate trade Trade between states. *European Union competition rules apply only when an anti-competitive agreement or abuse of a dominant position will affect trade between member states. Whether or not interstate trade is affected is therefore crucial to any competition analysis. Agreements relating to imports or exports are most likely to affect interstate trade, but so might an agreement between two businesses situated in one member state, depending on the terms or effect of the agreement.

intertemporal law The law that international courts apply when a long time has elapsed since the conclusion of a *treaty, to take into account changes that have taken place in *international law since the treaty was formulated and changes in the meaning of the expressions in the treaty. The existence of a *right (e.g. to a territorial claim) should be based not only on the law in effect at the time the right was created, but also on the international law as applied to the continued existence of that right. The legitimacy of a *title to territory must be renewed by the claimant state.

intervention order *See* DRUG INTERVENTION ORDER.

intestacy The state in which a person dies without having made a will disposing of all his *property.

intimate sample A sample of bodily fluid or tissue, dental impression, or swab from a body orifice (other than the mouth) taken in the course of a criminal investigation. The taking of the samples is regulated by s 65 of the Police and Criminal Evidence Act 1984. Such samples can only be taken by a doctor or nurse.

intimate search A physical examination of a body orifice (except the mouth) in accordance with s 65 of the Police and Criminal Evidence Act 1984.

intimidated witness *See* SPECIAL MEASURES.

intimidation 1. The act of frightening someone into doing something. Intimidation is not in itself a crime, but it may constitute part of a crime. For example, it is a crime to have sexual intercourse with a woman if her agreement was obtained by intimidation. It is a crime to intimidate a *juror or witness in relation to proceedings with which he is connected (*see* CONTEMPT OF COURT). If one intimidates someone into handing over money or *property, this may amount to *theft, and in some cases to *blackmail. There are also special statutory offences of threatening to *destroy or *damage someone else's property and threatening to kill someone. A person who commits a crime when intimidated by others may sometimes have a *defence of *duress. *See also* THREAT.

Under s 51 of the Criminal Justice and Public Order Act 1994 it is also an offence to intimidate a person whom the offender believes to be a potential or actual witness or juror. The offender must, however, have an intention to obstruct an investigation or the course of justice, although this will be presumed where it is proved that he did an act that intimidates. Similar offences exist with regard to reprisals against potential witnesses or jurors. On *summary conviction the maximum *penalty is six months' imprisonment and/or a *fine up to the statutory maximum of £5000, and on *indictment it is five years' imprisonment and/or an unlimited fine. *See also* JURY TAMPERING. **2.** A *tort in which A, with the intention of injuring B, either directly threatens B with some unlawful act or threatens C with an unlawful act in order to make him cause damage to B. Thus if A threatens to do an unlawful act to B's *employer (C) unless he dismisses B, and C succumbs to the threat, B has an action for intimidation against A for causing the loss of his job. It is irrelevant that C was entitled to dismiss B and did not act unlawfully: the essence of the tort is A's unlawful threat. The operation of the tort in trade disputes is limited by statute.

intoxicating liquor *See* ALCOHOL; LICENSING OF PREMISES.

intoxication The condition of someone who is drunk or under the influence of drugs. Although intoxication itself is not an offence (*but see* DRUNKENNESS), it is an element in a number of offences. These include *drunken driving, being found drunk in a *public place, being drunk and disorderly in a public place, and being drunk in a public place while possessing a loaded *firearm. Where drunkenness is an element of an offence, *alcohol must be present but may not be the only intoxicant. It is also an offence to supply or offer to supply to a person under 18 a substance (e.g. a glue or solvent) whose fumes are likely to be inhaled by that person for the purpose of causing intoxication.

When a person is so intoxicated that he is incapable of forming the **mens rea* required to be *guilty of a particular crime, he is usually entitled to be acquitted if the crime is one that requires a specific intention (but not if it requires a basic intention). A crime is one of **basic intent** if the *mens rea* required does not go beyond the **actus reus* of the crime (e.g. *rape, in which the *actus reus* is sexual intercourse without the woman's consent and the *mens rea* is intention to have sexual intercourse without her consent, or *recklessness whether she consents or not). A crime is one of **specific intent** if the *mens rea* required goes beyond the *actus reus* (e.g. *theft, in which the *actus reus* is merely appropriating someone else's property, but the *mens rea*—in addition to the intention of appropriating it—requires an intention to deprive the owner of it for good). Intoxication will not be a defence, however, if the crime is one of specific intent that can be committed by being reckless and the *indictment is framed in terms of recklessness. For example, if a drunken person sets fire to a building and endangers the lives of people in it, he may be *guilty of destroying *property being reckless as to whether life would be endangered, even though he was unaware of the risk. He could not, however, be guilty of damaging property intending to endanger life. Intoxication is not a defence if a person deliberately drinks or takes drugs in order to give himself **Dutch courage** to commit a crime.

In *international law, the Statute of the *International Criminal Court generally excludes *liability for the commission of an offence where the defendant is unable to appreciate the unlawfulness or nature of his conduct or control his conduct. *Immunity will not arise where the defendant has become voluntarily intoxicated in circumstances where he knew or disregarded the risk that as a result of the intoxication he was likely to commit a crime.

intracerebral Inside the brain.

intracranial Inside the skull.

intrapulmonary Inside the lungs.

intrastat offences The method of collecting information and producing statistics on the export and import of *goods between *European Union member states. It is regulated, *inter alia*, by the Statistics of Trade (Customs and Excise) (Amendment No 2) Regulations 1993 (SI 1993/3015). A person who trades with any of the other EU member states must report that trade to *Her Majesty's Revenue and Customs. How detailed that report is required to be depends on the value of the trade with other EU Member States for either purchases (arrivals) or sales (dispatches). A trader who fails to make such a report commits an offence.

intrauterine Inside the uterus.

intra vires [Latin: within the powers] Describing an act carried out by a body (such as a public authority or a company) that is within the limits of the powers conferred on it by statute or some other constituting *document (such as the *memorandum and *articles of association of a company). *Compare* ULTRA VIRES.

intrusive surveillance *See* SURVEILLANCE.

investigating officer An *employee of a *police authority, other than a *constable, designated under s 38 of the Police Reform Act 2002 to investigate offences and have certain police powers in relation to such an investigation.

investigation of a company An inquiry into the running of a company made by inspectors appointed by the Department of Trade and Industry acting under pt XIV of the Companies Act 1985 or the Financial Services Act 1986. It may be ordered by the Secretary of State, on his own initiative or upon application by the shareholders or the company itself, or by the court. Such an inquiry may be held to supply *company members with information or to investigate *fraud, unfair prejudice, nominee shareholders, or *insider dealing. The inspectors' report is usually published.

investigative interview A conversation between an investigator and victims, witnesses, and suspects intended to elicit information. The nationally accepted model of investigative interviewing has five phases and is usually referred to by the acronym *PEACE. *See also* COGNITIVE INTERVIEW; CONVERSATION MANAGEMENT.

The questioning of suspects is sometimes termed **interrogation**, although there are negative connotations associated with the term. Suspects are not obliged to answer such questions (*see* RIGHT OF SILENCE), and the right of the police to question suspects is governed by the Police and Criminal Evidence Act 1984 and the Codes of Practice made under it. The Codes deal with such matters as the rights of the suspect to communicate with third parties, rights to legal advice and to medical treatment, and advice to the police on the administering of a *caution, the provision of *interpreters, and the keeping of records concerning all these matters. There are special provisions applying to interviews with juveniles, the mentally ill, and the mentally handicapped. The provisions of the 1984 Act and its Codes must now be read subject to the requirements of the *Human Rights Act 1998. *See also* CONFESSION.

investment company A public listed company with a business of investing its funds mainly in *securities in order to spread investment risk and give *company members the benefit derived from the management of its funds. Investment companies must give notice in prescribed form to the Companies Registry. Under the Companies Act 1985 they are subject to special provisions in relation to dividends.

invitation to treat *See* OFFER.

invitee A person permitted to enter *land or *premises for a purpose in which the *occupier of the land has a material interest. An example of an invitee is a customer in a shop. *See* OCCUPIER'S LIABILITY.

in vitro fertilization (IVF) *See* HUMAN ASSISTED REPRODUCTION.

involuntary conduct Conduct that cannot be controlled because one is suffering from a physical or mental condition or is acting under *duress. Involuntary conduct will often give rise to a *defence of *automatism, although it may not be a defence if one is aware of one's condition or induced it oneself. Sometimes conduct may be regarded as involuntary if one is in control of one's faculties; e.g. when the brakes of a car suddenly fail, this will also afford a defence to a driving offence charge.

involuntary manslaughter An offence of *homicide that lacks the *malice aforethought required for *murder. *Compare* *voluntary manslaughter where the defendant has the malice aforethought for murder but has a partial defence which reduces the offence to manslaughter. The categories of involuntary manslaughter are: unlawful act manslaughter, gross negligence manslaughter, and reckless manslaughter.

irrebuttable presumption *See* PRESUMPTION.

irresistible impulse An uncontrollable urge to do something. Irresistible impulse is not usually a defence in law and it will not afford a defence of *insanity, unless it arises out of a disease of the mind as defined by the McNaghten Rules. When, however, an impulse is irresistible in that the body reacts in an instinctive way to it, there may be a defence of *involuntary conduct. An irresistible impulse may also constitute *diminished responsibility. *See also* PROVOCATION.

irrevocable Incapable of being revoked. For example, powers of appointment may be made irrevocable.

ischaemic Lacking blood, as in *ischaemic heart disease.

ischaemic heart disease (IHD) A disease caused by narrowing of the blood vessels in the heart caused by deposits of fat in the arteries.

issue 1. The matter in dispute in a court action. **2.** The children or other lineal descendants of a person. **3.** The total of bank notes in circulation within a country.

issued capital *See* AUTHORIZED CAPITAL.

jactitation of marriage A false assertion that one is married to someone to whom one is not in fact married.

jejunum The middle part of the small intestine between the *duodenum and *ileum.

jetsam *See* WRECK.

jettisoned at sea, drugs The throwing overboard of drugs. If drugs are jettisoned at sea and remain outside the limits of a port no offence of importation is committed under the Customs and Excise Management Act 1979. However if the tide were to carry them into the limits of a port then importation would be complete.

Jobseeker's Agreement An agreement that must be signed by a claimant for the *jobseeker's allowance and his Employment Service adviser. The agreement sets out any restrictions on the claimant's availability for work and outlines the type of work being sought and the plans the claimant has made for seeking work.

jobseeker's allowance (JSA) A taxable benefit introduced by the Jobseekers Act 1995 that replaced both unemployment benefit and income support for jobseekers from 7 October 1996. Those with national insurance contributions can claim contribution-based JSA, which is paid for up to six months. Those without NI contributions can claim income-based JSA, which is payable for as long as the claimant satisfies the rules. JSA is only paid to those who are available for work, are actively seeking work, and who have signed a *Jobseeker's Agreement.

joinder of causes of action The combination in one *action of several causes of action against the same defendant. Although any number of causes of action may be joined in the first instance, the court may order that they be severed if the joinder would cause procedural difficulties.

joinder of charges The joining of more than one charge of a criminal offence together in the same *indictment. This may be done when the charges are based on the same facts or are part of a series of offences of the same or similar character.

joinder of defendants Mentioning two or more defendants in one count of an *indictment and trying them together. It is possible to join two or more defendants even if one of them is the principal offender and the other an *accessory; if they are separately indicted, however, they cannot subsequently be tried together. Sometimes (e.g. in cases of *conspiracy) it is usual to join two or more defendants; one may be convicted even if all his co-conspirators named in the count are acquitted and even though conspiracy by definition requires more than one participant. Two or more defendants may also be joined in one indictment if they are charged with different offences, if the interests of justice require this; e.g. if two witnesses commit *perjury in relation to the same facts in the same proceedings. Defendants who have been jointly indicted will normally only be tried by separate *trials if a joint trial might prejudice one or more of them; e.g. when evidence against one accused is not admissible against the other or when the prosecution wish to call one of the defendants to give evidence against another.

joinder of documents The connecting together of two or more *documents so that, jointly, they fulfil statutory requirements when one of the documents alone would be insufficient.

joinder of parties (in civil law) The combination as claimants or defendants of two or more persons in a single *action. Joinder may take place with the permission of the court or when separate actions would result in some common question of law or fact arising in all the actions, and all claims in the action are in respect of or arise out of the same transaction or series of transactions. *See also* JOINDER OF DEFENDANTS.

joint and several Together and in separation. If two or more people enter into an obligation that is said to be joint and several, their liability for its breach can be enforced against them all by a joint action or against any of them by individual action. *See also* JOINT TORTFEASORS.

Joint Asset Recovery Database (JARD) A computer database established by the *Concerted Inter-Agency Criminal Finance Action Group in April 2004 to ensure better day-to-day management of asset recovery. Over 2 500 individuals have access to the system in the various agencies involved in asset recovery. The agencies that use the database are obliged to keep it updated by entering data about the progress of *confiscation order enforcement. Importantly, JARD records the date the confiscation order was made and the deadline the court sets for the defendant to satisfy the order.

joint investigation team A team set up under formal *mutual legal assistance agreements to carry out joint investigations into particular offences with cross-border elements, with a view to improving and speeding up investigation of the offences. Teams are made up of investigators (and sometimes *magistrates, *prosecutors, and specialist advisers) from two or more states who may carry out investigations in any of those states. Members working in a state other than their own are regarded as seconded to the national authorities of that state and, with the consent of their hosts, may undertake certain investigative measures or be present when such measures take place. *See also* ASSAULT; OBSTRUCTING A POLICE OFFICER, ETC.

joint tortfeasors Two or more people whose wrongful actions in furthering a common design cause a single injury.

joule burn A burn caused by electricity.

journalistic materials Materials acquired or created for the purpose of journalism (which includes radio and television and other media). Police cannot search for or seize such material except under powers created by s 9 of the Police and Criminal Evidence Act 1984 (PACE). Journalistic material that is held in confidence is *'excluded material', which can only be obtained under the second set of access conditions in sch 1 PACE. The circumstances would be extremely rare. Such material must have been held in confidence from the time of its creation or acquisition; it cannot be given confidential status later. Journalistic material which is not held in confidence is *'special procedure' material and can be obtained by police by way of a production order or *warrant granted under the first set of access conditions in sch 1.

Journals The authentic record of proceedings in *Parliament, as opposed to the verbatim record of debates (*see* HANSARD). There are two series published annually: *Journals of the House of Lords* (beginning in 1509) and *Journals of the House of Commons* (beginning in 1547).

joyriding *See* AGGRAVATED VEHICLE-TAKING; TAKING A CONVEYANCE WITHOUT CONSENT.

judge A state official with power to adjudicate on disputes and other matters brought before the courts for decision. In English law all judges are appointed by the *Crown, on the advice of the *Lord Chancellor in the case of *circuit judges and *High Court *puisne judges and on the advice of the Prime Minister in the case of judges of the *Court of Appeal and the *Lords of Appeal in Ordinary. The independence of the higher judiciary is ensured by the principle that they hold office during good behaviour and not at the pleasure of the Crown (with the exception of the Lord Chancellor). They can only be removed from office by a resolution of both Houses of Parliament assented to by the Queen. Circuit judges may be removed by the Lord Chancellor for *incapacity or misbehaviour. All judicial appointments are pensionable and there is a compulsory retirement age of

70 years, but this can be extended to 75 if considered to be in the public interest. *See also* JUDICIAL IMMUNITY. *Compare* MAGISTRATE.

judge advocate A *barrister or *solicitor who advises a *court martial on questions of law.

Judge Advocate-General's Department A department that advises the Secretary of State for Defence and the Defence Council on matters relating to the administration of military law and reviews proceedings of *courts martial.

judge in his own cause *See* NATURAL JUSTICE.

Judges' Rules Formerly, rules of practice drawn up by the *High Court governing the questioning and charging of suspects by the police. They were replaced by a *code of practice issued under the provisions of the Police and Criminal Evidence Act 1984. *See also* INVESTIGATIVE INTERVIEWING.

judgment 1. A decision made by a court in respect of the matter before it. **2.** The process of reasoning by which the court's decision was arrived at. In English law it is the normal practice for judgment to be given in open court or, in some appellate tribunals, to be handed down in printed form. If the judgment contains rulings on important questions of law, it may be reported in the *law reports.

judicial cognizance *See* JUDICIAL NOTICE.

Judicial Committee of the Privy Council A tribunal, created by the Judicial Committee Act 1833, consisting of the *Lord Chancellor, Lord President of the Council and ex-Lords President, *Lords of Appeal in Ordinary, and other members of the *Privy Council who have been Lords of Appeal in Ordinary or who have held high judicial office. Certain judges of Commonwealth countries who are Privy Counsellors are also members. The Committee's jurisdiction is to hear *appeals from courts in *dependent territories and those Commonwealth countries that have retained appeals to the Privy Council since attaining independence; it also hears appeals under certain statutes. The Judicial Committee also has jurisdiction to hear and determine 'devolution issues', that is questions relating to the powers and functions ofthe legislative and executive authorities established in Scotland and Northern Ireland and questions as to the competence and functions of the *Welsh Assembly. The Committee's decisions are not technically judgments but merely advice to the *Crown: they do not become final until incorporated into an *Order in Council. For this reason also, until 1966 dissenting opinions were not disclosed. The Committee's decisions are not binding as *precedents upon English courts but are merely of *persuasive authority. However the Privy Council's advice in *Attorney-General for Jersey v Holley* [2005] 2 AC 580 was followed by the Court of Appeal in a number of cases in preference to the House of Lords in *R v Smith (Morgan)* [1999] QB 1079. *See also* SUPREME COURT.

judicial dictum *See* OBITER DICTUM.

judicial discretion The power of the court to take some step, grant a remedy, or admit evidence or not as it thinks fit. Many rules of procedure and evidence are in discretionary form or provide for some element of discretion. In criminal cases, under s 78 of the Police and Criminal Evidence Act 1984, the court may exclude prosecution evidence if its admission would have such an adverse effect on the fairness of the proceedings that the court ought not to admit it. The *Court of Appeal is reluctant to review the exercise of discretion by *trial *judges.

judicial immunity The exemption of a *judge or *magistrate from personal actions for *damages arising from the exercise of his judicial office. The immunity is absolute in respect of all words or actions of the judge while acting within his *jurisdiction and extends to acts done without jurisdiction provided that they were done in *good faith.

judicial notice (judicial cognizance) The means by which the court may take as proven certain facts without hearing evidence. **Notorious facts** (i.e. matters of common knowledge) may be judicially noticed without inquiry; some other facts (e.g. matters that can easily be checked in a standard work of reference and are reasonably indisputable) may be noticed after inquiry. When judicial notice has been taken, *evidence in rebuttal is not permitted.

judicial precedent *See* PRECEDENT.

judicial review The supervisory function of the *Queen's Bench Division of the *High Court over inferior courts and official bodies such as government ministers or *chief constables. It is not an *appeal against the decision of the court or official body but a review of the decision making process or policy to see whether the applicant has been fairly treated (see *Chief Constable of North Wales Police v Evans* [1982] 1 WLR 1155). It is available where the court or authority has: exceeded its power; committed an error in law; committed a breach of *natural justice; reached a decision which no reasonable tribunal could have reached; abused its power; or committed a procedural impropriety.

It is no longer necessary to have a Divisional Court and the review may be conducted by a single judge. On finding for the applicant the court may grant a *quashing order, *mandatory order, *prohibition order, *declaration, or *injunction; it may also award *damages.

jugular veins The veins draining blood from the head and neck.

junior barrister Any barrister who is not a *Queen's Counsel. The word 'junior' does not necessarily imply youth or lack of seniority: many members of the Bar remain juniors throughout their careers.

jure gestionis [Latin: management authority] Describing commercial transactions by bodies that are owned by the state but are not regarded as organs of the state. In *international law the state accepts responsibility for such transactions and does not claim *immunity. *Compare* JURE IMPERII.

jure imperii [Latin: sovereign authority] Describing transactions by state bodies or representatives, such as diplomats. In *international law the state maintains *immunity from such transactions. *Compare* JURE GESTIONIS.

jurisdiction 1. The power of a court to hear and decide a case or make a certain order. (For the limits of jurisdiction of individual courts, see entries for those courts.) **2.** The territorial limits within which the jurisdiction of a court may be exercised. In the case of English courts this comprises England, Wales, Berwick-upon-Tweed, and those parts of the sea claimed as *territorial waters. Everywhere else is said to be **outside the jurisdiction**. **3.** The territorial scope of the legislative competence of *Parliament. *See* SOVEREIGNTY OF PARLIAMENT.

In *international law, jurisdiction can be exercised on a number of grounds, based on the following principles: (1) the territorial principle (that the state within whose boundaries the crime has taken place has jurisdiction, irrespective of the *nationality of the transgressor); (2) the nationality principle (that a state has the power of jurisdiction over one of its nationals for an offence he has committed in another state); (3) the protective principle (that a potentially injured state can exercise jurisdiction in all cases when its national security is threatened); (4) the passive personality principle (that a state has jurisdiction if the illegal act has been committed against a national of that state); and (5) the universality principle (when the accused has committed a crime in breach of a rule of **jus cogens*, i.e. a crime against humanity, any party having *custody of the alleged lawbreaker is permitted to bring criminal proceedings against him).

juris et de jure [Latin: of law and from law] An irrebuttable *presumption is so described.

juristic person (artificial person) An entity, such as a *corporation, that is recognized as having legal personality, i.e. it is capable of enjoying and being subject to legal rights and duties. It is contrasted with a human being, who is referred to as a **natural person**.

juror A member of a *jury. Each juror must swear that he will faithfully try the case and give a true *verdict according to the evidence; failure to do so is *contempt of court.

A defendant is entitled to challenge individual jurors (*see* CHALLENGE TO JURY); if he succeeds in his challenges, another person takes the place of the challenged juror. A person who appears to be suffering from a disability that could impair performance of his duties as juror must now be brought before the judge so that he may form an opinion as to the person's suitability.

jury A group of *jurors (usually twelve) selected at random to decide the facts of a case and give a *verdict. Most juries are selected to try crimes but juries are also used in coroner's *inquests and in some civil cases (e.g. *defamation actions). The judge directs the jury on points of law (*see* DIRECTION TO JURY) and sums up the evidence of the *prosecution and *defence for them, but he must leave the jury to decide all questions of fact themselves. He must also make it clear to them that they are the only *triers of fact and must acquit the defendant unless they feel sure that he is *guilty beyond reasonable doubt. The verdict of a jury should, if possible, be unanimous, but when there are at least ten people on the jury and they cannot reach a unanimous verdict, a *majority verdict is acceptable. Many offences must be tried by a jury; many others may be tried by a jury or by *magistrates (*see* INDICTABLE OFFENCE). *See also* CHALLENGE TO JURY.

It is a criminal offence to attempt to influence a jury's discussions or to question them about their discussions when the case is over. *See also* CONTEMPT OF COURT; INTIMIDATION; JURY TAMPERING.

jury tampering The act of influencing or attempting to influence, either directly or through a third party, the deliberations or decisions of a *jury during the course of a *trial, by bribery, *intimidation, or any other unlawful means. Part 7 of the Criminal Justice Act 2003, which came into effect on 24 July 2006, provides for a trial to be conducted without a jury where there is a real and present danger of jury tampering, or continued without a jury where the jury has been discharged because of it. In either event, the court must be satisfied that, notwithstanding any steps that could reasonably be taken to prevent it (including police protection), the risk of jury tampering is so substantial as to make it necessary in the interests of justice for the trial to be conducted in that way. Section 44(6) of the Act provides three examples where the provisions might be invoked: where a jury in a previous trial of the accused was discharged because jury tampering had taken place; where such tampering has taken place in previous criminal proceedings in which the accused was involved; and in cases where there has been intimidation, or attempted intimidation, of any person likely to be called as a witness in the proceedings. It is clear, then, that evidence of a wider threat to the integrity of the process may found an application. The rationale for this is that if there is evidence that the accused is prepared to attack the process, there must be a real and present danger that the jury is also at risk. Where a trial is conducted or continued without a jury and a defendant is convicted, the court is required to give its reasons for the conviction. *See also* INTIMIDATION; TRIAL BY CROWN COURT JUDGE ALONE.

jus [Latin: law] A law or right.

jus ad bellum [Latin: right to war] The right to wage war.

jus civile [Latin: civil law] **1.** *Municipal law. **2.** The whole body of Roman law.

jus cogens [Latin: coercive law] A rule or principle in *international law that is so fundamental that it binds all states and does not allow any exceptions. Such rules (sometimes called **peremptory norms**) will only amount to *jus cogens* rules if they are recognized as such by the international community as a whole. A *treaty that conflicts with an existing *jus cogens* rule is void, and if a new *jus cogens* rule emerges, any existing treaty that conflicts with it automatically becomes void. States cannot create regional customary international law that contradicts *jus cogens* rules. Most authorities agree that the laws prohibiting *slavery, *genocide, *piracy, and acts of aggression or illegal use of force are *jus cogens* laws. Some suggest that certain *human rights provisions (e.g. those prohibiting *racial discrimination) also come under the category of *jus cogens*.

jus gentium [Latin: the law of peoples] *See* INTERNATIONAL LAW.

jus in bello [Latin: the law of war] The method and means of waging war.

jus naturale [Latin: natural law] The fundamental element of all law. *See* NATURAL LAW.

just and equitable winding-up A *compulsory winding-up on grounds of fairness. This may occur, for example, when the purpose of the company cannot be achieved, when the management is deadlocked or has been *guilty of serious irregularities, or, in small companies run on the basis of mutual trust between members, when the majority have exercised their legal rights in breach of a common understanding between the members when the company was formed. No order will be made if another form of *minority protection would be more appropriate.

justice A moral ideal that the law seeks to uphold in the protection of *rights and *punishment of wrongs.

justice of the peace (JP) A person holding a commission from the *Crown to exercise certain judicial functions for a particular **local justice area**. JPs are appointed on behalf of and in the name of the *Queen by the *Lord Chancellor and may be removed from office in the same way. On reaching the age of 70 they are placed on a supplemental list and cease to be able to exercise any judicial functions. Their principal function is to sit as *magistrates in the *magistrates' courts but they may also sit in the *Crown Court when it is considering *committals for sentence and *appeals from magistrates' courts, sign *warrants of arrest and search warrants, and take statutory declarations. All *High Court judges are *ex officio* justices of the peace for the whole of England and Wales.

justices' clerk *See* CLERK TO THE JUSTICES.

justification 1. The defence to an action for *defamation that the defamatory statement made was true. Truth is a complete defence to a civil action for defamation, except where true statements about *spent convictions are proved to have been made maliciously. **2.** The defence that interference with the contractual or business relations of another was justified. The scope of the defence is uncertain, but the fact that the wages of chorus girls were so low that they were compelled to resort to *prostitution has been held to justify a theatrical performers' protection society inducing theatre owners to break their contracts with the girls' *employer (*Brimelow v Casson* [1924] 1 Ch 302).

justifying bail Demonstrating to a court granting *bail that one is capable of meeting the *surety specified in the bail (e.g. disclosing one's financial resources). A person standing surety for bail must be able to provide the bail out of his own resources.

just satisfaction The basis for *damages awarded by the *European Court of Human Rights (and thus in respect of claims under the *Human Rights Act 1998). In many cases where the Court finds a violation it has declined to award any damages on the basis that this finding is in itself sufficient just satisfaction. Subject to this discretion, damages can be obtained for pecuniary loss, non-pecuniary loss, and costs and expenses.

juvenile court *See* YOUTH COURT.

juvenile offender A person between the ages of 10 and 17 who has committed a crime (*see* DOLI CAPAX); an offender between the ages of 14 and 17 is known as a **young offender**: s 70, Children and Young Persons Act 1969. A person who has not attained the age of 18 may not be tried on *indictment unless: (a) he is charged with *homicide (which includes *murder and *manslaughter but does not include *causing death by dangerous driving) or an offence where the mandatory minimum sentence for certain *firearms offences applies; (b) he is charged with a violent or *sexual offence specified in sch 15 to the Criminal Justice Act 2003 that is punishable in the case of an adult by imprisonment for life or a determinate period of ten years or more and the court believes that if he is found *guilty the criteria for the imposition of a sentence of detention for life or for public protection (s 226, Criminal Justice Act 2003) or for an extended sentence of detention (s 228, Criminal Justice Act 2003) would be met; (c) the offence is one that is mentioned in s 91(1) or (2) of the Powers of Criminal Courts (Sentencing) Act 2000 (under which young persons convicted on indictment of certain crimes may be sentenced to be detained for long periods) and the court considers that if he is found guilty of the offence it ought to be possible to sentence him in pursuance of s 91(3); or (d) he is charged jointly with a person who has attained the age of 18 years and the court considers it necessary in the interests of justice that they be tried together. In all other cases, juvenile offenders must be tried summarily by an adult *magistrates' court or a *youth court (s 24(1), Magistrates' Courts Act 1980).

Where a juvenile has been convicted on indictment for an offence other than murder, the *Crown Court 'shall unless satisfied that it would be undesirable to do so, remit the case to a youth court' (s 8(1), Powers of Criminal Courts (Sentencing) Act 2000). In practice, the great majority of juveniles convicted in the Crown Court are also sentenced there. All of the sentences and other orders provided for use in respect of juvenile offenders are at the disposal of the Crown Court following conviction of a juvenile on indictment. Other than a custodial sentence (*see* CUSTODY FOR OFFENDERS UNDER 21) and a *youth community order (for offenders under 16) or a *community sentence (for offenders aged 16 and 17), these are principally a *fine; a *reparation order, a conditional or absolute *discharge; a *bind over; and a *compensation order. Section 150 of the 2000 Act places the court under a duty to bind over the *parents of an offender under the age of 16 if it is satisfied that it will help to prevent him from committing further offences. *See also* PARENTING ORDER.

Before passing sentence on a juvenile, the court must consider all available information regarding his conduct, school record, home circumstances, and medical history and must give both the offender and a parent or *guardian the chance to make representations about the appropriate sentence. *See also* PRE-SENTENCE REPORT; YOUTH COURT.

keeping (of property) *See* THEFT.

keeping the peace *See* BREACH OF THE PEACE; BIND OVER.

keloid An excessive scar formation seen most often in African-Caribbean people.

keratin A fibrous protein found in nails, hair, and skin.

kerb crawling The offence, contrary to s 1 of the Sexual Offences Act 1985, by a man of *soliciting a woman for prostitution in a *street or *public place either from a *motor vehicle or having just alighted from one, when the soliciting is persistent or likely to cause annoyance to the woman or nuisance to other people in the vicinity. In respect of offences of persistent soliciting, the *prosecution must prove more than one act of soliciting: either more than one invitation to one person or invitations to different people (*R v Tuck* [1994] Crim LR 375). The term 'street' is defined by s 4 (4) of the 1985 Act in language identical to that of the Street Offences Act 1959 (*see* STREET). However, there is no statutory definition of 'public place'. The offence is non-imprisonable. Home Office Circular 59/2003 suggests that courts should consider *disqualification from driving for this offence (*see* DISQUALIFICATION). *Anti-social behaviour orders can also be imposed in appropriate cases to exclude an offender from a specific location.

ketamine (*slang*: special K, vit K, kit kat, purple, super C) A Class C controlled drug from 1 January 2006. It can be taken alone by smoking or snorting but is more commonly mixed with ephedrine or caffeine. The mixture is then passed off as *ecstasy or another drug.

kidnapping Carrying a person away, without his consent, by means of force, threats, or fraud. Kidnapping is a *common-law offence punishable with a maximum sentence of *life imprisonment. A man may be *guilty of kidnapping his wife. Disputes between *parents about the right to their children are dealt with in family proceedings. A parent with care of the child may obtain a *warrant for the *arrest of the other parent if he or she takes the child away. Failure to comply with an order for the return of the child amounts to *contempt of court. *See also* ABDUCTION; HOSTAGE.

kleptomania A *mental disorder leading to the irresistible impulse to steal.

knock-out agreement An agreement by dealers not to bid against each other at an *auction. Such an agreement is illegal (*see* AUCTION RING).

knowledge For some criminal offences, it must be shown that the accused did an act knowing or believing that a certain state of affairs existed. These are subjective concepts and the question is what the defendant knew. The difference between knowing something to be the case and believing it to be so depends simply on whether it turns out to be true: if it was true then the defendant knew it to be so; if it was false then he believed it to be true. Knowledge requires a positive belief and a mere suspicion may not be sufficient (*R v Forsyth* [1997] 2 Cr App R 299, 320 (CA)). This does not mean, however, that the defendant must be absolutely certain that a particular state of affairs existed or would exist. It is sufficient that he has no serious doubt in that regard. If the defendant was aware that there was a risk that the state of affairs existed but deliberately chose not to make any reasonable inquiry to ascertain the truth then he is presumed to have the requisite degree of knowledge: *Westminster CC v Croyalgrange Ltd* [1986] 2 All ER 353 (HL). This is known as the doctrine of 'wilful blindness'.

laceration A break in the skin or organ in the body caused by blunt force (*compare* INCISIONS, which are caused by sharp instruments).

land 1. Those parts of the surface of the earth that are capable in law of being owned and are within the court's *jurisdiction. Generally, *ownership of land includes the *airspace above it and the subsoil below. For the purposes of land law, the Law of Property Act 1925 defines land as including mines and minerals (whether or not owned separately from the surface), buildings, and most interests in land. *Chattels fixed to the land so that they become part of it are also treated in law as land, under the maxim *quicquid plantatur solo, solo cedit* (*see* FIXTURE). **2.** In the *bore of a *firearm, one of several uncut portions of the surface left after the grooves have been cut into the metal to form the rifling (*see* RIFLE).

land certificate A *document issued by the *Land Registry to the proprietor of registered *land as proof of his *ownership of it. *See* LAND REGISTRATION.

land charge An interest in unregistered *land that imposes an obligation on the landowner in favour of some other person (the **chargee**). If validly created and registered where appropriate under the Land Charges Act 1972 at the *Land Charges Department, land charges will normally bind purchasers of the land. Important examples of land charges created by act of the *parties include mortgages not protected by deposit of title deeds, binding contracts for sale (including options and rights of pre-emption), restrictive covenants that affect freehold land, and equitable *easements. Some land charges arise under statute; e.g. a spouse's right to occupy the matrimonial home under the Matrimonial Homes Act 1983 (a Class F land charge) and the Inland Revenue charge for unpaid inheritance tax (a Class D land charge). **Local land charges**, which arise in favour of *local authorities from the exercise of their statutory powers, are registered by the local authority itself and apply to registered land as well as to unregistered land.

Land Charges Department A department of the *Land Registry, maintained under the Land Charges Act 1972 to keep registers of certain interests affecting the rights of persons owning unregistered *land (called **estate owners**). Registration of land charges against the name of the estate owner constitutes notice to everyone of their existence and generally renders them binding upon purchasers of any interest or estate in the land affected. A person contemplating taking such an interest may apply to the Department for an *official search certificate, which will reveal all interests registered against the estate owner's name.

landlord A person who grants a *lease or *tenancy. He need not be the outright owner of the tenanted *premises (he may, for example, be a *lessee himself or even a *licensee). A landlord may be an individual, a *local authority, a *trustee, a personal representative, or a *corporation (such as a company). The person who receives the rent is obliged to reveal the landlord's identity on the tenant's request. When there is a change of *ownership the new landlord must inform the tenant within two months or when rent is next due, whichever is the later.

land registration The system of registering, at local branch offices of the *Land Registry, certain *legal estates or interests in *land. Most transactions in land, including sale, gift, legal mortgage, etc., now trigger registration by the new or existing owner. If he fails to do so he does not acquire the legal estate and therefore runs the risk that the *vendor or *landlord may sell to someone else who can acquire a better *title by registration.

Upon registration of a title the Land Registry allocates a title number. Evidence of title is provided by the issue of a **land certificate** to the owner (who is known as the **registered proprietor**) or, if the land is in mortgage, a **charge certificate** to the mortgagee. The certificate represents the registered title, which is in three parts, comprising: (1) The **property register**. This describes the land and any additional rights incidental to it, such as *rights of way over adjoining land. The **filed plan** shows the location of the land, usually with a general indication of the position of the boundaries. Registration of precise boundaries is possible under a special procedure involving notice to adjoining owners and hearing their objections. (2) The **proprietorship register**. This names the registered proprietor(s) of the land and notes any restriction on their powers to dispose of it (e.g. restrictions, inhibitions, etc.). (3) The **charges register**. This details interests adverse to the proprietor, such as mortgages, restrictive covenants, or *easements to which the land is subject.

The land certificate fulfils a similar function to title *deeds to unregistered land, but if a more up-to-date record of the state of the registered title is required (e.g. by a prospective purchaser or mortgagee), the Land Registry will issue office copies or a certificate of *official search on application by the registered proprietor or any person with his authority to inspect the register. A registered proprietor's title is guaranteed by the state subject to overriding interests, which are not registrable in the charges register.

Land Registry A statutory body established under the Land Registration Act 1925 to maintain registers of certain *legal estates in *land. *See also* LAND REGISTRATION.

larceny Formerly (before 1969), *theft. Larceny was more limited than theft and required an **asportation** (carrying away of the property).

larva The second stage in the life cycle of an insect (egg—larva (maggot)—pupa (chrysalis)—imago (adult)). Depending on the time of year, insects lay their eggs in a dead body soon after death. These hatch into larvae and the presence of the various stages of development of the insects can be interpreted by a *forensic entomologist to give an indication of the post-mortem interval.

larynx (Adam's Apple) A cartilaginous box at the top of the *trachea (windpipe) containing the vocal chords. The *hyoid, which is part of the larynx, is often fractured in strangulation.

latent defect *See* DEFECT.

law 1. The enforceable body of rules that govern any society. *See also* COMMON LAW; NATURAL LAW. **2.** One of the rules making up the body of law, such as an *Act of Parliament.

Law Commission A body established by the Law Commissions Act 1965 to take and keep the law under review with a view to systematically developing and reforming it. In particular, it considers the codification of the law, the elimination of anomalies, the repeal of obsolete and unnecessary *enactments, a reduction in the number of separate enactments, and simplification and modernization generally. The Commission consists of a chairman and four other members, appointed by the *Lord Chancellor from among the holders of judicial office, *barristers, *solicitors, and academic lawyers. There is a separate Commission for Scotland.

Law Lords *See* LORDS OF APPEAL IN ORDINARY.

law officers of the Crown The *Attorney-General, *Solicitor General, *Lord Advocate, Solicitor General for Scotland, and Attorney-General for Northern Ireland.

law of nations *See* INTERNATIONAL LAW.

law of the sea The rules of *international law governing rights over the seas. The seas are divided into several different areas. (1) The *internal waters of a state (e.g. rivers, lakes, *ports, and harbours). A state may usually apply its laws to any merchant *ship within its internal waters. It may also apply navigation or health regulations to foreign warships in such waters and exclude foreign warships from its ports. (2) The *territorial waters. (3) The *high seas, beyond the territorial waters, which are open to all nations for such purposes as navigation, fishing, laying of submarine cables, and over-flying. Ships on the high seas are usually subject only to international law (e.g. in relation to acts of *piracy) and the law of the *flag state (usually dependent on registration in that state). There is also a limited right of *hot pursuit. (4) The *continental shelf, which—although geographically part of the high seas—is subject to specific rules.

The law of the sea is contained in customary international law and in the four Geneva Conventions of 1958. Since 1982, when the *United Nations Convention on the Law of the Sea came into force, there is a comprehensive code governing the whole of this law, which includes some completely new rules. To date (2006), 152 countries have established their consent to be bound by this Convention; the UK acceded to the treaty on 25 July 1997. In addition, many nations have subscribed to the related 1994 Agreement Regarding the United Nations Convention on the Law of the Sea. Even though some states chose not to ratify the 1982 Convention, many of the Convention's principles have now passed into the corpus of customary international law.

Law Reform Committee A body established by the *Lord Chancellor to consider particular areas of law that may need reform.

law reports Reports of cases decided by the courts, comprising a statement of the *facts of every case and the reasons the court gave for *judgment. The earliest reports were contained in the *Year Books*, which were published annually between 1283 and 1535. Their authors were anonymous and may have been student lawyers. The *Year Books* were superseded by personalized reports, i.e. reports written privately by lawyers (e.g. Chief Justice Coke) who appended their names to them. In 1865 the Incorporated Council of Law Reporting was established, a semi-official body that publishes *The Weekly Law Reports* (formerly *Weekly Notes*). These are reports of important cases selected by the Council, written by lawyers, and approved by the judges involved. A system of citation, called **neutral citation**, has been phased in and now applies to all cases so that all judgments in every division of the *High Court and the *Court of Appeal will be issued as approved judgments in a standard form with single spacing, paragraph numbering (in the margins), but no page numbers. Under these arrangements, paragraph 69 in Phoenix v Chatfield, the fifth numbered judgment of the year in the Civil Division of the Court of Appeal, would be cited as: *Phoenix v Chatfield* [2001] EWCA Civ 5 at [69]. The neutral citation always appears as the first citation in front of the citation from the law report series. The paragraph number must be the number allotted by the court in all future versions of the judgment.

The citation indicates the court:

UKHL	House of Lords
UKPC	Privy Council
EWCA Crim	England and Wales Court of Appeal, Criminal Division
EWCA Civ	England and Wales Court of Appeal, Civil Division
EWHC	England and Wales High Court

The division of the High Court is indicated after the case number, e.g. EWHC 123 (QB):

QB	Queen's Bench Division
Fam	Family Division
Ch	Chancery Division
Pat	Patents Court
Admin	Administrative Court
Comm	Commercial Court
Admlty	Admiralty Court
TCC	Technology and Construction Court

Neutral citations will not be automatically assigned to judgments delivered by judges in the High Court outside London, because they appear much less frequently in published reports.

There are in addition still a number of commercially published reports, e.g. the *All England Law Reports*, but the Court of Appeal and the House of Lords will cite the neutral citation in preference to other reports where there is a choice.

Law Society The professional body for *solicitors in England and Wales, incorporated by royal charter in 1831. The Society exists both to further the professional interests of solicitors and to discharge important statutory functions in relation to the admission to practice, the conduct, and discipline of solicitors. It issues annual *practising certificates to solicitors, without which they may not practise, and through its disciplinary committee may strike a solicitor's name off the roll or take other disciplinary action, subject to an *appeal to the *High Court. The Society is responsible for the examination of intending solicitors and organizes educational and training courses both through the College of Law and recognized universities.

laying an information Giving a *magistrate a concise statement (an **information**), verbally or in writing, of an alleged offence and the suspected offender, so that he can take steps to obtain the appearance of the suspect in court. Information can be laid by any member of the public, although it is usually done by the police. If an *arrest *warrant is required, the information must be in writing and on oath. An information may allege only one offence (r 12, Magistrates' Courts Rules 1981 (SI 1981/552)) and must be laid in the name of an individual rather than a body (*Rubin v DPP* [1990] 2 QB 80). It must state: the name and address of the informant and the accused, the brief facts of the case as alleged by the informant, and the statutory provision (if any) allegedly contravened by the accused. Objections cannot normally be made to information laid, on the grounds of formal defects or discrepancies between it and the *prosecution's subsequent evidence. But if the defect is fundamental to the charge the information will be dismissed, and if the defendant was misled by a discrepancy, he may be granted an adjournment of the *trial.

lay magistrate *See* MAGISTRATE.

leader A *Queen's Counsel or any *barrister who is the senior of two *counsel appearing for the same party.

Leader of the House *See* HOUSE OF COMMONS; HOUSE OF LORDS.

lead evidence To call or *adduce evidence.

leading case A case, the legal reasoning in which establishes an important principle of law. *See* PRECEDENT.

leading question A question asked of a witness in a manner that suggests the answer sought by the questioner (e.g. 'You threw the brick through the window, didn't you?') or that assumes the existence of disputed facts to which the witness is to testify. Leading questions may not be asked during *examination-in-chief (except relating to formal matters, such as the witness's name and address) but may normally be asked in *cross-examination.

leads and lags The custom amongst international traders deliberately to delay payment in certain currencies and accelerate payment in others as a way of protecting themselves from currency fluctuations.

leapfrog procedure **1.** (*House of Lords) The procedure for *appealing direct to the House of Lords from the *High Court or a *Divisional Court, bypassing the *Court of Appeal. The procedure is only allowed in exceptional cases. All *parties must consent and the case must raise a point of law of public importance, which either relates wholly or partly to the *interpretation of a statute or of a *statutory instrument or is one in respect of which the *trial *judge is bound by a previous decision of the Court of Appeal or the House of Lords. The trial judge must certify that he is satisfied as to the importance of the case and the House of Lords must give permission to appeal in this way. **2.** (Court of Appeal) The procedure by which a High Court judge or the *Master of the Rolls may transfer an appeal from a decision of a *district judge or *master to the Court of Appeal. Under the Access to Justice Act 1999 and the *Civil Procedure Rules, which substantially revised *appellate jurisdiction in the civil courts, such an appeal would normally be to a *circuit judge or a High Court judge. However, if the appeal is considered to raise an important point of principle or practice, or if there is some other compelling reason for the Court of Appeal to hear it, it may be transferred.

lease A contract under which an owner of *property (the *landlord or ***lessor**) grants another person (the *tenant or ***lessee**) exclusive possession of the property for an agreed period, usually (but not necessarily) in return for rent and sometimes for a capital sum known as a premium.

leasehold Held under a *lease, i.e. for a period of fixed minimum duration.

leasehold ownership Ownership of *property under a *lease.

leave Permission given by the court to take some procedural step in *litigation. Situations in which permission is required include *service out of the *jurisdiction and *appeals to higher civil courts (*see* APPELLATE JURISDICTION). Some items of evidence may be admissible only upon permission being granted by the *trial *judge.

legacy A gift of *personal property effected by will.

legal advice, right to The right of everyone in police *detention to free legal advice. The fact that the detained person has been informed of the right must be recorded on the *custody record (Police and Criminal Evidence Act 1984).

legal adviser *See* CLERK TO THE JUSTICES.

legal aid Free legal assistance provided to those unable to afford *representation. Under the Access to Justice Act 1999 (which repealed and replaced the Legal Aid Act 1988), the Legal Services Commission (which replaced the Legal Aid Board) is responsible for the *Community Legal Service, which provides legal aid in civil matters; and the *Criminal Defence Service, which provides advice and representation in criminal cases through a mix of contracts with private lawyers and salaried defenders. Private practice *solicitors' firms must hold a General Criminal Contract to carry out publicly funded criminal *defence work. Firms are audited against the Contract to ensure they continue to meet quality assurance standards.

legal easement *See* EASEMENT.

legal estate *Ownership of *land or an interest in land.

legal fiction *See* FICTION.

legal memory The period over which the law's recollection extends. Its commencement was arbitrarily fixed at 1189 by the Statute of Westminster I 1275. Time before legal memory is referred to as **time immemorial**. *Compare* LIVING MEMORY.

legal person A *natural person (i.e. a human being) or a *juristic person. It can include international bodies such as the *European Community (EC) and *Euratom, which can make *treaties in their own right. Where the EC has exclusive competence in a particular area, member states cannot conclude treaties on their own account.

legal privilege (in criminal investigations) Material to which legal privilege attaches cannot be seized or intercepted and no production order or search *warrant can be obtained for such material. Section 10 of the Police and Criminal Evidence Act 1984 defines legal privilege. Protection is given to communications between a professional legal adviser and his *client or a person representing his client, in connection with giving legal advice. It also attaches to communications between a professional legal adviser and any person in connection with or contemplation of legal proceedings. It also attaches to items enclosed in or referred to in the foregoing. Legal privilege is for the benefit of the client, not the lawyer, and can be waived only by the client. If the item is not legally privileged in the hands of the client then neither is it privileged in the hands of the *solicitor. Legal privilege does not attach to items held with the intention of furthering a criminal purpose or items that are part of commercial activity and not legal advice, such as house conveyancing *documents.

legal rights 1. *Rights recognized by the *common law courts, as distinct from *equitable rights or interests recognized by the Court of Chancery. In their developed form, legal rights affect everyone whether or not they know (or ought to know) of their existence (hence the expression 'legal rights bind the world'). **2.** Generally, all rights recognized by the law (both common law and *equity) as having legal existence and effect, as distinguished from moral rights.

Legal Services Commission (LSC) *See* COMMUNITY LEGAL SERVICE; CRIMINAL DEFENCE SERVICE; LEGAL AID.

Legal Services Ombudsman An official, appointed by the *Lord Chancellor under the Legal Services Ombudsman (Jurisdiction) Order 1990 (SI 1990/2485), who is responsible for hearing complaints against *solicitors, *barristers, and licensed conveyancers made by their professional bodies.

legislation 1. The whole or any part of a country's written law. In the UK the term is normally confined to *Acts of Parliament, but in its broadest sense it also includes law made under powers conferred by Act of Parliament (*see* DELEGATED LEGISLATION), law made by virtue of the *royal prerogative, and Church of England Measures. **2.** The process of making written law.

legislature The body having primary power to make written law. In the UK it consists of *Parliament, i.e. the *Crown, the *House of Commons, and the *House of Lords.

legitimacy The legal status of a child born to *parents who were married at the time of his conception or birth (or both). (*See also* LEGITIMATION.) There is a **presumption of legitimacy** in all cases when the mother is married, so that children of the marriage are presumed to be the offspring of the mother's husband. This may be rebutted, however, either by showing that the husband was impotent or absent on the date on which the child must have been conceived or by blood tests showing that he could not be the father. The Family Law Reform Act 1987 provides that a child conceived, by a party to a marriage, through artificial insemination by a donor, is to be treated as a legitimate child of that marriage. *See also* ILLEGITIMACY.

legitimate aim A prerequisite for interference with a *qualified right as set out in the *European Convention on Human Rights: a signatory state will be able to interfere with a qualified right only if that interference is designed to pursue a legitimate aim and the interference is a proportionate one (*see* PROPORTIONALITY). Legitimate aims include national security, public order, the prevention of crime, etc.

legitimation The process of replacing the status of *illegitimacy by that of *legitimacy. A living child may be legitimated if his parents marry one another, provided that the father is domiciled in England or Wales at the date of the marriage. Evidence that the husband recognized the child as his own may be sufficient to establish his paternity for purposes of legitimation. Legitimation takes effect from the date of the marriage and the child is treated thereafter as if he had been born legitimate. Under the Family Law Act 1986, a person may seek a court declaration that he is a legitimated person.

leonine A leonine *treaty or *convention is one that is forced upon a weaker state by a stronger one. In some *jurisdictions the adjective is applied to contracts which are manifestly unfair.

lessee The person to whom a *lease is granted. *See also* TENANT.

lessor The person by whom a *lease is granted. *See also* LANDLORD.

letter of attorney *See* POWER OF ATTORNEY.

letter of credence (*lettre de créance*) A formal *document by which the head of an accredited state presents its newly appointed *diplomatic agent to the head of state of the host country.

letter of credit A *document whereby a bank, at the request of a customer, undertakes to pay money to a third party (the **beneficiary**) on presentation of *documents specified in the letter (e.g. *bills of lading and policies of *insurance). The obligation of the bank to pay is independent of the underlying contract of sale and so is not affected by any *defects in the *goods supplied under the contract of sale. A contract of *sale of goods may require the *buyer to open an **irrevocable letter of credit** in favour of the *seller. This cannot be revoked by the issuing bank or the purchaser of the goods before its expiry date, without the consent of the beneficiary. A **confirmed letter of credit** is one in which the negotiating bank guarantees payment to the beneficiary should it not be honoured by the issuing bank.

letter of request (LOR; *commissions rogatoires*; letters rogatory; rogatory letter) A legal *document requesting assistance under *mutual legal assistance agreements in obtaining evidence from outside the UK for use in legal proceedings or a criminal investigation. In other *jurisdictions, they are generally referred to as '*commission rogatoires*' or 'letters rogatory'.

A LOR must comply with the relevant provisions of the Crime (International Cooperation) Act 2003 (which replaced similar provisions in the Criminal Justice (International Cooperation) Act 1990). It must also have regard to any relevant *treaties or *conventions that exist between the UK and the state to which it is addressed. These usually set out the form in which the request should be made, the information that must be included in the request, any type of material that may be requested and the use to which such material can be put. A request made outside the legal framework, or including inquiries not permitted thereby, is susceptible to *judicial review and any evidence obtained in consequence stands to be excluded by the courts. Where an offence has been committed in the UK or there are reasonable grounds for suspecting that such an offence has been committed, and the offence is being investigated or proceedings in respect of it have been instituted, then s 7 of the 2003 Act allows a judicial authority (*judge or *justice of the peace) or designated prosecuting authority to issue a LOR. There is no provision for a LOR to be issued by any law enforcement agency. The designated prosecuting authorities are: the *Attorney-General; the *Director of Public Prosecutions; the Directors of the *Revenue and Customs Prosecutions Office, *Serious Fraud Office, and the Financial Services Authority. Some countries will not accept letters issued other than by a judicial authority. These include the Hong Kong Special Administrative Region, the Channel Islands, Gibraltar, the Bahamas, and Bermuda.

A LOR is generally required in all cases in which the assistance sought is likely to involve judicial approval or order (e.g. a search *warrant or production order) or the exercise of compulsive powers provided for by the law of the country concerned (e.g. to answer questions or to produce information). However, other evidence (e.g. a statement provided voluntarily by a witness) often may be obtained under less formal *mutual assistance agreements.

Section 9 of the 2003 Act requires a domestic court, when considering the *admissibility in a court in England and Wales of a statement that is obtained from abroad, to have regard to (1) whether it was possible to challenge the person making it by questioning that person and (2) whether the law of the foreign state allowed for the *parties to the proceedings to be legally represented when the evidence was being obtained. Otherwise, the Act does not deal in any detail with issues of admissibility. Essentially, then, the admissibility of evidence obtained in another jurisdiction stands to be determined in accordance with domestic law.

letters of administration Authority granted by the court to a specified person to act as an administrator of a deceased person's estate when the deceased dies intestate.

letters rogatory *See* LETTER OF REQUEST.

leucomalachite green (LMG) A chemical used to detect the presence of blood.

levée en masse [French: mass uprising] A body of civilians who spontaneously take up arms against an advancing enemy. They are permitted to participate in hostilities and are protected by the Geneva Conventions.

lex ferenda [Latin: the law that should be borne] What the law ought to be. *Compare* LEX LATA.

lex lata [Latin: the law that has been borne] What the law is. *Compare* LEX FERENDA.

lex loci celebrationis [Latin: the law of the place of celebration] Generally used in relation to the celebration of a marriage. In *private international law, this law governs such questions as the formalities required for a marriage (subject to four special exceptions), whether or not such a marriage is monogamous or polygamous, and possibly what law governs impotence or wilful refusal to consummate a marriage.

lex loci contractus [Latin: the law of the place of contract] The law of the place where a contract was made. In *private international law, this law governs such matters as the formal requirements of a contract and the capacity to incur *liability as a *party to a *bill of exchange. Most other matters relating to contracts are governed by the proper law of the contract.

liability **1.** An amount owed. **2.** A legal duty or obligation. *See* OCCUPIER'S LIABILITY; PARENTS' LIABILITY; PRODUCT LIABILITY; STRICT LIABILITY; VICARIOUS LIABILITY.

liaison magistrate A *judge responsible for facilitating and advising on matters concerning *mutual legal assistance in relation to the investigation and *prosecution of transnational and cross-border crime; representing UK criminal justice; identifying good practice and lessons learnt from other national *jurisdictions; and liaising with UK and other liaison officers (*see* MUTUAL ASSISTANCE) on matters concerning *organized crime, counter-terrorism, and other serious crime. The *Crown Prosecution Service supports liaison magistrates in Washington, Paris, Rome, and Madrid.

libel A defamatory statement made in permanent form, such as writing, pictures, or film (*see* DEFAMATION). Radio and television broadcasts, public performance of plays, and statements posted on the Internet are treated as being made in permanent form for the purposes of the law of defamation. A libel is actionable in *tort without proof that its publication has caused special damage (actual financial or material loss) to the person defamed. Libel can also be a crime (**criminal libel**). Proof of publication of the statement to third parties is not necessary in criminal libel and truth is a defence only if the statement was published for the public benefit.

liberty and freedom from arbitrary detention A right set out in Article 5 of the *European Convention on Human Rights and now part of UK law as a consequence of the *Human Rights Act 1998, which provides that all *detentions must be prescribed by law and detentions must only be for one of the specified purposes set out in Article 5. Those detained must promptly be given reasons for their detention and then at regular intervals have access to a court to test the lawfulness of their continued detention. Those remanded in *custody pending a criminal *trial must be released on *bail unless their detention is justified and they shall be entitled to trial within a reasonable time. There is an enforceable right to *compensation for unlawful detention.

licence **1.** Formal authority to do something that would otherwise be unlawful. Examples include a *driving licence, a licence for selling intoxicating liquor (*see* LICENSING OF PREMISES), and a licence by the owner of a patent to manufacture the patented *goods. **2.** (in *land law) Permission to enter or occupy a person's *land for an agreed purpose.

licensable activity An activity that is licensable for the purposes of the Licensing Act 2003, which includes the following: (a) the sale by retail of *alcohol, (b) the supply of alcohol by or on behalf of a *club to, or to the order of, a member of the club, (c) the provision of regulated entertainment, and (d) the provision of late night refreshment. The following licensable activities are also qualifying club activities: (a) the supply of alcohol by or on behalf of a club to, or to the order of, a member of the club, (b) the sale by retail of alcohol by or on behalf of a club to a guest of a member of the club for consumption on the *premises where the sale takes place, and (c) the provision of regulated entertainment where that provision is by or on behalf of a club for members of the club or members of the club and their guests.

licensed premises *See* LICENSING OF PREMISES.

licensee 1. A person who has been granted a *licence, most commonly used of one who has been granted a licence by a *local authority to sell *alcohol (*see* LICENSING OF PREMISES) or one who has been granted a licence to use *intellectual property, such as *patents. **2.** A person with permission to do what would otherwise be unlawful. In relation to *land, a licensee is one who enters land with the express or implied permission of the *occupier. *See* LICENCE; OCCUPIER'S LIABILITY.

licensing authority A local authority which issues licences for *licensable activities under the Licensing Act 2003: (a) the council of a district in England, (b) the council of a county in England in which there are no district councils, (c) the council of a county or county borough in Wales, (d) the council of a London borough, (e) the Common Council of the City of London, (f) the Sub-Treasurer of the Inner Temple, (g) the Under-Treasurer of the *Middle Temple, or (h) the Council of the Isles of Scilly.

licensing of business The licensing of financial businesses by a *local authority under the Consumer Credit Act 1974. The seven types of financial business required to be licensed are: consumer credit; consumer hire; credit brokerage; debt counselling; debt adjusting; debt collecting; and credit reference agency. It is an *either way criminal offence punishable on indictment with up to two years' imprisonment and a *fine to operate such a business without a *licence.

licensing of premises The licensing of any *premises on which a *licensable activity is to be carried out, under the provisions of the Licensing Act 2003. Any person intending to sell or supply *alcohol by retail must obtain a *licence to do so from the *licensing authority. *See also* EXCLUSION ORDER.

lien [via Old French from Latin *ligamen*: a binding] The right of one person to retain *possession of *goods owned by another until the possessor's claims against the owner have been satisfied.

lie on the file *See* TERMINATION OF PROCEEDINGS.

life assurance *Insurance providing for the payment of a sum on the occurrence of an event that is in some way dependent upon a human life.

life imprisonment *Punishment of a criminal by imprisonment for the rest of his life. The only crime that always carries a sentence of life imprisonment is *murder: an offender aged 21 or over who has been convicted of murder must be sentenced to life imprisonment (s 1(1), Murder (Abolition of Death Penalty) Act 1965). For an offender aged 18 but under 21 the sentence is one of 'custody for life' and for offenders aged under 18 'to be detained during Her Majesty's pleasure' (ss 94 and 90, Powers of Criminal Courts (Sentencing) Act 2000). *See also* CUSTODY FOR OFFENDERS UNDER 21; DETENTION IN A YOUNG OFFENDER INSTITUTION; LONG TERM DETENTION.

However, the term 'life imprisonment' does not normally mean that the offender will stay in prison for the whole of his natural life. For offences committed prior to 4 April 2005, the *Home Secretary may order the release of a life prisoner on licence, on the advice of the Parole Board (*see* PAROLE), and after consulting the *Lord Chief Justice (and, if possible, the *trial *judge). For offences committed after that date, a minimum term of imprisonment must be set in accordance with the detailed statutory scheme introduced by ss 269 to 277 of and sch 21 to the Criminal Justice Act 2003. Whilst *common law offences (unless there is a statutory provision to the contrary) and some of the more serious statutory offences (e.g. *rape, *robbery) carry a maximum sentence of life imprisonment, that sentence is a discretionary one. For offences committed prior to 4 April 2005, such a sentence must be justified on the ground of seriousness or public protection (s 80(2)(a) and (b), Powers of Criminal Courts (Sentencing) Act 2000). A court which imposes a sentence of imprisonment for public protection must fix a minimum term to be served in accordance with s 82A of the Powers of Criminal Courts (Sentencing) Act 2000. For offences committed after 4 April 2005, ch 5 of pt 12 of the Criminal Justice Act 2003 establishes a new scheme of custodial sentences for *dangerous offenders, including life sentences for serious offences for those aged 18 or over (s 225) and detention for life for serious offences committed by those under 18 (s 226).

Section 109 of the Powers of Criminal Courts (Sentencing) Act 2000, which imposed a mandatory life sentence on any offender, aged 18 or over, convicted of a second 'serious offence' (including *manslaughter, rape, and *wounding with intent) was repealed on 4 April 2005 when the provisions dealing with dangerous offenders contained in ch 5 of pt 12 of the Criminal Justice Act 2003 came into effect. *See also* MANDATORY MINIMUM SENTENCES.

life peerage A non-hereditary peerage of the rank of baron or baroness created by the *Crown by letters patent under the Life Peerages Act 1958. The purpose of the Act was to strengthen the composition of the *House of Lords, and there is no limit to the number of peerages that may be created. The peerage of a *Lord of Appeal in Ordinary is also for life but is not customarily included among life peerages.

lifestyle offence *See* CRIMINAL LIFESTYLE.

lifting the veil The act of disregarding the veil of *incorporation that separates the personality of a *corporation from the personalities of its members. This exceptional course is occasionally sanctioned by statute, e.g. in relation to *wrongful trading or *fraudulent trading and inaccurate use of company names, when it may result in members of a *limited company losing their limited liability. It is also employed by the courts, e.g. if incorporation has been used to perpetrate *fraud or gives rise to un
pany and its s
never so as to defea
occasionally the courts
corporate personality but mor
evade its inconvenient consequen
deciding that the acts were performed b
the corporation acting as agent or *trustee for the *company members, to whom therefore they should be attributed.

ligature A rope or band of material used to constrict part of the body. Most often seen round the neck causing strangulation.

limitation of actions Statutory rules limiting the time within which civil actions can be brought. The present law is contained in the Limitation Act 1980, the Latent Damage Act 1986, and the Consumer Protection Act 1987. In *strict liability actions for defective products (*see* PRODUCT LIABILITY), the period is three years from accrual of the cause of action or (if later) the date when the claimant knew or should have known the material facts, but not later than ten years from when the product was put into circulation.

limited company A type of company incorporated by registration under the Companies Act 1985 whose members have a limited liability towards their company. Most companies are in this category. In a company limited by *shares, members must pay the nominal value (*see* AUTHORIZED CAPITAL) of their shares either upon allotment or subsequently (*see* CALL). In a company limited by *guarantee (a **guarantee company**) members must pay an agreed nominal amount (the guarantee), usually £1 to £5, to their company in the event of a *winding-up. The guarantee fund is intended to be for the benefit of company *creditors when the company is wound up and members' liability to contribute to it cannot be reduced or extinguished by the company. Because payment of the guarantee is postponed, guarantee companies often lack a working capital and are therefore more appropriate for charitable or social purposes than for trading.

The name of a limited company must end with the words 'Limited' (or 'Ltd') in

gally
e Lim-
, which
acts in its
ngly liable
for ... acts. Any two
or mo... ed for carrying
on a lawf... a view to profit
may set up su... tnership under the
Act. This type o... ness organization is intended to combine the flexibility of a traditional partnership with the corporate notion of limited liability. Under the provisions of the Act there is power to apply sections from both the Partnership Act 1890 and the Companies Act 1985, as appropriate, when dealing with the internal relations of the partners and limited liability, respectively. Persons intending to set up a limited liability partnership must register it with the *Companies Registry. There are also several *disclosure requirements that are similar in nature to those required by companies.

Lincoln's Inn An *Inn of Court situated between Carey Street and Holborn. The records of the Inn, the *Black Books*, survive in a continuous series from 1422 to the present. By tradition, *barristers practising in the *Chancery Division of the *High Court normally belong to Lincoln's Inn.

linked transaction (under the Consumer Credit Act 1974) A transaction (except one for the provision of security) that is linked to, but not part of, a *regulated agreement (the **principal agreement**) and is entered into by a *debtor or hirer with any other person. A linked transaction may comply with a term of the principal agreement (e.g. if the principal agreement requires that the *goods be insured with X) or it may be financed by the principal agreement if the latter is a *debtor-creditor-supplier agreement. Alternatively it may be suggested by a creditor or owner to the debtor or hirer. The latter then enters into the linked transaction ...r to induce the creditor or owner to ...er into the principal agreement, or ...r some other purpose related to the principal agreement, or—when the principal agreement is a restricted use credit agreement—for a purpose related to a transaction financed by the principal agreement.

liquidation *See* WINDING-UP.

liquidation committee A committee set up by *creditors of a company being wound up in order to consent to the *liquidator exercising certain of his powers. When the company is unable to pay its *debts, the committee is usually composed of creditors only; otherwise it consists of both creditors and contributories. *See also* COMPULSORY WINDING-UP; VOLUNTARY WINDING-UP.

liquidator A person who conducts the *winding-up of a company. Unless he is the *official receiver, he must be a qualified *insolvency practitioner. *See also* COMPULSORY WINDING-UP; LIQUIDATION COMMITTEE; PROVISIONAL LIQUIDATOR; VOLUNTARY WINDING-UP.

listed company A company that has satisfied the **listing rules** of the *Stock Exchange and whose *shares may therefore be quoted and traded on the Listed Market. Listed companies are subject to continuing obligations of disclosure to the Stock Exchange.

Listed Market *See* STOCK EXCHANGE.

lists Calendars of cases awaiting *trial. A court may maintain several lists comprising different types of case. Thus in the *High Court there is the *Queen's Bench non-jury list, the jury list, the short cause list, etc. A case enters the list after it has been allocated for trial.

literal rule *See* INTERPRETATION OF STATUTES.

litigant A person who is a *party to a court action. A litigant may present his case personally to the court. If he does so, he may be assisted by a friend who can take notes and advise but cannot assist in the actual presentation of the case (a **McKenzie friend**). Alternatively, a litigant may be represented by a *barrister or, where appropriate, a *solicitor.

litigation 1. The taking of legal action by a *litigant. **2.** The field of law that is concerned with all contentious matters.

litigation friend An adult responsible for the conduct and cost of legal proceedings instituted on behalf of, or against, a child or a mentally disordered person. Before the introduction of the *Civil Procedure Rules in 1999 such a person was called a **next friend**. *See also* OFFICIAL SOLICITOR.

live link *See* LIVE TELEVISION LINK.

livestock *See* CLASSIFICATION OF ANIMALS.

live television link One of the special measures allowed for by the Youth Justice and Criminal Evidence Act 1999, which provides for *vulnerable and intimidated witnesses to give evidence (both *examination-in-chief and *cross-examination) by means of a live television link. By s 24(8) of the Act, 'live link' means a live television link or other arrangement whereby a witness, while absent from the courtroom or other place where the proceedings are being held, is able to see and hear a person there, and to be seen and heard by the *judge and/or *magistrates, the *jury (if there is one), legal representatives acting in the proceedings, and any *interpreter appointed to assist the witness. Child witnesses are normally cross-examined using live link, the main exception being where the case is sexual, when the cross-examination is normally pre-recorded. The measure has been available since 24 July 2002 to witnesses eligible by virtue of either ss 16 (vulnerable witnesses) or 17 (intimidated witnesses) of the Act in the *Crown Court and to child witnesses in need of special protection in the *magistrates' courts. From 3 October 2005, live link facilities were extended to all magistrates' courts in England and Wales for all eligible witnesses. *See also* SPECIAL MEASURES.

When s 51 of the Criminal Justice Act 2003 comes into force (expected to be late 2006 or early 2007), a criminal court may grant leave for any witness (other than the defendant) to give evidence-in-chief, and to be cross-examined and re-examined, through a closed circuit television or video conferencing link. The court may only allow evidence in such a form if it is in the interests of the efficient or effective administration of justice (e.g. because the witness lives in a different part of the country). The provision will replace s 32 of the Act, which provides, in certain circumstances, for a witness who is out of the *jurisdiction to give evidence via a video conferencing link.

In civil proceedings, a court may allow any witness to give evidence through a video link or by other similar means (r 32.3, *Civil Procedure Rules).

lividity *See* HYPOSTASIS.

living memory The period over which the recollection of living people extends. *Compare* LEGAL MEMORY.

living on immoral earnings Using money obtained from prostitution for one's livelihood or upkeep. Under ss 30 and 31 of the Sexual Offences Act 1965, it was an offence for a man (but not for a woman) to knowingly live on the proceeds of female prostitution and for a woman to exercise control, direction, or influence over a female prostitute for the purposes of gain. These offences, together with the little-used offence provided by s 5 of the Sexual Offences Act (person knowingly living on the proceeds of male prostitution), were repealed and replaced with non-gender specific offences by the Sexual Offences Act 2003: see CAUSING OR INCITING OR CONTROLLING PROSTITUTION.

Lloyd's A society of *underwriters that was incorporated by Act of Parliament in 1871. Originally Lloyd's only provided marine *insurance but they now also provide other kinds. The insurance is undertaken by syndicates of private underwriters (**names**), each of which is managed by a professional underwriter; since 1992 limited companies have been allowed to become names. Each name underwrites a percentage of the business written by the syndicate and has to deposit a substantial sum with the corporation before being admitted as an underwriter. The public deals with the underwriters only through Lloyd's brokers.

loan capital Money raised by a company issuing debentures. The aggregate amount borrowed by the company with each issue is sometimes referred to as **stock**.

loan creditor A *creditor of a company, such as a person who holds redeemable *loan capital issued by the company. For the purposes of tax law, loan creditors (other than banks) are participators in close companies.

local Act *See* ACT OF PARLIAMENT.

Local Authorities Coordinators of Regulatory Services (LACORS) A local government central body created by the UK local authority associations to coordinate the enforcement activities of trading standards departments and other regulatory services enforcing such things as: metrology, petroleum and explosives, consumer credit, product safety, underage sales, fair trading, animal health and welfare, consumer advice and education and Civil Registration (including the registration of births, deaths, and marriages and other related services such as citizenship ceremonies, partnership registration, etc.), food safety and standards including labelling, sampling, and analysis, food imports and exports, health and safety at work, alcohol and public entertainment licensing, and gambling reform.

local authority A body of **councillors** elected by the inhabitants of a local government area (*see* FRANCHISE) to exercise local government functions. In England (except *Greater London and the metropolitan county areas) county areas are governed either by *county councils and *district councils (in a two-tier system) or by *unitary authorities (single-tier system); this mixed system of local government was introduced between 1996 and 1998, which resulted in the reorganization of some local government areas. There are in addition *parish councils for parishes with 200 or more electors. In Wales the local authorities are the county council, the county borough council, and the community council. The Welsh county and county borough councils are unitary authorities.

Local Criminal Justice Board (LCJB) A board set up to manage the *criminal justice system at a local level. It comprises the chief officers of police, *probation, and the *Crown Prosecution Service as well as the magistracy and judiciary. They report to the National Criminal Justice Board.

local government A form of government in which responsibility for the regulation of certain matters within particular localities (*local government areas) is delegated by statute to locally elected councillors (*see* LOCAL AUTHORITY).

local government area An area constituting a unit for local government purposes. The local government areas in England (except *Greater London) are the *county, the *district, and the *parish. In certain parts of England *unitary authorities replaced non-metropolitan county and district councils between 1996 and 1998, which resulted in the reorganization of some local government areas. In Wales the areas are the county, the county borough, and the community; counties and county boroughs, which are administered by unitary authorities, replaced the two-tier system of counties and districts in April 1996.

local investigation (of complaint) The investigation of a *complaint against police by the local *police force without control or supervision by the *Independent Police Complaints Commission.

local justice area An area specified by the *Lord Chancellor under s 8 of the Courts Act 2003. Local justice areas replace the commission areas and petty sessions areas provided for by ss 1 to 5 of the Justices of the Peace Act 1997. *See also* MAGISTRATE; MAGISTRATES' COURT.

local knowledge Knowledge of local circumstances, the use of which is implicit in the concept of local, lay *magistrates. In *Chesson v Jordan* [1981] Crim LR 333, the *Divisional Court held that such knowledge could not and should not be excluded from the court's mind when drawing inferences. However, in *Bowman v DPP* (1990) 154 JP 524 the same court held that magistrates should make known to the *prosecution and *defence that local knowledge was being relied upon and give the parties the opportunity to make representations regarding the knowledge which they claim to have.

local laws Laws applying in only one locality, such as the area of a *local authority (*see* BYELAW). In 1996 the Law Commission published a four-volume Chronological Table of Local Legislation to help those wanting to find out whether a local Act has been passed that affects them or their *property. The table lists all 26,500 or so local Acts passed since 1797 and states whether or not they are in force and how they have been amended.

local resolution The resolution of a *complaint against police at the police station or *Basic Command Unit.

Local Strategic Partnership (LSP) A non-statutory partnership coterminous with a *local authority area set up for the purpose of identifying common objectives for the local community, including road safety and anti-social behaviour. Membership includes representatives of the public and private sectors, business and voluntary organizations. LSPs are obligatory in designated neighbourhood renewal areas but many have been set up in other areas.

Locard's Principle The principle described by Dr Edmond Locard (1877–1966) in 1920, that when two objects come into contact with each other something is exchanged and taken away by both objects. This is the basis of the transfer and recovery of all scientific evidence.

locomotive A *mechanically propelled vehicle (e.g. a steam-roller) which is not constructed itself to carry a load other than water, fuel, accumulators and other equipment used for the purpose of propulsion, loose tools, and loose equipment, and the weight of which unladen exceeds 7 370 kg (reg 3(2), Road Vehicles (Construction and Use) Regulations 1986 SI 1986/1078)).

locus standi [Latin: a place to stand] The right to bring an *action or challenge some decision. Questions of *locus standi* most often arise in proceedings for *judicial review.

lodger A person who is given occupation of part of a house in return for rent, where the *premises remain under the close control of the owner. A lodger normally has a mere *licence rather than a *tenancy.

London *See* GREATER LONDON.

London Assembly A component of the *Greater London Authority, created by the Greater London Authority Act 1999, consisting of 25 members, of whom fourteen are *Constituency Members and eleven are London Members. The principal functions of the Assembly are to review and investigate actions and decisions of the Mayor of London and to submit proposals to the Mayor. It may amend the Mayor's budget and it provides members to serve on the Metropolitan Police Authority, the London Fire and Emergency Planning Authority, and the London Development Agency.

London borough *See* GREATER LONDON.

London Interbank Offered Rate (LIBOR) The base interest rate for lending in Eurocurrency markets.

long-term detention The *detention of an offender aged from 10 to 17 inclusive who is convicted on *indictment of an offence punishable in the case of a person aged 18 or over with imprisonment for fourteen years or more, certain offences under the Sexual Offences Act 2003, and certain offences under the Firearms Act 1968 (s 91, Powers of Criminal Courts Sentencing Act 2000). Before imposing such an order, the court must be satisfied that none of the other methods of dealing with the juvenile (including a *detention and training order) is appropriate. Usually, the term of the *sentence will be for more than two years and may be anything up to the maximum sentence for the offence. *See also* DETENTION IN A YOUNG OFFENDER INSTITUTION; JUVENILE OFFENDER.

long title *See* ACT OF PARLIAMENT.

looked-after children Children (under 18) may be 'looked after' by *local authorities under a number of legal arrangements:

- children who are subject to a *care order (s 31, Children Act 1989), interim care order (s 38, Children Act 1989), or *emergency protection order (s 44, Children Act 1989) where the local authority has acquired *parental responsibility for that child;
- children under a (criminal law) *supervision order with a *residence requirement to live in local authority accommodation;
- children who have appeared in court and have been *bailed to reside where the local authority directs—and are being provided with a local authority funded placement;
- children who are remanded to the local authority where release on bail has not been granted;
- children under a court ordered secure remand and held in council accommodation;
- children who are subject to a *secure accommodation order where the local authority is funding the cost of the secure placement. A child is not looked after if he is in secure accommodation due to his offending, and the cost of the placement is funded by the *Home Office.

Lord Advocate The chief law officer of the *Crown in Scotland, corresponding to the *Attorney-General in England. He has ultimate responsibility for criminal prosecutions in Scotland, being assisted by a Solicitor General, advocates depute, and *procurators fiscal. He is normally a supporter of the ruling party and resigns his office upon a change of government, but he is not always a Member of *Parliament.

Lord Chancellor The head of the judiciary, a government minister (in charge of the Lord Chancellor's Department), and member of the *House of Lords. He thus combines judicial, executive, and legislative functions. He is entitled to preside over the House when it sits as a final court of *appeal; he appoints *magistrates, and oversees such matters as the *Community Legal Service, law reform, *data protection, and *human rights. He is appointed by the Crown on the advice of the Prime Minister and (since 1974) may be a Roman Catholic.

Lord Chief Justice (LCJ) The chief judge of the *Queen's Bench Division of the *High Court. He ranks second only to the *Lord Chancellor in the judicial hierarchy. It was formerly the practice to appoint the Attorney-General when a vacancy in the office occurred but this practice has now been abandoned and recent LCJs have been either *Lords Justices of Appeal or *Lords of Appeal in Ordinary on appointment. The LCJ is *ex officio* a member of the *Court of Appeal and is President of its Criminal Division.

Lord Justice of Appeal (LJ) An ordinary judge of the *Court of Appeal. The Lord (and Lady) Justices (LJJ) are normally appointed from those holding the post of a *High Court judge or those possessing a ten-year High Court qualification under the Courts and Legal Services Act 1990. They become members of the *Privy Council on appointment.

Lords, House of *See* HOUSE OF LORDS.

Lords of Appeal in Ordinary (Law Lords) Up to eleven persons, holders of high judicial office or practising *barristers of at least fifteen years' standing, who are appointed to *life peerages under the Appellate Jurisdiction Act 1876 to carry out the judicial functions of the *House of Lords.

loss leader A product or service offered for sale by an organization at a loss in order to attract customers. The Competition Act 1998 prohibits *predatory pricing by dominant companies, as does Article 82 of the *Treaty of Rome. Non-dominant companies, however, are largely free to set their own resale pricing policy. *See also* RESALE PRICE MAINTENANCE.

lottery A game of chance in which the participants buy numbered tickets and the prizes are distributed by drawing lots. Under the Gambling Act 2005, lotteries are usually illegal (*see also* GAMING) unless they are: (1) on behalf of registered *charities or sports, (2) restricted to members of a private *club, (3) **local lotteries**, promoted in accordance with schemes approved by *local authorities and registered with the Gambling Commission, or (4) small lotteries that take place as part of an entertainment (e.g. in a bazaar or at a dance). The **National Lottery** was established by statute (the National Lottery Act 1993).

low copy number A method of obtaining a DNA profile from extremely small sources of DNA such as sweat.

lysergic acid diethylamide (LSD) (*slang*: acid, doses, hits, microdot, sugar cubes, tabs, trips) A hallucinogenic drug. It may appear on pieces of blotting paper, usually with a colourful design on them, on tabs or pieces of gelatine. It is taken by licking the LSD from the blotting paper. It derives from lysergic acid, which is produced by a fungus found on grains of rye. It is a potent mind-altering drug. The results of taking it are unpredictable and can include delusions and hallucinations. It is a Class A drug under the Misuse of Drugs Act 1971.

Maastricht Treaty The Treaty on European Union, which was signed at Maastricht (in the Netherlands) in February 1992 and came into force on 1 November 1993. The Treaty amended the founding treaties of the three *European Communities by establishing a *European Union based on these Communities. It required the defining and eventual implementation of a common foreign and security policy, cooperation in justice and home affairs, and—under certain conditions—the introduction of a single currency (*see* EUROPEAN MONETARY UNION). It also introduced the principle of *subsidiarity and increased the powers of the *European Parliament. It has since been amended by the *Amsterdam Treaty.

maceration The process of softening of tissue by soaking, e.g. to remove flesh from bones to allow examination of the bones. The destruction of tissue by decomposition.

machine gun An *automatic *firearm designed to fire a *cartridge from an ammunition belt or large-capacity *magazine, usually at rates of several hundred *rounds per minute.

magazine An *ammunition storage and feeding device. It may be integral to the *firearm or, more commonly in modern weapons, detachable.

maggot The larval stage of a fly. Flies, like all insects, have four stages in their life cycle: egg, *larva, *pupa (chrysalis), and imago (adult). Depending on the season and conditions, flies lay their eggs in a body soon after death. The insect develops through its stages at a known pace dependent on species. Thus by examining the various stages reached by insects in dead bodies an *entomologist can calculate the time since death.

magistrate A *justice of the peace sitting in a *magistrates' court. Most magistrates are lay persons and have no formal legal qualifications: they receive no payment for their services but give their time voluntarily. The Courts Act 2003 provides magistrates with national *jurisdiction, although they must be assigned to a particular *local justice area. *See also* DISTRICT JUDGE (MAGISTRATES' COURT).

magistrates' clerk *See* CLERK TO THE JUSTICES.

magistrates' court An inferior criminal court which usually consists of two or more lay *magistrates (*but see* EARLY ADMINISTRATIVE HEARING) or a single *district judge (magistrates' court) (formerly called stipendiary magistrate) exercising the *jurisdiction conferred by the Magistrates' Courts Act 1980 and other statutes. The principal function of magistrates' courts is to provide the forum in which all criminal *prosecutions are initiated. The guiding principle governing which magistrates' court should hear a case is that it should be heard either at a magistrates' court for the *local justice area in which (i) the offence is alleged to have been committed or where the subject of complaint originated or (ii) the person charged with the offence resides or where the person subject of the complaint resides or has their principal place of business.

In the case of an *offence triable either way in which the court declines jurisdiction or the defendant elects *trial on indictment (*see* MODE OF TRIAL), the court sits as *examining justices to consider whether or not there is sufficient evidence to justify committing the defendant to the *Crown Court (*see* COMMITTAL FOR TRIAL). For a *summary offence or an offence triable either way in which the court accepts jurisdiction and the defendant consents to *summary trial, the court sits as a **court of summary jurisdiction**, i.e. as a criminal court of trial without a *jury in which justices, assisted by the *clerk to the justices, decide all questions of law and fact. *See also* EARLY FIRST HEARING; PLEA BEFORE VENUE; COMMITTAL FOR SENTENCE.

Magistrates' courts also have a limited jurisdiction in civil matters relating to *debt and *family proceedings.

Magna Carta The Great Charter of Runnymede, acceded to by King John in 1215 after armed rebellion by his barons. It guaranteed the freedom of the church, restricted taxes and fines, and promised justice to all. Confirmed frequently by subsequent feudal kings, it has since been largely repealed as having only symbolic significance.

magnetic stripe The magnetic stripe on the back of all *payment cards issued by banks and other financial institutions. The stripe carries information about the account and customer and can be read by a card reader.

magnetometry A method of finding buried bodies or objects. An electric current is passed through the soil and the resistance to the current is measured. Anomalies in the conductivity indicate the possibility of a buried object.

majority (full age) The age of 18 years. The state of being below that age is a state of **minority** (*see* INFANT). The age of majority was originally 21 years, but was reduced to 18 by the Family Law Reform Act 1969. This majority applies for the purposes of any relevant legal rule and for the interpretation of any relevant statute, whenever it was made. It does not apply, however, to *deeds, wills, and other private *documents made before 1969, in which reference is made to majority or minority.

majority verdict The *verdict of a *jury reached by a majority. The verdict need not be unanimous if there are no fewer than eleven *jurors and ten of them agree on the verdict or if there are ten jurors and nine of them agree on the verdict. The jury must be given at least two hours in which to reach a unanimous verdict and the foreman of the jury must state in open court the number of jurors who respectively agreed to and dissented from the majority verdict. Majority verdicts can be taken in both criminal and civil cases.

making off without payment Leaving without paying for *goods or services received and with the intention of avoiding payment, when payment on the spot is expected. This is an offence contrary to s 3 of the Theft Act 1978, punishable by up to two years' imprisonment, but it must be proved that the person who made off knew that payment on the spot was expected. It will usually cover such behaviour as walking out of a restaurant, after having had a meal, without paying (even if there was originally no intention not to pay for the meal, and therefore no *theft, and no *deception when the meal was ordered); taking a taxi and disappearing without paying; and collecting any items from a shop that has repaired or cleaned them, without paying.

malfeasance An unlawful act. *Compare* MISFEASANCE.

m

malice 1. (in criminal law) A state of mind (*see* MENS REA) usually taken to be equivalent to *intention or *recklessness: it does not require any hostile attitude. Malice is said to be **transferred** when someone intends to commit a crime against one person but in fact commits the same crime against someone else (e.g. if he intends to shoot X but misses, and instead kills Y). Malice is **universal** (or **general**) when the accused has no particular victim in mind (e.g. if he shoots into a crowd intending to kill anyone). In both cases this constitutes *mens rea*. **2.** (in *tort) A constituent element of certain torts. In the English law of tort, the general rule is that a malicious motive cannot make conduct unlawful if it would otherwise be lawful. For example, a right to take water from under one's own *land can lawfully be exercised solely in order to cause *damage to a neighbour. However, in some cases malice can be relevant. An action for *malicious prosecution requires proof that the prosecution was instigated maliciously, i.e. without reasonable and probable cause. In *defamation, a malicious motive invalidates the *defences of fair comment and *qualified privilege.

Malice is also relevant to liability for *conspiracy to injure someone.

malice aforethought The **mens rea* (state of mind) required for a person to be *guilty of *murder. It is unnecessary for there to be any element of hostility (*see* MALICE) or for the intention to kill to be 'forethought' (i.e. premeditated). The term covers (1) intention to kill (**direct express malice aforethought**), (2) intention to cause *grievous bodily harm (**direct implied malice aforethought**), (3) realizing while doing a particular act that death would almost certainly or very probably result (**indirect express malice**), and (4) realizing that grievous bodily harm would very probably result from the act, e.g. shooting at someone without intending to kill him, but realizing that he may at least suffer a serious injury (**indirect implied malice**). The *prosecution must prove one of these four types of malice aforethought to secure a conviction of murder.

malicious damage Formerly (before 1971), *criminal damage.

m

malicious communication *See* OBSCENE AND THREATENING COMMUNICATIONS.

malicious prosecution The malicious institution of legal proceedings against a person. Malicious prosecution is only actionable in *tort if the proceedings were initiated both maliciously and without reasonable and probable cause and they were unsuccessful. No one who has been convicted of a criminal charge can sue for malicious prosecution. *See also* ABUSE OF PROCESS.

malicious wounding *See* WOUNDING.

malware A generic term (short for 'malicious software') covering a range of *software programs and types of programs designed to attack, degrade, or prevent the intended use of a *computer or network. Types of malware include *viruses, *worms, *Trojan horses, and *denial of service attacks. The term can also be used to refer to software that passively tracks the use of a computer system for the purposes of *fraud or the *theft of identity. *See also* SPYWARE.

managerialism The political ethos for the *criminal justice system since the 1980s, the purpose being to introduce private sector disciplines of value-for-money, performance targets, and discipline.

mandate 1. (in *private law) An authority given by one person (the **mandator**) to another to take some course of action. A mandate is commonly revocable until acted upon and is terminated by the death of the mandator. A *cheque is a mandate from the customer to his bank to pay the sum in question and to debit his account. **2.** (in *international law) The system by which dependent territories (such as the former German colonies in Africa) were placed under the supervision (but not the sovereignty) of mandatory powers by the League of Nations after World War I. After World War II, all remaining mandated territories became trust territories under the *United Nations (UN) with the exception of South-West Africa (now Namibia) and a strategic trust area consisting of a number of Pacific Islands north of the equator, which were administered by the USA. The mandate over Namibia was terminated by the General Assembly of the UN in 1966, which placed the territory under the direct responsibility of the UN; it became an independent state in 1990. The Pacific Islands territories are also now independent states.

mandatory minimum sentence A minimum *sentence, imposed under ss 110 and 111 of the Powers of Criminal Courts (Sentencing) Act 2000, applied to a person aged 18 years of age or over who is convicted of a third offence of Class A drug trafficking (*see* CONTROLLED DRUGS) or *burglary of a dwelling. The Act lays down a minimum sentence of seven years' and three years' imprisonment, respectively. The court need not impose the minimum term if it is of the opinion that there are specific circumstances which relate to any of the offences or the offender which would make it unjust to do so in all the circumstances. Section 152(3) of the Criminal Justice Act 2003 allows the court to give a discount for a *guilty *plea by reducing the actual sentence passed to 80 per cent of the statutory minimum.

Section 51A of the Firearms Act 1968 (as inserted by s 287, Criminal Justice Act

2003) provides for minimum custodial sentences for certain serious *firearms offences committed on or after 22 January 2004. The specified minimum sentences are five years' imprisonment in the case of an offender aged 18 or over and three years' detention (*see* LONG-TERM DETENTION) for any offender aged at least 16 but under 18 at the time of the offence.

Section 109 of the Powers of Criminal Courts (Sentencing) Act 2000, which imposed a mandatory life sentence on any offender, aged 18 or over, convicted of a second 'serious offence' (including *manslaughter, *rape, and *wounding with intent) was repealed on 4 April 2005 when the provisions dealing with *dangerous offenders contained in ch 5 of pt 12 of the Criminal Justice Act 2003 came into effect.

mandatory order A *prerogative order from the *High Court instructing an inferior tribunal, public official, *corporation, etc., to perform a specified public duty relating to its responsibilities (*see also* JUDICIAL REVIEW); e.g. an instruction to a statutory tribunal to hear a particular dispute. Formerly called **mandamus** (from Latin: we command), it was renamed in 1999 under pt 54.1 of the *Civil Procedure Rules.

mandatory referral A complaint against the police or serious incidents that could damage public confidence in the police which must be referred to the *Independent Police Complaints Commission for a decision on how the matter should be investigated.

mandible The lower jaw.

manslaughter *Homicide that does not amount to the crime of *murder but is nevertheless neither lawful nor accidental. Manslaughter may be committed in several ways. It may arise if the accused is charged with murder and had the **mens rea* required for murder (*see* MALICE AFORETHOUGHT), but mitigating circumstances (*diminished responsibility, a *suicide pact, or *provocation) reduce the offence to manslaughter; this is known as **voluntary manslaughter**. It may also be committed when there was no *mens rea* for murder in one of two situations: (1) if the accused committed an act of *gross negligence or (2) if the act, although not negligent, was criminally illegal and also involved an element of danger to the victim. For example, it would be manslaughter to knock some bricks off a bridge into the path of a train (*criminal damage), killing the driver, even if one had no idea that there was a train in the area. Such cases are known as **involuntary manslaughter**. There are generally three types of involuntary manslaughter, although the distinction between them remains unclear: **gross negligence manslaughter**, **unlawful act manslaughter**, and **reckless manslaughter**. The maximum *punishment for manslaughter is *life imprisonment, although this is rarely imposed; however, the Crime (Sentences) Act 1997 provides for a mandatory life sentence for those convicted of manslaughter for a second time (*see* REPEAT OFFENDER). Most cases of *causing death by dangerous driving and *causing death by careless driving whilst under the influence of drink or drugs are usually not charged as manslaughter but as special statutory offences under the Road Traffic Act 1991. However, in certain circumstances causing death by dangerous driving may amount to manslaughter.

mansuetae naturae [Latin: tame by nature] *See* CLASSIFICATION OF ANIMALS.

Mareva injunction *See* FREEZING INJUNCTION.

marquis test A test used to spot-test some illegal drugs. A small quantity of the suspected drug is added to a reagent, which changes colour in the presence of opiate drugs and amphetamine.

Martens clause A clause that was included in the *Hague Conventions of 1899 and 1907 by the Russian delegate, Friedrich von Martens (1845–1909), and has since then been included in many other *treaties. It states that anything not proscribed by the regulations of the treaty will be subject to *international law and will therefore not necessarily be permissible; it also allows the regulations of the treaty to keep pace with the consequences of modern developments in warfare.

martial law Government by the military authorities when the normal machinery of government has broken down as a result of invasion, civil war, or large-scale insurrection. The constitution of the UK does not provide for a declaration (with specified consequences) of martial law: it is no more than a situation capable of arising. While the military authorities are restoring order, their conduct could not be called into question by the ordinary courts of law. After the restoration of order, the legality of their actions would be theoretically capable of examination, but the standards that would be applied by the courts are unknown. Martial law should not be confused with military law (*see* SERVICE LAW); any courts held by the military authorities to try civilians during a state of martial law would not enjoy the status of *courts martial.

Marxist criminology A school of criminology that sees crime and deviance as defined by the ruling class and used as a means of social and to an extent economic control. This would include making traditional activities, such as collecting firewood in a forest, criminal offences to fulfil the needs of capitalists and to the detriment of the lower classes. Institutions such as the police, the justice system, prisons and schools, the family, and religion are regarded as being instruments of the ruling class, there to enforce conformity. Marxist criminology evolved via neo-Marxist criminology to New Criminology which was largely replaced by *Realist (Left) criminology.

master 1. One of the *Masters of the Supreme Court or the Masters of the Bench. **2.** The person having command or charge of a vessel. **3.** Formerly, an *employer. *See also* EMPLOYER; EMPLOYEE.

Master of the Rolls (MR) The *judge who is president of the Civil Division of the *Court of Appeal. The office is an ancient one and was originally held by the keeper of the public records. Later the holder was a judge of the Court of Chancery and assistant to the *Lord Chancellor, with his own court, the **Rolls Court**. Since 1881 he has been a judge of the Court of Appeal only, but retains important duties in relation to public records. He also admits *solicitors to practice.

Master of the Supreme Court An inferior judicial officer of the *Queen's Bench and *Chancery Divisions of the *High Court. Their principal function is to supervise *interim (interlocutory) proceedings in litigation and (especially in the Chancery Division) to take accounts. By convention, Chancery Masters are usually *solicitors and Queen's Bench Masters are usually *barristers. In the provinces a comparable jurisdiction is exercised by *district judges of the High Court.

maxilla The upper jaw.

McKenzie friend (from the case *McKenzie v McKenzie* [1970] 3 All ER 1034) A person who sits beside an unrepresented *litigant in court and assists him by prompting, taking notes, and quietly giving advice.

McNaghten Rules (M'Naghten Rules) *See* INSANITY.

mechanically propelled vehicle A *motor vehicle driven by petrol, oil, steam, or electricity (s 185, Road Traffic Act 1988 or s 136, Road Traffic Regulation Act 1984). The term includes a *locomotive.

medial The side of any part of the body nearer to the centre line, e.g. the inner aspect of an arm.

mediation (in *international law) A method for the peaceful settlement of an international dispute in which a third party, acting with the agreement of the disputing states, actively participates in the negotiating process by offering substantive suggestions concerning terms of settlement and, in general, by trying to reconcile the opposing claims and appeasing any feeling of resentment between the parties involved. *See also* GOOD OFFICES.

medical experiments It is an offence under the Statute of the *International Criminal Court and the *Geneva Convention to carry out medical experiments that are not for therapeutic purposes on persons in the power of an opposing party.

medical personnel *See* PROTECTED PERSONS.

meeting a child following sexual grooming An offence under s 15 of the Sexual Offences Act 2003 whereby an adult, after meeting or communicating with a child on at least two previous occasions, intentionally meets or goes to meet the child for the purpose of committing a *child abuse offence.

Member of Parliament (MP) *See* HOUSE OF COMMONS.

Members' interests Interests of *Members of Parliament that might affect their conduct as MPs; e.g. employments, company directorships, shareholdings, substantial property holdings, and financial sponsorships. By a 1975 resolution of the House, these must be registered for public information.

memorandum of association A constitutional *document of a *registered company that must be drawn up by the person(s) wishing to set it up. Under the Companies Act 1985 certain compulsory clauses must be inserted into the memorandum. These clauses deal with and outline the company's identity (**names clause**); its registered address (**registered office clause**); the amount of its authorized *share capital (**capital clause**); the purpose(s) for which the company has been formed (**objects clause**); and (if applicable) whether it is a *limited company or a *public company. The Companies Act 1985 contains specimen examples of such clauses for different types of company. The memorandum is said to be the 'superior constitutional document' of the company; in the event of a conflict between it and the *articles of association, the memorandum prevails.

menace *See* THREAT.

menacing communication *See* OBSCENE AND THREATENING COMMUNICATIONS.

meninges The tough membrane covering the brain. It has three layers,*dura mater, *arachnoid, and *pia mater. *Inflammation of the meninges is called meningitis. The form of this disease caused by bacteria is a very serious and often fatal disease. Viral meningitis is far less serious and commonly gets better without treatment.

mens rea [Latin: a guilty mind] The state of mind that the *prosecution must prove a defendant to have had at the time of committing a crime in order to secure a *conviction. *Mens rea* varies from crime to crime; it is either defined in the statute creating the crime or established by *precedent. Common examples of *mens rea* are *intention to bring about a particular consequence, *recklessness as to whether such consequences may come about, and (for a few crimes) *negligence. Some crimes require knowledge of certain circumstances as part of the *mens rea* (e.g. the crime of receiving stolen *goods requires the knowledge that they were stolen). Some crimes require no *mens rea*; these are known as crimes of *strict liability. Whenever *mens rea* is required, the prosecution must prove that it existed at the same time as the **actus reus* of the crime (coincidence of *actus reus* and *mens rea*). A defendant cannot plead ignorance of the law, nor is a good *motive a defence. He may, however, bring evidence to show that he had no *mens rea* for the crime he is charged with; alternatively, he may admit that he had *mens rea*, but raise a general defence (e.g. *duress) or a particular defence allowed in relation to the crime.

mental disorder (under the Mental Health Act 1983) Mental illness, incomplete or *arrested development of mind, *psychopathic disorder, and any other disorder or disability of mind. A person suffering (or appearing to be suffering) from mental disorder can be detained in hospital either for assessment or for treatment. *Detention for assessment normally takes place on an application for his admission made by his nearest relative or an approved social worker. This is supported in either case by the recommendation of two doctors that it is desirable in the interests of the patient's own health and safety or for the protection of others. The application authorizes detention for up to 28 days. In a case of emergency, however, detention may be for up to 72 hours on an application supported by one doctor only and made by an approved social worker or the patient's nearest relative. The procedure for detention for treatment is the same as the normal procedure for detention for assessment. The application authorizes detention for six months, renewable for a further six months, initially, and then for periods of one year on a report to the hospital managers by the doctor in charge. Discharge of a person detained may be effected by the managers or the doctor in charge and, within certain limits, the nearest relative; in the case of detention for treatment, discharge may also be directed by a *Mental Health Review Tribunal. The National Health Service and Community Care Act 1990 provided for more care in the community for patients who previously may have been treated in secure hospitals. *See also* HOSPITAL ORDER; SPECIAL HOSPITAL.

Mental Health Review Tribunal A tribunal, constituted under the Mental Health Act 1983, to which applications may be made for the discharge from hospital of a person detained there for assessment or treatment of *mental disorder or under a *hospital order or a *guardianship order. When a patient is subject to a *restriction order or direction an application may only be made after his first six months of detention. Such tribunals include legally and medically qualified members appointed by the *Lord Chancellor and are under the supervision of the Council on Tribunals.

mental health treatment requirement A requirement that may be imposed by a court dealing with an offender aged 16 or over as part of a *community order or *suspended sentence order, which requires the offender to submit, during a period or periods specified in the order, to treatment by or under the direction of a registered medical practitioner or a chartered psychologist (s 207, Criminal Justice Act 2003). Such a requirement may not be imposed unless the offender expresses a willingness to comply with the requirement.

mental impairment *See* ARRESTED DEVELOPMENT.

mercantile agent A commercial agent who has authority either to sell *goods, to consign goods for the purpose of sale, to buy goods, or to raise money on the security of goods on behalf of his principal.

mercenary A person who is paid to serve with armed forces other than those of the state of which he is a national. British officers undertaking such service (e.g. in Oman) were commonly known as **contract officers**. *See also* FOREIGN ENLISTMENT.

merchantable quality An *implied condition now replaced by *satisfactory quality.

merchant bank A bank and investment house which works as a financial intermediary, offering such services as *takeover and *merger assistance, and the placing of new *share and *bond issues.

merger An amalgamation between companies of similar size in which either the members of the merging companies exchange their *shares for shares in a new company or the members of some of the merging companies exchange their shares for shares in another merging company. It is usually effected by a *takeover bid. *Compare* TAKEOVER.

mesentery The sheet of tissue that supports the intestine.

metaphysis The zone at which the shaft and epiphysis of a bone come together. It is an area of growth in children.

methadone A drug used as a replacement for heroin in the treatment of addiction. It is supplied as syrup. It is frequently abused and is said by some to be more addictive than heroin.

methylenedioxymethamphetamine (MDMA) *See* ECSTASY.

MI5 *See* SECURITY SERVICE.

MI6 *See* SECRET INTELLIGENCE SERVICE.

middle meningeal artery An artery that runs near the inner surface of the skull and is often ruptured by fractures of the skull causing extradural haemorrhage.

Middle Temple One of the four *Inns of Court, situated in the Temple between the Strand and the Embankment. The earliest recorded claim for its existence is 1404.

Military Aid to Civil Authorities (MACA) The use of military personnel in support of various civil functions: *Military Aid to the Civil Community, *Military Aid to the Civil Power, *Military Aid to Government Departments.

Military Aid to Civil Power (MACP) The use of military personnel and equipment to support the forces of law and order, particularly in operations aimed at preventing and combating *terrorism, e.g. guarding airports or resolving sieges. The military can also assist in other criminal situations where criminals have military type weapons. It also includes Explosive Ordnance Disposal (bomb disposal) of *war time weapons or terrorist devices.

Military Aid to Government Departments (MAGD) The use of military personnel and equipment to assist government departments in time of emergency. For example, the provision of a fire and rescue service at times when the civilian fire services take strike action. Military forces were extensively used in an outbreak of foot and mouth disease in logistic roles.

Military Aid to the Civil Community (MACC) The use of military personnel and equipment to provide rescue and assistance to the public, particularly in natural disasters such as flooding.

military court A *court martial. *See also* SERVICE LAW; STANDING CIVILIAN COURT.

military law *See* SERVICE LAW. *Compare* MARTIAL LAW.

military stores Any *chattel belonging to the *Crown that is issued, or stored for the purpose of being issued when required, for military purposes. *Compare* NAVAL PROPERTY.

minimum term *See* LIFE IMPRISONMENT.

minister A person (by constitutional convention a member of either House of *Parliament) appointed to government office by the *Crown on the advice of the *Prime Minister. He may be a senior minister in charge of a department (normally styled Secretary of State but sometimes Minister), a senior minister without specific departmental responsibilities (e.g. the Lord Privy Seal or a Minister without Portfolio), or a junior minister assisting in departmental business (a Minister of State or a Parliamentary Secretary or Under-Secretary). In the Treasury the ministerial ranks are Chancellor of the Exchequer, Chief Secretary, Financial Secretary, and Ministers of State.

ministerial responsibility The responsibility to *Parliament of the *Cabinet collectively and of individual *ministers for their own decisions and the conduct of their departments. A minister must defend his decisions without sheltering behind his civil servants; if he cannot, political pressure may force his resignation.

minor *See* INFANT.

minority The state of being an *infant (or minor). *Compare* MAJORITY.

minority clauses Clauses in *treaties between states that make special provision for *ethnic minorities. For example, in the Greco-Bulgarian Convention of 1919 there was a minority clause that allowed for free migration of minorities between the signatory powers.

minority protection *Remedies evolved to safeguard a minority of *company members from the abuse of majority rule. They include *just and equitable winding-up, applying for relief on the basis of unfair prejudice, bringing a derivative action or a representative action, and seeking an *investigation of the company.

miscarriage 1. A failure of justice or a failure in the administration of justice. **2.** A spontaneous *abortion, i.e. one that is not induced.

mischief rule *See* INTERPRETATION OF STATUTES.

misconduct Incorrect or erroneous conduct. *See* WILFUL MISCONDUCT.

misconduct in public office A *common law offence when the holder of a public office, e.g. a *constable, does anything that amounts to malfeasance.

misdemeanour Formerly (before 1967), any of the less serious offences, as opposed to *felony.

misdescription An *either way offence under s 1 of the Property Misdescription Act 1991, punishable with a *fine, for *estate agents and property developers to make false or misleading statements about property in the course of their business. Misdescription in this case relates to what purports to be fact and not to mere expressions of opinion.

misdirection An incorrect direction by a *judge to a *jury on a matter of law. In such cases the *Court of Appeal may quash the *conviction.

m

misfeasance 1. The *negligent or otherwise improper performance of a lawful act. **2.** (in company law) An act by an officer of a company in the nature of a breach of trust or breach of duty, particularly relating to the company's assets. *Compare* MALFEASANCE.

misleading prices An offence under the Consumer Protection Act 1987 to give a *consumer who is buying *goods, services or accommodation misleading information about the price, conditions attached to the price, future price, or price comparison.

misprision Failure to report an offence. The former crime of misprision of *felony has now been replaced by the crime of *compounding an offence. However, the *common-law offence of misprision of *treason still exists; this occurs if a person knows or reasonably suspects that someone has committed treason but does not inform the proper authorities within a reasonable time. The *punishment for this offence is *forfeiture by the offender of all his *property during his lifetime.

mistake A misunderstanding or erroneous belief about a matter of fact (**mistake of fact**) or a matter of law (**mistake of law**). In civil cases, mistake is particularly important in the law of contract. Mistakes of law have no effect on the validity of agreements, and neither do many mistakes of fact. When a mistake of fact does do so, it may render the agreement void under *common-law rules (in which case it is referred to as an **operative mistake**) or it may make it voidable, i.e. liable, subject to certain limitations, to be set aside by rescission under more lenient rules of *equity.

In criminal cases, a mistake or accident may mean that a person lacked **mens rea*. If a defendant makes a mistake as to the civil law that prevents him having the *mens rea* required to be *guilty of the crime, he will normally be acquitted of the crime, even if his mistake is unreasonable (e.g. if he damages someone else's *property in the belief that it is his own, and this belief is caused by a mistake as to the law of property). *See also* GENERAL DEFENCES; INTOXICATION.

If someone commits a crime in ignorance that the law forbids it, he is usually *guilty (**ignorantia juris non excusat*: ignorance of the law is no excuse).

mistrial A *trial that is vitiated by some fundamental defect.

mitigation 1. Reduction in the severity of some *penalty. Before *sentence is passed on someone convicted of a crime, the *defence may make a *plea in mitigation, putting forward reasons for making the sentence less severe than it might otherwise be. These might include personal or family circumstances of the offender, and the defence may also dispute facts raised by the *prosecution to indicate aggravating circumstances. In raising mitigating factors, *hearsay evidence and *documentary evidence of *character are accepted. **2.** Reduction in the loss or injury resulting from a *tort or a *breach of contract. The injured party is under a duty to take all reasonable steps to mitigate his loss when claiming *damages.

mitochondrial DNA (mtDNA) DNA contained in the mitochondria, which are bodies in a cell but not in the nucleus. The DNA is inherited only from the mother. It is useful for tracing matrilineage and in forensic cases for elimination, but it cannot give a positive identification.

mock auction An *auction during which (1) any lot is sold to someone at a price lower than his highest bid for it; (2) part of the price is repaid or credited to the bidder; (3) the right to bid is restricted to those who have bought or agreed to buy one or more articles; or (4) articles are given away or offered as gifts. Under the Mock Auction Act 1961 it is an offence to promote or conduct a mock auction of plate, plated articles, linen, china, glass, books, pictures, prints, furniture, jewellery, articles of household or personal use, ornaments, or any musical or scientific instrument.

mode of trial (MOT) The decision made by a *magistrates' court in an either way case (*see* OFFENCE TRIABLE EITHER WAY) as to whether an offence is more suitable for *summary trial or *trial on indictment. It follows once the defendant has entered a *not guilty *plea or has not indicated a plea (*see* PLEA BEFORE VENUE) and the court has heard an outline of the *prosecution case and representation from both the prosecution and defence *advocates regarding the appropriate venue. The court is also required to have regard to guidelines issued by the *Sentencing Guidelines Council.

molestation Behaviour that has the effect or intention of annoying or pestering one's spouse (or cohabitant) or children. Such an act need not involve violence or physical *assault; *harassment (e.g. by threatening letters or telephone calls) may constitute molestation. Under the Family Law Act 1996, spouses (and in some cases unmarried cohabitants) can apply for a court *injunction to prevent molestation (*see* NON-MOLESTATION ORDER). *Magistrates' courts have similar powers under the Domestic Proceedings and Magistrates' Courts Act 1978, but only if there is violence and only in relation to married couples. There are procedures for protecting children in an emergency (*see* EMERGENCY PROTECTION ORDER). *See also* BATTERED CHILD; BATTERED SPOUSE OR COHABITANT.

money Bill A *Bill that, in the opinion of the Speaker of the *House of Commons, contains only provisions dealing with taxation, the Consolidated Fund, public money, the raising or replacement of loans by the state, and matters incidental to these subjects. Such a Bill can become an Act without the *House of Lords' consent (*see* ACT OF PARLIAMENT).

money laundering The process by which criminal proceeds are sanitized to disguise their illicit origins. Acquisitive criminals will attempt to distance themselves from their crimes by finding safe havens for their profits where they can avoid *confiscation orders, and where those proceeds can be made to appear legitimate. Money laundering schemes generally involve three stages:

- placement—the process of getting criminal money into the financial system;
- layering—the process of moving money in the financial system through complex webs of transactions, often via offshore companies; and
- integration—the process by which criminal money ultimately becomes absorbed into the economy, such as through investment in real estate.

Part 7 of the Proceeds of Crime Act 2002 creates various money laundering offences. *European Union measures exist to control, on an EU-wide basis, the laundering of money, especially that resulting from organized crime.

moneylender A person whose business it is to lend money. The Moneylenders Acts 1900–27 contained provisions for the control of moneylenders, including the form of their contracts. Under the Acts, the term 'moneylender' did not include pawnbrokers, friendly or building societies, corporate bodies with special powers to lend money, those carrying on a banking or insurance business, or businesses whose primary object is not the lending of money. The more extensive provisions of the Consumer Credit Act 1974 have replaced the provisions of the Moneylenders Acts.

monism The theory that national and *international law form part of one legal structure, in which international law is supreme. It is opposed to **dualism**, which holds that they are separate systems operating in different fields. The UK is a dualist state. Thus, when the UK signs a *treaty with other states it does not become part of the domestic law of the UK unless *Parliament passes an *Act to make it so, e.g. the Nuclear Explosions (Prohibitions and Inspections) Act 1998.

monoamine oxidase inhibitors Drugs used as anti-depressants. May have serious side effects if taken with certain foods such as cheese, red wine, and food containing yeast.

monopoly A situation in which a substantial proportion of a particular type of business is transacted by a single enterprise or trader. Provisions to prevent any adverse effects of monopolies are contained in the Fair Trading Act 1973 and the Competition Act 1998.

Monroe doctrine The declaration in 1823 by President Monroe that the USA would consider any attack by a European power on any part of North or South America, not just its own territory, as an attack on the USA and they would act in self-defence.

Montero's Aim The principle of keeping a person in *custody for his own protection from others.

moot A mock *trial, often held in university law schools and at the *Inns of Court, for students as practice for future advocacy. A hypothetical case is presented to students for preparation and then argued before the judge(s) at the moot. This practice originates in the formal moots held in the medieval Inns of Court, which were considered an essential part of legal education.

moral panic A mass movement based on the false or exaggerated perception that some cultural behaviour or group of people is dangerously deviant and poses a threat to society's values and interests. Moral panics are generally fuelled by media coverage of social issues. The phenomenon was first described in 1972 in relation to the 'Mods & Rockers' groups of the 1960s. Since then moral panics have occurred in relation to 'ritual satanic abuse', that was perceived to be widespread in the 1980s, and paedophilia, which led to vigilante action against innocent people.

morphine An opiate drug with strong analgesic (pain relieving) properties. It is classified as a Class A drug under the Misuse of Drugs Act 1971. When two molecules of morphine are linked, the drug *diamorphine (heroin) is produced.

motive The purpose behind a course of action. Motive is not normally relevant in deciding guilt or innocence (e.g. killing to save someone from suffering is still *murder or *manslaughter), although it may be of some relevance in the crime of *libel. Nor is a bad motive relevant in deciding legal guilt. However, a good motive may be invoked as a reason for *mitigating a *punishment upon *conviction, and a bad motive may provide *circumstantial evidence that the defendant committed the crime with which he is charged.

motor car *See* MOTOR VEHICLE.

motor caravan *See* MOTOR VEHICLE.

motor cycle *See* MOTOR VEHICLE.

motoring offences *See* OFFENCE RELATING TO ROAD TRAFFIC.

motor insurance *See* THIRD-PARTY INSURANCE.

Motor Insurers' Bureau A body set up by the *insurance industry, by agreement with the Department of Transport. It provides cover if someone has been injured or killed in a motor accident and in respect of a liability required by the Road Traffic Act to be covered by a contract of insurance when either (1) a *judgment against the party liable is unsatisfied, e.g. because the party is (in breach of the Road Traffic Act 1988) uninsured, or (2) the wrongdoer cannot be identified.

motor tractor A *mechanically propelled vehicle which is not constructed itself to carry a load, other than water, fuel, accumulators and other equipment used for the purpose of propulsion, loose tools, and loose equipment, and the weight of which unladen does not exceed

7370 kg (reg 3(2), Road Vehicles (Construction and Use) Regulations 1986 (SI 1986/1078)). *See also* MOTOR VEHICLE.

motor vehicle (for the purposes of the Road Traffic Acts) Any *mechanically propelled vehicle intended or adapted for use on the *roads (reg 3(2), Road Vehicles (Construction and Use) Regulations 1986 (SI 1986/1078)). This includes **motor cars** (vehicles of not more than 3 050 kg in unladen weight, designed to carry loads or up to seven passengers); **motor cycles** (vehicles of not more than 410 kg in unladen weight and having less than four wheels); and **motor caravans** (vehicles which are constructed or adapted for the carriage of passengers and their effects and which contain, as permanently installed equipment, the facilities which are reasonably necessary for enabling them to provide mobile living accommodation for their users). A car from which the engine has been removed may still be considered to be mechanically propelled if the removal is temporary, but if so many parts have been removed that it cannot be restored to use at a reasonable expense, it ceases to be mechanically propelled. A dumper used for carrying materials at a building site is not intended for use on roads, even if it is in fact used on a road near the building site; and a go-kart is not intended or adapted for use on the roads (even though it is capable of being used on the roads). *See also* CONVEYANCE; HEAVY MOTOR CAR.

motorway driving Contravention of the regulations relating to driving on a motorway, as outlined in the Highway Code, is an offence punishable by *endorsement (carrying between three and six points) and, in respect of some offences, discretionary *disqualification.

MOT test An annual test carried out on all *motor vehicles over a certain age to ensure that they comply with certain legal requirements relating to vehicle maintenance. The test covers brakes, steering, lights and indicators, windscreen wipers and washers, the exhaust system, horn, tyres (and to some extent, the wheels), bodywork and suspension (in so far as they affect the brakes and steering), and seat belts. It is an offence to use a motor vehicle that has been registered for over three years (five years in Northern Ireland) without a valid test certificate. A certificate is issued for twelve months and must be renewed annually; a vehicle that is subject to a test cannot be licensed without a test certificate (*see* ROAD TAX). It is not an endorsable offence not to have an MOT certificate. An MOT certificate does not indicate that the vehicle is roadworthy in all respects and is not a defence to charges brought under the *vehicle construction and maintenance regulations.

movables *Tangible items of property other than *land and *goods fixed to the land (i.e. *immovables).

multiple admissibility The principle of the law of evidence that if evidence is admissible for one purpose it may not be rejected solely because it is inadmissible for some other purpose. However, the *trier of fact may have to be directed not to consider the evidence when deciding those issues in respect of which it is inadmissible.

mummification The dehydration of a dead body associated with it lying in warm, dry conditions. The body is well preserved. Sometimes only part of the body is mummified and the rest decomposed in a more conventional way.

Munchausen's Syndrome A psychiatric condition whereby the sufferer falsely claims to have illness with a view to receiving treatment, often surgical operations. 'Munchausen's Syndrome by Proxy' occurs when parents describe symptoms or give the child poisons to induce symptoms in the child in order to get unnecessary treatment for the child. It is a controversial area of medicine.

municipal law The national, or internal, law of a state as opposed to *international law.

munitions of war Vessels, aircraft, fighting vehicles, arms, *ammunition, *explosive devices, or any other articles, materials, or devices intended or adapted for use in *war.

murder *Homicide that is neither accidental nor lawful and does not fall into the categories of *manslaughter or *infanticide. The **mens rea* for murder is traditionally known as *malice aforethought, which means an intention to kill or cause *grievous bodily harm. The *punishment (since 1965) is *life imprisonment. Murder is subject to the special *defences of *diminished responsibility, *suicide pact, and *provocation. (*See also* DANGEROUS OFFENDERS.)

mute *See* STANDING MUTE.

mutilation The infliction of serious bodily injury so as to disfigure or disable. It is a *war crime so classified by Article 8 of the Rome Statute of the *International Criminal Court.

mutiny An offence against *service law committed by any member of HM forces who combines with one or more other members (whether or not civilians are also involved) to overthrow or resist lawful authority in those forces or any forces cooperating with them. If a civilian is involved, his conduct will be a matter for the ordinary criminal law. The offence is also committed if the aim of the combination is to disobey lawful authority in a manner subversive of discipline, or for the purpose of avoiding any duty connected with operations against the enemy, or generally to impede the performance of any duty in HM forces or any cooperating forces.

mutual administrative assistance (MAA) *See* MUTUAL ASSISTANCE.

mutual assistance Mutual assistance (often referred to as 'mutual administrative assistance' or 'police-to-police inquiries') is the process whereby information, intelligence, and non-coercive evidence may be obtained from foreign authorities with which the UK has concluded a mutual assistance agreement. These come in several forms: *European Community Conventions (e.g. the 1959 Convention on Mutual Assistance in Criminal Matters), directives and regulations; other binding international agreements; Memoranda of Understanding (generally between one agency and its foreign counterpart); and Multi-agency Memoranda of Understanding (normally between all the relevant law enforcement agencies of the parties to the memoranda). Unlike the more formal *letter of request process, requests for mutual assistance do not require a formal letter of request in each case, but the extent to which countries are willing to assist without a formal request varies from country to country. Dependent upon the nature of the *inquiry, there may be a requirement for the request to be channelled through the Crime and Drug Liaison Officer Network in Europe, the Crime Liaison Officer in the United States,*Europol liaison officers, or Interpol.

It is impossible to list definitively the types of inquiries that can be made under mutual assistance arrangements although, generally, they are limited to routine inquiries and those that do not require the exercise of a coercive power. These include: obtaining public records, such as *Land Registry *documents and papers relating to the *registration of companies; taking a witness statement from a voluntary witness; obtaining details of previous *convictions; and obtaining basic subscriber data from communication service providers. In some instances, mutual assistance requests will provide information rather than evidence and will then need to be followed up by a formal letter of request to obtain evidence in an admissible form. *Compare* MUTUAL LEGAL ASSISTANCE.

mutual legal assistance (MLA) Formal measures and agreements for obtaining evidence in a foreign *jurisdiction. Generally, only those states obliged by *convention, scheme, *treaty, bilateral agreement, or other international instrument (e.g. European Convention on Mutual Assistance in Criminal Matters, 1959; European Convention on Mutual Assistance in Criminal Matters between the Member States of the European Union, 2000; Scheme Relating to Mutual Assistance in Criminal Matters within the Commonwealth (The Harare Scheme); Treaty Between the Government of the United Kingdom of Great Britain and Northern Ireland and the Government of the United States of America on Mutual Legal Assistance in Criminal Matters, 1994) can be requested to provide mutual legal assistance. Generally, the state from which the assistance is requested is entitled to refuse that assistance in certain situations. These include requests that concern an offence which the requested state considers to be a political offence or an offence connected with a political offence; conduct that would not constitute an offence under the law of the requested state; or those where the requested state is of the opinion that the request, if granted, would impair its *sovereignty, security, or other essential interests or would be contrary to important public policy. *Compare* MUTUAL ASSISTANCE. *See also* JOINT INVESTIGATION TEAM; LETTER OF REQUEST.

muzzle The end of the *barrel of a *firearm, from which the *bullet leaves the weapon.

myocardial Relating to the muscles of the heart.

myocardial infarction The death of a clump of muscle in the heart caused by a blocked blood vessel. This is the classic 'heart attack'.

myocardium Muscle of the heart.

Nacro An organization originally established in 1966 as the 'National Association for the Care and Resettlement of Offenders', or 'NACRO'. The aim of the charity was to set up practical services to help ex-offenders resettle, work with individuals at risk of getting involved in crime, and with communities to help prevent crime. In 1999 it changed its name to 'Nacro' usually described as 'Nacro, the crime reduction charity', to better reflect the whole work of the charity—around 50 per cent of its activity concerns the resettlement of offenders, 45 per cent concerns crime prevention, and 5 per cent concerns criminal justice reform. The resettlement of prisoners and ex-offenders is still central to its work and vision of how to make society safer but it also offers services across the spectrum of crime reduction—from youth activity and parenting projects to helping develop and deliver initiatives to tackle crime.

National Assembly for Wales *See* WELSH ASSEMBLY.

National Association for the Care and Resettlement of Offenders (NACRO) *See* NACRO.

National Asylum Support Service Part of the Immigration and Nationality Directorate at the Home Office. It was established in April 2000 to provide housing and financial support for destitute *asylum seekers and their dependants whilst they are awaiting the results of their claim for asylum status.

National Automated Fingerprint Identification System (NAFIS) A central *fingerprint database that can be addressed by any *police force in England and Wales. As a result each force now maintains its own records and possesses the fingerprints taken by the force.

National Crime Squad A body of *police officers organized on a national basis to tackle serious and organized crime. The organization was disbanded and replaced on 1 April 2006 by the *Serious Organized Crime Agency.

National Criminal Intelligence Service (NCIS) A non-departmental public body whose role was to gather, store, and analyze information in order to provide criminal intelligence to *police forces throughout the UK. Since 1 April 2006 it has been part of the *Serious Organized Crime Agency.

National Identification Service (NIS) A service operated by the Metropolitan Police Service on behalf of all UK *police forces (previously known as the National Identification Bureau). It is responsible for the national collection of *fingerprints and criminal records, and other search and disclosure services. The National Fingerprint Office in NIS provides a fingerprint service to the armed services police forces, States of Jersey Police, Ministry of Defence Police, Royal Mail, Interpol, Scottish police forces, and the Prison Service who are not part of the *National Automated Fingerprint Identification System. The NFO also maintains the national fingerprint hardcopy collection.

nationality The state of being a citizen or subject of a particular country. *See* BRITISH CITIZENSHIP; BRITISH DEPENDENT TERRITORIES CITIZENSHIP; BRITISH OVERSEAS CITIZENSHIP; BRITISH SUBJECT; BRITISH NATIONAL (OVERSEAS); BRITISH OVERSEAS TERRITORIES CITIZENSHIP.

National Occupational Standards A national framework that specifies the standards of performance that staff are expected to achieve in their work and the knowledge and skills they need to perform effectively. They have been agreed by *employers and trade unions and approved by the Qualifications and Curriculum Authority (QCA) and the

Scottish Qualifications Authority (SQA). Skills for Justice is responsible for the standards in the justice sector. The standards are also used in the Integrated Competency Framework (ICF).

National Policing Plan A three-year plan drawn up by the Home Office showing how it intends to implement the Government's vision of policing in England and Wales as set out in the Home Office Strategic Plan 2004–08.

National Register of Public Service Interpreters (NRPSI) *See* INTERPRETER.

national treatment standard The doctrine that a state is only bound to treat *aliens and their property in the same way as it would treat its own citizens. Opposed to the *international minimum standard, it is seen by its proponents (originally Latin American countries) as counteracting the attempts of economically and politically powerful Western states to use *international law to impose their will on less well-developed states. Its effect, however, has been to expose foreign nationals to objectionable standards in states that regularly maltreat their own nationals.

natural child A child of one's body, as opposed to an adopted child.

naturalization The legal process by which a person acquires a new *nationality. In the UK, *British citizenship or *British Overseas Territories citizenship is acquired by means of a certificate of naturalization. This is granted by the Secretary of State to an applicant who has satisfied statutory requirements as to residence, character, language, sufficient knowledge of life in the UK, and intentions and taken an *oath of allegiance.

natural justice Rules of fair play, originally developed by the courts of *equity to control the decisions of inferior courts and then gradually extended (particularly in the 20th century) to apply equally to the decisions of administrative and domestic tribunals and of any authority exercising an *administrative power that affects a person's status, rights, or liabilities. Any decision reached in contravention of natural justice is void as **ultra vires*. There are two principal rules. The first is the **rule against bias** (i.e. against departure from the standard of even-handed justice required of those who occupy judicial office)—*nemo judex in causa sua* (or *in propria causa*) (no man may be a judge in his own cause). This means that any decision, however fair it may seem, is invalid if made by a person with any financial or other interest in the outcome or any known bias that might have affected his impartiality. The second rule is known as *audi alteram partem* (hear the other side). It states that a decision cannot stand unless the person directly affected by it was given a fair opportunity both to state his case and to know and answer the other side's case.

natural law The permanent underlying basis of all law. The philosophers of ancient Greece, where the idea of natural law originated, considered that there was a kind of perfect justice given to man by nature and that man's laws should conform to this as closely as possible. Theories of natural law have been an important part of jurisprudence throughout legal history. Natural law is distinguished from **positive law**, which is the body of law imposed by the state. Natural law is both anterior and superior to positive law.

natural person A human being. *Compare* JURISTIC PERSON.

naval law *See* SERVICE LAW.

naval property Any *chattel belonging to the *Crown that is issued, or stored for the purpose of being issued when required, for naval purposes. *Compare* MILITARY STORES.

Naval Prosecuting Authority (NPA) An authority which provides advice to *service police on the investigation and prosecutions of offences and determines whether there is sufficient evidence for the case to proceed and if it is in the public interest to proceed. The NPA was established under the Armed Forces Act 1996 and came into existence on 1 April 1997. It acts independently of the military chain of command and is subject to the general superintendence of the Attorney-General. The Armed Forces Act will see the establishment of a joint-service prosecuting authority that will combine the *Army Prosecuting Authority, the *Royal Air Force Prosecuting Authority, and the Naval Prosecuting Authority. *See also* SERVICE LAW.

necessaries *Goods or services suitable to the condition in life and actual requirements of a minor or a person subject to incapacity, e.g. essential clothing. Although such a person's legal *capacity to contract is limited, he must pay a reasonable price for necessaries sold and delivered to him.

necessary in a democratic society An expression set out in a number of the articles of the *European Convention on Human Rights: it makes that particular right a *qualified right and provides a signatory state with a defence of *proportionality.

necessity Pressure of circumstances compelling one to commit an illegal act. The extent to which English law accepts a defence of necessity to a criminal charge is unclear (*compare* DURESS; SELF-DEFENCE). There have, however, been acquittals on this basis when (1) a prisoner escaped from a burning gaol; and (2) the crew of a ship jettisoned the cargo (not belonging to them) to save the ship from sinking. Necessity is not, however, a defence to charges of *theft or *murder (e.g. when ship-wrecked victims kill and eat one of their number) and it is not usually a defence to driving offences. The definitions of some statutory offences incorporate such expressions as 'unlawfully' or 'without lawful authority or excuse' and so should admit necessity defences. Other statutory provisions (1) authorize police and fire officers, if necessary, to break into *premises when a fire has broken out and do everything necessary to extinguish it; and (2) provide qualified exemption from compliance with traffic lights for fire engines, ambulances, and police vehicles.

The *International Criminal Court includes the defence of necessity within its definition of duress.

Necessity is in some circumstances a defence to an action in tort, but it is probably limited to action taken to protect life or property in an emergency not caused by the defendant's *negligence. The steps taken in the emergency must be reasonable.

necrophilia An offence created by s 70 of the Sexual Offences Act 2003 of sexual penetration of a corpse.

necropsy *See* AUTOPSY.

necrosis The death of body tissue.

necrotic Relating to dead body tissue.

neglect A criminal offence under s 1 of the Children and Young Persons Act 1933 whereby a *parent or *guardian neglects their child in a way that is likely to cause unnecessary suffering or injury to health, when the parent is aware of (or reckless as to) the likely consequences of the neglect. Neglect may also be evidence of *negligence and may give rise to a charge of *manslaughter if the neglected person dies. *See also* CHILD CRUELTY.

negligence 1. Carelessness amounting to the culpable breach of a duty: failure to do something that a *reasonable man (i.e. an average responsible citizen) would do, or doing something that a reasonable man would not do. In cases of professional negligence, involving someone with a special skill, that person is expected to show the skill of an average member of his profession. Negligence may be an element in a few crimes, e.g. *careless and inconsiderate driving, and various regulatory offences, which are usually punished by *fine. The main example of a serious crime that may be committed by gross negligence is *manslaughter (in one of its forms). When negligence is a basis of criminal liability, it is no defence to show that one was doing one's best if one's conduct still falls below that of the reasonable man in the circumstances. *See also* GROSS NEGLIGENCE. **2.** A *tort consisting of the breach of a *duty of care resulting in damage to the claimant. Negligence in the sense of carelessness does not give rise to civil liability unless the defendant's failure to conform to the standards of the reasonable man was a breach of a duty of care owed to the claimant, which has caused damage to him. *See also* RES IPSA LOQUITUR.

negligent misstatement (negligent misrepresentation) A false statement of fact made honestly but carelessly. A statement of opinion may be treated as a statement of fact if it carries the implication that the person making it has reasonable grounds for his opinion. A negligent misstatement is only actionable in *tort if there has been breach of a duty to take care in making the statement that has caused damage to the claimant. There is no general *duty of care in making statements, particularly in relation to statements on financial matters.

negotiable instrument A *document that constitutes an obligation to pay a sum of money and is transferable by delivery so that the holder for the time can sue upon it in his own name. The transferee can enforce the obligation even if the transferor's *title is defective, provided that he accepted the document in good faith and for value and had no notice of the defect. The most important classes of negotiable instruments are *bills of exchange (including cheques) and *promissory notes.

negotiation (in *international law) A diplomatic procedure by which representatives of states, either by direct personal contact or through correspondence, engage in discussing matters of mutual concern and attempt to resolve disputes that have arisen in relations between themselves.

negotiation of a bill The transfer of a *bill of exchange from one person to another so that the transferee becomes the holder. A bill payable to bearer is negotiated by *delivery; a bill payable to order is negotiated by the *endorsement of the holder completed by delivery. The issue of a bill to the payee is not a negotiation.

nemo dat quod non habet [Latin: no one can give what he has not got] The basic rule that a person who does not own property (e.g. a thief) cannot confer it on another except with the true owner's authority (i.e. as his agent). Exceptions to this rule include sales under statutory powers and cases in which the doctrine of *estoppel prevents the true owner from denying the authority of the seller to sell.

nemo debet bis vexari [Latin: no man ought to be twice vexed] No person should be twice sued or prosecuted upon the same set of facts if there has been a final decision of a competent court (*but see* DOUBLE JEOPARDY).

nemo judex in causa sua **(*nemo judex in propria causa*)** *See* NATURAL JUSTICE.

nemo tenetur seipsum accusare [Latin: no one is bound to incriminate himself] A maxim reflecting the policy underlying the *privilege against self-incrimination.

nervous shock A recognizable psychiatric illness caused by shock, as distinct from normal grief, sorrow, or anxiety. Psychiatric illness may amount to *actual bodily harm or *grievous bodily harm for the purposes of offences under the Offences Against the Person Act 1861. Those involved in an accident, who are known as **primary victims**, can recover damages for shock. Recovery by others (e.g. relatives of the accident victims), known as **secondary victims**, is strictly limited.

neurone A nerve cell.

neutrality The legal status of a state that adopts a position of impartiality toward two other states who are at *war with each other. The impartial state accords recognition of the state of belligerency between the two warring parties and this, in turn, creates rights and duties that fall upon all concerned.

neutralization The guarantee of the independence and political and territorial integrity of (usually) a small power by a collective agreement of great powers, subject to the condition that it will not take up arms against another state, except in self-defence, or enter into any treaty that may compromise its neutrality.

Newton hearing If following a *plea of *guilty there is a factual dispute between *prosecution and *defence versions so that it affects the appropriate *sentence in the case, the court must hear evidence on the disputed points.

new trial (retrial) A second *trial of a case ordered by an appellate court. In civil cases the *Court of Appeal may order a new trial on grounds including misconduct by the *judge (such as a serious *misdirection), serious procedural irregularity, or (in rare cases) because fresh evidence has come to light. (In criminal cases) *See* DOUBLE JEOPARDY. *See also* VENIRE DE NOVO.

next friend *See* LITIGATION FRIEND.

next of kin A person's closest blood relations. *Parents and children (including those of unmarried parents) are treated as being closer than grandparents, grandchildren, or siblings.

NHS Trust A self-governing body within the National Health Service that operates a local hospital. NHS Trusts, which are independent of Health Authority control, have their own budgets and are responsible for their own policies and priorities.

ninhydrin A chemical reagent that reacts with amino acids and possibly some other components in *fingerprints producing visible latent fingerprints on surfaces such as cheques, paper *documents, bank notes, etc. It reacts with blood and may be used for developing blood-contaminated fingerprints on porous and non-porous surfaces. Fingerprints developed with ninhydrin can be made fluorescent by application of zinc chloride. If used after DFO (1,8 Diazafluoren-9-one) additional fingerprints may be developed.

nisi [Latin: unless] Not final or absolute.

nitrazepam A *benzodiazepine drug.

no case to answer A submission by the defending party in a court action that the claimant's or *prosecution's case is not sufficient for the defendant to need to make any reply, either because of insufficient legal grounds or because of insufficient factual evidence.

noise *See* NUISANCE; NUISANCE NEIGHBOURS.

nolle prosequi [Latin: to be unwilling to prosecute] A procedure by which the *Attorney-General may terminate criminal proceedings before the *Crown Court at any time after the *bill of indictment is signed but before *judgment is entered. That decision is not subject to any control by the courts. It is most commonly employed when the accused cannot be produced in court to plead or stand his *trial owing to physical or mental incapacity that is expected to be permanent and, less often, when the Attorney-General considers that a prosecution is not in the public interest. Unlike an acquittal, a *nolle prosequi* does not bar a further prosecution, although that is most unlikely to occur in practice. *See also* TERMINATION OF PROCEEDINGS

nominal capital *See* AUTHORIZED CAPITAL.

nominal damages A token sum of *damages awarded when a legal right has been infringed but no substantial loss has been caused.

nominee shareholder A *company member who holds the *shares registered in his name for the benefit of another. The identity of the person with the true interest may be subject to *disclosure and to investigation under the Companies Act.

nonage The period during which someone is under the age of majority (18 years). *See* INFANT.

non-commercial agreement A *consumer-credit agreement or a *consumer-hire agreement that is made by a *creditor or owner but not in the course of a business carried on by him. Such an agreement is outside certain of the provisions of the Consumer Credit Act 1974.

non-consensual DNA analysis It is an offence contrary to s 45 of the Human Tissue Act 2004 (which repealed and replaced the Human Tissue Act 1961, the Anatomy Act 1984, and the Human Organ Transplants Act 1989) for a person to have any bodily material (that is, any material which has come from a human body and which consists of or contains human cells) intending to analyze the DNA unless the analysis has been consented to or the results are to be used for excepted purposes (including criminal justice purposes). The offence is triable *either way and carries a *penalty, on conviction on *indictment, of three years' imprisonment.

Consent may be given by the person from whose body the material came or, in the case of a child, by someone with parental responsibility. If the material originates from a deceased person then consent must be obtained from the spouse, partner, or qualifying relative (as listed in s 54(9) of the Act). Certain material is outside the scope of the offence altogether. This includes material from a person who died more than 100 years ago and embryos outside the body (to which the Human Fertilisation and Embryology Act 1990 applies).

non-disclosure (in contract law) The failure by one party, during negotiations for a contract, to disclose to the other a fact known to him that would influence the other in deciding whether or not to enter into the contract. A full duty of disclosure exists only in the case of contracts **uberrimae fidei*, which are usually contracts of *insurance. If the person to be insured tells an untruth, the contract will (like any other) be voidable for *misrepresentation; if this person also suppresses a material fact, it will be voidable for non-disclosure. In the case of other contracts, there is no general duty to volunteer information and mere silence cannot constitute misrepresentation. There is, however, a very limited duty of *disclosure. A person who does volunteer information must not tell only a partial truth and must correct any statement that subsequently becomes to his knowledge untrue; breach of this duty will render the contract voidable for misrepresentation.

non-governmental organization (NGO) A private international organization that acts as a mechanism for cooperation among private national groups in both municipal and international affairs, particularly in economic, social, cultural, humanitarian, and technical fields. Under Article 71 of the *United Nations Charter, the Economic and Social Council is empowered to make suitable arrangements for consultation with NGOs on matters within its competence.

non-intimate samples Samples taken from a suspect for evidential purposes. Under the provisions of the Police and Criminal Evidence Act 1984 as amended: a sample of hair (other than pubic hair); a sample taken from a nail or under a nail; a swab taken from any part of the body including the mouth but no other bodily orifice; saliva; a footprint or similar impression of any part of the body except the hand (which is dealt with by separate regulation).

non-molestation order A wide-ranging order under the Family Law Act 1996 restraining a person (the *respondent) from attacking or going near someone associated with the respondent (such as a cohabitant, spouse, or *parent) or from otherwise doing what the court orders him not to do. *See also* BATTERED SPOUSE OR COHABITANT; MOLESTATION.

non-provable debt A *debt that cannot be claimed in the course of *bankruptcy proceedings. Examples are *statute-barred debts and debts that cannot be fixed or estimated.

Northern Ireland Assembly A body established under the Northern Ireland Act 1998. It consists of 108 elected members and has limited primary legislative powers in such areas as agriculture, the environment, economic development, health, education, and social security.

nose The point of a *projectile.

notary (notary public) A legal practitioner, usually a *solicitor, who attests or certifies deeds and other *documents. Diplomatic and consular officials may exercise notarial functions outside the UK.

not guilty 1. A denial of the *charges by an accused person in court. If there is more than one charge, the accused may plead *guilty to some and not guilty to others. **2.** A *verdict finding that an accused person has not committed the offence with which he was charged. However, he may, at the same time, be found guilty of other offences. *See also* ACQUITTAL; INSANITY.

notice of discontinuance (in civil proceedings) Notice served by a claimant (or by a defendant in respect of a counterclaim) under r 38 of the Civil Procedure Rules, voluntarily giving up all or part of a claim. In general, a claimant may discontinue by filing a notice of discontinuance with the court and serving copies on all parties. Discontinuance does not require the permission of the court except in the following circumstances: (1) when an *interim injunction has been granted; (2) when an *undertaking to the court has been given; (3) when the claimant has received an interim payment; or (4) when there is more than one claimant.

(In criminal proceedings) Under s 23 of the Prosecution of Offences Act 1985, in criminal proceedings before the *magistrates' court the *prosecutor may give notice of discontinuance at any time evidence is called in a *summary trial, or any time before the committal or sending of the case to the *Crown Court for trial. The consent of the court is not required, however, the notice must explain the reasons for discontinuing the proceedings. If the defendant gives notice to the court within 35 days that he wishes the proceedings to continue, they must be reinstated. In the Crown Court, the only proceedings that can be discontinued are those that have been sent for trial under s 51 of the Crime and Disorder Act 1998 (s 23A, Prosecution of Offences Act 1985), and only until such time as the indictment is preferred. In both the magistrates' courts and the Crown Court, discontinuance is no bar to a further prosecution for the same offence, although, as a general rule, a decision to discontinue proceedings on the ground of public interest is final. Section 36(3) of the Commissioners for Revenue and Customs Act 2005 provides that ss 23 and 23A of the Prosecution of Offences Act 1985 apply to proceedings conducted by the Director of the *Revenue and Customs Prosecutions Office in the same way that they apply to proceedings conducted by the *Director of Public Prosecutions.

notice of intended prosecution A written notice issued to someone charged with any of certain specified driving offences stating that he or she will be prosecuted. These offences are: *speeding, *dangerous driving, *careless and inconsiderate driving, *ignoring traffic signals, and leaving a car in a dangerous position (*see* OBSTRUCTION). If the offender was not warned when he committed the offence that he might be prosecuted for it, he cannot normally be subsequently prosecuted unless he is served with either a *summons or a notice of intended prosecution within 14 days of committing the offence. If he is prosecuted nonetheless, he may *appeal against his *conviction. If the notice was posted by registered or recorded mail so that it would normally have arrived within the 14 days, the motorist cannot plead that he did not receive it within that time. It is not necessary to serve a notice of intended prosecution when: (1) an accident happened at the time of the alleged offence owing to the presence on the road of the car involved in the alleged offence; (2) it was not possible to find out the name and address of the accused (or registered owner) in time; or (3) the motorist is charged with *causing death by dangerous or *careless driving or *drunken driving.

notice of transfer A method by which an *either way offence may be transferred from the *magistrates' court in order that it may be tried in the *Crown Court (*see also* COMMITTAL FOR TRIAL; SENDING OFFENCES FOR TRIAL). Section 4 of the Criminal Justice Act 1987 and s 53 of the Criminal Justice Act 1991 provide, respectively, that in cases involving complex *fraud or specified offences of a violent or sexual nature where there is a child witness (either the victim of the offence or a witness to its commission) who will be called at *trial, the *prosecution may bypass the need for committal proceedings by serving a notice on the defendant and the magistrates' court transferring the case to the Crown Court. The notice must be accompanied by written witness statements which establish that there is sufficient evidence to commit the defendant for trial. The defendant may apply to a Crown Court judge to dismiss the charge(s) on the ground that there is *no case to answer (s 6, Criminal Justice Act 1987 and sch 6, Criminal Justice Act 1991). When brought into force, sch 3 to the Criminal Justice Act 2003 will repeal these provisions and replace them with ss 51B and 51C of the Crime and Disorder Act 1998.

not negotiable Words marked on a crossed cheque indicating that a transferee for value of the cheque gets no better *title to it than his transferor had. Since the Cheques Act 1992 most banks have printed cheques that are not negotiable. A *bill of exchange so marked is not transferable.

not proven A *verdict used in Scottish courts when the *prosecution's case has not reached a sufficient standard of proof to establish the accused person's guilt, but there is some doubt about his innocence. The effect is the same as a *not guilty verdict: the accused is released and cannot be tried again for the same offence.

novus actus interveniens **(*nova causa interveniens*)** [Latin: a new intervening act (or cause)] An act or event that breaks the causal connection between a wrong or crime committed by the defendant and subsequent happenings and therefore relieves the defendant from responsibility for these happenings. *See* CAUSATION.

'No Witness, No Justice' project A project introducing dedicated Witness Care Units across England and Wales, bringing police and the *Crown Prosecution Service together for the first time to jointly meet the individual needs of victims and witnesses in criminal court cases. The project recognizes that victims and witnesses play a fundamental role in the delivery of criminal justice.

nucleus The central body in every body cell, except red blood cells, that contains the cell's DNA and controls the cell's growth and reproduction.

nuisance An activity or state of affairs that interferes with the use or enjoyment of *land or rights over land (**private nuisance**) or with the health, safety, or comfort of the public at large (**public nuisance**). Private nuisance is a *tort, protecting occupiers of land from damage to the land, buildings, or vegetation or from unreasonable interference with their comfort or convenience by excessive noise, dust, fumes, smells, etc. An action is only available to persons who have property rights (e.g. owners, *lessees) or exclusive occupation. Thus, for example, lodgers and members of a property owner's family cannot sue in private nuisance.

Public nuisance is a crime. At *common law it includes such activities as *raves, *obstruction of the highway, carrying on an offensive trade, and selling food unfit for human consumption. The *Attorney-General or a *local authority may bring a civil action for an *injunction on behalf of the public, but a private citizen may obtain damages in tort only if he can prove some special damage over and above that suffered by the public at large.

Statutory nuisances are created by provisions dealing with noise, public health, and the prevention of pollution and permit a local authority to control neighbourhood nuisances by the issue of an *abatement notice.

nuisance neighbours People who disturb the lives of those living nearby by interfering with their *quiet enjoyment of their homes. The Protection from Harassment Act 1997, Crime and Disorder Act 1998, and the Anti-Social Behaviour Act 2003 (*see* ANTI-SOCIAL BEHAVIOUR ORDER) provide protection for those suffering *nuisance (including noise) from their neighbours. Offenders threatening violence can be jailed for up to five years and/or be subjected to an unlimited fine under s 4 of the 1997 Act; even if the *harassment does not give rise to fear for safety, the offender faces up to six months in jail and/or a fine of up to £5000 under s 2 of the Act.

nullity of marriage The invalidity of a marriage due to some defect existing at the time the marriage was celebrated (or, sometimes, arising afterwards).

nullum crimen sine lege [Latin: no crime without a law] The principle that conduct does not constitute crime unless it has previously been declared to be so by the law; it is sometimes known as the **principle of legality** and is enshrined in Article 7 of the *European Convention on Human Rights. Some serious offences are well-defined *common-law offences (although the details relating to their definition may often be unclear until ruled upon by the *judges); many regulatory offences (e.g. those involving road traffic and the manufacture of products) are constantly being created by statute. The principle is violated by the power occasionally attributed to judges to create new offences in order to punish morally harmful conduct (such as *conspiracy to outrage public decency).

oath A pronouncement swearing the truth of a statement or promise, usually by an appeal to God to witness its truth. An oath is required by law for various purposes, in particular for *affidavits and giving evidence in court if the witness is over the age of 14 years. The usual **witness's oath** is: 'I swear by Almighty God that the evidence which I shall give shall be the truth, the whole truth and nothing but the truth'. Those who object to swearing an oath, on the grounds that to do so is contrary to their religious beliefs or that they have no religious beliefs, may instead *affirm.

oath of allegiance An oath to be faithful and bear true allegiance to the *Crown. It is taken by members of both Houses at the opening of every new *Parliament, by certain officers of the Crown on their appointment, and by those who become *British citizens by *naturalization.

obiter dictum [Latin: a remark in passing] Something said by a *judge while giving judgment that was not essential to the decision in the case. It does not form part of the *ratio decidendi* of the case and therefore creates no binding *precedent, but may be cited as *persuasive authority in later cases.

objection to indictment A procedure in which the accused in a *trial on indictment attempts to prove some objection to the indictment on legal grounds (e.g. that it contravenes, or fails to comply with, an enactment). The objection is raised by application to quash the indictment.

objects clause *See* MEMORANDUM OF ASSOCIATION; *ULTRA VIRES*.

obligation A legal duty.

obscene and threatening communication A *summary offence, contrary to s 1 of the Malicious Communications Act 1988,to send to another person (a) a letter, electronic communication, or article of any description which conveys: a message which is indecent or grossly offensive; a threat; or information which is false and known or believed to be false by the sender; or (b) any article or electronic communication which is, in whole or part, of an indecent or grossly offensive nature. If the material contains a threat, there is a defence similar to that available on a *blackmail charge. Section 127 of the Communications Act 2003 makes it an offence to send by means of a public electronic communications network a message or other matter that is grossly offensive or of an indecent, obscene, or menacing character; or to cause any such message or matter to be so sent. The maximum *punishment for both offences is six months' imprisonment and/or a *fine at level 5.

obscene publication Material that tends to deprave or corrupt. Under the Obscene Publications Acts 1959 and 1964 (as amended) it is an offence to publish an obscene article or to have an obscene article for publication for gain. For the purposes of the Acts, obscenity is not limited to pornographic or sexually corrupting material: a book advocating drug taking or violence, for instance, may be obscene. Whether or not particular material is obscene is a question of fact in each case, to be decided by the *trier of fact, and *expert evidence is not usually permitted. Material that merely tends to shock or disgust is not obscene. The intention or motive of the author in writing or depicting the material is irrelevant.

Section 1 of the 1959 Act provides that a person 'publishes an 'article' who: (a) distributes, circulates, sells, lets on hire, gives, or lends it, or who offers it for sale or for letting on hire; or (b) in the case of an article containing or embodying matter to be looked at or a record, shows, plays, or projects it, or, where the matter is data stored electronically, transmits that data. The definition encompasses transmission of data electronically, including the uploading or downloading of a web page. An 'article' may be material that is to be looked at or played over, rather than read, and can also include, for instance, a negative of a film or any article used to reproduce material to be read or looked at. The term includes a video cassette (*Attorney-General's Reference (No 5 of 1980)* 72 Cr App R 71 (CA)) and also a computer disc (*R v Fellows and Arnold* [1997] 1 Cr App R 244 (CA)). This offence is one of *strict liability, but there is a defence of **lack of knowledge**, if the defendant can show he had not examined the article and had no reason to suspect that publishing it would constitute an offence. There is also a special defence of **public good**, which applies when the defendant shows that publication of the article was justified as being in the interests of science, literature, art, or learning. The offence of possessing an obscene article in the expectation that it will be published for financial gain is also subject to the defences of lack of knowledge and public good. If a *magistrate suspects that obscene articles are kept in any *premises for this purpose, he may issue a *warrant authorizing the police to search for and seize the articles. If they prove to be obscene, the magistrate may order them to be forfeited. The offences are triable *either way: the maximum *penalty on *indictment is three years' imprisonment, a *fine, or both.

Although the broadcasting and screening of obscene programmes and films was brought within the ambit of the Acts by the Broadcasting Act 1990 and the Criminal Law Act 1977 (subject to the rule that prosecutions in such cases require the consent of the *Director of Public Prosecutions), the obscene performance of a play is considered to be a transient thing. Hence, unlike the written script, it cannot amount to an 'article' for the purposes of the Obscene Publication Acts. Nor does the performance of an obscene play amount to the publication of its script. However, s 2 of the Theatres Act 1968 makes it an offence, subject to the public good defence, 'if an obscene performance of a play is given, whether in public or private'. Proceedings may not be commenced without the consent of the *Attorney-General. The offence is committed by 'anyone who (whether for gain or not) presented or directed' the performance. The penalty is the same as under the Obscene Publications Act 1959.

There are also various special offences relating to obscenity. Section 2 of the Children and Young Persons (Harmful Publications) Act 1955 provides that a person who prints, publishes, sells, or lets on hire any book, magazine, or other like work which is of a kind likely to fall into the hands of children or young persons and consists wholly or mainly of stories told in pictures portraying (a) the commission of crimes; or (b) acts of violence or cruelty; or (c) incidents of a repulsive or horrible nature; in such a way that the work as a whole would tend to corrupt a child or young person into whose hands it might fall, or has any such work in his possession for the purpose of selling it or letting it on hire, commits an offence and is liable, on *summary conviction, to imprisonment for a term not exceeding four months or to a fine not exceeding level 3 on the standard scale, or to both. Proceedings for the offence require the consent of the Attorney-General. Section 1 of the Indecent Displays (Control) Act 1981 provides that if any indecent matter is publicly displayed the person making the display and any person causing or permitting the display to be made shall be *guilty of an offence. The offence is triable *either way: on indictment the maximum penalty is two years or a fine or both. Prosecution requires the consent of the Director of Public Prosecutions. It is an offence contrary to s 85 of the Postal Services Act 2000 to send by post a postal packet which encloses 'any indecent or obscene print, painting, photograph, lithograph, engraving, cinematograph film or other record of a picture or pictures, book, card or written communication', or 'any other indecent or obscene article' or which has on it 'any words, marks or designs which are of an indecent or obscene character'. This offence is triable either way. The maximum penalty is twelve months' imprisonment. *See also* OBSCENE AND THREATENING COMMUNICATIONS.

Section 42 of the Customs Consolidation Act 1876 prohibits the importation of 'indecent or obscene prints, paintings, photographs, books, cards, lithographic or other engravings, or any other indecent or obscene articles'. The issue of obscenity or indecency is for the *jury. Importation in breach of that prohibition is an offence contrary to s 170(2) of the Customs and Excise Management Act 1979. The offence is triable either way: an offender convicted on indictment is liable to a penalty of any amount, or to imprisonment for a term not exceeding seven years, or to both. It is an offence to take, make, distribute, or possess indecent photographs or pseudo-photographs of a child (*see* INDECENT PHOTOGRAPHS OF CHILDREN).

obstructing a police officer, etc. **1.** The offence under s 89(2) of the Police Act 1996 of hindering a police officer who is in the course of doing his duty. 'Obstruction' includes any intentional interference, e.g. by physical force, threats, telling lies or giving misleading information, refusing to cooperate in removing an obstruction, or warning a person who has committed a crime so that he can escape detection (e.g. keeping lookout for a street game). It is not, however, an offence merely not to answer, or to advise someone not to answer, police questions that he does not have to answer. A police officer is acting in the course of his duty if he is preventing or detecting crime (in particular, *breaches of the peace) or obeying the orders of his superiors. However, he is not acting in the course of his duty when he is merely assisting the public in some way unconnected with crime. When the obstruction amounts to an *assault, the offence is punishable by imprisonment and/or a *fine. One may be *guilty of this offence even if the police officer was in plain clothes. **2.** The offence under the Misuse of Drugs Act 1971 of intentionally obstructing a police officer in the exercise of his powers under the Act to search for *drugs. **3.** There are a number of statutory offences which deal with obstructing other particular categories of public servant. These include:

- an officer of *Her Majesty's Revenue and Customs: s 31, Commissioner for Revenue and Customs Act 2005;
- designated staff of the *Serious Organized Crime Agency: s 51, Serious Organized Crime and Police Act 2005;
- a member of an international *joint investigation team: s 57, Serious Organized Crime and Police Act 2005;
- a trading standards officer: s 29, Trade Descriptions Act 1968;
- a court officer executing process against unauthorized occupants: s 10, Criminal Law Act 1977;
- a *Community Support Officer: s 46, Police Reform Act 2002;
- a Traffic Officer: s 10, Traffic Management Act 2004;
- a Court Security Officer: s 57, Courts Act 2003.

obstructing the highway An offence under s 137 of the Highways Act 1980 for a person without lawful authority or excuse in any way to wilfully obstruct the free passage along a *highway.

obstruction The offence of causing or allowing a *motor vehicle, *trailer, or other object to stand on a *road in such a way that it is likely to impede other road users or to use a vehicle on the road in a similar way (e.g. by driving unreasonably slowly). It is unnecessary to show that any other vehicle or person has in fact been obstructed. This offence is punishable by a *fine. It is also an offence under s 22 of the Road Traffic Act 1988 to leave a motor vehicle on a road in such a position or in such circumstances that it is likely to cause danger to other road users. This offence requires a *notice of intended prosecution and is punishable by a fine, *endorsement (which carries three penalty points under the totting-up system), and discretionary *disqualification.

occupation 1. Under the Family Law Act 1996, spouses have rights of occupation in the matrimonial home by virtue of marriage. **2.** (in *international law) The act of taking control of territory belonging either to no one (**peaceful occupation**) or to a foreign state in the course of a *war (**belligerent occupation**). Peaceful occupation is one of the methods of legally acquiring territory, provided the occupier can show a standard of control superior to that of any other claimant. Denmark acquired Greenland in this way, and the UK acquired Rockall. A belligerent occupant cannot acquire or annex the occupied territory during the course of the war. Certain provisions for the protection of enemy civilians in the Hague and Geneva Conventions are applied to those parts of the enemy territory that have been effectively occupied. A belligerent occupier must retain in force the ordinary penal laws and tribunals of the occupied power, but may alter them or impose new laws to ensure the security and orderly government of the occupying forces and administration. The government in exile is also regarded as continuing to represent the occupied state in international law without any special recognition being necessary. *See also* SUCCESSION.

occupation order Any of various orders under the Family Law Act 1996 relating to occupation of the matrimonial home in cases of *domestic violence. The orders can enforce the rights of co-owning spouses or spouses with matrimonial home rights to occupy the home and provide for the exclusion of the *respondent from the home or from any part of it. The orders can also extend similar rights to non-owning ex-spouses, whether or not they are actually in occupation, and also—under certain circumstances—to cohabitants or ex-cohabitants. *See also* BATTERED SPOUSE OR COHABITANT.

occupier 1. A person in possession of *land or buildings as owner, *tenant, or *trespasser. If he is a trespasser he may obtain a right to lawful occupation if the owner accepts money from him as rent, in which case a *tenancy may be created, or through *adverse possession for a sufficient period. **2.** For the purposes of the Misuse of Drugs Act 1971, a person who has the requisite degree of control over the *premises to exclude from them those who might otherwise intend to carry on forbidden activities. It would thus apply to a student in a room in a hall of residence because he has sufficient exclusivity of possession to be an occupier. (See *R v Tao* [1977] QB 141.)

occupier's liability The *liability of an *occupier of *land or *premises to persons on the land for the condition of the premises and things done there. The occupier for this purpose is the person or persons exercising control over the premises. At *common law the extent of an occupier's liability varied according to whether the person on the land entered under a contract, as an *invitee, as a *licensee, or as a *trespasser. The common law rules have been replaced by statutes. The English statutes distinguish between visitors and other persons on land. The Occupiers' Liability Act 1957 imposes on an occupier a *common duty of care to all his visitors (i.e. those who enter by his invitation or with his permission) to see that they will be reasonably safe in using the premises for the purpose for which they were invited or permitted to be there. Under the Occupiers' Liability Act 1984, an occupier only owes a duty to persons other than visitors (i.e. trespassers and persons who enter lawfully but without the occupier's permission) if the occupier is aware or has reasonable grounds to know of a danger on the premises and that a person may be in the vicinity of the danger and the risk is one against which he may reasonably be expected to offer some protection. The duty, if any, is confined to taking such care as is reasonable in all the circumstances to see that the danger does not cause death or personal injury to the person concerned. The duty may be discharged by taking such steps as are reasonable to give warning of the danger or to discourage persons from incurring the risk.

odontologist A person who studies and practises odontology.

odontology The scientific study of structure of teeth. (In forensic science) The study of teeth and teeth marks to identify people and to link bite marks to suspects.

offence A crime. The modern tendency is to refer to crimes as offences. Offences may be classified as *indictable only, *summary only, or *either way (i.e. triable either summarily or on indictment).

offence against designated and accredited persons A *summary offence under s 46 of the Police Reform Act 2002 of assaulting or obstructing *designated or *accredited persons, such as *Community Support Officers. *See also* ASSAULT; OBSTRUCTION.

offence against international law and order A crime that affects the proper functioning of international society. Some authorities regard so-called international crimes as crimes of individuals that all or most states are bound by treaty to punish in accordance with national laws passed for that purpose. Examples of this type of crime are *piracy, *hijacking, and *war crimes. *See also* INTERNATIONAL CRIMINAL COURT.

offence against property A crime that affects another person's rights of ownership (or in some cases possession or control). The main offences against property are *theft, offences of *deception and *making off without payment, *criminal damage, *arson, *forgery, and *forcible entry. Some offences against property, such as *burglary, *robbery, and *blackmail, may also contain elements of *offences against the person.

offence against public order A crime that affects the smooth running of orderly society. The main offences against public order are *riot, *violent disorder, *affray, *threatening behaviour, stirring up *racial hatred, public *nuisance, and *obstruction of highways. *See also* RACIALLY AGGRAVATED OFFENCES; RAVE; TRESPASS.

offence against the person A crime that involves the use or threat of physical force against another person. The main offences against the person are *homicide, *infanticide, illegal *abortion, *causing death by dangerous driving, and *causing death by careless driving (fatal offences against the person); and *torture, *wounding, causing or inflicting *grievous bodily harm, *assault, *aggravated assault, *battery, *kidnapping, and *rape and other *sexual offences (non-fatal offences against the person). *See also* POISON.

offence against the state A crime that affects the security of the state as a whole. The main offences against the state are *treason and *misprision of treason, *sedition (and incitement to *mutiny), offences involving *official secrets, and acts of *terrorism.

offence relating to road traffic A crime that is associated with using vehicles on public *roads and related acts. The main offences in this category are *careless and inconsiderate driving, *causing death by careless driving whilst under the influence, *dangerous driving, *causing death by dangerous driving, *drunken driving, *driving while disqualified, *driving without insurance, *driving without a licence, *speeding, *ignoring traffic signals, *parking offences, and *obstruction. Some road traffic offences require *notice of intended prosecution. Road traffic offences carry various penalties or combinations of penalties, such as *fines, *endorsement of driving licence, *disqualification from driving, and in some circumstances imprisonment. The court may also make a *driving-test order. Many road traffic offences (especially the minor ones) are offences of *strict liability. *See also* DRIVING LICENCE; MOT TEST; ROAD TRAFFIC ACCIDENT/COLLISION; ROAD TAX; VEHICLE CONSTRUCTION AND MAINTENANCE.

offence triable either way A crime that may be tried either as an *indictable offence or a *summary offence. These include offences of *deception, *theft, *burglary, and *sexual assault.

When an offence is triable either way, the *magistrates' court must decide, on hearing the initial facts of the case, if it should be tried on indictment rather than summarily, for example, because it appears to be a serious case (*see* MODE OF TRIAL). However, if the case concerns *criminal damage and the damage appears to be less than £5000, and does not involve endangering life or arson, the case must be tried summarily. *See also* JUVENILE OFFENDER; NOTICE OF TRANSFER; VOLUNTARY BILL PROCEDURE.

offender One who has committed a *crime. *See also* DANGEROUS OFFENDER; FIRST OFFENDER; FUGITIVE OFFENDER; JUVENILE OFFENDER.

offender profiling A type of investigative psychology in which the practitioner describes the characteristics of an offender by analyzing crime scenes and other known behaviour of an offender. Profilers can also give advice on the most appropriate methods of interviewing suspects. The findings of offender profilers are not admissible evidence in English courts.

offensive weapon Any object that is made, adapted, or intended to be used to cause physical injury to a person. Examples of objects made to cause injury are *revolvers, coshes, and daggers; objects adapted to cause injury include bottles deliberately broken to attack someone with, and sawn-off shotguns. In theory any object may be intended to be used to cause injury, but articles commonly intended for such use include sheath knives (or any household knife), pieces of wood, and stones.

It is an offence under s 1 of the Prevention of Crime Act 1953 to have an offensive weapon in one's possession in a *public place. This offence is punishable summarily by up to six months' imprisonment and/or a *fine at level 5 on the standard scale or on *indictment with up to two years' imprisonment and/or a fine, and the court may order the weapon to be forfeited. There are special exceptions for those (such as soldiers or *police officers) who carry offensive weapons in the course of duty and in cases of 'reasonable excuse', but the defendant must prove that he comes within these categories. *Self-defence is not usually a reasonable excuse unless there is an imminent and particular threat.

It is also an offence (finable only), under the Criminal Justice Act 1988, to possess in a public place (s 139) or on school *premises (s 139A) a bladed or sharply pointed article (other than a folding penknife with a blade of three inches or less). It is a defence to prove that the article was for use at work, for religious reasons (e.g. a Sikh's dagger), or part of a national costume, or that there was authority or good reason for its possession. The 1988 Act also gives the *Home Secretary power to prohibit the manufacture, sale, hire, and importation of certain offensive weapons.

See also FIREARM; WEAPON OF OFFENCE; PROHIBITED WEAPON.

offer An indication of willingness to do or refrain from doing something that is capable of being converted by *acceptance into a legally binding contract. It is made by an **offeror** to an **offeree** and is capable of acceptance only by an offeree who knows of its existence. Thus, a person giving information cannot claim a reward if he did not know that a reward was being offered. An offer must be distinguished from an **invitation to treat**, which is an invitation to others to make offers, as by displaying *goods in a shop window; and a **declaration of intention**, which is a mere statement of intent to invite offers in the future, as by advertising an auction.

offering no evidence In proceedings before the *magistrates' courts and the *Crown Court, the *prosecution may offer no evidence at any stage before the close of its case. Leave of the court is not required, although in the Crown Court the *judge has a discretion whether to accept the prosecution's decision. Where no evidence is offered in the Crown Court, a verdict of *not guilty is recorded and no further proceedings are possible for the offence unless the verdict is set aside under the procedure provided for in pt 10 of the Criminal Justice Act 2003 (*see* DOUBLE JEOPARDY). Where the matter is before the magistrates' court for *trial, the charge is dismissed and cannot be revived in the future. If no evidence is offered prior to *committal to the Crown Court for trial, the defendant is discharged (under s 6, Magistrates' Courts Act 1980), but there is no bar to a future charge for the same offence.

Office for the Supervision of Solicitors (OSS) The body that deals with complaints about *solicitors; it was previously called the **Solicitors Complaints Bureau.**

Office of Fair Trading A public body established on a statutory basis by the Enterprise Act 2002 that regulates the commercial supply of goods and services to consumers.

official receiver The person appointed by the Department of Trade and Industry who acts in *bankruptcy matters as interim receiver and manager of the estate of the *debtor, presides at the first meeting of *creditors, and takes part in the debtor's public examination. In the *compulsory winding-up of a company, he often becomes *provisional liquidator when a winding-up order is made.

official search A search, in response to an applicant's *requisition, into the registers of local *land charges, the Land Charges Department, or HM *Land Registry (as appropriate) in order to disclose any registered matter relevant to the requisition. A certificate is issued by the registrar giving details of encumbrances that the search has revealed.

official secret Information that is categorized as a secret code or password or is intended to be (or might be) useful to an enemy (for the purpose of the Official Secrets Acts 1911–89). It is an offence to make a sketch, plan, model, or note that might be useful to an enemy. It is also an offence to obtain, record, or communicate to anyone else a secret official code or password or any information or *document that is intended to be useful to an enemy. It is also an offence to enter, approach, inspect, or pass over (e.g. in an aircraft) any prohibited place. Such places include naval, military, or air-force establishments, national munitions factories or depots, and any places belonging to or used by the *Crown that an enemy would want to know about. For all three offences the *prosecution must prove that the act was done for a purpose that prejudices the safety or interests of the state. Even if no particular prejudicial act can be proved, someone may be convicted if it appears from the circumstances of the case, his conduct, or his known and proven character that his purpose was prejudicial to the interests of the state. There is also a presumption (which may be disproved by the defendant) that any act done within the scope of the three offences without lawful authority is prejudicial to the state's interests. All three offences are punishable by up to fourteen years' imprisonment.

Under the Official Secrets Act 1989 a member or former member of the security and intelligence services, or a person notified that he is subject to the Act, commits an offence, punishable with up to two years' imprisonment and/or a fine, if without lawful authority he discloses or purports to disclose any information, document, or other article relating to security or intelligence. Similarly, Crown servants and government contractors are prohibited from making disclosures that damage security services' operations, endanger UK interests abroad, or result in the commission of an offence, and from negligently failing to prevent such disclosures. Other offences relate to the disclosure by an ordinary citizen of protected information communicated in confidence by a Crown servant.

See also SABOTAGE; SPYING; TREASON.

Official Solicitor An officer of the *Supreme Court of Judicature who, when directed by the court, acts as *litigation friend (next friend) or *children's guardian for those under a disability who have no one else to act for them; he may also be called upon to intervene and protect the interests of children. He can be appointed judicial trustee in proceedings relating to disputed *trusts.

Old Bailey *See* CENTRAL CRIMINAL COURT.

oligopoly Control of a market by a small number of suppliers, which may or may not lead to the operation of a *cartel.

omission A failure to act. It is not usually a crime to fail to act; e.g. it is not usually a crime to stand by and watch a child who has fallen into a river drown. Sometimes, however, there is a duty on a person to act, either because of the terms of a contractual duty, or because he is a *parent or *guardian of a minor, or because he has voluntarily assumed a duty (e.g. looking after a disabled relative), or through a statutory imposition of such a duty. In such cases, omission may constitute a crime. Usually this will be a crime of *negligence (e.g. *manslaughter, if the victim dies because of the defendant's omission); if it is a deliberate omission with a particular intention (e.g. the intention of starving someone to death) it will amount to *murder. *See also* NEGLECT.

Similarly, there is no general liability in the law of *tort for failing to act, but there are some situations where the law imposes a duty to take action to prevent harm to others. Thus *occupiers of *premises are under a duty to see that their visitors are reasonably safe (*see* OCCUPIER'S LIABILITY).

onus of proof *See* BURDEN OF PROOF.

opening speech 1. A speech made by the *prosecution at the beginning of a criminal *trial, briefly outlining the case against the accused and summarizing the evidence that the prosecution intends to call to prove its case. **2.** The speech made by or on behalf of the claimant at the beginning of a civil trial.

operative mistake *See* MISTAKE.

opinio juris [Latin, from *opinio juris sive necessitatis*: whether the opinion of law is compulsory] An essential element of *custom, one of the four sources of *international law as outlined in the Statute of the *International Court of Justice. *Opinio juris* requires that custom should be regarded as state practice amounting to a legal obligation, which distinguishes it from mere usage.

opinion 1. A judgment by the *House of Lords or *Privy Council. **2.** (counsel's opinion) A *barrister's advice on a particular question. **3.** Advice on a case given by an *Advocate General before a final judgment of the *European Court of Justice.

opinion evidence (in the law of evidence) Any inference from observed facts. Generally, a witness can only give evidence of matters which happened in his presence or within his hearing (*but see* HEARSAY). Opinions, beliefs, and inferences are inadmissible to prove the truth of the matters believed or inferred as, questions of relevance and reliability aside, such evidence usurps the function of the *trier of fact to form an opinion on the issues before the court on the basis of the evidence placed before it. However, there are three exceptions to that *common law rule: an opinion as to general reputation is admissible to prove the pedigree or character of a person; *expert evidence is admissible to prove matters of specialized knowledge; and non-expert evidence of opinion may be received on matters within the experience of lay persons generally (e.g. the speed of a vehicle, the age of a person, the state of the weather, and the passage of time) or on matters with which the witness has a particular familiarity (e.g. the handwriting or voice of a person known to him).

opium A Class A narcotic *drug obtained from the unripe seed capsule of the opium poppy. The drugs can be used by smoking or can be used to prepare many different drugs including *morphine, *diamorphine, and pharmaceutical drugs. It is unique in that it is the only drug which it is an offence to use. It is also an offence to frequent a place used for the purpose of opium smoking or to possess articles for use in connection with smoking or preparing opium.

oppression Section 76 of the Police and Criminal Evidence Act 1984 defines oppression as including *torture, *inhuman or *degrading treatment, and the use of threat of violence. This has been widened by the courts which have adopted a dictionary definition as the exercise of authority or power in a burdensome, harsh, or wrongful manner; unjust or cruel treatment of subjects, inferiors, etc; the imposition of unreasonable or unjust burdens.

option A right to do or not to do something, usually within a specified time. An enforceable option may be acquired by contract (i.e. for *consideration) or by *deed to accept or reject an *offer within a specified period. An option to acquire *land or an interest in it on specified terms will only bind third parties if it is registered. If an option to buy does not specify the price it will only be valid if it specifies a means for determining the price, e.g. by a valuation to be made by a specified third party who is or will be under a duty to act. Thus an option to buy at a price to be agreed is *void for uncertainty.

On the London *Stock Exchange, options to sell or to buy quoted *securities are purchased for a certain sum of money, which is forfeited if they are not taken up. An option to sell is known as a **put option**, that to buy is a **call option**, and an option to either sell or buy is a **double option**. Under the Companies Act 1985, *directors, shadow directors, and the spouses or children of either are prohibited from buying or selling options in the shares of their own company.

oral agreement A contract made by word of mouth, as opposed to one made in writing. *See also* IMPLIED CONTRACT.

oral evidence Spoken evidence given by a witness in court, usually on *oath.

order 1. A direction or command of a court. In this sense it is often used synonymously with *judgment. **2.** The *document bearing the seal of the court recording its judgment in a case.

Order in Council A government order of a legislative character made by the *Crown and members of the *Privy Council either under statutory powers conferred on Her Majesty in Council (see DELEGATED LEGISLATION; STATUTORY INSTRUMENT) or in exercise of the *royal prerogative.

order of discharge A court order resulting in the *discharge of a bankrupt.

ordinance One of the forms taken by *legislation under the *royal prerogative, normally legislation relating to UK dependencies.

ordinary resolution A decision reached by a simple majority (i.e. more than 50 per cent) of *company members voting in person or by proxy. It is appropriate where no other type of resolution is expressly required by the Companies Acts or the *articles of association. *Compare* EXTRAORDINARY RESOLUTION; SPECIAL RESOLUTION.

ordinary share *See* SHARE.

ordnance Military stores or supplies, especially weapons, *ammunition, and *explosives.

organ, human Material taken from the body of a living (except hair or nails) or deceased person. The Human Tissue Act 2004 creates a number of offences in connection with possession of or dealing with human organs and tissue.

Under s 32 of the Act it is an offence to: give or receive a reward for the supply of, or for an offer to supply, any controlled material; seek to find a person willing to supply any controlled material for reward; offer to supply any controlled material for reward; initiate or negotiate any arrangement involving the giving of a reward for the supply of, or for an offer to supply, any controlled material; takes part in the management or control of a body of persons corporate or unincorporate whose activities consist of or include the initiation or negotiation of such arrangements, or to advertise for such material.

Section 16 of the Act prohibits without a *licence a number of activities except for the prevention or detection of crime, or the conduct of a *prosecution. These activities are: the carrying-out of an anatomical examination; the making of a post-mortem examination; the removal from the body of a deceased person; the storage of an anatomical specimen; the storage of the body of a deceased person, or relevant material which has come from a human body.

organized crime Criminals working with others in continuing serious criminal activities for substantial profit, whether based in the UK or overseas. The activities are mainly concerned with the supply of illicit *goods and services but may extend to suborning local or national government. The *European Union identifies eleven characteristics of a criminal organization. To amount to 'organized crime' for EU purposes six of the characteristics must be present; four mandatory plus two optional. The mandatory characteristics are:

- collaboration among more than two people;
- extending over a prolonged or indefinite period;
- suspected of committing serious offences punishable with at least four years' imprisonment;
- the goal is profit and/or power.

The optional characteristics are:

- specialized division of labour among participants;

- exercise of a measure of discipline or control;
- employing violence or other means of intimidation;
- employing commercial or business-like structures;
- participating in money-laundering;
- operational across national borders;
- exerting influence over legitimate social institutions (polity, government, justice, or the economy).

In the USA the main *legislation that 'seeks the eradication of organized crime in the United States' is the 'RICO' Act (Racketeer-Influence Corrupt Organizations Act) which has been a model for laws in other jurisdictions.

origin system A system for protecting products in which each is identified by means of an **appellation of origin**, which is similar to a *trade mark but may only be used for a product from a particular region. The regulations, which cover many products, were agreed in March 1996. The scheme stops manufacturers, etc., from other regions from using local names, such as Stilton cheese, Newcastle Brown Ale, and Jersey Royal potatoes.

outer Bar (utter Bar) Junior *barristers, collectively, who sit outside the *bar of the court, as opposed to *Queen's Counsel, who sit within it.

outraging public decency It is an offence at *common law to outrage public decency. The act must be done in a place where at least two members of the public might see it. Where the act is plainly indecent and likely to disgust and annoy, the *jury are entitled to infer such disgust and annoyance without evidence that anyone was disgusted or annoyed. It may be committed in a number of ways, e.g. by engaging in or simulating a sexual act, displaying earrings made of human foetuses, or publishing outrageously indecent material. It is a matter for the jury as members of the public to decide whether the conduct is outrageously indecent and disgusts and annoys them. By s 320 of the Criminal Justice Act 2003, the offence is triable *either way. The maximum *penalty on conviction on *indictment is imprisonment and/or a *fine at large. On *summary conviction, the maximum is six months or a fine not exceeding level 5, or both. *See also* CONSPIRACY.

overdraft A form of borrowing from a bank whereby the customer is allowed to draw more than he has in his account and thereby have a negative balance up to an amount set by the bank. The customer is charged interest on the amount borrowed. It is an offence under the Theft Act 1968 to obtain an overdraft by deception.

overrule To set aside the decision of a court in an earlier case. Because of the doctrine of *precedent, a court can generally only overrule decisions of courts lower than itself. The setting aside of the *judgment of a lower court on *appeal is called a **reversal**.

overseas company A *foreign company with an established place of business in Great Britain. Such companies are obliged to comply with certain formalities, such as filing their constitution or charter at the *Companies Registry and giving details of their *directors and of who is authorized to accept service of legal proceedings and notices in the UK.

overseas divorce A *divorce, annulment, or legal separation obtained overseas. There are different rules for the recognition of overseas divorces in the UK, according to whether or not they are obtained through judicial proceedings. An overseas divorce obtained through proceedings is recognized if: it is effective under the law of the country in which it was obtained; and either party to the marriage was habitually resident in, domiciled in, or a national of the country where it was obtained. An overseas divorce obtained otherwise than through proceedings is recognized if: it is effective under the law of the country where it was obtained; both parties were domiciled in that country, or one party was domiciled in that country and the other party was domiciled in another country that recognizes the divorce as valid; and neither party was habitually resident in the UK in the year preceding the divorce. *See also* EXTRAJUDICIAL DIVORCE.

ownership The exclusive right to use, possess, and dispose of property, subject only to the rights of persons having a superior interest and to any restrictions on the owner's rights imposed by agreement with or by act of third parties or by operation of law. Ownership may be **corporeal**, i.e. of a material thing, which may itself be a *movable or an *immovable; or it may be **incorporeal**, i.e. of something intangible, such as of a copyright or patent. Ownership involves enjoyment of a number of rights over the property. The owner can alienate (i.e. sell or give away) some of these rights while still retaining others; e.g. an owner of *land may grant a *right of way or a *patent owner may grant a *licence to manufacture the patented *goods. More than one person can own the same property at the same time.

pact *See* TREATY.

pacta sunt servanda [Latin: pacts must be respected] Agreements are to be kept; *treaties should be observed. *Pacta sunt servanda* is the bedrock of the customary *international law of treaties and, according to some authorities, the very foundation of international law. Without such an acceptance, treaties would become worthless.

pacta tertiis nec nocent nec prosunt [Latin: a treaty binds the parties and only the parties; it does not create obligations for a third state] Treaties do not create either obligations or rights for third states without their consent.

paedophile A person who is sexually attracted to children (of either sex). Sexual activity with children is criminalized by the Sexual Offences Act 2003. *See also* CHILD ABUSE; FOREIGN TRAVEL ORDER; PAYING FOR SEXUAL SERVICES OF A CHILD; SEXUAL OFFENCE; SEXUAL OFFENCES PREVENTION ORDER.

paid-up capital The amount actually paid to a company for *shares allotted or issued to a shareholder. If a shareholder makes a full payment of the purchase price of the share, the amount received is referred to as **fully paid-up capital**. If the company permits the shareholder to make only partial payment of the total purchase price, such shares are referred to as **partly paid-up shares**, with the remaining balance recorded in the company's accounts as an amount that the company may call upon in the future (**uncalled capital**).

pancreas An organ in the abdomen which produces enzymes that aid digestion and insulin which regulates level of sugar in the blood—lack of insulin is the cause of *diabetes.

panopticism A theoretical concept in criminology which uses Jeremy Bentham's (1748–1832) design for a prison, the Panopticon, as a metaphor for the exercise of control in other institutions such as factories and offices by the use of visibility and inspection.

paperless trading *See* ELECTRONIC DATA INTERCHANGE.

paracetamol A very common pain killing drug. Overdose causes liver failure and death. It is a common means of suicide. It has also been seen in cases of *Munchausen's by Proxy where children have been overdosed with a liquid version of the drug to produce symptoms that cause the child to be admitted to hospital.

parallel import A product bought in one state and imported into another by the purchaser, often to take advantage of price differences between states; such products are also known as **grey market** *goods. Parallel importation usually takes place outside supplier-authorized official distribution networks. Within the *European Union measures taken to prevent parallel imports in the *Single Market will infringe Article 81 of the *Treaty of Rome (*see* EXPORT BANS). While it is permitted to restrict an exclusive distributor from soliciting sales outside his exclusive area, absolute territorial protection may not be given, either by contract terms or by conduct or oral arrangements.

paraquat A herbicide which causes serious lung damage and possibly death if ingested. It is readily available and has been used in poisoning cases and product *contamination.

pardon The withdrawal of a *sentence or *punishment by the sovereign under the *prerogative of mercy. Once a pardon is granted, the accused cannot be tried, and if he has already been convicted, he cannot be punished. The responsibility is upon him, however, to plead the pardon as a bar to *prosecution or *punishment;

if he does not do so as soon as possible, he may be held to have waived it. A person may also be granted a **reprieve**, i.e. the temporary suspension of a punishment (e.g. if he becomes *insane after sentence is passed).

parent The mother or father of a child. The term also includes adoptive parents but does not usually include *step-parents. *See also* PARENTS' LIABILITY; SECTION 8 ORDER; SECTION 30 ORDER.

parental order *See* SECTION 30 ORDER.

parental responsibility All the rights, duties, powers, and responsibilities that by law a *parent of a child has in relation to the child and his or her *property. The concept was introduced by the Children Act 1989, replacing *custody. Parental responsibility is automatically conferred on both parents if married, and on the mother alone if not. An unmarried father can acquire parental responsibility either by agreement with the mother or by applying to court for a *parental responsibility order. In determining whether to grant such an order the court must treat the child's welfare as its paramount consideration. Both parents retain parental responsibility on *divorce. Other persons may acquire parental responsibility by virtue of being granted other orders. For example, anyone in whose favour a residence order (*see* SECTION 8 ORDER) is made acquires parental responsibility for the duration of that order, and a *care order or an *emergency protection order confer parental responsibility on the relevant *local authority. In all these cases, parental responsibility is shared with the parents. *See also* STEP-PARENT.

parental responsibility agreement A formal agreement between the mother and unmarried father of a child conferring *parental responsibility on the father. The agreement must be made on a set form, be signed and witnessed, and be registered in the Principal Registry of the Family Division in London. Once made, the agreement cannot be revoked by either party. Only a court may bring a parental responsibility agreement to an end—on the application of either party with parental responsibility or by the child himself if he has been given permission by the court to apply.

parental responsibility order An order made by a court conferring *parental responsibility on an unmarried father. In determining whether or not to make such an order, the court must treat the child's welfare as its paramount consideration. Courts will usually grant a parental responsibility order to a father who is able to demonstrate some degree of commitment and attachment to his child. A parental responsibility order may be revoked by a court.

parenting order An order under s 8 of the Crime and Disorder Act 1998 (as amended by ss 25 to 29, Anti-Social Behaviour Act 2003 and s 324, Criminal Justice Act 2003) that requires the *parent or *guardian of a *juvenile offender to comply, for a period not exceeding twelve months, with such requirements as the court considers necessary for preventing offences being committed by this child. The rationale behind the introduction of such orders was that inadequate parental supervision is thought to be strongly associated with youth offending.

Such an order can be made in respect of a child or young person who has been made the subject of a *child safety order, or *anti-social behaviour order, or who has been convicted of an offence, or where there has been a *conviction for truancy. An order can only be made if the court considers that it would prevent a repetition of the anti-social behaviour, truancy, or offending behaviour, although there is a presumption that the court will make such an order where a person under the age of 16 is convicted of an offence. The order may be for a period of up to twelve months and may impose certain requirements upon the parent in question during that period, e.g. to ensure that the child is kept at home from a certain hour in the evening. The order must include a requirement that the parent attends specified counselling or guidance sessions.

parents' liability The *liability of *parents for their own *negligence in failing to supervise or train young children, where the absence of supervision or training has led a child to cause *damage to others. Parents are not liable for their children's *torts, but in the case of older children, a parent can be vicariously liable for the torts of a child employed as a servant or agent on ordinary principles of *vicarious liability. There is no fixed age determining a child's liability for its own torts. A child may, however, be too young to form the *intention necessary for a particular tort. In cases in which the negligence or contributory negligence of a child is in question, the test applied is whether the child's conduct measured up to the standard of care to be expected from an average child of that age.

Parents are not legally responsible for their children's crimes, although they may have to pay their *fines.

parish A *local government area in England (outside Greater London) consisting of a division of a district (though not all districts are so divided). All parishes have meetings and many have an elected parish council, which is a *local authority with a number of minor local governmental functions (e.g. the provision of allotments, bus shelters, and recreation grounds). A parish council may by resolution call its area a town, itself a town council, and its chairman the town mayor. The Local Government and Rating Act 1997 (effective from 19 May 1997) gives extra powers to parish councils in relation to rights of transport and crime prevention.

parking offences Offences relating to parking a *motor vehicle. These include parking a vehicle within the limits of a pedestrian crossing or wherever signs or kerb markings indicate that parking is prohibited or restricted and failing to comply with the regulations associated with the use of parking meters. If the accused can show that road markings or signs indicating parking restrictions were absent or deficient, he may be acquitted. Parking offences are punishable by *fine only; apart from the offence of leaving a vehicle in a dangerous position under s 22 of the Road Traffic Act 1988 they are not subject to *endorsement. *See also* OBSTRUCTION.

parlementaire [from French *parlementer*: to discuss terms; parley] An agent employed by a commander of a belligerent force in the field whose function is to go in person within the enemy lines for the purpose of communicating or negotiating openly and directly with the enemy commander.

Parliament The *legislature of the UK, consisting of the sovereign, the *House of Lords, and the *House of Commons. Under the Parliament Act 1911, the maximum duration of any particular Parliament is five years, after which its functions expire. In practice, a Parliament's life always ends by its earlier **dissolution** by the sovereign under the *royal prerogative; this proclamation also summons its successor. The date of dissolution is chosen by the Prime Minister. The life of a Parliament is divided into sessions, normally of one year each, which are ended when Parliament is prorogued (also under the prerogative) by a royal commission. Each House divides a session into sittings, normally of a day's duration, which end when a motion for adjournment is passed. The functions of Parliament are the enactment of *legislation (*see* ACT OF PARLIAMENT), the sanctioning of taxation and public expenditure, and the scrutiny and criticism of government policy and administration. *See also* SOVEREIGNTY OF PARLIAMENT.

parliamentary papers Papers published on the authority of either House of *Parliament. They include *Bills, the Official Reports of Parliamentary Debates (*see* HANSARD), and reports of parliamentary committees.

parliamentary privilege Special rights and immunities enjoyed by the Houses of *Parliament and their members to enable them to carry out their functions effectively and without external interference. They are conferred mainly by the *common law but partly by statute; they can be extended by statute but not by the resolution of either House.

The Commons have five main privileges. (1) The right of collective access to the sovereign through the Speaker. (2) The right of individual members to be free from civil (but not criminal) arrest. Since the abolition of imprisonment for *debt, this privilege has been of only minor significance, but it would still shield a member against (for example) imprisonment for disobeying a court order in civil proceedings. (3) The individual right to freedom of speech. This substantial privilege means that a member cannot be made liable either civilly (e.g. for *defamation) or criminally (e.g. for breach of the *Official Secrets Acts) for anything said by him in the course of debates or other parliamentary proceedings. Under the Parliamentary Papers Act 1840 members are also not liable for statements repeated in reports published on the authority of the House. (4) The collective right to exclusive control of its own proceedings, so that it can (for example) exclude the public, prohibit reporting, and expel any member whom it may consider unfit to sit. (5) The collective right to punish for any **breach of privilege** or other **contempt**. Examples of breaches of privilege are initiating defamation proceedings in respect of privileged words and the reporting of secret proceedings. Other contempts include any conduct prejudicial to the proper functioning or dignity of the House, e.g. by refusing to give evidence to a committee, bribing members, or insulting the House. Members may be punished for contempt by expulsion, suspension, or imprisonment; others by reprimand or imprisonment. Imprisonment is terminated by prorogation. Whether or not particular conduct amounts to a contempt, and if so what *punishment (if any) is appropriate, is considered by the Committee of Privileges, whose report the House is free to accept or reject after debate.

The privileges of the Lords are similar, except that members have an individual right of access to the sovereign and the House can *fine for contempt and imprison for a fixed term, which is not affected by prorogation.

parole (release on licence) The release on licence of a prisoner serving his *sentence. If a prisoner on parole commits an offence during the period of his original sentence, he may have to serve any part of the original sentence still outstanding. In such cases limitations are imposed on his right to be considered again for parole.

parol evidence Evidence given orally, as opposed to *documentary evidence.

parry fracture A fracture, usually of a bone in the forearm, caused by the victim trying to ward off a blow from a weapon.

Part 1 warrant *See* EXTRADITION.

Part 3 warrant *See* EUROPEAN ARREST WARRANT.

parties 1. Persons who are involved together in some transaction, e.g. the parties to a *deed or a contract. **2.** Persons who are involved together in *litigation, either civil or criminal. *See also* JOINDER OF PARTIES.

partition 1. The division of a territory into two or more units, each under a different government. **2.** The division of supreme power over a territory between different governments (e.g. federal and state). **3.** The transfer to different companies of parts of a trade or *undertaking (or two or more trades or undertakings) of a company. This is usually by means of a distribution agreement or a demerger under the Income and Corporation Taxes Act 1988.

partnership An association of two or more people formed for the purpose of carrying on a business with a view to profit. Partnerships are governed by the Partnership Act 1890. Unlike an incorporated company, a partnership does not have a legal personality of its own and therefore partners are liable for the *debts of the firm. On leaving the firm they remain liable for debts already incurred; they cease to be liable for future debts if proper notice of retirement has been published. A **limited partnership** is governed by the Limited Partnership Act 1907. It consists of **general partners**, who are fully liable for partnership debts, and **limited partners**, who are liable to the extent of their investment. Limited partners lose their limits of *liability if they take part in management. A **partnership at will** is one for which no fixed duration has been agreed. Any partner may end the partnership at any time provided that he gives notice of his intention to do so to all the other partners, subject to any restriction in the partnership deed. *See also* LIMITED LIABILITY PARTNERSHIP.

passenger vehicle A vehicle constructed solely for the carriage of passengers and their effects (reg 3(2), Road Vehicles (Construction and Use) Regulations 1986 (SI 1986/1078)).

passing off Conducting one's business in such a way as to mislead the public into thinking that one's *goods or services are those of another business. The commonest form of passing off is marketing *goods with a design, packaging, or trade name that is very similar to that of someone else's goods. It is not necessary to prove an *intention to deceive: innocent passing off is actionable.

passport A *document, issued under the *royal prerogative by the *Home Office through its executive agency, the Passport Agency, that provides *prima facie evidence of the holder's *nationality. It is not required by law for leaving the UK, but it is required for entry into most other countries.

patent The grant of an exclusive *right to exploit an invention. In the UK, patents are granted by the *Crown through the Patent Office, which is an executive agency of the Department of Trade and Industry. An applicant for a patent (usually the inventor or his *employer) must show that the invention is new, is not obvious, and is capable of industrial application. An expert known as a **patent agent** often prepares the application, which must describe the invention in considerable detail. The Patent Office publishes these details if it grants a patent. A patent remains valid for twenty years from the date of application (the **priority date**) provided that the person to whom it has been granted (the **patentee**) continues to pay the appropriate fees. During this time, the patentee may assign his patent or grant *licences to use it. Such transactions are registered in a public register at the Patent Office. If anyone infringes his monopoly, the patentee may sue for an *injunction and *damages or an account of profits. However, a patent from the Patent Office gives exclusive rights in the UK only: the inventor must obtain a patent from the European Patent Office in Munich and patents in other foreign countries if he wishes to protect the invention elsewhere.

patent agent *See* PATENT.

patent defect *See* DEFECT.

patentee A person who has been granted a *patent.

pathologist A medical practitioner who studies diseases of the body. Pathologists examine dead bodies to determine the cause of death for medical purposes or on the orders of a *coroner so he can determine whether an inquest should be held. *Forensic pathologists examine dead bodies in cases where the death may be suspicious and give the evidence of their findings to a court. In *homicide cases it is now usual for the defendant to engage another pathologist to carry out another *autopsy to obtain a second opinion. If nobody is charged in a homicide case the coroner may order a second autopsy by a different pathologist before the body is released for burial. In cases of suspicious death only the coroner can order an autopsy and the police must seek his authority before calling a pathologist to examine a body.

pathology The scientific study of diseases of the body.

patrial *See* IMMIGRATION.

pawn (pledge) An item of *goods transferred by the owner (the **pawnor**) to another (the **pawnee**) as *security for a *debt. (The word is also used for the transfer itself.) A pawn involves a *bailment and the pawnor remains owner of the goods; the pawnee is liable for failure to take reasonable care of them. If the pawnor fails to repay the loan at the agreed time, the pawnee has the right at *common law to sell the pawn; he must account to the pawnor for any surplus after discharging his debt. **Pawnbrokers** are dealers licensed to lend money at a specified rate of interest on the security of a pawn. Pawnbroking is regulated by provisions of the Consumer Credit Act 1974 (replacing the Pawnbrokers Acts 1872 and 1960) with regard to such matters as pawn receipts, rates of interest, redemption period and procedure, consequences of failure to redeem, and realization of the pawn.

paying for sexual services of a child An offence under s 47 of the Sexual Offences Act 2003 whereby a person intentionally obtains for himself the sexual services of a person under 18 years of age. Such services may or may not involve *penetration. Before obtaining such services, the accused must have made or promised payment either to the child or to a third person. Alternatively he must know that another person has either made or promised such a payment. Payment is defined widely in terms of financial advantage including the discharge of an obligation to pay or the provision of *goods or services (including sexual services) gratuitously or at a discount. Provided that the child is over 18 years of age, it is a *defence for the offender to show that he reasonably believed the child was aged 18 or over. The offence is triable *either way; on *conviction on *indictment it carries a maximum *sentence of seven years' imprisonment.

payment card *Debit cards, *credit cards, and other cards issued by banks or other financial institutions, which can be used to purchase *goods and services.

p

PEACE A system of investigative interview developed and promulgated as *Association of Chief Police Officers policy. It is a guide to interviewing victims, witnesses, and suspects. The system has five phases:

- Planning and Preparation
- Engage and Explain
- Account
- Closure
- Evaluation.

peaceful assembly *See* FREEDOM OF ASSOCIATION.

peaceful enjoyment of possessions A right set out in Article 1 of the First Protocol to the *European Convention on Human Rights and now part of UK law as a consequence of the *Human Rights Act 1998. This right is a *qualified right; as such, the public interest can be used to justify an interference with it providing that this is prescribed by law, designed for a legitimate purpose, and proportionate. Therefore the state may deprive individuals of their possessions and control the use of property providing that this is prescribed by law, in the public interest, and proportionate.

pedestrian controlled vehicle A *motor vehicle which is controlled by a pedestrian and not constructed or adapted for use or used for the carriage of a *driver or passenger (reg 3(2), Road Vehicles (Construction and Use) Regulations 1986 (SI 1986/1078)).

pelvis The bones that form the pelvic girdle (the hips).

penal statute A statute that creates a criminal offence or provides for any *penalty (e.g. a *forfeiture) enforceable in civil proceedings. It is subject to strict construction (*see* INTERPRETATION OF STATUTES).

penalty A *punishment for a crime. A penalty must be clearly stated before it can be enforced. Article 7 of the *European Convention on Human Rights forbids the use of retrospective criminal penalties, and this prohibition is now part of UK law as a consequence of the *Human Rights Act 1998.

penalty notice for disorder (PND) A scheme provided for by ss 1 to 11 of the Criminal Justice and Police Act 2001 which deals specifically with disorderly behaviour and is part of the wider *fixed penalty notice scheme. Penalty notices for disorder can be issued to anyone aged 16 years and over. They carry a tariff of £80 or £50 according to the offence. They can be used in place of an informal/formal *caution or *charge for low-level offending and anti-social behaviour. An authorized officer, who has reason to believe that a person has committed a penalty offence, may issue a penalty notice for that offence. The officer must have sufficient evidence for a successful *prosecution before a notice can be issued. The notice may be issued either on the spot by an officer in uniform in public or in private; or at a police station by an authorized officer. The person awarded the penalty notice for disorder has 21 days from the date of issue either to: pay the penalty, thereby discharging their *liability to *conviction for the offence, or request a court hearing. Failure to pay the penalty or request a hearing may result in a *fine of one-and-a-half times the penalty amount or, exceptionally, proceedings commenced for the penalty offence. Although the *parent/legal *guardian of 15 to 16 year olds is expected to pay the penalty, only the young person who is the recipient of the penalty notice can choose whether or not to go to court.

penalty points *See* DISQUALIFICATION FROM DRIVING.

penetrating injuries Injuries that penetrate the skin. These are wounds in the languages of the Offences Against the Person Act 1861.

penetration 1. The depth to which a *bullet or other *projectile will penetrate a material before exploding or coming to rest. **2.** The insertion of a part of the body or anything else into the *vagina, *anus, or mouth of another. Penile penetration of those orifices without *consent constitutes the **actus reus* of *rape. Penetration of the vagina or anus is the basis of the offence of *assault by penetration. Section 79(2) of the Sexual Offences Act 2003 provides that penetration is a continuing act from entry to withdrawal. It follows that an accused can commit the offences if consent is withdrawn and he does not withdraw immediately.

penology A branch of criminology concerned with the management of prisons and the treatment of offenders.

people trafficking '[T]he recruitment, transportation, transfer, harbouring or receipt of persons, by means of the threat or use of force or other forms of coercion, or abduction, of fraud, of deception, of the abuse of power or of a position of vulnerability or of the giving or receiving of payments of benefits to achieve the consent of a person having control over another person, for the purposes of exploitation. Exploitation shall include, at a minimum, the exploitation of the prostitution of others or other forms of sexual exploitation, forced labour or services, slavery or practices similar to slavery, servitude or the removal of organs', as defined by the UN Protocol to Prevent, Suppress and Punish Trafficking in Persons, especially Women and Children, supplementing the UN Convention against Transnational Organized Crime (2000) (to which the UK is a signatory). Sections 57 to 59 of the Sexual Offences Act 2003 create offences of trafficking into, within, and out of the UK for the purpose of sexual exploitation (reproducing and extending the offence of trafficking first created in s 145 of the Nationality, Asylum and Immigration Act 2002). *See also* SEXUAL OFFENCES.

per capita [Latin: by heads] For each person.

per curiam **(per cur.)** [Latin] By the court.

peremptory challenge *See* CHALLENGE TO JURY.

peremptory pleas *See* PLEAS IN BAR.

perfidious killing or wounding A *war crime under the Statute of the *International Criminal Court whereby the perpetrator kills or wounds the victim by taking advantage of the victim's belief that he is in a state of protection under *international law. In international conflicts it protects the armed forces and civilians of an opponent. In non-international conflict it does not apply to civilians. Guerrilla fighters dressed in civilian clothes would always be *guilty of perfidious killing or wounding by pretending to have civilian status, but they are *not guilty if they carry their weapons openly.

performance of contract The carrying out of obligations under a contract. Performance by both parties discharges the contract completely; performance by one party discharges him alone.

performers' rights The *rights of performers, such as musicians, in the live performance of their works, to prevent others recording their performances. The rights are also infringed if anyone broadcasts a qualifying performance under the Copyright, Designs and Patents Act 1988 without consent or imports a recording of such a performance knowing that it was an illicit recording.

pericardium The cavity in which the heart is located.

perimortem At or close to the moment of death.

per incuriam [Latin: through lack of care] A decision of a court is made *per incuriam* if it fails to apply a relevant statutory provision or ignores a binding *precedent. In criminal cases a decision made *per incuriam* will usually result in the *conviction being *quashed.

periorbital haematoma A *'black eye'.

periosteum The thin membrane that covers bones.

perished goods (under the Sale of Goods Act 1979) *Goods under a contract of sale that have been either totally destroyed or so damaged that they no longer fit the contract description.

peritoneum The sheet of tissue that lines the abdominal cavity.

peritonitis Inflammation of the abdominal lining or its contents.

perjury The offence of giving false evidence or evidence that one does not believe to be true (even if it is in fact the truth). It is punishable by up to seven years' imprisonment and/or a *fine. The offence may be committed by any witness who has taken the *oath or affirmed, by the defendant at any stage of the *trial, and by an *interpreter. Perjury is only committed, however, in judicial proceedings, which include any proceedings before a court, tribunal, or someone with the power to hear evidence on oath. The evidence given must be relevant to the proceedings and must be given with knowledge that it is false or *reckless.

The Perjury Act 1911 also creates various offences related to perjury. These include making a **false statement** on oath in non-judicial proceedings and making a false statement or declaration relating to marriage (e.g. to obtain a licence to marry or make an entry in a register of marriage) or to the registration of a birth or death. These offences are punishable by up to seven years' imprisonment on *indictment. The offences of making a false statement in a statutory declaration or in any *account, *balance sheet, or *document required to be made by *Act of Parliament are punishable by up to two years' imprisonment. *See also* SUBORNATION.

permitted temporary event A category of event under the Licensing Act 2003 which replaces events for which an occasional licence would have been issued under the previous *legislation. In this category are events which will last for less than four days and will be attended by fewer than 500 people. *Alcoholic liquor may be sold but no *licence is required for these events. They may be staged by any person aged 18 or over provided that notice is given to the police and council at least ten days before the event. There are restrictions on the number of events a person can stage and the number of events that can be held at a particular venue. A person can stage five events per year unless he holds a *personal licence in which case he can stage 50 such events. A venue can usually hold a maximum of twelve events per year with 24 hours between events, but can hold 15 events if each is for only one day. Only the police can object and the only ground permitted for objection is crime prevention. If the council wishes to support the police objection it must serve an objection notice on the applicant and hold a hearing which must be complete at least 24 hours before the event.

persecution A *crime against humanity under the Statute of the *International Criminal Court prohibiting the persecution of identifiable groups or communities including individuals who are representatives of a group.

persistent offender Formerly, a person whose previous criminal record made him liable to be given an *extended sentence of imprisonment. *See* DANGEROUS OFFENDER; PERSISTENT YOUNG OFFENDER.

persistent young offender In the case of an offender under the age of 15 at the time of *conviction, the court may not make a *detention and training order unless it is satisfied that he is a 'persistent offender'. The term is not defined in the *legislation. The *Home Office defines the term to mean 'a young person aged 10 to 17, who has been sentenced by any criminal court in the UK on three or more occasions, for one or more *recordable offence, and within three years of the last sentencing occasions is subsequently arrested or has information laid against them for a further recordable offence'. However, the courts have declined to follow that definition. In *R v B (D) (A Juvenile)* [2001] 1 Cr App R(S) 113, the *Court of Appeal held that it is not necessary to establish a pattern of offences of the same or similar character in order to categorize a person as a persistent offender. *See also* CUSTODY FOR OFFENDERS UNDER 21.

personal Act *See* ACT OF PARLIAMENT.

personal-credit agreement An agreement made between an individual (the *debtor) and any other person (the *creditor) by which the creditor provides the debtor with credit of any amount. Personal-credit agreements (a concept under the Consumer Credit Act 1974) exclude loans, etc., to companies. *See also* CONSUMER-CREDIT AGREEMENT.

Personal Identification Number (PIN) A four-digit number used by a *payment card holder to establish identity at point of sale or a remote terminal such as an *automatic teller machine. The number is issued by the card issuer but can be changed by the card holder.

personal licence The *licence a person must hold to permit him to sell *alcohol. The licence is issued by the *district council and lasts for ten years. Applicants must be 18 years of age and have a recognized licensing qualification, must not have forfeited a licence within the last five years, and be subject to a *Criminal Records Bureau check. Unless the police object, the council must grant the licence. If the police do object, the council will refuse the licence unless there are 'exceptional and compelling circumstances' for doing so.

personal property (personalty) All *property that does not comprise *land or incorporeal *hereditaments.

personal records Defined in s 11 of the Police and Criminal Evidence Act 1984 (PACE) as records concerning an individual who can be identified from them and which relate to: his physical or mental health; spiritual counselling or assistance given or to be given to him; or the counselling or assistance given or to be given to him, for the purposes of his personal welfare, by any voluntary organization or by any individual who by reason of his office or occupation has responsibility for his welfare or has responsibility for his supervision by order of a court. Under s 9 PACE they are *excluded material.

personal service The *service of a *document effected by leaving a copy of the document with the person to be served.

personalty *See* PERSONAL PROPERTY.

persona non grata [Latin: an unacceptable or unwelcome person] A *diplomatic agent who is unacceptable to the receiving state. The sending state should recall such an agent; if this fails to occur, the host state may ignore the presence of the agent or expel him from its territory.

personation Passing oneself off as another person. It is an offence if done fraudulently for certain purposes: for the purpose of casting a vote; sitting on a *jury; or personation of a *surety—an offence under the Forgery Act 1834 of purporting to be another person in acknowledging any *recognizance or *bail.

persuading to murder The statutory offence, under s 4 of the Offences Against the Person Act 1861, which is punishable by a maximum sentence of *life imprisonment, of persuading or encouraging any person to *murder anyone else. This offence is committed even by a foreigner temporarily in England who persuades someone to commit a murder abroad (such a person would not normally be *guilty of *incitement), and thus applies to the activities of international terrorist organizations (*see* TERRORISM).

persuasive authority A decision or other pronouncement of law that, under the doctrine of *precedent, a court may, but need not, apply when deciding the case before it. Persuasive authorities include decisions of courts of equal or lesser standing, decisions of courts outside the English legal system (particularly, courts of *Commonwealth countries having systems based on the *common law), **obiter dicta*, and the opinions of eminent *textbook writers.

perverse verdict A *verdict of a *jury that is either entirely against the weight of the evidence or contrary to the *judge's direction on a question of law.

perverting the course of justice Carrying out an act that tends or is intended to obstruct or defeat the administration of public justice. Common examples are inventing false evidence to mislead a court (in either civil or criminal proceedings) or an arbitration tribunal, making false statements to the police, stealing or destroying evidence, threatening witnesses, and attempting to influence *jurors. The *common-law offence of perverting the course of justice overlaps with certain forms of *contempt of court, and with the separate offences of interfering with witnesses or jurors. It is not an offence, however, to offer money to someone to persuade him not to proceed with an action in the civil courts; nor is it an offence to offer to pay reasonable compensation to the victim of a crime, if he will agree not to take criminal proceedings. However, once he has made a statement to the police in connection with possible proceedings, it is an offence to attempt to induce him to withdraw or alter his statement.

petechial haemorrhages Tiny pinpoint haemorrhages frequently seen in cases of strangulation but that can be caused by non-suspicious events. They are seen in the tissue around the eyes, the lining of the mouth, and on some internal organs.

pethidine A member of a group of medicines called opioid analgesics (painkillers). Opioids have similar effects to naturally occurring pain relieving chemicals (endorphins). They work by blocking transmission of pain signals in the brain and spinal cord. They are used as medicinal drugs for relieving the pain of child birth and surgery but can be abused and become addictive.

petition A written application for a legal *remedy or relief that is only available if statute or rules of *procedure permit it.

petty sessions A court of summary jurisdiction now known as a *magistrates' court. The term was formerly used to denote a meeting of two or more *justices of the peace other than a general or *quarter sessions. *See also* LOCAL JUSTICE AREA.

pharming A form of *hacking in which a *Trojan horse program, *worm, or other form of *malware is introduced to a *computer in order to redirect Internet traffic from a legitimate website address to one controlled by the hacker without the knowledge of the computer user. The process is often used to gather information such as passwords and *credit card numbers to facilitate online *fraud. *See also* PHISHING.

pharynx The back of the throat.

phishing A form of identity *theft. In a phishing attack, emails apparently originating from a legitimate financial institution are sent randomly to end-users, with the intention of gathering sensitive personal information, such as passwords or credit card details, for fraudulent use. *See also* PHARMING.

phreaking The unauthorized intrusion into a public or private telecommunications system in order to obtain free telephone calls. *See also* HACKING.

pia mater The thin innermost layer of the *meninges.

picketing Attendance by *employees and their trade union representatives at or near a place of work for the purpose of persuading others to work or not to work, or to exchange information, in contemplation or furtherance of a trade dispute. There is no specific legal right to picket, nor any prohibition on picketing, but there is a concept of lawful picketing in the Trade Union and Labour Relations (Consolidation) Act 1992. Pickets have no *immunity from *prosecution for committing criminal offences and they have no right to compel others to stop or to listen to the pickets' views. However, employees and their trade union representatives picketing their own place of work are immune from civil legal action for inducing others to break commercial or employment contracts with the *employer involved in the dispute. Such immunity extends to persons engaged in secondary picketing in certain circumstances. **Secondary picketing** occurs when the *premises of an employer who is not an immediate party to the dispute are picketed.

'Flying pickets', who are neither employees nor trade union representatives of employees at the workplace picketed, have no immunity. The courts will grant injunctions to stop or prevent unlawful picketing. A *code of practice on picketing is published by the Department for Work and Pensions.

pillage To plunder, loot, or sack a place. A *war crime, the pillaging of towns and places is prohibited in international and non-international conflicts.

PIN pad An electronic device with a key pad into which a payment chip card is placed and verified by the card holder entering his *Personal Identification Number on the key pad.

piracy 1. (piracy *jure gentium*) Any illegal act of violence, *detention, or *robbery committed on a private *ship for personal gain or revenge, against another ship, people, or property on the high seas. Piracy may also be committed on or against an aircraft. Piracy also includes operating a pirate ship or aircraft and inciting or assisting any other act of piracy. However, acts committed for political purposes are not piracy; nor are any acts committed by a warship or government ship or aircraft. Piracy is an *international crime and all nations may exercise *jurisdiction over pirates, regardless of the *nationality of the ship or aircraft or the pirates. A ship or aircraft involved in piracy is also subject to seizure by any state. British courts have traditionally exercised such jurisdiction, and the power to do so is confirmed in the Tokyo Convention Act 1967.

English *municipal law has created certain offences of piracy that are not covered by *international law, but they are not subject to the jurisdiction of the English courts unless committed on board a British ship or within British *territorial waters. Examples of such offences are revolt by the crew of a ship against their master and *hijacking of the ship by the crew. These offences, if tried as piracy, are subject to *life imprisonment (the death penalty for piracy accompanied by acts endangering life, or by an assault with intent to *murder, has been abolished; *see* CAPITAL PUNISHMENT). **2.** (in marine *insurance) One of the risks covered by a marine insurance policy, which extends beyond the criminal offence to include a revolt by the crew or passengers and plundering generally. **3.** Infringement of *copyright, *trade marks, or other *intellectual property rights. The owner's usual remedy is to obtain an *injunction to end the infringement, although piracy is often also a criminal offence.

pistol A small, concealable *handgun that incorporates a single *chamber and a single *barrel which remain in a fixed linear orientation relative to each other while being fired and reloaded. Technically, the term does not include a *revolver, although this distinction is often ignored in colloquial usage. A semi-automatic pistol holds its *rounds in a *magazine, normally inserted into the grip of the weapon, and fires a single cartridge each time the *trigger is pressed. It automatically extracts the spent casing and chambers a new cartridge in preparation for firing. Their compact size, rate of fire and ease of operation make them a common weapon amongst the criminal fraternity. *See also* SEMI-AUTOMATIC WEAPON.

pistol-grip A handle or grip shaped like the butt of a *pistol, often found on *assault rifles and similar weapons.

place of safety order *See* EMERGENCY PROTECTION ORDER.

plaintiff *See* CLAIMANT.

plea A formal statement in court by or on behalf of a defendant as a response to the *charge made against him. If the defendant is a *corporation, a representative of the corporation may indicate the plea (s 33(6), Criminal Justice Act 1925 and sch 3, Magistrates' Courts Act 1980). That representative must have a written statement, signed by the managing *director or other person having the management of its affairs, appointing the representative to act for the corporation (s 33(6), Criminal Justice Act 1925). *See also* GUILTY; NOT GUILTY; PLEA BEFORE VENUE; PLEAS IN BAR.

plea and case management hearing (PCMH) A procedure in the *Crown Court at which the defendant enters his *plea and the *judge makes directions for the management of the case in accordance with the *Criminal Procedure Rules. Prior to the issue of those rules, the procedure was known as a **plea and directions hearing**.

plea and directions hearing (PDH) *See* PLEA AND CASE MANAGEMENT HEARING.

plea bargaining An agreement between the *prosecution and the *defence by which the accused changes his *plea from *not guilty to *guilty in return for an offer by the prosecution (e.g. to drop a more serious *charge against the accused). In *mode of trial proceedings, the defendant may request an indication from the court as to whether a *sentence will be custodial or non-custodial should the case be dealt with summarily and the defendant plead *guilty. In the *Crown Court, the defendant may request the court to indicate the maximum sentence that would be imposed should he plead guilty: *R v Goodyear* [2005] All ER (D) 266.

plea before venue (PBV) A procedure in the *magistrates' court where, in an *either way case, a defendant is given the opportunity to indicate his or her likely *plea, although he is not compelled to do so. If he pleads *guilty the court may proceed to *sentence or may commit him for sentence at the *Crown Court if, given the seriousness of the offence, the court considers that its powers of *punishment are insufficient. If he pleads *not guilty or declines to indicate a plea, then the court will proceed to determine *mode of trial. *See also* PLEA BARGAINING.

plead To make a *plea.

pleading (in colloquial usage) The claim form, *defence, or any other *document used in civil proceedings. The *Civil Procedure Rules have rendered this term obsolete, and it no longer has any formal meaning; pleadings are now called statements of case. However, it continues to be used informally by both lawyers and lay people.

pleading guilty by post In proceedings for a *summary offence brought by way of *summons in an adult *magistrates' court or in respect of a defendant aged 16 or 17 in the *youth court, the *prosecution may give the defendant the option of pleading *guilty by post (s 12, Magistrates' Courts Act 1980). The limitation which excluded offences punishable with more than three months' imprisonment was removed in April 2005 by s 308 of the Criminal Justice Act 2003. The defendant may send details of any mitigating circumstances and these are read out to the court. The court cannot sentence a person who has pleaded guilty by post to imprisonment in his absence or *disqualify him from driving without warning him of the possibility and giving him the opportunity to appear.

The procedure, although used most commonly for minor road traffic offences, applies to both *specified offences and those non-specified offences that are triable summarily only. In the event of a *not guilty *plea, the *Crown Prosecution Service must take over the proceedings.

pleas in bar (peremptory pleas) *Pleas in *trials on indictment setting out some special ground for not proceeding with the *indictment. There are four such pleas: **autrefois acquit*, **autrefois convict*, *pardon, and special liability to repair a road or bridge.

pledge *See* PAWN.

pleura Double sheet of tissue covering the lungs and their cavity.

pneumothorax Air between the two layers of the pleura often caused by injury (collapsed lung).

poaching Taking *game without permission from private *land or from land on which the killing of game is restricted. Wild animals cannot usually be stolen; there are, however, various statutory offences to cover poaching that do not amount to *theft: poaching by day and poaching by day in company (s 30, Game Act 1831); night poaching by unlawfully entering land and night poaching by unlawfully being on land (s 1, Night Poaching Act 1828); and poaching of deer (s 1, Deer Act 1991). Further, it is an offence to take or destroy fish from water which is private property or in which there is a private right of fishery (sch 1, para 2(1), Theft Act 1968).

point-of-sale A checkout, till, or other physical location where a customer pays for *goods or services.

poison A substance that, if ingested, is capable of endangering life or injuring health. It is an offence under s 24 of the Offences Against the Person Act 1861 (punishable by up to five years' imprisonment) to cause someone to consume a poison or any other noxious substance (which can include drugs or *alcohol administered in such quantities as to be harmful) with the intention of injuring or annoying them, even if no injury results. It is also an offence under s 23 of the Offences Against the Person Act 1861 (punishable by up to ten years' imprisonment) to cause someone to consume such substances so that their life is endangered or they suffer *grievous bodily harm as a result, even if this was not intended. Administering poison with the intention of killing someone or causing them serious harm may amount to an attempt to *murder or to cause grievous bodily harm. In both cases the attempt will be punishable with a maximum sentence of *life imprisonment.

The sale of poisons is controlled by various statutes, principally the Medicines Act 1968 and Poisons Act 1972.

The use of poison or poison gas in international or non-international conflicts is a *war crime contrary to the Statute of the *International Criminal Court.

police authority An authority responsible for one of the 43 areas into which England and Wales are divided for policing purposes, each coterminous with a county or group of counties. London has the Metropolitan Police Authority, and Northern Ireland has the Police Authority for Northern Ireland. Police authorities consist of local councillors, *magistrates, and independent members. They are responsible for maintaining adequate and efficient forces and (except in London), subject to the Home Secretary's approval, for appointing *chief constables. (The London forces have Commissioners, and the appointment of the Commissioner of Police of the Metropolis is technically by the *Crown.) Police authorities, do not, however, exercise operational or managerial control, although they are responsible for ensuring that authorities comply with their statutory duties of best value.

police bail *See* BAIL.

Police Complaints Authority An independent body established under the Police and Criminal Evidence Act 1984 to supervise the investigation of complaints against the police; now replaced by the *Independent Police Complaints Commission.

police court (*archaic*) A court of summary jurisdiction, renamed *magistrates' court following *legislation in 1949.

police force A body of *constables maintained for a police area by a *police authority. The chief officer of a police force is a *chief constable in provincial police forces and a Commissioner in the City of London and Metropolitan Police Service in London. Police forces are arranged on a geographical basis, being coterminous with a county or group of counties. Governance of police forces is by a tripartite system consisting of the chief constable, the *police authority, and the *Home Secretary. Appointments to a police force, and the direction of its operations, are matters for the chief constable or Commissioner, and its detailed management is largely determined by regulations made by the Home Secretary.

Police forces are also operated by various *undertakings to police: railways (British Transport Police), nuclear installations (Civil Nuclear Constabulary), ports (e.g. Port of London Authority); and by *local authorities (mainly parks police).

Police Information and Technology Organization (PITO) A non-departmental public body that provides expertise and advice on the best practice in the use of information and communication technology to the police and its other external customers. It also advises on local purchasing, legal, and contractual issues, and can negotiate with suppliers on their behalf. From April 2007 it will become part of the National Policing Improvement Agency, a new body which will support forces to improve the way they work across many areas of policing.

Police National Computer (PNC) A national information system, available to the police, criminal justice agencies, and a variety of other non-policing organizations. It holds comprehensive details of people, vehicles, crimes, and property on its database. Its functions include: QUEST (Querying Using Enhanced Search Techniques)—this enables the search of the names database to identify suspects by searching for physical description and personal features; VODS (Vehicle Online Descriptive Search)—this allows users to search the vehicles database by search criteria such as registration, postcode, and colour details to narrow the list to potential suspect vehicles; ANPR (Automatic Number Plate Recognition)—this is used to scan the number plates of motor vehicles and check them against entries on the PNC, alerting police to any that are of interest; Property—an index of items which are lost and found such as *firearms, *trailers, marine equipment, plants, and animals; CRIMELINK—an enhanced, web-based version of the *Comparative Case Analysis Tool, which can be used to help solve serious serial-type crimes by searching for similarities in incidents, helping investigators to identify patterns and links.

police officer A person who, whatever his rank within a *police force, holds the ancient office of *constable, i.e. one who has undertaken to serve the *Crown as an officer of the peace. His office is, in law, independent. He is not technically a Crown servant, since the Crown neither appoints him nor pays him, nor is he a *local authority *employee.

police protection order An order of the court enabling the police to remove a child to suitable accommodation if there is reasonable cause to believe that the child would otherwise be likely to suffer significant harm. No child may be kept in police protection for more than 72 hours and the police do not acquire *parental responsibility as a result of the order. *See also* SECTION 47 INQUIRY.

Police Scientific Development Branch (PSDB) *See* HOME OFFICE SCIENTIFIC DEVELOPMENT BRANCH.

police service A term for all the police in the country. It is now used by some *police forces in preference to the term 'police force'.

police-to-police inquiries *See* MUTUAL ASSISTANCE.

political asylum *See* ASYLUM.

political offence *See* EXTRADITION.

pollution Any action rendering the environment impure. Statutes relating wholly or partly to **air pollution** include the Clean Air Acts 1956 and 1968, the Health and Safety at Work Act 1974, the Control of Pollution Act 1974, the Environmental Protection Act 1990 as amended by the Clean Neighbourhoods and Environment Act 2005, and the Environment Act 1995, which control the emission of smoke into the atmosphere, the emission of noxious or offensive substances, and the composition of petrol and other fuels. **Water pollution** generally is governed by the Control of Pollution Act 1974 and the Environmental Protection Act 1990 as amended by the Clean Neighbourhoods and Environment Act 2005, under which it is an offence (among other things) to allow polluting matter to enter rivers or other inland waters or to impede their flow so as to aggravate pollution due to other causes. Control of pollution by oil is covered by the Prevention of Oil Pollution Act 1971. Pollution by the deposit of waste on *land is governed primarily by the Control of Pollution Act 1974, which permits household, commercial, and industrial waste to be deposited only on licensed sites. *Local authorities are required by the Act to collect and dispose of household waste free of charge; for the purposes of **refuse disposal** by their residents, they are also, by the Refuse Disposal (Amenity) Act 1978, obliged to provide free refuse dumps.

polydipsia Excessive thirst commonly seen in diabetics, but it *may be a symptom of internal bleeding*. Medical advice should be sought.

polygamy The practice of having more than one spouse. A polygamous marriage may be recognized by the English courts in the circumstances laid down by s 47 of the Matrimonial Causes Act 1973.

polymerase chain reaction (PCR) A widely used technique for the selective amplification of particular DNA sequences, such as individual genes. It is quick and sensitive and is particularly useful when the amount of starting material is limited or poorly preserved. Examples of PCR applications include cloning DNA from single cells, and the analysis of DNA sequences for *forensic purposes in samples such as *fingerprints, blood stains, semen, or hairs.

polyuria The excessive passing of urine. It is a common symptom of *diabetes, but may be a symptom of renal (kidney) failure or sickle cell disease. Medical advice should be sought.

pons An area at the base of the brain above the spinal cord.

pontine Relating to the *pons.

port A place or town with access to the sea to which *ships may conveniently come and at which they may load and unload. Under the Customs and Excise Management Act 1979 a port for the purposes of the Act means any port defined as such by the Commissioners for *Her Majesty's Revenue and Customs. The Commissioners also determine the 'limits of a port' and have done so in such a way that the entire coast of the UK is within the limits of a port.

position of trust A person is in a 'position of trust' for the purposes of ss 16 to 19 of the Sexual Offences Act 2003 (the *'abuse of position of trust' offences), when he is over the age of 18, looks after a person under that age, and falls within one of the categories of carer laid down in s 21 of the 2003 Act. As enacted, those categories are exhaustive as regards professional carers, such as teachers, medical personnel, and workers in care homes and the like, but do not include familial carers or other non-professional carers such as scout and guide leaders, members of the clergy, and school caretakers. However, the Act provides that the Secretary of State may add to the categories at a later date (s 21(1)(b)).

positivism A school of criminology that believes criminality is the result of biological, psychological, or social factors that are outside the control of the offender.

possession For the purposes of the Misuse of Drugs Act 1971 'possession' has two elements: the physical element and the mental element. The physical element involves proof that the thing is in the custody of the defendant or subject to his control. The mental element involves proof of knowledge that the thing exists and that it is in his possession. Proof of knowledge that the thing is an article of a particular kind, quality, or description is not required. For *firearms a person may be in possession of a firearm if it is under his control even though he does not have physical possession of it. In the case of *land possession may be actual, when the owner has entered onto the land, or possession in law, when he has the right to enter but has not yet done so. Possession includes receipt of rent and profits, or the right to receive them.

post-mortem [Latin: after death] *See* AUTOPSY.

powder Any of several mixtures used as a propellant in *firearm *ammunition. Generally, powder used in modern *small arms ammunition consists of either nitrocellulose alone or a combination of nitrocellulose and nitroglycerin.

power A legal *discretion (as opposed to a *duty) to carry out or refrain from carrying out any act. *See also* ULTRA VIRES.

power of arrest 1. A power to detain and restrain a person for a criminal offence. Such a power may arise from a *warrant issued by a *magistrate or *judge or, in certain circumstances, at *common law or under the Police and Criminal Evidence Act 1984 (as amended by the Serious Organized Crime and Police Act 2005). *See also* ARREST. **2.** (in cases of *domestic violence) A power attached to, for example, a *non-molestation order or an *occupation order, which enables a police *constable to arrest without warrant a person whom he has reasonable cause for suspecting of being in breach of the order to which it is attached, even though that person might not be committing a criminal offence.

power of attorney (letter of attorney) A formal instrument by which one person empowers another to act on his behalf, either generally or in specific circumstances.

power of search The legal right to search people or property. Private people have no powers of search, but various statutes, notably the Police and Criminal Evidence Act 1984, confer such powers on police or other officials, often on the authority of a **search warrant** issued by a *magistrate or a *High Court *judge. Section 1 of the 1984 Act empowers the police to stop and search any person or vehicle found in a *public place for stolen or prohibited articles and to detain a person or vehicle for such a search. (An article is 'prohibited' if it is either an *offensive weapon including bladed or sharply pointed items except folding pocket knives with a blade of less than three inches, or made or adapted for use in connection with *burglary, *theft, *taking a conveyance, or obtaining property by *deception or items made, adapted, or intended for use in *destroying or *damaging property.) Before such a search the *police officer must state his station and object. If out of uniform, he must produce evidence of his status. He must always give his grounds for the search if asked and must record details of it. A magistrate may issue a search warrant to an officer if he is satisfied that there are reasonable grounds for believing that an *indictable offence has been committed and material evidence is to be found on the *premises. Under the Theft Act 1968, for example, police may obtain a warrant to search for stolen *goods when there are reasonable grounds for believing that they are in someone's possession or on his premises. Under certain circumstances the police are given powers of search without requiring either a warrant or any superior authorization; e.g. under the Misuse of Drugs Act 1971 (*see* CONTROLLED DRUGS) and the Terrorism Act 2000 (*see* TERRORISM). The police also have a general power, when arresting someone for an indictable offence, to enter and search any place in which the suspect is believed to be. Statutes sometimes give powers of search to public officials, e.g. customs officers, Department of Trade and Industry officials, or Inland Revenue officers.

Police powers of stop and search were extended under the Criminal Justice and Public Order Act 1994. Where a senior police officer reasonably believes that an incident involving serious violence may take place in his area he may issue an authorization (valid for 24 hours, extendable for up to six hours) for persons and vehicles (which can include caravans, *ships, aircraft, and hovercraft and their passengers) to be stopped and searched if he thinks it expedient to do so to prevent violence. A *constable in uniform may stop and search any person for the purpose of seeing whether that person is carrying an offensive weapon or an instrument that has a blade or a sharp point. Failure to stop is a *summary offence punishable by one month's imprisonment and/or a *fine on level 3. Failure to cooperate might amount to *obstructing a police officer in the execution of his duty. Similar powers are available to senior police officers to authorize searches for periods of 28 days to prevent acts of terrorism connected with the affairs of Northern Ireland or international terrorism. Both failure to stop and wilful obstruction of a constable are summary offences for the purpose of this power and are punishable by six months' imprisonment and/or a fine at level 5.

practice 1. The mode of proceeding to enforce a legal right. It is virtually synonymous with *procedure, but is sometimes used to denote informal rules of procedure as distinct from those derived from rules of court. **2.** A book or code on practice and procedure, such as the *Civil Procedure Rules and *Criminal Procedure Rules.

Practice Directions Published statements, usually issued by the head of the court or division to which they relate, indicating the procedure to be followed in particular matters or the court's intended policy in certain cases. Unlike *rules of court, they have no statutory authority. They are normally published in the *law reports. *See also* CONSOLIDATED CRIMINAL PRACTICE DIRECTION.

practising certificate An annual certificate issued by the *Law Society to a *solicitor entitling him to practise. The fee chargeable includes the premium of an *insurance policy indemnifying the solicitor against the consequences of professional *negligence. *Barristers obtain a practising certificate from the *Bar Council after they have successfully completed a twelve-month pupillage and have attended further education courses required by the Bar Council.

preamble The part of a statute that sets out its purposes and effects. It follows immediately after the long title and date of royal assent. Preambles are now virtually confined to statutes originating in private *Bills.

precedent A *judgment or decision of a court, normally recorded in a *law report, used as an authority for reaching the same decision in subsequent cases. In English law, judgments and decisions can represent **authoritative precedent** (which is generally binding and must be followed) or **persuasive precedent** (which need not be followed). It is that part of the judgment that represents the legal reasoning (or **ratio decidendi*) of a case that is binding, but only if the legal reasoning is from a superior court and, in general, from the same court in an earlier case. Accordingly, *ratio decidendi* of the *House of Lords are binding upon the *Court of Appeal and all lower courts and are normally followed by the House of Lords itself. The *ratio decidendi* of the Court of Appeal are binding on all lower courts and, subject to some exceptions, on the Court of Appeal itself. *Ratio decidendi* of the *High Court are binding on inferior courts, but not on itself. The *ratio decidendi* of inferior courts do not create any binding precedent.

precept A lawful demand or direction, particularly a demand from a rating authority to another authority to levy a community charge for the benefit of the former. For example, a *district council's community charge includes an amount that it collects as a result of a precept from such bodies as its *county council, *parish council, and *police authority.

predatory pricing The practice, undertaken largely by dominant businesses, of pricing *goods or services at such a low level that competitors are forced to leave the market. While small companies are entitled to price as they wish, provided this is not in collusion with other companies, dominant businesses must comply with Article 82 of the *Treaty of Rome and the Competition Act 1998; predatory pricing may be an abuse of a dominant position contrary to these provisions. Companies can be fined for engaging in predatory pricing.

preference 1. The favouring by an insolvent *debtor of a particular *creditor (e.g. by paying one creditor in full when there is no prospect of paying the others). If the debtor subsequently becomes *bankrupt (in the case of an individual) or goes into insolvent liquidation (in the case of a company), and was motivated by a desire to improve the position of the creditor, the court can order that the position be restored to what it would have been had that creditor not been given preference. The court can also make orders when the debtor has given property away or sold it at an undervalue. **2.** A floating *charge created within one year before the commencement of *winding-up in favour of an existing creditor. It is invalid if the company was insolvent at the time it was created unless the creditor provided some fresh benefit to the company at that time, e.g. by way of loan or *goods supplied. If the charge was created in favour of a person connected with the company, the period is two years and it is not necessary to show that the company was insolvent at the time of its creation.

preference share *See* SHARE.

preferential debts The *debts of a company on *winding-up or of an individual on *bankruptcy that have priority over unsecured debts and those secured only by floating *charge. They are defined in the Insolvency Act 1986 and include various debts to government departments and to *employees.

preferment **1.** The submission to the court of a statement or *information. **2.** The act of bringing a *bill of indictment before an appropriate court.

prejudice A preconceived judgment. *See also* WITHOUT PREJUDICE.

preliminary hearing In a case triable only on *indictment in which the accused has indicated a *guilty *plea before the *magistrates' court and it is known that there is an issue as to the basis or acceptability of that plea, the court may determine that there should be a preliminary hearing in the *Crown Court prior to the *plea and case management hearing.

premature closure The drawing of conclusions from limited information prior to an interview, thereby discounting information that does not fit the hypothesis and placing undue weight upon information that does fit the hypothesis.

premises *Land or buildings; a parcel of land.

premises licence The *licence required under the Licensing Act 2003 for each *premises where any *'licensable activity' is to take place. A licence is also required for premises which are hired out for *'regulated entertainment'. The Act does not restrict the permitted opening hours but the council must decide within its published licensing policy and the licensing objectives.

preparatory hearing A hearing before a *judge of the *Crown Court, before the *jury are sworn, in a case of serious or complex *fraud or other complex or lengthy cases for the purpose of identifying issues likely to arise in the case and assisting in their comprehension and management. It is governed by pt 15 of the *Criminal Procedure Rules.

prerogative of mercy The power of the *Crown, on the *Home Secretary's advice, to pardon a criminal offence absolutely (thereby relieving the defendant of all the consequences of *conviction), to commute a *sentence to a milder form, or to remit a sentence in part.

prerogative orders Orders issued by the *High Court for the supervision of inferior courts, tribunals, and other bodies exercising judicial or quasi-judicial functions. They comprise *quashing orders, *mandatory orders, and *prohibition orders. Until 1938 they were **prerogative writs**, but since the Administration of Justice Act 1938 the only remaining prerogative writ is *habeas corpus.

prescribed by law To be 'prescribed by law' there must be a legal regime governing the interference in question. This is a prerequisite for interference with any right in the *European Convention of Human Rights: any such interference will be unlawful if it is not prescribed by law (or 'in accordance with the law'). Moreover, that law must be both adequately accessible (in that citizens must be able to understand whether or not the law applies in a given case) and formulated with sufficient precision to enable citizens to regulate their conduct.

prescribed limit The maximum amount of *alcohol a person is legally allowed to have in his blood if he is driving or in charge of a *motor vehicle on a *road or *public place (*see* DRUNKEN DRIVING). The level is currently fixed at 80mg of alcohol per 100mls of blood or 35μgs of alcohol per 100mls of breath.

prescription (in *international law) The acquisition of *title to territory through an uncontested exercise of *sovereignty over an extended period of time. Prescription presupposes a prior sovereign authority whose control and administration over the territory in question has lapsed through:

- failure to occupy,
- failure to administer,
- abandonment or neglect,
- a wrongful original claim, or
- failure to contest a new claim.

pre-sentence report A report ordered by the court prepared by a *probation officer, social worker, or member of a *youth offending team, which provides the court with information about an offender. It is prepared according to National Standards set by the *Home Office. Section 156 of the Criminal Justice Act 2003 reproduces the combined effect of ss 81 and 36 of the Powers of Criminal Courts (Sentencing) Act 2000 (relating to custodial and *community sentences, respectively), modified to take into account the provisions of the 2003 Act. A court must obtain and consider a pre-sentence report before deciding that the case is sufficiently serious to warrant a custodial or community sentence, unless it is of the opinion that, in the circumstances of the case, it is unnecessary. In the case of an offender under the age of 18, a court can only form that opinion if it has had regard to information contained in an earlier report obtained in respect of the offender.

presiding judge A *puisne judge appointed by the *Lord Chancellor to supervise the work of a circuit (*see* CIRCUIT SYSTEM). Each circuit has two presiding judges with the exception of the South-Eastern circuit, which has the *Lord Chief Justice and two puisne judges. There is a Senior Presiding Judge for England and Wales.

pressing social need A concept that has been used by the *European Court of Human Rights as the basis for assessing whether or not an interference with a *qualified right is necessary in a democratic society.

presumption A supposition that the law allows or requires to be made. Some presumptions relate to people, e.g. the *presumption of innocence and *presumption of sanity. Others concern events, e.g. the presumption of legality (*omnia praesumuntur rite et solemniter esse acta*: all things are presumed to have been done correctly and solemnly). Most relate to the interpretation of written *documents, particularly statutes (*see* INTERPRETATION OF STATUTES). Almost every presumption is a **rebuttable presumption**, i.e. it holds good only in the absence of contrary evidence. Thus, the presumption of innocence is destroyed by positive proof of guilt. An **irrebuttable presumption** is one that the law does not allow to be contradicted by evidence, as, for example, the presumption that a child below the age of 10 is incapable of committing a crime (*see* DOLI CAPAX). *See also* CONSENT.

presumption of death A *common-law *presumption that someone has died. The presumption will be made if a spouse has been missing for at least seven years (with nothing to indicate that he or she is still alive) or by proof of other reasonable grounds (e.g. that the spouse was on a ship that sank). The courts are empowered to grant a decree of **presumption of death and dissolution of marriage**, enabling the other spouse to remarry; the remarriage will be valid even if the first spouse later reappears.

presumption of innocence The legal *presumption that every person charged with a criminal offence is innocent until proved *guilty. Although this is termed a 'presumption', it is in fact a fundamental principle underlying the criminal law, which has been reinforced by the *Human Rights Act 1998 (*see* FAIR TRIAL). *See* BURDEN OF PROOF.

presumption of sanity The legal *presumption that every person charged with a criminal offence was sane (and therefore responsible in law) at the time he is alleged to have committed the crime. *See* INSANITY.

pre-trial review *See* CASE MANAGEMENT HEARING.

preventing births A crime of *genocide under the Statute of the *International Criminal Court of preventing births within a group with the intention of causing the extinction of that group. The offence may be committed by forcible sterilization, forcible birth control, prohibition of marriage, and physical segregation of the sexes.

previous convictions *See* ANTECEDENTS; CHARACTER; CREDIT.

previous statements (in the law of evidence) If a witness has on some previous occasion made a statement that is inconsistent with his present *testimony, this may be put to him in *cross-examination in order to impeach (discredit) him; if he denies having made the statement, it may be proved by *secondary evidence. Evidence of the previous consistent statements of a witness is not in general admissible. It may, however, be given in order to rebut the suggestion that his present testimony is a recent fabrication or when it concerns the *complaint of the victim of a *sexual offence. *See also* CREDIT.

price (in a contract of sale) The money *consideration given in exchange for the transfer of *ownership. In a contract of *sale of goods the price may be fixed by the contract, it may be left to be fixed in a manner agreed by the contract, or it may be determined by the course of dealing between the parties. If the price is not determined in any of the above ways, the buyer must pay a reasonable price. Under the Consumer Protection Act 1987, it is a criminal offence to give a misleading indication of the price of *goods, services, accommodation, or facilities; e.g. when the consumer might reasonably expect the price indicated to cover matters for which an additional charge is in fact made.

prima facie [from Latin *prima facies*: first appearance] At first sight; on the face of things.

prima facie case A case that has been supported by sufficient evidence for it to be taken as proved in the absence of adequate evidence to the contrary.

prima facie evidence 1. (presumptive evidence) Evidence that is sufficient to discharge any evidential *burden of proof borne by a party and that may be sufficient to discharge the persuasive burden of proof if no evidence in rebuttal is tendered. **2.** Evidence of a *fact that is of sufficient weight to justify a reasonable inference of its existence but does not amount to conclusive evidence of that fact.

primary detection An offence cleared up by charging a person with the offence or administering an official *caution or *final warning.

primary evidence Evidence, such as the original of a *document, that by its nature does not suggest that better evidence is available. *See also* BEST-EVIDENCE RULE; SECONDARY EVIDENCE.

primary fact A *fact found by the *trial court to be established on the basis of the *testimony of witnesses and the production of real or documentary evidence. Appellate courts are generally unwilling to change the trial court's findings concerning primary facts, but may reverse its decisions concerning the inferences to be drawn from them.

Prime Minister The head of the UK government, who is appointed by the *Crown to select and preside over the *Cabinet and bears ultimate responsibility for the policy and machinery of government. The Prime Minister also advises the Crown on such matters as the dissolution of *Parliament, the creation of peerages, and the making of senior appointments (e.g. the Ombudsman). Like the Cabinet, the office derives from constitutional convention, which requires that the person appointed is the leader of the party with the greatest number of Members of Parliament.

primer A detonating mixture which when struck by the *firing pin, ignites the propellant *powder. The primer is generally contained in either a 'primer pocket' contained in the base of the *cartridge case (centrefire cartridge) or within the rim of the case (rimfire cartridge).

principal 1. (in criminal law) The person who actually carries out a crime. (Formerly, the actual perpetrator was known as the **principal in the first degree** and a person who *aided and abetted was called **principal in the second degree**, but the former is now known as the principal and the latter as the secondary party.) A person can be a principal even if he does not carry out the act himself; e.g. if he acts through an innocent agent, such as a child, or if he is legally responsible for the acts of another (e.g. because of *vicarious liability). *See also* ACCESSORY. **2.** (in the law of agency) The person on whose behalf an agent acts. **3.** (in finance) The sum of money lent or invested, as distinguished from the interest.

prison breach The offence at *common law that is committed when force is used against a person or property in order to *escape.

prisoner custody officer A person who is not a *constable or prison officer, employed to transport and guard prisoners. There are two classes of prisoner custody officer: one is employed by the prisoner escort service to escort prisoners between police stations, courts, and prisons; the second is employed as a prison officer in a privately managed prison. Their powers and duties are laid down in ss 82 and 86 of the Criminal Justice Act 1991.

privacy The right to be left alone. The right to a private life as set out in Article 8 of the *European Convention on Human Rights is now part of UK law as a consequence of the *Human Rights Act 1998. The right includes privacy of communications (telephone calls, correspondence, etc.); privacy of the home and office; environmental protection; the protection of physical integrity; and protection from unjustified *prosecution and *conviction of those engaged in consensual non-violent sexual activities. This right is a *qualified right; as such, the public interest can be used to justify an interference with it providing that this is prescribed by law, designed for a legitimate purpose, and proportionate. Public authorities have a limited but positive duty to protect privacy from interference by third parties.

private company A residuary type of *registered company defined under the Companies Act 1985 as any company that is not a *public company. This form of company is prohibited from offering its *shares to the public at large. Although not a strict requirement under the Act, it is common to find such companies placing restrictions on the transfer of shares and confining them to other (often family) members. Unlike a public company, a private company can consist of only one *company member (**single-member company**), and many of the other restrictions that apply to public companies (such as those relating to financial assistance) may be relaxed provided that the company complies with a specified procedure under the Act.

private defence Action taken in reasonable defence of one's person or *property. It can be pleaded as a *defence to an action in *tort. The right of private defence includes the defence of one's family, and probably of any other person, from unlawful force.

private international law (conflict of laws) The part of the national law of a country that establishes rules for dealing with cases involving a foreign element (i.e. contact with some system of foreign law). *Compare* INTERNATIONAL LAW.

private law The part of the law that deals with such aspects of relationships between individuals that are of no direct concern to the state. It includes the law of *property and of trusts, family law, the law of contract, mercantile law, and the law of *tort. *Compare* PUBLIC LAW.

private life *See* PRIVACY.

private member's Bill *See* BILL.

private nuisance *See* NUISANCE.

privilege 1. A special *right or *immunity in connection with legal proceedings conferred upon a person by virtue of his rank or office. For example, Members of Parliament enjoy certain privileges in relation to *arrest, which, however, do not extend to arrest in connection with *indictable offences (*see* PARLIAMENTARY PRIVILEGE). *See also* ABSOLUTE PRIVILEGE; QUALIFIED PRIVILEGE. **2.** (in the law of evidence) The right of a witness when testifying to refuse to answer certain types of question or of a party when disclosing *documents (*see* DISCLOSURE AND INSPECTION OF DOCUMENTS) to refuse to produce certain types of document on the ground of some special interest recognized by law. Privileges are divided into two groups: **public-interest privilege** and **private privilege**. The *Crown has always been able to claim public-interest privilege in relation to secrets of the state and other matters whose confidentiality is essential on grounds of public interest (*see* PUBLIC INTEREST IMMUNITY). Private privileges include the **privilege against self-incrimination**, according to which a witness may not be asked a question the answer to which might tend to incriminate him; **legal professional privilege**, which protects confidential communications between lawyers and their clients and between lawyers and third parties with a view to advising their clients; and a privilege attaching to *without prejudice communications in the course of *litigation. Under *European Union law there is no professional privilege between a lawyer working for a company and members of that company, only between a lawyer not employed by the company concerned and the company.

privity of contract The relationship that exists between the *parties to a contract. The *common-law doctrine of privity of contract established that only the parties to the contract, i.e. those that provided *consideration, could *sue or be sued under the contract. Third parties could not derive *rights from, nor have *obligations imposed on them by, someone else's contract. This position has now been modified by the Contracts (Rights of Third Parties) Act 1999. By the provisions of the Act, a person can enforce a term of a contract to which he is not a party provided that the term purports to confer a benefit on him or the contract expressly provides for such enforcement.

Privy Council (PC) A body, headed by the President of the Council, that formerly advised the *Crown on government policy but has been superseded in that role by the *Cabinet. Its functions are now mainly formal (e.g. a few members are summoned to make *Orders in Council), but it has limited statutory powers of *legislation and it also advises the sovereign, through committees, on certain judicial matters (*see* JUDICIAL COMMITTEE OF THE PRIVY COUNCIL) and other matters of a non-political nature (e.g. the grant of university charters). There are about 350 Privy Counsellors, who include members of the royal family, all Cabinet ministers, the Speaker, other holders of high non-political office, and persons honoured for public services. A Privy Counsellor is addressed as 'Right Honourable'.

probation 1. A trial period in a job or rank. **2.** The first two years of a *constable's service during which time training is undertaken and the constable can be discharged if he is unlikely to become an efficient constable.

probation centre A place at which non-residential facilities are provided for the rehabilitation of offenders. A court may order a person subject to a *community rehabilitation order to attend such a centre for up to 60 days (unless he was convicted of a *sexual offence, in which case the 60-day maximum does not apply).

probation hostel A residential home run by the National Probation Service of England and Wales. They are there to provide homes for people who have been recently discharged from prison and have nowhere to go, or those serving probation orders who have been ordered to remain in probation accommodation. They are also used to house people on *bail when it is a condition of their bail that they reside at a probation hostel.

probation officer An officer whose duties include supervising persons subject to a *community sentence. A probation officer advises, assists, and befriends these and others (e.g. persons who have been released from prison or are on *bail) and inquires into the circumstances of offenders in order to assist the court to determine how best to deal with them.

probation order *See* COMMUNITY REHABILITATION ORDER.

Problem Oriented Policing (POP) A method of policing based on problem solving. It was developed in the USA and has been adopted by *police forces and other agencies in England and Wales. Its aim is to identify and solve underlying problems within communities, rather than simply responding to individual incidents. Police, communities, and local agencies are encouraged to work together to identify specific problems that cause incidents and tackle them together. POP is implemented by a systematic way of managing crime reduction work. This approach is known by the acronym SARA, representing the four stages of the process:

- Scanning: problems are identified using local knowledge and data from a wide range of organizations.
- Analysis: the data are used to identify the problems caused.
- Response: solutions are devised to solve the problem using situational and social approaches.
- Assessment: review to see if the solution worked and what lessons can be learnt.

procedure (in court proceedings) The formal manner in which legal proceedings are conducted. *See also* ADJECTIVE LAW; PRACTICE; RULES OF COURT.

procès-verbal [French: oral proceedings] An informal record or memorandum of international understandings arrived at in negotiations. It is frequently a preliminary step in concluding a *treaty.

procurator fiscal In Scotland, an officer of the sheriff court (roughly equivalent to the English *county court). Appointed by the *Lord Advocate, he must be a qualified *advocate or *solicitor. The Crown Office and Procurator Fiscal Service is responsible for the *prosecution of crime in Scotland, the investigation of sudden or suspicious deaths, and the investigation of complaints against the police.

procurement Persuading or inviting a woman to have sexual intercourse. Prior to the enactment of the Sexual Offences Act 2003, the Sexual Offences Act 1956 provided the following offences: (1) ss 2 and 3—procuring a woman to have sexual intercourse with oneself or anyone else, anywhere in the world, by means of *threats or *false pretences; (2) s 9—procuring a severely mentally retarded woman (who is incapable of guarding herself against exploitation) to have sexual intercourse anywhere in the world; (3) s 22—procuring a woman to become a *prostitute or to leave the UK with the intention that she should join or frequent a *brothel; (4) s 23—procuring a girl under the age of 21 to have sexual intercourse with a third person anywhere in the world. The first two of these offences were repealed by the 2003 Act without replacement. Although rarely used, the failure to provide replacement offences has been the subject of criticism as the offences did allow for the *prosecution of cases in which threats or *deceptions falling short of that which is sufficient to vitiate *consent (and, accordingly, not sufficient for the offence of *rape) had been used to procure sexual intercourse. The offences contained within ss 30 to 41 of the 2003 Act replace and expand upon the offences relating to 'defectives' in the 1956 Act, including the s 9 'procurement' offence'; ss 22 and 23 of the 1956 Act were replaced by s 52 of the 2003 Act (*see* CAUSING OR INCITING OR CONTROLLING PROSTITUTION).

procuring disclosure of personal data An offence committed by someone who obtains personal information about an individual that is stored on a *computer when he knows or believes that he is not a person to whom the data user is registered to disclose this data (*see* DATA PROTECTION). Other offences are committed when the data procured in this way is offered for sale or sold. In each case the offences under s 5 of the Data Protection Act 1984 were added by s 161 of the Criminal Justice and Public Order Act 1994.

production of documents The act of a party in making available *documents in his *possession, custody, or power either for inspection by the other party (*see* DISCLOSURE AND INSPECTION OF DOCUMENTS) or for use as evidence at *trial in accordance with a notice to produce.

product liability The *liability of manufacturers and other persons for defective products. Under the Consumer Protection

Act 1987, passed to conform with the requirements of *European Community law, the producer of a defective product that causes death or personal injury or *damage to *property is strictly liable for the damage.

profit-and-loss account A *document presenting in summary form a true and fair view of the company's profit or loss as at the end of its financial year. It must show the items listed in one of the four formats set out in the Companies Act 1985. Its function is to show as profit or loss the difference between revenue generated and the expenditure incurred in the period covered by the account. *See also* ACCOUNTS.

profit *à prendre* The right to take soil, minerals, or produce (such as wood, turf, or fish) from another's *land (the servient tenement) or to graze animals on it. It may exist as a legal or equitable interest. The right may be enjoyed exclusively by one person (a **several profit**) or by one person in common with others (a **common**). A profit may exist **in gross** (i.e. existing independently of any ownership of land by the person entitled) and may be exercisable without any limit on the amount of produce taken. It may be sold, bequeathed, or otherwise dealt with. Profits existing for the benefit of the owner's land (the dominant tenement) are generally exercisable only to the extent to which the dominant tenement can benefit. They may be appurtenant, when the nature of the right depends on the terms of the grant; or *pur cause de vicinage* (Norman French: because of vicinity), in respect of cattle grazing the dominant tenement and straying onto the unfenced adjacent servient tenement. Profits may be created by express or implied grant or by statute; profits appurtenant may also arise by *prescription (or presumed grant). They may be extinguished (1) by an express release; (2) by the owner occupying the servient tenement; or (3) by implied release (e.g. through abandonment, which may be presumed through long non-use, through changes to the dominant tenement that make enjoyment of the right unnecessary or impossible, or through an irreversible alteration of the servient tenement).

Programme Management Organization An organization set up by the banking and retail industries to coordinate the chip-and-pin project.

programme requirement A requirement that may be imposed by a court dealing with an offender aged 16 or over as part of a *community order, *custody plus order, *suspended sentence order, or an intermittent custody order. It requires the offender to participate in a systematic set of activities, accredited by the local probation board (in the case of an offender aged 18 or over) or *youth offending team for a number of days specified in the order (s 202, Criminal Justice Act 2003).

prohibited activity requirement A requirement that may be imposed by a court dealing with an offender aged 16 or over as part of a *community order, *custody plus order, *suspended sentence order, or an intermittent custody order. It requires the offender to refrain from participating in activities specified in the order (including that the offender does not possess, use, or carry a *firearm) on a day or days or during a period specified in the order. Before imposing such a requirement, the court must consult the local probation board (in the case of an offender aged 18 or over) or *youth offending team (s 203, Criminal Justice Act 2003).

prohibited degrees of relationships Family relationships within which marriage is prohibited (and, if celebrated, is void), although sexual intercourse within such a relationship may not amount to a familial *sexual offence under the Sexual Offences Act 2003. A man, for example, may not marry his grandmother, aunt, or niece; a woman may not marry her grandfather, uncle, or nephew.

prohibited weapon A weapon suitable only for use by the armed forces and having no normal function in civilian life. Prohibited weapons include automatic *firearms, weapons designed or adapted to discharge a poisonous liquid or gas, and *ammunition containing poisonous substances. It is an offence (punishable with up to two years' imprisonment) to produce, sell, buy, or possess any prohibited weapon without the permission of the Defence Council. *See also* OFFENSIVE WEAPON.

prohibition notice A notice under the Health and Safety at Work Act 1974 specifying activities that, in the opinion of an inspector, involve a risk of serious personal injury, and prohibiting them until specified safeguards have been adopted.

prohibition order A *remedy in which the *High Court orders an ecclesiastical or inferior court, tribunal, or administrative authority not to carry out an **ultra vires** act (e.g. hearing a case that is outside its *jurisdiction). It is available in cases in which, had the act been carried out, the remedy would have been a *quashing order, and it is governed by broadly similar rules.

prohibitory injunction *See* INJUNCTION.

projectile A *bullet or any other object projected by force and continuing in motion by its own inertia. A bullet is not a projectile until it is in motion. *See also* AMMUNITION.

prolixity Excessive length or repetitiveness in statements of case, *affidavits, or other *documents.

promise An *undertaking given by one person (the **promisor**) to another (the **promisee**) to do or refrain from doing something. It is legally binding only if contained in a contract or made by *deed.

promissory note An unconditional promise in writing, made by one person to another and signed by the maker, engaging to pay a specified sum of money to (or to the order of) a specified person or to the bearer, either on demand or at a fixed or determinable future time. Promissory notes are *negotiable instruments and many of the provisions in the Bills of Exchange Act 1882 apply with necessary modifications to promissory notes. Promissory notes are not presented for acceptance and the party primarily liable is the maker of a note. A bank note is a promissory note issued by a bank; the sum of money mentioned on the note is payable to the bearer on demand.

promoter 1. A person engaged in the formation or *flotation of a company. A promoter stands in a *fiduciary relationship to the company; his functions may include drafting a *prospectus, negotiating preliminary agreements, instructing *solicitors, and obtaining *directors. *Solicitors, bankers, and other professionals involved in the company, but acting merely in their professional role, are not regarded as promoters. **2.** One who introduces a private *Bill.

prone Lying face down.

proof 1. The means by which the existence or non-existence of a *fact is established to the satisfaction of the court, including *testimony, *documentary evidence, *presumptions, and *judicial notice. Since most facts with which a court is concerned are not capable of being tested empirically, proof in the legal sense is quite different from proof in the context of mathematics or science. The uncorroborated evidence of one credible witness is sufficient proof for most purposes in the law. *See* STANDARD OF PROOF. **2.** (*informal*) The written statement of a prospective witness obtained by a *solicitor. A witness is said not to have **come up to proof** if he fails to testify in accordance with his proof.

proof beyond reasonable doubt The *standard of proof required in criminal proceedings. If the *jury has any reasonable (even if unlikely) doubts about the guilt of the accused, it may not convict him. It is often paraphrased by the *judge instructing the jury that they must be 'satisfied so that they are sure' of the guilt of the accused. It is disputed whether this standard is ever applicable in civil proceedings (e.g. when there is an allegation of *fraud): it is generally held that it is not. *See also* BURDEN OF PROOF.

proof in absence A *summary trial may take place in the absence of the defendant, under s 11 of the Magistrates' Courts Act 1980, provided that the court is satisfied that he has received notice of the proceedings and there is no good reason for his absence. In cases commenced by *summons, unless the defendant has appeared on a previous occasion in answer to the summons it must be proved to the satisfaction of the court that it was served on him in 'reasonable' time before the hearing. In cases tried in the absence of the defendant, the burden remains on the *prosecution to prove its case to the normal criminal standard, whether by calling oral evidence or by reading statements served on the accused under s 9 of the Criminal Justice Act 1967. If the case is proved, the court may either proceed immediately to sentence or, in certain circumstances, it may adjourn to give the defendant notice that he should attend for sentencing or issue a *warrant for his *arrest.

In the *Crown Court, the accused must be present at the start of his *trial in order to plead. If he subsequently voluntarily absents himself by escaping from custody or by failing to surrender to *bail, then the *judge has a discretion to complete the trial and pass *sentence in his absence: *R v Jones (No 2)* [1972] 1 WLR 887.

proof of age The age of a person may be proved by *direct evidence, such as the *testimony of someone present at the person's birth, and in some cases from his appearance. It is usually proved by producing a birth certificate, under the exception to the *hearsay rule relating to statements in *public documents, and evidence that the person in question is the one referred to in the birth certificate.

proof of birth Birth is usually proved by the production of a birth certificate, which is admissible under the exception to the *hearsay rule relating to statements in *public documents, coupled with evidence identifying the person in question with the person referred to in the birth certificate.

proof of handwriting Handwriting may be proved by the *testimony of the person whose handwriting it is or by that of someone who saw him execute the *document in question. It may also be proved by the opinion of someone familiar with the handwriting of the alleged writer or by comparison with a proved example of the writer's handwriting. Expert testimony is also admissible.

proof of marriage Legally valid evidence that a marriage was celebrated. This will usually be shown by possession of a marriage certificate and proof of identity, but may also be shown by other forms of evidence.

proof of service *See* SUMMONS.

propellant The chemicals which, when ignited, propel a *projectile from a weapon. *See also* AMMUNITION; POWDER.

property Anything that can be owned. A distinction is made between ***real property** (*land and incorporeal *hereditaments) and ***personal property** (all other kinds of property) and between ***tangible property** (that which has a physical existence, e.g. *chattels and *land) and ***intangible property** (*choses in action, including *intellectual property, and incorporeal *hereditaments). For purposes of the law of *theft, property includes all real, personal, and intangible property, although land can only be stolen under certain specified conditions. For purposes of the offences of *criminal damage, property does not include intangible property.

property in goods A right of *ownership in *chattels.

property interference The entry into or other interfering with property without the knowledge or consent of the owner for the purpose of installing listening, video, or other surveillance device. Authority must be given by a chief *police officer or equivalent in the *Serious Organized Crime Agency or *Her Majesty's Revenue and Customs. Under the Police Act 1997, proper authorization absolves those concerned from liability for *trespass, *criminal damage, or unlawful interference with wireless telegraphy.

proponent The party who bears the evidential, and in some cases the persuasive, *burden of proof in relation to an issue in *litigation.

proportionality 1. A principle of the *European Union ensuring that a legislative measure is introduced at EU level only when it is appropriate to have a measure at that level, and that when local *legislation is all that is needed, this will be encouraged. *See also* SUBSIDIARITY. **2.** A central provision of the *European Convention on Human Rights. It applies particularly to the *qualified rights and where the expression 'necessary in a democratic society' is contained within the article. Whether or not such a right has been violated will depend on whether the interference with the right is proportionate to the legitimate aim pursued by that interference. Thus even if a policy that interferes with a Convention right might be aimed at securing a legitimate purpose (e.g. the prevention of crime), this will not in itself justify the violation if the means adopted to secure the purpose are excessive in the circumstances.

prorogation *See* PARLIAMENT.

proscribed organization An organization or association declared to be forbidden by the *Home Secretary under the Terrorism Act 2000, because it appears to be concerned with terrorist activities (*see* TERRORISM).

prosecution The pursuit of legal proceedings, particularly criminal proceedings. The term is also used for the party instituting the proceedings (*see also* PROSECUTOR). Criminal prosecutions on *indictment are in the name of the *Crown; summary prosecutions commenced by *information and *summons are in the name of an individual (*see* LAYING AN INFORMATION). Although a private individual may bring a prosecution (most private prosecutions are for *assault), the *Director of Public Prosecutions can intervene either to take it over or terminate it. Many government departments and other authorities have power to prosecute; e.g. the Department for Work and Pensions, and *local authorities. Under the Prosecution of Offenders Act 1985, the duty of conducting prosecutions falls principally upon the *Crown Prosecution Service. The consent of the *Attorney-General or Director of Public Prosecutions is required before proceedings may be commenced for some offences, e.g. in cases involving *official secrets. *See also* ARMY PROSECUTING AUTHORITY; NAVAL PROSECUTING AUTHORITY; REVENUE AND CUSTOMS PROSECUTIONS OFFICE; ROYAL AIR FORCE PROSECUTING AUTHORITY; SPECIFIED OFFENCE; STATUTORY CHARGING SCHEME.

prosecutor The person who institutes and/or conducts criminal proceedings on behalf of the *Crown. *See also* CROWN PROSECUTOR; PROSECUTION; REVENUE AND CUSTOMS PROSECUTOR.

prosecutor's statement *See* STATEMENT OF INFORMATION.

prospectus A *document inviting the public to invest in *shares or debentures of a *public company (*see* FLOTATION). The prospectus of a *listed company (called the **listing particulars**) must contain the information required by the *Stock Exchange; the prospectus of an unlisted company must comply with the Financial Services Act 1986.

prostitute '[A] person who on at least one occasion and whether or not compelled to do so, offers or provides sexual services to another person in return for payment or a promise of payment', as defined by the Sexual Offences Act 2003. Prostitution itself is not a crime, but various activities related to it are (*see* BROTHEL; CAUSING OR INCITING OR CONTROLLING PROSTITUTION; COMMON PROSTITUTE; KERB CRAWLING; SOLICITING).

protected emblems The emblems of the Red Cross, Red Crescent, and Red Lion and Sun give those authorized to bear them protection against attack in international and non-international armed conflicts. It is a *war crime under the Statute of the *International Criminal Court to attack the bearer of a protected emblem. Those entitled to bear the symbol are medical personnel and orderlies, chaplains, Red Cross and Red Crescent workers, *employees of aid organizations of neutral states. Emblems also protect buildings, vehicles, *ships, and aircraft used for medical purposes.

It is a summary offence under the Geneva Convention Act 1957 to use a red cross emblem unless authorized or on a toy when the emblem must be not more than 1.5 inches across.

protected goods (under the Consumer Credit Act 1974) *Goods that are the subject matter of a regulated *hire purchase or *conditional sale agreement of which the *debtor is in breach, but under which he has already paid to the *creditor one-third or more of the total price of the goods, which remain in the ownership of the creditor. The creditor may not recover possession of the goods except on an order of the court, which may allow the debtor further time to pay. The restriction does not apply if the debtor has terminated the agreement.

protected person A head of state (or a member of a corporate head of state), head of government, or minister for foreign affairs, or any member of his family accompanying him; or a representative or official of a state or of an intergovernmental international organization who is entitled under *international law to special protection from personal injury or any member of his family who is also a member of his household. The Internationally Protected Persons Act 1978 incorporates into English law the provisions of the 1974 New York Convention on Crimes against Internationally Protected Persons. The Act gives jurisdiction to English courts to try those charged with committing certain serious acts against protected persons (e.g. *rape, *assault, causing *actual bodily harm, *wounding or inflicting *grievous bodily harm, *kidnapping, and certain attacks on *premises), even if the alleged acts were committed outside the UK. It also creates offences of threatening to commit any of the above acts anywhere in the world, and extends *jurisdiction to various types of attempts and assistance. It is no defence to any of these offences that the defendant did not know that the victim was a protected person.

protected state A state that, although nominally sovereign, is under the protection of another state. Usually the protected state allows the protector full control over its external affairs but retains control over its internal affairs. Examples are the Kingdom of Bhutan under the protection of India and the State of Brunei under British protection. A protected state is sometimes called a **protectorate**.

protocol 1. The original draft of a *document. **2.** An international agreement of a less formal nature than a *treaty. It is often used to amend treaties. It may also be an instrument subsidiary or ancillary to a *convention, in which case it may deal with points of interpretation and reservations. **3.** A code of procedure. **4.** Minutes of a meeting setting out matters of agreement.

provisional liquidator A person appointed by the court to conduct the *compulsory winding-up of a company pending the appointment of a *liquidator. Either the *official receiver or a qualified *insolvency practitioner may be appointed.

proviso 1. A clause in a statute, *deed, or other legal *document introducing a qualification or condition to some other provision, frequently the one immediately preceding the proviso itself. **2.** Prior to the substitution of s 2(1) of the Criminal Appeal Act 1968 by the Criminal Appeal Act 1995, the section provided that the court should allow an *appeal if it thought that (a) the *conviction was unsafe or unsatisfactory, (b) that the *judgment of the court of *trial should be set aside on the ground of a wrong decision of any question of law, or (c) that there had been a material irregularity in the course of the trial, provided that the court could dismiss the appeal, notwithstanding that it was of the opinion that the point raised might be decided in favour of the appellant, if it was satisfied that no miscarriage of justice had occurred (known as '**applying the proviso**'). There is now a single basis for allowing an appeal, namely that the court thinks that the conviction is unsafe. However, the law in this area is presently under review.

provocation Conduct or words causing someone to lose his self-control. Provocation is not recognized as a *general defence to a criminal charge in English law, though what otherwise would have been *murder may be reduced to *manslaughter if provocation is shown (it is not, however, a defence to a charge of attempted murder).

The test for provocation is whether the acts or words involved did in fact make the defendant lose his self-control, and if so, whether they would also have made a reasonable man in the defendant's position do the same. This is a question of fact for the jury to decide in each case. Since *Attorney-General for Jersey v Holley* [2005] 2 AC 580, a reasonable man for these purposes must be a person of the same sex and age as the defendant. Other characteristics of the defendant may only be taken in consideration in deciding the gravity of the provocation.

pseudo-photograph *See* INDECENT PHOTOGRAPHS OF CHILDREN.

psychopathic disorder (for the purposes of the Mental Health Act 1983) A form of *mental disorder consisting of a persistent disorder or disability of mind (which may or may not include significant impairment of intelligence) that results in abnormally aggressive or seriously irresponsible conduct and requires, or is susceptible to, medical treatment.

psychopathology Abnormal psychology.

psychosis A mental illness or disorder in which the sufferer may suffer from delusions, hallucinations, disorganized speech, or catatonia. There is considerable dispute as to whether people suffering from psychoses are more or less likely to commit crime.

psychotropic drugs *Drugs that produce mind-altering effects that may appear to be *psychosis. These drugs include *lysergic acid diethylamide, 'angel dust', and psilocin. These drugs are not addictive but produce mental disturbance, and the user may suffer from 'flashbacks' some time after the initial taking.

public Act *See* ACT OF PARLIAMENT.

publication 1. (in the law of *defamation) The communication of defamatory words to a person or persons other than the one defamed. In the English law of *tort, publication to at least one other person must be proved. Communication between husband and wife does not amount to publication, but communication by the defendant to the spouse of the claimant is sufficient. Dictation of a defamatory statement to a secretary or typist is publication. Publication to persons other than the one defamed is not required in Scottish law or in criminal *libel. **2.** (in *copyright law) The issuing of reproductions of a work or edition to the public. Protection under the Copyright, Designs and Patents Act 1988 may depend on whether the work has been published. *See also* OBSCENE PUBLICATIONS.

public body Any body, corporate or otherwise, that performs its duties and exercises its powers for the public benefit, as opposed to private gain. Under the Local Government Act 1972, public bodies include *local authorities, *trustees, commissioners, and those who have duties to provide cemeteries and markets and act for the improvement of any place, or who have powers to issue or levy *precepts.

public company A type of *registered company that can offer its *shares to the public (*compare* PRIVATE COMPANY). Its *memorandum of association must state that it is a public company, that its name ends with the words 'public limited company' (or plc), and that its *authorized capital is at least the authorized minimum (£50000). It cannot do business until it has allotted shares with a nominal value corresponding with the authorized minimum. It cannot allot shares except upon payment of one-quarter of their nominal value plus any *share premium. £12500 is therefore its minimum capital. It thus may not have much wealth or substance, although many assume the contrary. Under the Companies Act 1985 an *undertaking to do work or perform services is not an acceptable *consideration for shares in a public company, and other non-cash considerations are subject to independent valuation and must be transferred to the company within five years of allotment. *See also* FLOTATION; STOCK EXCHANGE.

public corporation A body established to perform a public function, frequently commercial but not necessarily so (it may be social, advisory, or of any other character). Thus bodies established to manage nationalized industries are public corporations, as are such bodies as English

Nature. A public corporation is normally a **statutory corporation**, i.e. established by *Act of Parliament; exceptions include the British Broadcasting Corporation, which was established by royal charter.

Public Defender Service (PDS) A component part of the *Criminal Defence Service, with offices in Birmingham, Liverpool, Middlesbrough, Swansea, Cheltenham, Chester, Darlington, and Pontypridd. Its stated objectives are to provide legal advice and representation to individuals under investigation or charged with criminal offences; facilitate the fair, efficient, and effective operation of the *Criminal Justice System (CJS) and influence positive improvements in it; and to help individuals address the causes of their offending behaviour and reduce that offending through effective links with other CJS initiatives and the *Community Legal Service. *See also* LEGAL AID.

public document A *document concerned with a public matter, made under a public duty to inquire into all the circumstances recorded and meant for public inspection. Statements in public documents are admissible as an exception to the general rule against *hearsay evidence.

public duties The official duties of certain public officers, including *magistrates, councillors, school and college governors, and members of health authorities. Under s 50 of the Employment Rights Act 1996, officers are entitled to time off work to fulfil their official duties. An *employee entitled to time off work for public duties does not have a statutory right to be paid for his periods of absence.

public examination (in *bankruptcy proceedings) An investigation into the conduct, dealings, and property of a *debtor. It takes place in a court and the debtor is compelled to attend and answer questions on *oath. The *official receiver has a discretion whether or not to apply to the court for a public examination after a bankruptcy order is made. He must apply (unless the court directs otherwise) if the *creditors request it.

public good A special *defence to some *charges under the Obscene Publications Act. *See* OBSCENE PUBLICATIONS.

public house A *premises *licensed for the sale of *alcohol under the Licensing Act 2003.

public interest immunity The law governing the protection of information, which, if disclosed, would damage the public interest (formerly *Crown privilege). In *R v Chief Constable of West Midlands, ex p Wiley* [1994] 3 WLR 433 it was defined thus: 'public interest immunity is a ground for refusing to disclose a *document which is relevant and material to the determination of issues involved in civil or criminal proceedings. A claim to public interest immunity can only be justified if the public interest in preserving the confidentiality of the document outweighs the public interest in securing justice'.

In cases where unused sensitive material is identified as meeting the test for disclosure (*see* DISCLOSURE OF UNUSED MATERIAL) and disclosure of that material would create a real risk of serious prejudice to an important public interest, then, under ss 3 (6), 7A(8), or 8(5) of the Criminal Procedure and Investigations Act 1996, the *prosecution may apply to the court for an order that the material be withheld on public interest grounds. Common examples of instances where such applications are made are to protect the identity of an informant (see *R v Turner* [1995] 1 WLR 264) or the location of an observation point (see *R v Johnson* [1988] 1 WLR 1377). Rule 25(1) of the *Criminal Procedure Rules provides that, wherever possible, the prosecution should notify the *defence that it is making such an application and the nature of the material to which the application relates. The defence may then attend the hearing and make representations (the **inter partes* procedure). However, where the *prosecutor has reason to believe that to reveal to the accused the nature of the material to which the application relates would have the effect of disclosing that which the prosecutor contends should not in the public interest be disclosed, the prosecutor need only notify the defence that an application to which this rule applies has been made. The defence is not permitted to be present at the hearing of the application (the *ex parte* with notice procedure). In exceptional cases where the prosecutor has reason to believe that to reveal to the accused the fact that an application is being made would have the effect of disclosing that which the prosecutor contends should not in the public interest be disclosed, the application may be brought without notifying the defence (the *ex parte* without notice procedure). *See also* SPECIAL ADVOCATE.

public law The part of the law that deals with the constitution and functions of the organs of central and local government, the relationship between individuals and the state, and relationships between individuals that are of direct concern to the state. It includes constitutional law, administrative law, tax law, and criminal law. *Compare* PRIVATE LAW.

public limited company (PLC) *See* LIMITED COMPANY; PUBLIC COMPANY.

public morals *See* CORRUPTION OF PUBLIC MORALS.

public nuisance *See* NUISANCE.

public place A place to which the public has access. The main offences relating to public places are: (1) being found drunk or being drunk and disorderly in a public place; (2) carrying a *firearm, *offensive weapon, or bladed article in a public place; (3) *soliciting in a public place; and (4) displaying support for a *proscribed organization in a public place. *See also* OFFENCE AGAINST PUBLIC ORDER.

public policy The interests of the community. If a contract is (on *common-law principles) contrary to public policy, this will normally make it an *illegal contract.

Pubwatch A community based crime prevention scheme organized by pub *licensees to afford each other confidence and support, as well as some form of protection. The scheme is a message-passing link between licensees, the object of which is to combat violence and other criminal conduct. It also provides better communication between licensees and police and provides a forum for the discussion and solution of problems relating to violence on *licensed premises.

pugilistic attitude When a body has been in fire or other extreme heat the muscles contract and the arms take on the appearance of the stance of a boxer.

puisne [from Old French *puisné*: later born] Inferior; of lesser rank.

puisne judge Any ordinary *judge of the *High Court. Puisne judges are referred to as (for example) 'Mr Justice Smith', even though they are knighted upon appointment. They must be *barristers of at least ten years' standing.

pulmonary Relating to the lungs.

pulmonary embolism The blocking of a blood vessel in the lungs by a blood clot that has often moved from the legs. A frequent cause of sudden death.

punishment A *penalty imposed on a defendant duly convicted of a crime by an authorized court. The *European Convention on Human Rights (signed 1950) forbids the use of 'inhuman or degrading' punishment; this prohibition is now part of UK law as a consequence of the *Human Rights Act 1998 (*see* DEGRADING TREATMENT OR PUNISHMENT; INHUMAN TREATMENT OR PUNISHMENT). Similarly, the prohibition on the use of **arbitrary punishment**, as set out in Article 7 of the Convention, is now incorporated into the 1998 Act. This provision makes unlawful the use of criminal penalties that are not prescribed by law.

pupa A stage in the development of insects (egg—*larva—pupa—imago). The pupa is the penultimate stage from which the imago (adult) emerges, leaving a hard pupal case. Soon after death insects lay their eggs in the body. By examining the stages reached by insects in the body, including pupae or their cases, a *forensic entomologist can give an indication of post-mortem interval (time since death).

purchaser for value *See* BONA FIDE PURCHASER FOR VALUE.

putative father A man alleged to be the father of an *illegitimate child.

putrefaction Decomposition of a body.

qualified privilege The defence that a statement cannot be made the subject of an action for *defamation because it was made on a privileged occasion and was not made maliciously, for an improper motive. Qualified privilege covers statements made fairly in situations in which there is a legal or moral obligation to give the information and the person to whom it is given has a corresponding duty or interest to receive it and when someone is acting in defence of his own property or reputation. Qualified privilege also covers fair and accurate reports of public meetings and various other public proceedings. The privilege attaching to professional communications between solicitor and client is probably qualified, rather than absolute. *Compare* ABSOLUTE PRIVILEGE.

qualified right A right set out in the *European Convention on Human Rights that will only be violated if the interference with it is not proportionate (*see* PROPORTIONALITY). An interference with a qualified right that is not proportionate to the *legitimate aim being pursued will not be lawful. *Compare* ABSOLUTE RIGHT.

qualifying distribution Formerly, a distribution of profits by a company on which *advance corporation tax had to be paid.

quango A quasi-autonomous non-governmental organization: a body appointed wholly or partly by the government (but not constituting a department of government) to perform some public function, normally administrative or advisory and frequently involving the distribution of public moneys.

quantum (of damages) The amount of money awarded by way of *damages.

quarantine A period of isolation of people or animals that have been in contact with a communicable disease. The period was originally 40 days (hence the name, which is derived from the Italian *quarantina*), but is now approximately the incubation period of the suspected disease. Quarantine is imposed, for example, by public health regulations relating to ships and aircraft or by orders made under the Animal Health Act 1981 and the Rabies (Importation of Dogs, Cats and other Mammals) Order 1974 (SI 1974/2211), as amended.

quarter sessions Originally, a *court of record with quarterly meetings of the *justices of the peace for a county. City and borough quarter sessions were presided over by the *Recorder sitting alone. In modern times quarter sessions became a court for the *trial of offences triable on *indictment, other than those that had to be tried at *assizes. Quarter sessions were abolished by the Courts Act 1971 and their jurisdiction is now exercised by the *Crown Court.

quash To invalidate a *conviction made in an inferior court or to set aside a decision subject to *judicial review. *See also* QUASHING ORDER.

quashing order A discretionary remedy, obtained by an application for *judicial review, in which the *High Court orders decisions of inferior courts, tribunals, and administrative authorities to be brought before it and quashes them if they are **ultra vires* or show an *error on the face of the record. The claimant must apply for it within three months. As it is discretionary, a quashing order may be refused if alternative remedies exist. Originally called *certiorari*, it was renamed in 1999 under pt 54 of the *Civil Procedure Rules.

quasi-easement A right in the nature of an *easement enjoyed over a plot of *land for the benefit of another plot owned by the same person: it would be an easement if the two plots of land were owned and occupied by different persons.

quasi-judicial Describing a function that resembles the judicial function in that it involves deciding a dispute and ascertaining the facts and any relevant law, but differs in that it depends ultimately on the exercise of an executive discretion rather than the application of law.

queen 1. The sovereign if female (*see* CROWN). **2.** The wife of the sovereign (**queen consort**). **3.** The widow of a sovereign (**queen dowager**).

Queen By the Royal Titles Act 1953, 'Elizabeth II by the Grace of God of the United Kingdom of Great Britain and Northern Ireland and of Her other Realms and Territories Queen, Head of the Commonwealth, Defender of the Faith'. The Act empowers Her Majesty to adopt by proclamation such other style and titles as she may think fit. *See also* CROWN.

Queen's Bench Division (QBD) The division of the *High Court of Justice whose principal business is the *trial of civil actions based upon contract or *tort. It also has important appellate functions in relation to *appeals from *magistrates' courts on points of law and from certain tribunals, and exercises supervisory jurisdiction over all inferior courts. The Admiralty Court and Commercial Court are part of the QBD.

Queen's Bench Master *See* MASTER OF THE SUPREME COURT.

Queen's Counsel (QC) A senior *barrister of at least ten years' practice who has received a patent as 'one of Her Majesty's counsel learned in the law'. Recommendations for appointment are made by the Independent Selection Panel, which includes a substantial lay membership and a retired senior judge. Their recommendations are passed to the Secretary of State for Constitutional Affairs and *Lord Chancellor who put the recommendations to the Queen. The Lord Chancellor has no power to veto or add names. In court they sit within the bar and wear silk gowns (hence they are also known informally as **silks**). If the monarch is a king these barristers are known as **King's Counsel** (**KC**).

Queen's evidence Evidence given on behalf of the *prosecution by an accused person who has confessed his own guilt and who then acts as a witness against his accomplices. Such evidence is generally considered less reliable than other evidence because the witness is likely to minimize his own role and exaggerate that of his accomplices. If it is not corroborated, the *judge must warn the *jury of the danger of convicting on the basis of this evidence alone. *See also* CORROBORATION.

Queen's Regulations *See* SERVICE LAW.

Queen's Speech (Speech from the Throne) A speech prepared by the Government and read by the *Queen to *Parliament (assembled in the *House of Lords) at the beginning of a parliamentary session. It outlines the Government's principal legislative and policy proposals for the session.

que estate [Norman French: whose estate] A claim to have acquired by *prescription an *easement or *profit *à prendre* by virtue of the continuous use of the right both by the claimant and by those whose estate he has, i.e. those who owned the dominant tenement before him.

questioning of suspects *See* INVESTIGATIVE INTERVIEW; RIGHT OF SILENCE.

quiet enjoyment One of the obligations of a *landlord, which is implied in every *lease unless specifically excluded. It entitles the *tenant to possess and enjoy the *land he leases without interference from the landlord or anyone claiming rights through the landlord.

quorum The minimum number of people who must be present at a meeting in order for business to be transacted. The required number is usually laid down in the *articles of association, constitution, or rules of the company or other body concerned. *See also* GENERAL MEETING.

quotation A listing of a *share price on the *Stock Exchange. A price may be obtained by accessing the **Stock Exchange Automated Quotations System**. A quotation can be cancelled or suspended if the company does not comply with the Rules of the Stock Exchange or if it becomes impossible to rely on market forces to arrive at a price for the securities (e.g. because of inaccurate accounts or manipulation of the market).

R Abbreviation for *Rex* or *Regina* [Latin: King or Queen]. Criminal *prosecutions on *indictment are brought in the name of the *Crown, since a crime is viewed as a wrong against the public at large, or the state, represented by the monarch. Hence the formula *R v Defendant* (the Crown versus the defendant).

racial and religious hatred Hatred against a group of people because of their colour, race, *nationality (including citizenship), or ethnic or national origins (s 17, Public Order Act 1986). Hatred against a religion is thus not directly covered (*see* BLASPHEMY). The definition was extended by s 37 of the Anti-terrorism, Crime and Security Act 2001 and now includes hatred directed against a relevant group of persons anywhere in the world. 'Hatred' is not defined by the 1986 Act. It is much stronger than ridicule or contempt; it is not enough to cause offence or to mock a racial group. According to the *Crown Prosecution Service *charging standards, 'hatred' connotes an element of hostility.

The Act contains six offences of stirring up racial hatred, which all require proof of words, behaviour, or material that are threatening, abusive, or insulting; there must be an *intention of stirring up racial hatred or the likelihood that this will happen. All offences are punishable with up to two years' imprisonment and/or a *fine and require the Attorney-General's consent before proceedings can be instituted.

The offences are as follows. (1) s 18—Using *threatening behaviour or words or displaying threatening written material. This offence may be committed in a public or private place, but it is a defence for the accused person to prove (*see* BURDEN OF PROOF) that he was inside a dwelling and had no reason to believe that his behaviour or display would be seen or heard by someone outside that or another dwelling. Even if the intention to stir up racial hatred is not proved, the accused can still be *guilty of the offence if he is proved to have either intended his behaviour or material to be threatening or been aware that it might be so. The offence does not extend to behaviour or written material that is used solely for inclusion in a radio or television programme. (2) s 19—Publishing or distributing to the public threatening written material. It is a *defence for the accused to prove that he was unaware of the material's contents and did not suspect that it was threatening. (3) s 20—Presenting or directing the public performance of a play that involves the use of threatening words or behaviour. The actual performers do not commit or *aid and abet the offence, and recordings or broadcasts of plays can only involve the offence if outsiders attend. It is a defence for the accused to prove that he was unaware and had no reason to suspect that (a) the performance would involve use of the threatening words, or (b) the offending words were threatening, or (c) racial hatred would be likely to be stirred up during the performance. (4) s 21—Distributing, showing, or playing a recording of visual images or sound to the public. It is a defence for the accused to prove that he was unaware of the recording's content and did not, and had no reason to, suspect that it was threatening. (5) s 22—Providing, producing, or directing a radio or television programme involving threatening images or sounds. The offence is limited to broadcasts by satellite, community radio services, cable, pirate stations, and the like; it does not extend to BBC or IBA programmes. It is a defence if the accused can prove either of the following: (a) that he was unaware and had no reason to suspect that the offending material was threatening; or (b) that he was unaware and had no reason to suspect that (i) the programme would involve the offending material and that it was not reasonably practicable for him to remove the material or (ii) the programme would be broadcast or that racial hatred would be likely to be stirred up by it. Defence b(ii) is unavailable to those providing the broadcasting service. A broadcaster who uses the offending words can also commit the offence; defences (a) and b(ii) are available to him. (6) s 23—Possessing threatening written material or a sound or visual recording with a view to its being distributed or broadcast, or (written material only) published, or (a recording only) shown or played. The offence does not extend to the BBC or IBA, and defence (a) above is available. Courts can order *forfeiture of offending material after *conviction.

The Racial and Religious Hatred Act 2006 amended the Public Order Act 1986 by creating new offences of stirring up hatred against persons on religious grounds. Religious hatred is defined (s 29A) as hatred against a group of persons defined by reference to religious belief or lack of religious belief. The offences apply to the use of words or behaviour or display of written material (s 29B), publishing or distributing written material (s 29C), the public performance of a play (s 29D), distributing, showing, or playing a recording (s 29E), broadcasting or including a programme in a programme service (s 29F) and the possession of written materials or recordings with a view to display, publication, distribution, or inclusion in a programme service (s 29G). For each offence the words, behaviour, written material, recordings, or programmes must be threatening and intended to stir up religious hatred. Section 29J provides that the offences of stirring up religious hatred are not intended to limit or restrict discussion, criticism, or expressions of antipathy, dislike, ridicule, or insult or abuse of particular religions or belief systems or lack of religion or of the beliefs and practices of those who hold such beliefs or to apply to proselytization, evangelism, or the seeking to convert people to a particular belief or to cease holding a belief. The offences are triable *either way and carry a maximum sentence of seven years' imprisonment. Proceedings required the consent of the *Attorney-General. Courts can order forfeiture of offending material after conviction.

The Protection from Harassment Act 1997 provides additional remedies for those harassed on racial grounds (*see* HARASSMENT); offenders may receive jail sentences of up to five years. *See also* RACIALLY AND RELIGIOUSLY AGGRAVATED OFFENCE.

racial discrimination *Discrimination on the grounds of colour, race, *nationality, or ethnic origins. It is dealt with by the Race Relations Acts of 1965, 1968, and 1976. The 1965 Act created an offence of *incitement to racial hatred and made racial discrimination illegal in *public places. The 1968 Act prohibits discrimination in respect of *goods, services, facilities, employment, accommodation, and advertisements. The 1976 Act prohibits indirect racial discrimination, as well as discrimination in *clubs with more than 25 members. It also prohibits the types of discrimination dealt with by the 1975 Sex Discrimination Act. The Race Relations (Amendment) Act 2000 extends coverage of the 1976 Act by prohibiting racial discrimination in the functions of the police and other public authorities not previously covered by that Act. It also places a general duty on public authorities to eliminate discrimination and promote racial equality. The *Commission for Racial Equality has the power to conduct formal investigations into complaints. Individual complaints in the field of employment are dealt with by *employment tribunals; other complaints are dealt with in specified *county courts. *See also* RACIAL SEGREGATION.

racial harassment *See* RACIALLY AND RELIGIOUSLY AGGRAVATED OFFENCE; THREATENING BEHAVIOUR.

racialization A process whereby the idea of 'race' is introduced to identify and give meaning to some particular group, its characteristics and actions.

racially and religiously aggravated offence A criminal offence created by ss 29 to 32 of the Crime and Disorder Act 1998. The provisions take a number of *summary or *either way offences and substantially increase the *penalty if at the time of committing the offence or immediately before or after the offender demonstrates towards the victim racial or religious hostility. Religious aggravation was added by the Anti-Terrorism Crime and Security Act 2001. The offences that can be racially or religiously aggravated are: common *assault, assault occasioning *actual bodily harm, unlawful *wounding, *criminal damage, certain Public Order Act 1986 offences, and *harassment.

racial segregation An offence committed in the context of an institutionalized regime of systematic oppression and domination by one racial group over any other racial group or groups. It is a *crime against humanity under the Statute of the *International Criminal Court, which puts into effect *United Nations resolutions on apartheid.

rape At *common law, rape was defined as sexual *penetration of a woman forcibly and against her will. However, the law contained a number of legal and procedural requirements that made the prosecution of rape difficult. Under the utmost resistance doctrine, a man could be found *guilty of rape only if his victim could demonstrate that she had physically attempted to fight off the rape but had been overpowered. A woman who was not physically bruised had little hope of proving a case of rape. If a woman did not promptly complain of a rape, under the fresh complaint rule, seemingly based on the theory that a delayed report was more likely to be fabricated, her case could not be heard. Rape was first enacted as a statutory crime in the Offences Against the Person Act 1861. The Act simply provided that 'it is a felony for a man to rape a woman', leaving the judiciary to establish the elements of the offence and to develop the factors that might vitiate *consent. Its statutory successor, s 1 of the Sexual Offences Act 1956, failed to provide a definition that was any more substantive. It was not until 1976 that s 1(1) of the Sexual Offences (Amendment) Act defined rape as 'unlawful sexual intercourse with a woman who at the time of the intercourse does not consent to it'.

Prior to the Criminal Justice Act 1994, rape could only be committed by penetration of the complainant's *vagina. It followed that only females could be the victims of the offence. Non-consensual anal penetration of either a male or a female (and also unlawful consensual anal penetration) was charged as *buggery, an offence contrary to s 12 of the Sexual Offences Act 1956. Section 142 of the 1994 Act extended the definition of rape to include penetration of the *anus, which meant that both males and females could be the victims of the offence. By removing the word 'unlawful' from the term 'unlawful sexual intercourse', that provision also gave statutory effect to the decision in *R v R* [1993] 1 All ER 747. In that landmark case, an exercise in judicial law-making which was criticised by some jurists at the time, the *House of Lords rejected the common law *fiction that on marriage a wife gave irrevocable consent to sexual relations at any time during the marriage and therefore marital rape was an impossibility, except in very limited circumstances.

Section 1 of the Sexual Offences Act 2003 redefined the offence of rape, extending it to cover non-consensual oral sex with both a male and a female, and the controversial 'defence' of genuine or mistaken belief in consent, however unreasonable, was removed. The offence remains one that can only be committed by a man as it requires penile penetration of the vagina, anus, or mouth. However, a woman can be charged with rape as an accessory. The common law presumption that a boy under the age of 14 is incapable of sexual intercourse was abolished by s 1 of the Sexual Offences Act 1993. It follows that boys under that age (but not under the age of 10: *see* DOLI CAPAX) can be convicted of rape. An unsuccessful rape can be treated as a *sexual assault or as an *assault occasioning bodily harm or causing *grievous bodily harm, depending on the circumstances. The maximum *penalty for rape or attempted rape is *life imprisonment. (*See also* ANONYMITY; ASSAULT BY PENETRATION; CONSENT; DANGEROUS OFFENDERS; SEXUAL OFFENCES.)

ratification 1. (in *international law) The approval of a *treaty, usually by the head of state (or by the head of state and *legislature). This takes place when *documents of ratification are either exchanged or deposited with a named depositary. Normally a treaty states expressly whether it will bind a party as soon as it is signed by that party's representative or whether it requires ratification. The Vienna Convention on Treaties (1969) provides that when a treaty does not specify whether or not ratification is required, reference will be made to the party's intention. Performance of a treaty may amount to implicit ratification. **2.** (in company law) A resolution of a *general meeting sanctioning some irregularity in the running of a company. Some irregularities cannot be sanctioned, such as acts that are **ultra vires* or a *fraud on the minority.

ratio decidendi [Latin: the reason for deciding] The principle or principles of law on which the court reaches its decision. The *ratio* of the case has to be deduced from its *facts, the reasons the court gave for reaching its decision, and the decision itself. It is said to be the statement of law applied to the material facts. Only the *ratio* of a case is binding on inferior courts, by reason of the doctrine of *precedent.

rational choice theory A theory in criminology which holds that offenders make rational decisions to seek advantage for themselves by criminal behaviour.

rave An assembly, unlicensed by the *local authority, of 100 or more people, partly or entirely in the open air, at which amplified music is played during the night, and which is likely to cause serious distress to local inhabitants. Under s 63 of the Criminal Justice and Public Order Act 1994, a *police officer of at least the rank of superintendent may issue directions to participants to leave if it is reasonably believed that two or more people are preparing for a rave or ten or more people are waiting for one to start or are already participating in an event that will attract 100 or more participants. A *summary offence is committed by anyone (excluding the occupier, a member of his family, and an *employee or agent) who fails to leave as soon as reasonably practicable or who re-enters within seven days; it is punishable by up to three months' imprisonment and/or a *fine at level 4. He may also stop and turn back within five miles of a rave anyone whom he believes to be travelling to the rave. Failure to comply is a summary offence punishable by a fine at level 3.

There are supplementary powers of entry for the purpose of clearing the *land and seizing and removing vehicles and sound equipment. Any sound equipment under the control of a person convicted under these provisions may be made the subject of a *forfeiture order.

real 1. Relating to *land. *See also* REAL PROPERTY. **2.** Relating to a thing, rather than to a person. *See also* REAL EVIDENCE.

real evidence Evidence in the form of material objects (e.g. weapons). When an object is admitted in evidence, it is usually marked as an *exhibit. *Documents are not usually classified as real evidence, but may be treated as such if the physical characteristics of the document (rather than its content) are of significance (*see also* COMPUTER DOCUMENTS). Some authorities include *evidence of identification and the demeanour of witnesses within the classification of real evidence.

realist criminology Modern theories of criminology of the left and right which, from their own perspectives, seek pragmatic policies for crime reduction rather than utopian solutions.

real property (realty) *Land and incorporeal *hereditaments. *See* PROPERTY.

realty *See* REAL PROPERTY.

reasonable doubt *See* PROOF BEYOND REASONABLE DOUBT.

reasonable force At *common law a person may use reasonable force in *self-defence and, in extreme circumstances, may be justified in killing an attacker. Reasonable force may be used in defending one's *property, and if someone intrudes on one's property at night, one might be justified in treating this as a threat not merely to property, but to personal safety. An *occupier of *premises (even if he is not the owner) and possibly even a *licensee (such as a lodger) may use reasonable force against a *trespasser. Section 3 of the Criminal Law Act 1967 permits the use of reasonable force in order to prevent crime, to lawfully arrest a criminal or suspected criminal (or to help in arresting him), or to capture someone who has escaped from lawful detention. The Act extends to both police and private citizens. *See also* FORCIBLE ENTRY; MISTAKE.

reasonable man An ordinary citizen, sometimes referred to as 'the man on the Clapham omnibus'. The standard of care in actions for *negligence is based on what a reasonable person might be expected to do considering the circumstances and the foreseeable consequences. The standard is not entirely uniform: a lower standard is expected of a child, but a higher standard is expected of someone, such as a doctor, who purports to possess a special skill.

rebuttable presumption *See* PRESUMPTION.

recall of witness The further examination of a witness after his evidence has been completed. The court may permit the recall of a witness even after the close of a party's case to allow *evidence in rebuttal or to remedy an omission in the party's case: *Malcolm v DPP* [2007] EWHC 363.

recaption The retaking of *goods that have been wrongfully taken or are being wrongfully withheld. It is a form of *self-help.

receiver 1. One who receives stolen *goods. *See* HANDLING STOLEN GOODS. **2.** A person appointed under the terms of a debenture or by the court to realize assets charged and apply the proceeds for the benefit of those entitled. Notice of appointment must be given to the *Companies Registry and must appear upon business *documents. The receiver may have power to manage the company. *See also* ADMINISTRATIVE RECEIVER; OFFICIAL RECEIVER. **3.** Of a *rifle, the metal housing to which the *barrel is attached and in which the *bolt mechanism, the *magazine, and the *trigger assembly are contained. Also, the frame of an *automatic or *semi-automatic pistol.

recent complaint At common law, evidence that the victim of a sexual offence made a voluntary complaint at the first reasonable opportunity was admissible (as an exception to the rule against *hearsay) as evidence of the consistency of the victim's conduct with the account given by her in court. The common law rule has now been superceded by s 120 of the Criminal Justice Act 2003, which extends the 'recent complaint' exception to any offence and provides that such evidence may be admitted not just to show consistency but also as evidence of the facts stated.

recent possession, doctrine of The 'doctrine of recent possession' is a misnomer as it is not a doctrine and does not refer to recent possession—it refers to *possession of *property that has been recently stolen. The 'doctrine' is simply part of the principles of *circumstantial evidence. It applies only to offences of *handling stolen goods and is relevant to proving the **mens rea* of the offence. The 'doctrine' was explained in the case of *R v Abramovitch* [1914–15] All ER 204 and lays down that when a person charged with handling stolen goods is found in possession of, or dealing with, goods that have recently been stolen, a *jury may infer that he is *guilty if he offers no explanation of his possession or they do not believe the explanation given. The jury is not bound to draw such an inference and must only do so if they are satisfied that he has committed the offence charged.

recidivism The habit of repeated offending.

reciprocity The principle that one will treat someone in a particular way if one is so treated by them. This is relevant under *European Union law in relation to agreements that the EU has with non-EU countries, particularly in relation to public procurement and free trade.

recklessness A form of **mens rea* that amounts to less than *intention but more than *negligence. Many *common-law offences can be committed either intentionally or recklessly, and it is now common for statutes to create offences of recklessness. Recklessness has generally been held to have a subjective meaning of being aware of the risk of a particular

r

consequence arising from one's actions but deciding nonetheless to continue with one's actions and take the risk.

recognizance An *undertaking by an offender (or by *sureties on his behalf) to forfeit a sum of money under certain conditions. Where the recognizance is taken to ensure the attendance of a defendant at a criminal court a recognizance can only be taken from a surety and not from the defendant. Recognizances may be entered into to answer to *judgment, i.e. to appear before the court for pronouncement of judgment on a specified date. This procedure may be appropriate if the accused wishes to *appeal against *conviction. Alternatively, recognizances may be used in addition to or in place of any other *sentence or judgment, the offender being obligated to keep the peace and be of good behaviour. *See* BREACH OF THE PEACE; BIND OVER.

recommendation for deportation on conviction A recommendation by a court that a convicted offender should be *deported. The power of the *Home Secretary to deport a convicted person is conferred by s 3(6) of the Immigration Act 1971. A person can be deported where he has been convicted of an offence punishable with imprisonment (whether or not he is actually sentenced to imprisonment), has attained the age of 17 years before the date of *conviction, and is not a *British citizen. Exemptions apply in certain circumstances to citizens of *Commonwealth countries or the Republic of Ireland who are resident in the UK, and to diplomatic personnel and their families (ss 7 and 8 of the Act). On the coming into force (on 30 April 2006) of the Immigration (European Economic Area) Regulations 2006 SI 2006/1003) and the consequent implementation of EU Directive 2004/38, nationals of EU member states (other than those of Norway, Iceland, Liechtenstein, and Switzerland and dependent on their particular circumstances) have certain rights of residence in the UK. Nonetheless, such a person can be deported if the Home Secretary decides that his removal is justified on the grounds of public security, provided that the decision is 'proportionate'.

The power of the court to recommend deportation is conferred by s 6(1) of the Act. Such a recommendation can only be made if the defendant has been served with a 'Notice as Regards Liability to Deportation' (Form IM3) at least seven days beforehand, although the court can adjourn the case to allow the notice to be given or the seven days to elapse (s 6(2) and (4)). The recommendation can be combined with any other *sentence, including *life imprisonment (s 6(4)).

When considering whether to make a recommendation for deportation, the question that must be asked by the court is 'whether the continued presence of the offender is to the detriment of this country'; i.e. whether it is in the public interest for him to be deported. One serious offence is liable to lead to the conclusion that continued presence is detrimental. A less serious offence may also justify a recommendation when combined with a likelihood of reoffending, whether demonstrated by previous convictions or other cogent material. Although, apparently, the Home Secretary applies an unpublished rule of thumb to the effect that he will not normally order deportation of a non-EU national where the sentence is less than one year's imprisonment, or two years in the case of an EU national; nonetheless, the court may recommend deportation if satisfied that the continued presence of the person in the UK is against the public interest, but should be cautious when doing so (*R v Carmona* [2006] 1 WLR 2264).

Since the order of the court is merely a recommendation, and not a decision to deport, the court does not have to take account of the person's rights under Articles 2 (*right to life), 3 (prohibition on *torture), and 8 (right to respect for *family life) of the *European Convention on Human Rights, or the rights of anyone else. In particular, the conditions and the regime in the country to which the person would be deported, and any effect on his family or dependents, are not relevant considerations for the court. They are matters for the Home Secretary to take into account when deciding whether to act on the recommendation.

record The *documents constituting an authentic account of the proceedings before a court, including the *claim form or other originating process, the statements of case, and the *judgment or order, but usually not the evidence tendered.

recordable offence An offence specified in the National Police Records (Recordable Offences) Regulations 2000 (SI 2000/1139) (as amended). In addition to the offences specified in the Regulations, any offence which is punishable with imprisonment in the case of an adult is a recordable offence. The offences specified by Regulations as at 1 September 2006 are listed at **Appendix 2**.

recorder 1. A *barrister or *solicitor appointed as a part-time *judge. **2.** Formerly, a member of the *Bar appointed to preside at City or borough *quarter sessions.

Recovered Assets Incentivization Fund (RAIF) A fund set up by the Government in 2004 to incentivize asset recovery by relevant law enforcement agencies and prosecuting authorities and to fund multi-agency *Regional Asset Recovery Teams. From 2006–07 a new incentive scheme will operate under which all agencies involved in asset recovery will get back 50 per cent of the assets they recover.

recovered memory A controversial subject surrounding memory of events, often from childhood, including such traumatic events as *child abuse. Most of the memories are retrieved during psychotherapy. There are strong arguments against the reliability of such memories. *See also* FALSE-MEMORY PARADIGM.

recovery of premises The right to regain *possession of *property from which one has been unlawfully dispossessed (*see* FORCIBLE ENTRY) or the right of a court officer to enforce a *judgment for this. It is a *summary offence, punishable by up to six months' imprisonment and/or a *fine at level 5 on the standard scale, to resist or intentionally obstruct a court officer in the process of enforcing such a judgment, whether or not one knows that he is a court officer. There is, however, a specific *defence if one can show that one believed that he was not a court officer. This offence covers most action taken by *squatters to resist *eviction, such as physical *assaults, boarding up doors, or merely refusing to leave.

Red Crescent *See* PROTECTED EMBLEMS.

Red Cross *See* PROTECTED EMBLEMS.

Red Lion and Red Sun *See* PROTECTED EMBLEMS.

re-examination The questioning of a witness by the *party who originally called him to testify, following the *cross-examination of the witness by the opposite party. *Leading questions may not be asked in re-examination. Re-examination must be confined to matters arising out of the cross-examination; new matter may only be introduced with the permission of the *judge.

reference The referral by a court of a case (or an issue arising in a case) to a higher court.

refreshing memory A procedure in which a witness may, while testifying, remind himself of events that he has forgotten by referring to a *document that was made at the same time as the occurrence of the events in question and was accepted as accurate by the witness while the facts were fresh in his memory. At *common law the document itself did not become evidence in the case, but it is now admissible in civil and criminal cases.

refuse disposal *See* POLLUTION.

Regional Asset Recovery Teams (RART) Teams brought about as a product of the Government's *Assets Recovery Strategy to disrupt organized crime groups, confiscate more criminal assets, and tackle *money laundering. Five teams have been formed (West Midlands, North West, North East, London, and Wales), made up from officers and staff seconded from various *police forces, *Her Majesty's Revenue and Customs, the *Assets Recovery Agency, *Crown Prosecution Service, and *Serious Organized Crime Agency. They are funded from the *Recovered Assets Incentivization Fund.

registered (in relation to *motor vehicles) The fact of being registered under any of the following enactments: (a) the Roads Act 1920, (b) the Vehicles (Excise) Act 1949, (c) the Vehicles (Excise) Act

1962, or (d) the 1971 Act and, in relation to the date on which a vehicle was registered, the date on which it was first registered under any of those enactments (reg 3(2), Road Vehicles (Construction and Use) Regulations 1986 (SI 1986/1078)).

registered company A company incorporated by registration under the Companies Act 1985 (*see* REGISTRATION OF A COMPANY). There are several types of registered company (*see* LIMITED COMPANY; PRIVATE COMPANY; PUBLIC COMPANY; UNLIMITED COMPANY).

registered design A design registered at the Designs Registry, which is part of the Patent Office (*see* PATENT). Registration gives monopoly rights over the outward appearance of an article, including its shape, configuration, pattern, or ornament, but not over the underlying idea. Works of sculpture, wall plaques, medals, and printed matter primarily of a literary or artistic character cannot be registered. *See* DESIGN RIGHT.

registered office The official address of a *registered company. It must be notified to the *Companies Registry before *registration of the company and it must appear on company letter-heads and order forms. *Documents may be served to a company's registered office and various registers and records may be inspected there.

register of members A record of the names, addresses, and shareholdings of members of a *registered company, which is kept at the *registered office or wherever it is compiled. The register must be kept open for public inspection (members free) for at least two hours daily; it may not be closed for longer than 30 days in any year.

registrar 1. An official responsible for compiling and keeping a register, e.g. the Registrar of Companies. The office of Registrar of the *Chancery Division of the *High Court has now been abolished. **2.** (in the *Court of Appeal) The officer (Registrar of Civil Appeals) responsible for superintending the pre-hearing stages of *appeals in the Civil Division of the court. **3.** (district registrar) *See* DISTRICT JUDGE.

registration as citizen or subject A method by which minors can, either by right or at the Secretary of State's discretion, acquire *British citizenship. *See also* NATURALIZATION.

registration of a company The most usual method of forming an incorporated company (*see* INCORPORATION). Under the Companies Act 1985 the following *documents must be delivered with the appropriate fee to the *Companies Registry: the *memorandum of association signed by at least two *company members, *articles of association (if any), statements relating to the *directors, secretary, and the *registered office, and a statutory declaration that the Companies Act has been complied with. The Registrar will then enter the company's name in the *companies register and issue a *certificate of incorporation.

registration of birth The recording of a birth by a Registrar of Births and Deaths under the Births and Deaths Registration Act 1953. Information for this purpose must be supplied to him within 42 days of the birth by a *parent of the child, the *occupier of the *premises in which the birth takes place, a person present at the birth, or a person having charge of the child. The informant must supply details of the date and place of birth, the name and sex of the child, and its parentage, which are entered on the **birth certificate**; an unmarried father's name may be included on the birth certificate in certain circumstances. A birth certificate may be obtained from the Registrar, the Superintendent Registrar, or the General Register Office; a short form of the certificate, relating to the child's name, sex, and date of birth but not parentage, may also be obtained (*see* ILLEGITIMACY). Children may consult the birth register to discover who their registered parents are and adopted children over the age of 18 have a right to see their original birth certificate.

registration of death The recording of a death by the Registrar of Births and Deaths under the Births and Deaths Registration Act 1953. This must take place within five days of the death or, if written notice of the death is given to the Registrar within that period, within 14 days. It may be effected by any relative of the deceased present at the death or during the last illness, by any other relative, by any person present at the death, or by the *occupier or any inmate of the *premises on which the death occurred. The informant must supply details of the date and place of death, the name, sex, address, and occupation of the deceased, and the cause of death. A **death certificate** may be obtained from the Registrar, the Superintendent Registrar, or the General Register Office.

registration of marriage The official recording of details relating to a marriage after it has been solemnized. (It is not to be confused with registration of notice of an intended marriage.) The details usually registered include the names, ages, occupations, and addresses of the parties, names and occupations of their fathers, and place of solemnization of the marriage. Certified copies of the details may be issued on request.

regular forces Generally, the armed forces of the *Crown other than *reserve forces or auxiliary forces.

regulated agreement Any *consumer-credit agreement or *consumer-hire agreement under the Consumer Credit Act 1974, other than one specifically exempted by the Act. Exempted agreements include *debtor-creditor-supplier agreements secured by a *land mortgage, in which the *creditor is a *local authority or building society who finances the purchase of that land or the provision of dwellings on the land, and *debtor-creditor agreements secured by a land mortgage. The Act also enables the Secretary of State to exempt other consumer-credit agreements in which the number of payments to be made by the debtor does not exceed a specified number, the rate of the total charge for credit does not exceed a specified rate, or the agreement has a connection with a country outside the UK.

regulated entertainment An activity that requires a *licence under the Licensing Act 2003. It is defined as: plays and films; indoor sport, boxing, and wrestling; live and recorded music; or dancing. Normal pub games, such as darts, are not covered because they are not provided for the entertainment of an audience, merely for the private enjoyment of the participants. The Act also exempts video advertising, incidental music, TV broadcasts, church services, garden fetes, private parties, Morris dancing, spontaneous events, and moving vehicles.

regulations of the EU *See* COMMUNITY LEGISLATION.

regulatory agency Any of the non-ministerial government departments with statutory duties of control over privatized industries.

rehabilitation *See* PUNISHMENT; SPENT CONVICTION.

rehearing 1. A second hearing of a case already adjudicated upon, e.g. an *appeal to the *Crown Court from *conviction by a *magistrates' court. All the evidence is heard again and either side may introduce fresh evidence without leave. **2.** The hearing of an *appeal by the *Court of Appeal, in which the Court will consider all the evidence presented to the *trial court (if it is relevant to the appeal) by reading the verbatim transcript of the trial; it will not usually permit fresh evidence to be given. The Court of Appeal will usually not disturb the trial judge's findings on *primary facts, as opposed to the inferences to be drawn from those facts.

rejection of offer The refusal of an offer by the offeree. Once an offer has been rejected, it cannot subsequently be accepted by the offeree. A counter-offer ranks as a rejection, but a mere inquiry as to the possibility of varying some term does not.

release The freeing of a person formerly detained, either upon *discharge when sentencing him or at the end of a prison *sentence.

release on licence *See* PAROLE.

relevance (relevancy) (in the law of evidence) The relationship between two facts that renders one probable from the existence of the other, either taken by itself or in connection with other facts. Although most relevant facts are admissible in evidence, relevance is not the same as *admissibility, since even relevant evidence must be excluded if it falls within one of the *exclusionary rules. If no exclusionary rule is involved, all facts that have logical relevance to a fact in issue may be proved even though they are not in issue themselves.

relevant evidence *See* RELEVANCE.

relevant facts *See* RELEVANCE.

relief *See* REMEDY.

remand To commit an accused person to *custody or release him on *bail during an *adjournment.

remedy (redress, relief) Any of the methods available at law for the enforcement, protection, or recovery of rights or for obtaining redress for their infringement. A **civil remedy** may be granted by a court to a party to a civil action.

remission Cancellation of part of a prison *sentence. Formerly, a prisoner could earn remission of one-third of his sentence by *good behaviour in prison and was released upon remission without any conditions. However, a prisoner serving an *extended sentence, or a prisoner serving more than 18 months' imprisonment, who was under the age of 21 when sentenced, could only be released on licence (*see* PAROLE). Remission of a sentence for good conduct was abolished by the Criminal Justice Act 1991, which specifies the conditions now required for the early release of prisoners.

reparation order An order imposed by the court (under ss 73 and 74 of the Powers of Criminal Courts (Sentencing) Act 2000) that requires an offender to make reparation to the victim of the offence or someone otherwise affected by it. Such an order can only be imposed on offenders aged under 18. It is not a *community sentence and, accordingly, is not subject to the general provisions relating to such sentences. 'Reparation' consists of a period of unpaid work, up to a maximum of 24 hours.

reparations (in *international law) **1.** Compensation for injuries or international *torts (breaches of international obligations). Whenever possible, international courts or arbitration tribunals will rule that reparations be made by means of restitution in kind; if this is not possible, compensation is by payment of a sum equivalent to the value of restitution in kind. The aim of reparations is to eradicate the consequences of the illegal act. It is not clear, however, whether there is an obligation to make reparations for all breaches of international law. **2.** Payments made by a defeated state to the conquering state to compensate for damage suffered by the victor.

repatriation A person's voluntary return from a foreign country to that of which he is a national. *Compare* DEPORTATION.

repeal The total or partial revocation of a statute by one passed subsequently. A statute is normally repealed by express words, but if provisions of a later statute are inconsistent with those of an earlier one this will imply that *Parliament intended repeal. Repeal does not affect any transaction that has been completed under the repealed statute.

repeat offender An offender who commits the same offence on more than one occasion. *See also* DANGEROUS OFFENDER; MANDATORY MINIMUM SENTENCE.

repeat victimization The incidence of a person or place becoming the victim of crime on more than one occasion. Studies suggest that 4 per cent of victims account for about 40 per cent of crimes.

reporting an accident *See also* STOPPING AND REPORTING.

reporting restrictions Statutory limitations on making public certain information relating to a case. Section 8(1) of the Magistrates' Courts Act 1980 makes it unlawful to publish a report (written or broadcast) of any information other than the identity of the court; the names of examining justices and legal representatives; the names, addresses, ages, and occupations of *parties and witnesses, *charges; and decisions on the grant of *bail or publicly funded *representation. The restriction applies to all stages of the case in the *magistrates' court, including the *committal, and, unless lifted, applies in the *Crown Court until the *trial is over. Breach of the restriction carries a maximum *fine of £5000. Section 39 of the Children and Young Persons Act 1933 empowers an adult court to order that the media shall not reveal the name, address, school, or any other identifying details of a *juvenile offender or any juvenile who is a witness in a case that is brought before it. Section 49 of the 1933 Act imposes a similar reporting restriction in the *youth court, although the restriction is automatic. The court has the power to lift the restriction if it is appropriate to do so in order to avoid injustice; in respect of a child or young person who has been charged or convicted of a violent or *sexual offence or an offence punishable (in the case of an adult) with imprisonment for 14 years or more and is unlawfully at large; and in relation to a child or young person who has been convicted of an offence if it is in the public interest to do so. Breach of an order made under the 1933 Act carries a maximum fine of £5000.

Sections 44 and 45 of the Youth Justice and Criminal Evidence Act 1999 contain provisions intended to clarify the law restricting the reporting of information on a person under the age of 18 involved in the legal process and to extend that restriction back to the investigative stage of the offence. However, those provisions have not yet been brought into force. *See also* ANONYMITY.

representation 1. The state of being represented, e.g. by an elected representative in the *House of Commons (*see also* PARLIAMENT), by a defending *counsel in court, or by an agent acting on behalf of his principal. **2.** (in contract law) A statement. A person who has been induced to enter into a contract on the basis of a statement that is untrue or misrepresents a material fact may *sue for *damages or for rescission of the contract. Under the Consumer Credit Act 1974 a representation includes a *condition, *warranty, or any other statement or *undertaking, either oral or in writing. Many contracts exclude all prior representations from terms of the contract, although in consumer contracts such an exclusion may be void if unfair.

reprimand A formal warning to a person under the age of 18 years who has admitted an offence, which replaces the *caution for young offenders. Usually an offender will be reprimanded on only one occasion.

reprisals Retaliatory measures taken by one state against another to settle a dispute occasioned by the other's illegal or unjustified conduct. Reprisals include boycotts, *embargoes, and limited military action. A military reprisal, if otherwise than for the purpose of lawful *self-defence under Article 51 of the *United Nations Charter, is now illegal under *international law, other than within very narrow exceptions to the general principle.

reputation The estimation in which a person is generally held. *See* CHARACTER.

requisition (in military law) The compulsory acquisition of *property for use by the armed forces. The Army Act 1955 and the Air Force Act 1955, for example, contain provisions that, if brought into force by a government order made in the public interest, enable commanding officers to issue requisitioning orders authorizing the acquisition (in return for payment and *compensation for *damage) of vehicles, horses, food, and stores.

rescue 1. Action to save people or *property from danger. There is no general duty to rescue people or property from danger, though a master of a *ship is bound by statute to render assistance to people in danger at sea. Voluntary attempts to rescue people in danger are encouraged by the law. Someone injured in such a rescue attempt may recover *damages from the person whose *negligence created the danger. The rescuer is not regarded as having assumed the risk of being injured and courts are reluctant to find that his injuries were due to contributory negligence. Attempts to rescue property may not be treated so sympathetically. **2.** The forcible removal of a person in the *custody of the law, which is a criminal offence.

reservation (in *international law) A unilateral statement made by a state, when signing, ratifying, accepting, approving, or acceding to a *treaty, in order to exclude or modify the legal effect of certain provisions of the treaty in their application to that state. This device is used by signatory states to exempt particular policies from challenge. The UK has made one reservation in relation to the *right to education in Article 2 of the First Protocol to the *European Convention on Human Rights. The *Human Rights Act 1998 also excludes public authorities from duties under Article 2 where this reservation applies.

reserve forces Forces not in active service. They include the Army Reserve, the Territorial Army, the Air Force Reserve, the Royal Auxiliary Air Force, the Royal Naval Reserve, the Royal Naval Special Reserve, and the Royal Marines Reserve. The Reserve Forces Act 1996 provides a new power allowing call-out of reserve forces for humanitarian disaster relief and operations and introduced two new categories of reserve. The **high readiness reserve** will consist of about 3000 volunteers who have agreed, with their *employers' consent, to accept increased liability for being called out. These volunteers will be people with special skills, such as linguists and public information specialists. The **sponsored reserve** will undertake some support tasks currently restricted to regular personnel. The *legislation also makes provision to allow reservists to volunteer to undertake productive tasks other than training without being called out. There are powers to increase the military pay of reservists called out for operations if this pay is less than their civilian pay would be. There are also powers to pay employers for additional costs when the reservists are called out. A **Reserve Forces Appeal Tribunal**, set up under the 1996 Act, hears *appeals from reservists and employers who are dissatisfied.

res gestae [Latin: things done] The events with which the court is concerned or others contemporaneous with them. In the law of evidence, *res gestae* denotes: (1) a rule of *relevance according to which events forming part of the *res gestae* are admissible; (2) an exception to the rule against *hearsay evidence under which statements forming part of the *res gestae* are admissible, for example if they accompany and explain some relevant act or relate to the declarant's contemporaneous state of mind or his contemporaneous physical sensations.

residence 1. The place in which a person has his home. The term has been defined in various ways for different purposes in *Acts of Parliament. For example, the Income and Corporation Taxes Act 1988 provides that, for the purposes of *tax, a person is resident in the UK even if he has left the UK for occasional residence abroad. Temporary residents are chargeable to tax in the UK if they stay in the UK for a period (or periods adding up to) six months in any year. It is possible to be a resident of more than one country at the same time. **2.** In the case of a company not incorporated in the UK, the country in which central management and control is located; companies incorporated in the UK are deemed to reside there irrespective of the location of central management and control. Residence determines the company's liability to corporation tax.

residence requirement A requirement that may be imposed by a court dealing with an offender aged 16 or over as part of a *community order or *suspended sentence order, which requires the offender to reside at a specified place for the period specified in the order. Before imposing such a requirement, the court is obliged to consider the home surroundings of the offender (s 206, Criminal Justice Act 2003).

residential occupier A person who is living in a property as a result of his contractual *rights, his statutory rights, his rights under a rule of law, or because other people are restricted by law from removing him. It is an offence to force a residential occupier to leave the property without complying with the proper procedure. *See* ADVERSE OCCUPATION; EVICTION; FORCIBLE ENTRY; HARASSMENT OF OCCUPIER.

resilience The personal quality of a person exposed to high *risk factors that often lead to delinquent behaviour, but they do not do so.

res ipsa loquitur [Latin: the thing speaks for itself] A principle often applied in the law of *tort of *negligence. If an accident has occurred of a kind that usually only happens if someone has been negligent, and the state of affairs that produced the accident was under the control of the defendant, it may be presumed in the absence of evidence that the accident was caused by the defendant's negligence.

resistance survey A method of searching for clandestine *graves by passing an electric current though the soil and looking for inconsistencies in the electrical resistance.

resisting arrest Taking any action to prevent one's *arrest. A person may use *reasonable force to resist an illegal arrest. If he resists a legal arrest, however, he lays himself open to a charge under s 89 of the Police Act 1996 of assaulting or *obstructing a police officer in the course of his duty. The fact that the *police officer was in plain clothes is no defence to such a charge. The *House of Lords has ruled that it is the right and duty of every citizen to take reasonable steps to prevent a *breach of the peace by detaining the offender. The offender therefore has no right to resist such an arrest on the grounds of *self-defence; if he uses force to do so, he may be *guilty of an *assault. It is an offence under s 38 of the Offences Against the Person Act 1861 to assault anyone with intent to resist or prevent arrest or detainer.

resolution 1. A decision reached by a majority of the members at a company meeting. **2.** The decision of a meeting of any other assembly, such as the *United Nations.

respondeat superior [Latin: let the principal answer] The doctrine by which an *employer is responsible for certain wrongs committed by his *employee in the course of his employment. *See* VICARIOUS LIABILITY.

respondent The defending *party in an *appeal or *petition to the courts. *Compare* DEFENDANT.

restitution The return of *property to the owner or person entitled to *possession. If one person has unjustifiably received either property or money from another, he has an obligation to restore it to the rightful owner in order that he should not be unjustly enriched or retain an unjustified advantage. This obligation exists when, for example, *goods or money have been transferred under compulsion (*duress), under *mistake, or under a transaction that fails because of illegality, lack of formality, or for any other reason or when the person who has taken the property has acquired a benefit through his actions without justification.

In certain circumstances the courts may make a **restitution order** in respect of property. Under the Theft Act 1968, if someone is convicted of any offence relating to stolen *goods the court may order that the stolen goods or their proceeds should be restored to the person entitled to recover them. The court will only exercise this power, however, in clear cases that do not involve disputed questions of fact or law. Under the Police (Property) Act 1897, *magistrates' courts are empowered to make a restitution order in favour of a person who is apparently the owner of property that has been obtained by the police in connection with any crime, even when no charge can be brought or the goods are seized under a search warrant. If the owner cannot be found, the court may make any order it thinks fit (usually an order for sale by *auction).

restorative justice An umbrella term for a *criminal justice system that brings victims, offenders, and communities together to decide on a response to a particular crime. The Government's aim is to put victims' needs at the centre of the criminal justice system and to find positive solutions to crime by encouraging offenders to face up to their actions.

restraining order 1. A court order forbidding a person to do something or to be in a certain place. Under ss 5 and 5A of the Protection from Harassment Act 1997 (as amended by the Domestic Violence, Crime and Victims Act 2004), a court before which a person is acquitted of a criminal offence or which is sentencing or otherwise dealing with a person convicted of any criminal offence may, if it considers it necessary to do so to protect a person from *harassment, make an order prohibiting the person acquitted or convicted from doing anything described in the order. The order may have effect for a period specified or until further order. Breach of the order amounts to a criminal offence. **2.** An order under the Sex Offenders Act 1997, as amended, that enabled a *Crown Court to place restrictions following release from prison on a person who had been sentenced to imprisonment for twelve months or more for a sexual offence. It is now replaced by a *sexual offences prevention order.

restraint of trade A contractual term that limits a person's right to exercise his trade or carry on his business. An example is a term in an employment contract or *partnership agreement prohibiting a party from engaging in a similar business for a specified period after the relationship ends. Such a term is void unless the party relying on it shows that it does not offend *public policy; it must also be reasonable as between the parties. Many such terms are reasonable and therefore valid.

restraint order An order made by a criminal court to preserve specified *assets to prevent the defendant disposing of them to prevent a *confiscation order being satisfied.

restricted byway A *right of way along which the public can travel on foot, on or leading a horse, or on a vehicle other than a *mechanically propelled vehicle. The category was created by the Countryside and Rights of Way Act 2000.

restriction order An order placing special restrictions (for a specified period or without limit of time) on the discharge from hospital of a person detained there by a *hospital order. It may be made by the *Crown Court (but not a *magistrates' court) when this appears necessary for the public protection, and its principal effects are that discharge may be authorized only by the *Home Secretary and may be subject to conditions (e.g. subsequent supervision by a mental welfare officer).

retirement of jury The withdrawal of the *jury from the court at the end of the *trial so that they may decide on their *verdict in private. The jury members are not allowed contact with the public until they reach (or fail to reach) a verdict. They may not afterwards disclose the content of their discussions in reaching a verdict.

retorsion (retortion) A lawful means of retaliation by one state against another. It is usually provoked by an equally lawful, but discourteous, act of the other state, such as trade discrimination measures that single out foreign nationals or by hostile propaganda produced via government-controlled sources of information. *See also* REPRISALS; SANCTION; SELF-HELP.

retrial *See* NEW TRIAL.

retribution *See* PUNISHMENT.

return 1. A formal *document, such as an annual return or the document giving particulars of *shares allotted and to whom (**return of the allotment**), which must be delivered to the *Companies Registry within one month of allotment. **2.** The official result of the votes cast in an election.

return day The day specified in a *summons for the hearing of the summons.

Revenue and Customs Prosecutions Office (RCPO) An independent prosecuting authority, established by the Commissioners for Revenue and Customs Act 2005, that is responsible for conducting criminal prosecutions (and related proceedings such as the restraint and confiscation of assets) in England and Wales where there has been an investigation by *Her Majesty's Revenue and Customs and for providing legal advice in relation to such investigations. It does so under the superintendence of the *Attorney-General and in accordance with the *Code for Crown Prosecutors. The RCPO coordinates its efforts with those of the *Crown Prosecution Service and the *Serious Organized Crime Agency.

Revenue and Customs Prosecutor A *barrister or *solicitor appointed pursuant to s 37 of the Commissioners for

Revenue and Customs Act 2005. Their function, duties, and responsibilities are similar to those of a *Crown Prosecutor.

revenue statute An *Act of Parliament concerning taxation.

revocation of offer The withdrawal of an *offer by the offeror so that it can no longer be accepted. Revocation takes effect as soon as it is known to the offeree (from whatever source); offers can be revoked at any time before acceptance unless they are coupled with an *option. *See also* REJECTION OF OFFER.

revolver A *handgun with a fixed *barrel and revolving coaxial *cylinder composed of *chambers holding *ammunition to be presented successively before the barrel. A single action revolver must be cocked manually; pressure on the *trigger will not cock the weapon. Conversely, applying pressure to the trigger of a double action revolver revolves the cylinder to align a chamber with the *bore and cock the weapon. Further pressure releases the hammer to discharge the bullet. With a *semi-automatic revolver, the force of the recoil revolves the cylinder, aligns the chamber, and cocks the weapon. Trigger pressure will then discharge the weapon and repeat the process.

rifle A long barrelled weapon intended to be fired from the shoulder. The *bore carries longitudinal spiral grooves to impart spin (and, hence, gyroscopic stabilization) to the *bullet in flight, thereby increasing accuracy. A **repeating rifle** (or **magazine rifle**) is capable of discharging several *rounds with a single loading of the *magazine by manual operation of the bolt. A **self-loading rifle** is designed so that extraction of the fired *cartridge and reloading are performed automatically by the action of recoil. *See also* SEMI-AUTOMATIC WEAPON.

right 1. *Title to or an interest in any *property. **2.** Any other interest or privilege recognized and protected by law. **3.** Freedom to exercise any power conferred by law. *See also* HUMAN RIGHTS.

right of abode *See* IMMIGRATION.

right of audience The right of an *advocate to be heard in legal proceedings. *Barristers have the right of audience in all courts. *Solicitors have a right of audience in *county courts and *magistrates' courts and some solicitors are qualified to appear in the higher courts. Many administrative tribunals have no rules concerning rights of audience and a party may be represented by any person he chooses.

right of establishment The right under the *Treaty of Rome of a national of a member state of the *European Community to engage in and manage businesses in any other member state.

right of silence The right of someone charged with an offence or being tried on a criminal *charge not to make any statement or give any evidence. However, under the Criminal Justice and Public Order Act 1994, if a suspect fails to mention something at the time of his *arrest or charge that is later relied on in his *defence, this may result in a court at a subsequent *trial drawing such inferences as appear proper (*see* CAUTION). *See also* COMPULSORY POWERS.

Failure of an accused aged 14 or over to give evidence in his own defence or refusal to answer questions without good cause will also allow such inferences to be drawn. Inferences may also be drawn from a suspect's failure to account for any object, mark, or substance found on his person, in his clothing or footwear, or otherwise in his possession at the time of arrest. The *police officer must reasonably believe that such items are attributable to an offence and inform the suspect accordingly. Inferences may also be drawn from a suspect's failure to account for his presence at a particular place.

right of way The right to pass over another's *land. It may exist as a public right exercisable by anyone; as an *easement for the benefit of a particular piece of land; or as a *licence, purely personal to the person to whom it is granted.

rights issue A method of raising *share capital for a company from existing members rather than from the public at large. Members are given a right to acquire further shares, usually in proportion to their existing holding and at a price below the market value of existing shares. This right may be sold (**renounced**) to a third party.

right to begin The right of a *party at *trial to present his case to the court first (i.e. to **open the case**) by making the opening speech and presenting his evidence. The right to begin usually belongs to the party who carries the persuasive *burden of proof. Thus, in a criminal case the *prosecution always has the right to begin; in civil cases the claimant normally begins, but the defendant may do so when he has the burden of proving all issues.

right to life A right set out in Article 2 of the *European Convention on Human Rights and now part of UK law as a consequence of the *Human Rights Act 1998. The right to life is not an absolute right and the Article does not make the use of the death sentence unlawful (*but see* CAPITAL PUNISHMENT). Deprivation of life is not in contravention of the Convention if it is absolutely necessary in defence of a person from unlawful violence; in order to effect a lawful *arrest or to prevent the *escape of a person lawfully detained; or, in action lawfully taken for the purpose of quelling a *riot or insurrection. Article 2 makes unlawful the use of lethal force where the use of force was greater than that which was absolutely necessary (this is a higher test than imposed by s 3 of the Criminal Law Act 1967). The right to life also imposes a positive obligation on public authorities to take reasonable measures to protect life from threats from third parties. Article 2 also imposes a duty to ensure that any investigation of a death caused by a public body is independent and effective.

right to marry A right set out in Article 12 of the *European Convention on Human Rights and now part of UK law as a consequence of the *Human Rights Act 1998. The right is not a particularly strong one; it only exists subject to the national laws governing the exercise of this right.

rigid vehicle A *motor vehicle which is not constructed or adapted to form part of an *articulated vehicle or *articulated bus (reg 3(2), Road Vehicles (Construction and Use) Regulations 1986 (SI 1986/1078)).

rigor mortis The stiffening of muscles after death causing the joints to become rigid. The process may start soon or several hours after death depending on several factors including *temperature. If the body is cooled rapidly the onset of rigor may be delayed. Maximum stiffness is reached usually between twelve and 24 hours after death. The rigor remains for one to three days then the muscles relax due to decomposition. Rigor does give an indication of time of death, but is rather inaccurate.

riot An offence committed when twelve or more persons, present together, intentionally use or threaten unlawful violence (*see* VIOLENT DISORDER) for a common purpose. The collective conduct must be such as would have caused a reasonable person to fear for his safety, though no one else need be present. A person is only *guilty of riot if he intended to use violence or was aware that his conduct might be violent. The offence of riot is found in s 1 of the Public Order Act 1986, though it can be committed in private as well as in *public places. It replaces the *common-law offence of riot and is punishable with up to ten years' imprisonment and/or a *fine. Under the Riot (Damages) Act 1886, when property has been destroyed, damaged, or stolen in the course of a tumultuous riot, the owner is entitled to compensation out of public funds. *See also* AFFRAY.

risk factor An element of an environmental situation that generally is thought to increase the likelihood of offending.

risk of sexual harm order An order under the Sexual Offences Act 2003 made by a *magistrates' court on application of a chief officer of police, that prevents the defendant from doing anything described in the order. The order can only be made against a person aged 18 or over on grounds of behaviour prescribed in the Act and can only prohibit activity when it is necessary for the protection of children from harm from the defendant.

road (in road traffic law) Any *highway or other route to which the general public has access. A road must be a route leading from one place to another, and this is always a question of fact. It may include a hotel forecourt, a road privately owned but to which the public has access, or a bridge over which a road passes, but a *car park is usually not regarded as a road. Some traffic offences are defined to cover roads and 'other public places'.

road rage Aggressive behaviour while driving *motor vehicles on *roads. Although there is no specific road rage offence, such behaviour may involve breach of other laws. If the aggressor causes injury he may face a *conviction for *dangerous driving or for some other similar offence.

road tax A *tax (formally called **vehicle excise duty**) that must be paid in respect of any *mechanically propelled vehicle used, parked, or kept on a public road. It is an offence to fail to pay it. Electrically propelled vehicles and invalid vehicles do not have to be taxed, and no tax is required when a motorist is driving to and from a prearranged *MOT test. It is also an offence to fail to display a tax disc showing that the vehicle has been taxed, unless one has applied for a new disc before the old one expired and it is within fourteen days from the date of expiry. The tax disc must be displayed on the nearside lower corner of the windscreen. Failure to pay road tax or display the tax disc is punishable by *fine, but is not subject to *endorsement. Vehicles over 25 years old are exempt from paying the tax but a tax disc must be obtained and displayed.

road traffic accident/collision An *accident involving a *motor vehicle on a *road. If an accident has been caused by the presence of a motor vehicle on a road and results in injury to anyone or damage to anyone else's vehicle or to property on the road or neighbouring *land (e.g. someone's garden wall), it is an offence for the *driver of the vehicle not to stop, unless he can show that he did not know that the accident happened. It is also an offence to refuse to give one's name and address to anyone who reasonably requires it (e.g. a *police officer or another driver or pedestrian involved in the accident), unless one reports the accident to the police as soon as possible (not later than 24 hours after it occurred). If a person has been injured in a road accident, it is an offence not to produce one's *certificate of insurance (*see* THIRD-PARTY INSURANCE) for a police officer or anyone else with reasonable grounds for asking for it, unless one reports the accident to the police not later than 24 hours after it occurred and, at the same time or within five days, produces the certificate of insurance at any police station one specifies. *See also* ACCIDENT RECORD BOOK.

Failure to stop after an accident or give particulars is an endorsable offence (carrying five to ten penalty points under the totting-up system) and is subject to a *fine at level 5 on the standard scale and to discretionary *disqualification.

robbery The offence under s 8 of the Theft Act 1968 of using force against any person, or putting them in fear of being subjected to force, in order to commit a *theft, either before the theft or during the course of it. It is also robbery to threaten to use physical force in these circumstances, even if the person threatened is not frightened by the threats. The degree of force required is a question of fact in each case to be decided by the jury; nudging someone so that he loses his balance may constitute sufficient force. The force must, however, be directed against the person, rather than his *property. Robbery and *assaults with intent to rob are punishable by a maximum sentence of *life imprisonment.

rogatory letter *See* LETTER OF REQUEST.

Rome Conference The *United Nations Conference held in 1998 at which the Statute of the *International Criminal Court was drawn up.

round A military term used to describe one complete *cartridge.

rout An old public-order offence approximating to *riot, now repealed.

Royal Air Force Prosecuting Authority (RAFPA) A body established under the Armed Forces Act 1996 which came into existence on 1 April 1997. It acts independently of the military chain of command and is subject to the general superintendence of the *Attorney-General. The Authority provides advice to *service police on the investigation and *prosecution of offences and determines whether there is sufficient evidence for the case to proceed and if it is in the public interest to proceed. The Armed Forces Act will see the establishment of a joint-service prosecuting authority that will combine the *Army Prosecuting Authority, the Royal Air Force Prosecuting Authority, and the *Naval Prosecuting Authority. *See also* SERVICE LAW.

royal assent The agreement of the *Crown, given under the *royal prerogative and signified either by the sovereign in person or by royal commissioners, that converts a *Bill into an *Act of Parliament or gives a Measure the force of an Act. It is the duty of the Clerk of the Parliaments to endorse the date on which it was given immediately after the long title.

royal prerogative The special *rights, *powers, and *immunities to which the *Crown alone is entitled under the *common law. Most prerogative acts are now performed by the Government on behalf of the Crown. Some, however, are performed by the sovereign in person on the advice of the Government (e.g. the dissolution of *Parliament) or as required by constitutional convention (e.g. the appointment of a *Prime Minister). A few prerogative acts (e.g. the granting of certain honours, such as the Order of the Garter) are performed in accordance with the sovereign's personal wishes.

The Crown has limited powers of legislating under the prerogative, principally as respects the civil service and UK *dependent territories. It does so by *Order in Council, *ordinance, letters patent, or royal *warrant. The dissolution and prorogation of Parliament and the granting of the *royal assent to *Bills take place under the prerogative. Originally the fountain of justice from which the first courts of law sprang, the Crown still exercises (through the *Home Secretary) the *prerogative of mercy and retains the right (through the *Attorney-General) to stop a *prosecution by entering *a *nolle prosequi*. In foreign affairs, the sovereign declares *war, makes peace and international *treaties, and issues *passports under the prerogative. Many appointments (e.g. the higher judiciary, archbishops, and diocesan bishops) are made under the prerogative, and a variety of honours, including new hereditary peerages, are conferred by the Crown as the fountain of honour. The sovereign is head of the armed forces, and, although much of the law governing these is now statutory, their disposition generally remains a matter for the prerogative. There is a prerogative power, subject to the payment of *compensation, to *expropriate or *requisition private *property in times of war or apprehended war. Miscellaneous prerogative rights include the rights to *treasure trove and to *bona vacantia*. An important immunity of the sovereign is the prerogative of perfection. The common-law maxim that 'the King can do no wrong' resulted in the complete immunity of the sovereign personally from all civil and criminal proceedings for anything that he or she might do. This personal immunity remains, but actions may now be brought against the Crown under the Crown Proceedings Act 1947.

If a statute confers on the Crown powers that duplicate prerogative powers, the latter are suspended during the existence of the statute unless it either abolishes them or preserves them as alternative powers.

royal proclamation A *document by which the sovereign exercises certain prerogative powers (e.g. the summoning and dissolution of *Parliament) and certain legislative powers conferred on the sovereign by statute (e.g. the declaration of a state of emergency; *see* EMERGENCY POWERS).

royal title *See* QUEEN.

royalty A sum payable for the right to use someone else's *property for the purpose of gain. Royalties are paid on wasting assets, which have a limited lifespan. For example, the royalty paid by a *licensee to mine someone's *land is a fixed sum per tonne of the mineral he extracts, and an author's royalty is similarly determined by the total number of his books the publisher sells. Royalties are paid generally for the licensing of *intellectual property.

rule of law 1. The supremacy of law. **2.** A feature attributed to the UK constitution by Professor AV Dicey (1835–1922) (*Law of the Constitution*, 1885). It embodied three concepts: the absolute predominance of regular law, so that the government has no arbitrary authority over the citizen; the equal subjection of all (including officials) to the ordinary law administered by the ordinary courts; and the fact that the citizen's personal freedoms are formulated and protected by the ordinary law rather than by abstract constitutional declarations.

Rule of Nines Wallace's Rule of Nines is a way of approximating the area of skin affected by burns. It divides the body into areas divisible by nine. In an adult, the following are the respective percentages of the total body surface area: head and neck total for front and back 9 per cent: each upper limb total for front and back 9 per cent; thorax and abdomen front 9 per cent; thorax and abdomen back 18 per cent; perineum 18 per cent (ignored for the 'nine' rule); each lower limb total for front and back 18 per cent.

A rough guide for investigating officers dealing with burns cases is that if the total area of the body burnt plus the age of the victim adds up to more than 100, that person is likely to die (usually of septicaemia). The investigating officer should take appropriate steps to take a statement from the person.

rules of court Rules regulating the practice and procedure of a court, usually made by a rule committee acting under a statutory power. *See also* CIVIL PROCEDURE RULES; CRIMINAL PROCEDURE RULES.

running-account credit (under the Consumer Credit Act 1974) A facility under a *personal-credit agreement that enables a *debtor to receive periodically from the *creditor or a third party cash, *goods, or services to an amount or value that does not exceed the *credit limit (if any), taking into account payments made by or to the credit of the debtor. Examples are bank overdrafts and *credit cards.

ruses of war Deception of an opponent in armed conflict that is permitted in *international law (*compare* PERFIDIOUS KILLING OR WOUNDING, which is not permitted).

s (plural ss) The recognized abbreviation used in citing a particular section of a statute, as in 's 4', 'ss 70 to 73'.

sabotage *Damage to or destruction of *property, especially the property of an *employer during a *strike or of the state for political reasons. Sabotage as such is not an offence, although it may be treated as *criminal damage. The courts have, however, interpreted the phrase 'prohibited place' in the Official Secrets Act 1911 to bring sabotage against the state within the scope of that Act, even though it is clear that *Parliament's intention was only to prohibit spying. *See* OFFICIAL SECRETS.

safe haven A zone of territory within a sovereign state demarcated by the *United Nations (or other international organization) as a refuge to which a persecuted *ethnic minority can choose to retire. While within such a zone the ethnic minority is afforded military protection by the body that established the zone. The international community set up safe havens in Iraq and the former Yugoslavia in response to acts of systematic persecution carried out by the government of the sovereign state concerned against part of its own population. *See also* HUMANITARIAN INTERVENTION.

safety at work Every *employer has a *common-law duty to take reasonable care for his *employees' health, safety, and welfare at work: he may be *sued in the courts for *damages if an employee is injured through the employer's *negligence or failure to observe the safety regulations. The employer cannot contract out of this *liability and, under the Employers' Liability (Compulsory Insurance) Act 1969, must insure against his liability for employees' injuries and diseases sustained or contracted at work. The Health and Safety at Work Act 1974 further requires employers to ensure, as far as is reasonably practicable, that their working methods, equipment, *premises, and environment are safe and to give such training, information, and supervision as will ensure their employees' health and safety (*see* HEALTH AND SAFETY COMMISSION). Anyone employing more than five persons must maintain a written statement of his general policy concerning his employees' health and safety (dealing, for example, with safety rules and protective clothing) and must keep them informed of it. He must also give relevant information to the *safety representatives of his employees' trade unions and establish a safety committee where appropriate.

Employees also have a duty to take reasonable care for their own health and safety, e.g. by complying with safety regulations and using protective equipment supplied to them. Employers and employees who fail to comply with the requirements of the Health and Safety at Work Act 1974 face prosecution in the criminal courts. An employee dismissed for health and safety reasons is under certain circumstances regarded as having been unfairly dismissed. It is also regarded as automatically unfair to select an employee for redundancy on certain grounds connected with health and safety.

safety representatives *Employees appointed by trade unions to represent the interests of their colleagues regarding their health, safety, and welfare at work. Regulations made under the Health and Safety at Work Act 1974 give a trade union recognized as having negotiating rights on behalf of a group or class of employees the right to appoint at least one of those employees as a safety representative. The representatives' statutory powers include the investigation of *accidents and industrial diseases occurring at the workplace and inspection of the *premises to determine their causes. The *employer must allow them time off work with pay to train for and perform their duties and to attend meetings of safety committees.

salafism A branch of Islam whose adherents believe in a pure interpretation of the Koran and Islamic law. Salafists are orthodox Muslims who consider the Islam practiced by Mohammed and his companions as the only true version of the religion. Salafist Islam is used as a base ideology for several major *terrorist organizations including Osama Bin Laden's al-Qaeda network.

sale A contract involving the *sale of goods or a similar contract involving the transfer of *land.

sale of goods A contract by which a *seller transfers or agrees to transfer the *ownership of goods to a *buyer in exchange for a money price. If ownership is to pass at a future time the contract is called an **agreement to sell**. The contract, which need not be in writing, may contain *express terms. Terms may also be implied by law (*see also* IMPLIED CONDITION); e.g. that the seller has a right to sell, that the goods correspond with the description under which they are sold, and that the goods are of *satisfactory quality and are reasonably fit for the buyer's purpose. Unless the parties agree otherwise, the seller must hand over the goods in exchange for the price and the buyer must pay the price in exchange for the goods. Much of the law governing the sale of goods is codified in the Sale of Goods Act 1979.

salicylate Aspirin. A drug originally derived from the bark of willow trees. It is an analgesic and also slows the clotting of blood. It can be fatal in very high overdose.

salvage The service rendered by a person who saves or helps to save maritime property. Property saved in a non-tidal river cannot be subject to a salvage claim.

sanction 1. A *punishment for a crime. *See* NULLA POENA SINE LEGE. **2.** A measure taken against a state to compel it to obey *international law or to punish it for a breach of international law. It is often said that international law is deficient because it lacks the power to impose sanctions or even to compel states to accept the jurisdiction of courts (*see* INTERNATIONAL COURT OF JUSTICE). There are, however, certain sanctions that can be applied. A state may, in certain cases, use force in *self-defence, or as a sanction against an act of aggression, or as a *reprisal (e.g. by *expropriating *property belonging to citizens of a country that had previously carried out unlawful acts of expropriation). It may also act by way of *retorsion. There are also certain powers of sanction available under the *United Nations system, such as economic (and, at least in theory, military) sanctions, although the powers of the Security Council to impose sanctions are subject to veto. *See also* ANGARY.

sanity *See* PRESUMPTION OF SANITY.

satisfactory quality An *implied condition that *goods sold in the course of business will meet the standard that a reasonable person would regard as satisfactory. In assessing this, account is taken of any description of the goods, the price (if relevant), and all other circumstances. The quality of goods includes their state and condition, taking account of their fitness for purpose, appearance and finish, freedom from minor defects, safety, and durability. Most commercial agreements exclude the implied conditions and replace them with express *warranties, although unreasonable exclusions in standard-form contracts, even between two businesses, may be void under the law relating to *unfair contract terms. Satisfactory quality replaced the term **merchantable quality** by the Sale and Supply of Goods Act 1994, with effect from 3 January 1995.

scald A 'burn' caused by hot liquid or steam.

scalp The skin over the skull.

scapegoating The placing of blame for social, economic, or other ills on an innocent person or community.

scapula The shoulder blade.

scar Fibrous tissue produced by the body to repair damage.

Scenes of Crime Officer A *police officer or member of police support staff employed to examine scenes of crime and record and recover scientific evidence. They are now usually titled Crime Scene Investigators.

schedule An appendix to an *Act of Parliament or other *legislation that deals with points of detail supplementary to the main part.

Schengen Agreement The agreement between most member states of the *European Union (but not the UK) to abolish internal border controls. It came into force on 26 March 1995. *See also* PASSPORT.

scienter rule *See* CLASSIFICATION OF ANIMALS.

sclera The white of the eye.

scorched earth tactics Military tactics which involve destroying anything that might be useful to the enemy when advancing through or withdrawing from an area. It is a *war crime when used by a passing army to destroy all crops and food supplies. However it is permissible for a party to armed conflict to clear its own territory; it is also permissible in some cases of 'imperative military necessity'.

scratch Minor linear abrasion.

scuttling Sinking a ship (particularly with a view to making a fraudulent *insurance claim) by making or opening holes in its hull to allow the entry of water.

S

seal Wax impressed with a design and attached to any *document as a sign of its authenticity; alternatively, an adhesive wafer or anything else intended to serve the purpose of a seal may be used.

sear The part of a *firearm, usually a tooth on a lever on the *trigger, which holds back the hammer or *firing pin and releases it when the trigger is pulled. In some firearms, the firing mechanism is simplified to integrate the trigger and sear as one part.

search of ship The right that a belligerent power has during wartime, under public *international law, to search any *ship of a neutral power on the *high seas in order to discover whether it is carrying *contraband.

search order An order made by the *High Court (usually the Chancery Division) under s 7 of the Civil Procedure Act 1997 (amplified by pts 23 and 25 of the *Civil Procedure Rules) requiring a defendant to permit a claimant or his representatives to enter the defendant's *premises to inspect or take away material evidence that the defendant might wish to remove or destroy in order to frustrate the claimant's claim, or to force a defendant to answer certain questions. Formerly (until 1999) known as an **Anton Piller order**, from the case *Anton Piller KG v Manufacturing Processes* (1976) Ch 55 (CA), the order is commonly used in cases where the *copyright of video films or tapes or *computer *software is alleged to have been infringed. By statute the *privilege against self-incrimination does not apply.

search warrant *See* POWER OF SEARCH.

seat belt A belt fitted in a *motor vehicle, designed to restrict the forward movement of a *driver or passenger in the event of an accident. All passenger vehicles with seating for fewer than 13 passengers and most four-wheeled *goods vehicles registered after 1 January 1965 must comply with statutory regulations governing seat belts, although the details of these regulations vary according to the date when the vehicle was first registered. There are some exceptions: (1) drivers carrying out any manoeuvre that includes reversing (passengers must still wear their seat belts during such manoeuvres); (2) drivers making local delivery or collection rounds in specially adapted vehicles (e.g. milkmen in milk vans); (3) anyone whose seat belt has become faulty during the course of the journey on which he is engaged or who has already arranged to have a faulty belt repaired; (4) anyone whose belt has locked on a steep hill; (5) anyone supervising a learner who is reversing; (6) certain categories of people with a special exemption certificate on medical grounds. Particular regulations apply to children.

Failure to wear a seat belt carries a *fine at level 2 on the standard scale and may also be regarded as *contributory negligence in a claim for injuries sustained in a *road traffic accident, leading to a reduction in *damages.

sea waybill A receipt for *goods that contains or evidences the contract for the *carriage of goods by sea and also identifies the person to whom delivery of the goods is to be made by the *carrier in accordance with that contract. A sea waybill is not a *bill of lading: it is commonly used in container transport and, unlike a bill of lading, does not have to be produced at the *port of discharge in order to obtain delivery.

seaworthy 1. Having at the start of a voyage the degree of fitness (as respects the *ship, her crew, and her equipment) for that particular voyage that a careful owner might be expected to require of his ship. **2.** The suitability of a particular ship to carry a particular cargo. Obligations relating to seaworthiness are implied by law in charterparties and imposed by the Hague Rules in bills of lading. A marine *insurance policy incorporates by statute a *warranty that the insured ship is seaworthy.

secession The action of breaking away or formally withdrawing from an alliance, a federation, a political or religious organization, etc. An example of secession is the attempted withdrawal of the Confederate States from the United States in the War of Secession (1861–5).

secondary detection An offence cleared-up by the offender having the offence taken into consideration or otherwise admitted by a convicted offender.

secondary evidence Evidence that by its nature suggests the existence of better evidence and might be rejected if that better evidence is available (e.g. a copy of a *document). Secondary evidence is generally admissible if the absence of the *primary evidence is explained. *See also* BEST-EVIDENCE RULE.

secondary party An *accessory to a crime.

Secretary of State *See* MINISTER.

Secret Intelligence Service (SIS; MI6) A government organization that provides the British Government with a global covert capability to promote and defend the national security and economic well-being of the UK. It operates worldwide to collect secret foreign intelligence in support of the British Government's policies and objectives. It assists the Government to meet the challenges of regional instability, *terrorism, the proliferation of weapons of mass destruction, and illegal narcotics.

sectarianism A narrow-minded adherence to a particular sect (political, ethnic, or religious), often leading to conflict with those of different sects or possessing different beliefs. Sectarian conflicts are often breeding grounds for acts of *terrorism and the formation of terrorist groups.

section 8 order A court order under the Children Act 1989 that settles practical details concerning the child's care and upbringing in any *family proceedings in which the child's welfare is a matter for consideration (such as matrimonial, *wardship, or adoption proceedings). Section 8 orders, which replace the old access, custody, and care and control orders, include residence, contact, prohibited steps, and specific issues orders. A **residence order** settles arrangements about where a child is to live. Such an order is typically made when *parents live apart and cannot agree where the child is to live. Residence orders may also be made in respect of non-parents: in such a case, the order would confer *parental responsibility on those in whose favour the order is made. A **contact order** defines the extent and nature of the contact the child is to have with other individuals. A contact order cannot be made in favour of a *local authority or while the child is in care. A **prohibited steps order** prohibits certain specified steps (e.g. taking a child abroad) being taken without the consent of the court and can be made against anyone regardless of whether he or she has parental responsibility for the child. A **specific issue order** deals with any specific issues concerning the child's upbringing, such as education or medical treatment.

Section 8 orders are only necessary when there is a dispute between the parents or others in relation to a child and are usually only made in respect of children up to the age of 16. In determining whether or not to make such an order, the court must treat the child's welfare as paramount.

section 30 order (parental order) An order of the court made under s 30 of the Human Fertilization and Embryology Act 1990, which provides for a child to be treated in law as the child of the parties to a marriage if the child has been carried by a woman other than the wife as a result of *human assisted reproduction. Application must be made within six months of the child's birth and the child's home must be with the husband and wife at the time of the application.

section 37 investigation An investigation of a child's circumstances ordered by the court to be carried out by a *local authority when the court has cause for serious concern about the child's upbringing (s 37, Children Act 1989). The order may be made in any *family proceedings, e.g. when an application for a residence or contact order is being made by a *parent (*see* SECTION 8 ORDER). The local authority carrying out the investigation must consider whether it should apply for a *care order or a *supervision order or assistance for the child or its family or take any other action with respect to the child.

section 47 inquiry An inquiry carried out by a *local authority in order to enable it to decide whether or not it should take any action to safeguard and promote the welfare of a particular child (s 47, Children Act 1989). The local authority is under a duty to carry out such an investigation if it has reasonable cause to suspect that a child is suffering or likely to suffer significant harm, or is the subject of an *emergency protection order, or is in police protection (*see* POLICE PROTECTION ORDER). As a result of its inquiries a local authority might decide that no action is required; alternatively, it may decide that the family in question is in need of support and provide the appropriate services, or it may apply for an emergency protection order, a *care order, a *supervision order, or a *child assessment order. If, in the course of its inquiries, a local authority is denied access to a child, it should immediately apply to court for an emergency protection order.

secure accommodation order An order that allows a *local authority to restrict the liberty of a child whom it is looking after by placing him in secure accommodation. Under the Children Act 1989 such orders may only be sought in respect of a child who has a history of absconding from unsecure accommodation and who, if he does abscond, is likely to suffer significant harm.

secure training centre An institution for young offenders up to the age of 17. They are run by private operators according to *Home Office contracts, which set out detailed operational requirements. They house vulnerable young people who are sentenced to *custody in a secure environment where they can be educated and rehabilitated. They differ from Young Offender Institutions (YOIs) in that they have a higher staff to young offender ratio (a minimum of three staff members to eight trainees) and are smaller in size, so that individuals' needs can be met more easily. The regimes are constructive and education-focused. They provide programmes tailored for young offenders that give them the opportunity to develop as individuals which, in turn, will help stop them reoffending. Trainees are provided with formal education 25 hours a week, 50 weeks of the year. All services are provided on-site, including all education and training, primary healthcare, dentistry, and services to address the young person's offending behaviour (including input from mental health and social care professionals). They can also be used to house people remanded to *local authority accommodation.

securities Loosely, *stocks, *shares, *bonds, or any other rights to receive dividends or interest.

Securities and Investment Board (SIB) The agency set up under the Financial Services Act 1986 to ensure that those who are engaged in investment business (including dealing in, arranging deals in, and managing investments and also giving investment advice) are honest, competent, and solvent. It is an offence, unless exempt, to carry on investment business without SIB authorization (which may be obtained directly or via membership of a recognized self-regulatory organization or professional body). Those in contravention may be unable to enforce transactions, and investors who suffer loss may be entitled to compensation. The composition of the Board must reflect a proper balance between the interests of those who carry on investment business and the interests of the public.

Security Council (of the UN) *See* UNITED NATIONS.

Security Service (MI5) A government organization responsible for protecting the country against covertly organized threats to national security. These include *terrorism, espionage, and the proliferation of weapons of mass destruction. In addition the Security Service provides security advice to a range of other organizations, helping them reduce their vulnerability to the threats. Its aims are to:

- frustrate terrorism;
- prevent damage to the UK from foreign espionage and other covert foreign state activity;
- frustrate procurement by proliferating countries of material, technology, or expertise relating to weapons of mass destruction;
- watch out for new or re-emerging types of threat;
- protect the Government's sensitive information and assets, and the Critical National Infrastructure;
- assist the *Secret Intelligence Service and the *Government Communications Headquarters in the discharge of their statutory functions;
- build Service capability and resilience.

sedition The speaking or writing of words that are likely to incite ordinary people to public disorder or insurrection. Sedition is a *common-law offence (known as **seditious libel** if the words are written) if it is committed with the intention of (1) arousing hatred, contempt, or disaffection against the sovereign or her successors (but not the monarchy as such), the Government of the UK, or either House of *Parliament or the administration of justice; (2) encouraging any change of the law by unlawful means; or (3) raising discontent among Her Majesty's subjects or promoting ill-will and hostility between different classes of subjects. There must be an intention to achieve these consequences by violence and disorder. An agreement to carry out an act to further any of these intentions is a criminal *conspiracy.

seduction The offence under the Incitement to Disaffection Act 1934 of maliciously and advisedly endeavouring to persuade any member of HM forces to abandon his duty or allegiance to the *Crown.

select committee A committee appointed by either House of *Parliament or both Houses jointly to investigate and report on a matter of interest to them in the performance of their functions. Examples are the committees of the *Commons that examine government expenditure or the activities of government departments and the nationalized industries, and the Joint Committee on Statutory Instruments.

self-defence 1. A *defence at *common law to charges of *offences against the person (including *homicide) when *reasonable force is used to defend oneself, or one's family, or anyone else against attack or threatened attack. The scope of the defence often overlaps with the statutory right to use reasonable force to prevent a crime (*see* USE OF FORCE), but also extends to cases in which the statutory right is inapplicable (e.g. when the attacker is for some reason *not guilty of a crime). There is no rule of law that a person must retreat before acting in self-defence. If a person acting in self-defence mistakenly uses more force than was necessary in the circumstances and kills his attacker, he has no defence of self-defence (since the force was not reasonable) and the killing will therefore amount to *murder, unless he can show that there was also *provocation. However, in deciding whether the force used was justified or reasonably thought to be justified, the jury must bear in mind the difficulty of quickly assessing the correct amount of force to be used. *See also* GENERAL DEFENCES. **2.** One of the very few bases for a legal use of force under *international law. Under *Chapter VII (Article 51) of the *United Nations Charter, the inherent right of self-defence is preserved. Reference to 'inherent right' has promoted the belief that the pre-Charter right of self-defence in customary international law is specifically preserved by the Charter. However, the pre-existing right is arguably wider in scope than that allowed for by the terms of Article 51 and may arguably also allow for anticipatory self-defence. *See also* SELF-HELP; USE OF FORCE.

self-determination (in *international law) The right of a people living within a non-self-governing territory to choose for themselves the political and legal status of that territory. They may choose independence and the formation of a separate state, integration into another state, or association with an independent state, with autonomy in internal affairs. The systems of *mandates and trusteeship marked a step towards recognizing a legal right of self-determination, but it is not yet completely recognized as a legal norm. It is probably illegal for another state to intervene against a liberation movement and it may be legal to give assistance to such a movement. *See also* ERGA OMNES OBLIGATIONS.

self-employed In business on one's own account, i.e. not engaged as an *employee under a contract of employment. Statutory employment provisions do not apply to the self-employed. A self-employed person may nevertheless be the *employer of others.

S

self-help 1. Action taken by a person to whom a wrong has been done to protect his *rights without recourse to the courts. Self-help is permitted in certain *torts, such as *trespass and *nuisance. A trespasser may be *evicted provided only reasonable force is used. A nuisance may be abated (*see* ABATEMENT). *See also* RECAPTION. **2.** Independent and self-directed action taken by an injured state against the transgressing state in order to gain redress. Until the middle of the 20th century the right of self-help was claimed by states as one of the essential attributes of *sovereignty. In the absence of an international executive agency, an injured state undertook on its own account the *defence of the claim it was making. Forcible measures falling short of *war might prove sufficient; failing these, war might be resorted to as the ultimate means of self-help. Since self-help was regarded at *international law as a legal remedy, the results secured by it were recognized by the international community as a final settlement of the case. Since the establishment of the *United Nations, self-help with regard to *use of force can only be legal in so far as it forms part of a legitimate claim to *self-defence. The remaining forms of self-help are countermeasures, such as *retorsion and *reprisals.

self-loading rifle *See* RIFLE.

self-loading weapon *See* SEMI-AUTOMATIC WEAPON.

self-policing 1. A method of enforcing regulations without intervention by authorities, e.g. a 20mph speed limit enforced by traffic calming methods rather than detection. **2.** Control by members of the community without involving law enforcement agencies. A controversial concept, which can lead to non-policing at one extreme and vigilantism at the other.

self-reporting A system in most English *police forces whereby victims of crime can report offences on the Internet or by post without speaking to a *police officer. The scheme is particularly aimed at reporting hate crime. Self-reporting forms are usually available at post offices, doctors' surgeries, Citizen Advice Bureaux and other public buildings. Victims can report crimes anonymously which means they cannot be detected but it does help by showing the pattern of crime in an area.

seller The party to a contract of *sale of goods who transfers or agrees to transfer *ownership of the goods to the *buyer. The term may also be used in the context of the transfer of the ownership of *land, but a seller of land is more usually called a **vendor**.

semi-automatic weapon Any of a variety of weapons which upon being manually loaded and fired, will eject the fired case, load the next *cartridge from the *magazine, and cock the gun ready for re-firing. Pressure on the *trigger must be released and reapplied after each shot for the next shot to fire. Gas expansion, recoil, and mechanical spring action are used to perform ejection and reloading operations. It is also called auto-loading or self-loading.

semi-conductor topography Etching on a *computer chip otherwise known as a **mask work** or **right**: an *intellectual property right protecting the layout of a semiconductor chip or integrated circuit. Such rights are protected in the *European Union under Directive 87/54.

semi-trailer A trailer which is constructed or adapted to form part of an *articulated vehicle (reg 3(2), Road Vehicles (Construction and Use) Regulations 1986 (SI 1986/1078)).

sending distressing letters *See* OBSCENE AND THREATENING COMMUNICATIONS.

sending offences for trial A statutory procedure which automatically brings certain cases within the *jurisdiction of the *Crown Court. Section 51 of the Crime and Disorder Act 1998 abolished committal proceedings for cases triable on *indictment only and provided for such offences, together with certain related offences, to be sent automatically by the *magistrates' court directly to the Crown Court. With the coming into force of sch 3 to the Criminal Justice Act 2003 (which inserted ss 51B and 51C of the Crime and Disorder Act 1998, replacing similar provisions previously found in the Criminal Justice Act 1987 and Criminal Justice Act 1991), designated cases of serious and complex *fraud and certain cases involving children will also be sent automatically to the Crown Court. The 2003 Act also abolished committal proceedings for cases triable *either way, although the relevant provisions have yet to be brought into force. In such cases, once the accused has pleaded *not guilty, the magistrates' court will consider *mode of trial under s 19 of the Magistrates' Courts Act 1980. Where *jurisdiction is declined, the court will then send the case directly to the Crown Court. *See also* NOTICE OF TRANSFER.

sentence The *judgment of a court stating the *punishment to be imposed on a defendant who has pleaded *guilty to a crime or been found guilty by the *jury. Before the sentence is imposed, the *prosecution must present the *judge with the accused's *antecedents and the *defence may then make a *plea in *mitigation of the sentence. The court may also request, and in some circumstances must request, that a *pre-sentence report be prepared by a *probation officer or, in the case of an offender aged under 13, a *local authority social worker and may adjourn the case (and remand the accused) until the report is obtained (s 10(3), Magistrates' Courts Act 1980). The court may also obtain reports from non-legal specialists on the mental, physical, social, or personal circumstances of the offender.

Sentence must be pronounced in open court by the presiding judge and is almost always pronounced in the presence of the accused (*but see* PROOF IN ABSENCE). The sentence may be altered (or rescinded) within 28 days by the *trial court, and the *Crown Court also has a further (*common-law) power to postpone sentence for more than 28 days when circumstances require this (e.g. when intending to impose a *disqualification from driving under the **totting-up** provisions, if the driving licence is not available). There is a power to postpone sentence for up to six months (*see* DEFERRED SENTENCE).

Courts have very wide discretionary powers of sentencing in all crimes (except *murder and *treason). The *penalties prescribed by law are maximum penalties, to be imposed in the most serious cases, and the judge must decide what is the appropriate sentence in each case. However, *mandatory minimum sentences apply for persistent burglars (*see* BURGLARY) and dealers in hard drugs (*see* CONTROLLED DRUGS) and for certain serious *firearms offences.

Apart from imprisonment (which may be a *concurrent sentence or a *suspended sentence) and *fines, the courts can impose a *community sentence, a *confiscation order, and a *hospital order, as well as an absolute or conditional *discharge. (For the sentencing of young offenders, *see* JUVENILE OFFENDER.) *Magistrates' courts have less extensive powers of sentencing, but may sometimes, upon convicting an offender, remit him to the Crown Court for sentence (e.g. when he has been tried summarily for an offence triable *either way). They are not empowered to sentence first offenders to imprisonment unless satisfied there is no other appropriate way of dealing with them. There is usually a right of *appeal against sentence to the *Court of Appeal. The *Attorney-General may refer cases to the Court of Appeal (with its permission) when Crown Court sentences appear unduly lenient. The Court of Appeal may then *quash the sentence and substitute any sentence that they think appropriate and that the Crown Court had power to pass. *See also* NULLA POENA SINE LEGE.

Sentencing Advisory Panel An independent body originally set up to provide advice to the *Court of Appeal, when it was the Court's responsibility to issue sentencing guidelines. It now provides advice to the *Sentencing Guidelines Council following consultation.

Sentencing Guidelines Council An independent body whose role is to issue sentencing guidelines to assist all courts in England and Wales. It took over responsibility for developing sentencing and allocation guidelines from the *Court of Appeal and the Magistrates' Association. Its aims are to: give authoritative guidance on sentencing; give a strong lead on the approach to allocation and sentencing issues based on a principled approach which commands general support; and enable sentencers to make decisions on sentencing that are supported by information on effectiveness of sentences and on the most effective use of resources.

separate trials *See* JOINDER OF DEFENDANTS.

separation of powers The doctrine that the liberty of the individual is secure only if the three primary functions of the state (legislative, executive, and judicial) are exercised by distinct and independent organs. It was propounded by Montesquieu (1689–1755) (*De l'Esprit des Lois*, 1748), who regarded it as a feature of the UK constitution. In fact, however, while the judiciary is largely independent, the legislature and the executive depend on one another and their members overlap. The doctrine had a great influence over the form adopted for the *constitution of the USA and many other countries.

Serious Organized Crime Agency (SOCA) A law enforcement agency that became operational on 1 April 2006 with the aim of reducing the harm caused to people in the UK by serious *organized crime. It took over the functions of the *National Crime Squad, the *National Criminal Intelligence Service, the drug trafficking investigation role of *Her Majesty's Revenue and Customs, and the role of the UK Immigration Service in investigating organized *immigration crime.

Serious Fraud Office (SFO) A body established in 1987 to be responsible for investigating and prosecuting cases of serious or complex *frauds in England and Wales and Northern Ireland. The Director (*see also* DIRECTOR OF THE SERIOUS FRAUD OFFICE) is empowered to investigate any suspected offence that appears to involve serious fraud and may employ any suitable person to help in the investigation. The aims of the SFO are to reduce fraud and the cost of fraud; to deliver justice and the *rule of law; and to maintain confidence in the UK's business and financial institutions. Extensive powers of investigation are given to the Director and other delegated members of the office by s 2 of the Criminal Justice Act 1987 (*see* COMPULSORY POWERS). Serious and complex fraud cases can be transferred to the *Crown Court without *committal for trial (*see* NOTICE OF TRANSFER).

serology A blood test to determine blood group or the presence of antibodies.

servant An *employee.

service The delivery of any *document relating to court proceedings. Service may be made by physically handing the document to the person concerned (*see*

PERSONAL SERVICE) or it may be delivered to the *address for service supplied by that person. Once the document has been formally issued by the court, it must be served within twelve months (or, in the case of *claim forms, four months) unless the court allows this period to be extended. In the case of certain motoring offences, such as *speeding and *careless and inconsiderate driving, the police must serve a *summons within fourteen days unless the accused was warned at the time of the offence that he might be prosecuted or unless they serve a *notice of intended prosecution within fourteen days.

service civilian court *See* STANDING CIVILIAN COURT.

service discipline Acts *See* SERVICE LAW.

service law The law that regulates the conduct of members of the armed forces. It consists of **naval law**, **military law**, and **air-force law** (military law is the branch relating to the army, but the expression is frequently used to describe all three branches). Its primary sources are the Naval Discipline Act 1957, the Army Act 1955, and the Air Force Act 1955 (the 'service discipline Acts'); supplementary sources are Admiralty Instructions and the **Queen's Regulations** both for the Army and for the Royal Air Force. The three Acts concerned require annual renewal. Every fifth year an Armed Forces Act enables them to continue in force for one year and provides that for each of the following four years they may be continued in force by an Order in Council that has been approved by resolution of each House of *Parliament The purpose of this procedure (which did not apply to the Naval Discipline Act 1957 until this was provided by the Armed Forces Act 1971) is to ensure that Parliament has an annual opportunity of debating matters relating to the armed forces.

Service law is a specialized code of criminal law. Its essential concern is the maintenance of discipline and it embodies a variety of offences (including *desertion, malingering, and insubordination) that have no counterpart in the ordinary criminal law. Since 1 April 1997 it has been an offence against service law to refuse to take a service compulsory drug test; in addition, the service authorities have been empowered to take *fingerprints or DNA samples from those convicted of service offences, for criminal records purposes. A commanding officer (CO) is empowered to deal with minor offences summarily. With effect from 2 October 2000, an *appeal against the commanding officer's finding and/or award may be brought to a **Summary Appeal Court**. The Summary Appeal Court, consisting of a *judge advocate and two officers, may uphold, *quash, or vary the commanding officer's finding or award. But the tribunals primarily responsible for the *trial and *punishment of offences are the *courts martial. Service law applies to a member of the armed forces wherever he may be. In the UK he is subject both to service law and to the ordinary criminal law. When he is not in the UK, the ordinary criminal law does not in general apply to him; the relevant Acts therefore provide that it is an offence under service law for any serviceman to do anything that constitutes an offence under the ordinary criminal law. The effect of this general provision is to create, in the case of a member of the armed forces who is in the UK, a duality of offences. If, for example, a soldier in the UK steals, he commits an offence against both the ordinary criminal law and service law. He cannot, however, be punished under both.

Although service law applies primarily to members of the armed forces, certain classes of civilians are also subject to it. These include civilians employed outside the UK within the limits of the command of any officer commanding a body of the regular forces and the families of members of the armed forces residing with them outside the UK. The inclusion of the latter has had the effect of extending the jurisdiction of courts martial to cases with which they are manifestly not equipped to deal. This has led to the establishment of *standing civilian courts.

The Armed Forces Act 2006 replaces the service discipline Acts and harmonizes the tri-services approach to service discipline. The Act creates offences and provides for the investigation of alleged offences, the *arrest, holding in *custody and *charging of individuals accused of committing an offence and for them to be dealt with summarily by a CO or tried by court martial. Instead of (as at present) courts-martial being set up to deal with particular cases, the Act provides for a standing court martial, called the 'Court Martial', which may sit in more than one place at the same time. More serious cases must be notified to the service police and passed direct to the independent Director of Service Prosecutions (DSP) for a decision on whether to prosecute. In other cases the CO will consider whether to deal with the matter summarily or to refer the case to the DSP with a view to proceeding to a *trial by the Court Martial. In all cases that are tried by the Court Martial, the DSP takes the decision to prosecute and determines the charge(s). Those charged with offences under the Act that the CO intends to deal with summarily have a right to elect trial by the Court Martial and to appeal the outcome of a summary hearing to the Summary Appeal Court or the outcome of a court martial to the Court Martial Appeal Court. *See also* SERVICE POLICEMAN.

service policeman A member of the Royal Navy Regulating Branch, the Royal Marines Police, the Royal Military Police, or the Royal Air Force Police. They have many of the functions of civilian police but are members of the armed forces with no constabulary powers. This means that service police cannot exercise statutory powers conferred on *constables; any powers they require must be specifically applied to them. Prior to the Armed Forces Act 2001, powers, which might need to be exercised by a service policeman during the investigation of offences allegedly committed by members of the armed forces (or other persons who are subject to the *service discipline Acts) were exercised on the authority of the commanding officer under his inherent powers. However, the 2001 Act provides the service police with statutory powers of entry, search, and seizure based on those available to the civilian police. By virtue of the Police and Criminal Evidence Act 1984 (Application to the Armed Forces) Order 2006 (SI 2006/2015), the relevant provisions of the Police and Criminal Evidence Act 1984 apply to the investigation of offences conducted by a service policeman and to persons held in arrest in connection with such an investigation.

The Armed Forces Act 2006 defines the powers of *arrest in relation to service offences, powers to search arrested persons, to stop and search persons and vehicles, and to enter *premises for the purpose of search and seizure. It also sets out the regime governing the holding in *custody (before or after *charge) of a person arrested by a service policeman and covers such matters as time limits for custody and review of custody. The requirements include review of that custody by a *judge advocate. *See also* SERVICE LAW.

setting aside An order of a court cancelling or making void some other order or *judgment or, in civil proceedings, some step taken by a *party in the *action.

settled Ordinarily resident in the UK and not subject under *immigration law to any restriction on length of stay there. *See* BRITISH CITIZENSHIP; IMMIGRATION.

several Separate (in contrast to 'joint'), as in *joint and several.

severance An order amending an *indictment so that the accused is tried separately on any count or counts of the indictment.

severe mental impairment *See* ARRESTED DEVELOPMENT.

sex change A change in a person's sexual characteristics, usually by means of surgical operation and hormone treatment. For the purposes of marriage, the law does not recognize the validity of such a change; sex is deemed to be determined at birth and cannot be changed. For the purposes of employment, however, English law now recognizes the validity of a sex change (*see* GENDER REASSIGNMENT). *See also* TRANSSEXUAL.

sex offender *See* DANGEROUS OFFENDERS; SEXUAL OFFENCE.

sex offender order *See* SEXUAL OFFENCES PREVENTION ORDER.

sex offenders register A national register created by the Sex Offenders Act 1997, on which the name of an offender convicted of any of a range of *sexual offences is entered. Relevant offenders were obliged to tell the police every time they moved. Part 2 of the Sexual Offences Act 2003 extends the provisions of the 1997 Act, reducing the time in which the offender has to notify the police of any change to his name, whereabouts, or address (from fourteen days to three days) or of any plans to travel abroad. It also introduces a requirement to re-notify the police of his notified details at least once a year. The length of the period during which the offender is subject to the notification requirements varies between two years (for an offender cautioned for a relevant offence) to an indefinite period (for an offender sentenced to a term of imprisonment of 30 months or more). Section 91 of the Act makes it an offence to fail to comply with any notification requirement without reasonable excuse. The maximum *sentence is five years' imprisonment.

sextasy A mixture of *methylenedioxymethamphetamine (commonly known as 'E' or 'ecstasy') and a drug such as sildenafil citrate (Viagra™), used for erectile dysfunction. The combination is generally taken in capsule form or may be 'snorted' nasally as a powder. It is also known as 'trail mix' and 'cocktail pills'. Using the cocktail is sometimes referred to as 'hammer heading'.

sexual Relating to sex. For the purposes of the Sexual Offences Act 2003, *penetration, touching, or any other activity is sexual if a reasonable person would consider that whatever its circumstances or any person's purpose in relation to it, it is because of its nature sexual; or because of its nature it may be sexual and because of its circumstances or the purpose of any person in relation to it (or both) it is sexual.

sexual assault An offence under the Sexual Offences Act 2003 which replaced the offence of **indecent assault**. The offence criminalizes all non-consensual *sexual touching which is not penetrative, and includes touching over clothing for sexual gratification. The offence is triable *either way and carries a maximum *penalty of ten years' imprisonment. *See also* ASSAULT BY PENETRATION.

sexual history Previous sexual behaviour. Sections 41 to 43 of the Youth Justice and Criminal Evidence Act 1999 impose wide restrictions on evidence and questioning about the sexual history of a *complainant in a *sexual offence case. The *legislation is intended to offer such complainants better protection against unnecessary *cross-examination on their sexual behaviour; to provide a more structured approach to decision-taking; and to set out more clearly when evidence of previous sexual history can be admitted. Evidence of previous sexual behaviour (defined in s 42(1)(c) of the 1999 Act) can only be adduced if the court grants leave pursuant to an application made in accordance with pt 36 of the *Criminal Procedure Rules (as inserted by the Criminal Procedure (Amendment No 2) Rules 2006 (SI 2006/2636)).

Under s 41 of the 1999 Act, courts may now only grant such leave if: the evidence or questions rebut evidence led by the *prosecution; or the evidence or questions relate to a relevant issue at *trial and that issue is not one of *consent; or if the issue is one of consent, the behaviour to which they relate is either alleged to have taken place at or about the same time as the alleged offence; or is so similar to the complainant's alleged behaviour at that time that it cannot reasonably be explained as a coincidence. The court must also be satisfied that to refuse leave would result in the *jury, or the court, reaching an unsafe conclusion on a relevant issue at trial. The courts will also refuse permission if they believe that the real main aim of evidence claimed to relate to a relevant issue is simply to undermine the complainant's credibility.

sexual offence Any crime that involves sexual intercourse or any other *sexual act. The Sexual Offences Act 2003 provided a complete revision of the former law on sexual offences, extending many pre-existing offences and setting out new categories of offences involving abuse of trust, internet grooming, with a view to committing a sexual offence, and *people trafficking, amongst others. Sexual penetration of a *cadaver is also criminalized for the first time. The protection of children was one of the primary objectives of the Act and, accordingly, offences against children constitute a major part of the *legislation. Under the Act, children under the age of 13 are not capable in law of giving consent to any form of sexual activity and any such conduct is treated as an offence of *strict liability. The Act also repeals a number of archaic offences: in particular, the offences of ***buggery** and ***gross indecency** between consensual male adults are repealed in full. *See also* ANONYMITY; CHILD ABUSE; DANGEROUS OFFENDERS.

sexual offences prevention order A civil order introduced by s 104 of the Sexual Offences Act 2003 to replace *restraining orders and **sex offender orders** provided for by the Sex Offenders Act 1997. The order prohibits the person against whom it is made from doing anything described in the order. It may be imposed by a court dealing with an offender convicted of an offence listed in schs 3 or 5 to the 2003 Act (which include offences other than *sexual offences) where it is satisfied that such an order is necessary to protect the public or any particular person from serious sexual harm from the defendant; and that the prohibitions contained in the order will have that effect. An order may be sought by the police by way of *complaint to a *magistrates' court in cases where a person has been convicted of one of the scheduled offences (or an equivalent offence committed outside the UK) and has since acted in such a way as to give reasonable cause to believe that the order is necessary to protect the public or any particular person from serious sexual harm from the defendant. *See also* FOREIGN TRAVEL ORDER.

shadow director A person who is not a *director of a company but who gives instructions (rather than professional advice) upon which the directors are accustomed to act. Certain statutory provisions (e.g. those relating to put and call *options) apply to both shadow directors and directors proper.

shaming Method of *punishment whereby the offender is identified and stigmatized and ostracized. The method is commonly used in Japan and there are calls in England for offenders to be 'named and shamed'.

sham marriage A marriage entered into for some ulterior motive, without the intention of cohabiting with the other party. Such marriages will usually nonetheless be deemed valid, unless one of the parties (e.g. a person trying to escape *extradition) deceives the other party as to his identity or the marriage is entered into to escape a threat to life, limb, or liberty (e.g. to enable a person imprisoned under harsh conditions to leave his or her country) or to escape imprisonment.

share A unit that measures the holder's interest in and *liability to a company. Because an incorporated company is in law a separate entity from the company membership, it is possible to divide and sell that entity in specified units. In the case of a company limited by shares (*see* LIMITED COMPANY) the liability of shareholders is confined to the purchase price of the shares. Once purchased, these units of the company become intangible property in their own right and can be bought and sold as an activity distinct from the trading activities of the company in question. While the company is a going concern, shares carry rights in relation to voting and sharing profits. When a limited company is wound up the shareholders have rights to share in the *assets after *debts have been paid. If there are no such assets shareholders lose the amount of their investment but are not liable for the company's debts (see FRAUDULENT TRADING; WRONGFUL TRADING).

Preference shares usually carry a right to a fixed percentage dividend, e.g. 10 per cent of the nominal value (*see* AUTHORIZED CAPITAL), before ordinary shareholders receive anything and holders also have the right to the return of the nominal value of their shares before ordinary shareholders (but after *creditors). Holders of **participating preference shares** have further rights to share surplus profits or assets with the ordinary shareholders. Preference shares are generally **cumulative**, i.e. if no dividend is declared in one year, holders are entitled to arrears when eventually one is paid. Usually preference shareholders can vote only when their class rights are being varied.

Ordinary shares constitute the risk capital (also called equity capital), as they carry no prior rights in relation to dividends or return of nominal value. However, the rights they do carry are unlimited in extent: if the company is successful, the ordinary shareholders are not restricted to a fixed dividend (unlike the preference shareholders) and the high yield upon their shares will cause these to increase in value. Similarly, if there are surplus assets on a *winding-up, the ordinary shareholders will take what is left after the preference shareholders have been satisfied. Because ordinary shareholders carry the risk of the enterprise, they generally have full voting rights in a *general meeting (though some companies issue non-voting ordinary shares to raise additional capital without diluting the control of the company).

Redeemable shares are issued subject to the proviso that they will or may be bought back (at the option of the shareholder or the company) by the company. They cannot be bought back unless fully paid-up and then only out of profits or the proceeds of a fresh issue of shares made for the purpose.

A **golden share** enables the holder, usually the Government, to outvote all other shareholders on certain types of company *resolution.

share certificate A *document issued by a company evidencing that a named person is a *company member and stating the number of *shares registered in his name and the extent to which they are paid up. The certificate must normally be produced on a transfer of shares. *Compare* SHARE WARRANT.

share premium The amount by which the price at which a *share was issued exceeds its nominal value (*see* AUTHORIZED CAPITAL). Share premiums must be credited by the company to a **share premium account**, which is subject to the rules relating to reduction of capital and can only be used for certain purposes, e.g. paying up bonus shares.

share transfer A *document transferring registered *shares, i.e. shares for which a *share certificate has been issued, usually on a **stock transfer form**. A share transfer in proper form must usually be delivered to the company before it places the transferee's name on the register of members (Stock Transfer Act 1963). *See also* TRANSFER OF SHARES.

share warrant A *document issued by a company certifying that the bearer is entitled to the shares specified in it. The name of the bearer will not appear on the register of members until he surrenders the warrant to the company in return for *transfer of the shares, but he may be regarded as a *company member under the provisions of the *articles of association. The company is contractually bound to recognize the bearer as shareholder. *Compare* SHARE CERTIFICATE.

sheriff The principal officer of the *Crown in a county. In relation to the administration of justice, his functions (in practice discharged by the under-sheriff) include the execution of process issuing from criminal courts, levying *forfeiture of *recognizances, and the enforcement of *judgments of the *High Court by *writs of *fieri facias* (Latin: you should cause to be done), possession, and delivery.

ship For the purposes of the Merchant Shipping Act 1995 (which provides among other things for the registration of British ships), any vessel used in navigation and not propelled by oars. For the purposes of *ownership, a British ship is notionally divided into 64 shares. Each share may be in different ownership, but no share may be in the ownership of an alien or a foreign company.

shipwreck *See* WRECK.

shock A serious medical condition caused by actual or functional loss of body fluids—mainly blood. It may be caused by injury causing serious bleeding, heart attack, or infection. The victim will suffer from one or more of the following symptoms: anxiety or agitation; confusion; pale, cool, clammy skin; lightheadedness, or faintness; profuse sweating; moist skin; rapid but weak pulse; shallow breathing; chest pain; blue lips (Cyanosis); unconsciousness. Medical aid should be sought immediately. *See* NERVOUS SHOCK.

shoplifting A euphemism for stealing from shops. Shoplifters could be charged with *making off without payment under the Theft Act 1978, but it is more usual to charge them with *theft under the Theft Act 1968. It is not legally necessary to remove the *goods from the shop precincts in order to be *guilty of shoplifting, but in practice it is advisable to wait until the accused has left the shop before stopping him, as it is then easier to prove the *intention to steal (*see also* ARREST). A cashier in the shop who deliberately rings up a price lower than the true price may be guilty of *aiding and abetting theft.

short tandem repeat A class of polymorphisms in DNA that occurs when a pattern of two or more nucleotides are repeated and the repeated sequences are directly adjacent to each other. The techniques using short tandem repeat enable scientists to produce DNA profiles from very small amounts of bodily material.

short title *See* ACT OF PARLIAMENT.

S

shotgun A smooth bore gun (not being an *air weapon) which has a *barrel not less than 24 inches long and not more than 2 inches in diameter, is not a *revolver and does not a have a *magazine other than a non-detachable magazine that holds not more than two *cartridges.

sight Any of a variety of devices designed to aim a *firearm.

signature of treaty The formal and official affixing of names to the text of a *treaty by the representatives of the negotiating states, either as a means of expressing the definitive consent of the state to be bound by the terms of the treaty or as an expression of provisional consent subject to *ratification, acceptance, or approval.

silence *See* RIGHT OF SILENCE.

silencer A device attached to the *muzzle of a *firearm to reduce the noise of discharge. It has a volume many times greater than the *barrel, thereby allowing the propellant gases to escape at a much lower pressure and, hence, with far less noise.

silk *See* QUEEN'S COUNSEL.

similar-fact evidence Formerly, evidence that a party, especially the accused, had on previous occasions misconducted himself in a way similar to the misconduct being alleged against him in the proceedings before the court. (It is now part of 'bad character' under the Criminal Justice Act 2003; *see* CHARACTER). The evidence frequently took the form of a previous conviction. In general, the *prosecution could not offer similar-fact evidence as part of its case unless it could be shown to be relevant to an issue before the *jury, e.g. by rebutting some *defence advanced by the accused. Thus, if a person charged with *fraud contended that he was honestly mistaken, the fact that he had committed similar frauds on previous occasions may be admissible. The judge may in his discretion exclude otherwise admissible similar-fact evidence under s 78 of the Police and Criminal Evidence Act 1984 if he considers that it would have an adverse effect on the fairness of the proceedings.

sine die [Latin] Without a date. To adjourn a case *sine die* is to adjourn it without setting a date for a future hearing.

single action *See* REVOLVER.

Single European Act The *legislation passed in 1986 in the *European Community (in force from 1 July 1987) that committed all member states to an integrated method of trading with no frontiers between countries by 31 December 1992. It was the first Act to amend the principles of the *Treaty of Rome. In practice, some of its terms on harmonization, such as the *insurance market, have taken considerably longer to implement. The main creation of the Single European Act is the

*Single Market for trading in *goods and services within the *European Union.

Single Market The concept that underlies trading in the *European Union, as codified in the *Single European Act 1986. The Single Market came into force on 1 January 1993 with between 90 and 95 per cent of the necessary *legislation enacted by all member countries. The measures covered by the *legislation include: the elimination of frontier controls (the full measures have been repeatedly delayed); the acceptance throughout the market of professional qualifications; the acceptance of national standards for product harmonization; open tendering for public supply contracts; the free movement of capital between states; a reduction of state aid for certain industries; and the harmonization of VAT and excise duties throughout the market.

sittings (in the *Supreme Court of Judicature) The four periods of the legal year during which the full range of judicial business is transacted. The sittings are Michaelmas, Hilary, Easter, and Trinity. Sittings were substituted for *terms by the Judicature Act 1873. *See also* VACATIONS.

situational crime prevention An approach to crime reduction developed during the 1980s in which the environment of crime hot spots is altered by measures such as physical security, property marking, surveillance, and the design of buildings, walkways, cars, etc.

skeletal Relating to the skeleton.

skimming A common form of *fraud in which the *magnetic stripe on a *payment card is copied (usually by a rogue trader) without the knowledge of the cardholder and put onto another card.

skin The multi-layered covering of the body, all the layers of which must be breached to amount to a *wound.

skull The group of bones that surround the brain.

slander A defamatory statement made by such means as spoken words or gestures, i.e. not in permanent form. Generally slander is only actionable on proof that its publication has caused special damage (actual financial or material loss), not merely loss of reputation. Proof of special damage is not necessary when the slander implies the commission of a criminal offence punishable by imprisonment, infection with a contagious disease, unchastity in a woman, or is calculated to disparage a person in his office, business, trade, or profession. *See* DEFAMATION.

slavery The condition of being a servant completely divested of freedom and personal rights. The prohibition on slavery or *forced labour as set out in Article 4 of the *European Convention on Human Rights is now part of UK law as a consequence of the *Human Rights Act 1998. There are exceptions to this prohibition for prisoners, military service, normal civic obligations, and in emergencies.

small agreement 1. (under the Consumer Credit Act 1974) A regulated *consumer-credit agreement for credit not exceeding £50, other than a *hire purchase or *conditional sale agreement, or a regulated *consumer-hire agreement that does not require the hirer to make payments exceeding £50. In both cases the agreement is either unsecured or secured by a *guarantee or *indemnity only. Some small agreements are outside certain provisions of the Act. **2.** (under the Competition Act 1998) An agreement in which the parties are exempt from the imposition of *penalties (*fines) for anticompetitive practices. Section 39 of the Act provides the exemption, and the Competition Act 1998 (Small Agreements and Conduct of Minor Significance) Regulations 2000 (SI 2000/262) define an anticompetitive agreement as 'small' when both parties to it have a total turnover of under £20m. However, no exemption applies for a price-fixing agreement. Moreover, small agreements are not exempt from other provisions of the 1998 Act, and thus restrictive clauses in them may still be void.

small arm Any weapon designed to be carried on the person for use against personnel and lightly armoured or unarmoured equipment. Generally, the term is applied to individual weapons, although it may also include crew-served weapons, such as smaller *machine guns.

small premises A *licensed premises with an occupancy limit of fewer than 200.

smoke A product of combustion containing particles and hot gases. Inhalation of smoke ('fumes of fire') is the most frequent cause of death in fires.

smother To cover the mouth and nose to prevent breathing.

smuggling The offence contrary to s 170 of the Customs and Excise Management Act 1979 of importing or exporting specified *goods that are prohibited or are subject to customs or excise duties without having paid the requisite duties. Smuggled goods are liable to confiscation and the smuggler is liable to pay treble their value or a sum laid down by the law (whichever is the greater); offenders may alternatively, or additionally, receive a term of imprisonment.

social control An overall term including all means by which conformity to social norms might be achieved.

social exclusion The process whereby an individual, class of person, or community is excluded from all or part of the social, economic, or political system thus preventing their integration into society. There may be exclusion from specific provisions such as policing, information, education, housing, and health.

S

social justice The fair distribution of social goods such as housing, income, food, health, education, etc. For some criminologists social justice is the value base for criminology. They tend to favour social policy rather than penal policy as a way of reducing crime.

social policy rule *See* INTERPRETATION OF STATUTES.

sodomy *See* BUGGERY.

soft law (in *international law) Guidelines of behaviour, such as those provided by *treaties not yet in force, resolutions of the *United Nations, or international conferences, that are not binding in themselves but are more than mere statements of political aspiration (they fall into a legal/political limbo between these two states). Soft law contrasts with **hard law**, i.e. those legal obligations, found either in treaties or customary international law (*see* CUSTOM), that are binding in and of themselves.

software *Computer programs, which are protected by *copyright under the Copyright, Designs and Patents Act 1988. EU Directive 91/250 on the legal protection of computer programs provides that all member states must protect computer programs by copyright law. The directive also provides a right to make back-up copies of software and a very limited *decompilation right. A right to repair is also included, unless a software *licence prohibits this. The UK implemented the directive by the Copyright (Computer Programs) Regulations 1992 (SI 1992/3233).

soliciting 1. The offences, contrary to s 1 of the Street Offences Act 1959, by a *common prostitute, whether male or female, of loitering or soliciting in a *street or *public place in an attempt to obtain clients. The maximum *penalty is a *fine at level 2 on the standard scale on a first *conviction and at level 3 on a subsequent conviction. Any act committed by the prostitute (even smiling provocatively) may constitute soliciting. If a prostitute in a private house attracts the attention of men in the street (e.g. by tapping on the window and inviting them in, or even merely by sitting at the window illuminated by a red light), this may amount to soliciting: *Behrendt v Burridge* [1976] 3 All ER 285. However, a prostitute does not 'solicit' if she advertises her services on a card in a phone box or in a shop window. Depending on the content, such advertising may amount to a *common law conspiracy to outrage public decency (*but see* CONSPIRACY) or contravene the Obscene Publications Act 1959 (*see* OBSCENE PUBLICATIONS) or the Indecent Displays (Control) Act 1981. Section 1 of the 1981 Act provides that if any indecent matter is publicly displayed (i.e. visible from any public place), the person making the display and any person causing or permitting the display to be made shall be *guilty of an offence. The word 'indecent' is not defined by the Act so in each case it will be for the *trier of fact to decide whether the matter is indecent. The offence is triable *either way and on conviction on *indictment carries a maximum penalty of two years' imprisonment and a level 5 *fine. Section 46 of the Criminal Justice and Police Act 2001 makes it a particular offence to place an advertisement relating to prostitution on or in the vicinity of a public telephone with the intention that the advertisement should come to the attention of any other person or persons. For the purposes of the Act, an advertisement relates to prostitution if it is for the services of a prostitute, whether male or female, or indicates that such services are available at any *premises. It is a *summary offence and carries a maximum penalty of six months' imprisonment and a level 5 *fine. *See also* PROSTITUTE. **2.** The offence, contrary to the Sexual Offences Act 1985, by a man of persistently accosting a woman in a public place for the purpose of prostitution (*see also* KERB CRAWLING) or persistently accosting anybody in a public place for immoral purposes. 'Persistently' requires either a number of single invitations to different people or more than one invitation to the same person.

solicitor A legal practitioner admitted to practise under the provisions of the Solicitors Act 1974. With some statutory exceptions, practising solicitors must possess a *practising certificate. Solicitors form much the larger part of the English legal profession (*compare* BARRISTER), undertaking the general aspects of giving legal advice and conducting legal proceedings. They have *rights of audience in the lower courts but may not act as *advocates in the *Supreme Court (except in chambers) or the *House of Lords unless they have acquired a relevant advocacy qualification under the terms of the Courts and Legal Services Act 1990. A solicitor may be sued for professional *negligence and owes the duties of a *fiduciary to his client; these include the duty to preserve the confidentiality of the client's affairs.

Solicitor General A law officer of the *Crown immediately subordinate to the *Attorney-General. The Solicitor General is usually a Member of *Parliament of the ruling party. He acts as deputy to the Attorney-General and may exercise any power vested by statute in the latter (unless the statute otherwise provides) if the office of Attorney-General is vacant or the Attorney-General is unable to act through illness or has authorized him to act.

Solicitors' Disciplinary Tribunal A tribunal established under the Solicitors Act 1974 for hearing applications and complaints against *solicitors. It has the power to strike the name of a solicitor off the roll and to restore the name of a solicitor previously struck off, suspend a solicitor from practice, and order the payment of a *penalty. The members of the tribunal are practising solicitors of not less than ten years' standing and some lay members. They are appointed by the *Master of the Rolls. Appeals from decisions of the tribunal can be brought to the High Court of the Master of the Rolls. *See also* OFFICE FOR THE SUPERVISION OF SOLICITORS.

somatotype To assign behavioural tendencies, such as delinquency, to individuals by measuring their physiological features

sovereign *See* CROWN.

sovereign immunity The exemption of the sovereign or other head of a foreign state and foreign governmental departments from the *jurisdiction of the English courts. The principles governing this exemption are now contained in the State Immunity Act 1978 and are consistent with the European Convention on State Immunity. The immunity granted is no longer absolute; it is subject to numerous exceptions outlined in the Act. Subject to modifications, the Diplomatic Privileges Act 1964 extends to foreign sovereigns the same privileges and immunities as are granted to heads of *diplomatic missions. It is now clear under English law that such immunity does not apply to former heads of state who are alleged to have committed *crimes against humanity.

sovereignty Supreme authority in a state. In any state sovereignty is vested in the institution, person, or body having the ultimate authority to impose law on everyone else in the state and the power to alter any pre-existing law. How and by whom the authority is exercised varies according to the political nature of the state. In many countries the executive, legislative, and judicial powers of sovereignty are exercised by different bodies. One of these bodies may in fact retain sovereignty by having ultimate control over the others. But in some countries, such as the USA, the powers are carefully balanced by a constitution. In the UK sovereignty is vested in *Parliament (*see* SOVEREIGNTY OF PARLIAMENT).

In *international law, it is an essential aspect of sovereignty that all states should have supreme control over their internal affairs, subject to the recognized limitations imposed by international law. These limitations include, in particular, the international law of *human rights and the rules forbidding the use of force. However, no state or international organization may intervene in matters that fall within the domestic jurisdiction of another state. The concept of state sovereignty was outlined, among other things, in a declaration on Principles of International Law (Resolution 2625), proclaimed by the General Assembly of the *United Nations in 1970.

sovereignty of Parliament The constitutional principle that the legislative competence of *Parliament is unlimited. No court in the UK can question its power to enact any law that it pleases. In practice, however, Parliament does not assume unlimited authority; it can legislate only for territories that are recognized by *international law to be within its competence, i.e. the UK, the Channel Islands and the Isle of Man, and UK dependencies. The *Welsh Assembly, Scottish Parliament, and *Northern Ireland Assembly have devolved power in certain areas.

Speaker *See* HOUSE OF COMMONS; HOUSE OF LORDS.

Speaking Up For Justice The report of the Interdepartmental Working Group on the treatment of vulnerable or intimidated witnesses in the *Criminal Justice System published in June 1998. The term is used in some agencies to refer to the vulnerable and intimidated witness provisions introduced by the Youth Justice and Criminal Evidence Act 1999. *See also* SPECIAL MEASURES.

special advocate An *advocate appointed by the court to protect the interests of a party against whom an adverse order may be made and who cannot (either personally or through his legal representative), for reasons of national security, be fully informed of all the material relied on against him. The advocate may not disclose to the subject of the proceedings the material disclosed to him. This procedure was first introduced by s 6 of the Special Immigration Appeals Commission Act 1997 and r 7 of the Special Immigration Appeals Commission (Procedure) Rules 1998 (SI 1998/1881), in proceedings concerned with exclusion or removal of a person as conducive to the public good or in the interests of national security. Similar provision was made by s 91 of the Northern Ireland Act 1998; s 5 of the Terrorism Act 2000 and r 10 of the Proscribed Organizations Appeal Commission (Procedure) Rules 2001 (SI 2001/443); and s 70 of the Anti-Terrorism, Crime and Security Act 2001 and r 8 of the Pathogens Access Appeal Commission (Procedure) Rules 2002 (SI 2002/1845). Although there is no similar statutory provision that relates to the appointment of a special advocate to represent the interests of the accused in an application brought by the *prosecution to withhold unused material (*see* DISCLOSURE OF UNUSED MATERIAL; PUBLIC INTEREST IMMUNITY) on public interest grounds, their use has been sanctioned by the courts in appropriate cases (see *R v H; R v C* [2004] 2 AC 134).

special constable An unpaid volunteer *police officer with all the powers and privileges of a *constable in the police area for which he is appointed and surrounding police areas. Special constables undertake routine uniformed police work, including patrolling, crime scene preservation, and crime prevention work.

Special Constabulary A body of *special constables set up within each *police force.

special hospital A hospital (e.g. Broadmoor or Rampton) for persons suffering from *mental disorder who require *detention under special security conditions, because of their dangerous, violent, or criminal propensities.

speciality The principle that the state requesting the *extradition of a fugitive from another state must, in order for the request to succeed, specify the crime for which the accused is to be extradited. Further, the requesting state must only try the individual for the crime specified in the extradition request, unless the consent of the requested state is obtained or the individual is first given the opportunity to return to the country from which he was extradited. *See also* DUAL CRIMINALITY.

special measures Measures contained in ss 16 to 33 of the Youth Justice and Criminal Evidence Act 1999 to help witnesses (other than the defendant) who might otherwise have difficulty giving evidence in criminal proceedings or who might be reluctant to do so. There are three categories: children under the age of 17; those who suffer from a mental or physical disorder, or have a disability or impairment that is likely to affect their evidence; and those whose evidence is likely to be affected by their fear or distress at giving evidence in the proceedings. Under pt 29 of the *Criminal Procedure Rules, both the *prosecution and *defence may apply, normally before the *trial, for the court to make a *special measures direction authorizing the use of such measures for a witness they are calling. Courts may also decide to make a direction even if no such application has been made. The measures include: screening the witness from the defendant; taking the evidence of a witness by *live television link, allowing *video-recorded evidence of an interview conducted with the witness at the investigative stage of the case to be shown as the witness's evidence-in-chief at trial; video-recording the *cross-examination or *re-examination of such a witness; and, in a *sexual case or where there is a fear that the witness might be intimidated, taking evidence in private. With the commencement on 1 July 2005 of s 143 of the Serious Organized Crime and Police Act 2005, special measures now apply to applications for *anti-social behaviour orders under ss 1, 1C, and 1D of the Crime and Disorder Act 1998 in the *Crown Court and *magistrates' courts. *See also* SPECIAL PROTECTION.

special measures direction The order by which the court states which, if any, of the *special measures provided by the Youth Justice and Criminal Evidence Act 1999 will be used to assist a particular witness. In deciding which measures may be appropriate, the court must aim to maximize the quality of the witness's evidence whilst still allowing the party challenging the evidence to test it effectively. In the case of a child witness, there is a presumption that their evidence-in-chief will be received in the form of a *video-recorded interview, with live link being used for *cross-examination and *re-examination. *See also* SPECIAL PROTECTION.

special plea A *plea in bar of arraignment, e.g. **autrefois acquit* or **autrefois convict*.

special procedure material Confidential material (other than *legally privileged or *excluded material) acquired or created in the course of a trade, business, profession, or unpaid office. Under the Police and Criminal Evidence Act 1984, production orders and *warrants to search for such material can only be obtained by following a special procedure laid down in sch 1 to the Act and require the authority of a *district judge (magistrates' court), *recorder, *circuit judge, or *High Court judge.

special protection The Youth Justice and Criminal Evidence Act 1999 provides that a child witness is in need of special protection where the crime is a *sexual offence, as defined by s 35(3)(a) or an offence of *assault or a related offence as defined by s 35(3)(b). In the former category are offences under pt 1 of the Sexual Offences Act 2003; in the latter are offences involving *kidnapping, *false imprisonment, *child abduction, cruelty, *neglect, and any offence involving injury or the threat of injury to any person. Where an offence of either sort is involved the court cannot decline to make a *special measures direction on the grounds that it believes that to apply it will not maximize the quality of the child's evidence. In addition, where the offence is sexual, the court must include in the direction a provision for *video-recorded cross-examination, unless the child does not want that measure to apply.

special reasons Reasons why a court might decide not to impose a period of mandatory *disqualification or not to *endorse a *driver's *licence with penalty points (s 34(2), Road Traffic Offenders Act 1988). A special reason is one which is a mitigating circumstance, is not a *defence to the *charge in law, is directly connected with the circumstances in which the offence was committed and not to the personal circumstances of the driver, and is a factor which the court ought properly to take into consideration. In the *Crown Court, special reasons hearings are held by a *judge alone.

special resolution A decision reached by a majority of not less than 75 per cent of *company members voting in person or by proxy at a *general meeting. At least 21 days' notice must be given of the meeting.

special verdict 1. A *verdict of *not guilty by reason of *insanity. **2.** A verdict on particular questions of *fact, without a general conclusion (in criminal cases) as to guilt or (in civil cases) in favour of the claimant or the defendant. The *judge asks the *jury their opinion on the facts, but decides the general question himself. Such verdicts in criminal cases are very rare. *Compare* GENERAL VERDICT.

specific intent crime A criminal offence that requires the *prosecution to prove that the defendant had a particular *intention. That particular intention will vary according to the offence. Intention must be proved, *recklessness is not sufficient **mens rea*.

specific performance A court order to a person to fulfil his obligations under a contract. For example, when contracts have been exchanged for the sale of a house, the court may order a reluctant *seller to complete the sale. The *remedy is a discretionary one and is not available in certain cases; e.g. for the enforcement of a contract of employment or when the payment of *damages would be a sufficient remedy.

specified offence An offence specified in the Prosecution of Offences Act 1985 (Specified Proceedings) Order 1999 (SI 1999/904). Under s 3 of the Prosecution of Offences Act 1985, the *Director of Public Prosecutions must take over the conduct of all criminal proceedings instituted on behalf of a *police force, whether by a member of that force or any other person. An exception is made in proceedings for specified offences. These include a number of minor road traffic and other offences, the routine nature of which do not require independent review.

specimen of blood A sample of blood for analysis, used as an alternative to a *specimen of breath in cases involving *drunken driving. A *police officer may require a specimen of blood if he reasonably believes that he cannot demand a breath specimen for medical reasons, if an approved and reliable device for taking a breath specimen is unavailable or cannot be used, or if the defendant is suspected of being unfit to drive and a doctor believes that his condition is due to a drug. A police officer may also ask for a blood specimen if the suspect is in hospital (subject to the consent of the doctor treating him). A suspect may be asked to give a blood specimen under these conditions even if he has already given a breath specimen.

A blood specimen may only be taken with the defendant's consent and by a medical practitioner, otherwise it cannot be used as evidence in any proceedings. It must be analyzed by a qualified analyst, who must sign a certificate stating how much *alcohol he found. The suspect may ask to be given half the specimen for his own analysis, which may be used to contradict the *prosecution's evidence; if he has asked for but was not given half of the sample, the other half may not be used in evidence against him. A *specimen of urine may sometimes be taken as an alternative to a blood specimen.

It is an offence contrary to s 7 of the Road Traffic Act 1988 not to provide a specimen without a reasonable excuse, and the police officer should warn a suspect of this when asking for the specimen. This offence is punishable by *fine or imprisonment, *endorsement (ten penalty points), and discretionary *disqualification (in cases of being in charge of a vehicle) or compulsory disqualification (in cases of driving or attempting to drive).

specimen of breath A sample of breath for analysis taken from a person suspected of *drunken driving. It is this specimen that usually forms the evidence for a *prosecution and *conviction for offences of drunken driving and should not be confused with the preliminary *breath test. The specimen may be required whenever the police are investigating any of these offences, but only if the suspect is at the police station. Usually he will have been brought to the station under *arrest as a result of a positive breath test or refusal to undergo such a test. It is an offence contrary to s 7 of the Road Traffic Act 1988 not to provide a specimen without a reasonable excuse, and the *police officer should warn a suspect of this when asking for the specimen. This offence is punishable by *fine or imprisonment, *endorsement (ten penalty points), and discretionary *disqualification (in cases of being in charge of a vehicle) or compulsory disqualification (in cases of driving or attempting to drive).

The suspect must give two breath specimens, which should be measured by means of an *evidential breath test device (not the *breathalyzer used for the preliminary breath test) that automatically prints out the level of *alcohol in the breath. A print-out of the lower of the two readings is used as evidence in a subsequent *trial, together with a signed certificate by a police officer that it refers to the defendant's specimen given at the stated time. The defendant must be given a copy of these *documents at least seven days before his trial, and he may serve notice not later than three days before the trial that he requires the police officer who signed it to attend the hearing. At his trial, a defendant may bring evidence to show that he drank more alcohol between the time of the alleged offence and giving the specimen and that this accounted for his exceeding the prescribed limit. It is an offence, however, to deliberately drink more alcohol in order to make it difficult to prove his guilt.

Under certain circumstances the suspect can provide either a *specimen of blood or a *specimen of urine instead of a breath specimen. If the breath specimen records a reading of more than 35 but less than 50 micrograms of alcohol per 100ml of breath (and prosecution is intended), the suspect is entitled to ask that it should be replaced by a blood or urine specimen.

Once a suspect has given a specimen he is free to leave the police station, but the police may detain him if they reasonably suspect that he is likely to continue driving with an excess alcohol level or while unfit to drive.

specimen of urine A sample of urine for analysis, used as an alternative to a *specimen of breath in cases involving *drunken driving. A specimen of urine may be required when there are objections to taking a breath specimen and when a medical practitioner thinks that a *specimen of blood should not be taken for medical reasons. A urine specimen must be provided within one hour after it has been asked for; two specimens are asked for, and it is the second specimen that is used as evidence in a subsequent *trial. In all other respects the law relating to urine specimens is the same as the law relating to blood and breath specimens.

speeding Driving a *motor vehicle at a speed in excess of that permitted. The maximum speed for most classes of vehicle in a built-up area (with street lights) is 30mph. The maximum speed for cars and car-derived vans up to 2 tonnes maximum laden weight is 60mph on undivided carriageways and 70mph on dual carriageways and motorways. Cars towing caravans and *trailers are restricted to 50mph on undivided carriageways and 60mph on dual carriageways and motorways. Buses, coaches, and *goods vehicles not exceeding 7.5 tonnes maximum laden weight (unless articulated or towing a trailer) are restricted to 50mph on undivided carriageways, 60mph on dual carriageways, and 70mph on motorways. Goods vehicles exceeding 7.5 tonnes maximum laden weight are restricted to 40mph on undivided carriageways, 50mph on dual carriageways, and 60mph on motorways.

The *penalty for speeding is a *fine, *endorsement (carrying three penalty points), and discretionary *disqualification. A person cannot be convicted of a speeding offence on the evidence of one witness alone, but the evidence of a single *police officer reading his speedometer may be enough to secure a *conviction. Speeding may itself be evidence of *careless and inconsiderate driving or *dangerous driving, but it is an offence in its own right even if it caused no danger and the *driver was not in any way at fault. Speeding offences are subject to the requirement of a *notice of intended prosecution.

spent conviction A *conviction that, after a specified number of years known as the **rehabilitation period**, may in all subsequent civil proceedings be treated as if it had never existed. The length of the rehabilitation period depends on the gravity of the offence, and some convictions are not subject to rehabilitation (e.g. when the sentence was *life imprisonment). Dismissal from a job on the grounds of an undisclosed spent conviction may amount to unfair dismissal. Similarly, to deny that one has been convicted if the conviction is spent does not amount to *perjury or *deception. Malicious publication of statements about a person's spent convictions can make the publisher liable for *defamation, even if the statements are true. The provisions relating to spent convictions do not apply in criminal proceedings, but *counsel and the court should, as far as possible, avoid referring to a spent conviction and references to it in open court may only be made with express leave of the *judge in the interests of justice. A spent conviction in a record should be marked as such. *See also* CRIMINAL RECORDS BUREAU.

spying (espionage) Obtaining or passing on to an enemy information that might prejudice the safety or interests of the state or be useful to an enemy. *See* OFFICIAL SECRETS.

spyware A term used to describe any *software that covertly gathers information from a *computer user through the computer's Internet connection. Typically, spyware applications are introduced to the user's computer as hidden components of some programs that are downloaded from the Internet. Once installed, the spyware monitors user activity and transmits that information in the background to someone else. Although generally used to gather marketing information, spyware can also be used to gather information such as passwords and *credit card numbers to facilitate online *fraud.

squatter A person unlawfully occupying *land. *See* TRESPASS.

stag A speculator who applies for a new issue of *securities in a *public company with the intention of making a quick profit by reselling them if they increase in value within a few days of issue. This will only occur if the issue is oversubscribed, i.e. if there are more applicants for *shares than there are shares available.

stalking Persistent threatening behaviour by one person against another. (*See* HARASSMENT; HARASSMENT OF A PERSON IN HIS HOME; MOLESTATION.) In Scotland the *common law has always provided protection against stalking through the offence of *breach of the peace.

standard of proof The degree of *proof required for any *fact in issue in *litigation, which is established by assessing the evidence relevant to it. In criminal cases the standard is *proof beyond reasonable doubt (*see also* BURDEN OF PROOF); in civil cases (including *divorce petitions) the standard is proof on a balance of probabilities.

standing civilian court A court, provided for by the Armed Forces Act 1976, for the *trial outside the UK of lesser offences committed by certain civilians, e.g. the families of servicemen (*see* SERVICE LAW). The range of offences which may be dealt with is limited to those which could be dealt with by a *magistrates' court had the offences been committed in the UK and the powers of *punishment available to the court are limited to up to six months' imprisonment and/or a *fine of £5000. The Secretary of State for Defence (with the approval of the *Lord Chancellor) specifies which areas such courts serve and draws up panels of serving officers and civilians to sit as assessors. The Lord Chancellor appoints legally qualified persons to act as *magistrates in the courts. The court consists of a magistrate sitting alone, unless the accused is under 17 years old, in which case up to two members or assessors will also sit. The Armed Forces Act 2006 will replace this court with the service civilian court.

standing mute The refusal of the defendant in a *trial on indictment to plead to the indictment. *See also* UNFIT TO PLEAD.

stare decisis [Latin: to stand by things decided] A maxim expressing the underlying basis of the doctrine of *precedent, i.e. that it is necessary to abide by former precedents when the same points arise again in *litigation.

state A sovereign and independent entity capable of entering into relations with other states (*compare* PROTECTED STATE) and enjoying *international legal personality. To qualify as a state, the entity must have: (1) a permanent population (although, as in the case of the Vatican or Nauru, this may be very small); (2) a defined territory over which it exercises authority (although its borders, as in the case of Israel, need not be defined or undisputed); (3) an effective government. There are currently over 180 states. When a new state comes into existence, it is automatically bound by the principles of *international law.

For some purposes, entities that do not normally qualify as fully fledged states may nonetheless be treated as such. Liechtenstein, for example, was refused admission as a state to the League of Nations (and did not become a member of the *United Nations until 1990), but is a party to the Statute of the *International Court of Justice, which is only open to states. *See also* BOUNDARY; JURISDICTION.

state crime Crimes committed by states on their own citizens or other states as a means of furthering domestic or foreign policy.

statement of affairs 1. A *document that must be prepared by a *debtor after a *bankruptcy order has been made against him except when the bankruptcy order was made on his own petition or when the court excuses him. It gives details of his *assets, *debts and *liabilities, the names and addresses of his *creditors, and what *securities they hold. The debtor must send the statement to the *official receiver, and the creditors are entitled to inspect it. A debtor who wrongly fails to submit a statement of affairs is *guilty of *contempt of court. *See also* BANKRUPTCY. **2.** *See* VOLUNTARY WINDING-UP.

statement of case A formal written statement in a civil action served by each party on the other, containing the allegations of *fact that the party proposes to prove at *trial and stating the *remedy that the party claims in the action.

statement of information A statement prepared by the prosecuting authority in support of an application for a *confiscation order. In cases where the *prosecutor or the Director of the *Assets Recovery Agency has asked the *Crown Court to proceed under s 6 of the Proceeds of Crime Act 2002 (*see* CONFISCATION ORDER), s 16 of the Act requires the prosecutor or the Director to give the court a statement of information within a period specified by the court. If the court is acting on its own initiative, it may order the prosecutor (but not the Director) to give such a statement within a specified period. If the prosecutor or Director alleges that the defendant has a *criminal lifestyle, the statement must include matters that are relevant to the determination as to whether the defendant has such a lifestyle, and whether he has benefited from his general criminal conduct, and the amount of his benefit from that conduct, together with information relevant to the making of the four assumptions that the court is required to make by s 10 of the Act. This will normally consist of information relating to the defendant's *assets or his expenditure and receipts during the six-year period specified in the section. Otherwise, the statement should not contain information other than that relating to whether the defendant has benefited from his particular criminal conduct, and the amount of that benefit. Under the statutory predecessors of the 2002 Act, the Criminal Justice Act 1988 and the Drug Trafficking Act 1994, such statements were known as **prosecutors' statements**.

state of emergency *See* EMERGENCY POWERS.

status A person's legal standing or capacity. The term derives from Roman law, in which it referred to a person's freedom, citizenship, and family rights. Status is an index to legal rights and duties, powers, and disabilities.

status frustration *See* STRAIN THEORY.

statute *See* ACT OF PARLIAMENT.

statute book The entire body of existing statutes.

statute law The body of law contained in *Acts of Parliament. *Compare* CASE LAW.

statutory charging scheme A scheme introduced by pt 4 of the Criminal Justice Act 2003 (amending s 37 of the Police and Criminal Evidence Act 1984 and inserting s 37A into the Act) in response to recommendations made by Lord Justice Auld in his review of the *criminal justice system. Under the scheme, the *Crown Prosecution Service (CPS) will determine whether a person is to be charged in all *indictable only, *either way, or *summary offences, subject to certain exceptions (*see* SPECIFIED OFFENCE) which the police may continue to charge without reference to the CPS. In deciding how a person is to be dealt with, a police *custody officer must comply with the guidelines issued by the *Director of Public Prosecutions pursuant to s 37A(1)(a) of the Police and Criminal Evidence Act 1984, as inserted by the Criminal Justice Act 2003.

statutory declaration A *declaration made in a prescribed form before a *justice of the peace, *notary public, or other person authorized to administer an *oath. Statutory declarations are used in extrajudicial proceedings and not in court, but have similar effects to declarations made on oath.

statutory instrument Any *delegated legislation (not including *sub-delegated legislation) to which the Statutory Instruments Act 1946 applies. This includes (1) delegation made under powers conferred by an Act passed after 1947, either on the *Crown or on a Government minister, and expressed by that Act to be exercisable by *Order in Council in the former case or by statutory instrument in the latter; or (2) delegation made after 1947 under powers conferred by an earlier Act and formerly governed by the Rules Publication Act 1893 (which was replaced by the 1946 Act and provided for the publication of delegated legislation to which it applied in an official series known as **statutory rules and orders**). Regulations or orders made before the 1946 Act came into force may still be statutory instruments if the power they exercise was a power to make statutory rules within the meaning of pre-existing legislation, which was duly conferred on a rule-making authority under that legislation.

statutory interpretation *See* INTERPRETATION OF STATUTES.

statutory power of removal A power conferred by or under any enactment to remove or move a vehicle from any *road or from any part of a road.

statutory rules and orders *See* STATUTORY INSTRUMENT.

step-parent A person who is married to the father or mother of a child but is not the natural *parent of the child. A step-parent has no automatic legal status in relation to his or her step-children, but will usually qualify to apply, as of right, for a *section 8 order in respect of the child by virtue of being married to the child's natural parent. Step-parents may acquire *parental responsibility either by applying to court for a residence order (which automatically confers parental responsibility) or by applying to adopt the child together with the child's natural parent. There is, however, a policy of discouraging step-parent adoption since the effect will be to irrevocably sever the child's legal ties with its other natural parent.

For the purposes of the familial child *sexual offences introduced by ss 25 and 26 of the Sexual Offences Act 2003 (sexual activity with a child family member; inciting a child family member to engage in sexual activity), a step-parent falls within the category of person who can commit the offences, provided that he lives or has lived in the same household as the child or had been regularly in sole charge or responsible for training, supervising, or caring for the child.

stereotype A preconceived and oversimplified idea of the characteristics which typify a person, race, or community which may lead to treating them in a particular way.

stipendiary magistrate *See* DISTRICT JUDGE (MAGISTRATES' COURT).

stock 1. A fixed-interest loan raised by the Government or a *local authority. **2.** *Shares in a *registered company that have been converted into a single holding with a nominal value equal to that of the total of the shares. For example, a holder of 100 shares of £1 each will have £100 stock after conversion. **3.** *See* LOAN CAPITAL. **4.** That part of a *rifle, *shotgun, or other *firearm intended to be fired from the shoulder that is attached to the *receiver and enables the weapon to held, aimed, and fired. It is made of wood, metal, plastic, or some other rigid material; its quality and design is of great importance in increasing the accuracy of the weapons.

Stock Exchange The International Stock Exchange of the UK and the Republic of Ireland Ltd: the body responsible for regulating the issue and marketing of company *securities.

stopping and reporting A *driver is required by s 170 of the Road Traffic Act 1988 (as amended) to stop his vehicle if an *accident has occurred owing to the presence of a *mechanically propelled vehicle on a *road or other *public place, in which either personal injury is caused to someone other than the driver of the vehicle, or damage is caused to another vehicle, or to an animal (other than one being carried by the driver), or to any property attached to *land on which the road is situated or adjacent to the road. If so required by a person having reasonable grounds, the driver must give his own name and address, the name and address of the owner of the vehicle, and the registration number of his vehicle. If the driver does not give his name and address to any such person, he must report the accident to a police station or to a *constable as soon as is reasonably practicable and, in any event, within 24 hours. The offences are punishable by up to six months' imprisonment and a level 5 *fine and are *endorsable. A court also has the discretion to *disqualify the offender from driving for a period.

It is also an offence under s 168 of the 1988 Act for a person alleged to have committed the offence of dangerous or careless driving or cycling (*see* CARELESS AND INCONSIDERATE DRIVING; CARELESS AND INCONSIDERATE CYCLING; DANGEROUS CYCLING; DANGEROUS DRIVING) to refuse, on being so required by a person having reasonable grounds to do so, to give his name and address to that person or to give a false name and address. The offences are punishable by a level 3 *fine.

stowaway A person who secretes himself upon a *ship and goes to sea. This is a criminal offence under the Merchant Shipping Act 1894.

strain theory A cause of criminality where people suffer from status frustration whereby they cannot achieve the social and economic status that they think they deserve and turn to other means of achieving that status.

street 1. A public *road in a city, town, or village usually running between two lines of houses or other buildings. **2.** (in law) A term that is variously defined in statute. For the purposes of the Street Offences Act 1959 and the Sexual Offences Act 1985 a 'street' 'includes any bridge, road, lane, footway, subway, square, court, alley or passage, whether a thoroughfare or not, which is for the time being open to the public; and the doorways and entrances of premises abutting on a street...and any ground adjoining and open to a street, shall be treated as forming part of the street'. The New Roads and Street Works Act 1991 defines a 'street' as the whole or any part of any *highway, road, lane, *footway, alley, or passage; any square or court; and any *land laid out as a way, irrespective of whether they are a thoroughfare. The term has the same meaning in the Highways Act 1980. **3.** Of or relating to the sub-culture of fashionable urban youth.

street offence Any offence relating to the use of public *streets. Examples are *obstruction, failing to obey police regulations about movement of traffic or pedestrians, *kerb crawling, and *soliciting.

strict liability 1. (in criminal law) *Liability for a crime that is imposed without the necessity of proving **mens rea* with respect to one or more of the elements of the crime. There are few crimes of strict liability at *common law but such crimes are often created by statute, particularly to control or regulate daily activities; examples include offences relating to the production and marketing of food and *offences relating to road traffic. Most crimes of strict liability do, however, require *mens rea* in respect of at least some of the elements of the crime. In some cases statute provides for strict liability, but then allows a *defence if the accused can prove (*see* BURDEN OF PROOF) that he had no reason to know of or suspect certain facts, so that, in effect, the crime becomes one of *negligence. *Automatism is a defence to all crimes, including crimes of strict liability. **2.** (in *tort) Liability for a wrong that is imposed without the claimant having to prove that the defendant was at fault. Strict liability is exceptional in the law of tort, but is imposed for torts involving dangerous animals (*see* CLASSIFICATION OF ANIMALS) and dangerous things (the rule in *Rylands v Fletcher* (1868) LR 3 HL 330), *conversion, *defamation, *product liability, and some cases of *breach of statutory duty. It is no defence in these torts that the defendant took reasonable care to prevent *damage, but various other defences are admitted.

strike A cessation of work or refusal to work by *employees acting together in connection with a trade dispute to secure better terms and conditions of employment for themselves and/or other workers. A trade union cannot call its members out on strike unless it has held a secret ballot and the majority agree to the action.

sub-delegated legislation *Legislation made under powers conferred by *delegated legislation or by sub-delegated legislation itself (in which case it is technically sub-sub-delegated legislation). Sub-delegated legislation is very common (as when the parent Act authorizes a minister to make regulations and these in turn authorize others to make orders), but sub-sub-delegated legislation is rare (though examples have existed in wartime); the chain has not in practice been further extended. Sub-delegated legislation is not subject to any form of parliamentary control but it is subject to judicial control by means of the doctrine of **ultra vires*.

***sub judice* rule 1.** A rule limiting comment and *disclosure relating to judicial proceedings, in order not to prejudge the issue or influence the *jury. *See* CONTEMPT OF COURT. **2.** A parliamentary practice in which the Speaker prevents any reference in questions or debates to matters pending decision in court proceedings (civil or criminal). In the case of civil proceedings, he has power to waive the rule if a matter of national interest is involved.

submachine gun An *automatic firearm that fires pistol *ammunition. It is lighter, shorter, and, hence, more concealable than an automatic *rifle.

subordinate legislation *See* DELEGATED LEGISLATION.

subornation Procuring another to commit an offence. Normally subornation is included in the offence of aiding, abetting, or procuring (*see* ACCESSORY), but there is a special statutory offence of **subornation of perjury**.

subpoena *See* WITNESS SUMMONS.

subsidiarity A principle of the *European Union, introduced by Article 3A of the *Maastricht Treaty, ensuring that in areas which do not fall within the exclusive competence of the EU, it shall not take action unless the objectives of the proposed action cannot be adequately achieved by individual member states. Thus it provides for *legislation at national level when EU measures are not required.

substantive law The part of the law that deals with *rights, *duties, and all other matters that are not matters purely of practice and procedure. *Compare* ADJECTIVE LAW.

succession (in *international law) The transfer of *sovereignty over a territorial entity from one subject of international law (i.e. one state) to another. As a result of succession, an existing state becomes totally extinguished (as when Tanganyika and Zanzibar ceased to exist in 1964 on the formation of Tanzania) or a state transfers part of its territory to another state.

sue To make a claim for a *remedy in the civil courts by issuing court proceedings.

suicide The act of killing oneself intentionally. Since 1961 suicide itself is not a crime, but s 2 of the Suicide Act 1961 provides that it is an offence (punishable by up to fourteen years' imprisonment) to aid, abet, counsel, or procure a suicide. In practice very few *prosecutions are brought for this offence. Doing nothing to stop someone else from committing suicide is not abetting it, but *euthanasia (mercy killing) in the form of giving assistance to the sufferer (rather than actually killing him) may amount to aiding. Where there is 'a common agreement between two or more persons having for its object the death of all of them, whether or not each is to take his own life' (a **suicide pact**), any one of them who does the killing is *guilty, if he survives, not of *murder but of *manslaughter (s 4, Homicide Act 1957).

sui generis [Latin: of its own kind] Forming a class of its own; unique.

sui juris [Latin: of his own right] Describing the status of a person who is of full age and capacity.

suit A court claim. The term is commonly used for any civil court proceedings although originally it denoted a suit in *equity as opposed to an action at law.

summary conviction A *conviction in a *magistrates' court. The *magistrates are the judges of both *fact and law and must either convict the accused or dismiss the case.

summary offence An offence that can only be tried summarily, i.e. before *magistrates. Most minor offences (e.g. common *assault and *battery) are summary. *Prosecutions for all summary offences must be started within six months of the commission of the offence, unless the statute creating the offence expressly provides otherwise (s 127, Magistrates' Court Act 1980). For example, if the offence is one contrary to the customs and excise Acts, s 146A of the Customs and Excise Management Act 1979 provides that proceedings for a summary offence shall not be commenced after the end of the period of three years beginning with the day on which the offence was committed but, subject to that, may be commenced at any time within six months from the date on which sufficient evidence to warrant the proceedings came to the knowledge of the prosecuting authority. Other relevant provisions include: ss 47 and 50, Vehicle Excise and Registration Act 1994; s 731, Companies Act 1985; s 34, Health and Safety at Work etc. Act 1974; s 41, Game Act 1831; s 274, Merchant Shipping Act 1995. *Compare* INDICTABLE OFFENCE; OFFENCE TRIABLE EITHER WAY.

summary trial *Trial by *magistrates without a *jury. All summary offences are tried in this way, as well as some *offences triable either way. The main procedural principles followed in *trial on indictment also apply to summary trial, but there are some differences of which the most important are as follows. (1) The accused does not usually have to be present at the hearing. (2) Objections cannot usually be made either to *information laid before the magistrates or to a *summons or *warrant served on the defendant on the grounds of 'defects of substance or form' (unless they are fundamental defects). (3) Under s 12 of the Magistrates' Courts Act 1980, in proceedings for summary offences commenced by way of summons in an adult magistrates' court or in respect of a person aged 16 or 17 in a *youth court, the defendant may send in a written *plea of *guilty, together with a statement of *mitigation, and the case may then be disposed without the *prosecution or *defence appearing (*see* PLEADING GUILTY BY POST). *See also* PROOF IN ABSENCE.

summing up A *judge's speech at the end of a *trial by *jury, in which he explains to the jury what its functions are, directs the members of the jury on any relevant points of law, and summarizes all the evidence that has been given in the trial.

summons A court order to an individual to appear in court at a specified place and time. The term is used in criminal cases for appearance at a *magistrates' court. Proof of service of a summons is governed by r 99(1) of the Magistrates' Courts Rules 1981 (SI 1981/552), which provides that service may be effected by (a) hand delivery to the defendant, or (b) by leaving the summons with a person at the last known or usual address, or (c) by posting it to that address. It is not necessary for the person who delivered the summons or, as the case may be, posted it to the defendant's address to attend court to give oral evidence since proof of those matters may be provided by a signed certificate. See also WITNESS SUMMONS.

Sunday trading The opening of shops for trading on a Sunday, which is governed by the Sunday Trading Act 1994 as consolidated in the Employment Rights Act 1996. Small shops may open at will on a Sunday. Large shops with a floor area over 280 square metres may now open on Sunday if notice is given to the *local authority, provided that they open for no more than six hours beginning no earlier than 10am and ending no later than 6pm. These rules do not include Easter Sunday or Christmas Day when it falls on a Sunday. Local authorities may keep registers of large shops open for Sunday trading; these are open to inspection. Certain large shops can open on a Sunday without the need to register, including farm shops, off-licences, motor and cycle suppliers, pharmacies, airport shops, shops at railway stations, motorway service areas, petrol-filling stations, shops supplying ships or aircrafts, stores selling at exhibitions, and shops occupied by people who observe the Jewish Sabbath (Saturday). *Fines can be levied for breach of the requirements. The Act also controls noisy unloading on a Sunday.

Shopworkers who were taken on before 25 August 1994 (other than those employed for Sunday working only), and those who were taken on after that date who are not required by their contracts to work on Sundays, have a legal right to refuse to work on Sundays unless they have agreed to do so (e.g. by signing an 'opting-in notice').

superglue fuming A method of revealing *fingerprints on non-porous surfaces. The item to be examined is placed in a humidified chamber and superglue is heated in it. The vaporised glue then forms on the fingerprint and reveals its pattern.

superior court Any of the higher courts of the legal system, whose *jurisdiction is not limited, for example, by geography or by value of the subject matter of the claim and whose decisions have weight as *precedents. In English law, the superior courts are the *House of Lords, the *Court of Appeal, the *High Court, and the *Crown Court, together with the *Judicial Committee of the Privy Council. Decisions of superior courts are not subject to *judicial review by the High Court. *Compare* INFERIOR COURT.

superior orders A *plea that certain conduct does not constitute a crime because it was committed in obedience to the orders of a superior (usually a superior officer in the armed forces). It could arise, for example, on the unjustified shooting of a rioter when the military are restoring order. UK law does not recognize the plea as a *defence in itself. If an order is unlawful, a soldier's duty is to disobey it. If, however, an unlawful order is not manifestly so, the plea could be raised as establishing that the soldier did not have the necessary *mens rea.

In *international law it was a defence until the end of World War II. The law now is not entirely clear but seems to be that the defence will only relieve the defendant of *liability if the order was not manifestly unlawful, he did not know that the order was unlawful, and he had a duty to obey the order.

supervision order **1.** An order of the court made under s 63 of the Powers of Criminal Court (Sentencing) Act 2000, placing an offender who has attained the age of 10 but is under 18 under the supervision of a *local authority social worker, a member of the *youth offending team, or a *probation officer whose duty it is to 'advise, assist and befriend' the child. The order may last for up to three years. Subject to various limitations, a range of additional requirements may be added to a supervision order. These include:

- residence with a named individual, in local authority accommodation or with *foster parents;
- compliance with arrangements made by his *parents and approved by the local education authority for his education;
- compliance with any directions given by the court or a supervisor to live at a specified place, present himself to a specified person at a specified time and date, and participate in activities specified by the supervisor;
- making reparation for the offence to the victim or the community at large;
- remaining in a specified place between 6pm and 6am;
- participate in a drug treatment and testing programme (introduced by s 279, Criminal Justice Act 2003).

Breach of a supervision order is punishable with a fine of up to £1000 or by a *curfew order or *attendance centre order. The court can also revoke the supervision order and re-sentence the offender for the original offence. **2.** An order made by the family court under s 31 of the Children Act 1989. The court can make a supervision order only if certain *threshold criteria are satisfied. The order does not confer *parental responsibility and initially lasts only for one year with a possible extension for up to a maximum of three years. *Compare* CARE ORDER.

supervision requirement A requirement that may be imposed by the court as part of a *community order, *custody plus order, *suspended sentence order, or an intermittent custody order where to do so would promote the offender's rehabilitation. It requires the offender to attend appointments with a *probation officer (s 213, Criminal Justice Act 2003, replacing a similar provision in s 41, Powers of Criminal Court (Sentencing) Act 2000).

suppression of documents The dishonest destruction, hiding, or defacing of any valuable security (i.e. almost any *document creating, extinguishing, or transferring a right in money or *property), will or similar document, or any original document (but not a copy) belonging to or filed in any court or governmental department. If done with the purpose of gaining as a result, or causing loss to someone else, it is an offence under s 20 of the Theft Act 1968 punishable by up to seven years' imprisonment. *See also* FORGERY.

supremacy The prevalence of one law or *document over another that conflicts with it. Within the *European Union, EU law prevails over national law; there are many instances of national law being overturned by the *European Court of Justice when a member state has ignored provisions of the *Treaty of Rome. However, in certain areas, e.g. competition law, national laws may be permitted when they are stricter than provisions in EU law.

Supreme Court The Court which will function as the highest court in the UK, on the coming into effect of the relevant provisions of the Constitutional Reform Act 2005, taking over from the *House of Lords and the *Judicial Committee of the Privy Council. It will comprise a President,

Deputy President, and ten Justices of the Supreme Court. Initially, the exiting *Lords of Appeal in Ordinary will fill the positions. In any proceedings, the Court will normally be properly constituted if it consists of an uneven number of judges and at least three judges.

Supreme Court of Judicature A court created by the Judicature Acts 1873–5 to take over the *jurisdiction of all the higher courts, other than the *House of Lords, existing at that time. It does not sit as a single court but comprises the *High Court of Justice, the *Court of Appeal, and the *Crown Court. It will be renamed the Senior Courts of England and Wales on the coming into effect of the relevant provisions of the Constitutional Reform Act 2005. Its practice and procedure are regulated by the *Civil Procedure Rules.

surety 1. Security in the form of money to be forfeited upon non-appearance in court, offered either by the defendant himself or by other people of suitable financial resources, character, and relationship to the defendant. **2.** Any person who offers security for another.

See also BAIL; RECOGNIZANCE.

surname A family name. Upon marriage a wife is entitled to take her husband's surname (and title or rank) and to continue using it after his death or *divorce (unless she uses it for fraudulent purposes), although she is not obliged to do so. A *legitimate child, by custom, takes the name of his father and an *illegitimate child that of his mother (although the father's name may be entered on the birth registration if both *parents agree or an affiliation order names the man as the putative father). Upon adoption a child automatically takes the name of his adoptive parents. *See also* CHANGE OF NAME.

surrender to custody To give oneself into the *custody of the court or police at an appointed time and place (*see* BAIL). Failure to surrender to custody is an offence (*see* ABSCONDING). The police may *arrest without *warrant anyone whom they reasonably believe is not going to surrender to custody or anyone whom they have been informed by a *surety (who wishes to be relieved of his *undertaking) is not going to surrender.

surrogacy The role of a woman (a **surrogate mother**) who is commissioned to bear a child by a married couple unable to have children themselves. The Surrogacy Arrangements Act 1985 prohibits commercial agencies from engaging women to act as surrogate mothers. Breach of the prohibition is punishable with a *fine of up to £2000 or three months' imprisonment. Surrogate mothers and commissioning *parents are exempt from *liability. Advertising surrogacy services is punishable with a similar maximum fine. *See also* SECTION 30 ORDER.

surveillance The systematic observation, either overtly or covertly, of places, persons, or things, by visual, aural, electronic, photographic, or other means. For law enforcement purposes, the term is defined by s 48(1) of the Regulation of Investigatory Powers Act 2000 to include monitoring, observing, or listening to persons, their movements, their conversations, or their other activities or communications and recording anything so monitored, observed, or listened to. It may also include the interception of a communication in the course of its transmission by means of a postal service or telecommunication system but does not include the use of a *covert human intelligence source for obtaining or recording any information which is disclosed in the presence of that source.

Surveillance is regulated by the 2000 Act and the *codes of practice issued thereunder. The Act is designed to ensure that surveillance by the police and other agencies is carried out without breaching the *European Convention on Human Rights, and provides that there will be no civil liability arising out of conduct that is carried out in accordance with the authorization to which it relates or is incidental to the authorized conduct.

Three types of activity are covered: 'directed surveillance', 'intrusive surveillance', and the conduct and use of covert human intelligence sources.

'Directed surveillance' is covert surveillance that is undertaken in relation to a specific investigation or operation that is likely to result in the obtaining of private information about a person, unless it is an immediate response to events or circumstances the nature of which is such that it would not be reasonably practicable for an authorization to be sought for the carrying out of the surveillance. This deals with situations where suspicious activity is observed spontaneously and the officer continues to keep observation. 'Private information' includes any information relating to his private or family life. Surveillance is covert where it is carried out in a manner calculated to ensure that the person or persons subject to the surveillance are unaware that it is or may be taking place. Directed surveillance includes the interception of communications where there is no interception *warrant and where the communication is sent by or is intended for a person who has consented to the interception. It is available to the police and a long list of other public authorities shown in sch 1 to the Act. Directed surveillance may be authorized by a superintendent or, in other bodies, as set out in the Regulation of Investigatory Powers (Prescription of Offices, Ranks and Positions) Order 2000 (SI 2000/2417).

'Intrusive surveillance' is covert surveillance carried out in relation to anything taking place on residential *premises or in any private vehicle. It is available only to the police and other law enforcement agencies. This kind of surveillance may take place by means either of a person or device located inside residential premises or a private vehicle of the person who is subject to the surveillance or by means of a device placed outside which consistently provides a product of equivalent quality and detail as a product which would be obtained from a device located inside. A tracking device that only provides information about the location of the vehicle is not intrusive. The authorization is given by a Chief Officer, or equivalent, who must be satisfied that it is to prevent serious crime or is in the interests of national security or the economic well-being of the UK. The prior approval of a Surveillance Commissioner is required before taking effect (except in cases of urgency). The authorization is normally for three months and can be renewed. If given orally, or by someone other than the recognised authorizing officer, the authorization lasts for 72 hours. It needs to be regularized if it is to extend beyond that. *See also* COVERT HUMAN INTELLIGENCE SOURCE; PROPERTY INTERFERENCE.

sus law The law that formerly empowered the police to arrest any reputed thief or suspected person found loitering with intent to commit an *arrestable offence. This law caused much public concern and was abolished by the Criminal Attempts Act 1981.

suspended sentence A prison *sentence that does not take effect immediately. A new form of suspended sentence was introduced by ss 189 and 190 of the Criminal Justice Act 2003 (CJA). The key changes were that there must be 'exceptional circumstances' before the court can suspend a sentence of imprisonment and the inclusion of a supervisory element intended to increase the rehabilitative effect of the sentence.

Under the new provisions, a court that passes a prison sentence of between 28 and 51 weeks (or between 28 and 65 weeks in the case of consecutive sentences for two or more offences) may suspend the sentence for a period of between six months and two years and order the offender to undertake one or more of the following community requirements:

- *unpaid work requirement (s 199, CJA 2003);
- *activity requirement (s 201, CJA 2003);
- *programme requirement (s 202, CJA 2003);
- *prohibited activity requirement (s 203, CJA 2003);
- *curfew requirement (s 204, CJA 2003), generally in conjunction with an *electronic monitoring requirement (s 177 (3), CJA 2003);
- *exclusion requirement (s 205, CJA 2003), generally in conjunction with an *electronic monitoring requirement (s 177(3), CJA 2003);
- *residence requirement (s 206, CJA 2003);

- *mental health treatment requirement (s 207, CJA 2003);
- *drug rehabilitation requirement (s 209, CJA 2003);
- *alcohol treatment requirement (s 212, CJA 2003);
- *supervision requirement (s 213, CJA 2003);
- (in the case of an offender aged under 25) *attendance centre requirement (s 214, CJA 2003).

The custodial part of the sentence only takes effect if the offender either commits a further offence during the period of suspension or fails to comply with community requirements imposed by the court.

The powers to make a **suspended sentence supervision order** and to make an order for a **partially suspended sentence** have been repealed.

tache noire Dark post-mortem staining in the *sclera of the eye. It has no *forensic significance.

tachycardia Fast heart rate.

takedown A *rifle or *shotgun designed to allow the *barrel to be disassembled from the buttstock and receiver without the use of tools, thus allowing it to be carried and concealed more easily.

takeover The acquisition of control by one company over another, usually smaller, company (the **target company**). This is usually achieved (1) by buying *shares in the target company with the agreement of all its members (if they are few) or of only its controllers; (2) by purchases on the *Stock Exchange; or (3) by means of a *takeover bid. *Compare* MERGER.

takeover bid A technique for effecting a *takeover or a *merger. The bidder makes an offer to the members of the target company to acquire their *shares (either for cash or in exchange for shares in the bidding company) in the hope of receiving sufficient acceptances to obtain voting control of the target company. Unless there is a *scheme of arrangement—and providing that the court does not order otherwise—if members holding not less than 90 per cent in value of the shares involved in the bid accept the offer, the bidding company can compulsorily acquire the shares of the remaining members.

taking a conveyance without consent (TWOC) It is an offence, under s 12 of the Theft Act 1968, punishable by up to six months' imprisonment and/or a fine, for a person to take a conveyance for his own or someone else's use (albeit temporary) without the permission of the owner, or to drive or be transported in a conveyance knowing that it has been taken without the owner's consent. *See also* AGGRAVATED VEHICLE-TAKING; INTERFERING WITH VEHICLES.

talaq An Islamic *divorce, usually effected by a triple declaration ('I divorce you') by the husband to the wife in front of witnesses. In some Muslim countries this may be done informally; in other countries it must be pronounced before an authorized officer of the court. It may also be effected by a written **talaqnama**. *See also* EXTRAJUDICIAL DIVORCE.

talesman A person added to a *jury to make up the numbers if insufficient have been summoned to court. Any passerby can be called provided they meet the jury qualifications.

tangible property *Property that has a physical existence, e.g. *chattels and *land but not *choses in action nor incorporeal *hereditaments (which are **intangible property**).

Tardieu spots *Petechial haemorrhages found on *pleura and usually indicative of strangulation or suffocation.

target hardening Crime prevention by improving the physical security of the protected person or property.

tax A compulsory contribution to the state's funds. It is levied either directly on the taxpayer by means of income tax, capital gains tax, *inheritance tax, and corporation tax; or indirectly through tax on purchases of *goods and services (*see* VALUE-ADDED TAX) and through various kinds of duty, e.g. *road tax, stamp duty, and duties on betting and gaming.

taxable person *See* VALUE-ADDED TAX.

taxable supply *See* VALUE-ADDED TAX.

tax avoidance The lawful arrangement or planning of one's affairs so as to reduce liability to tax. *Compare* TAX EVASION.

tax credit A form of benefit available to families with children, single *parents, and those on low incomes. The Tax Credits Act

2002, which received royal assent on 8 July 2002, makes provision for two tax credits: the **child tax credit** for families with children and the **working tax credit** for working households with a low income, including those in which a worker has a disability. The scheme, which is administered by *Her Majesty's Revenue and Customs (HMRC), replaced the child-related elements of *income support and income-based *jobseeker's allowance; child dependency increases paid as additions to some non-means tested benefits; the pre-existing tax credits, working families' tax credit, disabled person's tax credit, and the children's tax credit; and the New Deal 50plus employment credit.

Sections 31 to 36 of and sch 2 to the Act provide for sanctions to be imposed in certain cases and for information powers in cases of suspected *fraud in relation to tax credits. These cases include: where incorrect statements or declarations have been made in a claim or incorrect information has been submitted in support of a claim; where there has been a failure to provide required information or evidence; where there has been a failure to tell HMRC about certain prescribed changes in circumstances which might affect entitlement to the credits (e.g. changes in child care costs); or where a person is knowingly concerned in fraudulent activity with a view to obtaining tax credits. Penalties may also be imposed on *employers for failing to maintain and provide accurate information or *documents and for failure to make payments of working tax credit.

tax evasion Any illegal action taken to avoid the lawful assessment of taxes; e.g. by concealing or failing to declare income. *Compare* TAX AVOIDANCE.

tax point The date on which a taxable supply becomes liable for *value-added tax. The rate of tax chargeable on the supply is the rate in force at the tax point, and the supply must be accounted for in the tax period in which the tax point occurs. If the supply is a straightforward *sale of goods, the tax point is normally the date on which the customer takes possession of the goods. For the supply of services, the tax point is normally the date on which the service is completed. In the case of hirings, rentals, continuous or metered supplies (e.g. electricity), and supplies that are subject to progress payments, the tax point is either the date on which an invoice is issued or the date on which payment is received, whichever is earlier. If the supplier issues a tax invoice, this must show the tax point.

technical bail Bail granted to a defendant who is in *custody for another matter, either on remand or as a convicted prisoner, and therefore will not actually be released from custody.

telephone tapping Secretly listening to telephone conversations by interfering with the line. *See also* ELECTRONIC SURVEILLANCE.

temazepam (Restoril™) (*slang*: tems, temazzies, eggs, green eggs, jellies, norries, rugby balls) A *benzodiazepine drug used pharmaceutically for treatment of insomnia. It is abused and taken in higher doses. It is a Class B drug and when prepared for injection is a Class A drug. It is very dangerous if intravenously injected because the gel from the capsule may reform in the blood vessel.

temperature The level of heat within a body. The temperature of a body can give an estimate of the time since death until the body reaches ambient temperature. When a body is found it is important to take the temperature of the surrounding air/water as this will affect the rate at which the body cools.

temporal bone A thin bone making up part of the side of the skull.

temporary activity *Licensable activity including the sale of *alcohol, by unlicensed persons and on unlicensed *premises, which is permitted if it is an event at which not more than 500 people will attend and will not last for more than 96 hours (Licensing Act 2003). The person wishing to organize such an event must serve a temporary event notice on the *licensing authority. A person who does not hold a licence can stage five such events per year and a licensed person can stage 50. A venue can only hold twelve such events in a year. The police can object to an event on the grounds of crime prevention.

temporary event notice *See* TEMPORARY ACTIVITY.

tenancy Broadly, the interest of one who holds *land by any *right or *title. The term is often used in a more restricted sense, however, for the arrangement in which the owner allows another person (the tenant) to take possession of the land for an agreed period, usually in return for rent. A person who has a tenancy is in possession of the land for the purposes of s 4 of the Theft Act 1968.

tenant A person who is granted a *lease or a *tenancy. A tenant need not be an individual; e.g. a company can be a tenant.

tender offer An offer of a company's *securities to the public (*see* FLOTATION) at a uniform price (above a specified minimum) that is determined by the bids received and ensures that all the securities are taken up.

term 1. Originally, any of four periods of the year during which judicial business had to be transacted. For this purpose terms were abolished by the Judicature Acts 1873–5, and the legal year is now divided into *sittings and *vacations. In the *Inns of Court the year is still divided into terms that have the same names as the court sittings but are shorter. **2.** Any provision forming part of a contract. A term may be either a *condition, a *warranty, or an *innominate term, depending on its importance, and either an *express term or an *implied term, depending on its form.

termination of proceedings There are three methods by which summary proceedings may be terminated: by service of a *notice of discontinuance, by application to the court to withdraw the *summons or *charge (*see* WITHDRAWAL OF PROCEEDINGS), and by *offering no evidence in court. In the *Crown Court, the only proceedings that can be discontinued are those that have been sent for *trial under s 51 of the Crime and Disorder Act 1998 (*see* SENDING OFFENCES FOR TRIAL). Otherwise, proceedings may be terminated only by offering no evidence or by the entry of a **nolle prosequi*. The *prosecution may also apply to the court to leave an *indictment or a count on an indictment to '**lie on the file**'. In such cases, there is no *verdict, so the proceedings are not formally terminated. However, there can be no further proceedings against the defendant on those matters without the leave of the Crown Court or *Court of Appeal.

territoriality (in *international law) The principle that states should not exercise their *jurisdiction outside the area of their territory. They are entitled, however, to exercise jurisdiction within their territory over acts committed by their citizens outside their territory, and all states have jurisdiction over *offences against international law and order. The territory of a state for purposes of jurisdiction includes its ships and aeroplanes. A state may exercise jurisdiction over crimes that are either originated within its territory but completed outside or originated outside its territory and completed inside.

territorial limits The geographical limits within which an *Act of Parliament operates, which include, in the UK, the territorial sea up to the twelve-mile limit. The limits are restricted by *international law (*see* SOVEREIGNTY OF PARLIAMENT).

territorial waters The band of sea between the limit of the *internal waters of a state (*see* BASELINE) and the *high seas, over which the state has certain specified rights. These rights are governed by a 1958 Geneva Convention, which is taken to represent the position under customary *international law. A coastal state exercises *sovereignty over its territorial waters, which includes, in particular, the following: (1) an exclusive right to fish and to exploit the resources of the seabed and subsoil of the seabed and exclusive use of the *airspace above the territorial sea; (2) the exclusive right to use the territorial waters to transport people and *goods from one part of the state to another; (3) the right to enact laws concerning navigation, immigration, customs dues, and health, which bind all foreign ships; (4) the right to ask a warship that ignores navigation regulations to leave the territorial waters; (5) certain powers of arrest over merchant ships and people on board, and *jurisdiction to try crimes committed on board such ships within the territorial waters; (6) the right to exclude fighting in the territorial waters during a *war in which the coastal state is neutral. All foreign ships, however, have a right of **innocent passage** through the territorial sea, i.e. the right to pass through, provided they do not prejudice the peace, security, or good order of the coastal state (submarines must navigate on the surface). *See also* HOT PURSUIT, RIGHT OF; LAW OF THE SEA.

The extent of the territorial sea is usually measured from the low tide mark on the shore, but in estuaries and small bays it is measured from a **closing line** between two points on the shore, which delimits the state's internal waters. The width of the territorial sea is a matter of dispute in international law. Traditionally it has been fixed at three nautical miles (*see* CANNON-SHOT RULE), but many states have claimed twelve miles or more, and this will probably become the normal width. The Territorial Sea Act 1987 fixes the territorial waters of the UK at twelve nautical miles. Beyond the territorial sea, states have a **contiguous zone**, not exceeding 24 nautical miles, in which they may exercise jurisdiction over certain infringements of their customs, fiscal, immigration, or sanitary regulations. In recent years many states (including the UK) have also claimed **exclusive fishery zones** extending 200 miles beyond the low tide mark. The UK is subject to the EU's Common Fisheries Policy in relation to fishing.

terrorism The use or threat of violence for political ends, including putting the public in fear. The Terrorism Act 2000 has abolished all the previous statutory provisions relating to terrorism, apart from a number of specific provisions that continue to exist under the Northern Ireland (Emergency Provisions) Act 1996, the Terrorism (Temporary Provisions) Act 1989, and the Criminal Justice (Terrorism and Conspiracy) Act 1998. The Terrorism Act 2000 defines terrorism in s 1 as (a) the use or threat of action that involves serious violence against a person or serious damage to property, endangers a person's life, creates a serious risk to the health or safety of the public or a section of the public, or is designed to interfere with or disrupt an electronic system, or (b) the use or threat of violence designed to influence the government or intimidate the public or a section of the public: in both cases the use or threat of such action or violence is made for the purpose of advancing a political, religious, or ideological cause. The Act also provides that the action referred to includes that taken within as well as outside the UK. The Act contains provisions that allow for certain organizations to be declared as **proscribed organizations**. It then becomes an offence to be a member of such an organization. The Act also contains detailed provisions as to property defined as being 'terrorist property' and the *forfeiture of such property. There are detailed provisions relating to the investigation of terrorist activities that grant the police and security services special and extra powers. These include special powers to stop and search, detain, and interrogate those suspected of involvement in terrorist activities.

The Act was a further attempt at bringing UK *legislation into line with the 1977 European Convention on the Suppression of Terrorism. This was needed in order to ensure that persons within the UK who were suspected of terrorist activity in other parts of Europe could be successfully extradited to face *trial in those other states.

The Terrorism Act 2006 (which came into effect on 13 April 2006) created a number of new and serious criminal offences in respect of things done in the course of or in connection with the commission of an act of terrorism or for the purposes of terrorism, notably: encouragement of terrorism (s 1); dissemination of terrorist publications (s 2); preparation of terrorist acts (s 5); training for terrorism (s 6); attendance at a place used for terrorist training (s 8); making and possession of radioactive devices or materials (s 9); misuse of radioactive devices or material and misuse and damage of facilities (s 10); making demands or threats relating to devices, materials, or facilities (s 11). Section 17 of the Act significantly extends

English (and other UK) criminal jurisdiction over terrorist conduct abroad, irrespective of whether the alleged offender is a British citizen or, in the case of a company, a company incorporated in a part of the UK.

test case A case brought to test a principle of law that, once established, can be applied in other cases. Thus when there are a number of claimants with similar claims, a test case may be brought by one of them, after which the remainder of the claims can be settled out of court on the same basis.

testimony (testimonial evidence) A statement of a witness in court, usually on *oath, offered as evidence of the truth of what is stated.

textbook A book used as a standard work for the study of a particular subject. Textbooks are sometimes cited in court to assist in the *interpretation of the law. They have no authority as a source of law but merely provide an expert opinion as to the current state of the law. There was formerly a convention that only the works of dead authors could be cited, but modern practice also allows citation of living authors. The **Books of Authority**, i.e. the works of Glanvil, Bracton, Littleton, Coke, and Blackstone, are treated as having the same authority as cases of the same period.

thallium One of the heavy metals. It is a *poison which causes the hair to fall out and fatally damages the nervous system.

theft The offence contrary to s 1 of the Theft Act 1968 of dishonestly appropriating property belonging to another with the intention of permanently depriving the other of it (*see* DISHONESTY). 'Appropriation' is defined by s 3 of the Act as the assumption of the rights of the owner of the property and includes any act showing that one is treating the property as one's own, which need not necessarily involve taking it away. For example, switching price tags from one item to another in a shop to enable one to buy *goods at a lower price could amount to an appropriation, as could purporting to sell someone else's property. If a person acquires property without stealing it, but later decides to keep the property unlawfully, he may be regarded as having appropriated it. For example, if A lends his golf clubs to B for a week and B subsequently decides to keep the clubs or sell them, this indicates that B has assumed the rights of the owner unlawfully. Under s 4 of the Act, 'property' includes all *tangible and *intangible objects and *choses in action (e.g. bank balances) but there are special provisions in the Act governing *land and wild plants and animals (*see* POACHING). Property belongs to anyone who either owns it or has physical possession or control of it. Section 2 of the Act expressly states that a person is not dishonest if he believes (even if unreasonably) that he is legally entitled to appropriate the property or that the owner would consent or could not be discovered by taking reasonable steps. The *punishment for theft is up to seven years' imprisonment. Theft involving the use of force may amount to *robbery. *See also* BURGLARY; DECEPTION; TAKING A CONVEYANCE WITHOUT CONSENT.

thing *See* CHOSE.

third-party insurance *Insurance against risks to people other than those that are parties to the policy. It is an offence under s 143 of the Road Traffic Act 1988 to use, or allow anyone else to use, a *motor vehicle on a *road unless there is a valid insurance policy (or security under s 146) covering death, physical injury, or damage caused by the use of the vehicle in Great Britain. It also covers any *liability resulting from the use of a vehicle (or a *trailer) that is compulsorily insurable in EU countries. The policy is only considered valid when a *certificate of insurance has been issued.

There is a duty upon anyone driving a motor vehicle to give his name and address and that of the car owner and to produce the certificate of insurance whenever asked to do so by a *police officer. He may, however, produce it within seven days at any police station he specifies at the time he was asked to produce it. Where a motor vehicle is involved in an accident that causes injury to a person other than the *driver of that vehicle, the driver must produce evidence of the insurance or security to any person having a reasonable cause to demand to see it. Breach of any of these duties is punishable by *fine, *endorsement, and *disqualification. *See also* DRIVING WITHOUT INSURANCE.

thorax The chest.

threat The expression of an intention to harm someone with the object of forcing them to do something. A threat (or **menace**), or the action of threatening someone (*see* INTIMIDATION), is an ingredient of many crimes. *See* BLACKMAIL; BOMB HOAX; CRIMINAL DAMAGE; DURESS; FORCIBLE ENTRY; INTIMIDATION; OBSCENE AND THREATENING COMMUNICATIONS; RACIAL AND RELIGIOUS HATRED; RAPE; THREATENING BEHAVIOUR; VIOLENT DISORDER.

threatening behaviour The offence, contrary to s 4 of the Public Order Act 1986 and punishable with up to six months' imprisonment and/or a *fine, of using towards another person threatening, abusive, or insulting words or behaviour. It is a similar offence to distribute or display anything that is threatening, abusive, or insulting. In both cases it must be proved either that the accused person had the specific intent (*see* INTOXICATION) to cause the other person to believe that immediate unlawful violence would be used against him or, simply, that the threatened person was likely to believe that violence would be used against him. A further offence of intentionally causing harassment, alarm, or distress, contrary to s 4A of the 1986 Act, was introduced by the Criminal Justice and Public Order Act 1994; it is punishable by a fine and/or six months' imprisonment.

It is also an offence, contrary to s 5 of the 1986 Act, punishable with a fine, to use threatening or disorderly behaviour, or to display anything that is threatening, abusive, or insulting, within the hearing or sight of anyone likely to be harassed, alarmed, or distressed by it. Here, it is a *defence if the accused person proves (*see* BURDEN OF PROOF) either that he had no reason to believe that there was anyone within hearing or sight who was likely to be harassed, alarmed, or distressed, or that he was inside a dwelling (any living accommodation, including a hotel bedroom) and had no reason to believe that the behaviour or display would be heard or seen by someone outside, or that his conduct was reasonable.

The offences may be committed in private as well as *public places unless the behaviour or display took place inside a dwelling. *See also* RACIAL AND RELIGIOUS HATRED; STALKING; VIOLENT DISORDER.

three-tier system A system for allocating cases between *Crown Court centres. First-tier centres deal with both criminal and *High Court civil cases and are served by High Court *puisne judges, *circuit judges, and *recorders. Second-tier centres deal only with criminal cases, but are served by the same kinds of judge as first-tier centres. Third-tier centres deal only with criminal cases and are served by circuit judges and recorders only.

threshold criteria The minimum preconditions that must be met before the court is able to make a *care or *supervision order. These are set out in the Children Act 1989 and are that the child is suffering or likely to suffer significant harm either caused by the care or lack of care given to it by its *parents or because the child is beyond parental control.

threshold test A test, under the *Code for Crown Prosecutions, applied by a *prosecutor in cases in which it would not be appropriate to release a suspect on *bail after *charge, but the evidence to apply the *full code test is not yet available. The prosecutor must decide whether there is at least a reasonable suspicion that the suspect has committed an offence, and if there is, whether it is in the public interest to charge that suspect. Where a prosecutor makes a charging decision in accordance with the threshold test, the case must be reviewed in accordance with the full code test as soon as reasonably practicable, taking into account the progress of the investigation.

throat 1. The forward section of a *firearms chamber tapering to coincide with the diameter of the *bore. **2.** The enlargement of the bore of a *revolver at the *breech end, designed to centre the *bullet in the *barrel as it passes from the *cylinder when the weapon is fired.

thrombosis A blood clot that forms inside a blood vessel and can move after it is formed. It can be fatal, depending upon where it forms or moves to.

thyroid cartilage A cage of cartilage in the neck seen as the 'Adam's apple'. It becomes ossified and brittle in old age and may be injured by strangulation.

tibia The shin bone.

time immemorial *See* LEGAL MEMORY.

time limits *See* SUMMARY OFFENCE; INDICTABLE OFFENCE.

time provisions in contracts Provisions in contracts that relate to the time within which acts are to be performed. The question often arises whether or not a time provision constitutes a *condition of the contract. If it does, it is said that time is **of the essence**. In general, time is of the essence only if the contract says so or if an intention that it should be so is to be inferred from the nature of the transaction or the circumstances surrounding it. Most suppliers' contracts, however, include an express term that time is not of the essence.

tit for tat (in consumer protection law) The strategy of enforcement bodies not to prosecute as long as the offending body complies with regulations and mends its ways.

title 1. A person's right of *ownership of property. Someone with a **good title** has adequate evidence to establish his right. **2.** The heading of an *Act of Parliament, which may be a **long title** or a **short title**. **3.** The name of a particular court action, which is derived from the heading of the originating *process that initiated it.

toluene An aromatic hydrocarbon chemical used extensively in the chemical industry and as a solvent. It is a substance abused by 'glue sniffers'. Frequent use can lead to irreversible brain damage and damage to teeth.

tools of trade A workman's tools, which he is entitled to keep if he is made *bankrupt. They include all tools, books, vehicles, and other items of equipment necessary for the bankrupt's personal use in his employment, business, or vocation.

tort [Old French: harm, wrong; from Latin *tortus*: twisted or crooked] A wrongful act or omission for which *damages can be obtained in a civil court by the person wronged, other than a wrong that is only a *breach of contract. The law of tort is mainly concerned with providing compensation for personal injury and property damage caused by *negligence. It also protects other interests, however, such as reputation (*see* DEFAMATION), personal freedom (*see* ASSAULT; FALSE IMPRISONMENT), title to property (*see* CONVERSION; TRESPASS), enjoyment of property (*see* NUISANCE), and commercial interests (*see* INTIMIDATION; CONSPIRACY; PASSING OFF). It must usually be shown that the wrong was done intentionally or negligently, but there are some torts of *strict liability. Most torts are actionable only if they have caused damage, but torts whose main function is to protect rights rather than to compensate for damage (such as trespass) are actionable without proof of damage. The person principally liable is the one who committed the tort (the **tortfeasor**) but under the rules of *vicarious liability one may be liable for a tort committed by another person. The main remedy for a tort is an action for damages, but in some cases an *injunction can be obtained to prevent repetition of the injury. Other remedies are *self-help and orders for specific *restitution of property.

Some torts are also breaches of contract. Negligent driving by a taxi-driver that causes injury to his passenger is both the tort of negligence and breach of the contract to carry the passenger safely to his destination. The passenger may sue either in tort or for breach of contract, or both. Many torts are also crimes. Assault is both a crime and a tort. *Dangerous driving is a crime and may give rise to an action in tort if it causes injury to another person. The crime is prosecuted by agents of the state in the name of the *Crown. It is left to the injured person to seek *compensation from the wrongdoer by means of an action in tort.

tortfeasor One who commits a *tort. *See also* JOINT TORTFEASORS.

tortious Having the nature of a *tort; wrongful.

torture Deliberate *inhuman treatment or punishment causing very serious and cruel suffering. Under s 134 of the Criminal Justice Act 1988, the offence committed by a public official (or someone with the official's acquiescence) of intentionally inflicting severe physical or mental suffering on any person anywhere in the world. It carries a maximum *sentence of *life imprisonment. Under this Act, the accused had a *defence if he proved that his conduct was legally authorized, justified, or excusable. However, the prohibition on torture as set out in Article 3 of the *European Convention on Human Rights is now part of UK law as a consequence of the *Human Rights Act. This right is an *absolute right, and torture can never be justified as being in the public interest, no matter how great that public interest might be. Public authorities have a limited but positive duty to protect this right from interference by third parties.

totting up *See* DISQUALIFICATION FROM DRIVING.

touting Seeking business by approaching potential customers. Under s 166 of the Criminal Justice and Public Order Act 1994 it is a *summary offence (punishable by a fine) for unauthorized persons to offer or display for sale, in a *public place, a ticket for a designated football match or other sporting event for which more than 6000 tickets are issued. Similarly, under s 167 of the 1994 Act it is a summary offence (punishable by a fine) for taxi operators to solicit persons to hire vehicles to carry them as passengers unless they are licensed operators within an authorized scheme that permits such soliciting.

toxicology The detection and study of *poisons.

trachea The windpipe which runs from the throat to the lungs.

trade description Any direct or indirect indication of certain characteristics of *goods or of any part of them, such as their quantity, size, fitness for their purpose, time or place of origin, method of manufacture or processing, and price. Under the Trade Descriptions Act 1968, it is a criminal offence to apply a trade description to goods that is false or to supply or offer to supply any goods to which such a description is applied (*see* FALSE TRADE DESCRIPTION).

trade mark A distinctive symbol that identifies particular products of a trader to the general public. The symbol may consist of a device, words, or a combination of these. A trader may register his trade mark at the Register of Trade Marks, which is at the Patent Office (*see* PATENT). He then enjoys the exclusive right to use the trade mark in connection with the *goods for which it was registered. Any person or firm that has a trade connection with the goods may register a trade mark. For example, he may be the manufacturer, a dealer, importer, or retailer. Under the Trade Marks Act 1994 (and EU Directive 89/104), registration is initially for ten years; it is then renewable. Trade marks can be registered for ever. However, the right to remain on the register may be lost if the trade mark is not used or is misused. The owner of a trade mark may assign it or allow others to use it. If anyone uses a registered trade mark without the owner's permission, or uses a mark that is likely to be confused with a registered trade mark, the owner can sue for an *injunction and *damages or an *account of profits. Unregistered marks are protected by *passing off. Since 1 April 1996 *Community Trade Marks can now be obtained. These are cheaper than trade marks obtained by registration in several individual EU states. Trade marks are an example of *intellectual property.

trade mark at common law A *trade mark that is not registered in the Register of Trade Marks but is identified with particular *goods through established use. The trade mark's owner may bring an action for *passing off in the case of infringement.

trade secret Some process or product belonging to a business, disclosure of which would harm the business's interests. The courts will generally grant injunctions to prohibit any threatened disclosure of trade secrets by *employees, former employees, and others to whom the secrets have been disclosed in confidence. There is a relationship of trust and confidence between *employer and employee that may be destroyed if the employee discloses a trade secret, providing a reason for dismissal; such a dismissal may be fair if the procedure adopted complies with the necessary requirements. *See* RESTRAINT OF TRADE.

traffic offence *See* OFFENCE RELATING TO ROAD TRAFFIC.

trailer A vehicle drawn by a motor vehicle (reg 3(2), Road Vehicles (Construction and Use) Regulations 1986 (SI 1986/1078)).

trajectory The path a *bullet takes in flight.

transfer of children An offence under the Statute of the *International Criminal Court of transferring children from one group to another with the intention of destroying the original group's existence. It is a form of *genocide. The transfer must be permanent and forcible. Forcible includes threat of force, duress, psychological oppression, or abuse of power.

transfer of party's own civilian population An offence under the Statute of the *International Criminal Court where in *armed conflict an occupying power transfers part of its own population to the occupied territory usually for the purpose of colonizing the territory.

transfer of risk The passing from the *seller of *property to the *buyer of the incidence of the loss if the property is damaged or destroyed. The Sale of Goods Act 1979 provides that, unless it is otherwise agreed, *goods remain at the seller's risk until *ownership passes to the buyer. After that they are at the buyer's risk, whether or not delivery has been made.

transfer of shares A transaction resulting in a change of *share ownership.

transferred malice *See* MALICE.

transferring cases to the Crown Court *See* NOTICE OF TRANSFER; SENDING OFFENCES FOR TRIAL.

transmission of shares A *transfer of shares that occurs automatically, by operation of law, upon *bankruptcy (from the bankrupt to his *trustee in bankruptcy) or upon death (to the personal representatives of the deceased). The transferees do not become *company members until the company enters their names upon the register of members; in the meantime they are unable to attend or vote at company meetings.

transnational corporation An enterprise consisting of commercial entities in more than one state that are linked by *ownership or otherwise. Transnational corporations operate in such a way that they exercise a uniform, cohesive, and common policy in order to further their economic interests. This policy can allow them to wield significant influence over the activities of those states in which they carry out their commercial activities, i.e. by exerting pressure over the direction of domestic policy of the host states.

transparency An essential condition for those operating in a market, which ensures that the rules to which they are subject are made obvious. Generally, it ensures that the reasons behind measures and the applicable regulations are clear to all, so that all are treated fairly.

transsexual A person who believes he or she belongs to the sex opposite to his or her gender at birth; transsexuals may undergo surgery and drug treatment to alter the external appearance of their bodies to conform with their view of themselves (*see* SEX CHANGE). *See also* VAGINA.

Under English law, for the purposes of marriage transsexuals are regarded as belonging to the sex determined at their birth and registered on their birth certificates. For the purposes of employment, however, the law now recognizes the validity of sex changes in transsexuals (*see* GENDER REASSIGNMENT).

trauma Physical injury or mental stress.

traumatic asphyxia Asphyxia caused by restriction of the movement of the chest wall as happens when a person is crushed or buried.

treachery Conduct that assists an enemy. This was defined under the Treachery Act 1940 as an offence relating to World War II, which was punishable by death. There is now, however, no specific crime of treachery: acts of this sort are usually dealt with under the Official Secrets Acts (*see* OFFICIAL SECRETS) or, in some cases, as *treason.

treason Conduct comprising a breach of allegiance owed to the sovereign or the state. Under the Treason Act 1351, high treason included violating the king's wife, eldest unmarried daughter, or wife of the king's eldest son; openly attempting to prevent the heir to the throne from succeeding; and killing the chancellor or any *judge while performing their duties. Treason was redefined by the Treason Act 1795 and the principal forms now include: (1) compassing the death or serious injury of the sovereign or his (or her) spouse or eldest son; (2) levying *war against the sovereign in his (or her) realm, which includes any insurrection against the authority of the sovereign or of the government that goes beyond *riot or *violent disorder; (3) giving aid or comfort to the sovereign's enemies in wartime. The *penalty for treason (fixed by law) was formerly death but is now *life imprisonment.

treasure trove Formerly, items of gold and silver found in a concealed place, having been hidden by an owner who was untraceable. Under medieval law they belonged to the *Crown, but only if it could be proved at a *coroner's inquest that the owner had intended to retrieve the items and had not merely abandoned them. If the items were lost or abandoned, the finder acquired a right to possess them. The Treasure Act 1996 altered the law in this field; the Act and the Code of Practice made under it apply only to England, Wales, and Northern Ireland. The definition of treasure now includes any object at least 300 years old and containing more than 5 per cent precious metal (excluding single coins). The Crown is now entitled to receive *all* treasure and will pay a reward to the finder. The Act creates a new offence of failing to report the discovery of treasure, with a maximum *penalty of a £5000 fine or three months' imprisonment (or both). The Code of Practice sets out guidelines on such matters as which objects should be reported; how finders can seek advice from museums and archaeologists in the event of a large find; government policy on the payment of *ex gratia* rewards, including rewards to landowners and rewards for finds resulting from trespass; and policy and procedures for reaching valuations, including the commissioning of reports from independent experts and provisions for finders to submit their own valuations.

Treasury Counsel Treasury Counsel to the *Crown at the *Central Criminal Court: a group of *barristers, nominated by the *Attorney-General, who receive briefs from the *Director of Public Prosecutions to appear for the *prosecution in *trials at the Central Criminal Court (Old Bailey). There are six Senior Counsel (who, despite the name, are not *Queen's Counsel) and ten Junior Counsel.

treaty An international agreement in writing between two states (a **bilateral treaty**) or a number of states (a **multilateral treaty**). Such agreements can also be known as *conventions, **pacts**, *protocols, *final acts, **arrangements**, and **general acts**. Treaties are binding in *international law and constitute the equivalent of the municipal-law contract, conveyance, or *legislation. Some treaties create law only for those states that are parties to them, some codify pre-existing customary international law, and some propound rules that eventually develop into customary international law, binding upon all states (e.g. the Genocide Convention). Federal states, colonial states, and public international organizations are sometimes also able to enter into treaty obligations. The Vienna Convention on the Law of Treaties (1969) defines in detail the rules relating to inter-state treaties and is itself generally considered to declare or develop customary international law in this area. Treaties are normally concluded by the process of *ratification. *See also* HIGH CONTRACTING PARTIES; RESERVATION; SIGNATURE OF TREATY.

In England the power to make or enter into treaties belongs to the monarch, acting on the advice of government ministers, but a treaty does not become part of English *municipal law until brought into force by an *Act of Parliament.

Treaty of Rome The treaty founding the European Economic Community (now known as the *European Community) and the European Atomic Energy Community (*see also* EUROPEAN UNION). The treaty was signed in Rome on 25 March 1957 by its founder members, i.e. Belgium, West Germany, France, Italy, Luxembourg, and the Netherlands. It has since been amended (*see* SINGLE EUROPEAN ACT; AMSTERDAM TREATY) and is now known as the **European Community Treaty** (Treaty Establishing the European Community as Amended by Subsequent Treaties).

Treaty on European Union *See* MAASTRICHT TREATY.

tree preservation order An order made by a local planning authority prohibiting, in the interests of amenity, the felling, lopping, uprooting, or other wilful damage or destruction of a tree (or trees) without its consent. The term 'tree' is not defined by statute, but in *Kent County Council v Batchelor* (1976) 3 P & CR 185 it was said that it 'ought to be something over seven or eight inches in diameter'. Hence, bushes, hedges, and shrubs may not be the subject of such an order.

trespass A wrongful direct interference with another person or with his *possession of *land or *goods. In the Middle Ages, any wrongful act was called a trespass, but only some trespasses, such as trespass by force and arms (*vi et armis*), were dealt with in the King's Courts. The distinguishing feature of trespass in modern law is that it is a direct and immediate interference with person or property, such as striking a person, entering his land, or taking away his goods without his consent. Indirect or consequential injury, such as leaving an unlit hole into which someone falls, is not trespass. Trespass is actionable per se, i.e. the act of trespass is itself a *tort and it is not necessary to prove that it has caused actual damage.

There are three kinds of trespass: to the person, to goods, and to land. **Trespass to the person** may be intentional or negligent, but since negligent physical injuries are remedied by an action for *negligence, the action for trespass to the person is now only brought for intentional acts, in the form of actions for *assault, *battery, and *false imprisonment. **Trespass to goods** includes touching, moving, or carrying them away (*de bonis asportatis*). It may be intentional or negligent, but *inevitable accident is a *defence. **Trespass to land** usually takes the form of entering it without permission. It is no defence to show that the trespass was innocent (e.g. that the trespasser honestly believed that the land belonged to him). Trespass to land or goods is a wrong to possession rather than to *ownership. Thus a *tenant of rented property, for example, has the right to sue for trespass to that property. Trespass to land is a tort but not normally a crime: the notice 'Trespassers will be prosecuted' is therefore usually misleading.

However, trespass may sometimes constitute a crime. Thus squatters may be *guilty of a crime (*see* ADVERSE OCCUPATION). It is also an offence to trespass on diplomatic or consular *premises or premises similarly protected by immunity (s 9, Criminal Law Act 1977); to enter and remain on any premises as a trespasser with a *weapon of offence for which one has no authority or reasonable excuse (s 8, Criminal Law Act 1977); or to be on any premises, land, or water as a trespasser with a *firearm for which one has no reasonable excuse (s 20, Firearms Act 1968). Under the Sexual Offences Act 2003 it is an *either way offence to trespass with intent to commit a *sexual offence.

The *summary offence of **aggravated trespass** (s 68, Criminal Justice and Public Order Act 1994) occurs when a trespasser in the open air seeks to intimidate, obstruct, or disrupt a lawful activity; an offender can be arrested and failure to leave the land on the direction of a senior *police officer is also an offence (s 69, Criminal Justice and Public Order Act 1994). **Collective trespass** occurs when two or more people are trespassing with the purpose of residing on land belonging to another person. The police have powers, under s 61 of the 1994 Act, to direct collective trespassers to leave if they have caused damage, used threatening or abusive words towards the occupier, or brought six or more vehicles (which may be caravans) onto the land (*see also* UNAUTHORIZED CAMPING). Failure to leave or re-entry within three months is also a summary offence.

Under s 39 of the Civil Aviation Act 1982, it is an offence to trespass on any land forming part of an aerodrome licensed in pursuit of an Air Navigation Order. Trespassing on any railway lines, sidings, embankments, tunnels, or similar railway works is an offence contrary to s 55 of the British Transport Commission Act 1949. *See also* AIRSPACE; BURGLARY; TRESPASSORY ASSEMBLY.

trespass *ab initio* [Latin: trespass from the beginning] A form of trespass that occurs when a person enters *land with authority given by law, e.g. to *arrest a criminal or search for stolen *goods, and subsequently commits an act that is an abuse of that authority. The authority is cancelled retrospectively and the entry is deemed to have been a trespass from the beginning. Following *R v Collins* [1973] QB 100, the doctrine does not apply to trespass in cases of *burglary.

trespassory assembly An assembly of more than 20 people in the open air on *land to which the public has no right, or a limited right, of *access, when the *occupier has not consented to the event and it is likely to result in serious disruption to the life of the community or significant damage to land, monuments, or buildings of historical, architectural, archaeological, or scientific importance. Under s 14A of the Public Order Act 1986, a chief officer of police may apply to prohibit such an assembly if he reasonably believes it is going to be held. Knowingly organizing or inciting a trespassory assembly are *summary offences contrary to s 14B of the Act, punishable by a *fine at level 4 and/or three months' imprisonment; knowingly taking part attracts a fine on level 3. Under s 14C of the Act, a uniformed *police officer is empowered to stop people proceeding to such an assembly.

trial The hearing of a civil or criminal case before a court of competent *jurisdiction. Trials must, with rare exceptions (*see* IN CAMERA), be held in public. At the trial all issues of law and fact arising in the case will be determined. *See also* SUMMARY TRIAL; TRIAL ON INDICTMENT.

trial by Crown Court judge alone Provisions for *trial by *Crown Court *judge alone are contained within the Criminal Justice Act 2003 (in relation to cases of *jury tampering) and in the Domestic Violence, Crime and Victims Act 2004 (in relation to counts which are samples of other counts upon which a jury has convicted).

trial on indictment The *trial of a person charged with an *indictable offence, which is by *jury in the *Crown Court. The *indictment is read out to the accused at the start of the trial. There are a number of differences between trial on indictment and *summary trial (i.e. by *magistrates). The courts have power to impose greater penalties on indictment and there is no time limit before which indictable offences must be tried (most summary offences must be tried within six months).

tribunal *See* ADMINISTRATIVE TRIBUNAL; DOMESTIC TRIBUNAL; TRIBUNAL OF INQUIRY.

tribunal of inquiry A tribunal appointed under the Tribunals of Inquiry (Evidence) Act 1921 to investigate a matter of public importance. The Act provides machinery for the thorough examination of any matter (e.g. a national disaster or alleged corruption in government) that is a source of public disquiet but is not the subject of ordinary proceedings in the ordinary courts. A tribunal is appointed on resolutions of both Houses of *Parliament, its chairman is normally a senior judge, and it has all the powers of the *High Court concerning the summoning and examination of witnesses and the production of *documents.

trier of fact A member of a court who has the duty to decide questions of fact. In criminal *trials on *indictment and civil trials with a *jury, the jury is the trier of fact; in civil trials by *judge alone and in *summary trials, the judge and *magistrates, respectively, decide all issues both of law and fact.

trigger Any of a variety of devices which, by acting on a *sear, causes the firing mechanism to discharge the weapon.

Trojan horse A form of *computer *virus that allows a *hacker to access a user's computer covertly when the user connects to the Internet. Typically, Trojan programs are introduced to the user's computer as hidden components of some programs that are downloaded from the Internet or as a program or other executable file attached to unsolicited email messages. The name refers to the wooden horse the Greeks reputedly used to gain access to the city of Troy.

trustee A person having a nominal *title to property that he holds for the benefit of one or more others, the beneficiaries. Trustees may be individuals or corporate bodies and can include such specialists as judicial trustees and the Public Trustee. A trustee must show a high standard of care towards his beneficiaries, must not allow his interests to conflict with those of his beneficiaries, and must not profit from his trust. In the exercise of his duties he is answerable to the court.

trustee *de son tort* [from French: of his own wrongdoing] A person unconnected with a trust who takes upon himself to act as a *trustee. He is thereafter liable as if he had been appointed a trustee.

trustee in bankruptcy A person in whom the property of a *bankrupt is vested for the benefit of the bankrupt's *creditors. The trustee in bankruptcy must collect the bankrupt's *assets, sell them, and distribute the proceeds among those with valid claims against the bankrupt. Some claims (e.g. by the Inland Revenue) take preference over others.

trust property Property subject to a trust, normally held by *trustees (it may include trust *documents, which affect the trust). If trust property is wrongfully disposed of, it may be recovered by the beneficiaries.

tu quoque [Latin: you as well] A response to an accusation by accusing the accuser. In *international law it is not a *defence to point out the opponent's breaches of international law.

turning Queen's evidence *See* QUEEN'S EVIDENCE.

t

uberrimae fidei [Latin: of the utmost good faith] Describing a class of contracts in which one party has a preliminary duty to disclose material facts relevant to the subject matter to the other party. *Non-disclosure makes the contract voidable (*see* VOIDABLE CONTRACT). Examples of this class are *insurance contracts, in which knowledge of many material facts is confined to the party seeking insurance.

ulna The thicker of the two long bones in the forearm.

ulterior intent An element of the **mens rea* for certain crimes that requires an intention to bring about a consequence beyond the criminal act (*see* ACTUS REUS) itself. Crimes of ulterior intent include *burglary with intent and *wounding with intent. In the former, the ulterior intent is the intention held at the time of entering a building as a *trespasser, to commit one of three crimes (*theft, causing *grievous bodily harm, or causing *criminal damage) or committing or attempting to commit one of two crimes (theft or causing grievous bodily harm) having entered the building as a trespasser (the *actus reus*).

ultraviolet light Light from beyond the blue end of the spectrum. It has many uses in crime investigation. In *forensic medicine it is used to identify old injuries, particularly bite marks which can be detected after several weeks. It is a useful indicator of the presence of semen, which fluoresces under UV light. It is also used to detect property markers, which are invisible in ordinary light.

ultra vires [Latin: beyond the powers] Describing an act by a public authority, company, or other body that goes beyond the limits of the powers conferred on it. *Ultra vires* acts are invalid (*compare* INTRA VIRES). The *ultra vires* doctrine applies to all powers, whether created by statute or by a private *document or agreement (such as a trust deed or contract of agency).

In the field of public (especially administrative) law it governs the validity of all *delegated and *sub-delegated legislation. This is *ultra vires* not only if it contains provisions not authorized by the enabling power but also if it does not comply with any procedural requirements regulating the exercise of the power. Sub-delegated legislation that is within the terms of the delegated legislation authorizing it may still be invalid if the power to make that legislation did not include the power to sub-delegate. The individual can normally establish the invalidity of delegated or sub-delegated legislation by raising the point as a defence in proceedings against him for contravening it.

The doctrine also governs the validity of decisions made by inferior courts or administrative or domestic tribunals and the validity of the exercise of any *administrative power. The decision of a court or tribunal is *ultra vires* if it exceeds *jurisdiction, contravenes procedural requirements, or disregards the rules of *natural justice (the power conferring jurisdiction being construed as requiring the observance of these).

The exercise of an administrative power is *ultra vires* not only if unauthorized in substance, but equally if (for example) it is procedurally irregular, improperly motivated, or in breach of the rules of natural justice. The remedies available for this second aspect of the doctrine are *quashing orders, *prohibition orders, *declaration, and *injunction (the first two of these are public remedies, not available against decisions of domestic tribunals whose jurisdiction is based solely on contract).

Acts by a registered company are *ultra vires* if they exceed the objects clause of the *memorandum of association. A *company member can restrain such acts prior to performance; thereafter they are treated as valid (though they may be a breach of *directors' duties). Section 35 of the Companies Act 1985 (as amended in 1989) made it much harder to challenge *ultra vires* acts of a company.

unauthorized camping The summary offence, contrary to s 77 of the Criminal Justice and Public Order Act 1994, of camping in vehicles on *land without the consent of the *occupier, or on land forming part of a *highway, or on any other unoccupied land, and failing to comply with a direction to leave by the *local authority. It is also an offence to re-enter the land within three months. The local authority may direct the removal of vehicles or any other property; it may also apply to a *magistrates' court for an order authorizing removal. A vehicle does not have to be fit for use on the roads and includes any body or chassis, with or without wheels, and any caravan. The offences are punishable by a *fine at level 3. Defences of illness, mechanical breakdown, or immediate emergency may be available. Local authorities may establish caravan sites for *gipsies but are no longer under a duty to do so. *See also* TRESPASS.

unconditional surrender *See* CAPITULATION.

undertaking 1. A promise, especially in legal proceedings, that creates an *obligation. A *solicitor who breaks such a promise will be in breach of disciplinary rules. **2.** A business, such as a company, *partnership, or sole trader. Article 81 of the *Treaty of Rome applies to agreements between undertakings. EU case law has established that some state bodies of a trading nature, as well as charities and trade associations, may under certain circumstances be classed as undertakings.

underwriter 1. A member of an *insurance company or a *Lloyd's syndicate who decides whether or not to accept a particular risk for a specified premium. In general, the public only deal with underwriters through a broker. **2.** An individual, finance company, or issuing house who undertakes for a commission to acquire a specified number of *shares in a company if those shares are not taken up by the public during a *flotation. In both cases the underwriter may relieve himself of part of his liability by effecting similar arrangements with **sub-underwriters**.

undischarged bankrupt A person who has been made bankrupt and who has not yet received an *order of discharge from the court. Such a person is disqualified from holding certain offices, which include *justice of the peace, councillor, and Member of Parliament. He must not obtain credit for more than £250 without informing the *creditor that he is an undischarged bankrupt, and he must not carry on a business without disclosing the name under which he was made bankrupt to those who deal with him. *See also* BANKRUPTCY.

unfair consumer practices *See* CONSUMER PROTECTION.

unfair contract terms Contractual terms relating to the exclusion or restriction of a person's liability that, under the Unfair Contract Terms Act 1977 and Unfair Terms in Consumer Contracts Regulations 1999 (SI 1999/2083), are either ineffective or effective only so far as is reasonable. *See* EXCLUSION AND RESTRICTION OF NEGLIGENCE LIABILITY; EXEMPTION CLAUSE; INTERNATIONAL SUPPLY CONTRACT.

unfavourable witness An *adverse witness who is not *hostile towards the party who called him to testify. An unfavourable witness may not be cross-examined by that party.

unfit to plead Describing an accused person who is under a disability (e.g. mental incapacity) that would constitute a bar to his being tried. When the question of fitness to plead arises, the *judge decides whether the defendant is unfit. If the judge so decides, a *jury is empanelled to determine whether the defendant did the *actus reus* of the offence charged. If the jury determines that the defendant did the act the judge may order: the defendant to be detained in a *special hospital; a *supervision order; or an absolute *discharge. The court may postpone consideration of the question of the accused's fitness to plead until the *defence case is opened so that (for example) the strength of the *prosecution case may be tested. The procedure is governed by the Criminal Procedure (Insanity) Act 1964, as amended by the Criminal Procedure (Insanity and Unfitness to Plead) Act 1991 and the Domestic Violence, Crime and Victims Act 2004.

unilateral contract A contract in which one party (the promisor) undertakes to do or refrain from doing something if the other party (the promisee) does or refrains from doing something, but the promisee does not undertake to do or refrain from doing that thing. An example of a unilateral contract is one in which the promisor offers a reward for the giving of information. *Compare* BILATERAL CONTRACT.

unincorporated body An association that has no legal personality distinct from those of its members (*compare* CORPORATION). Examples of unincorporated bodies are *partnerships and *clubs.

unitary authority An all-purpose *local authority created under the Local Government Act 1992 and subsequent *legislation to replace the two-tier system of local government by *county and *district councils. Unitary authorities were established in Wales (and Scotland) in April 1996 and in certain non-metropolitan counties in England between 1996 and 1998; single-tier authorities also administer *Greater London and the former metropolitan county areas (since 1986) and the Isle of Wight (since 1995).

United Nations (UN) An international organization, based in New York and Geneva, set up by the United Nations Charter in 1945 to replace the League of Nations. The main aims of the UN are: (1) to maintain international peace and security and to bring about settlement of international disputes by peaceful means; (2) to develop friendly relations among nations; and (3) to achieve international cooperation in solving international problems of an economic or cultural nature and in promoting respect for human rights. The Charter sets out certain fundamental principles, which include the *undertaking to refrain from using or threatening force against the territory or political independence of any state.

The Charter established six principal organs, of which the most important are the General Assembly, the Security Council, the Economic and Social Council, and the *International Court of Justice. The **General Assembly** is the debating forum of the UN, consisting of all the member states; it can pass *resolutions, but these are not legally binding upon member states. The **Security Council** has five permanent members (China, France, Russia, the UK, and the USA), and ten temporary members elected for two-year periods. Its resolutions are binding on member states, but each permanent member has the right to *veto a resolution. It is empowered, under certain conditions, to make recommendations and take measures to maintain the peace, including the establishment of peacekeeping military forces in sensitive areas.

In certain policy areas the UN operates through subsidiary organs; e.g. the United Nations High Commissioner for Refugees (UNHCR) and the United Nations Children's Fund (UNICEF).

unity of personality Formerly, the *common-law doctrine that husband and wife were one person in the eyes of the law. This doctrine has now been almost entirely abolished. However, the court still has jurisdiction to stay proceedings in *tort brought by one spouse against another if there will be no substantial benefit from it; a husband and wife may not be convicted of criminal conspiracy together with each other (unless a third person is involved); and there are certain limitations on criminal proceedings in relation to *theft of property belonging to one's spouse.

Universal Declaration of Human Rights (UDHR) A declaration adopted by the *United Nations General Assembly outlining the organization's view on the *human rights guaranteed to all people. It was referred to by Eleanor Roosevelt who chaired the United Nations Human Rights Commission, which drew up the declaration, as 'a Magna Carta for all mankind'.

unladen weight The weight of a vehicle or *trailer inclusive of the body and all parts (the heavier being taken where alternative bodies or parts are used) which are necessary to or ordinarily used with the vehicle or trailer when working on a *road, but exclusive of the weight of water, fuel, or accumulators used for the purpose of the supply of power for the propulsion of the vehicle or, as the case may be, of any vehicle by which the trailer is drawn, and of loose tools and loose equipment (reg 3(2), Road Vehicles (Construction and Use) Regulations 1986 (SI 1986/1078)).

unlawful assembly *See* VIOLENT DISORDER.

unlawful possession of drugs *See* CONTROLLED DRUGS.

unlawful sexual intercourse Prior to the coming into force of the Sexual Offences Act 2003, this referred to sexual intercourse that occurred in any of the former sexual offences involving intercourse, including intercourse with a girl under the age of 16 or a mentally defective woman. In this context 'unlawful' implied extramarital intercourse. It applies only to offences committed before 1 May 2004.

unlimited company A type of *registered company whose members have an unlimited *liability. Thus on *winding-up, the company can make demands upon its members until it has sufficient funds to meet the *creditors' claims. The risk that members of unlimited companies assume is balanced by certain advantages: an unlimited company (unless it is a parent or subsidiary of a *limited company) does not have to deliver its *accounts to the *Companies Registry and it has more freedom to deal with its capital than a limited company. Unlimited companies may be formed with an *authorized capital, thus enabling them to issue *shares and raise working capital, but members' liability is not limited to the nominal value of these shares.

unnatural offence *Buggery. Other 'unnatural' forms of intercourse, however, are not included in the term. *See also* ABOMINABLE CRIME.

unpaid seller A *seller of *goods who has not been paid in full for them or who has received a cheque or other *negotiable instrument that has not been honoured. Although *ownership of the goods may have passed to the buyer, an unpaid seller has certain rights against the goods themselves. Under the Sale of Goods Act 1979, these rights are: (1) a possessory *lien (particular, not general); (2) a right of stoppage *in transitu*; and (3) a right of resale.

unpaid vendor's lien An *equitable right arising in favour of a *vendor of *land against the purchaser (and those taking title through him as volunteers) if the vendor has given *possession of the land to the purchaser before receiving the whole of the purchase price. This form of *lien gives the vendor no right to possession of the land but entitles him to seek a court order for the sale of the property to ensure that he is paid the money owing by the purchaser.

unpaid work requirement A requirement that may be imposed by a court dealing with an offender aged 16 or over as part of a *community order, *custody plus order, *suspended sentence order, or an *intermittent custody order. It requires the offender to perform between 40 and 300 hours of unpaid work during a 12 month period (s 199, Criminal Justice Act 2003).

unregistered company A company that is incorporated otherwise than by registration under the Companies Acts. Unregistered companies, which include *statutory companies and *foreign companies, are subject to some provisions of the Companies Act 1985.

unsolicited goods *Goods sent to someone (other than a trader) who has not asked for them to be sent. It is not in itself an offence to send unsolicited goods (except for matter describing human sexual techniques or advertisements for such matter), but it is a criminal offence to demand payment for them. The Consumer Protection (Distance Selling) Regulations 2000 (SI 2000/2334) amended the Unsolicited Goods and Services Act 1971 and removed any rights of the sender in respect of unsolicited goods and services and any obligations on the *consumer. As such, consumers can retain unsolicited goods or dispose of them as they wish. They are under no obligation to keep them safe or to return them. It is an offence to demand payment from consumers for unsolicited goods or services.

unsworn evidence Evidence given by a child under the age of 14 in a criminal case in accordance with the provisions of the Youth Justice and Criminal Evidence Act 1999. The child must be sufficiently intelligent to justify the reception of his evidence and understand the duty of speaking the truth. Formerly, the child's evidence had to be supported by some *corroboration, but this requirement has now been abolished.

unsworn statement A statement made from the dock by an accused person while not on *oath. The evidentiary effect of such a statement was much disputed, but the right to make one, which had been preserved when the accused was made a competent witness by the Criminal Evidence Act 1898, was abolished by the Criminal Justice Act 1982.

usage A long-established and well-known practice in a particular market or trade. It may affect the interpretation of, and the nature of *implied terms in, a contract made in that market or trade.

use [possibly from Latin *opus*: benefit] Formerly, a right, recognized only in Chancery, of a beneficiary (the *cestui que use*) against the legal owner of *land. The medieval *common law recognized only legal rights, which were often restricted in nature, but the Chancery protected those to whose use or benefit land was given, although they were not the legal owners. If A held property to the use of B, A was the legal owner (**feoffee to uses**) and B was the beneficiary (*cestui que use*). Uses gave flexibility and helped the evasion of feudal incidents (the medieval equivalent of tax liability). In 1535 the Statute of Uses executed the use, i.e. converted the rights of a *cestui que use* to legal rights, but the statute proved ineffective; it was repealed and uses were abolished in 1925.

use of force A person may lawfully use such force as is reasonable in the circumstances for the purposes of *self-defence, defence of another, defence of property, the prevention of crime or in effecting a lawful *arrest. A *constable may, if necessary, use reasonable force for the purpose of exercising a power conferred on him by the Police and Criminal Evidence Act 1984, such as in the execution of a search *warrant issued by a court.

The use of offensive military action, whether amounting to *war or not, is prohibited under Article 2(4) of the United Nations Charter. The only exceptions to this strict rule are as follows: (1) when the use of force is by way of an *enforcement action (Article 39 within *Chapter VII of the UN Charter); (2) when force is used for the purposes of self-defence under Chapter VII (Article 51); and (3) controversially, when a state uses force for the purposes of self-defence under customary *international law (arguably preserved by Article 51). Resort to force upon any other basis is illegal under international law.

user The use or enjoyment of property.

uti possidetis [Latin: as you possess] A principle usually applied in *international law to the delineation of borders. When a colony gains independence, the colonial boundaries are accepted as the boundaries of the newly independent state. This practice, first adopted for the sake of expediency by the Spanish American colonies when they declared independence, has since been employed elsewhere in the world following the withdrawal of empire.

The principle of *uti possidetis* is also applied to the status of movable public property of belligerent states. Unless a peace *treaty provides to the contrary, each party will retain such property as was in its possession on the day the hostilities ceased.

utter Bar *See* OUTER BAR.

vacations The periods between the end of any of the *sittings of the *Supreme Court of Judicature and the beginning of the next sitting, i.e. the Long Vacation, Christmas Vacation, Easter Vacation, and Whitsun Vacation.

vagal inhibition Stopping the heart by stimulation of the vagus nerve in the neck. This can be caused by pressure on the neck.

vagina Part of the female sexual organs extending from the *vulva to the neck of the womb. By the Sexual Offences Act 2003 vagina includes a surgically constructed vagina, particularly as part of gender reassignment surgery.

vagrant A person classified under the Vagrancy Act 1824 as an 'idle and disorderly person', a 'rogue and vagabond', or an 'incorrigible rogue'. The first of these groups includes pedlars who trade without a licence, *prostitutes who behave indecently in a *public place, and those who beg in a public place. Rogues and vagabonds include those with a second conviction for being idle and disorderly, those who collect charity under false pretences, and tramps who do not make use of available places of shelter. Incorrigible rogues include those with a second conviction for being rogues and vagabonds. Schedule 2 to the Criminal Justice Act 2003 reduced the penalties for offences under the 1824 Act from imprisonment to *fines.

valium *See* DIAZEPAM.

valuable consideration *See* CONSIDERATION.

value Valuable *consideration.

value-added tax (VAT) A *tax payable on a wide range of supplies of *goods and services by way of business. As well as straightforward sales, **taxable supplies** include hirings, rentals, the granting of rights, and the distribution of promotional gifts. VAT is also payable on imports. The amount of tax payable is a percentage of the value of the supply (at present 17.5 per cent for the majority of supplies) and the liability for the tax arises at the time of the supply (*see* TAX POINT). Any person, firm, or organization that makes regular taxable supplies above a certain, regularly revised annual value must register with *Her Majesty's Revenue and Customs, who administer the tax. A registered person (known as a **taxable person**) must collect from his customers the tax due on the supplies that he makes. This is known as his **output tax**. He pays the tax on a periodic basis (usually quarterly), but in doing so he may reclaim any VAT that he has himself paid in the course of his business (his **input tax**). The entire tax is therefore borne by the ultimate consumer. VAT came into force on 1 April 1973, replacing purchase tax and selective employment tax. *See also* EXEMPT SUPPLY; ZERO-RATED SUPPLY.

vandalism Defacing or damaging property. There is no offence of vandalism as such, but it will usually constitute an offence of *criminal damage.

vehicle construction and maintenance The manufacture and subsequent maintenance of *motor vehicles are governed by detailed rules, failure to comply with which may constitute a criminal offence. The main rules deal with such matters as the brakes and steering system, mirrors, windscreen wipers and washers, petrol tanks, door hinges and latches, silencers, pollution prevention, indicators, speedometers, lights, and tyres. There are also regulations governing the use of a motor vehicle. Breach of the regulations relating to brakes, steering system, or tyres or breach of any of the regulations relating to construction, maintenance, or use in a manner that causes or is likely to cause danger is an offence punishable by *endorsement and discretionary *disqualification. Other breaches are subject to *fines but not to endorsement. There are also special offences relating to the sale or attempted sale of vehicles whose use on the *roads would be a breach of the regulations, to the fitting of parts to a vehicle in such a way that its subsequent use would be in breach of the regulations, and to selling or supplying parts whose fitting would cause the vehicle's subsequent use to be in breach of the regulations. These offences do not apply, however, if the defendant proves that the vehicle was sold for export or that he reasonably believed that it would not be used in Britain in an unlawful condition. *See also* MOT TEST.

vehicle insurance *See* THIRD-PARTY INSURANCE; DRIVING WITHOUT INSURANCE.

vehicle interference *See* INTERFERING WITH VEHICLES.

vehicle in the service of a visiting force or of a headquarters A vehicle so described in Article 8(6) of the Visiting Forces and International Headquarters (Application of Law) Order 1965 (SI 1965/1536) (reg 3(2), Road Vehicles (Construction and Use) Regulations 1986 (SI 1986/1078)). *See also* VISITING FORCES.

vehicle used in manner causing alarm, distress or annoyance Where a *constable in uniform has reasonable grounds for believing that a *motor vehicle is being driven carelessly or inconsiderately (*see* CARELESS AND INCONSIDERATE DRIVING); in contravention of the prohibition of off-road driving imposed by s 34 of the Road Traffic Act 1988; or has been used on any occasion in a manner which is causing, or is likely to cause, alarm, distress, or annoyance to members of the public, then he may (a) order the person driving it to stop the vehicle; (b) seize and remove the motor vehicle; (c) enter any *premises (other than a private dwelling house) on which he has reasonable grounds for believing the motor vehicle to be; and (d) use reasonable force, if necessary, in the exercise of those powers. Except in certain circumstances, the power to seize the vehicle is only exercisable if the constable has warned the person using the vehicle that he will seize it if the unlawful use continues or is repeated; and the use has continued or been repeated thereafter (s 59, Police Reform Act 2002).

velocity Of a *projectile, the speed, usually expressed in feet per second.

vendor A *seller, particularly one who sells *land.

venereal disease Any infectious disease transmitted through sexual contact (such as HIV infection, syphilis, or gonorrhoea). If a spouse at the time of marriage was, unknown to his (or her) partner, suffering from a venereal disease, this constitutes a ground for annulment of the marriage. Evidence of a venereal disease contracted since the marriage, when neither partner was previously suffering from it, may be prima facie evidence of adultery. Intentionally or recklessly infecting a sexual partner with such a disease may amount to inflicting *grievous bodily harm under the Offences Against the Person Act 1861.

venire de novo [Latin: to come anew] An order made by the *Court of Appeal (Criminal Division) annulling a *trial on indictment and ordering a *new trial on the ground of some fundamental flaw in the proceedings (e.g. failure to obtain a necessary consent to the institution of proceedings). Originally, it was a writ (*venire facias de novo juratores*) addressed to the *sheriff, ordering him to cause new *jurors to try the case afresh.

ventricle One of the two main pumping areas in the heart.

ventricular fibrillation An irregular uncoordinated contraction of the fibres in the muscles of the heart preventing the pumping of blood. It is corrected by application of electric shock (defibrillation).

venture capital trust (VCT) An *investment company listed on the London Stock Exchange that specializes in investing in companies of the same kind as those that can qualify under the Enterprise Investment Scheme. This enables individuals to spread the risk over a number of qualifying companies. The investor buys shares in the VCT, and fund managers invest the money raised in trading companies; the profits are paid out as dividends. The investor is entitled to relief from income tax and capital gains tax.

venue of trial *See* MODE OF TRIAL.

verbals Any remarks that an accused person has made in the presence of the police. These are written down by the police and may be read out as evidence at the *trial. *See also* CAUTION.

verdict 1. A *jury's finding on the matters referred to it in a criminal or civil *trial. The jury is asked to give its decision to the court separately for each of the questions it was asked to consider (e.g. when there are several charges on the *indictment). The reply is usually given by the foreman. A jury reaches its verdict in secret and no subsequent inquiry can be made as to how it was reached. The jury must try to reach a unanimous verdict but a *majority verdict is accepted in certain circumstances. If the jury cannot agree a verdict at all they are discharged and there is a new trial. Verdicts are either *general or *special. The usual form of verdict is general (such as a finding of *guilty or *not guilty); special verdicts are exceptional. A jury may decide that the accused is not guilty of the offence charged but guilty of some lesser offence (*see* ALTERNATIVE VERDICT). *See also* PERVERSE VERDICT. **2.** The finding of a *coroner's inquest. *See* INQUISITION.

vertebra One of the bones of the spine.

very pistol A weapon designed to discharge flares for signalling purposes.

vest 1. To confer legal *ownership of *land on someone. **2.** To confer legal rights on someone.

veto 1. (in *international law) The power given to any permanent member of the Security Council of the *United Nations to refuse to agree to any non-procedural proposal (there is no such power in relation to procedural matters) and thereby defeat it. An abstention is not equivalent to a veto. The President of the Security Council has power to determine which questions are non-procedural. The General Assembly of the UN passed a Uniting for Peace Resolution in 1950, providing for the Assembly to take over some of the functions of the Security Council when the Council's work has been paralysed by use of the veto. This resolution, however, was only a political gesture and failed to overcome the veto power. **2.** (in EU law) The power of a member state in the *Council of Europe to block *legislation when a unanimous decision in favour of a measure is required. Although much EU legislation only requires a qualified majority decision of the Council, unanimity votes are required in such areas as taxation, budgets, foreign policy, and the admission of new member states. The power of the *European Parliament to reject legislation proposed by the Commission operates by means of the codecision procedure.

vexatious action An *action brought for the purpose of annoying the opponent and with no reasonable prospect of success. A **vexatious litigant** is a person who regularly brings such actions. The actions may be struck out and the court may order, on an application made by the Attorney-General, that no legal proceedings may be begun or continued by the vexatious litigant without the leave of the court.

vicarious liability (vicarious responsibility) Legal *liability imposed on one person for *torts or crimes committed by another (usually an *employee but sometimes an *independent contractor or agent), although the person made vicariously liable is not personally at fault. An *employer is vicariously liable for torts committed by his employees when he has authorized or ratified them or when the tort was committed in the course of the employees' work. Thus negligent driving by someone employed as a *driver is a tort committed in the course of his employment, but if the driver were to assault a passing pedestrian for motives of private revenge, the assault would not be connected with his job and his employer would not be liable. The purpose of the doctrine of vicarious liability is to ensure that an employer pays the costs of damage caused by his business operations. His vicarious liability, however, is in addition to the liability of the employee, who remains personally liable for his own torts. The person injured by the tort may sue either or both of them, but will generally prefer to sue the employer.

Vicarious criminal liability may effectively be imposed by statute on an employer for certain offences committed by an employee in relation to his employment. Thus it has been held that an employer is *guilty of selling unfit food under the Food Act 1984 when his employee does the physical act of selling (the employee is also guilty, though in practice is rarely prosecuted). Likewise, an employer may be guilty of supplying *goods under a false trade description when it is his employee who actually delivers them. For an offence that normally requires **mens rea*, an employer will only be vicariously liable if the offence relates to licensing laws. For example, if a *licensee has delegated the entire management of his *licensed premises to another person, and that person has committed the offence with the necessary *mens rea*, the licensee will be vicariously liable.

Vicarious liability for crimes may be imposed in certain other circumstances. The registered owner of a vehicle, for example, is expressly made liable by statute for *fixed-penalty and excess parking charges, even if the fault for the offence was not his. If the offence is a regulatory offence of *strict liability, the courts often also impose vicarious liability if the offence is defined in the statute in a way that makes this possible.

Vice Chancellor (VC) 1. A judge who is vice president of the *Chancery Division of the *High Court (the *Lord Chancellor is the president but in practice rarely, if ever, sits in the Division). The Vice Chancellor is by statute responsible to the Lord Chancellor for the organization and management of the business of the Division and is *ex officio* a member of the *Court of Appeal. **2.** Formerly, a judge of the palatine courts. The title is still held by the judge assigned to exercise Chancery jurisdiction in Lancashire.

victim (in human rights law) A person who is actually and directly affected by an act or omission that is incompatible with the *European Convention on Human Rights, or a person who is at risk of being directly affected. Only victims have a right to take proceedings. *See* HUMAN RIGHTS ACT.

victimless crimes A term used to describe criminal offences where there is no *complainant and no readily recognizable victim. Such crimes include drug abuse and prostitution and this 'victimless' status is used by some to support calls for legalisation of these activities: others oppose this view.

victimology An area of criminology which studies the victims of crime and their relationship with offenders; the *criminal justice system; the media; the cost of crime; and social movements.

Victim Support The independent national charity that helps people to cope with the effects of crime. It has a network of local branches across England, Wales, and Northern Ireland. Its trained volunteers offer: someone to talk to in confidence; information on police and court procedures; help in dealing with other organizations; information about compensation and insurance; links to other sources of help.

Anyone affected by crime can contact Victim Support directly for help. In some police areas details of reported crimes are passed to Victim Support who will offer their services to victims and others affected by the crime. The services are free and available to everyone, whether or not the crime has been reported and regardless of when it happened. *See also* WITNESS SERVICE.

victim surveys Surveys of victims of crime are carried out by many bodies for different reasons. *Police forces frequently conduct surveys of people who are reported victims of crime in order to monitor their performance in responding to the report. Other surveys, such as the *British Crime Survey, are directed at the public at large to gauge the level of crime as against the level of reported crime. The accuracy of such surveys in showing the extent of crime is doubtful as *'victimless crimes' are not unlikely to be revealed whereas crimes such as domestic violence and sexual offences may not be mentioned.

video conferencing link *See* LIVE TELEVISION LINK.

video evidence *See* LIVE TELEVISION LINK; VIDEO-RECORDED EVIDENCE.

video identification A method of testing the ability of a witness to identify an offender by picking him out from a number of similar video clips showing the suspect and a number of other people of broadly similar appearance in similar circumstances. The method has taken over from identification parades as the primary method of identification. The procedures to be used are laid down in the Codes of Practice to the Police and Criminal Evidence Act 1984.

Video Identification Parade Electronic Recording (VIPER) A national centre for the storage of the images of suspects and volunteers for use in video identification procedures.

video-recorded evidence A court may grant leave for a video recording of an interview with any witness (other than the defendant) to be admitted as evidence-in-chief in *trials of indictable only offences and those *either way offences prescribed by order of the *Home Secretary (under s 137 of the Criminal Justice Act 2003, expected to come into force late 2006 or early 2007). The court may only allow evidence in such a form if it is satisfied that the witness's recollection of events is likely to be significantly better at the time the recording was made than at the time of trial and that it is in the interests of justice to use it. Where a video-recording is admitted, it will be treated as the final statement of any matters adequately dealt with in it. *See also* SPECIAL MEASURES.

Vienna Single Convention A *United Nations Convention signed in 1961, which brought together a number of earlier *treaties. The convention lays down obligations on signatories, which obliges them to take measures against production, trafficking, and possession of drugs. Calling it the 'single' convention was unfortunate because there have been two more since: the 1971 Convention on Psychotropic Substances and the 1988 Convention Against the Illicit Traffic of Narcotic Drugs and Psychotropic Substances. Legalizing drugs would mean breaching these treaties.

view (in court proceedings) The inspection by a *judge, or judge and *jury, of any place or thing with respect to which any question arises in the course of litigation, including if necessary places or things outside the jurisdiction of the court. A view is part of the evidence in the case and the judge should not hold a private view of a *public place in the absence of the parties. The judge has discretion to decide whether or not to hold a view; he may decide to do so even if the parties are opposed.

violence for securing entry *See* FORCIBLE ENTRY.

violent disorder An offence contrary to s 2 of the Public Order Act 1986 that replaced the *common-law offence of UNLAWFUL ASSEMBLY. It is committed when three or more persons, present together, use or threaten unlawful violence. Their collective conduct must be such as would have caused a reasonable person to fear for his safety, though no one else need be present. 'Violence' includes violent conduct towards property as well as persons and extends to conduct causing or intended to cause injury or damage. It therefore includes throwing a missile at someone though it does not hit him or falls short. The offence can be committed in private as well as in *public places. It is punishable with up to five years' imprisonment and/or a fine. Violent disorder differs from *riot in the smaller minimum number of participants, the absence of need to prove community of purpose, and a lesser maximum *punishment. However, both are *indictable offences. As with *affray, a person is only *guilty if he intended to use or threaten violence or was aware that his conduct might be violent or threaten violence. For this purpose, an intoxicated person is taken to be aware of what a sober person would have been aware. If the police fear that a violent event may take place they may now exercise stop-and-search powers (*see* POWER OF SEARCH). *See also* THREATENING BEHAVIOUR.

It is also a summary offence, under s 241 of the Trade Union and Labour Relations (Consolidation) Act 1992, to do any of the following, without legal authority, in order to compel a person to do (or not to do) something he has a right to do (or not to do): use violence towards or intimidate that person, his wife, or children or injure his property; persistently follow him; hide his property or hinder his use of it; watch or beset him or his place of residence, work, or business; or follow him with two or more others in a disorderly manner in a street or road. It is punishable with six months' imprisonment and/or a fine. This offence is aimed mainly at disorderly *picketing. However, it is lawful to watch or beset a place (other than a residence) for the sole purpose of peacefully obtaining or communicating information or peacefully persuading any person to work or not to work.

violent offence/offender *See* DANGEROUS OFFENDERS.

virus A self-replicating *computer program with the ability to modify other programs, usually to the detriment of the computer. Whilst it may be intentionally destructive in itself, its predominant effect is uncontrolled self-reproduction, which wastes or overwhelms computer resources. It is so named because it behaves in a way similar to a biological virus, spreading itself throughout the programs on a computer as the biological version inserts itself into living cells. Extending the analogy, the insertion of a virus is known as an 'infection', and the infected file or program is called a 'host'. The term is sometimes used to refer to *worms, *trojan horses, and other sorts of *malware.

visiting forces Commonwealth forces stationed in the UK and any other forces from abroad designated by *Order in Council, including their civilian components. The Visiting Forces Act 1952 empowers the service courts of such forces to exercise *jurisdiction over their members according to their national law (but not to carry out the death penalty). It exempts their members from *trial by UK criminal courts in the case of offences committed on duty, against other members, or against the property of the force or other members. The Income and Corporation Taxes Act 1988 confers certain exemptions from UK taxation on members of visiting forces. *See also* VEHICLE IN THE SERVICE OF A VISITING FORCE OR OF A HEADQUARTERS.

visitor 1. A person appointed to visit and inspect an institution and, in particular, to inquire into internal irregularities. Many universities have a visitor (frequently the Crown), and *judges are visitors of the *Inns of Court. Boards of Visitors, appointed for prisons by the *Home Secretary, act as disciplinary tribunals for breaches of the Prison Rules. A Lord Chancellor's Visitor is appointed under the Mental Health Act 1983 to visit patients and inquire into their ability to manage their affairs. **2.** A member of the independent Board of Visitors appointed by the Secretary of State for Defence as visitors to the Military Correctional Training Centre (MCTC). They are people from the local community who have volunteered to be members of the Board. They are all civilians and have no other connection with the MCTC, but one member of the Board should be a retired Officer from one of the Armed Services. Their purpose is to: see that Service Persons Under Sentence (SUS) are properly and fairly treated; inspect the *premises, food, training, education, and all other parts of the MCTC; and receive complaints and requests from SUS in private. **3.** A person who enters *land or premises at the invitation or with the permission of the *occupier. *See* OCCUPIER'S LIABILITY.

visual display unit (VDU) A *computer monitor. The *European Union's Directive 90/270 on the minimum safety and health requirements for work with display screen equipment protects employees by setting out requirements for such matters as risk assessments of computers used at work and by providing for free sight tests and footstools for staff and regular breaks from VDU work.

vitreous humour The fluid inside the eyeball.

voice identification The identification of a suspect by reference to his voice as heard by a witness or by scientific analysis of a recorded voice by a voice recognition expert. The method of identification has been challenged a number of times but the *Court of Appeal has approved the method with the safeguards given to visual identification (e.g. *Turnbull* direction [1977] QB 224).

void Having no legal effect.

voidable Capable of being avoided (set aside).

voidable contract A contract that, though valid when made, is liable to be subsequently set aside (*compare* VOID CONTRACT). Voidable contracts may arise through *misrepresentation, some instances of *mistake, *non-disclosure, and *duress. Certain proprietary contracts entered into by minors are also voidable (*see* CAPACITY TO CONTRACT). The setting aside of a voidable contract is effected by rescission.

void contract A contract that has no legal force from the moment of its making (*compare* VOIDABLE CONTRACT). Void contracts occur when there is lack of *capacity to contract and by the operation in some instances of the doctrine of *mistake. An *illegal contract is void. In addition, certain contracts (e.g. *gaming and wagering contracts) are declared void but not illegal by statute, and certain contracts that are at *common law contrary to *public policy are merely void but not illegal. Under UK and EU *competition law on restrictive trade practices, clauses infringing those laws are void but usually the rest of the contract continues. Contracts that are void or, in certain cases, illegal may be saved by *severance.

voir dire **(*voire dire*)** [Norman French: to speak the truth] **1.** The preliminary examination by a *judge of a witness to determine his competence or of a *juror to determine his qualification for jury service. **2.** An inquiry conducted by the judge in the absence of the jury into the admissibility of an item of evidence (e.g. a *confession). It is sometimes called a **trial within a trial**. **3.** Formerly, a special oath taken by witnesses called to testify on the *voir dire*.

volenti non fit injuria [Latin: no wrong is done to one who consents] The defence that the claimant consented to the injury or (more usually) to the risk of being injured. Knowledge of the risk of injury is not sufficient; there must also be (even if only by implication) full and free consent to bear the risk. A claimant who has assumed the risk of injury has no action if the injury occurs. The scope of the defence is limited by statute in cases involving business liability and public and private transport.

voluntary accommodation Accommodation provided by a *local authority for children whose *parents are temporarily unable to look after them or for children who have been abandoned. (It is important to distinguish between a child who is being accommodated by a local authority and a child who is the subject of a *care order.) The purpose of a local authority in supplying accommodation is to support children in need and their families; it is not a means for the local authority to gain control of the child against the parents' wishes. The local authority does not acquire *parental responsibility for a child who is accommodated; parents with parental responsibility must consent to their child being accommodated and may remove the child without notice and without the consent of the local authority (before 1989 it was necessary to give 28 days' notice before removing the child from voluntary care). If a child is the subject of a care order, the local authority acquires parental responsibility for that child and may act against the parents' wishes.

voluntary arrangement **1.** An agreement between a *debtor and his *creditors concerning the payment of his *debts under the provisions of the Insolvency Act 1986. It takes the form of either a **scheme of arrangement** or a **composition**. It can be made either before *bankruptcy proceedings are initiated or between an *undischarged bankrupt and his creditors. The court makes an order, called an **interim order**, to protect the debtor from bankruptcy and other court proceedings while an agreement is worked out. The debtor presents his proposals to a creditors' meeting to which all his creditors must be invited. If the meeting agrees with the debtor's proposals, the **approved voluntary arrangement** becomes binding on all the debtor's creditors, whether or not they attended the meeting. The approved voluntary arrangement does not have to be registered as a deed of arrangement. The meeting's decision is reported to the court, which may discharge the interim order if no agreement has been reached. An *insolvency practitioner (the **supervisor**) is appointed to supervise the carrying out of an approved voluntary arrangement. He may petition for a *bankruptcy order if the debtor fails to comply with the terms of the arrangement. **2.** A similar agreement between a company in financial difficulties and its creditors. Under the Insolvency Act 1986 it must be approved by meetings of both the company and the creditors; if it affects the priority of *preferential debts, the consent of the preferential creditors is required. If the arrangement is approved it becomes binding from the date of the creditors' meeting; there is no interim order. It is supervised by a **nominee**, who must be a qualified *insolvency practitioner. An *administration order may be granted to assist the conclusion of a voluntary arrangement.

voluntary attendance at a police station A person who attends a police station for the purpose of assisting with an investigation is entitled to leave at will unless he is placed under *arrest. When a person attends voluntarily and at some stage the *police officer decides that the person cannot leave if he wishes, he must be placed under arrest, even if he was willing to stay.

voluntary bill procedure A procedure governed by s 2(2)(b) of the Administration of Justice (Miscellaneous Provisions) Act 1933 that enables the prosecution to apply to a *judge of the *High Court to obtain consent for preferring a *bill of indictment against a defendant. This procedure is usually used when a *magistrates' court has held committal proceedings but has refused to commit the defendant for *trial on indictment or in cases where a defendant has been committed for *trial and a second defendant is arrested shortly before that trial.

voluntary confession *See* CONFESSION.

voluntary intoxication A defendant who is of his own accord intoxicated to an extent where he cannot form the necessary intent has a defence to crimes of *specific intent, such as *murder, but not to other offences, such as assault occasioning *actual bodily harm. The defence does not apply where the *intoxication merely reduces inhibition or provides 'Dutch courage'.

voluntary liquidation *See* VOLUNTARY WINDING-UP.

voluntary manslaughter Unlawful killing with all the elements of *murder, including **mens rea*, but one of three special defences reduces the charge to manslaughter. The three partial defences are: *diminished responsibility; *provocation; or *suicide pact.

voluntary winding-up (voluntary liquidation) A *winding-up procedure initiated by a special or extraordinary *resolution of the company. In a **members' voluntary winding-up**, the *directors must make a statutory **declaration of solvency** within the five weeks preceding the resolution. This declaration states that the directors have investigated the affairs of the company and are of the opinion that the company will be able to pay its debts in full within a specified period, not exceeding 12 months from the date of the resolution. The *liquidator is appointed by the *company members. A **creditors' voluntary winding-up** arises when no declaration of solvency has been made or when the liquidator in a members' voluntary winding-up disagrees with the forecast made by the directors. In these circumstances the company must hold a meeting of its *creditors and lay before it a **statement of affairs** disclosing its *assets and *liabilities. A liquidator may be nominated by the company and by the creditors; the creditors' nominee is preferred unless the court orders otherwise. If the company nominee acts as liquidator prior to the creditors' meeting he can only exercise his powers with the consent of the court. The creditors can also appoint a *liquidation committee.

In both types of voluntary winding-up the powers of the directors are restricted after the resolution for voluntary winding-up has been passed and they cease when a liquidator has been appointed.

voting (in a registered company) The process of casting a vote on a motion proposed at a company meeting. Initially the vote is taken upon a show of hands, i.e. each *company member present in person has one vote. If the result is disputed, it is usually possible for the chairman or members (present in person or by *proxy) to demand a **poll**, in which votes are cast (in person or by proxy) in accordance with the number and class of *shares held. Particulars of these voting rights are usually stated in the *memorandum or *articles of association. The chairman usually has a casting vote in the event of an equality of votes. Members may agree among themselves how they will cast their votes in relation to particular types of resolution (**voting agreement**).

voyeurism An offence under s 67 of the Sexual Offences Act 2003 committed where a person observes another doing a private act for the purpose of sexual gratification.

vulnerable and intimidated witness A witness identified in s 16 of the Youth Justice and Criminal Evidence Act 1999 as: under the age of 17 at the time of the hearing; suffering from a mental disorder as detailed under the Mental Health Act 1983; significantly impaired in relation to intelligence and social functioning; or with a physical disability or suffering from a physical disorder. The Act provides for the making of *special measures directions to assist these vulnerable witnesses in giving evidence. Witnesses who qualify for such assistance under the Act are termed *eligible witnesses. *See also* SPECIAL MEASURES.

vulva The outer sexual organs of a woman consisting of the labia major and labia minor. The mutilation of these is a custom and common practice in some parts of Africa. It is an offence in this country to perform the mutilation or for a UK subject or resident to perform the act anywhere in the world.

wad A piece of paper or cardboard used to retain the charge in a *shotgun cartridge.

wagering contract *See* GAMING CONTRACT.

waiver 1. The act of abandoning or refraining from asserting a legal right. **2.** The instrument that declares the act of waiving. **3.** Variation of a contract.

waiver of privilege *See* ABSOLUTE PRIVILEGE.

war The legal state of affairs that exists when states use force to vindicate rights or settle disputes between themselves. States can engage in hostilities (e.g. reprisals) without being in a technical state of war, and they can be in a state of war without much fighting taking place. At *common law a state of war could not exist until there had been a formal declaration of war or commencement of hostilities by the *Crown. The legal condition of war automatically terminates diplomatic relations and certain types of *treaties between the participants. Normal intercourse and commerce between British subjects and those of a power with which the Crown is at war are prohibited.

In the Kellogg–Briand Pact (also known as the Pact of Paris) of 1928, the contracting parties renounced war as an instrument of national policy and undertook to settle their disputes by peaceful means. The *United Nations Charter declares that all parties to it 'shall refrain...from the threat or use of force against the territorial integrity or political independence of any state' or in a manner inconsistent with the Charter, and this is commonly accepted as an accurate statement of customary *international law. Nonetheless it appears that states still retain a right of *self-defence, at least if they have been the victims of armed attack and until the Security Council can act. The Security Council is also authorized to use force (or to call upon states to do so) under certain circumstances in order to protect the peace, although in practice this power has not been invoked (*see* USE OF FORCE). The right of self-defence includes a collective right to assist other states acting in self-defence.

The *Hague Conventions and *Geneva Conventions provide rules governing the conduct of wars and stating the rights and duties of both combatants and noncombatants during war. However, they do not deal with all aspects of warfare or all types of war. There have also been various specific conventions governing particular issues, including a 1972 convention on the use or possession of bacteriological and toxic weapons, a 1976 convention on the military use of environmental modification techniques, and a 1981 convention and three protocols on cruel or indiscriminate non-nuclear weapons. Civil wars are not usually illegal from the point of view of *international law, but it is uncertain whether or not other states may legally help either the insurgents or the established authorities (*see* BELLIGERENT COMMUNITIES, RECOGNITION OF; INSURGENCY). The 1977 First and Second Protocols to the Geneva Conventions of 1949, respectively, extend some of the laws of war to civil wars and wars of national liberation (*see* SELF-DETERMINATION).

See also AGGRESSION; HUMANITARIAN INTERVENTION; MARTENS CLAUSE; OCCUPATION; OFFENCE AGAINST INTERNATIONAL LAW AND ORDER; WAR CRIME.

war crime Any violation of the laws or customs of *war amounting to a criminal act. According to the Charter of the Nuremberg International Military Tribunal of 1946, war crimes include *murder, ill-treatment, or *deportation of civilian populations, murder or ill-treatment of prisoners of war, killing hostages, plundering property, and wanton destruction of population centres or devastation that is not justified by military necessity. The Nuremberg Tribunal also defined a new category of **crimes against humanity**, consisting essentially of murder, extermination, enslavement, deportation, and other inhumane acts committed against any civilian population before or during World War II and *persecution on political, racial, or religious grounds (but only if the persecution is connected with war crimes or crimes against peace); these acts are crimes against humanity whether or not they violate the domestic law of the country where the crime was committed. It is now arguable that this definition is of general application and is wider than that of war crimes. In consequence, the prohibition of crimes against humanity denies the right of any state to treat its citizens as it pleases. This has had major implications for the relationship between state *sovereignty and *humanitarian intervention.

The Tribunal also created a third category of **crimes against peace**, i.e. planning, preparing, or waging a war of aggression or a war in violation of international treaties. It is generally considered that these definitions now form part of customary *international law.

The Rome Statute of the *International Criminal Court made in 1998 and put into effect in 2003 creates a permanent International Criminal Court in The Hague and creates offences under the headings of; Genocide; Crimes Against Humanity; War Crimes; and the Crime of Aggression. The court can investigate and try individuals for a wide variety of offences committed in international armed conflict and some non-international conflicts. The Statute incorporates the Geneva Conventions of 1949 and subsequent conventions. In considering which law is applicable in any case the Court will first apply the Rome Statute; secondly, applicable *treaties and the principles and rules of international law including the established principles of the international law of armed conflict. Failing that, general legal principles of the laws of the legal system of the world, provided they do not conflict with the principles of the Statute.

war crimes tribunals Established at the end of World War II with *jurisdiction to try and punish those who allegedly committed war crimes while acting in the interests of the European Axis countries or Japan. More recently, under *Chapter VII of the UN Charter, the UN Security Council has set up ad hoc war crimes tribunals in relation to the conflicts in the former Yugoslavia (1993) and Rwanda (1994). *See also* INTERNATIONAL CRIMINAL COURT.

The War Crimes Act 1991 gives jurisdiction to UK courts to try those charged with war crimes committed in German-held territory during World War II, irrespective of the accused's *nationality at the time. Prosecutions may be brought with the consent of the Attorney-General for *homicide offences.

ward of court **1.** A minor under the care of a *guardian (appointed by the *parents or the court), who exercises rights and duties over the child subject to the general control and discretion of the court. **2.** A minor in respect of whom a *wardship order has been made and over whom the court exercises parental rights and duties. A child becomes a ward of court when a wardship order is made and remains a ward until he reaches the age of 18 or the court orders that he should cease to be a ward. Any child who is actually in England or Wales (or ordinarily resident in England or Wales) may be made a ward of court, even though he is neither domiciled there nor a British subject. Marriage of a ward does not necessarily terminate the wardship.

wardship The *jurisdiction of the *High Court to make a child a *ward of court and assume responsibility for its welfare. The jurisdiction is almost unlimited, although subject to consideration of the child's welfare and, to some extent, the rights of other persons and the public interest. The court exercises detailed control of the ward: it may appoint the *Official Solicitor to act as the child's *guardian and may order either *parent to make periodical payments for his maintenance. Wardship proceedings are heard in private and the usual rules of evidence may be relaxed (e.g. in respect of *hearsay evidence). The court may enforce its orders by *injunction; breach of this or tampering with the ward may constitute contempt of court.

Wardship proceedings are usually used (1) when there is a dispute between estranged parents but no *divorce proceedings have been started; (2) when a *foster parent or potential adopter wishes to prevent relatives interfering with the child or when a third party wishes to remove the child from parents who are considered unfit to have parental responsibility; (3) when a child has been 'kidnapped' by a parent; (4) to exercise control over a wayward child; and (5) to control medical treatment, such as sterilization, even when this is contrary to the wishes of the child. Any person who can establish a proper interest in the child may apply for wardship (including the child himself), but the Children Act 1989 restricts the right of *local authorities to use wardship proceedings. It also repeals the court's power to commit a ward to the care or supervision of a local authority. Since the Children Act came into force, use of wardship may be limited as the court may prefer to make a *section 8 order instead.

warning A warning under the Crime and Disorder Act 1998 given by police to a *young offender as an alternative to prosecution. Only one warning can be given (unless an earlier warning was more than two years before). The youth will also be referred to a *youth offending team for assessment.

warrant 1. A *document authorizing some action, especially the payment of money. A **warehouse** (or **wharfinger's**) **warrant** is issued when *goods are taken into a public warehouse and must be produced when they are removed. This document is negotiable and transferable by endorsement. *See also* SHARE WARRANT. **2.** A written document issued by a *magistrate for the *arrest of a person or the search of his property (*see* POWER OF SEARCH). When a suspect has fled abroad and there is an *extradition treaty covering the offence he is suspected of, the magistrate who has *jurisdiction over the place in which the offence was allegedly committed may issue an arrest warrant to enable the *Director of Public Prosecutions and the *Home Secretary to extradite the suspect. *See also* WRIT OF ASSISTANCE. **3.** An authority issued by a magistrate under the Police and Criminal Evidence Act 1984 allowing the police to detain a person who has been arrested for an *indictable offence for up to 96 hours. An application must be made before the person has been in detention for 36 hours. The magistrates can issue a warrant authorizing the further detention initially for up to 36 hours. On further application the warrant can be extended. In order to issue a warrant of further detention the magistrates must be satisfied that the person has been arrested for an indictable offence, that the inquiry is being conducted expeditiously, and it is necessary to detain the person to secure or preserve evidence or to obtain evidence by questioning him.

warrant backed for bail *See* BACKED FOR BAIL.

warrant card An identification card issued to all *police officers and signed by the chief officer of their force, certifying that he holds the office of *constable, which is the warrant for the execution of his duty. Similar *documents are issued to officers of *Her Majesty's Revenue and Customs and the *Serious Organized Crime Agency.

warranty 1. (in contract law) A term or promise in a contract, breach of which will entitle the innocent party to *damages but not to treat the contract as discharged by breach. *Compare* CONDITION. **2.** (in insurance law) A promise by the insured, breach of which will entitle the insurer to treat the contract as discharged by breach. The word therefore has the same meaning as *condition in the general law of contract. **3.** Loosely, a manufacturer's written promise as to the extent he will repair, replace, or otherwise compensate for defective *goods; a *guarantee.

wasted costs order An order for *costs made against the legal or other representative of a party on the ground that they were incurred by any improper, unreasonable, or negligent act or *omission of the representative or his *employee. In criminal cases, such orders are governed by s 19A of the Prosecution of Offences Act 1985.

wasting police time A *summary offence under s 5(2) of the Criminal Law Act 1967 committed by someone who causes wasteful employment of the police by making a false report tending to show an offence has been committed or by implying that a person or property is in danger or that he has information relevant to a police inquiry. The consent of the *Director of Public Prosecutions is required for prosecutions for this offence, which is punishable by a *fine and/or imprisonment.

waybill *See* SEA WAYBILL.

weapon of offence Any *offensive weapon or any article made, adapted, or intended for incapacitating someone (e.g. a rope to tie someone with, or pepper to make him sneeze). There are special offences of aggravated *burglary (s 10, Theft Act 1968) and of *trespass with a weapon of offence (s 8, Criminal Law Act 1977). *See also* FIREARM.

Welsh Assembly The National Assembly for Wales, a body established by the Government of Wales Act 1998. The Assembly has 60 elected salaried members. It does not have legislative or taxing powers, exercising instead a diverse range of functions, such as housing, education, economic development, and flood defence. In operation from 1999, the Assembly has taken over many of the powers and responsibilities of the Secretary of State for Wales. *See* DEVOLUTION.

wild animals *See* CLASSIFICATION OF ANIMALS; DANGEROUS ANIMALS; POACHING.

wilful Deliberate; intended: usually used of wrongful actions in which the conduct is intended and executed by a free agent.

wilful default The failure of a person to do what he should do, either intentionally or through recklessness; e.g. non-appearance at court.

wilful misconduct Intentionally doing something that is wrong, or wrongfully omitting to do something, or doing something or omitting to do something that shows reckless indifference as to what the consequences may be.

wilful neglect Deliberate or intentional failure to perform a duty.

winding-up (liquidation) A procedure by which a company can be dissolved. It may be instigated by members or *creditors of the company (*see* VOLUNTARY WINDING-UP) or by order of the court (*see* COMPULSORY WINDING-UP). In both cases the process involves the appointment of a *liquidator to assume control of the company from its *directors. He collects the assets, pays debts, and distributes any surplus to *company members in accordance with their rights.

withdrawal of issue from jury A procedure enabling a *judge, who is not satisfied that there is sufficient evidence to discharge the evidential *burden of proof borne by a party in relation to a particular issue, to prevent that issue being put before a *jury.

withdrawal of proceedings In criminal proceedings before the *magistrates' courts, a *prosecutor may seek leave of the court to withdraw a *charge or *summons at any time before the defendant is called upon to enter a *plea. The court should grant leave and discharge the defendant, unless there is bad faith on the part of the prosecutor or unfairness to the defendant. Withdrawal is no bar to future proceedings for the same offence.

without notice application A procedure in civil litigation by which one party may apply for an order of court to be made without the other party being aware of it. An example may occur when one party wishes to freeze the assets of the other party. Secrecy is essential to avoid the other party having the opportunity to dispose of the assets. In cases of this sort it is possible for a without notice application to be made for a *search order or a *freezing injunction. *See also* EX PARTE.

without prejudice A phrase used to enable parties to negotiate settlement of a *claim without implying any admission of *liability. Letters and other *documents headed 'without prejudice' cannot be adduced as evidence in any court action without the consent of both parties. However, they may be relevant when costs are discussed in courts—thus the phrase 'without prejudice save as to costs' is often added on settlement correspondence. Whether or not a discussion or letter is 'without prejudice' and therefore cannot be disclosed to the court depends on whether it was a genuine attempt to settle a dispute, not whether the words were written on a letter or said in a meeting. The reason such discussions are kept secret from the court is that the courts are keen to encourage settlement of disputes without recourse to the courts, and if settlement discussions could be disclosed it may deter people from settling disputes.

witness 1. A person who observes the signing of a legal *document in case it is subsequently necessary to verify the authenticity of the signature. He adds his own signature to the document as a witness. Many legal documents are only valid if properly witnessed (*see* DEED). **2.** A person who gives evidence to a court or tribunal. In court, witnesses are required either to give evidence on *oath or to *affirm that their evidence is true. At *common law, the general rule is that all persons are competent to give evidence, provided that they have sufficient mental understanding (*see also* COMPETENCE). In civil cases a child who is too young to understand the nature of an oath may be competent to give *unsworn evidence (s 96, Children Act 1989). Part II, Ch 5 of the Youth Justice and Criminal Evidence Act 1999 makes similar provision in criminal proceedings in relation to a child under the age of 14. Most competent witnesses can be compelled to give evidence (a witness who refuses to answer is in *contempt of court) but again there are exceptions. For example, a witness cannot be compelled to answer a question that may *incriminate him. A witness's evidence is usually given orally in open court. However in certain circumstances evidence is allowed by *affidavit (*see* COMMISSION) or by video link (*see* VIDEO RECORDED-EVIDENCE). The evidence of certain witnesses is considered to be unreliable and requires *corroboration. *See also* ADVERSE WITNESS; HOSTILE WITNESS; ZEALOUS WITNESS; INTERFERING WITH WITNESSES; PERJURY; QUEEN'S EVIDENCE; WITNESS SUMMONS.

Witness Service *Victim Support runs the Witness Service in every criminal court in England and Wales to give information and support to witnesses, victims, their families and friends when they go to court. They help witnesses who are called to give evidence, including defence witnesses, victims of crime and their families and friends attending court for any reason. Witness Service staff and volunteers can provide someone to talk to in confidence, a chance to see the court beforehand and learn about court procedures, a quiet place to wait, someone to go into the court room with the witness when giving evidence, practical help (e.g. with expense forms), easier access to people who can answer specific questions about the case (the Witness Service cannot discuss evidence or offer legal advice), and a chance to talk over the case when it has ended and to get more help or information. Like the rest of Victim Support, the Witness Service is free and independent of the police or courts.

witness's oath *See* OATH.

witness summons An order to a person to appear in court on a certain day to give evidence or to produce a *document to the court. The party calling the witness must pay his reasonable expenses. A witness who fails to comply with the order is in *contempt of court.

In criminal proceedings, where the prosecution or defence wish to secure the attendance of a witness, but are not satisfied that he will attend voluntarily, they can apply for a witness summons. In the *Crown Court, the procedure is set out in ss 2 to 4 of the Criminal Procedure (Attendance of Witnesses) Act 1965. In the *magistrates court, the attendance of both *prosecution and *defence witnesses for purposes of criminal proceedings may be secured by the issue of a *summons or *warrant under s 97 of the Magistrates' Courts Act 1980.

In civil proceedings, the procedure is governed by r 34.2 of the Civil Procedure Rules. Formerly, such an order was known as a **subpoena**. There are two kinds of witness summons: a summons requiring a person to give evidence (formerly called a **subpoena *ad testificandum***); and a summons requiring him to produce particular documents that are required as evidence (formerly called a **subpoena *duces tecum***).

words of art Words whose legal interpretation has been fixed so that the legal effect of their use is known.

worker An *employee.

working day 1. For banking and financial purposes, any day other than Saturday, Sunday, and *bank holidays. *See also* SUNDAY TRADING. **2.** (of a court) Any day other than Sunday or holidays, called a *dies juridicus*. A day on which no legal business can be carried on is called a *dies non*.

working hours The number of hours worked by *employees and office holders. The *European Union's Directive 93/104 concerning certain aspects of the organization of working time required all member states to limit the working week of workers to 48 hours (except when workers have agreed otherwise). The provisions of this Directive were enacted by the British Government in the Working Time Regulations 1998 (SI 1998/1833) and 2002 (SI 2002/3128). Key elements of the Regulations require a maximum working week of 48 hours, daily rest breaks, weekly rest periods, and annual paid leave of four weeks in each holiday year. The Regulations also contain protections with respect to night working. They are enforced by the Health and Safety Executive.

working tax credit *See* TAX CREDIT.

World Trade Organization (WTO) An international trade organization formed under the General Agreement on Tariffs and Trade (GATT). It began operating on 1 January 1995 and as at 11 December 2005 had 149 members. The WTO's aims are to agree international trading rules and further the liberalization of international trade. The WTO extends its jurisdiction into such aspects of trading as *intellectual property rights. WTO rules are very important in international trade contracts.

worm A self-replicating, self-contained *computer program that transmits itself from computer to computer via a network connection, often making use of the host computer's email program for the purpose. Its predominant effect is uncontrolled self-reproduction, which wastes or overwhelms computer resources.

wounding Breaking the continuity of the skin or of a membrane (such as that lining the cheeks or lips). Scratching, bruising, burning, or breaking a bone without tearing the skin do not constitute wounding. **Malicious wounding** is an *either way offence under s 20 of the Offences Against the Person Act 1861, punishable by up to five years' imprisonment. It requires an intention to cause some physical harm (not necessarily a wound) or foresight of the risk of causing physical harm. A person is *not guilty of this offence if he intended only to frighten his victim but in fact accidentally wounded him, although he would be *guilty of *assault or *battery. It is a specified *violent offence within sch 15 to the Criminal Justice Act 2003 (*see* DANGEROUS OFFENDERS).

wounding with intent The offence under s 18 of the Offences Against the Person Act 1861 of *wounding or causing *grievous bodily harm with the intention of causing grievous bodily harm (even if grievous harm does not in fact result) or wounding or causing grievous bodily harm with the intention of resisting a lawful arrest or preventing detainer. Wounding with intent is an *indictable only offence and carries a maximum *sentence of *life imprisonment. It is a specified *violent offence within sch 15 to the Criminal Justice Act 2003 (*see* DANGEROUS OFFENDERS). *See also* ULTERIOR INTENT.

wreck 1. (shipwreck) The destruction of a *ship at sea, as by foundering in a storm or being driven onto rocks. **2.** The remains of a wrecked ship. **3. Jetsam**: *goods cast overboard in order to lighten a vessel which is in danger of being sunk, notwithstanding that afterwards it perishes. **4. Flotsam**: goods lost from a ship which has sunk or otherwise perished which are recoverable by reason of their remaining afloat. **5. Lagan**: goods cast overboard from a ship which afterwards perishes, buoyed so as to render them recoverable. **6. Derelict**: property, whether vessel or cargo, which has been abandoned and deserted at sea by those who were in charge of it without any hope of recovering it. Most wreck which is reported to the *receiver falls under the heading of Derelict or occasionally Flotsam. Boats which have come off their moorings are not classified as wreck for the purposes of the Merchant Shipping Act 1995, as they have not been abandoned without hope of recovery.

writ An order issued by a court in the *sovereign's name that directs some act or forbearance. Originally, a writ was an instrument under seal bearing some command of the sovereign.

writ of assistance A documentary authorization to search unspecified *premises for *smuggled goods, first issued to English customs officials in 1662. They are issued by the *Queen's Bench Division of the *High Court at the beginning of the monarch's reign and remain valid until six months after the end of that reign, during which time they are lodged at various customs (now *Her Majesty's Revenue and Customs) offices, where the senior manager is responsible for their custody and use.

Following a decision of the *European Court of Human Rights in which a search by French Customs officials investigating currency offences was considered to be a breach of Article 8 of the *European Convention on Human Rights, as it was carried out under a statutory power of search without a *warrant, s 161 of the Customs and Excise Management Act 1979 was modified by s 25 of the Finance Act 2005 so that the use of the writ is limited to urgent situations where the delay caused by seeking a search warrant to search premises for smuggled goods is likely to result in such goods being destroyed or moved to another location. Where considerations of urgency do not apply, officers of HMRC, like *police officers, are required to apply for a search warrant. The power of entry conferred by the writ may not be exercised 'by night' (between the hours of 11pm and 5am) unless the HMRC officer is accompanied by a *constable.

writ of execution A *writ used in the *enforcement of a *judgment. It may be a writ of *fieri facias*, a *writ of possession, a writ of delivery, a writ of sequestration, or any further writ in aid of any of these writs.

writ of possession A writ directing the *sheriff to enter upon *land to give vacant possession to the claimant. It is used to enforce *judgments for the possession of land.

written order to search Where there are reasonable grounds for believing that there is material on *premises which is likely to be of substantial value, whether by itself or together with other material, to a *terrorist investigation, a *police officer of at least the rank of superintendent may, by a written order signed by him, give to any *constable the authority to enter the premises specified to search the premises and any person found there, and to seize and retain any relevant material which is found.

An order can only be made if the officer has reasonable grounds for believing that the case is one of great emergency, and that immediate action is necessary. Where such an order is made the Secretary of State shall be notified as soon as is reasonably practicable (sch 5, Terrorism Act 2000).

wrong An illegal or immoral act. A distinction must be drawn between moral wrongs and legal wrongs. Some moral wrongs, such as *murder or *theft, are also crimes punishable by law. Legal wrongs may be criminal or civil. Crimes are offences against society as a whole, not merely against the victim of the crime. Civil wrongs, such as *torts, *breaches of contract, and interferences with property rights, are wrongs to the individuals affected.

wrongful interference with goods (under the Torts (Interference with Goods) Act 1977) Any of various *torts to *goods. It includes *conversion, *trespass to goods, *negligence so far as it results in damage to goods or to an interest in goods, and any other tort that results in damage to goods or an interest in goods.

wrongful trading Carrying on business knowing that the company has no reasonable prospect of avoiding an insolvent *winding-up. Such knowledge may be implied if a reasonably diligent person would have realized the position. *Directors responsible may be ordered to contribute to the *assets of the company when the winding-up occurs unless they can prove that, after acquiring the relevant knowledge, they endeavoured to minimize loss to the company's creditors, e.g. by initiating a winding-up or *administration order. *See also* FRAUDULENT TRADING.

young offender *See* JUVENILE OFFENDER.

youth community order A non-custodial *penalty which may be imposed on a person aged under 16 who has been convicted of a criminal offence. The Criminal Justice Act 2003 brought together various forms of community orders available under the Powers of Criminal Courts (Sentencing) Act 2000. Section 147(2) of the 2003 Act defines a youth community order as a *curfew order, *exclusion order, *attendance centre order, *supervision order, or *action plan order. The orders continue to be made under the 2000 Act, although all the relevant provisions have been amended so as to make them available only in the case of offenders under 16 years of age. Section 36B of the 2000 Act (as amended) allows the court to include an *electronic monitoring requirement to ensure compliance with any requirement imposed under a youth community order. *See also* REPARATION ORDER.

youth court A *magistrates' court exercising jurisdiction over crimes committed by *juvenile offenders and other matters relating to children under 18. It was formerly called a **juvenile court**. The court consists of either three lay *magistrates (at least one of whom should normally be a man and one a woman) or a single *district judge (magistrates' court). All these magistrates are selected from the youth court panel, whose members are thought to be specially qualified to deal with juveniles and who have received additional training for this purpose. The proceedings of the court are not open to the general public, access being very restricted and determined by s 47(2) of the Children and Young Persons Act 1933. Generally, the media may not publish the identity of any juvenile concerned in the court's proceedings (*see* REPORTING RESTRICTIONS). Court proceedings are generally more informal than in the magistrates' court for adult offenders, and hearings can be heard in locations other than other court buildings, although generally they will be in existing magistrates' courts. A juvenile defendant can be 'found guilty' of an offence but may not be described as 'convicted'; and an 'order upon a finding of guilt' is made rather than a 'sentence' being handed down.

youth custody *See* CUSTODY FOR OFFENDERS UNDER 21.

youth detention *See* CUSTODY FOR OFFENDERS UNDER 21; DETENTION AND TRAINING ORDER; DETENTION IN A YOUNG OFFENDER INSTITUTION; LONG-TERM DETENTION.

Youth Justice Board A non-departmental body sponsored by the Home Office. It has two main roles: first to monitor performance of the youth justice system and report to the *Home Secretary; and secondly to purchase *secure accommodation for people under the age of 18 years who have been remanded or sentenced to *custody.

youth offending team (YOT) A team established in each borough with representatives of the police, Probation Service, social services, health, education, drugs and alcohol misuse and housing officers. The purpose of the YOT is to identify the needs of each young offender by assessing them with a national assessment. It identifies the specific problems that make the young person offend as well as measuring the risk they pose to others. The YOT then identifies a suitable programme to address the needs of the young person with the intention of preventing further offending.

zealous witness A witness who displays undue favouritism towards one party in the case.

zebra crossing An uncontrolled road crossing for pedestrians, identified by studs and alternating black and white stripes on the *carriageway and lighted yellow globes (normally flashing) at each end. Movement and behaviour of pedestrians and traffic on crossings is governed by Section IV of the Zebra, Pelican and Puffin Pedestrian Crossings Regulations and General Direction 1997 (SI 1997/2400). Pedestrians take precedence over vehicles on crossings uncontrolled by police or traffic wardens, and it is an offence to fail to accord precedence. Other offences include: waiting within the limits of a crossing and overtaking within the approach. Pedestrians may not stay on the crossing longer than is necessary to cross. Breaches of the Regulations are offences under s 25 of the Road Traffic Regulation Act 1984.

zemiology The branch of criminology studying the social harm caused by actions.

zephyr brush A brush with soft bristles used to apply fingerprint powders.

zero-rated supply A supply that is within the scope of *value-added tax but is charged at a nil rate. Examples are food (excluding restaurant and takeaway meals), books and journals, and children's clothes; all exports are also zero-rated. Unlike *exempt supplies, zero-rated supplies count towards the turnover limit above which registration for VAT is compulsory, and any input tax relating to them may be reclaimed by the registered trader.

zero tolerance A method of policing in which laws against even the most minor offences are enforced. The theory behind it is that if minor offences are prevented there will be a consequent decrease in major crime. This method of policing first came to prominence in New York from 1994. After the introduction of this method of policing major crime did reduce but this may have been due to other factors. Opponents of the system said that it led to oppressive policing.

Appendix 1. Abbreviations and acronyms

A list of commonly used abbreviations and acronyms. Entries followed by * have an entry in the dictionary under the fully spelled-out headword.

A&E	Accident and Emergency
AA	Ambulance Aid
AAIB	Air Accidents Investigation Branch
ABC	Acceptable Behaviour Contract*
ABH	Actual Bodily Harm*
ABI	Association of British Insurers
ABV	Alcohol By Volume
AC	Assistant Commissioner (MPS)
ACAS	Advisory, Conciliation and Arbitration Service*
ACC	1. Assistant Chief Constable 2. Anti-Corruption Command (MPS)
ACCESS	Assess, Collect, Collate, Evaluate, Survey, Summary*
ACCOLC	Access Overload Control: access and usage control protocols of the mobile phone network
ACF	Army Cadet Force
ACMD	Advisory Council on the Misuse of Drugs
ACOPS	Association of Chief Officers of Probation
ACPO	Association of Chief Police Officers*
ACPOD	Association of Chief Police Officers' Drivers
ACPO IM	ACPO Information Management
ACPORP	Association of Chief Police Officers' Road Policing Committee
ACPOS	ACPO of Scotland
ACSO	Accredited Community Support Officer
ADABAS	Manages the PNC database
ADP	Automatic Data Processing
ADR	Alternative Dispute Resolution*
AES	Advanced Encryption Standard
AFO	Authorized Firearms Officer
AG	Advocate General*
A-G	Attorney-General*
AIO	Ambulance Incident Officer
ALARP	As Low as Reliably Practicable
ALG	Association of London Governments
AML	Anti-Money Laundering
ANPR	Automatic Number Plate Recognition
APA	1. Army Prosecuting Authority* 2. Association of Police Authorities
ARA	Assets Recovery Agency*
ARCA	Asbestos Removal Contractors' Association
ARV	Armed Response Vehicle
ASA	Ambulance Service Association
ASAP	As Soon As Possible
ASBO	Anti-Social Behaviour Order*
ASLEF	Association of Locomotive Engineers and Firemen
ATM	Automatic Teller Machine*
ATO	Ammunition Technical Officer
ATOC	Association of Train Operating Companies
ATSAC	ACPO Strategic Advice Centre
AVLS	Automatic Vehicle Location System
AWB	Air Waybill
AWE	Atomic Weapons Establishment, Aldermaston
BAA	British Airports Authority
BACS	Bankers' Automated Clearing System
BBC	British Broadcasting Corporation
BBS	Bulletin Board System
BC	Basic Check (vetting)
BCG	Bronze Coordinating Group
BCP	Business Continuity Planning
BCS	British Crime Survey*
BCU	Basic Command Unit*
BDE	Brigade
BID	1. Burglary in Dwelling 2. Brought in Dead (alternative to DOA)
BIOS	1. Basic Input/Output System* 2. Basic Integrated Operating System

BIU	Business Information Unit
BoP	Breach of the Peace*
BPA	Black Police Association
BSIA	British Security Industry Association
BT	British Telecom
BTP	British Transport Police
BTWC	Biological and Toxic Weapons Convention
BVPI	Best Value Performance Indicator
C	Command Paper (1870–99)*
C&C	Command and Control
CA	Court of Appeal*
CAA	Civil Aviation Authority
CAB	Criminal Assets Bureau*
CAC	Central Ambulance Control
CACJ	Central American Court of Justice
CAD	1. Communities Against Drugs* 2. Computer Aided Despatch
CAFCASS	Children and Family Court Advisory and Support Service*
CAP	Common Approach Path
CARIN	Camden Assets Recovery Inter-Agency Network*
CARMS	Computer Aided Resource Management System
CAT	Convention Against Torture and other Cruel, Inhuman or Degrading Treatment or Punishment*
CATCHEM	Centralized Analytical Team Collating Homicide Expertise Management*
CBD	Chemical and Biological Defence, Porton Down
(CB)IED	(Chemical or Biological) Improvised Explosive Device
CBM	Confidence Building Measures
CBRN	Chemical/Biological/Radiological/Nuclear
CC	Crown Court*
CC&C	Command, Control and Communication
CCA	Comparative Case Analysis*
CCC	1. Central Criminal Court* 2. Central Command Complex 3. Colour Change Chemistry: detection method for CWAs 4. Civil Contingencies Committees 5. Customs Co-operation Council 6. Community Customs Code
CCC(CBRN)	Sub-Committee on Chemical, Biological, Radiological and Nuclear Consequence Management
CCC(LR)	Sub-Committee on London Resilience
CCC(P)	Civil Contingencies Committee, Policy
CCC(UK)	Sub-Committee on UK Resilience
CCCG	Chief Constable's Co-coordinating Group (Strategic Group)
CCC-IR	Central Command Complex Information Room, New Scotland Yard
CCC-SOR	Special Operations Room, New Scotland Yard
CCDC	Consultant in Communicable Disease Control
CCF	Combined Cadet Force
CCMF	Criminal Case Management Framework*
CCMP	Criminal Case Management Programme*
CCO	Casualty Clearing Officer
CCRC	Criminal Cases Review Commission*
CCRF	Civil Contingencies Reaction Force
CCS	1. Casualty Clearing Station 2. Civil Contingencies Secretariat
CCTV	Closed Circuit Television
CCU	Computer Crime Unit
CCV	Command and Control Vehicle
Cd	Command Paper (1900–18)*
CDF	Channel Data Format
CDI	Child Dependency Increase
CDRP	Crime and Disorder Reduction Partnerships*
CDS	Criminal Defence Service*
CEC	Commission for Environmental Cooperation
CEGB	Central Electricity Generating Board
CEHR	Commission for Equality and Human Rights
CEMA	Customs and Excise Management Act 1979
CENTREX	Central Police Training and Development Authority*
CEO	Chief Executive Officer
CEP	Civil Evasion Penalty
CEPU	Central Emergency Planning Unit
CERD	International Convention on the Elimination of All Forms of Racial Discrimination
CESG	Communications-Electronic Security Group

CETF	Confiscation Enforcement Task Force*
CFI	Court of First Instance*
CFSP	Common Foreign and Security Policy
CGT	Criminal Geographic Targeting
CHAPS	1. Chemical Hazards and Poisons (part of the HPA) 2. Clearing House Automated Payment System
CHAS	Contractors Health and Safety Assessment Scheme
CHI	Commission for Health Improvement
CHIS	Covert Human Intelligence Source*
CIC	Coalition Information Centre
CICA	Criminal Injuries Compensation Authority*
CICFA	Concerted Inter-Agency Criminal Finances Action Group
CID	Criminal Investigation Department*
CIDTP	Cruel, Inhuman or Degrading Treatment or Punishment
CIMAH	Control of Industrial Major Accident Hazard
CIMIC	Civil Military Cooperation
CIRS	Chemical Incident Response Service
CITOPS	Customs and International Trade Operations
CJA	Criminal Justice Act
CJB	Criminal Justice Board
CJCSA	Criminal Justice Court Service Act
CJIT	Criminal Justice Information Technology
CJS	1. Criminal Justice Support 2. Criminal Justice System*
CJSB	Central Jury Summoning Bureau*
CJU	Criminal Justice Unit*
CJX	Criminal Justice Extranet
CLI	Call Line Identification
CLO	Crime Liaison Officer*
CLS	Community Legal Service*
CM	Capability Management
Cm	Command Paper (1986–)*
CMB	Central Media Brief
CMC	Computer Mediated Communication
Cmd	Command Paper (1919–56)*
CMLO	Consequence Management Liaison Officer
Cmnd	Command Paper (1957–86)*
CMO	Chief Medical Officer
CMOS	Complementary Metal-Oxide Semi-Conductant
CMR	Convention Marchandises Routiers
CMT	Crisis Management Team
CNCD	Consignment Note and Customs Declaration
CNI	Critical National Infrastructure
CNN	Cable News Network
CNP	Card-Not-Present*
CO	1. Cabinet Office 2. Commanding Officer
COBR	Cabinet Office Briefing Room, aka COBRA
CODIS	Combined DNA Indexing System
COG	Chief Officer Group
COI	Central Office of Information
COLP	City of London Police
COMAH	Control of Major Accident Hazard Regulations
COPFS	Crown Office and Procurator Fiscal Service
CorDM	Corporate Data Model
COSHH	Control of Substances Hazardous to Health
COSLA	Convention of Scottish Local Authorities
COY	Company
CPA	1. Child Protection Agency 2. Crime Pattern Analysis*
CPAC	Consumer Protection Advisory Committee*
CPIA	Criminal Procedure and Investigations Act
CPO	1. Case Progression Officer* 2. Chief Petty Officer (RN) 3. Crime Prevention Officer
CPR	1. Cardio-Pulmonary Resuscitation 2. Civil Procedure Rules* 3. Criminal Procedure Rules*
CPS	Crown Prosecution Service*
CPTDA	Central Police Training and Development Authority*
CPU	1. Central Processing Unit* 2. Child Protection Unit
CRB	Criminal Records Bureau*
CRCA	Commissioners for Revenue and Customs Act 2005
CRFP	Council for the Registration of Forensic Practitioners
CRISP	Cross Region Information Sharing Project
CRO	Criminal Record Office
CRU	Civil Recovery Unit*
CS	Incapacitating agent

CSB	Correctional Services Board
CsCDC	Consultants in Communicable Disease Control
CSCE	Conference on Security and Cooperation in Europe
CSF	Cerebrospinal Fluid
CSI	1. Crime Scene Investigator* 2. Centralized System Information
CSIA	Central Sponsor for Information Assurance
CSM	Crime Scene Manager
CSO	Community Support Officer*
CSP	Communication Service Provider
CTLR	Channel Tunnel Rail Link
CTM	Community Trade Mark*
CTO	Central Ticket Office
CVA	Cerebrovascular Accident
CW	Chemical Weapons
CWA	Chemical Warfare Agent
D&I	Drunk and Incapable
DAC	Deputy Assistant Commissioner (MPS)
DAF	Data Acquisition Facility
DAT	Drugs Action Team
DC	Detective Constable
DCA	Department of Constitutional Affairs
D-Cable	Digital Cable
DCI	Detective Chief Inspector
DCMS	Department for Culture, Media and Sport
DCS	Detective Chief Superintendent
DDoS	Distributor Denial of Service Attack*
DDT	Digital Data Transmitter
DEFRA	Department for Environment, Food and Rural Affairs
DES	Data Encryption Standard
DfES	Department for Education and Skills
DfT	Department for Transport
DGN	Dangerous Goods Note
DH	Department of Health
DI	Detective Inspector
DIA	Diffuse Axonal Injury*
DIC	1. Driver Improvement Course 2. Drunk in Charge
DIO	1. Divisional Intelligence Officer 2. Drugs Intelligence Officer 3. Duty Intelligence Officer
DLO	Drug Liaison Officer*
DLR	Docklands Light Railway
DMS	Defence Medical Services
DNA	Deoxyribonucleic acid*
DOA	Dead on Arrival
DoB	Date of Birth
DoH	Department of Health
DOP(IT)	Defence and Overseas Policy: Sub-Committee on International Terrorism
DoS	Denial of Service Attack*
DP	Detained Person
DPA	Data Protection Act
DPH	Director Public Health
DPO	Documentary Proof of Origin
DPP	Director of Public Prosecutions*
DPTC	Disabled Person's Tax Credit
DRS	1. Direct Rail Services 2. Disaster Recovery System 3. Driver Rectification Scheme
DS	Detective Sergeant
D-Sat	Digital Satellite
DSL	Digital Subscriber
DSP	Director of Service Prosecutions
DsPH	Directors of Public Health
Dstl	Defence, Science and Technology Laboratory, Porton Down
D/Supt	Detective Superintendent
DTI	Department of Trade and Industry
DTO	Detention and Training Order
DTP	Digital TV Project
DTT	Digital Terrestrial Television
DTV	Digital Television
DV	Developed Vetting
DVD/DVD-R	Digital Versatile Disc/Digital Versatile Disc Recorder
DVI	Disaster Victim Identification
DVLA	Driver and Vehicle Licensing Agency
DWP	Department of Work and Pensions
EAH	Early Administrative Hearing*
EAT	Employment Appeal Tribunal*
EAW	European Arrest Warrant*
EBM	Evidential Breath Machine
EC	European Community*
ECB	European Central Bank*
ECG	Electrocardiogram
ECHR	European Convention on Human Rights*
ECI	Enhanced Cognitive Interview*
ECJ	European Court of Justice*
ECMA	1. European Convention on Mutual Assistance in Criminal Matters 1959 2. European Convention on Mutual Assistance in Criminal Matters between the Member States of the European Union 2000

ECN	Emergency Communications Network
ECSC	European Coal and Steel Community*
ECSR	European Committee of Social Rights
ECtHR	European Court of Human Rights*
ECU	European Currency Unit (Euro)*
EDI	Electronic Data Interchange*
EDU	Europol Drugs Unit*
EEC	European Economic Community*
EEG	Electroencephalogram
EFP	European Firearms Permit
EFQM	European Foundation for Quality Management
EFS	Encrypted File System (Microsoft)
EFTA	European Free Trade Association*
EFTPOS	Electronic Fund Transfer at Point of Sale*
EGT	Evidence Gathering Team
EHO	Environmental Health Officer
EIR	Equipment Identity Register
EKP	Economic Key Points
ELO	Europol Liaison Officers
ELVIS	Easy Link Vehicle Information System
EMS	European Monetary System*
EMU	European Monetary Union*
EN	Euro Norm
EOC	Emergency Operation Centre
EOD	Explosives Ordnance Disposal
EP	Emergency Planning
EPA	Environment Agency
EPC	Emergency Planning College
EPCU	Emergency Planning Coordination Unit
EPIC	Emergency Procedures Information Centre (British Airways)
EPLO	Emergency Planning Liaison Officer
EPO	Emergency Planning Officer
EPS	European Passenger Services (Eurostar)
EPU	Emergency Planning Unit
ESA	1. EFTA Surveillance Authority 2. Environmental Services Association
ESC	European Social Charter
ESE	Electronic Security Environment
ESDA	Electrostatic Detection Apparatus
ESLA	Electrostatic Lifting Apparatus
ET	Employment Tribunal*
ETMP	Effective Trial Management Programme*
EU	European Union*
Euratom	European Atomic Energy Community*
EWS	English, Welsh and Scottish Railways
FAC	Firearms Certificate
FANY	First Aid Nursing Yeomanry
FATF	Financial Action Task Force
FBO	Football Banning Order*
FBOA	Football Banning Order Authority
FCO	Foreign and Commonwealth Office
FCP	Forward Control Point
FDR	Firearms Discharge Residue*
FEL	Forensic Explosives Laboratory
FIB	Force Intelligence Bureau
FIELD	Foundation for International Environmental Law and Development
FIM	Force Incident Manager
FIND	Facial Image National Database
FIO	1. Field Intelligence Officer 2. Force Intelligence Officer
FIU	1. Force Intelligence Unit 2. Financial Investigation Unit
FLINTS	Forensic-Led Intelligence System
FLO	1. Family Liaison Officer 2. Football Liaison Officer
FMC	Forward Military Commander
FME	Forensic Medical Examiner
FMEA	Failure Mode and Effect Analysis
FOIA	Freedom of Information Act
FPN	Fixed Penalty Notice*
FPT	Family Protection Team
FSA	1. Financial Services Authority* 2. Food Standards Agency* 3. Football Supporters Association
FSC	1. Financial Securities Centre 2. Forward Scientific Controller
FSS	Forensic Science Service*
FSSoc	Forensic Science Society*
FTA	1. Failed to Appear 2. Freight Transport Association
FTS	Failed to Stop
GATT	General Agreement on Tariffs and Trade

GB Great Britain
GBH Grievous Bodily Harm*
GCG Gold Coordinating Group
GCHQ Government Communications Headquarters*
GCS Glasgow Coma Scale*
GEMAC Greeting, Explanation, Mutual Activity, and Close*
GICS Government Information Communications Service: part of the Cabinet Office
GIF Graphics Interchange Format
GIS Geographical Information System
GLA Greater London Authority*
GLO Government Liaison Officer
GLT Government Liaison Team: link between strategic decision-making by the GCG and COBR
GMC General Medical Council
GNER Great North Eastern Railway
GNN Government News Network
GO Government Offices
GOE Government Office for the East of England
GOEM Government Office for the East Midlands
GOL Government Office for London
GONE Government Office for the North East
GONW Government Office for the North West
GORs Government Offices in the Regions
GOSE Government Office for the South East
GOSW Government Office for the South West
GOWM Government Office for the West Midlands
GOYH Government Office for Yorkshire and Humberside
GP General Practitioner
GPMS Government Protective Marking System
GPR Ground Penetrating Radar
GPRS General Packet Radio System, often referred to as 2.5 Generation
GPS Global Positioning System
GSI Government Secure Intranet
GT New Scotland Yard Major Incident Room
GTPS Government Telephone Preference Scheme: landline priority access protocols
HA Health Authority
HAT Housing Action Trust*
HAZMAT Hazardous Materials
HCAER High Capacity Egress and Access Routes (evacuation routes)
HCEA High Capacity Emergency Access
HCO Hydrocarbon Oils
HDD Hard Disk Drive
HDU High Dependency Unit
HEPA Hospital Emergency Planners
HGV Heavy Goods Vehicle
HIV Human Immunodeficiency Virus
HMCE Her Majesty's Customs and Excise
HMIC Her Majesty's Inspectorate of Constabulary
HMIP Her Majesty's Inspectorate of Prisons
HMP Her Majesty's Prison
HMRC Her Majesty's Revenue and Customs*
HMRI Her Majesty's Railway Inspectorate
HMSO Her Majesty's Stationery Office
HMT Her Majesty's Treasury
HO Home Office
HOLAB Home Office Laboratory Form
HOLMES Home Office Large Major Enquiry System*
HORT/1 Home Office Road Traffic Form 1*
HOSDB Home Office Scientific Development Branch
HOTPU Home Office Terrorist Prevention Unit
HPA Health Protection Agency
HPD High Potential Development
HQ Headquarters
HQP&SS Headquarters, Provost and Security Services (RAF Police)
HR Human Resources
HRC Human Rights Committee (UN)
HSC Health and Safety Commission*
HSE Health and Safety Executive*
HTTP Hyper Text Transfer Protocol; the method to transfer or convey information on the world wide web
HTTPS As above, but the S indicates a default port and an additional encryption/authentication layer; used for secure transactions
IAHR Inter-American Commission on Human Rights
IATA International Air Transport Association

IBDS	Integrated Biological Detection Systems
IC	1. Identification Code 2. Information Commissioner
ICC	International Criminal Court*
ICC Court	International Court of Arbitration of the International Chamber of Commerce
ICD	Inland Clearance Depot
ICF	Integrated Competency Framework
ICJ	International Court of Justice
ICJS	Integrated Criminal Justice System
ICPO	International Criminal Police Organization*
ICRP	International Commission on Radiological Protection
ICT	Information and Communication Technology
ICTR	International Criminal Tribunal for Rwanda
ICTY	International Criminal Tribunal for former Yugoslavia
ICU	Intensive Care Unit
IDENT1	Platform to support wider identification capabilities, including the national automated fingerprint and palm print identification service
IECC	Integrated Electronic Control Centre
IED	Improvised Explosive Device
IEM	Integrated Emergency Management
IHCF	Industry Hot Card File
IHD	Ischaemic Heart Disease
ILC	International Law Commission*
ILO	1. Inter-Agency Liaison Officer 2. International Labour Organization
IMB	Independent Monitoring Boards
IMPACT	Intelligence Management Prioritization Analysis Coordination and Tasking
IMS	1. Information Management Strategy 2. Industrial Methylated Spirits
IND	Immigration and Nationality Directorate
Int Corps	Army Intelligence Corps
INTERIGHTS	International Centre for the Legal Protection of Human Rights
Interpol	International Criminal Police Organization*
INTSUM	Intelligence Summary
IO	Investigating Officer*
IPA	International Police Association
IPCC	Independent Police Complaints Commission*
IPE	Individual Protective Equipment
IPT	Integrated Project Team
IPV6	Internet Protocol Version Six
IR	1. Infra Red 2. Inland Revenue*
IRB	Incident Report Book
IS/IT	Information System and Information Technology
ISS	Information Systems Strategy
ISSP	Intensive Supervision and Support Programme
ISS4PS	Information Systems Strategy for the Police Service
IT/IM	Information Technology/ Information Management
ITLOS	International Tribunal for the Law of the Sea
IVF	In Vitro Fertilization*
JARD	Joint Asset Recovery Database*
JCE	Justices' Chief Executive
JESCC	Joint Emergency Services Control Centre
JHAC	Joint Health Advisory Cell
JIC	Joint Intelligence Committee
JIG	Joint Intelligence Group
JIO	Joint Intelligence Organization
JMC	Joint Military Commander
JP	Justice of the Peace*
JPAT	1. Joint Planning Advisory Team 2. Joint Planning and Assessment Team
JPEG	Joint Photographic Experts Group
JSA	Jobseekers' Allowance*
KPI	Key Performance Indicator
LA	Local Authority*
LACORS	Local Authorities Coordinators of Regulatory Services*
LAEPSC	Local Authority Emergency Planning Sub-Committee
LAGPA	Lesbian and Gay Police Association
LALO	Local Authority Liaison Officer
LAN	Local Area Network
LANTERN	Portable Livescan System
LAS	London Ambulance Service
LCJ	Lord Chief Justice*
LCJB	Local Criminal Justice Board*
LCN	Low Copy Number

LEC Local Emergency Centre
LGA Local Government Association
LGC Laboratory of the Government Chemist
LGV Light Goods Vehicle
LHR London Heathrow
LIBOR London Interbank Offered Rate*
LIO Local Intelligence Officer
LJ Lord Justice of Appeal*
LLAEPG London and Local Authority Emergency Planning Group
LMG Leucomalachite Green*
LOR Letter of Request*
LSC Legal Services Commission*
LSD Lysergic Acid Diethylamide*
LSP Local Strategic Partnership*
LUL London Underground Limited
MAA Mutual Administrative Assistance*
MACA Military Aid to Civil Authorities*
MACC Military Aid to the Civil Community*
MACP Military Aid to Civil Power*
MAGD Military Aid to Government Departments*
MAIB Marine Accident Investigation Branch
MAOI Monoamine Oxidase Inhibitors*
MAPPS Multi-Agency Public Protection Panel
MARPLE Multi-Agency Rendezvous Points for London Emergencies
MC Magistrates' Court*
MCA Maritime and Coastguard Agency
MCC Magistrates' Courts Committee
MCSI Magistrates' Courts Service Inspectorate
MCTC Military Correctional Training Centre
MCV Mobile Communications Vehicle
MDA Misuse of Drugs Act
MDAT Major Disaster Advisory Team
MDMA Methylenedioxymeth-amphetamine*
MEF Media Emergency Forum
MEP Member of the European Parliament
MFH Missing from Home
MHEG Multimedia Hypermedia Experts Group
MI Major Incident
MI5 Security Service (originally Military Intelligence 5)
MI6 Secret Intelligence Service
MICAF Mobile Industry Crime Action Forum
MIU Minor Injury Unit
MIRSAP Major Incident Room Standard Administrative Procedure
MLA Mutual Legal Assistance*
MLAT Mutual Legal Assistance Treaties
MMU Media Monitoring Unit
MO 1. Medical Officer
2. *Modus Operandi*
MoD Ministry of Defence
MODACE Management of Disaster and Civil Emergency
MOT 1. Ministry of Transport test for motor vehicles over three years old
2. Ministry of Transport (now Department for Transport)
3. Mode of Trial
MOU Memorandum of Understanding
MP 1. Member of Parliament*
2. Military Police
MPS Metropolitan Police Service
MPSOR/GT Metropolitan Police Special Operations Room: often referred to by its call sign 'GT'
MR Master of the Rolls*
MRCC Maritime Rescue Coordination Centre (HM Coastguard)
MRSC Maritime Rescue Sub-Centre (HM Coastguard)
mtDNA Mitochondrial DNA
MV Management Vetting
NACRO National Association for the Care and Resettlement of Offenders*
NACTSO National Counter Terrorism Security Office
NAFIS National Automated Fingerprint Identification System*
NAI Non-Accidental Injury
NAO National Audit Office
NART Nuclear Accident Response Team (MoD)
NASS National Asylum Support Service*
NATO North Atlantic Treaty Organization
NATS National Air Traffic Services
NBC Nuclear, Biological, Chemical
NCC 1. Network Control Centre (LUL)
2. News Coordination Centre
NCCDO News Coordination Centre Duty Officer

NCTT	National Community Tensions Team
NCEC	National Chemical Emergency Centre
NCIS	National Criminal Intelligence Service*
NCOF	National Crime and Operations Faculty
NCPE	National Centre for Policing Excellence
NCS	National Crime Squad*
NDPB	Non-Departmental Public Body
NDS	News Digital Systems
NEBR	Nuclear Emergency Briefing Room
NFA	1. No Fixed Abode 2. No Further Action
NFIU	National Football Intelligence Unit
NFLMS	National Firearms Licensing Management System
NFO	National Fingerprint Office
NGO	Non-Governmental Organization*
NHS	National Health Service
NI	Northern Ireland
NID	National Injuries Database
NIM	National Intelligence Model
NINO	National Insurance Number
NIP	Notice of Intended Prosecution*
NIS	National Identification Service*
NISCC	National Infrastructure Security Coordination Centre
Nitesun	Searchlight mounted on police helicopters
NJU	National Joint Unit
NMIS	National Management Information System
NOM	National Offender Management
NOMIS	National Offender Management Information System
NOMS	National Offender Management System
NORMACE	North Group mutual assistance plan to meet civil emergencies
NPA	Naval Prosecuting Authority*
NPD	National Probation Directorate
NPIA	National Policing Improvement Agency
NPS	National Probation Service
NRF	National Resilience Framework
NRPB	National Radiological Protection Board
NRPSI	National Register of Public Service Interpreters*
NSCWIP	National Steering Committee on Warning and Informing the Public
NSPCC	National Society for the Prevention of Cruelty to Children
NSPIS	National Strategy for Police Information Systems
NSY	New Scotland Yard
NVIS	National Video Identification Strategy
OASys	Offender Assessment System
ODPM	Office of the Deputy Prime Minister
OD Sec	Defence and Overseas Secretariat in the Cabinet Office
OFCOM	Office of Communications
OFGEM	Office of Gas and Electricity Markets
OGC	Office of Government Commerce
ONS	Office of National Statistics
OPS DO	CCS Operations Centre Duty Officer
OPSI	Office of Public Sector Information (formerly HMSO)
ORR	Office of the Rail Regulator
OSD	Open Systems Direction
OSS	Office for the Supervision of Solicitors*
OSU	Operational Standards Unit
PBV	Plea Before Venue*
PACE	Police and Criminal Evidence Act 1984
PC	1. Personal Computer 2. Police Constable 3. Privy Council*
PCIJ	Permanent Court of International Justice
PCL-R	Hare Psychopathy Checklist—Revised*
PCMH	Plea and Case Management Hearing*
PCR	Polymerase Chain Reaction*
PCT	Primary Care Trust
PDH	Plea and Directions Hearing*
PDS	Public Defender Service*
PEP	Politically Exposed Person
PFI	Private Funding Initiative
PGP	Pretty Good Privacy: a computer program for the encryption and decryption of data
PI	1. Participating Informant 2. Performance Indicator
PIA	Proved in Absence

PIC	Police Incident Commander	PTSD	Post Traumatic Stress Disorder
PII	Public Interest Immunity*	PVR	Personal Video Recorder
PIN	Personal Identification Number*	PYO	Persistent Young Offender*
PIO	Police Incident Officer	QAM	Quadrature Amplitude Modulation
PIR	Police Initial Recruitment	QBD	Queen's Bench Division*
PITO	Police Information Technology Organization	QC	Queen's Counsel*
PLA	Port of London Authority	QCA	Qualifications and Curriculum Authority
PLC	Public Limited Company*	QGM	Queen's Gallantry Medal
PLP	Press Liaison Point	QPM	Queen's Police Medal
PLX	Police Local Cross Referencing System	QUEST	Query Using Extended Search Techniques; a PNC application to identify criminal records from partial descriptive details
PM	Post-Mortem*	R	1. Regina 2. Rex
PMBS	Police Main Base Station	RA	Risk Assessment
PMO	Programme Management Organization	RAF	1. Royal Air Force 2. Recovered Assets Fund
PMR	Private Mobile Radio	RAIF	Recovered Assets Incentivization Fund*
PNC	Police National Computer*	RART	Regional Asset Recovery Team*
PND	Penalty Notice for Disorder*	RAS	Radioactive Substances Division (DEFRA)
PNICC	Police National Information and Coordination Centre	RAYNET	Radio Amateurs Emergency Network
PNN	Police National Network	RCCC	Regional Civil Contingencies Committee (GCG)
PNN2 and PNN3	The second and third implementation of the PNN	RCI	Revenue Control Inspector
PO	Public Order	RCPO	Revenue and Customs Prosecutions Office*
POA	Prosecution of Offences Act 1985	RCU	Regional Coordination Unit: part of ODPM
POCA	Protection of Children Act	RDPH	Regional Director of Public Health
POLSA	Police Search Adviser	RDS	Radio Data System
POP	Problem Oriented Policing*	RE	Royal Engineers
POS	Point-of-Sale*	Regt	Regiment
POT	Prevention of Terrorism	REPPIR	Radiation Emergency Preparedness and Public Information
POVA	Protection of Vulnerable Adults	RFS	Ready for Service
PPAF	Police Performance Assessment Framework	RFTU	Road Fuel Testing Unit
PPE	Personal Protection Equipment	RIDDOR	Reporting of Injuries, Diseases and Dangerous Occurrences Regulations
PPO	Prisons and Probation Ombudsman	RIO	Rail Incident Officer
PPP	Private Public Partnership	RIPA	Regulation of Investigatory Powers Act 2000
Pro	Provost	RMP	Royal Military Police
PSA	Public Service Agreement	RN	Royal Navy
PSD	Professional Standards Department	RNC	Regional Nominated Co-ordinator
PSDB	Police Scientific Development Branch (now HOSDB)	RO	Recovery Officer
PSNI	Police Service of Northern Ireland	ROA	Rehabilitation of Offenders Act
PSR	Pipeline Safety Regulation	ROM	Regional Offender Manager
PSSC	Police Support Staff Council	ROSPA	Royal Society for the Prevention of Accidents
PSSO	Police Skills and Standards Organisation		
PSTN	Public Services Telephone Network		
PSU	1. Police Support Unit 2. Professional Standards Unit		
PSV	Public Service Vehicle		
PTR	Pre-Trial Review*		

ROTI	Record of Taped Interview
ROVI	Record of Video Interview
RPE	Respiratory Protection Equipment
RRD	Regional Resilience Directors
RSHO	Risk of Sexual Harm Order*
RSPB	Royal Society for the Protection of Birds
R/T	Radio Telephony
RTC	Road Traffic Collision/Crash
RTP	Registered Tobacco Premises
RTRA	Road Traffic Regulation Act
RV	1. Rendezvous 2. Recruitment Vetting
RVP	Rendezvous Point
S	Section
SAMM	Support after Murder and Manslaughter
SAR	Search and Rescue
SARA	Scanning, Analysis, Response and Assessment
SAS	Special Air Service
SB	Special Branch
SBS	Special Boat Service
SC	Sub-committee
SCG	Silver Coordinating Group
SCG	Strategic Coordinating Group
SCOSS	Standing Committee on Structural Safety Sector Commander
SEAQ	Stock Exchange Automated Quotations System
SF	Special Forces
SFO	Serious Fraud Office*
SGC	Sentencing Guidelines Council*
SIB	1. Securities and Investment Board* 2. Special Investigation Branch (RMP)
SIDS	Sudden Infant Death Syndrome
SIM	Subscriber Identification Module
SIO	Senior Investigating Officer
SIPs	Service Insertion Points
SITREP	Situation Report
Skyshout	Public address system mounted on police helicopters
SLA	Service Level Agreement
SLP	Self-Loading Pistol
SLR	Self-Loading Rifle
SMC	Senior Military Commander
SME	Small and Medium-sized Enterprises
SMG	Sub-Machine Gun
SMS	Short Message Service
SOCA	Serious Organized Crime Agency*
SOCO	Scenes of Crime Officer*
SOCRATES	Integrated scientific support management system
SOFA	Status of Forces Agreement (NATO)
SOIT (officer)	Sexual Offence Investigative Techniques Trained Officer
SOLO	Sexual Offences Liaison Officer
SOPO	Sexual Offences Prevention Order
SPOC	Single Point of Contact
SQA	Scottish Qualifications Authority
SS	Sections
SSA	Senior Scientific Authority
SSM	Scientific Support Manager
SSN	Standard Shipping Note
SSSI	1. Site of Special Scientific Interest 2. Statutory Services
STIF	Standard Interface
STO	Specially Trained Officer
SUS	Service Person Under Sentence
TA	1. Territorial Army 2. Tactical Advisor
TAG	Technical Assessment Group, Dstl Chemical and Biological Science
TANU	Traffic Area Network Unit
TDN	The Digital Network: UK DDT Multiplex Operators Organization
TEG-C	Technology and Equipment Group—Converters subgroup
TETRA	Terrestrial Trunked Radio
TFT	Tit for Tat*
TIC	Taken into Consideration
TIR	Transports Internationaux Routiers
TPD	Tobacco Products Duty
TPM	Trusted Platform Module
TPU	Terrorism and Protection Unit (Home Office)
TRF	Technical Response Force (specialist military/scientific team)
TWOC	Taking Without Consent
UDHR	Universal Declaration of Human Rights*
UK	United Kingdom
UKCA	United Kingdom Central Authority
UKIS	United Kingdom Immigration Service
UKRP	United Kingdom Resident Permit
UMTS	Universal Mobile Telephone System—3rd generation platform
UN	United Nations*

UNCLOS United Nations Convention on the Law of the Sea
UNHCR United Nations High Commissioner for Refugees
UNICEF United Nations Children's Fund
UPSA Unified Police Security Architecture
URL Uniform Resource Locator
USB Universal Serial Bus
UTM Universal Transaction Monitor
UTMV Unauthorized Taking of a Motor Vehicle = TWOC
UXB Unexploded Bomb
VAS Voluntary Aid Service
VASCAR Visual Average Speed Camera and Recorder
VAT Value-Added Tax*
VC Vice Chancellor*
VCS Voluntary and Community Sector
VCT Venture Capital Trust*
VDR Vehicle Defect Rectification
VDU Visual Display Unit
VIPER Video Identification Parade Electronic Recording*
ViSOR Violent Offender and Sex Offender Register
VISTA Windows' upcoming operating system
VOD Video on Demand
VODS Vehicle Online Descriptive Search
VP/FPO Vehicle Procedures/Fixed Penalty Office
VRN 1. VAT Registration Number
2. Vehicle Registration Number
VVAPP Victims of Violence and Abuse Prevention Programme
WAP Wireless Application Protocol
WCO World Customs Organization
WFTC Working Families Tax Credit
WG Working Group
WNBFB Warrant Not Backed for Bail
WORM Write Once Read Many
WRVS Women's Royal Volunteer Service
WS Witness Service*
WTLS Wireless Transport Layer Security
WTO World Trade Organization*
WWB Warrant with Bail
WWW World Wide Web
XML Extensible Mark-up Language
YJB Youth Justice Board*
YOS Youth Offending Service
YOT Youth Offending Team*

Appendix 2. Recordable offences

Section 27(4) of the Police and Criminal Evidence Act 1984, as amended by para 61 of sch 8 to the Crime and Disorder Act 1998, allows the Secretary of State to designate offences for which convictions, cautions, reprimands, and warnings (but not a penalty notice for disorder issued under ss 1 to 11 of the Criminal Justice and Police Act 2001) may be recorded in national police records.

Additionally, any offence which is punishable with imprisonment in the case of an adult may be recorded.

By virtue of the National Police Records (Recordable Offences) Regulations 2000 (SI 2000/1139), as amended by the National Police Records (Recordable Offences) (Amendment) Regulations 2003 (SI 2003/2823) and the National Police Records (Recordable Offences) (Amendment) Regulations 2005 (SI 2005/3106), the following offences are specified:

1. Giving intoxicating liquor to children under 5 (s 5, Children and Young Persons Act 1933)
2. Exposing children under 12 to risk of burning (s 11, Children and Young Persons Act 1933)
3. Failing to provide for safety of children at entertainments (s 12, Children and Young Persons Act 1933)
4. Drunkenness in a public place (s 91, Criminal Justice Act 1967)
5. Touting for hire car services (s 167, Criminal Justice and Public Order Act 1994)
6. Purchasing or hiring a crossbow or part of a crossbow by person under the age of 17 (s 2, Crossbows Act 1987)
7. Possessing a crossbow or parts of a crossbow by unsupervised person under the age of 17 (s 3, Crossbows Act 1987)
8. Failing to deliver up authority to possess prohibited weapon or ammunition (s 5(6), Firearms Act 1968)
9. Possessing an assembled shotgun by unsupervised person under the age of 15 (s 22(3), Firearms Act 1968)
10. Possessing an air weapon or ammunition for an air weapon by unsupervised person under the age of 14 (s 22(4), Firearms Act 1968)
11. Possessing in a public place an air weapon by unsupervised person under the age of 17 (s 22 (5), Firearms Act 1968)
12. Throwing missiles (s 2, Football (Offences) Act 1991)
13. Indecent or racialist chanting (s 3, Football (Offences) Act 1991)
14. Unlawfully going on to the playing area (s 4, Football (Offences) Act 1991)
15. Trespassing in daytime on land in search of game (s 30, Game Act 1831)
16. Refusal of person trespassing in daytime on land in search of game to give his name and address (s 31, Game Act 1831)
17. Five or more persons being found armed in daytime in search of game and using violence, or refusal of such persons to give name and address (s 32, Game Act 1831)
18. Being drunk in highway or public place (s 12, Licensing Act 1872)
19. Obstructing an authorized person inspecting premises before the grant of a licence, etc. (s 59(5), Licensing Act 2003)
20. Failing to notify change of name or alteration of rules of club (s 82(6), Licensing Act 2003)
21. Obstructing an authorized person inspecting premises before the grant of a certificate (s 96 (5), Licensing Act 2003)
22. Obstructing an authorized person exercising a right of entry where a temporary event notice has been given (s 108(3), Licensing Act 2003)
23. Failing to notify licensing authority of convictions during application period (s 123(2), Licensing Act 2003)
24. Failing to notify court of personal licence (s 128(6), Licensing Act 2003)
24A. Keeping alcohol on premises for unauthorized sale, etc. (s 138(1), Licensing Act 2003)
24B. Allowing disorderly conduct on licensed premises, etc. (s 140(1), Licensing Act 2003)
24C. Selling alcohol to a person who is drunk (s 141(1), Licensing Act 2003)
24D. Obtaining alcohol for a person who is drunk (s 142(1), Licensing Act 2003)
24E. Failing to leave licensed premises, etc. (s 143(1), Licensing Act 2003)
24F. Keeping smuggled goods (s 144(1), Licensing Act 2003)

24G. Allowing unaccompanied children on certain premises (s 145(1), Licensing Act 2003)
24H. Selling alcohol to children (s 146(1) and (3), Licensing Act 2003)
24I. Allowing sale of alcohol to children (s 147(1), Licensing Act 2003)
24J. Purchasing alcohol by or on behalf of children (s 149(1), (3), and (4), Licensing Act 2003)
24K. Consumption of alcohol on relevant premises by children (s 150(1) and (2), Licensing Act 2003)
24L. Delivering alcohol to children (s 151(1), (2), and (4), Licensing Act 2003)
24M. Sending a child to obtain alcohol (s 152 (1), Licensing Act 2003)
24N. Allowing unsupervised sales by children (s 153(1), Licensing Act 2003)
24O. Making false statements (s 158(1), Licensing Act 2003)
24P. Allowing premises to remain open following a closure order (s 160(4), Licensing Act 2003)
24Q. Obstructing authorized person exercising rights of entry to investigate licensable activities (s 179(4), Licensing Act 2003)
25. Making false statement in connection with an application for a sex establishment licence (para 21, sch 3, Local Government (Miscellaneous Provisions) Act 1982)
26. *Revoked*
27. Falsely claiming a professional qualification, etc. (Article 44, Nursing and Midwifery Order 2001 (SI 2001/253))
28. Taking or destroying game or rabbits by night, or entering any land for that purpose (s 1, Night Poaching Act 1828)
29. Wearing police uniform with intent to deceive (s 90(2), Police Act 1996)
30. Unlawful possession of article of police uniform (s 90(3), Police Act 1996)
31. Causing harassment, alarm, or distress (s 5, Public Order Act 1986)
32. Failing to give advance notice of public procession (s 11, Public Order Act 1986)
33. Failing to comply with conditions imposed on a public procession (s 12(5), Public Order Act 1986)
34. Taking part in a prohibited public procession (s 13(8), Public Order Act 1986)
35. Failing to comply with conditions imposed on a public assembly (s 14(5), Public Order Act 1986)
36. Taking part in a prohibited assembly (s 14B(2), Public Order Act 1986)
37. Failing to comply with directions (s 14C(3), Public Order Act 1986)
38. Failing to provide specimen of breath (s 6, Road Traffic Act 1988)
39. Tampering with vehicles (s 25, Road Traffic Act 1988)
40. Kerb crawling (s 1, Sexual Offences Act 1985)
41. Persistently soliciting women for the purpose of prostitution (s 2, Sexual Offences Act 1985)
42. Allowing alcohol to be carried on public vehicles on journey to or from designated sporting event (s 1(2), Sporting Events (Control of Alcohol Etc.) Act 1985)
43. Being drunk on public vehicles on journey to or from designated sporting event (s 1(4), Sporting Events (Control of Alcohol Etc.) Act 1985)
44. Allowing alcohol to be carried in vehicles on journey to or from designated sporting event (s 1A(2), Sporting Events (Control of Alcohol Etc.) Act 1985)
45. Trying to enter designated sports ground while drunk (s 2(2), Sporting Events (Control of Alcohol Etc.) Act 1985)
46. *Revoked*
47. *Revoked*
48. *Revoked*
49. *Revoked*
50. Loitering or soliciting for purposes of prostitution (s 1, Street Offences Act 1959)
51. *Revoked*
52. Taking or riding a pedal cycle without owner's consent (s 12(5), Theft Act 1968)
53. Begging (s 3, Vagrancy Act 1824)
54. Persistent begging (s 4, Vagrancy Act 1824)

Appendix 3. Disclosure Code of Practice

The Disclosure Code of Practice, issued pursuant to s 23(1) of the Criminal Procedure and Investigations Act 1996, sets out the manner in which investigators are to record, retain, and reveal to the prosecutor material obtained in a criminal investigation and which may be relevant to the investigation.

The Disclosure Code of Practice is reproduced below:

Preamble

This code of practice is issued under Part II of the Criminal Procedure and Investigations Act 1996 ('the Act'). It sets out the manner in which police officers are to record, retain and reveal to the prosecutor material obtained in a criminal investigation and which may be relevant to the investigation, and related matters.

Introduction

1.1 This code of practice applies in respect of criminal investigations conducted by police officers which begin on or after the day on which this code comes into effect. Persons other than police officers who are charged with the duty of conducting an investigation as defined in the Act are to have regard to the relevant provisions of the code, and should take these into account in applying their own operating procedures.

1.2 This code does not apply to persons who are not charged with the duty of conducting an investigation as defined in the Act.

1.3 Nothing in this code applies to material intercepted in obedience to a warrant issued under section 2 of the Interception of Communications Act 1985 or section 5 of the Regulation of Investigatory Powers Act 2000, or to any copy of that material as defined in section 10 of the 1985 Act or section 15 of the 2000 Act.

1.4 This code extends only to England and Wales.

Definitions

2.1 In this code:

- a *criminal investigation* is an investigation conducted by police officers with a view to it being ascertained whether a person should be charged with an offence, or whether a person charged with an offence is guilty of it. This will include:
  —investigations into crimes that have been committed;
  —investigations whose purpose is to ascertain whether a crime has been committed, with a view to the possible institution of criminal proceedings; and
  —investigations which begin in the belief that a crime may be committed, for example when the police keep premises or individuals under observation for a period of time, with a view to the possible institution of criminal proceedings;
  —charging a person with an offence includes prosecution by way of summons;
- an *investigator* is any police officer involved in the conduct of a criminal investigation. All investigators have a responsibility for carrying out the duties imposed on them under this code, including in particular recording information, and retaining records of information and other material;
- the *officer in charge of an investigation* is the police officer responsible for directing a criminal investigation. He is also responsible for ensuring that proper procedures are in place for recording information, and retaining records of information and other material, in the investigation;
- the *disclosure officer* is the person responsible for examining material retained by the police during the investigation; revealing material to the prosecutor during the investigation and any criminal proceedings resulting from it, and certifying that he has done this; and disclosing material to the accused at the request of the prosecutor;
- the *prosecutor* is the authority responsible for the conduct, on behalf of the Crown, of criminal proceedings resulting from a specific criminal investigation;

- *material* is material of any kind, including information and objects, which is obtained in the course of a criminal investigation and which may be relevant to the investigation. This includes not only material coming into the possession of the investigator (such as documents seized in the course of searching premises) but also material generated by him (such as interview records);
- material may be *relevant to an investigation* if it appears to an investigator, or to the officer in charge of an investigation, or to the disclosure officer, that it has some bearing on any offence under investigation or any person being investigated, or on the surrounding circumstances of the case, unless it is incapable of having any impact on the case;
- *sensitive material* is material, the disclosure of which, the disclosure officer believes, would give rise to a real risk of serious prejudice to an important public interest;
- references to *prosecution disclosure* are to the duty of the prosecutor under sections 3 and 7A of the Act to disclose material which is in his possession or which he has inspected in pursuance of this code, and which might reasonably be considered capable of undermining the case against the accused, or of assisting the case for the accused;
    —references to the disclosure of material to a person accused of an offence include references to the disclosure of material to his legal representative;
    —references to police officers and to the chief officer of police include those employed in a police force as defined in section 3(3) of the Prosecution of Offences Act 1985.

General responsibilities

3.1 The functions of the investigator, the officer in charge of an investigation and the disclosure officer are separate. Whether they are undertaken by one, two or more persons will depend on the complexity of the case and the administrative arrangements within each police force. Where they are undertaken by more than one person, close consultation between them is essential to the effective performance of the duties imposed by this code.

3.2 In any criminal investigation, one or more deputy disclosure officers may be appointed to assist the disclosure officer, and a deputy disclosure officer may perform any function of a disclosure officer as defined in paragraph 2.1.

3.3 The chief officer of police for each police force is responsible for putting in place arrangements to ensure that in every investigation the identity of the officer in charge of an investigation and the disclosure officer is recorded. The chief officer of police for each police force shall ensure that disclosure officers and deputy disclosure officers have sufficient skills and authority, commensurate with the complexity of the investigation, to discharge their functions effectively. An individual must not be appointed as disclosure officer, or continue in that role, if that is likely to result in a conflict of interest, for instance, if the disclosure officer is the victim of the alleged crime which is the subject of the investigation. The advice of a more senior officer must always be sought if there is doubt as to whether a conflict of interest precludes an individual acting as disclosure officer. If thereafter the doubt remains, the advice of a prosecutor should be sought.

3.4 The officer in charge of an investigation may delegate tasks to another investigator, to civilians employed by the police force, or to other persons participating in the investigation under arrangements for joint investigations, but he remains responsible for ensuring that these have been carried out and for accounting for any general policies followed in the investigation. In particular, it is an essential part of his duties to ensure that all material which may be relevant to an investigation is retained, and either made available to the disclosure officer or (in exceptional circumstances) revealed directly to the prosecutor.

3.5 In conducting an investigation, the investigator should pursue all reasonable lines of inquiry, whether these point towards or away from the suspect. What is reasonable in each case will depend on the particular circumstances. For example, where material is held on computer, it is a matter for the investigator to decide which material on the computer it is reasonable to inquire into, and in what manner.

3.6 If the officer in charge of an investigation believes that other persons may be in possession of material that may be relevant to the investigation, and if this has not been obtained under paragraph 3.5 above, he should ask the disclosure officer to inform them of the existence of the investigation and to invite them to retain the material in case they receive a request for its disclosure. The disclosure officer should inform the prosecutor that they may have such material. However, the officer in charge of an investigation is not required to make speculative enquiries of other persons; there must be some reason to believe that they may have relevant material. That reason may come from information provided to the police by the accused or from other inquiries made or from some other source.

3.7 If, during a criminal investigation, the officer in charge of an investigation or disclosure officer for any reason no longer has responsibility for the functions falling to him, either his supervisor or the police officer in charge of criminal investigations for the police force concerned must assign someone else to assume that responsibility. That person's identity must be recorded, as with those initially responsible for these functions in each investigation.

Recording of information

4.1 If material which may be relevant to the investigation consists of information which is not recorded in any form, the officer in charge of an investigation must ensure that it is recorded in a durable or retrievable form (whether in writing, on video or audio tape, or on computer disk).
4.2 Where it is not practicable to retain the initial record of information because it forms part of a larger record which is to be destroyed, its contents should be transferred as a true record to a durable and more easily-stored form before that happens.
4.3 Negative information is often relevant to an investigation. If it may be relevant it must be recorded. An example might be a number of people present in a particular place at a particular time who state that they saw nothing unusual.
4.4 Where information which may be relevant is obtained, it must be recorded at the time it is obtained or as soon as practicable after that time. This includes, for example, information obtained in house-to-house enquiries, although the requirement to record information promptly does not require an investigator to take a statement from a potential witness where it would not otherwise be taken.

Retention of material

(a) Duty to retain material
5.1 The investigator must retain material obtained in a criminal investigation which may be relevant to the investigation. Material may be photographed, video-recorded, captured digitally or otherwise retained in the form of a copy rather than the original at any time, if the original is perishable; the original was supplied to the investigator rather than generated by him and is to be returned to its owner; or the retention of a copy rather than the original is reasonable in all the circumstances.
5.2 Where material has been seized in the exercise of the powers of seizure conferred by the Police and Criminal Evidence Act 1984, the duty to retain it under this code is subject to the provisions on the retention of seized material in section 22 of that Act.
5.3 If the officer in charge of an investigation becomes aware as a result of developments in the case that material previously examined but not retained (because it was not thought to be relevant) may now be relevant to the investigation, he should, wherever practicable, take steps to obtain it or ensure that it is retained for further inspection or for production in court if required.
5.4 The duty to retain material includes in particular the duty to retain material falling into the following categories, where it may be relevant to the investigation:

- —crime reports (including crime report forms, relevant parts of incident report books or police officer's notebooks);
- —custody records;
- —records which are derived from tapes of telephone messages (for example, 999 calls) containing descriptions of an alleged offence or offender;
- —final versions of witness statements (and draft versions where their content differs from the final version), including any exhibits mentioned (unless these have been returned to their owner on the understanding that they will be produced in court if required);
- —interview records (written records, or audio or video tapes, of interviews with actual or potential witnesses or suspects);
- —communications between the police and experts such as forensic scientists, reports of work carried out by experts, and schedules of scientific material prepared by the expert for the investigator, for the purposes of criminal proceedings;
- —records of the first description of a suspect by each potential witness who purports to identify or describe the suspect, whether or not the description differs from that of subsequent descriptions by that or other witnesses;
- —any material casting doubt on the reliability of a witness.

5.5 The duty to retain material, where it may be relevant to the investigation, also includes in particular the duty to retain material which may satisfy the test for prosecution disclosure in the Act, such as:

—information provided by an accused person which indicates an explanation for the offence with which he has been charged;

—any material casting doubt on the reliability of a confession;

—any material casting doubt on the reliability of a prosecution witness.

5.6 The duty to retain material falling into these categories does not extend to items which are purely ancillary to such material and possess no independent significance (for example, duplicate copies of records or reports).

(b) Length of time for which material is to be retained

5.7 All material which may be relevant to the investigation must be retained until a decision is taken whether to institute proceedings against a person for an offence.

5.8 If a criminal investigation results in proceedings being instituted, all material which may be relevant must be retained at least until the accused is acquitted or convicted or the prosecutor decides not to proceed with the case.

5.9 Where the accused is convicted, all material which may be relevant must be retained at least until:

—the convicted person is released from custody, or discharged from hospital, in cases where the court imposes a custodial sentence or a hospital order;

—six months from the date of conviction, in all other cases.

If the court imposes a custodial sentence or hospital order and the convicted person is released from custody or discharged from hospital earlier than six months from the date of conviction, all material which may be relevant must be retained at least until six months from the date of conviction.

5.10 If an appeal against conviction is in progress when the release or discharge occurs, or at the end of the period of six months specified in paragraph 5.9, all material which may be relevant must be retained until the appeal is determined. Similarly, if the Criminal Cases Review Commission is considering an application at that point in time, all material which may be relevant must be retained at least until the Commission decides not to refer the case to the Court.

Preparation of material for prosecutor

(a) Introduction

6.1 The officer in charge of the investigation, the disclosure officer or an investigator may seek advice from the prosecutor about whether any particular item of material may be relevant to the investigation.

6.2 Material which may be relevant to an investigation, which has been retained in accordance with this code, and which the disclosure officer believes will not form part of the prosecution case, must be listed on a schedule.

6.3 Material which the disclosure officer does not believe is sensitive must be listed on a schedule of non-sensitive material. The schedule must include a statement that the disclosure officer does not believe the material is sensitive.

6.4 Any material which is believed to be sensitive must be either listed on a schedule of sensitive material or, in exceptional circumstances, revealed to the prosecutor separately. If there is no sensitive material, the disclosure officer must record this fact on a schedule of sensitive material.

6.5 Paragraphs 6.6 to 6.11 below apply to both sensitive and non-sensitive material. Paragraphs 6.12 to 6.14 apply to sensitive material only.

(b) Circumstances in which a schedule is to be prepared

6.6 The disclosure officer must ensure that a schedule is prepared in the following circumstances:

— the accused is charged with an offence which is triable only on indictment;

— the accused is charged with an offence which is triable either way, and it is considered either that the case is likely to be tried on indictment or that the accused is likely to plead not guilty at a summary trial;

— the accused is charged with a summary offence, and it is considered that he is likely to plead not guilty.

6.7 In respect of either way and summary offences, a schedule may not be needed if a person has admitted the offence, or if a police officer witnessed the offence and that person has not denied it.
6.8 If it is believed that the accused is likely to plead guilty at a summary trial, it is not necessary to prepare a schedule in advance. If, contrary to this belief, the accused pleads not guilty at a summary trial, or the offence is to be tried on indictment, the disclosure officer must ensure that a schedule is prepared as soon as is reasonably practicable after that happens.

(c) Way in which material is to be listed on schedule
6.9 The disclosure officer should ensure that each item of material is listed separately on the schedule, and is numbered consecutively. The description of each item should make clear the nature of the item and should contain sufficient detail to enable the prosecutor to decide whether he needs to inspect the material before deciding whether or not it should be disclosed.
6.10 In some enquiries it may not be practicable to list each item of material separately. For example, there may be many items of a similar or repetitive nature. These may be listed in a block and described by quantity and generic title.
6.11 Even if some material is listed in a block, the disclosure officer must ensure that any items among that material which might satisfy the test for prosecution disclosure are listed and described individually.

(d) Treatment of sensitive material
6.12 Subject to paragraph 6.13 below, the disclosure officer must list on a sensitive schedule any material, the disclosure of which he believes would give rise to a real risk of serious prejudice to an important public interest, and the reason for that belief. The schedule must include a statement that the disclosure officer believes the material is sensitive. Depending on the circumstances, examples of such material may include the following among others:

—material relating to national security;
—material received from the intelligence and security agencies;
—material relating to intelligence from foreign sources which reveals sensitive intelligence gathering methods;
—material given in confidence;
—material relating to the identity or activities of informants, or undercover police officers, or witnesses, or other persons supplying information to the police who may be in danger if their identities are revealed;
—material revealing the location of any premises or other place used for police surveillance, or the identity of any person allowing a police officer to use them for surveillance;
—material revealing, either directly or indirectly, techniques and methods relied upon by a police officer in the course of a criminal investigation, for example covert surveillance techniques, or other methods of detecting crime;
—material whose disclosure might facilitate the commission of other offences or hinder the prevention and detection of crime;
—material upon the strength of which search warrants were obtained;
—material containing details of persons taking part in identification parades;
—material supplied to an investigator during a criminal investigation which has been generated by an official of a body concerned with the regulation or supervision of bodies corporate or of persons engaged in financial activities, or which has been generated by a person retained by such a body;
—material supplied to an investigator during a criminal investigation which relates to a child or young person and which has been generated by a local authority social services department, an Area Child Protection Committee or other party contacted by an investigator during the investigation;
—material relating to the private life of a witness.

6.13 In exceptional circumstances, where an investigator considers that material is so sensitive that its revelation to the prosecutor by means of an entry on the sensitive schedule is inappropriate, the existence of the material must be revealed to the prosecutor separately. This will apply only where compromising the material would be likely to lead directly to the loss of life, or directly threaten national security.
6.14 In such circumstances, the responsibility for informing the prosecutor lies with the investigator who knows the detail of the sensitive material. The investigator should act as soon as

is reasonably practicable after the file containing the prosecution case is sent to the prosecutor. The investigator must also ensure that the prosecutor is able to inspect the material so that he can assess whether it is disclosable and, if so, whether it needs to be brought before a court for a ruling on disclosure.

Revelation of material to prosecutor

7.1 The disclosure officer must give the schedules to the prosecutor. Wherever practicable this should be at the same time as he gives him the file containing the material for the prosecution case (or as soon as is reasonably practicable after the decision on mode of trial or the plea, in cases to which paragraph 6.8 applies).

7.2 The disclosure officer should draw the attention of the prosecutor to any material an investigator has retained (including material to which paragraph 6.13 applies) which may satisfy the test for prosecution disclosure in the Act, and should explain why he has come to that view.

7.3 At the same time as complying with the duties in paragraphs 7.1 and 7.2, the disclosure officer must give the prosecutor a copy of any material which falls into the following categories (unless such material has already been given to the prosecutor as part of the file containing the material for the prosecution case):

—information provided by an accused person which indicates an explanation for the offence with which he has been charged;
—any material casting doubt on the reliability of a confession;
—any material casting doubt on the reliability of a prosecution witness;
—any other material which the investigator believes may satisfy the test for prosecution disclosure in the Act.

7.4 If the prosecutor asks to inspect material which has not already been copied to him, the disclosure officer must allow him to inspect it. If the prosecutor asks for a copy of material which has not already been copied to him, the disclosure officer must give him a copy. However, this does not apply where the disclosure officer believes, having consulted the officer in charge of the investigation, that the material is too sensitive to be copied and can only be inspected.

7.5 If material consists of information which is recorded other than in writing, whether it should be given to the prosecutor in its original form as a whole, or by way of relevant extracts recorded in the same form, or in the form of a transcript, is a matter for agreement between the disclosure officer and the prosecutor.

Subsequent action by disclosure officer

8.1 At the time a schedule of non-sensitive material is prepared, the disclosure officer may not know exactly what material will form the case against the accused, and the prosecutor may not have given advice about the likely relevance of particular items of material. Once these matters have been determined, the disclosure officer must give the prosecutor, where necessary, an amended schedule listing any additional material:

—which may be relevant to the investigation,
—which does not form part of the case against the accused,
—which is not already listed on the schedule, and
—which he believes is not sensitive,

unless he is informed in writing by the prosecutor that the prosecutor intends to disclose the material to the defence.

8.2 Section 7A of the Act imposes a continuing duty on the prosecutor, for the duration of criminal proceedings against the accused, to disclose material which satisfies the test for disclosure (subject to public interest considerations). To enable him to do this, any new material coming to light should be treated in the same way as the earlier material.

8.3 In particular, after a defence statement has been given, the disclosure officer must look again at the material which has been retained and must draw the attention of the prosecutor to any material which might reasonably be considered capable of undermining the case for the prosecution against the accused or of assisting the case for the accused; and he must reveal it to him in accordance with paragraphs 7.4 and 7.5 above.

Certification by disclosure officer

9.1 The disclosure officer must certify to the prosecutor that to the best of his knowledge and belief, all relevant material which has been retained and made available to him has been revealed to the prosecutor in accordance with this code. He must sign and date the certificate. It will be necessary to certify not only at the time when the schedule and accompanying material is submitted to the prosecutor, and when relevant material which has been retained is reconsidered after the accused has given a defence statement, but also whenever a schedule is otherwise given or material is otherwise revealed to the prosecutor.

Disclosure of material to accused

10.1 If material has not already been copied to the prosecutor, and he requests its disclosure to the accused on the ground that:

—it satisfies the test for prosecution disclosure, *or*

—the court has ordered its disclosure after considering an application from the accused,

the disclosure officer must disclose it to the accused.

10.2 If material has been copied to the prosecutor, and it is to be disclosed, whether it is disclosed by the prosecutor or the disclosure officer is a matter of agreement between the two of them.

10.3 The disclosure officer must disclose material to the accused either by giving him a copy or by allowing him to inspect it. If the accused person asks for a copy of any material which he has been allowed to inspect, the disclosure officer must give it to him, unless in the opinion of the disclosure officer that is either not practicable (for example because the material consists of an object which cannot be copied, or because the volume of material is so great), or not desirable (for example because the material is a statement by a child witness in relation to a sexual offence).

10.4 If material which the accused has been allowed to inspect consists of information which is recorded other than in writing, whether it should be given to the accused in its original form or in the form of a transcript is matter for the discretion of the disclosure officer. If the material is transcribed, the disclosure officer must ensure that the transcript is certified to the accused as a true record of the material which has been transcribed.

10.5 If a court concludes that an item of sensitive material satisfies the prosecution disclosure test and that the interests of the defence outweigh the public interest in withholding disclosure, it will be necessary to disclose the material if the case is to proceed. This does not mean that sensitive documents must always be disclosed in their original form: for example, the court may agree that sensitive details still requiring protection should be blocked out, or that documents may be summarised, or that the prosecutor may make an admission about the substance of the material under section 10 of the Criminal Justice Act 1967.

Appendix 4. Attorney-General's Guidelines on Disclosure

The Attorney-General's Guidelines, reissued in April 1995, make it clear that the regime set out in the Criminal Procedures and Investigations Act 1996, as amended by the Criminal Justice Act 2003, must be scrupulously followed, and that those appointed as disclosure officers must have the requisite experience, skills, competence, and resources for the role.
The Attorney-General's Guidelines are reproduced below:

Disclosure of Unused Material in Criminal Proceedings

Introduction

1. Every accused person has a right to a fair trial, a right long embodied in our law and guaranteed under Article 6 of the European Convention on Human Rights (ECHR). A fair trial is the proper object and expectation of all participants in the trial process. Fair disclosure to an accused is an inseparable part of a fair trial.

2. What must be clear is that a fair trial consists of an examination not just of all the evidence the parties wish to rely on but also all other relevant subject matter. A fair trial should not require consideration of irrelevant material and should not involve spurious applications or arguments which serve to divert the trial process from examining the real issues before the court.

3. The scheme set out in the Criminal Procedure and Investigations Act 1996 (as amended by the Criminal Justice Act 2003) (the Act) is designed to ensure that there is fair disclosure of material which may be relevant to an investigation and which does not form part of the prosecution case. Disclosure under the Act should assist the accused in the timely preparation and presentation of their case and assist the court to focus on all the relevant issues in the trial. Disclosure which does not meet these objectives risks preventing a fair trial taking place.

4. This means that the disclosure regime set out in the Act must be scrupulously followed. These Guidelines build upon the existing law to help to ensure that the legislation is operated more effectively, consistently and fairly.

5. Disclosure must not be an open ended trawl of unused material. A critical element to fair and proper disclosure is that the defence play their role to ensure that the prosecution are directed to material which might reasonably be considered capable of undermining the prosecution case or assisting the case for the accused. This process is key to ensuring prosecutors make informed determinations about disclosure of unused material.

6. Fairness does recognise that there are other interests that need to be protected, including those of victims and witnesses who might otherwise be exposed to harm. The scheme of the Act protects those interests. It should also ensure that material is not disclosed which overburdens the participants in the trial process, diverts attention from the relevant issues, leads to unjustifiable delay, and is wasteful of resources.

7. Whilst it is acknowledged that these Guidelines have been drafted with a focus on Crown Court proceedings the spirit of the Guidelines must be followed where they apply to proceedings in the magistrates' court.

General principles

8. Disclosure refers to providing the defence with copies of, or access to, any material which might reasonably be considered capable of undermining the case for the prosecution against the accused, or of assisting the case for the accused, and which has not previously been disclosed.

9. Prosecutors will only be expected to anticipate what material might weaken their case or strengthen the defence in the light of information available at the time of the disclosure decision, and this may include information revealed during questioning.

10. Generally, material which can reasonably be considered capable of undermining the prosecution case against the accused or assisting the defence case will include anything that tends to show a fact inconsistent with the elements of the case that must be proved by the prosecution. Material can fulfil the disclosure test:

(a) by the use to be made of it in cross-examination; or
(b) by its capacity to support submissions that could lead to:
 (i) the exclusion of evidence; or
 (ii) a stay of proceedings; or
 (iii) a court or tribunal finding that any public authority had acted incompatibly with the accused's rights under the ECHR, or
(c) by its capacity to suggest an explanation or partial explanation of the accused's actions.

11. In deciding whether material may fall to be disclosed under paragraph 10, especially (b)(ii), prosecutors must consider whether disclosure is required in order for a proper application to be made. The purpose of this paragraph is not to allow enquiries to support speculative arguments or for the manufacture of defences.

12. Examples of material that might reasonably be considered capable of undermining the prosecution case or of assisting the case for the accused are:

i. Any material casting doubt upon the accuracy of any prosecution evidence.
ii. Any material which may point to another person, whether charged or not (including a co-accused) having involvement in the commission of the offence.
iii. Any material which may cast doubt upon the reliability of a confession.
iv. Any material that might go to the credibility of a prosecution witness.
v. Any material that might support a defence that is either raised by the defence or apparent from the prosecution papers.
vi. Any material which may have a bearing on the admissibility of any prosecution evidence.

13. It should also be borne in mind that while items of material viewed in isolation may not be reasonably considered to be capable of undermining the prosecution case or assisting the accused, several items together can have that effect.

14. Material relating to the accused's mental or physical health, intellectual capacity, or to any ill treatment which the accused may have suffered when in the investigator's custody is likely to fall within the test for disclosure set out in paragraph 8 above.

Defence statements

15. A defence statement must comply with the requirements of section 6A of the Act. A comprehensive defence statement assists the participants in the trial to ensure that it is fair. The trial process is not well served if the defence make general and unspecified allegations and then seek far-reaching disclosure in the hope that material may turn up to make them good. The more detail a defence statement contains the more likely it is that the prosecutor will make an informed decision about whether any remaining undisclosed material might reasonably be considered capable of undermining the prosecution case or of assisting the case for the accused, or whether to advise the investigator to undertake further enquiries. It also helps in the management of the trial by narrowing down and focussing on the issues in dispute. It may result in the prosecution discontinuing the case. Defence practitioners should be aware of these considerations when advising their clients.

16. Whenever a defence solicitor provides a defence statement on behalf of the accused it will be deemed to be given with the authority of the solicitor's client.

Continuing duty of prosecutor to disclose

17. Section 7A of the Act imposes a continuing duty upon the prosecutor to keep under review at all times the question of whether there is any unused material which might reasonably be considered capable of undermining the prosecution case against the accused or assisting the case for the accused and which has not previously been disclosed. This duty arises after the prosecutor has complied with the duty of initial disclosure or purported to comply with it and before the accused is acquitted or convicted or the prosecutor decides not to proceed with the case. If such material is identified, then the prosecutor must disclose it to the accused as soon as is reasonably practicable.

18. As part of their continuing duty of disclosure, prosecutors should be open, alert and promptly responsive to requests for disclosure of material supported by a comprehensive defence statement. Conversely, if no defence statement has been served or if the prosecutor considers that the defence statement is lacking specificity or otherwise does not meet the requirements of section 6A of the Act, a letter should be sent to the defence indicating this. If the position is not resolved satisfactorily, the prosecutor should consider raising the issue at a hearing for directions to enable the court to give a warning or appropriate directions.

19. When defence practitioners are dissatisfied with disclosure decisions by the prosecution and consider that they are entitled to further disclosure, applications to the court should be made pursuant to section 8 of the Act and in accordance with the procedures set out in the Criminal Procedure Rules. Applications for further disclosure should not be made as ad hoc applications but dealt with under the proper procedures.

Applications for non-disclosure in the public interest

20. Before making an application to the court to withhold material which would otherwise fall to be disclosed, on the basis that to disclose would give rise to a real risk of serious prejudice to an important public interest, rosecutors should aim to disclose as much of the material as they properly can (for example, by giving the defence redacted or edited copies or summaries). Neutral material or material damaging to the defendant need not be disclosed and must not be brought to the attention of the court. It is only in truly borderline cases that the prosecution should seek a judicial ruling on the disclosability of material in its possession.
21. Prior to or at the hearing, the court must be provided with full and accurate information. Prior to the hearing the prosecutor and the prosecution advocate must examine all material, which is the subject matter of the application and make any necessary enquiries of the investigator. The prosecutor (or representative) and/or investigator should attend such applications.
22. The principles set out at paragraph 36 of *R v H & C* should be rigorously applied firstly by the prosecutor and then by the court considering the material. It is essential that these principles are scrupulously attended to to ensure that the procedure for examination of material in the absence of the accused is compliant with Article 6 of ECHR.

Responsibilities

Investigators and disclosure officers

23. Investigators and disclosure officers must be fair and objective and must work together with prosecutors to ensure that disclosure obligations are met. A failure to take action leading to inadequate disclosure may result in a wrongful conviction. It may alternatively lead to a successful abuse of process argument, an acquittal against the weight of the evidence or the appellate courts may find that a conviction is unsafe and quash it.
24. Officers appointed as disclosure officers must have the requisite experience, skills, competence and resources to undertake their vital role. In discharging their obligations under the Act, code, common law and any operational instructions, investigators should always err on the side of recording and retaining material where they have any doubt as to whether it may be relevant.
25. An individual must not be appointed as disclosure officer, or continue in that role, if that is likely to result in a conflict of interest, for instance, if the disclosure officer is the victim of the alleged crime which is the subject of investigation. The advice of a more senior investigator must always be sought if there is doubt as to whether a conflict of interest precludes an individual acting as the disclosure officer. If thereafter a doubt remains, the advice of a prosecutor should be sought.
26. There may be a number of disclosure officers, especially in large and complex cases. However, there must be a lead disclosure officer who is the focus for enquiries and whose responsibility it is to ensure that the investigator's disclosure obligations are complied with. Disclosure officers, or their deputies, must inspect, view or listen to all relevant material that has been retained by the investigator, and the disclosure officer must provide a personal declaration to the effect that this task has been undertaken.
27. Generally this will mean that such material must be examined in detail by the disclosure officer or the deputy, but exceptionally the extent and manner of inspecting, viewing or listening will depend on the nature of material and its form. For example, it might be reasonable to examine digital material by using software search tools, or to establish the contents of large volumes of material by dip sampling. If such material is not examined in detail, it must nonetheless be described on the disclosure schedules accurately and as clearly as possible. The extent and manner of its examination must also be described together with justification for such action.
28. Investigators must retain material that may be relevant to the investigation. However, it may become apparent to the investigator that some material obtained in the course of an investigation because it was considered potentially relevant, is in fact incapable of impact. It need not then be retained or dealt with in accordance with these Guidelines, although the investigator should err on the side of caution in coming to this conclusion and seek the advice of the prosecutor as appropriate.

29. In meeting the obligations in paragraphs 6.9 and 8.1 of the Code, it is crucial that descriptions by disclosure officers in non-sensitive schedules are detailed, clear and accurate. The descriptions may require a summary of the contents of the retained material to assist the prosecutor to make an informed decision on disclosure. Sensitive schedules must contain sufficient information to enable the prosecutor to make an informed decision as to whether or not the material itself should be viewed, to the extent possible without compromising the confidentiality of the information.
30. Disclosure officers must specifically draw material to the attention of the prosecutor for consideration where they have any doubt as to whether it might reasonably be considered capable of undermining the prosecution case or of assisting the case for the accused.
31. Disclosure officers must seek the advice and assistance of prosecutors when in doubt as to their responsibility as early as possible. They must deal expeditiously with requests by the prosecutor for further information on material, which may lead to disclosure.

Prosecutors
32. Prosecutors must do all that they can to facilitate proper disclosure, as part of their general and personal professional responsibility to act fairly and impartially, in the interests of justice and in accordance with the law. Prosecutors must also be alert to the need to provide advice to, and where necessary probe actions taken by, disclosure officers to ensure that disclosure obligations are met.
33. Prosecutors must review schedules prepared by disclosure officers thoroughly and must be alert to the possibility that relevant material may exist which has not been revealed to them or material included which should not have been. If no schedules have been provided, or there are apparent omissions from the schedules, or documents or other items are inadequately described or are unclear, the prosecutor must at once take action to obtain properly completed schedules. Likewise schedules should be returned for amendment if irrelevant items are included. If prosecutors remain dissatisfied with the quality or content of the schedules they must raise the matter with a senior investigator, and if necessary, persist, with a view to resolving the matter satisfactorily.
34. Where prosecutors have reason to believe that the disclosure officer has not discharged the obligation in paragraph 26 to inspect, view or listen to relevant material, they must at once raise the matter with the disclosure officer and, if it is believed that the officer has not inspected, viewed or listened to the material, request that it be done.
35. When prosecutors or disclosure officers believe that material might reasonably be considered capable of undermining the prosecution case or assisting the case for the accused, prosecutors must always inspect, view or listen to the material and satisfy themselves that the prosecution can properly be continued having regard to the disclosability of the material reviewed. Their judgement as to what other material to inspect, view or listen to will depend on the circumstances of each case.
36. Prosecutors should copy the defence statement to the disclosure officer and investigator as soon as reasonably practicable and prosecutors should advise the investigator if, in their view, reasonable and relevant lines of further enquiry should be pursued.
37. Prosecutors cannot comment upon, or invite inferences to be drawn from, failures in defence disclosure otherwise than in accordance with section 11 of the Act. Prosecutors may cross-examine the accused on differences between the defence case put at trial and that set out in his or her defence statement. In doing so, it may be appropriate to apply to the judge under section 6E of the Act for copies of the statement to be given to a jury, edited if necessary to remove inadmissible material. Prosecutors should examine the defence statement to see whether it points to other lines of enquiry. If the defence statement does point to other reasonable lines of inquiry further investigation is required and evidence obtained as a result of these enquiries may be used as part of the prosecution case or to rebut the defence.
38. Once initial disclosure is completed and a defence statement has been served requests for disclosure should ordinarily only be answered if the request is in accordance with and relevant to the defence statement. If it is not, then a further or amended defence statement should be sought and obtained before considering the request for further disclosure.
39. Prosecutors must ensure that they record in writing all actions and decisions they make in discharging their disclosure responsibilities, and this information is to be made available to the prosecution advocate if requested or if relevant to an issue.
40. If the material does not fulfil the disclosure test there is no requirement to disclose it. For this purpose, the parties' respective cases should not be restrictively analysed but must be

carefully analysed to ascertain the specific facts the prosecution seek to establish and the specific grounds on which the charges are resisted. Neutral material or material damaging to the defendant need not be disclosed and must not be brought to the attention of the court. Only in truly borderline cases should the prosecution seek a judicial ruling on the disclosability of material in its hands.

41. If prosecutors are satisfied that a fair trial cannot take place where material which satisfies the disclosure test cannot be disclosed, and that this cannot or will not be remedied including by, for example, making formal admissions, amending the charges or presenting the case in a different way so as to ensure fairness or in other ways, they must not continue with the case.

Prosecution advocates

42. Prosecution advocates should ensure that all material that ought to be disclosed under the Act is disclosed to the defence. However, prosecution advocates cannot be expected to disclose material if they are not aware of its existence. As far as is possible, prosecution advocates must place themselves in a fully informed position to enable them to make decisions on disclosure.

43. Upon receipt of instructions, prosecution advocates should consider as a priority all the information provided regarding disclosure of material. Prosecution advocates should consider, in every case, whether they can be satisfied that they are in possession of all relevant documentation and that they have been instructed fully regarding disclosure matters. Decisions already made regarding disclosure should be reviewed. If as a result, the advocate considers that further information or action is required, written advice should be promptly provided setting out the aspects that need clarification or action. Prosecution advocates must advice on disclosure in accordance with the Act. If necessary and where appropriate a conference should be held to determine what is required.

44. The prosecution advocate must keep decisions regarding disclosure under review until the conclusion of the trial. The prosecution advocate must in every case specifically consider whether he or she can satisfactorily discharge the duty of continuing review on the basis of the material supplied already, or whether it is necessary to inspect further material or to reconsider material already inspected. Prosecution advocates must not abrogate their responsibility under the Act by disclosing material which could not be considered capable of undermining the prosecution case or of assisting the case for the accused.

45. Prior to the commencement of a trial, the prosecuting advocate should always make decisions on disclosure in consultation with those instructing him or her and the disclosure officer. After a trial has started, it is recognised that in practice consultation on disclosure issues may not be practicable; it continues to be desirable, however, whenever this can be achieved without affecting unduly the conduct of the trial.

46. There is no basis in law or practice for disclosure on a 'counsel to counsel' basis.

Involvement of other agencies

Material held by Government departments or other Crown bodies

47. Where it appears to an investigator, disclosure officer or prosecutor that a Government department or other Crown body has material that may be relevant to an issue in the case, reasonable steps should be taken to identify and consider such material. Although what is reasonable will vary from case to case, the prosecution should inform the department or other body of the nature of its case and of relevant issues in the case in respect of which the department or body might possess material, and ask whether it has any such material.

48. It should be remembered that investigators, disclosure officers and prosecutors cannot be regarded to be in constructive possession of material held by Government departments or Crown bodies simply by virtue of their status as Government departments or Crown bodies.

49. Departments in England and Wales should have identified personnel as established Enquiry Points to deal with issues concerning the disclosure of information in criminal proceedings.

50. Where, after reasonable steps have been taken to secure access to such material, access is denied the investigator, disclosure officer or prosecutor should consider what if any further steps might be taken to obtain the material or inform the defence.

Material held by other agencies

51. There may be cases where the investigator, disclosure officer or prosecutor believes that a third party (for example, a local authority, a social services department, a hospital, a doctor, a school, a provider of forensic services) has material or information which might be relevant to

the prosecution case. In such cases, if the material or information might reasonably be considered capable of undermining the prosecution case or of assisting the case for the accused prosecutors should take what steps they regard as appropriate in the particular case to obtain it.

52. If the investigator, disclosure officer or prosecutor seeks access to the material or information but the third party declines or refuses to allow access to it, the matter should not be left. If despite any reasons offered by the third party it is still believed that it is reasonable to seek production of the material or information, and the requirements of section 2 of the Criminal Procedure (Attendance of Witnesses) Act 1965 or as appropriate section 97 of the Magistrates Courts Act 1980[1] are satisfied, then the prosecutor or investigator should apply for a witness summons causing a representative of the third party to produce the material to the Court.

53. Relevant information which comes to the knowledge of investigators or prosecutors as a result of liaison with third parties should be recorded by the investigator or prosecutor in a durable or retrievable form (for example potentially relevant information revealed in discussions at a child protection conference attended by police officers).

54. Where information comes into the possession of the prosecution in the circumstances set out in paragraphs 51–53 above, consultation with the other agency should take place before disclosure is made: there may be public interest reasons which justify withholding disclosure and which would require the issue of disclosure of the information to be placed before the court.

Other disclosure

Disclosure prior to initial disclosure

55. Investigators must always be alive to the potential need to reveal and prosecutors to the potential need to disclose material, in the interests of justice and fairness in the particular circumstances of any case, after the commencement of proceedings but before their duty arises under the Act. For instance, disclosure ought to be made of significant information that might affect a bail decision or that might enable the defence to contest the committal proceedings.

56. Where the need for such disclosure is not apparent to the prosecutor, any disclosure will depend on what the accused chooses to reveal about the defence. Clearly, such disclosure will not exceed that which is obtainable after the statutory duties of disclosure arise.

Summary trial

57. The prosecutor should, in addition to complying with the obligations under the Act, provide to the defence all evidence upon which the Crown proposes to rely in a summary trial. Such provision should allow the accused and their legal advisers sufficient time properly to consider the evidence before it is called.

Material relevant to sentence

58. In all cases the prosecutor must consider disclosing in the interests of justice any material, which is relevant to sentence (e.g. information which might mitigate the seriousness of the offence or assist the accused to lay blame in part upon a co-accused or another person).

Post-conviction

59. The interests of justice will also mean that where material comes to light after the conclusion of the proceedings, which might cast doubt upon the safety of the conviction, there is a duty to consider disclosure. Any such material should be brought immediately to the attention of line management.

60. Disclosure of any material that is made outside the ambit of Act will attract confidentiality by virtue of *Taylor v SFO* [1998].

Applicability of these guidelines

61. Although the relevant obligations in relation to unused material and disclosure imposed on the prosecutor and the accused are determined by the date on which the investigation began, these Guidelines should be adopted with immediate effect in relation to all cases submitted to the prosecuting authorities in receipt of these Guidelines save where they specifically refer to the statutory or Code provisions of the Criminal Justice Act 2003 that do not yet apply to the particular case.

[1] The equivalent legislation in Northern Ireland is section 51A of the Judicature (Northern Ireland) Act 1978 and Article 118 of the Magistrates' Courts (Northern Ireland) Order 1981.

Oxford Paperback Reference

The Kings of Queens of Britain
John Cannon and Anne Hargreaves

A detailed, fully-illustrated history ranging from mythical and pre-conquest rulers to the present House of Windsor, featuring regional maps and genealogies.

A Dictionary of Dates
Cyril Leslie Beeching

Births and deaths of the famous, significant and unusual dates in history – this is an entertaining guide to each day of the year.

'a dipper's blissful paradise ... Every single day of the year, plus an index of birthdays and chronologies of scientific developments and world events.'

Observer

A Dictionary of British History
Edited by John Cannon

An invaluable source of information covering the history of Britain over the past two millennia. Over 3,600 entries written by more than 100 specialist contributors.

Review of the parent volume
'the range is impressive ... truly (almost) all of human life is here'

Kenneth Morgan, *Observer*

OXFORD